FOOD AND BEVERAGE SERVICES & OPERATIONS

FOOD AND BEVERAGE SERVICES & OPERATIONS

Manoj Kumar Yadav
Lecturer
Institute of Hotel Management,
Catering Technology & Applied Nutrition
Gwalior (MP)

NEW DELHI

Published and Printed by
Techsar Pvt. Ltd.
4435-36/7, Ansari Road, Daryaganj
New Delhi–110 002 (India)
E-mail: tech_info@techsarworld.com
Website: www.techsarworld.com

ISBN 978-93-85909-94-8

Reprint 2025

Preface

ORIGIN

The origin of this book lies in the absence of any one convenient source to which hospitality students and practitioners alike could refer for fundamental knowledge and information the food and beverage division.

CONTENTS

A comprehensive detail of food and beverage operations formulating in India as well as abroad has been provided, along with a brief description of their definitions, types, origins, nature, functions and so forth. Additionally, and most importantly, it identifies and defines many of the most commonly used terms and concepts within hospitality fields, especially in food and beverage division.

Hospitality education has undergone a drastic series of changes over the past years. Hospitality education today demands new approaches to teaching and new directions for learning. This manual is a practical-cum-theoretical text written to help make you more efficient and effective professional.

For whom is this book written?

This training manual is suitable for:

- Students undertaking various hospitality programmes at different hospitality educational institutes.
- Academicians and teachers involved in the field of hospitality industry.
- Consultants to hospitality industry
- Industry observers or other interested parties.

Structure

The manual is divided into two parts:

- Food and Beverage Service Operations (Part 1)
- Food and Beverage Production Operations (Part 2)

In addition to the above two sections, almost all the chapters are powered with a range of quick scroll boxes for the purpose of instant glance.

Manoj Kumar Yadav

Acknowledgements

I would like to give sincere thanks to all those professionals and individuals who have given me assistance and support in the preparation of this manual. The completion of this book has drawn upon a variety of experiences and literature. I also owe my sincere gratitude to the following people who have given their precious time for my book and assist a lot in its completion through their knowledge, experience and guidance.

First, I am full of gratitude to my institute that has always supported and inspired me for self-developmental activities.

Thanks to my all students who always raise excellent queries which force me to remain updated always.

After all, special thanks to my god (Shri Hanuman Ji), my parents (Father – R. S Yadav – always inspire me to move forward, think bigger, do right things in life and always help others) and my wife Poonam. Last but not the least, my good luck my two cute daughters, Aastha Yadav and Yashika Yadav because they didn't disturb me while I was developing the text, even when I utilized time meant for them.

Manoj Kumar Yadav

Contents

PART A

Food and Beverage Service Operations

Introduction

OBJECTIVES

Students will be able to:

- explore the nature and scope of the catering industry;
- evaluate the features of different food and beverage outlets; and
- analyze the major segments of the catering industry.

CATERING INDUSTRY

The industry which offers the provisions of food and beverages to captive and non-captive market segments is known as *catering industry*. The term captive market segment is used for restricted market segment (like commuters in transport catering) where guests face limited competitive caterers, therefore outlets under captive market result in higher prices and less diversity for guests. On the other side, non-captive market segment refers to general public.

Straightforwardly, all sectors whether commercial or non-commercial, residential or non-residential involved in the business of serving food and beverages, are collectively known as *catering industry* or *food and beverage industry*. If this catering business is run to earn profit then it is a component of commercial catering sector, but if it is for human welfare (like catering in temples) then it forms a part of non-commercial catering sector. The person/owner of a catering establishment is known as *caterer*, the facility/provision offer to guests known as *to cater* and the business of food and beverage known as *catering*. The catering industry can be broadly classified into various sectors that are listed in below given scroll box.

Catering Sectors

Sectors	Objective	Oriented Towards/Targeted Market Segment (Plus Examples)
Commercial (A)	Profit seeking	Captive (like transport) and non-captive (like hotel and restaurant) market
Non-commercial (B)	Cost seeking	Institutional, industrial, hospital, defence, temple and other welfare segments.

Residential (A or B)	Lodging based	Like hotels, resorts and motels. It may or may not have meal provision.
Non-residential (A or B)	Meal based	Like restaurants, bars, pubs, coffee shops, food courts and fast food outlets

TYPES OF FOOD AND BEVERAGE OUTLETS

The food and beverage service department is a crucial department of a hotel because, after the front office department, it comes in direct interaction with guests as well as also supports the food production department by selling their meals. For the purpose of effectual management and control, food and beverage department is further divided into different sections which are often called "outlets". Each *outlet* is headed by an outlet manager and has its own hierarchy and standard operational procedures. These outlets may be part of a hotel establishment/*hotel based* as well as independently operated. Some important types of food and beverage outlets are given below.

TYPES OF RESTAURANTS

Specialty	Ethnic cuisine
Multi-cuisine	Multiple cuisine
Franchised	Chain outlet
Dependent	Hotel based
Independent	Self governing
Theme	Subject based
Haute cuisine	High cuisine

Restaurant (FDH—Formal Dining Hall)

- ✓ These are formal establishments with elaborate cover layouts where only meals and beverages (sometimes restaurants may also have the provision of *dispense bar*) are served to the non-captive market segment or general public. Generally, restaurants are for commercial business, however, they never provide or offer an accommodation facility.
- ✓ A restaurant may be a part of hotel organization, franchised or an independent establishment. Restaurants also vary in standards from basic cafes to exclusive eateries in star hotels. Generally, restaurants are open during major *meal hours* only but most of independent and specialty restaurants do not offer breakfast (or serve only lunch and dinner).

Coffee Shop (A Component of QSR)

- ✓ It is a kind of restaurant where limited range of meals is served along with choice of beverages, most particularly tea and coffee. The service of food is mostly in American style, i.e., pre-plated service.

✓ Coffee shops are usually open for 24 hours. The concept of coffee shop originated in US and it is often distinguished by its quick service style. Table layouts are less elaborate than FDH, thus have basic essentials only.

Bar (or Permit Room)

✓ Bar means any establishment where one can purchase and consume beverages, especially alcoholic, thus a bar must be licensed. There is range of licences required to sell different categories of alcoholic beverages, for their storage and serving options.

✓ For instance, L-3 licence is required to serve IMFL liquor to the residents in their rooms (in hotels) whereas L-4 licence is granted to independent restaurants for service of IMFL liquor. Bars can be broadly classified into two major types i.e. *public bar* (display bar) and *service bar* (dispense bar). Often, bar is also called *permit room.*

Banquet (A Function Hall)

✓ Banquet is usually the highest revenue generating outlet in the *hotel based* food and beverage service department. It serves food and beverages to a gathering of people under one roof, who gather there for a function and for a specified period of time.

✓ Banquet can be an independent outlet as well as a part of a hotel establishment. It is mainly used for formal, semi-formal and informal banqueting functions. For instance, wedding, reception, ceremony, birthday party, exhibitions, concerts and so forth. But nowadays, due to the emergence of convention halls and conference centres, banquets are mainly rent out for informal functions only.

Room Service (or IRD—In Room Dining)

✓ It offers service of food and beverages in guest rooms of hotels, hence, also called as "in room dining". The menu is often a simplified version of what is available in the hotel, with slightly high price to compensate for the higher overheads in terms of staff and equipment.

✓ Small orders are served in trays; major meals are taken on trolleys. It is always a *hotel based* outlet; never independent and mostly works for 24 hours.

Grill Room (A Component of Live Kitchen)

✓ In French it is called "Rotisserie" which is a kind of restaurant or room in a hotel (or independent establishment) where grilled items such as meats and fishes are prepared and served.

- ✓ The service offered is faster and meals are less elaborate than those offered in the large dining room. These restaurants are casual dining halls where generally a live kitchen prepares food for its guests.

Kitchen Stewarding (KST)

- ✓ Actually, it is not an outlet; it is a back-of-house area which never comes in contact with guests but it is a vital section of food and beverage department. It is also known as *dish washing area* which works for both – food preparing (performs pot washing and floor cleaning) and for food serving outlets (performs dishwashing).
- ✓ Along with this, most of kitchen stewarding department also deals with keeping and maintaining the stock of food and beverages and kitchen equipment. Apart from this, it also involves garbage clearance, pest control, receiving kitchen raw materials and so forth activities.

Barbecue (BBQ or Barby)

- ✓ Barbecue means an unenclosed facility for barbecuing food. Here, the food items are prepared out of premises (or under open sky) directly over hot coals, heated tava, hot stones, gas flame, or other similar methods.
- ✓ A food service establishment can use stationary/mobile food preparation unit, table service unit or temporary food facility for the purpose of barbecuing. Remember, barbeque is different from grill. In grilling, cooking is hot and fast (usually at 500-550°F or higher) whereas in barbecuing, cooking is slow (usually at 200-225°F or lower).

Cafeteria (EDH—Employees Dining Hall)

- ✓ A small restaurant type outlet (but without table service provision) where patrons select their choice of food from items displayed along a counter. Patron passes through lines and receives food items from the serving staff.
- ✓ Cafeteria service is identical to buffet service except that the counter staff is responsible for serving meals to patrons in cafeteria provision. It is due to portion control purpose. Whereas in buffet guests serve to themselves or self-service provision is offered.

Discotheques (A Component of Record Library)

- ✓ The concept of discotheque originated in France. It is principally meant for dancing on recorded music; a live band (optional) may also perform in it. Bar is an essential part of a discotheque and food offered mainly consists of snack-like items.

- ✓ In simple terms, a discothèque is an entertainment venue or club where recorded music is played by disc jockeys through a public address (PA) system, rather than an on-stage band.

Steakhouse (A Component of Restaurant that Specializes in Serving Steaks)

- ✓ A steakhouse is a restaurant type outlet that specializes in beef steaks. Often, steakhouse is also known as a chophouse.
- ✓ The concept of steakhouse started in the USA in the late 19th century as a development of traditional inns and bars. Some famous steakhouses include Buffalo Grill, Mr. Steak, Outback Steakhouse and Mitchell's Steakhouse.

Fast Food Outlet (QSR—Quick Service Restaurant)

- ✓ It is a food service operation, which has limited or only basic menu. These establishments may be eat-in and/or takeaway. Many are chain operated, thus utilize similar standard operating procedures.
- ✓ The features of fast food outlets include moderately priced menu, less formal service, high guest turnover, high profit through volume business, low differential profit margin (or DPM) on every dish, moderately comfortable guest seating, etc.

Snack Bars (A Component of QSR)

- ✓ Snack bars may be licensed or unlicensed and often specialize in quick service or offer self-service. These outlets generally offer a variety of drinks, sandwiches, and quickly prepared dishes and specialize in providing snacks, soda fountain, ice cream, etc.
- ✓ Some snack bars also offer hotdogs, hamburgers, French fries, potato chips/corn chips, etc. The décor of snack bars is relatively inexpensive.

Nightclub (An Adaptation of Discotheque or Dance Club)

- ✓ An entertainment venue or outlet which is usually open during evening hours and often distinguished from bars, pubs or taverns by the inclusion of a dance floor and a DJ booth, where a DJ plays recorded music (for dance) and pop music.
- ✓ Usually, alcoholic drinks and occasionally food is also offered in these outlets. Its common features include membership based (or allow to enter only members) entry for guests, targeted to limited and restricted market segment, lavish décor, elaborate service, may impose dress code and so forth.

Others

✓ It includes sandwich bar, oyster bar, business centres, executive lounges, snug (or smoke room like hukka bar), pubs, pizzeria, club food service, bistro, brassieres, seafood restaurants, top restaurants, destinations, automats, K-minus outlets, confectionary and bakery shops.

KEY TERMS

Captive market	:	Specific market segment like transport catering that focuses particularly on commuters.
Permit room	:	Bar, especially public bar which caters to general public. It is also known as dispense bar.
Chop house	:	Steakhouse that specializes in steak preparations
Haute cuisine	:	High cuisine restaurants
Rotisserie	:	Grill room
IMFL	:	Indian Made Foreign Liquor
Dispense bar	:	Public bar that focuses on general public for business.
Catering	:	Business of food and drinks.
Display bar	:	Restaurant bar that focuses on restaurant patrons only.
K-minus	:	Food service outlets that do not contain a kitchen. Here, a centralized kitchen prepares the food and transports it to the respective outlets.

REVIEW QUESTIONS

1. Classify catering industry and enlist targeted sectors along with their objectives of catering.
2. Enlist different food and beverage outlets and briefly explain each outlet.
3. Differentiate between a restaurant and a specialty restaurant
4. Name two food and beverage outlets that are usually open for 24 hours. Explain each outlet briefly.

Food and Beverage Organizational Structure

Objectives
Students will be able to:

- develop organizational chart and illustrate influence of various levels on each other;
- introduce the value of departmentalization and job description of employees; and
- describe the traits, behaviour and grooming standards for serving staff.

ORGANIZATIONAL STRUCTURE

The term organizational structure is concerned with a diagram of chain of commands of people working in an organization and its various departments/sections. It shows how an organization or department/section is structured. It facilitates developing the work profile, duties, responsibilities, who reports to whom and so forth information.

In order to perform all tasks efficiently and effectively, department/section needs to design structured *span of control* system, so that authority and responsibility among all involved members can flow properly. This systematic relation among all distinct job positions and *flow of command* is collectively known as *organizational structure* or *hierarchy*. In luxury hotels, food and beverage director is primarily responsible for food production and food and beverage service department. Under *food and beverage director*, *food and beverage service manager* along with his/her team is accountable for all food and beverage service oriented activities whereas *executive chef* along with his/her team is accountable for all the kitchen related activities. Remember, organizational sturcture varies with the size of establishment, for instance large hotels always carry more job positions than medium and small establishments.

DUTIES AND RESPONSIBILITIES OF FOOD AND BEVERAGE SERVING STAFF

Managerial Level

It includes duties and responsibilities of departmental heads, associates, outlet heads and their assistants.

This level demands *conceptual* and *administrative* skills which are related with the ability to see beyond the technical aspects of a job. It includes skills like recognizing the interdependence of various departments and functional areas within the organization and understanding how the organization fits into the structure of the industry, the community and the wider world at large. *Departmental heads* require leadership qualities, to organize and motivate outlet heads, plan menus, perform production planning and develop standard operating procedures. *Outlet heads* make schedules, take briefing, instruct workers and control quality. Their general and specific duties and responsibilities include:

General duties and responsibilities (or standard job description)

- ✓ Principally, managers are responsible for managerial works like planning, organizing, staffing, directing, controlling and evaluating the performance of their staff. Apart from it, managers are also responsible for situation handling, for example, handling staff's and guests' grievances and disputes.
- ✓ During the peak hours/seasons, managers also help their supervisors and subordinates in dealing with groups and transient guests.

Specific duties and responsibilities (or standard job specifications)

- ✓ Outlet managers are responsible for preparing budget and other financial reports of their outlets and submit it to food and beverage manager. They develop budget (or *sub-budget*) for their outlets which are later submitted to food and beverage manager for approval.
- ✓ Subsequently, food and beverage manager prepares a *master budget* by compiling all outlet budgets (after thorough analysis and interpretation of sub-budgets). Heads are also responsible for arranging training schedules for their staff.
- ✓ They are accountable for developing and implementing "standard operating procedures" for their own outlets after coordinating with relevant departments/ outlet heads. Lastly, they *refine budget* before actual execution of it.

Food and beverage director (or food and beverage division manager)

- ✓ Food and beverage director is collectively responsible for the performance of food and beverage service and food production departments. He/she is responsible for planning, organizing, staffing, directing and controlling the entire food and beverage division. In addition, he assists in planning menus and production procedures. Thus, the director must have the knowledge of budget making, controlling cost, purchasing food supplies, equipment and so forth.
- ✓ Additionally, he/she is responsible for managing the staff, ensure proper coverage of differential profit margin (DPM), communicate goals and assign work to the staff. He/she should ensure that the staff is properly trained on quality and service standards and have the tools and equipment needed to carry out their job functions effectively. He/she also monitors food and beverage sales, costs, and departmental profitability against the stated goals.

✓ He/she supports sales and marketing team in system-wide food and beverage marketing programmes and promotions. In certain situations, he/she may participate in menu design and development with the director of catering and executive chef.

Food and beverage manager (chief of food and beverage department)

✓ He/she is accountable for the performance of all sub-divisions of food and beverage service department. He prepares *master budget* of food and beverage service department with the help of different sub-budgets from the outlets. He supervises all food and beverage outlets, evaluates performance of employees and arranges training programmes.

✓ In small establishments, he/she (or he/she can delegate to his assistant) conducts inventory counting task in accordance with established procedures and timeframes as assigned. He also assists the food and beverage director in the development and implementation of local food and beverage marketing programmes for the hotel.

✓ Food and beverage manager can often involve in activities like preparing staff duty schedule, conduct employee briefing and de-briefing session, instruct workers and control quality. Along with above-mentioned errands, the head must be able to work under the extreme pressure and maintain healthy relations with others.

Restaurant manager (directeur du restaurant)

✓ He/she has the overall responsibility of the organization and administration of a particular food and beverage service operation, i.e., restaurant outlet. Restaurant manager aids to food and beverage manager in setting standards of service and arranging training programmes for the staff (both on and off-the-job training).

✓ He/she makes duty ROTA, prepares holiday list, working hours, overtime hours, weekly offs and contributes to other operational duties.

Reception headwaiter (maître d'hôtel réception)

✓ Responsible for accepting booking and making its diary. They are also accountable for reserving tables then allocate the reservation to the particular station.

✓ In the absence of host/hostess, they greet the guests on arrival and take them to the allotted table and provide them comfortable seating by giving assistance.

Supervisory Level

It includes duties and responsibilities of senior captain and captain from different food and beverage outlets.

Supervisory level staff requires *soft skills, interpersonal* and *human relations skills* as well as thorough knowledge and experience in their respective fields. It indicates an ability to work, and understand and communicate with people. These skills also help the senior captain and captain to lead, motivate and develop *esprit-de-corps* (or team spirit). Remember, human relation skills are required by all levels of management, since all managers have to interact and work with employees. Along with the above-mentioned qualities, the head must be able to work under extreme pressure, concurrently needs to maintain healthy relations with others. His/her general and specific duties and responsibilities include:

General duties and responsibilities (or standard job description)

- ✓ Supervisors are generally responsible for their own outlets/sections/stations. They supervise their staff during the working hours. If the staff has any problems, supervisors assist and guide them. Supervisors also coordinate with their subordinates as well as their seniors.
- ✓ They are responsible for transferring the staff grievances, increment, promotion and training related information to their managers and passing instructions, notices, circulars of their managers to operational staff.

Specific duties and responsibilities (or standard job specifications)

- ✓ They are specifically responsible for taking *briefing* (meeting before starting of operation) as well as *de-briefing* (meeting after completing of operation) of their staff. In briefing sessions, they inform their subordinates about VIP guest arrival, special dish of the day and other relevant information of the outlet whereas during de-briefing sessions the captain resolves the problems of stewards.
- ✓ During the operational hours, if any server or steward is busy in serving guest table then he/she may assist them by taking meal orders from new arrivals. In peak hours, they also assist their subordinates in serving meals and beverages.

Head waiter/senior captain/supervisor (or maitre d' hotel)

- ✓ They are overall in-charge of the staff team (or of all stations) and responsible for receiving guests and supervising all the necessary duties for mise en place and ensure that nothing is forgotten. They also aid the reception headwaiter.
- ✓ In few situations they are held responsible for taking guests order like when the station waiter/headwaiter is busy. They help in compilation of duty ROTA and holidays list. They may relieve the restaurant manager or reception headwaiter during their offs.

Station headwaiter/captain or station captain/station supervisor/section supervisor

- ✓ Station headwaiters are responsible for serving meals and beverages to guests. He/she is the controller of his/her station (set of tables is called *station*). They must have good knowledge of food and drinks and its correct service and must be able to instruct the staff.

✓ They also offer menu card to take meal orders and carry out all food and beverage service related activities with the help of chef-de-rang. In French, this position is termed *"Maitre d' hotel de carre"*.

Operational Level

It includes duties and responsibilities of operational and supportive staff.

This level involves the intricacy of the service trade, techniques of food and beverage preparation, presentation and service. The operational level people are real players in the industry because all elementary activities are performed by them only. In the absence of these employees no establishment can survive. They generate business by performing good work; attract potential market segment by their positive attitude and behaviour, augment product sale through their salesmanship. Their general and specific duties and responsibilities include:

General duties and responsibilities (or standard job description)

✓ It includes a wide range of common duties and responsibilities of the operational level employees of food and beverage serving outlet. These duties and responsibilities are further divided into three groups, i.e.:

Before the shift

- Make side station ready for efficient and effective service.
- Read menu and check for any special or chef preparation of the day.
- Check for the items or dishes which are not available in the kitchen.
- Collect information about the prospective VIP and VVIP guests of the day.

During the shift

- Take guest order and place it with *aboyeur* (barker, announcer or in-charge of hot plate area) or directly route to kitchen section.
- Give the service of food and beverage to the guest after receiving from kitchen or bar section.
- Assist senior or junior at all times, especially during the serving sessions.
- Attend to guest while he/she is eating food in the restaurant.
- Attend to guest's special requirement and fulfil it, if possible.

After the shift

- Collect all washed equipment (like knives, spoons, forks, etc.) from the kitchen stewarding section and wipe them.

- Collect washed crockery (plates, tea and coffee cups, saucers, soup bowls, etc.) and glassware from the kitchen stewarding and wipe them.
- Make ready side station with all the required cutlery, crockery, glassware, linen, etc.
- Make ready the entire outlet and lay tables for the next shift/operation.
- Inform or make a note in the logbook or any special instruction for the next shift like handling the VIP guest coming on that day.

Specific duties and responsibilities (standard job specifications)

- It means explicit or specific duties and responsibilities of the operational level employees of a food and beverage serving outlet. The staff members are responsible for their specific areas of work and are entirely responsible for the successful completion of their work. All staff members must work in close coordination as well.

Station waiter/station steward/section steward (or chef de rang)

- ✓ Station waiters aid the station headwaiter and are responsible during the *offs* of the station headwaiter. He/she works in coordination with station headwaiter to give efficient and speedy service.

Assistant station waiter/Assistant station steward (or demi chef de rang)

- ✓ He/she is a person who is in-charge or next in seniority to chef de rang, thus assists wherever necessary.

Waiter/server (or commi de rang)

- ✓ He/she follows the instructions given by chef de rang. He is responsible for completing mise en place. He also fetches required things and may also do a little service of either vegetables or sauce, offer rolls, place plates on the table and so forth. Simultaneously, he helps clear the tables after each course.

Trainee/apprentice (or commis)

- ✓ He/she is a learner/trainee; keeps the sideboard ready at all times and carries out mise en place. He/she is principally responsible for arranging and serving hors d' oeuvres, cold sweets and assorted cheese from the counter or trolley.

Carver (trancheur)

- ✓ Carver is responsible for operating carving trolley and carving of joints at tableside, as and when required. In trolley service, carver should plate the dish with correct portion and offer appropriate accompanying condiments and accompaniments.

Cashier

- ✓ Cashier is especially responsible for billing and taking payments or making ledger and account entries for food and beverage operations into register or computer system.

Floor waiter (or floor service staff/room service staff/chef d'etage)

- ✓ Floor waiter may either be responsible for serving single floor or to all floors. It depends on the size of the property. In large establishments, floor service staff have to serve all meals and beverages throughout the day. In small establishments, the service may be limited to early morning tea and breakfast. Staff consists of a head floor waiter with appropriate number of floor waiters.
- ✓ Floor service staff normally works from floor pantry or from a central kitchen; they can also use staff lift and trolley to serve the guest.

Lounge staff (or chef de salle)

- ✓ In large establishments, they deal particularly with lounge service. But in small establishments, regular service staff is assigned (on ROTA basis) with the responsibility of lounge service. Lounge staff is responsible for morning coffee, afternoon teas, aperitifs and liqueurs, before and after the lunch and dinner and to serve any coffee required after meal.
- ✓ They are also responsible for setting up lounge in the morning and maintaining its cleanliness and presentable throughout the day.

Wine waiter (or wine butler or sommelier)

- ✓ In a *restaurant bar*, wine waiter is responsible for the service of wine, particularly during the meals. But in *public bar*, wine waiter is responsible for serving all wines throughout the operating hours.
- ✓ He is a key person for selling wines in the hotel. Thus, he must have a thorough knowledge of all drinks and of wines to go with certain foods. He must also have knowledge regarding the licensing laws in respect to particular establishment and area.

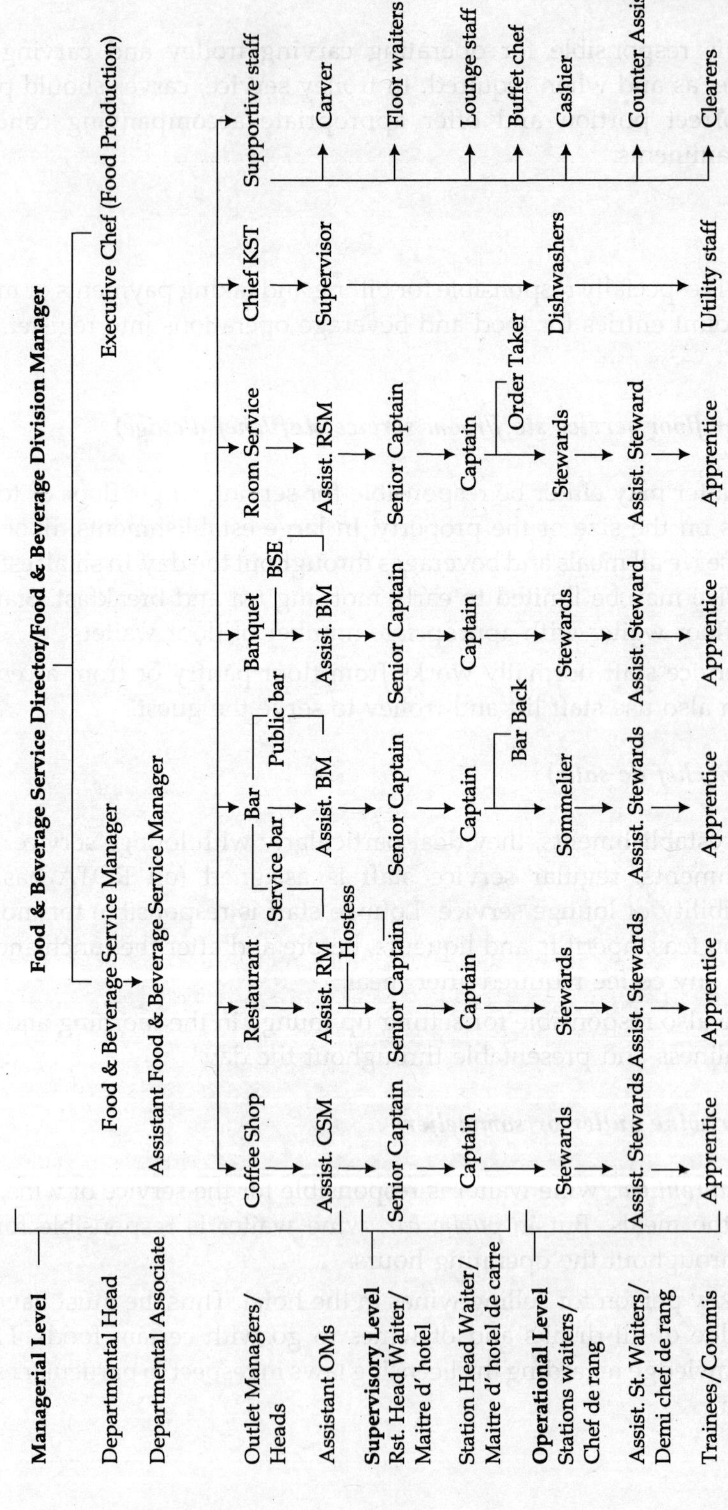
Managerial Level
Departmental Head
Departmental Associate
Outlet Managers/ Heads
Assistant OMs
Supervisory Level
Rst. Head Waiter/ Maitre d' hotel
Station Head Waiter/ Maitre d' hotel de carre
Operational Level
Stations waiters/ Chef de rang
Assist. St. Waiters/ Demi chef de rang
Trainees/Commis
Food & Beverage Service Director/Food & Beverage Division Manager
Food & Beverage Service Manager
Assistant Food & Beverage Service Manager
Executive Chef (Food Production)
Coffee Shop
Restaurant
Bar
Banquet
Room Service
Chief KST
Supportive staff
Service bar
Public bar
BSE
Assist. CSM
Assist. RM
Hostess
Assist. BM
Assist. BM
Assist. RSM
Supervisor
Senior Captain
Senior Captain
Senior Captain
Senior Captain
Senior Captain
Captain
Captain
Captain
Captain
Captain
Bar Back
Order Taker
Dishwashers
Stewards
Stewards
Sommelier
Stewards
Stewards
Assist. Stewards
Assist. Stewards
Assist. Stewards
Assist. Steward
Assist. Steward
Apprentice
Apprentice
Apprentice
Apprentice
Apprentice
Utility staff
Carver
Floor waiters
Lounge staff
Buffet chef
Cashier
Counter Assist.
Clearers

Cocktail bar staff

✓ They are responsible for making cocktails and serve them. Thus, thorough knowledge of all alcoholic and non-alcoholic drinks, their ingredients, method of making, licensing laws, etc., is necessary for the cocktail bar staff.

Buffet chef (or buffet assistant/chef de buffet)

✓ He/she is in-charge of buffet, its preparation and presentation, carving and portioning of food (optional). He/she is normally a member of kitchen brigade.

Counter assistant and table clearers

✓ *Counter assistants* are mostly found in cafeterias. They stock the counter and sometimes serve or portion food for the customer. Sometimes, they may also cook to call order items.

✓ The *table clearers* are usually found in seating areas. Clearers are responsible for clearing tables thereafter stacking washed crockery, glassware, cutlery, etc., at the designated place.

Function catering (or banqueting staff)

✓ In function catering only certain number of permanent staff is required like, banquet manager, assistant banquet manager, banquet sales executive, 1 or 2 banquet headwaiters and a dispense person. Remaining operating staff is usually engaged on a casual basis.

✓ Manager, assistant manager and headwaiter would undertake the necessary administrative and organizational work whereas operating staff is required to perform all operational works like serving of meals and drinks.

ATTRIBUTES

The term *attribute* indicates the personality traits of every individual employee. It is concerned with the quality of food and beverage service staff; it also reflects the quality of the establishment. If staff is well trained and efficient, they can, to a certain extent, make up for other shortcomings in the service provided. Up to some extent, serving and dining etiquettes are a fraction of attributes. These attributes are further classified as *work oriented* and *corporeal attributes*:

Work Oriented Attributes

It means the qualities, protocol and modus operandi which food and beverage service staff must possess while performing their duties and responsibilities. Few major work oriented attributes are as follows:

Punctuality

✓ The staff members should come and report to the concerned authority at right time or a few minutes before the starting of their shift operation.

Discipline

✓ All staff members must follow discipline/ code of conduct/laid rules and regulations of the organization, simultaneously ensure that subordinates must also follow it.

Sales ability

✓ The staff members must have good sales ability, i.e., up-selling ability as well as suggestive selling ability.

Knowledge

✓ The staff members must have complete knowledge of menu items, i.e., meals, their ingredients and preparation methods; beverage/cocktails, their ingredients and preparation methods; menu prices; prevailing beverage laws; local area knowledge and so forth.

Additional Attributes

- Appreciative
- Sense of urgency
- Committed
- Cooperative
- Positive attitude
- Empathy
- Flexible
- Helpful
- Honest
- Informative
- Innovative
- Observant
- Passionate
- Persuasive
- Professional
- Sense of humour
- Tactful
- Reliable
- Polite
- Presentable

Sharp memory

✓ The staff members must have sharp memory. They should remember names of offered menu items, their ingredients, price and who ordered what.

Diplomacy

✓ The staff members, especially managerial and supervisory level staff must have art of dealing with people (staff as well as customers) in a sensitive, professional and effective manner.

Loyal

✓ The staff members must be trustworthy for their organization. They should not adopt any wrong practice to earn money as well as not give opportunity to others (to staff or customers).

Problem solver

✓ Staff members should listen carefully to guest's complaints and take it as an opportunity to improve the quality of service and their sales skills and abilities.

Confident

✓ All staff members must be self-assured or full of confidence but this confidence should not be either over as well as under because both are harmful for an individual as well as for the organization.

Coordinator

✓ All the staff members must support and work in close coordination with each other so that excellent service can be offered to the patrons.

Others

✓ Attributes include motivation, positive attitude, decision making skills, interpersonal skills, conceptual skills, soft skills and other operational and managerial skills and abilities (in accordance to the level of employee's job position). Apart from these, one may also include lot of additional work oriented attributes.

Corporeal Attributes

The term *corporeal attributes* indicates to an individual employee's physical manifestation. It means how serving staff look and the first impression they create on others. All food and beverage service staff should be aware of their individual responsibilities to ensure that they are put into practice:

Daily bath

✓ All staff members should take bath/shower daily before coming on duty, so that they feel fresh while working in the shift.

Clean uniform

✓ Uniform should be neat, clean and well ironed. Badges should be on the left-hand side above the pocket, displayed eminently.

WAITER'S KIT

- Serviette
- Matchbox/ Lighter
- Writing pad/ KOT/BOT
- Wine opener
- Tic-toc pen
- Change money

Comb hair

✓ Men should have hair above ear level and women must tie their hair with French plait. Hair should be neatly combed and no sign of dandruff falling from the hair.

Shave daily

✓ Like daily bath, men should also shave (with no sign of stubble) on daily basis before coming on duty. For people who have beard as part of their religion, should wear a net over it.

Wear limited or no jewellery

✓ Wear minimum of jewellery while on duty. Women can wear ear rings and bangles. In many establishments, wedding ring is also allowed.

Ample sleep

✓ All staff members must take ample sleep because food service industry requires more labour intensive work (or standing work). Simultaneously, it usually does not offer or offer limited chair-around work.

Brush teeth

✓ All staff members should brush their teeth before coming on duty. Smokers must gargle and use mouth freshener before coming on the duty.

Simple shoes

✓ All staff members must wear simple, comfortable; rubber soul based footwear–Oxford style shoes are always preferable. Women should not wear high heel footwear.

Hands

✓ Do not touch food with bare hands; always wear gloves before handling food. Nails should be neatly trimmed, cut square and close. Regularly do dirt under fingernails. No nicotine, carbon, ink stains should be on the hand/palm.

Others

✓ It includes cut short nails, short side-locks, wear simple wrist watch, button-up shirt, properly tucked shirt, do not use too strong body odour, cover burns and scalds and so forth.

Serving and Dining Etiquettes	
Serving Etiquettes	**Dining Etiquettes**
• Serve food from correct side–if space allows	• Excuse yourself when requires to leave
• Do not disturb your guest/excuse yourself before serving	• Eat at leisure pace or speed
• Assists in seating and standing by pulling/pushing the chair	• Do not overfill your mouth while eating
• Always follow courtesy rules	• Do not talk while eating
• Do not delay in service	• Do not clatter or play with cutlery
• Do not pour food over the table or guest	• Follow courtesy rules
• Use correct equipment	• Handle knife with the right and fork with the left hand
• Never allot wrong table to the guest	• Use napkin to wipe the mouth and finger

KEY TERMS

Station : A specific part/section/segment of restaurant served from one side station.

ROTA : Duty allotment system in a cyclic pattern.

Attribute : Work oriented and personality traits of every individual employee.

Chef d'etage : Floor serving staff

Chef de salle : Lounge serving staff

Waiter's kit : Waiter's essentials while working

Sommelier : Wine steward or wine butler

Apprentice : Trainee

Briefing : A meeting session conducted before the starting of operation

Maitre d' hotel de carre : Section supervisor/station supervisor

REVIEW QUESTIONS

1. Describe the significance of departmentalization.
2. Enlist the work oriented attributes of food and beverage serving staff.
3. Write a short note on serving and dining etiquettes.
4. What are the duties and responsibilities of a restaurant station head waiter.

Food and Beverage Service Equipment

OBJECTIVES

Students will be able to:

- identify standard service equipment along with ideal size/shape/capacity or other specifications;
- recognize glassware, hollowware and other service equipment; and
- understand the process of care, cleaning and maintenance of equipment.

FOOD AND BEVERAGE SERVICE EQUIPMENT

There are varieties of equipment required in different outlets of food and beverage establishment but up to some extent all these equipment are same (although may with different pattern) in majority of outlets like spoons, forks, knives, plates, cups, saucers, chafing dishes, soup tureens, etc.

All these food and beverage service equipment can be broadly classified on different basis, for instance, on the basis of size and operating mode. In term of equipment size, it includes small vs large equipment such as cutlery, crockery, glassware, hollowware, etc., are a few examples of small equipment whereas trolleys, furniture (like chairs, tables and side stations), bar counter, etc., are examples of large equipment.

Similarly, ice cube making machine, blender, bain-marie, hot plate, commercial bread toaster, etc., are perfect examples of manual equipment whereas vending machines, property management system, dish washing machine, etc., are some examples of mechanical equipment. A broad classification with brief description of major food and beverage service equipment is given below.

Silverware

May be stainless steel or electroplated nickel silver (EPNS). It comprises 18% chromium and 08% nickel. It is a collective term for all EPNS cutlery and flatware. The word *cutlery* denotes all forms of knives and other cutting equipment. On the other side, *flatware* denotes all forms of spoons and knives.

Crockery (it can be bone china, earthenware, stoneware or porcelain)

✓ Crockery is also called *chinaware*. It is made up of silica, soda ash, china clay and dry glazed to give it a fine finish. It is available in different designs, colours, strengths and patterns. It mostly comprises plates, bowls and cups.

Glassware (can be soda lime, lead crystal, borosilicate or toughened)

✓ *Glassware* is a collective term for all assortments of glasses from non-alcoholic beverages to alcoholic beverages. These are available in four different forms, i.e., stem based, goblet, tumbler and mug style.

Hollowware

✓ The term hollowware indicates all forms of deepware (or deep vessels) that have some depth and volume. It can be made up of ceramic material as well as of EPNS (or SS). Hollowware is mainly used for serving dishes and beverages, such as entrée dish, serving bowls, tea pot, sugar pot and so forth.

Napkin Folds

- Bishop mâitre
- Cone shape
- Pyramid fold
- Rosette fold
- Lily fold
- Cock's comb

Linen (it can be Damask, cotton or denim)

✓ Linen means cloths, often the term *napery* is also used for linen. Actually, napery denotes table linen, particularly napkins. Linens come in a wide range and are made of different fabric materials. The restaurant linens are wiping cloth, dusters, napkins, tablecloth, slipcloth, etc.).

Furniture

✓ The structure of any equipment made of any kind of wood is called *furniture*. The restaurant furniture comprises table, chair, sideboard, cash counter or anything which is made up of wooden.

Special

✓ The term *special equipment* is used for all those silver and ceramic tableware that mainly accompany special dishes, such as snail set with snail preparation, fondue set with fondue dishes and so forth. Remember, the tableware comprises cover appointments and centre appointments.

Light (in balanced combination of natural and artificial light)

✓ The term *light* indicates to illumination that must match and support the interior décor. There are two sources of lighting, i.e., natural and artificial, and both must be in proper balance. Because natural light saves a lot of energy cost whereas artificial light is obligatory. Artificial light is available in two forms, i.e., incandescent and fluorescent. Ideally, these must be in the ratio of 30:70.

Trolleys (often found in function catering)

✓ Trolley is a kind of sideboard but with wheels. In French, it is called "cart or service cart". Various types of food and beverage provisions are delivered to guests from it. It ranges from mobile display cabinet to live cooking trolley. For example, soup, salad, pastry and Guéridon trolley. Salesmanship and showmanship are two basic essential attributes required in trolley service.

Technology (an appropriate provision to generate and maintain databank and to control misconduct)

✓ The term *technology* is used for available and upcoming software programs and hardware instruments. EPOS units, PMS, F&BMS and so forth are excellent examples of software whereas ESP (electronic server pad) is an excellent example of hardware.

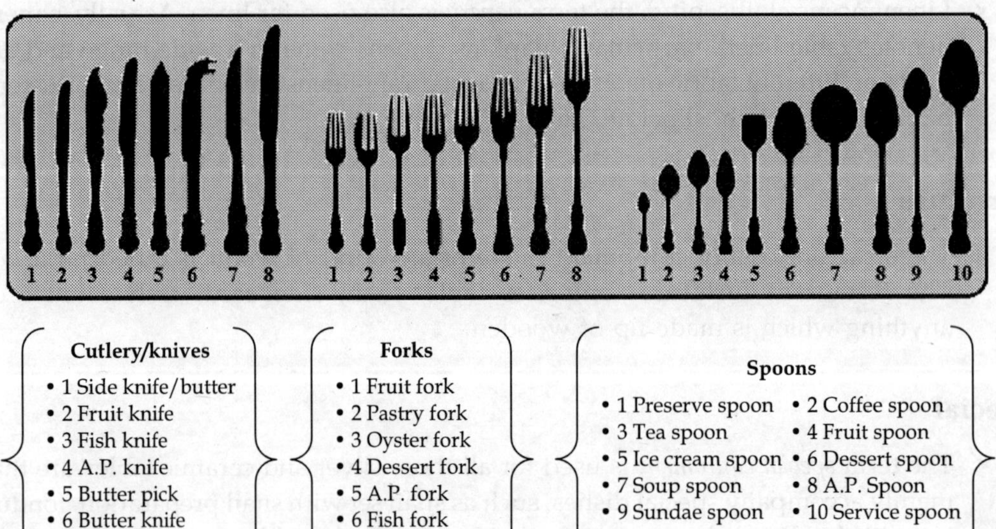

Cutlery/knives

- 1 Side knife/butter
- 2 Fruit knife
- 3 Fish knife
- 4 A.P. knife
- 5 Butter pick
- 6 Butter knife
- 7 Steak knife
- 8 Joint knife

Forks

- 1 Fruit fork
- 2 Pastry fork
- 3 Oyster fork
- 4 Dessert fork
- 5 A.P. fork
- 6 Fish fork
- 7 Joint fork
- 8 Service fork

Spoons

- 1 Preserve spoon
- 2 Coffee spoon
- 3 Tea spoon
- 4 Fruit spoon
- 5 Ice cream spoon
- 6 Dessert spoon
- 7 Soup spoon
- 8 A.P. Spoon
- 9 Sundae spoon
- 10 Service spoon

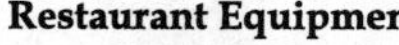

Restaurant Equipment

- Silverware
  - **Cutlery**
    - *Knives*
      - Fish
      - Joint
      - Side
      - Caviar
      - Steak
      - Fruit
  - **Flatware**
    - *Forks*
      - Fish
      - Joint
      - Dessert
      - Oyster
      - Fruit
      - Pastry
      - Service
      - Snail
      - Lobster
    - *Spoons*
      - Dessert
      - Tea/coffee
      - Preserve
      - Soup
      - Ice cream
      - Sundae
      - Service
      - Fruit
- Crockery
  - **Plates** (In D. inches)
    - Joint (12)
    - Full (10)
    - Half (08)
    - Side (06)
    - Base (10)
    - Saucer (04)
    - Soup (08)
    - Cereal (08)
  - **Cups** (fl. oz)
    - Tea (06)
    - Coffee (03)
    - Soup (08)
  - **Bowls**
    - Monkey
    - Cereal
    - Soup
- Glassware
  - **Beer** (in fl. oz)
    - Goblet (12-14)
    - Pilsner (10-12)
    - Mug (14-16)
    - Tanker (14-16)
  - **Wine** (06-08 fl. oz)
    - Red
    - White
    - Sherry
  - **Champagne** (06-08 fl. oz)
    - Flute
    - Tulip
    - Saucer (or bird bath)
  - Water (08-10 fl. oz)
    - Goblet
    - Tumbler
  - Others glasses (In fl. oz)
    - Martini —— (06-08)
    - Roly-poly —— (08-10)
    - Margarita —— (06-08)
    - Old-fashion —— (08-10)
    - Brandy —— (08-10)
    - Tequila —— (01-02)
    - Liquer —— (01-02)
    - Sundae -
    - Parfait —— (10-12)
    - Collin —— (10-12)
    - Pony —— (04-06)
- Hollowware
  - **Pots**
    - Milk
    - Coffee
    - Tea
  - **Bowls**
    - Portion
    - Sugar
    - Finger
  - **Others**
    - Creamer
    - Entrée
    - Jug
    - Sauce boat
- Linen & furniture
  - **Linen/Cloth**
    - Slip (03 ft. × 03 ft.)
    - Runner
    - Napkin (18-20 in sq.)
    - Buffet (06 ft. × 12 ft)
    - Waiters
    - Wiping
    - Placemat (10 in × 15 in)
    - Frill
    - Tea cozy (D shape)
    - Tray mats (As per tray)
    - Baize (Pre-fitted)
    - Table (Given later)
  - **Furniture**
    - Table (Given below)
      - Square
      - Round
      - Rectangular
    - Chairs (18 × 18 × 18 in)
    - Sideboard (30 × 66 × 18 in)
    - Counter
- Special
  - **Snail**
    - Dish
    - Tong
  - **Cracker**
    - Lobster
    - Nut
  - **Tong**
    - Pastry
    - Sandwich
    - Spaghetti
    - Asparagus
    - Ice
  - Others
    - Egg slicer
    - Skewer
    - Corn on the cob
    - Au gratin
    - Cocotte
    - Butter dish
    - Gourmet spoon
    - Grape fruit spoon
    - Grape scissor
    - Marmite
    - Cassolette
    - Terrine
    - Cloche
    - Soup tureen
    - Gateaux slicer
    - Ice cream scoop
    - Sauce ladle
    - Stilton scoop
- Light
  - **Natural**
    - Sunlight
  - **Artificial**
    - *Incandescent* (30%)
      - Bulb
      - Focus light
      - Flash light
    - *Fluorescent* (70%)
      - Tube light
      - CFL
      - LED
- Trolleys & other tools
  - **Trolleys**
    - Flambé
    - Carving
    - Guéridon
    - Dessert
    - Fruit
    - Room service
    - Appetizer
    - Bussing
    - Soup
    - Cheese
    - Wagon
    - Wine
    - Pastry
    - Liqueur
    - Snack
    - Liqueur
    - Salad
  - **Other tools**
    - Ash tray
    - Bud vase
    - Cruet set
    - Fruit stand
    - Salver
    - Tray
    - Candle stand
    - Table No.
    - Ice bucket (with stand)
    - Carving fork
    - Carving knife
- Technology
  - **Software**
    - F&BMS
    - PMS
  - **Hardware**
    - ESP
    - POS
    - ECR

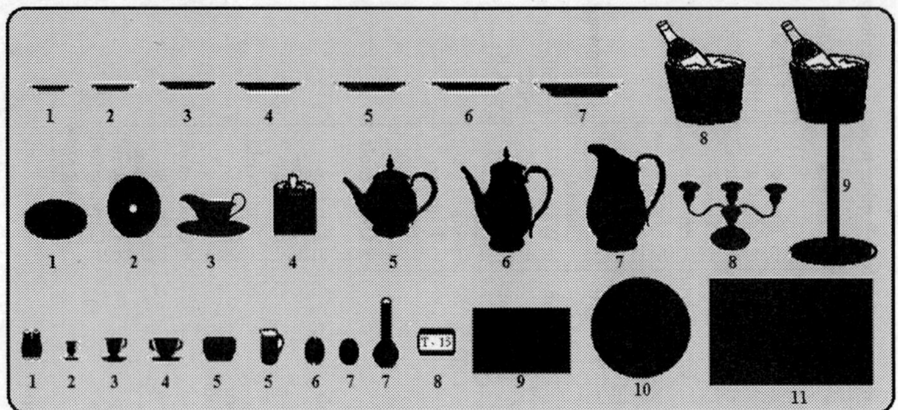

Row 1: Plates

- 1 Saucer
- 2 Side/cheese/ B&B/Quarter
- 3 Half plate
- 4 Fish plate
- 5 Dessert plate
- 6 Full plate
- 7 Joint plate
- 8 Ice bucket
- 9 Ice bucket with stand

Row: 2

- 1 Entrée dish
- 2 Portion bowl
- 3 Gravy boat
- 4 Sugar bowl/basin
- 5 Coffee pot
- 6 Tea pot
- 7 Water pitcher/Jug
- 8 Candle stand

Row: 3

- 1 Cruet set
- 2 Coffee/espresso cup
- 3 Consommé/soup cup
- 4 Soup bowl
- 5 Milk pot
- 6 Ashtray
- 7 Bud vase
- 8 Table number
- 9 Tea tray
- 10 Salvey
- 11 Full tray

Glassware

- 1 Beer mug
- 2 Beer goblet
- 3 Brandy ballon/sniffer
- 4 Champagne flute
- 5 Champagne saucer
- 6 Martini/cocktail
- 7 Water tumbler/high ball
- 8 Paris goblet
- 9 Margarita
- 10 Champagne tulip
- 11 Collin glass
- 12 Whiskey/old fashion
- 13 Parfait glass
- 14 Water goblet
- 15 Rolly polly
- 16 Pilsner
- 17 Slim jim glass
- 18 Irish coffee mug
- 19 Mason jar
- 20 Sundae glass
- 21 Juice/pony glass
- 22 Pool glass
- 23 Decanter
- 24 Pousse cafe
- 25 Red wine glass
- 26 Sherry glass
- 27 Tequila shot
- 28 White wine glass

Special Equipment

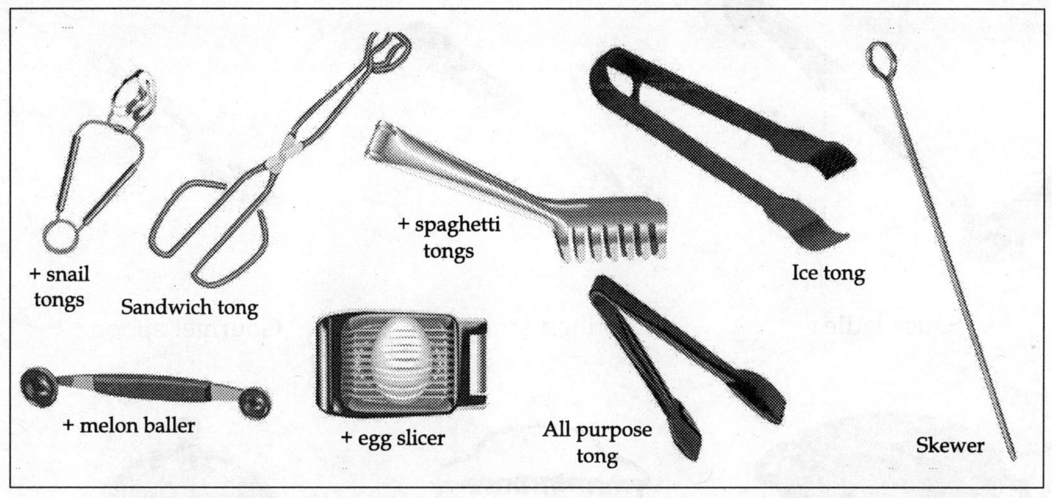

Courtesy: www.visualdictionaryonline.com

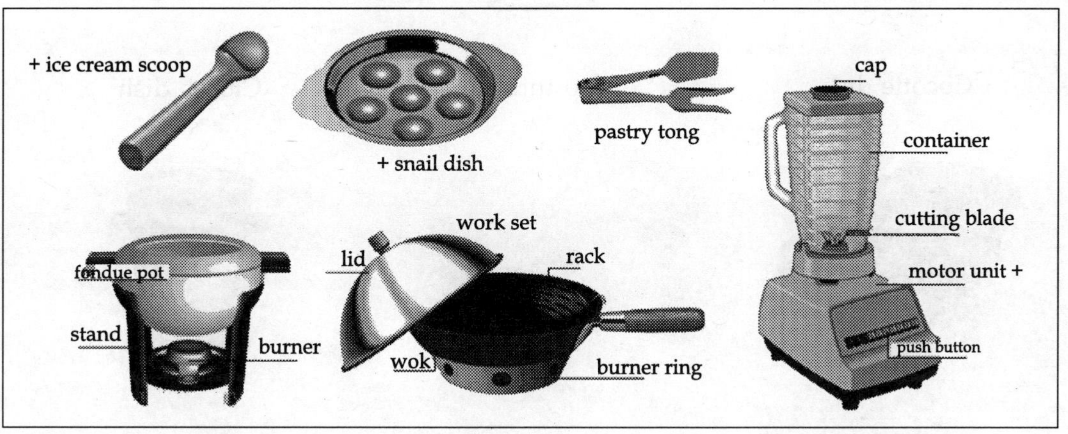

Courtesy: www.visualdictionaryonline.com

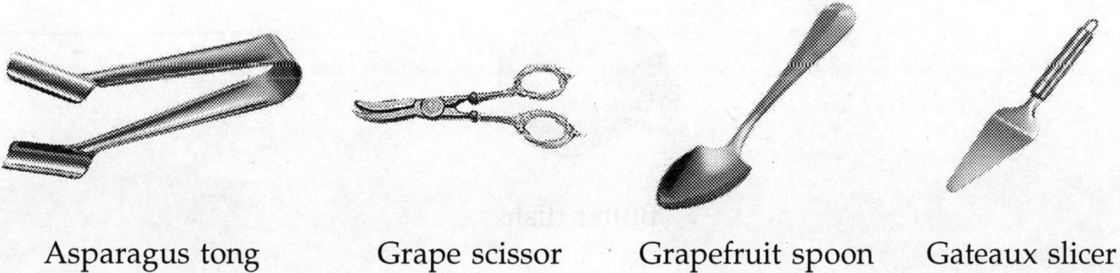

Asparagus tong Grape scissor Grapefruit spoon Gateaux slicer

Sauce ladle

Stilton scoop

Gourmet spoon

Cocotte dish

Soup turqeen

Cloche dish

Terrine dish

Salad bowl

Marmite dish

Butter dish

Table Style	Size, Description and Use		
	Table Size	Linen Size	Number of persons
Square table	28 inches × 28 inches	54 inches × 54 inches	For two people
	36 inches × 36 inches to 40 inches × 40 inches	62 inches × 62 inches or 64 inches × 64 inches	For four persons
	48 inches × 48 inches to 52 inches × 52 inches	72 inches × 72 inches or 74 inches × 74 inches	For six persons
Round table	36 inches in diameter	64 inches in diameter	For two people
	60 inches in diameter to 66 inches in diameter	81 inches in diameter to 84 inches in diameter	For four persons
	72 inches in diameter to 76 inches in diameter	90 inches in diameter to 94 inches in diameter	For six persons
Rectangular table	30 inches × 48 inches	54 inches × 72 inches	For two persons
	30 inches × 72 inches	54 inches × 96 inches	For four persons
	40 inches × 72 inches	64 inches × 96 inches	For six persons
	40 inches × 96 inches	64 inches × 120 inches	For eight persons
Sideboard	Size & design →	Varied	
	No. of section →	• Six or more slots (for soup spoon, AP spoon, AP knife, AP fork, service spoon, service fork and so forth) side by side. • Two big racks for keeping tablecloths and napkins. • Two or more big sections for keeping chinaware.	
	Height →	32 – 34 inches in height whereas length × width is 1.5 × 4.5 ft	
Chair	Chair seat height →	18 inches from the ground.	
	Chair back side height →	39 inches from ground to back side top.	
	Chair seat dimension →	18 inches in square	

CARE AND MAINTENANCE OF EQUIPMENT

Towards the end of every shift, it is crucial that all service items and equipment are left spotlessly clean. Although your workplace will have its own procedures, but yet there are some elementary rules for the cleaning of service items, these are:

Furniture

✓ Furniture is an expensive equipment as well as difficult to acquire the same or similar furniture in future. Thus, the following cleaning activities are important to consider:

- All chairs, tables and side stations should be dusted daily.
- Perform regular repair and maintenance work as well as *special cleaning* (like polishing of furniture).
- Properly stack and stock the furniture in the back area.
- Do not clean the wooden furniture with water.

Fixtures and Fitting

✓ The *fixture* and *fitting* are wall mounting appliances and decorative pieces, for instances, wall scones, wall frames, paintings and so forth. Often these are expensive, therefore their regular care and maintenance is vital. Major care and maintenance activities include the following:

- Do the dusting of all lights on regular basis, especially of guest seen (or guest seating area) areas like restaurant, guest rooms, corridors, lobbies and so forth.
- If lights, air conditioning, etc., are not working properly, immediately report to engineering and maintenance department.
- If there is any type of fault in the wiring cable like – short circuit, loose wiring, etc., immediately report to concerned department.
- Do the deep cleaning of air-conditioning and other fixtures regularly.

Chinaware

✓ The chinaware (also known as *crockery*) is the most expensive equipment of every food serving outlet; simultaneously highly breakable in nature. Thus, proper care and maintenance is also crucial. Precautions involve the following:

- Handle chinaware cautiously to avoid damage. Never stack or keep side plate (or *cheese plate*) on full plate followed by half plate or vice versa. Stack similar items together.
- Do not stack plates, saucers, cups or bowls too high.
- When filling dishwasher trays, stack items correctly so that they do not vibrate together, as this may cause damage.

- Check cleanliness of cups (like *demitasse*). Observe for tea or coffee stains at the bottom of the cup or lipstick stains on the rim of cups or bowls.
- Be careful when unloading hot rinsed crockery directly from the dishwasher onto a cold work surface. As sudden changes in temperature may cause crockery to crack.

Cutlery and Flatware

✓ The stainless steel and silver plated cutlery should look shiny and bright. If smears remain after washing, dip cutlery into very hot water (you may also add vinegar or lemon drops) and then polish with a clean and dry cloth. Clean silver cutlery according to the manufacturer's instructions and your workplace policy.

✓ EPNS (electroplated nickel silver) cutlery should be regularly polished with appropriate agents like pink powder, polivit, silver dip, etc., thereafter wash before using and placing on the cover.

Glassware

✓ All arrays of *glasses* should be handled carefully. If any glassware is chipped or cracked, it must be discarded. Care and maintenance of glassware involves the following activities:

- Reduce stress to the glasses, never overload them in dishwashing racks and never use glasses to scoop ice or to store or to carry cutlery in it. After the completion of glassware polishing, make sure to carry them by their stem.
- Glasses should not be stacked in each other. If they get stacked, place the outer one in warm water. It will expand and the inner one can be easily removed. Alternately, place ice blocks in the inner one to separate them.
- Do not put cold glass into hot water. As sudden temperature change can cause cracking of glassware. Never place glasses upside down or downside up in salver; always keep heavy pedestal of glass on salver.

Table Linen

✓ *Table linen* is of immense importance because it is an imperative component of internal décor of an outlet as well as makes the table attractive. Table linen generally belongs to a multipurpose product category.

✓ The utility of table linen varies from storing, decoration to cleaning. Table linen does not require intensive care; however, certain things (some of them mentioned below) need to be kept in mind to ensure their longevity.

- Follow the washing or dry cleaning instruction given by the manufacturer.
- Wash the table linen frequently.
- Do not store wet linen to prevent fungal/bacterial growth.
- Linen should be stored in a cool and dry place.

- Linen should be ironed, folded and neatly piled to retain their original shape.
- Avoid storing linen in plastic bags or directly on cardboards.
- Bleach (when required) linen to retain their 'new look'.

Trolleys

✓ Many considerations are kept in mind while providing any type of trolley service in any food and beverage organization It demands adequate space to move, skilled staff to prepare food in front of the guest, guest must have sufficient time to consume the meal and so forth.

✓ Trolleys also require daily dusting, scheduled deep cleaning, occasionally wheel greasing (or oiling). Some points in relation to care and maintenance of trolleys are as follows:

- Clean the trolley thoroughly.
- Check wheels are properly working or not.
- Stock only adequate number of equipment and supplies.
- Perform *deep cleaning* of trolley at scheduled intervals.
- Use trolley for designated purpose only.

CLEANING AND POLISHING OF EPNS

Burnishing method

✓ This method is mostly suitable for cutlery and other small articles of silver. The machine is equipped with a revolving drum half filled with ball bearings. The machine is lined with rubber so it does not damage or scratch the silverware.

✓ The cleaning agent must be used in accordance with manufacturer's instructions (generally a special powder of *refined soda* with hot water is preferred).

Polivit Method

✓ This method is used to clean large or heavy pieces of silverware. It consists of aluminium sheet with holes. Remember, utensils placed on aluminium sheet must be completely submerged in boiling water containing washing soda.

✓ The reaction of soda with aluminium removes the stains from the silverware. After this, the silverware is rinsed with fresh water.

Plate Powder Method

✓ It is an excellent method of dishwashing because it removes all types of grease spots and stains from the surface of utensils. However, it is a time consuming method.

- ✓ This method is mainly used when cutlery cannot be washed with the above-mentioned methods. All archetypal food and beverage items (like sauceboat, toast rack, etc.) are washed by this method.

Silver Dip Method

- ✓ This method is similar to plate powder method but in this method silver utensils are dipped in a pink liquid solution (solution usually made with Goddard's) instead of cleaning with dry pink powder.
- ✓ The cutlery is placed in the wire basket and then immerse this wire basket into pink liquid solution (for a few minutes). Afterwards drain and rinse cutlery into warm water and finally polish with wiping cloth.

Other Methods

- ✓ There are many other methods of cleaning cutlery, crockery and glassware. For instance, clean with appropriate detergent powder/soaps like Vim Bar, Bartan Bar liquid cleaners.

KEY TERMS

EPNS	:	Electroplated nickel silver
Goddard's	:	Pink liquid solution (or brand) used to clean silverware
Polivit	:	Polishing method for silver/EPNS utensils
Napery	:	Table linen, particularly napkins.
Bird bath	:	Champagne saucer glass
Flatware	:	All types of forks whereas *cutlery* specify to all cutting equipment including spoon
Cheese plate	:	Six inches side plate also known as quarter plate, or bread and butter plate
Demitasse	:	Three fl oz coffee cup, mainly used to serve espresso coffee.
Baize cloth	:	Silencer cloth that lays on the tabletop for protecting tabletop as well as tablecloth.

REVIEW QUESTIONS

1. Enlist any 20 glasses and write their capacity (in fl. oz) and their use.
2. Differentiate among cutlery, flatware, hollowware, chinaware and glassware.
3. Explain how care and maintenance of equipment is financially profitable for any outlet.
4. Briefly explain major silver/EPNS polishing methods.

Food and Beverage Department Coordination

Objectives

Students will be able to:

- explain the importance of coordination among all hotel departments;
- realize the importance of interrelationship of each department;
- explain the areas (or points) of coordination with other departments; and
- understand the importance of ancillary departments of food and beverage.

COORDINATION

Food and beverage service department is the foremost area of every residential hotel establishment which is predominantly responsible for serving meals and beverages to resident as well as non-resident guests, chiefly in general serving outlets and guest rooms.

Food and beverage service department requires close coordination with food production department because functions of both are unified and inter-reliant on each other. Similarly, food and beverage department acquires information from the front office to ascertain to whom meals and beverages can be offered by means of *charge privilege* provision (or on credit) thereafter transfer their signed bills to their respective room accounts (at front desk cashier). The role of coordination can also be identified here.

A hotel has many departments which may be classified as major, supportive, ancillary and internal sales outlets. The activities of these outlets and departments are intimately allied to each other and if one link is conked out then the entire hotel operation cycle collapses. Hence, coordination is imperative among all these internal outlets and departments.

Remember, the fundamental objective of the management is to assign work, organize people and resources to achieve the stated organizational goals. And it is extremely intricate to achieve these goals without cooperation and coordination of the staff. Employees from every level of management play a crucial role in managing this coordination and cooperation. Coordination is not only significant among employees but also among all interrelated as well as intrarelated departments and sections. An epigrammatic explanation of coordination among all these interrelated and intrarelated departments/sections is given below.

INTERDEPARTMENTAL COORDINATION

All departments of a hotel are so closely interlinked that none can do without the other. Therefore, it becomes imperative for everybody to understand what communication exists among these departments so that they may practise the same in their work experience. Coordination, as the word says, *"it is a process whereby work which has been subdivided is brought together and pre-unified into specific tasks or objectives"*. The need for coordination and synchronization of the work of individuals is one of the most important managerial activities. This is not a periodic activity, it is an ongoing process. If coordination is not achieved timely and appropriately then it will lead to guest dissatisfaction. Consequently, it will reflect in the form of loss of business/revenue, concurrently damage the reputation of organization too. Let us look into this area keeping in view the food and beverage department as the central focal point. Below the coordination of food and beverage service department with its relevant sections and other major departments is explained briefly.

Coordination of Food and Beverage Department with Other Major Departments

Coordination with food production

- ✓ In comparison to other major departments, food production department requires working in close association with food and beverage service department due to the interdependency or interrelated work of each other.
- ✓ Food production department relies on food and beverage service department with the intention to know numerous important information to prepare its routine meal planning and especially during banqueting functions.
- ✓ Generally, executive chef, sous chef, food and beverage manager and restaurant manager are responsible for developing the menu, hence lack of coordination may lead to a dangerous situation.
- ✓ The various outlets of food and beverage department must solidly be backed up with kitchen department for the production of food and their accompaniments. Staff of both the departments have to coordinate at different stages of interactions like receiving and placing food orders, dispatching of food orders and so on.

Coordination with front office

- ✓ All outlets of food and beverage department receive information regarding arrivals and expected departure dates of guests from the front office department. With the help of this information, food and beverage staff knows whether the guests are resident guests or walk-ins in the various outlets.
- ✓ All food and beverage bills of resident guests are needed to be sent (when not settled in cash) to the cashier at the front office for computing the *grand master bill* for the guest.

- ✓ Any outside reservation for dining in the food and beverage outlet are routed by the front office personnel to the respective outlets. Front office also provides information (via generating voucher) to room service, regarding placement of complementary item into guest rooms, like fruit basket, chocolate tray or champagne bottle.
- ✓ During group check-ins, front office assists the stewards in serving welcome drinks to GITs in hotel lobby.

Areas of Coordination

With Kitchen	
For…….	With……..
Cold starter	Garde manger
Hot starter	Hot kitchen
Soup	Soup kitchen
Milk shakes	Kitchen pantry
Fruit platters	Kitchen pantry
Roasted items	Tandoor
Hot dessert	Hot kitchen
Cold dessert	Cold kitchen
Tea/Coffee	Service pantry
Drinks	Service bar
With Front Office	
For……..	With……..
House count	Front desk
Room count	Front desk
Charge privilege	Cashier
Deferred payment	Cashier
Departure status	Front desk
Late payment	Cashier
With Housekeeping	
For……..	With……..
Flowers	Horticulture
Linens	Laundry
Cleaning	Control desk
Stitching	Sewing room
Uniform exchange	Uniform room
Linen exchange	Linen room

Coordination with housekeeping

- ✓ This department principally works in close coordination with the front office but also needs to coordinate with other departments especially food and beverage.
- ✓ This department plays a major role in keeping the various food and beverage outlets neat, hygienic and clean.
- ✓ Maintenance of furnishings and upholsteries, linen, electrical and electronic fixtures is normally the responsibility of housekeeping department.
- ✓ Staffs of both departments have to coordinate to maintain high standards of professional upkeep and maintain accurate room status chart/information. This room status information affects the total revenue of the hotel.

COORDINATION OF FOOD AND BEVERAGE DEPARTMENT WITH SUPPORTIVE DEPARTMENTS

Human Resource

- ✓ Food and beverage department assists human resource department in developing *job description* and *job specification* of every level job position. It provides information like, required qualification, experience, technical proficiency in relation to the job. And on the basis of this information human resource department proceeds with the recruitment.
- ✓ Coordination is also required during the interview, selection, training and placement of the selected employees. Food and beverage department also assists in conducting performance appraisal of employees.
- ✓ Coordination is also required between these two departments in order to deal with employees benefit program and monitor compliance with laws related to equal opportunity in hiring and promotion.

Engineering and Maintenance

- ✓ Food and beverage department requires coordinating with the engineering and maintenance department for the purpose of regular, preventive and breakdown maintenance work.
- ✓ Engineering and maintenance department provides relevant services such as repair to electronic appliances (if not working properly), *on* and *off* to restaurant music, regularly check and replace restaurant lights, especially during buffet setup. It assists buffet staff in making attractive buffet arrangement by fitting lights as demanded by the serving staff.
- ✓ During pool side party or in-lawn party, maintenance department again plays a central role with food and beverage department by arranging lights and fitting of electronic equipment at desired places and style.

Purchase Department

- ✓ Whenever food and beverage department requires anything from outside the hotel (often in large banqueting functions), it prepares a *requisition sheet* (or purchase specification) for store department. And store department prepares *purchase order* (on the basis of requisition sheet) for purchase department in order to purchase requisitioned items.
- ✓ It is the duty of purchase department to obtain the required things from market as per the given *specifications*. Thus, if there is no proper coordination between these two departments, purchase process will not be effectively fulfilled which will ultimately affect the entire hotel in the form of revenue loss and guest dissatisfaction.

Marketing and Sales

- ✓ Banquet sales executive works in close coordination with marketing department to facilitate banquet sale. Food and beverage department informs the marketing division regarding the restaurant and its menu, bar and its drinks, banquet and its pricing policy, banquet booking status, *happy hours* and so forth.
- ✓ On behalf of this information, marketing and sales department develops its marketing plan (for banquet sale, banquet menu sales) in order to attract potential market segment as well as regular customers.

Store Department

- ✓ Food and beverage department requires maintaining good relation with storekeeper as it receives all the required perishable (like jam, jelly, butter, honey, marmalade, etc.) and non-perishable (such as napkin, straws, coaster, matchbox, pen, writing pad, lighter, etc.) items from the storeroom.
- ✓ Food and beverage department prepares indent sheet/order and sends to store for obtaining the required items. This requisition sheet often supports in maintaining minimum-maximum stock level, reorder level, economic order quantity (EOQ) and updating bin card.
- ✓ Balance against their requirement is the need to keep the capital invested in stocks at a reasonable level. There is always a temptation to overstock against shortage, or to buy in large quantities to obtain a better price. Here, coordination plays a crucial role in maintaining minimum/maximum stock level.

Accounts

- ✓ Food and beverage department gives information about staff's *performance points* to accounts section, on the basis of which tips can be distributed in points and salary increments and other financial benefits (or rewards) are awarded to the employee. At the time of budget planning, food and beverage department requires the assistance of the accounts section.
- ✓ Cashiers of all food and beverage outlets deposit their daily collected cash, cheques, vouchers, etc. (along with *sales summary sheet*) to the head cashier (or may drop in *drop box* facility) then the head cashier prepares its report and sends/submits to the accounts section. Head cashier may also directly deposit the collected amount into organization's bank account.
- ✓ Both head cashier and accountant belong to the accounts department. Hence, one can say that the accounts office has the responsibility of overall financial management, thus coordination is paramount between account and food and beverage department.

Security Department

- ✓ Food and beverage department also requires coordination with the security department as it provides relevant information about the employee's attendance record and other necessary information such as any article captured during the staff checking process at time/security office.
- ✓ Security department assists the food and beverage department during any problem created by any resident or non-resident guests. It often involves dealing with drunken and misbehaving guests (if situation is out of control), guest creating problems with staff and other guests and so forth.

Points/Areas of Coordination	
Human resource	For acquiring skilled, qualified, experienced, talented and knowledgeable manpower.
Maintenance	For regular, preventive and break-down maintenance of outlet.
Purchase	For acquiring products in right quality, quantity, price and time.
Marketing	For generating business for banquets, restaurants, bar, coffee shops and so forth.
Storeroom	For receiving indented products regularly and as and when required (or in emergency).
Accounts	For maintaining and updating accounts in relation to salary/wages, meal charges and fringe benefits.
Security	For making property safe and secure, prevent theft and smuggling and employee in and out time entry.

INTRADEPARTMENTAL COORDINATION

The term *intradepartment* indicates to all sub-divisions of food and beverage division/ department. These subdivisions are often known as food and beverage outlets. Resembling to interdepartmental coordination, all these subdivisions must also have strong alliance among themselves, for instance coordination of IRD with bar (for obtaining beverage orders for in-room service). All these subdivisions require close coordination with ancillary sections as well (for supportive services like maintaining par stock, inventory restocking, to replenish condiments and other accompanying items, etc.) and kitchen stewarding, particularly with dishwashing area (to replenish clean serving utensils). Some of these outlets are mentioned below and their points/areas of coordination are briefly given in quick scroll box.

Room Service

✓ It is also known as in-room dining provision. Room service involves delivery of food and beverage items to guest rooms in any residential establishment.

Restaurant

✓ A food service establishment with a dining room for the general public where food can be purchased and consumed. Dozens of variations exist.

Bar (or *permit room*)

✓ Area within a hotel, motel or restaurant, or other place of business for which a liquor licence is required to serve alcohol, primarily by the glass to its customers. Commonly a counter (or bar) separates customers from the service personnel.

Barbecue

✓ It is also an outlet of food and beverage service department — usually popular in winters. This provision is offered in order to increase the revenue of the hotel. The food served here is barbecued over a direct fire.

Coffee Shop

✓ It is a type of restaurant where a limited range of meals are served along with an array of beverages, particularly, tea and coffee.

Banquet

✓ It is an outlet that caters food and beverage to a large gathering of people. This gathering can be for formal, semi-formal or informal functions.

Salon Bar

✓ It is an outlet that primarily serves alcoholic beverages in the lounge area. In simple terms, if bar is available in the lounge area and caters primarily to lounge guests then it is termed "lounge bar or salon bar".

Pantry

There can be two kinds of pantries in a hotel, i.e., *kitchen pantry* and *service pantry*. The former is a part of the kitchen department which is mainly responsible for providing the service of sandwiches, juices, milk shakes, etc., whereas *service pantry* or *restaurant pantry* works as still room and hot plate area for food and beverage supporting outlet, especially restaurants.

Points/Areas of Coordination	
Room service	For in-room dining and for placing in-room complementary items and their refilling.
Restaurant	For fine dining, booking restaurant table and transferring bills to respective room account.
Bar	For serving hard, mild and soft beverages at public bar as well as in restaurant bar.
Barbeque	For bonfire dining, in it vegetarian/non-vegetarian items are cooked over direct flame.
Coffee shop	For serving variety of tea/coffee and substantial meals round the clock.
Banquet	For arranging and organizing formal, semi-formal and informal banqueting functions.
Lounge bar	For serving beverages in lounge area.
Kitchen pantry	For serving running meals like shakes, fruit platters and sandwiches.

COORDINATION OF FOOD AND BEVERAGE DEPARTMENT WITH ANCILLARY DEPARTMENTS

The term *ancillary department* indicates to auxiliary or subsidiary departments which commonly work for all food and beverage outlets. These departments assist in serving meals and beverages to guests and providing endorsement for smooth running of outlets. Some major ancillary departments are given below along with their foremost work profile and points/areas of coordination.

Hot Plate (a meeting point between kitchen and serving employees)

- ✓ In small establishments, a *hot plate* is a specially designed heated table cabinet with a hot flat top, inside which a supply of hot plates, prepared meal orders, etc., can be kept. It forms an essential part of service equipment. In large food service establishments, there is a separate section for hot plate along with pick-up tables for meals.
- ✓ It is mainly a meeting point between the food and beverage service staff and food preparation staff. *Aboyeur*/barker/ announcer is the in-charge of this hot plate area.

Silver Room (a place for keeping and polishing SS/EPNS utensils)

- ✓ *Silver room* is also an essential section of the ancillary department as it has provision of keeping silvers as well as provision of cleaning and polishing of these utensils.

- ✓ In small establishments, it is often combined with wash-up area (or kitchen stewarding) or next to dishwashing, while in large establishments, it forms a separate place.

Pantry (responsible for serving running items)

- ✓ Generally, pantry is a part or section of food production department which works for restaurant or other outlets as well. It is a source for providing running items like sandwiches, fruit platters, juices, shakes, etc. Nowadays, restaurant pantry (or service pantry) is the area often found between the kitchen and restaurant (in large hotels) which works as a *still room*.
- ✓ Remember, restaurant pantry is different from kitchen pantry. *Restaurant pantry* is a part of ancillary division, alongside it following *ancillary sections* are situated – *hot plate* or *food pick up area*; place to keep soiled plates and glassware; place/box to keep soiled linens; place to keep clean plates and cups; a sink to wash small equipment such as glasses and cups; bar to serve IRD and so forth.

Still Room (a place to keep condiments, meal accompaniments, running meals and for serving tea/coffee)

- ✓ *Still room* is a place where tea, coffee and similar beverages are prepared. It also provides items like jam, jelly, honey, maple syrup, butter, cream, breakfast cereals, etc., which are not provided by any other section of hotel.
- ✓ Traditionally, the still room comes under the direct supervision of restaurant manager or maitre de hotel rather than chef-de-cuisine. Nowadays, many properties intermingle to both due to limited available space.

Linen Room

- ✓ Linen room (or also known as *spare linen room*) is important *back-of-the-house service area* in a hotel. This room is used to keep all types of service linen like tablecloth, napkins, naprons, tea cozy, slipcloth, tray mats, etc.
- ✓ The linen room should stock enough linen in order to facilitate the smooth running of the outlet. Regular linens (mainly tablecloth, napkin and slipcloth) are changed on daily basis (or as and when required) in restaurants and exchanged on the principle of *one-on-one basis* from the housekeeping department's linen room.

Storeroom

- ✓ It is an important area to keep all the required grocery items, stationery, dry goods, utensils, etc., of food and beverage service. This storeroom is a source to supply proprietary sauces, order pads, stationery items, bottle openers or any other supplies.

- ✓ In large establishments, they have separate stores like, food stores, beverage stores and perishable stores to keep items of different nature.

Plate Room

- ✓ Plate room and storeroom may be common as well as separate, depending on the size of organization and the available space.
- ✓ In both situations, this room is used for keeping tableware, especially crockery, hollowware and glassware. After polishing, silver utensils (like flatware and cutlery) are also placed in this room.

Kitchen Stewarding

- ✓ This department plays an important role in the smooth functioning of both food production and food and beverage service department. It is headed by a chief kitchen steward who reports to food and beverage manager.
- ✓ The main function of kitchen stewarding is to wash all cutlery, crockery, glassware, hollowware, etc., of the food and beverage outlet at dishwashing area, simultaneously kitchen equipment at pot washing area. It also looks towards the floor cleaning of kitchen department.
- ✓ Sometimes, kitchen stewarding also has to deal with keeping and maintaining the stock of food and beverage and kitchen department equipment.

Points/Areas of Coordination	
Hot plate	For placing cooked hot meal orders which afterwards are collected by food servers.
Silver room	For cleaning and polishing EPNS and other silver utensils
Service pantry	For serving running items like, milk shakes, fresh lime soda (sweet or salty), etc.
Still room	For supplementary items like, preserves, condiments and accompanying sauces.
Linen room	For obtaining/exchanging linens like, tablecloths, napkins, placemats, slipcloths, etc.
Plate room	For utensils back-up like, cutlery, crockery, glassware, hollowware, flatware after polishing.
Storeroom	For back-up of grocery, accompaniments, soft beverages, juices, preserves and dry goods.
Kitchen stewarding	For dish and pot washing, i.e., glassware, hollowware, cutlery, crockery, flatware, pot and so forth.

KEY TERMS

Aboyeur	: The head position of hot plate area which is also known as barker or announcer.
Running items	: *Easy-to-prepare and ready-to-serve preparations*. Mainly pantry section offers these items.
Silver room	: Ancillary section that is mainly responsible for cleaning, polishing and keeping service items.
Service pantry	: Restaurant pantry that supplies running preparations, especially to restaurant patrons.
Still room	: Ancillary section which provides supplementary (or accompanying) food and beverage items.
Salon bar	: Lounge bar that mainly caters to lounge guests.
Ancillary area	: Internal supportive areas/sections of food and beverage department.
Drop box	: The system whereby outlet cashiers drop (in sealed envelope) their outlet cash at the end of the shift.
Grand master bill	: Final bill or folio of resident guests.
Purchase specification	: Description that illustrates specific and distinctive features of an item to be purchased.

REVIEW QUESTIONS

1. Write down the effects of good coordination of food and beverage department with kitchen on revenue creation and guest satisfaction.
2. Classify ancillary outlets of food and beverage department, explain them briefly.
3. Kitchen stewarding is the backbone of every food and beverage outlet. Justify this statement with examples.
4. Hot plate area is a meeting point between food and beverage outlet and kitchen area. Enlist work description of hot plate area.

Restaurant Operations

OBJECTIVES

Students will be able to:

- explain step-by-step functioning of restaurant operations;
- inform the task required before the opening of restaurant and during the guest service; and
- recognize the sequential work order while dealing with restaurant guests.

RESTAURANT AND ITS OPERATIONAL CYCLE

A *restaurant* is a formal dining hall/area (FDH) for resident (in hotel based restaurants) as well as non-resident guests. Restaurants are predominantly open during major meal periods. However, it may also be open for supporting meal periods (or *day parts*) like during brunch, afternoon tea, evening tea and so forth. It chiefly depends on the guest turnover rate. See Figure 5.1.

So, to properly comprehend the work profile (and procedures) of a restaurant, their relations and effect, the entire restaurant operations are divided into different stages. Remember, the layout of restaurant also plays a crucial role in effective and efficient execution of activities, particularly during arrival, stay period and departure of guests. An ideal layout of a restaurant along with stations/sections is given in Figure 5.2.

The duties to be carried before the service commences are diverse in accordance to the particular food and beverage service area concerned. A series of elementary activities during different stages of guest and staff interaction is shown below (Figure 5.1), but it should be noted that not all of them are germane to every situation; it depends on the policy of the establishment.

ACTIVITIES BEFORE THE GUEST ARRIVAL

Stewards have plenty of work to be done before guests arrive. Therefore, food and beverage service staff should report on time or before the starting of the shift. It allows adequate time to the captain to conduct *briefing session* and intimate the staff about *soft lunch* (if any). Besides, it also allows the food serving staff to prepare restaurant for service. Major activities which are required before the guest arrival are explained below.

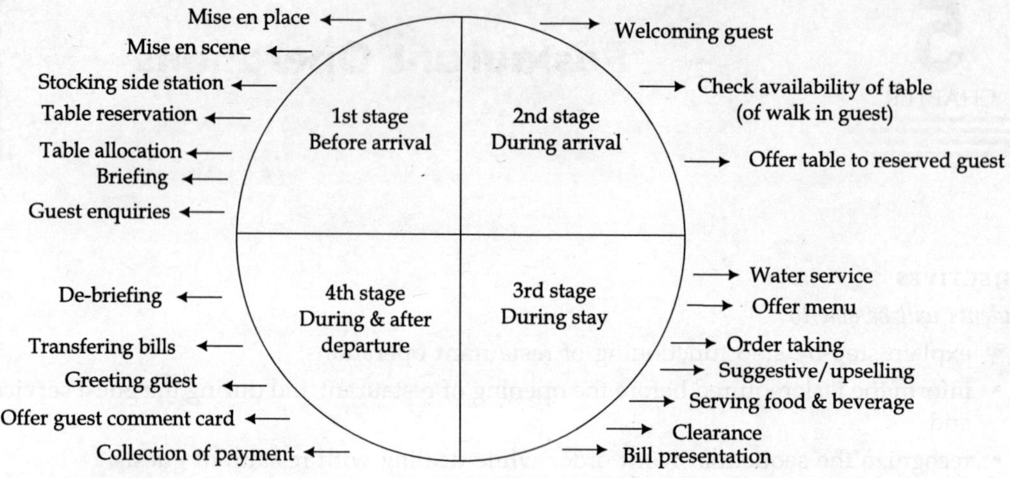

Note. Briefing (meeting before restaurant operation), de-briefing (meeting after completion of restaurant operation).

Fig. 5.1 Restaurant operational cycle

PREPARE RESTAURANT FOR SERVICE (MISE EN SCENE)

All works related to the convivial and pleasant restaurant environment is collectively known as *mise en scene* (a French term). In simple terms, it means "creating the restaurant environment" for service. It involves activities like to change stained curtains, shampoo carpet stains, clean service area, tables, chairs, side stations, trolleys and other service equipment. Steward must check all mise en scene tasks in his/her opening duty checklist. Generally, following duties are performed under mise en scene:

Furniture

✓ Ensure all furniture (like chair, table and side station) should be properly dusted and arranged in proper alignment. Steward should also check for the breakage, loose, cut and wobbling.

Linen

✓ Ensure all linen items (like tablecloths, slipcloths, napkins, placemats, curtains and drapery) should be neat and clean, ironed and laid/hung properly.

Lights and Fixtures

✓ Ensure all electric equipment (like bulb, AC, tubelight, music and wall scones) function properly. Fixtures should be dusted on daily basis, metal fixtures like door knob and door handles should be polished at regular intervals.

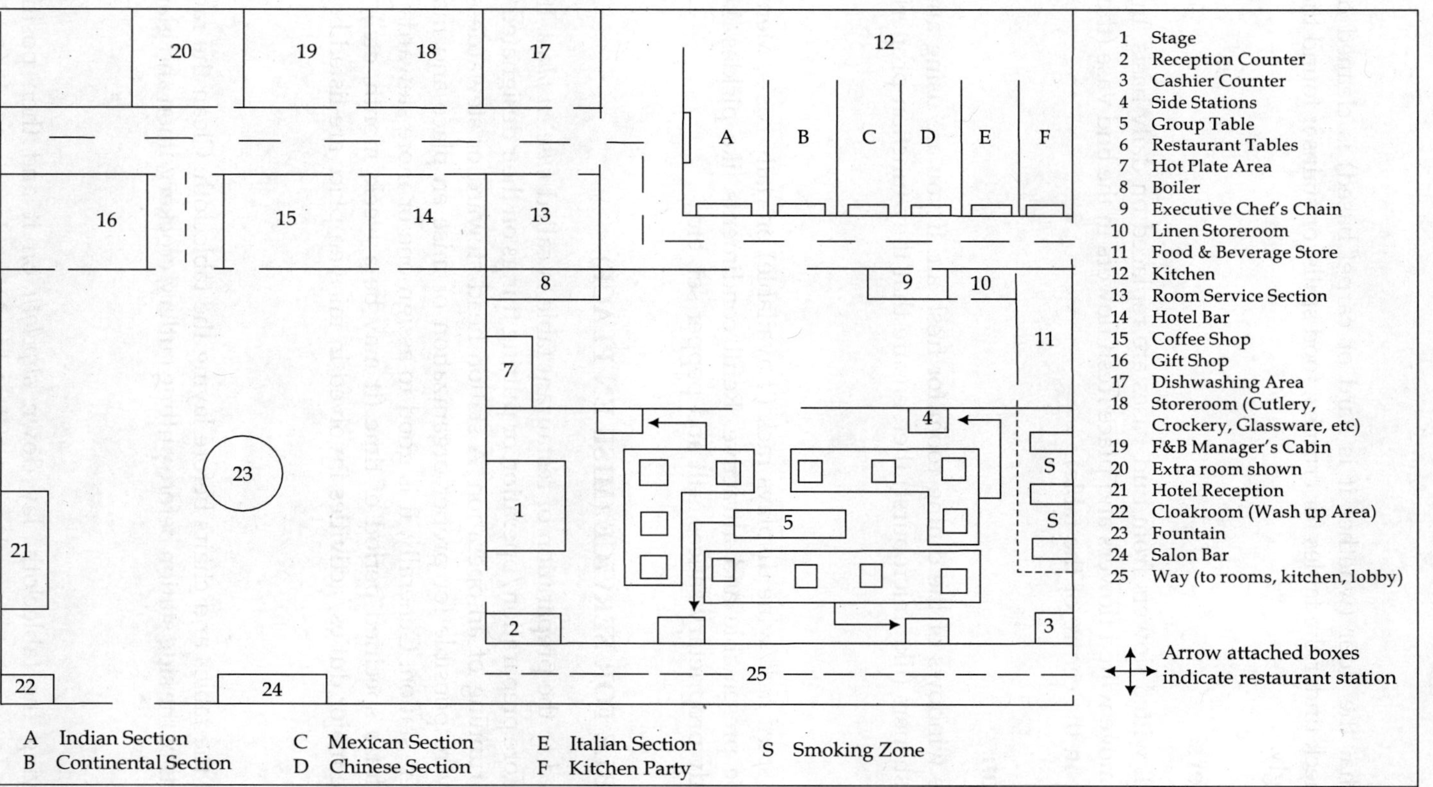

Fig. 5.2 Customary layout of a restaurant with receiving & serving areas.

Floors

✓ Ensure that the floor (whether it is hard or carpet based) is cleaned on daily basis. Check under the tables for crumbs, food spills, or stains if found then treat accordingly.

Change Flowers

✓ Ensure all wilted flowers from bud vases are replaced on daily basis. In simple terms, remove wilted flowers and place fresh flowers in the bud vase (then place bud vase in the centre of the table).

Air Circulation

✓ Open the windows of the dining room for fresh air. If you are using automatic room fresheners (like microburst) then ensure that they function properly.

Other Works

✓ Dust the *speed rack*/wine displays rack (if available) on daily basis. Menu cards should be presentable and attractive. Refill condiments like pickles, ketchup, keep ready proprietary sauces, salt and pepper set, etc.

PREPARE TABLE FOR SERVICE (MISE EN PLACE)

All works related to the preparation of restaurant table is called *mise en place*. It means "preparation before preparation/operation or putting things on their designated places" for the smooth running of an operation. A station head steward or stewardess of the outlet is usually responsible for proper organization of mise en place and managing duties of his/her station. Generally, it is good to assign one or more stewards to each of such duties for a specified period of time (it may be a week, month, etc.), i.e., on rota basis. Some major duties/activities involved in mise en place are listed below.

Furniture

✓ Clean all the tables and chairs before laying the tablecloth. Clean the racks and cupboards of the side station before putting cutlery, crockery, linen and glassware.

Linen

✓ After laying the tablecloth, lay down *slipcloth* on it and then position the placemats/cover-mats on each cover of the table. Nowadays, instead of tablecloths, placemats are used directly on the glass/wooden/marble tables. It also reduces the cost of laundering as placemats are mostly reversible. At last, keep the folded napkins in the centre of the cover or directly on the side plate.

Crockery (especially plates)

- ✓ First of all place *centre appointments* [ash tray (optional), bud vase and cruet set] on the table in the sequence of ABC. Place side plate on extreme left-hand side of the cover. Now place show plate in the centre of the cover, so that the steward can properly arrange or place the remaining equipment on the cover.

Crockery (especially cups)

- ✓ In breakfast session, steward may place sugar bowl in the centre of the table and tea/coffee cup with saucer and tea/coffee spoon on the right-hand side of the cover.

Cutlery

- ✓ First of all select only the required amount of cutlery for the cover layout, such as fish knife and fish fork for *à la carte* cover setup (ALC). And for *table d'hôte* (TDH) cover layout, steward needs to extend *à la carte* set-up with joint knife, joint fork, dessert indicators and soup spoon. Remember, every cover layout should start from inside to outside.
- ✓ For English breakfast cover layout, replace soup spoon with cereal spoon and dessert indicator with fruit spoon and fruit fork in table d'hôte cover layout.

Glassware

- ✓ In glassware, the steward should place either water tumbler or high ball glass/ water goblet (08-10 fl.oz) in the cover, whichever the organization uses. Water glass is placed on the right-hand side of the cover—on the tip of the first knife from inside the cover. Generally, a steward can place up to 3 glasses in any cover layout.

Napkin

- ✓ After placing all cover appointments, now it is the time to place napkins on the cover. First, correctly fold the napkins (cone shape, bishop maitre, book fold, etc.) then place it in the centre (on show plate) or on the side plate.

At last, steward needs to check the overall appearance of the table. He also requires a water jug ready for service on the side station. This jug should be filled with in-house water (or regular filtered water) and must be covered with a napkin.

Note.

- In general, the steward should place fruit knife and fruit fork on top of the cover in English breakfast. But if the outlet does not have fruit knife and fruit fork then the steward can replace it with a dessert indicator (dessert fork + dessert spoon) to eat fresh fruits.
- If the steward is placing more than one glass on the cover then place the remaining glasses (after water glass) in 45 degree angle below the water glass (in downward direction).
- Other glasses which may be placed on the cover include juice glass in the morning breakfast, wine glass (red or white wine) in lunch and dinner. Remember, one can place only up to three glasses at a time on the cover.

KEY TIPS

- Never place ceramic soup spoon on the cover. It should always be offered separately by placing on the under-liner beside the soup bowl.
- Never use salver to keep chinaware (or ceramic plates) while offer on the table or performing the clearance. Plates should always be carried directly with hands (gloves can be used).
- Cutlery and flatware should always be handled from the neck—never with spoon's bowl, fork's prongs and knife's edges or sharpness.
- Plates are always placed by carrying through the pile of the plates. Never place thumb or any other finger inside the plate.
- Tea or coffee cups should be carried with their handle, and soup bowl and water glass with their base; never with brim.

MAINTAINING SIDE STATION (OR STOCKING SIDE STATION)

The side station is also known as "side stand, dummy waiter, side section, working station, side table or service console". It is an important piece of furniture in a restaurant. It is used by the service staff for keeping all service equipment at one place. It is also used as a landing table for the dishes picked up from the kitchen *en route* to the guest table and to place soiled dishes from the guest's table *en route* to the wash-up area. For the convenience of service staff, the side station should be strategically located. It should be kept neat, clean and presentable as it is always in the direct view of the guests. Further details in relation to stocking side station are given below:

Stocking Side Station

✓ Always maintain *par level* in the side station. A par is the number of supplies steward will need to get through one work shift. Side station must stock in advance all the items which may be required during the dining operation, i.e., glasses, silverware, dishes, ashtrays, napkins, tablecloths, etc.

✓ Simultaneously, if the restaurant has limited utensils then the side station must be refilled regularly during the shift. Make sure that there is always a fresh supply of condiments also.

Maintain During Operation

✓ For the smooth running of an operation, it is important to maintain the side station throughout the shift. Regularly check the side work with the help of checklist. Common side work/task includes folding of napkins, wiping serving trays, refilling water jugs, replenishing condiments, etc. Recurrently, wipe up spills, bread crumbs, etc., as soon as possible, so that fresh order and soiled dishes can be easily placed on the side station.

✓ Check the side station throughout the meal service and keep the supplies and equipment orderly. A steward who is working or standing at the side station should never show his back to the guest.

Clean Side Station

✓ Take all soiled dishes, cutlery, crockery and glassware to the dishwashing area. Wipe the shelves and countertop with a clean and damp cloth.

✓ Throughout the service, clean the side station as needed.

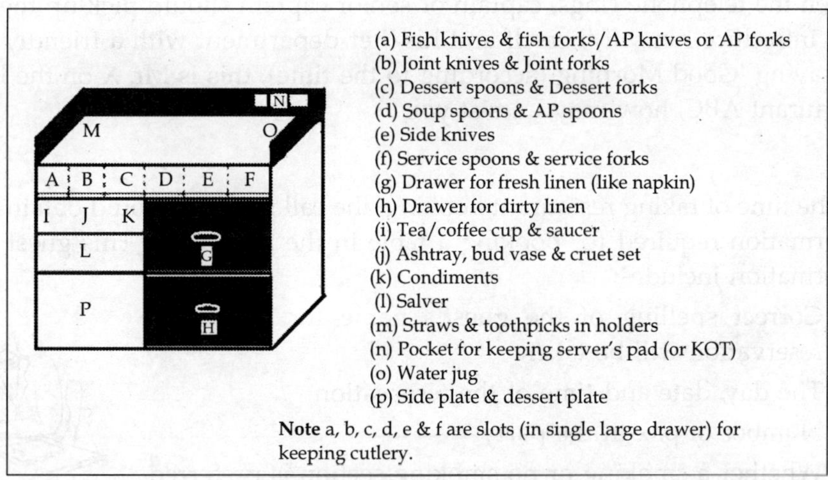

Fig. 5.3 Side station specimen

Note. The above shown slots are further partitioned into two or three sub-slots which are used to keep related cutlery and flatware. For example, slot *A* can be partitioned into two sections—first section for fish knives and the second section for fish forks.

TABLE RESERVATION AND ALLOCATION

Table Reservation

- ✓ When a guest arrives at a food and beverage outlet with prior information and confirmation of his or her seat, the case is called guest-with-*table-reservation*. In dictionary term, table reservation means the advance agreement by a guest to hold a seat in an outlet at an intending place/time. It is commonly referred to as *table booking*.

Table Allocation

- ✓ After accepting the *booking of table*, the next task is to reserve a particular table for that guest. Remember, table is allocated in accordance with the guest's preference. Finally, a reserve card should be placed in the centre of that table, so that no other guest sits on the table.

Table Reservation and Allocation Procedure

A standard procedure for table reservation in any restaurant consists of the following steps:

Step 1

- ✓ When the telephone rings, captain or senior captain should pick up the receiver and introduce himself/herself and his/her department with a friendly greeting by saying 'Good Morning (according to the time), this is Mr. X on the line from restaurant ABC, how may I assist you'.

Step 2

- ✓ At the time of taking restaurant booking, the call receiver should obtain essential information required for booking a table in the restaurant. This guest oriented information includes:
  - Correct spelling of the guest's name for whom the reservation will be taken
  - The day, date and time of the reservation
  - Number of pax in the party
  - Whether a smoking or no-smoking section is preferred
  - Whether the guest wants a table or a separate booth
  - Name of the person who is booking the table
  - Address and telephone number
  - Any special request
  - Mode of payment

Step 3

✓ Inform in advance about the holding time of reservation like "we will hold your reservation for 30 minutes". At the end of the telephone call for a booking, one should say "Thank you for your booking, we shall look forward to seeing you."

Step 4

✓ Record or transfer this information to the reservation diary of the restaurant. Afterwards, allocate the table to the guest in accordance with his preference (if possible). Finally, place reserved tag on that table.

Step 5

✓ If a cancellation request is received, confirm the earlier given details with the guest then proceed for cancellation. The steward can also request to book a table for any other meal/occasion in place of cancellation.

Restaurant Table Reservation Diary

Table for 2 persons ....

Table for 4 persons .... Meal ....

Table for 6 persons .... Date ....

Group table ....Day ....

Name of the guest	No. of guests	Time	Table allotted	Special requirement

Fig. 5.4 Pro forma of table reservation diary

CONDUCT BRIEFING SESSION

Task 1 Senior captain calls all the staff members and takes attendance. Afterwards, he checks their grooming standards and waiter's kit.

Task 2 Briefs staff members on menu, its *signature items, meal solutions*, today's special (or chef special)—about its ingredients, cooking method, etc. Senior captain should also intimate those dishes which the outlet cannot offer that day, if situation arises.

Task 3 Informs about the HWC guests, i.e., *guests handle with care* (or VIP guests), special order of any guests like wedding cake, table reservation status, group arrival/dining status and so forth.

Task 4 Obtain staff's feedback regarding qualms (or handle queries) and finally designates duties to all staff members. Staff duty schedule may also be displayed on the display board.

Task 5 Finally, disperses staff for meal taking because as often it has been seen that staff meal timing is around the briefing session and/or before the starting of actual restaurant operation/lunch/dinner.

ACTIVITIES DURING GUEST ARRIVAL AND STAY PERIOD

It is awfully significant that how guests are received because it sets the mood of the guest for the meal. Remember, it is difficult to recover from a first bad impression, no matter how good the food, beverage and service may be. Consequently, arrival stage activities play a crucial role in overall guest satisfaction and generating positive *meal experience*. This stage consists of several activities, which predominantly include:

Receiving and Seating the Guest

Step 1 Hostess/host/captain must give a warm greeting to the guest in compliance to the time of the day. If he/she knows the name of the guest then greet him/her with his/her name like "Good morning Mr. Yadav, welcome back to restaurant ABC."

Step 2 Check/confirm for advance table reservation with the guest. If he/she has reservation (refer reservation diary to check the allotted table) then escort them to the allotted seat.

Step 3 If the guest does not hold table reservation then check for the available table/seat in accordance with guest's preference and number of pax. If table/seat is available then allot, otherwise request him/her to wait for the turn and escort him/her to the waiting area and request/offer tea, coffee, juice, etc.

Step 4 Assist guests during their seating by pulling chair to ease the guest. Ensure children should be offered high chairs, next to their mother.

Step 5 Remove extra cover from the table, if any. It usually occurs when the table is allotted to less number of people than the covers such as four-cover table allotted to three people only.

Note.

- If the guest has any extra baggage or article (like packed items but not purse), it is good that hostess should take it on the entrance and keep it at her desk. So that the guest can freely enjoy to his/her meal. The same will be handed over to the guest during farewell.

WATER SERVICE

Task 1 After table allotment, the first step is to serve water to the guest. Steward should suggest mineral water first and if the guest does not want it then serve *house water* (or regular filtered water).

Task 2 Now, the steward can use his/her salesmanship by suggesting mineral water. He/she has an opportunity to provoke extra revenue (through suggestive selling) for his/her outlet just by selling mineral water.

Task 3 Steward can raise huge profit by selling mineral water only because if guest places order for mineral water then a single bottle is never sufficient for the entire meal; he will order more.

Task 4 Otherwise, serve *house water* or regular filtered water (from jug) from right-hand side (RHS) of the guest. For mineral water, steward generates BOT, collects bottle from the bar, shows to the guest and requests him to check temperature. Next take consent to open the cap of the bottle and lastly, serve it.

Task 5 Bottled mineral water is served from the RHS of the guest. If water remains in bottle, keep it on the guest table (after closing the cap).

PRESENTING MENU AND TAKING BEVERAGE ORDER

Task 1 In cover turnover situation, the server should bring fresh glasses of water on their first trip to the table then serve water. Afterwards, present menu to the guest from right-hand side.

Task 2 After presenting the menu card, give at least 5-10 minutes, so that the guest goes through the menu and selects whatever he/she would like to order. It is always inevitable to take beverage order first followed by food order.

Task 3 In small establishments, a common menu card is offered to the guests in which food as well as beverage items are written together.

Task 4 But in large establishments, there are separate menu cards for all assortment of items like starter menu, dessert menu, and wine list/ beverage menu. Here, wine list/beverage menu is preferred to offer first next food menu.

Task 5 While taking beverage order, the server should number the guest check so that he/she can recognize who ordered what. Nowadays, in most of food serving outlets steward uses *order wheel* for this purpose, specifically for table/seat recognition.

Task 6 Steward should write correct beverage order (and choice specification, if any) from each guest like choice of garnish and other preference such as whether the drink should be served with ice (like on the rocks) or without ice (or neat). Also pay attention for specific *call brand* or *premium brand* if any guest has requested.

Task 7 Steward should take all beverage orders from the right-hand side of the guest. He should maintain an appropriate distance from the guest while taking order (usually, steward should stand at 45 degree angle in analogous to the table corner).

PLACING BEVERAGE ORDERS AT THE BAR

Task 1 Procedure for obtaining beverages at the bar are frequently similar to procedure for ordering food in the kitchen.

Task 2 First, the steward should remember that beverage orders should be recorded on BOT (Beverage Order Ticket) instead of KOT (Kitchen Order Ticket).

Task 3 In some restaurants, server route and pick beverage orders from the *service bar* which is located in restaurant while in other outlets, the server goes to the *public bar* to obtain the drink orders.

Task 4 Next the steward will handover beverage order ticket to the *bar back* or bartender and obtain the drink instantly (if possible) or after 5 minutes.

Task 5 When receives beverage order from bar, steward should ensure to accept correct drink then directly move towards the restaurant, subsequently to the guest table and serve beverage. While routing from bar to the guest table, the steward may require additional items which he/she can collect from sideboard.

SERVING BEVERAGES

Task 1 In table service provision, especially in restaurants, drinks are carried on a salver whereas tray is used to serve drinks in guest rooms.

Task 2 Cocktails are prepared then portioned (at bar counter) in appropriate glassware by cocktail bar staff whereas spirits are pre-poured in correct glass at the bar counter. Thereafter, steward tops-up either with water, soda or both at the guest table.

Task 3 Beer and wine are first presented to guest then take approval to open it. Wine cork requires to present the guest for smelling whereas beers are directly served after removing the crown cap.

Task 4 Salver/tray should never rest on the guest table (and avoid jostling guests or against the outlet standards). Remember, beverages are always served from the right-hand side of the guest and their clearance is too done from the same side.

Task 5 Steward should serve drink in appropriate glassware like cocktails are mainly served in cocktail glasses, water in water tumbler or goblet, whisky in old fashioned glass, beer in beer goblet and so forth.

PRESENTING FOOD MENU AND TAKING ORDERS

Task 1 If a restaurant offers separate food menu then elementary procedure for menu presentation is same as for beverage menu, i.e., presenting the menu (in open position) from right-hand side of the guest.

Task 2 (optional) If the guest is busy with his/her right hand (like enjoying drink) then the steward may offer food menu from the left-hand side of the guest.

Task 3 When taking order, the steward should stand on the right-hand side of the host (or guest). Do not forget to maintain an appropriate distance with the host or guest. The steward must write the food order on KOT.

Task 4 Steward should verbally replicate the meal order during conversation as well as reiterate all the dishes after the completion of order.

Task 5 *Order wheel* is equipped in restaurants (or in back area) where guest turnover rate is high. Here, the steward hangs KOTs on *order wheel* to remember who ordered what in an attempt to recognize table/seat/cover to serve.

Task 6 During food service, it is always preferred to initiate with a woman then serve orders clockwise. Therefore, the server should write a KOT in such a way that he/she can recognize "who orders what".

PLACING AND RECEIVING ORDERS IN THE KITCHEN

Task 1 Procedure for placing food orders in the kitchen varies. In some restaurants, the server simply calls out the orders in the kitchen. In others, KOT is directly transferred to the kitchen personnel (or to *sous chef*).

Task 2 While in certain outlets, the KOT is given to *barker* who further transfers this to the kitchen personnel. *Barker* is the in-charge of *hot plate* area and also called "aboyeur or announcer". In small hotels, generally a common KOT is prepared for placing hot as well as cold food.

Task 3 In large establishments, KOT is prepared in five copies (especially in room service outlet) so that the entire meal order can be placed simultaneously. In it, KOT flows like, 1st copy to hot kitchen, 2nd copy to cold kitchen, 3rd copy to bar, 4th copy to cashier and the last copy remains with the steward.

Task 4 In large establishments, *aboyeur* aids the communication between the kitchen and restaurant. He receives the KOT/food order from the service staff and announces the order to the kitchen. Thereafter, hot plate area staff collects meal orders from the kitchen (remember that hot meals are kept in *pellet*), subsequently, picked up by restaurant steward.

Task 5 When picking food order, the server must know how to carry a loaded salver (or tray). For safety reason, the heaviest dishes and dishes containing liquid or semi-liquid preparations (such as seafood food cocktails, gravy dishes, etc.) should be placed in the centre of the salver (or tray).

Task 6 Nowadays, in order to avoid accident while transporting meal orders from kitchen to dining area or hot plate area, restaurants have swinging doors concept. These swinging doors are clearly marked with "In" and "Out" sign on respective faces.

SERVING ORDERS

Task 1 The restaurant's standard operating procedures determine how servers present and serve food to the guests. For instance, in many outlets the server places napkin on the laps of the guests.

Task 2 In general, servers place the (either on salver or tray) meal orders on side station (or *dummy waiter*) or on food service stands. Next they approach to guest to obtain permission to start meal service. Now steward returns to side station and remove lids/plate covers (if placed) from the dishes then moves towards the guest table to start meal serving.

Task 3 In fine dine restaurants, service rules dictate that guests should serve from the left-hand side (as dishes are served via platter-to-plate service). In other outlets like coffee shop and fast food, guests are served from the right-hand side (as ordered meals are served through pre-plated service).

Task 4 Usually, children are served first then the women (elder lady first followed by younger one) and finally men. (For more detail, please refer *Chapter-7 Handling Skills)*.

Task 5 After serving, the steward should reconfirm with the guests for any other requirements. Steward should ask "Is everything to your satisfaction?" or similar question.

Task 6 When several courses are being served, the steward should clear emptied dishes before serving the next course. For example, remove all emptied dishes and cruet set before serving dessert. Remember, clearance is done from the right-hand side of the guest.

How to Place Napkin on Guest Lap

Step 1 Stand at the right-hand side of the guest; pickup the napkin with your right hand.

Step 2 Shake the napkin from its fold into a triangle.

Step 3 Place the longest side of the triangle closest to the guest.

Step 4 Move anticlockwise around the table and open and place the napkins, offer to host at last.

Note. Nowadays, many guests choose to open and place their napkin by themselves (especially ladies), as soon as they sit on the table. Hence, a steward should be extremely careful while dealing with female guests (stewardess or hostess is usually preferred at here).

RULES FOR COVER CLEARANCE

Task 1 While clearing the table, do not put everything on a single tray; remove different articles in sequential order like soiled plates first followed by unused food containers (like butter and bread rolls) then condiments, sauces, cruet set and so forth centre appointments.

Task 2 Remove all unused cover appointments like cutlery and flatware in a separate tray or plate. Do not mix unused cutlery and flatware with the used ones. Water glasses and napkins are removed after the guest leaves.

Task 3 Remember, clearance of all beverages as well as of food items is done from the RHS of the guest. Used meal plates are cleared with right hand and then stacking on each other on your left hand.

Task 4 Do not stack plates of different dimensions on each other. Thus, while handling a table of multiple pax, remove full plates in the first round and side plates in the second round. Keep filthy flatware and cutlery in a separate plate/bowl.

Task 5 The salver is used to clear only emptied glassware, centre appointments and those items which accompanied under-liner like tea and coffee cups with saucer, soup bowl with saucer. Salver is never suggested for clearance of soiled plates. (For more detail, please refer Chapter 7: Handling Skills).

TABLE CRUMBING

Task 1 Table crumbing is essential after the completion of main course. So, when main course is over, the steward should remove unwanted cutlery (except dessert indicator), cruet set, sauce bottles, condiments, etc.

Task 2 Cutlery and flatware required for the next course may also be temporarily transfered to side station. But in certain situations, cutlery and flatware do not need to shift on the side station such as *dessert indicator* because it is kept on the top of the cover.

Task 3 Once again steward should remember not to mix unused cutlery and flatware with the soiled ones. Therefore, it is always desirable to remove unsullied cutlery and flatware separately. Otherwise, these may unnecessarily require washing and wiping again.

Task 4 Next, the steward starts crumbing down the table. For crumbing, he requires a folded waiter's cloth, side plate and uncommonly service gear. Folded napkin is used to gather food particles at one corner of the cover. This napkin can be either directly held with fingers or with service gear.

Task 5 Now swiftly move the side plate under the edge of table then carefully push down the gathered crumbs on side plate. This crumbing can be done from any side of the guest (but prefer from left-hand side).

Task 6 Steward should not keep this crumb collected side plate in front of the guest (or on side station) for long.

Task 7 After crumbing, place the dessert fork on left-hand side and dessert spoon on right-hand side of the cover. Lastly, serve the dessert.

DESSERT

Task 1 Before offering the dessert, remove (except napkin and water glass) the full plate, side plate, cruet set, accompaniments, portion bowl, etc.

Task 2 Now shift dessert cutlery (for those pre-plated desserts which will be offered in half plate) on the designated place in the cover – dessert fork on left-hand side and dessert spoon on right-hand side.

Task 3 For those desserts which are offered in cup, glass or bowl – offer them by placing on underliner. In addition, put spoon (either ice cream spoon, tea spoon or sundae spoon – in accordance with dessert type), on RHS of the underliner.

Task 4 At the end, take the clearance of dessert course. The clearance procedure for dessert course (which offered in half plate) will be same as for the clearance of the main course. But the clearance of pre-portioned desserts (which is offered in bowls) will be done in a similar way as tea and coffee cup clearance.

Order Taking Procedure

Step 1 Steward should ask for the food/beverage order in a courteous manner like "Excuse me sir/madam, May I have your order please".

Step 2 Concurrently, follow an order taking system like write order either on KOT or BOT pad.

Step 3 Finally, place food order with kitchen and beverage order with bar and cold dessert order with cold kitchen.

Some points to be observed while taking order from the guest. These are as follows:

- Steward should stand in the correct position and posture (don't lean over the guest) to take order.
- Steward should have good command over menu to answer guest enquiries.

- Suggest special or additional courses as and when required but never force the guest to order any specific dish.
- Suggest a bottle of wine. Or ask if the guest would like another beverage.
- Try to meet special request, if possible.
- Repeat food items or guest order and ask him whether he wants to order anything more.
- If the guest is in hurry and seeks your assistance then suggest him some "ready-to-serve" food items rather than "cook-to-order" items.

Important. It is vital to keep sequence while serving food. Steward should write down in his KOT/notepad the sequence of meal ordered and who order what. Generally, service is done in clockwise direction. First take order from the host then start following to his right and give an identification number to each guest. Steward should plan some coding method so that he can easily ascertain who ordered which food. He should never ask "who order what" simultaneously it will look worse if you place wrong food in front of any guest. Thus, write every order in a sequential order.

ACTIVITIES DURING AND AFTER THE GUEST DEPARTURE

Presenting Guest Checks

Towards the end of the meal, the steward requires to present the bill to the guest. If the bill is presented too soon, guest may be offended, feeling that the steward is trying to push them out. On the other hand, it is extremely annoying for diners, if they have limited time, and the steward keeps him/her to be waiting for the bill. Hence, at the request of the guest, the bill should be collected from the cashier and presented to the host in a bill folder. After the successful settlement of the bill, the steward should return the balance amount to the respective guest and never demand for any gratuity. A step-by-step guideline to present a guest check is given below.

Task 1 Firstly, opportune delivery of the guest bill (or guest check but never to KOT or BOT) is important because some guest may be in urgency; others may linger over their meals. Whereas bill of resident guests may require to post in their *room account*.

Task 2 The guest bill should be verified, totalled and ready before the guest demands it. Server should recheck the bill contents and amount before presenting it to the guest.

Task 3 The bill can be presented in several ways. Generally, if the bill is presented on a plate/tray/ folder, it means that server will collect the payments.

Task 4 Presenting the bill without plate/tray/folder generally means that the guest will pay at the cashier's counter. When presenting the check to a group, the server should present the bill to the group leader or the host.

Task 5 Server should ensure that guest must handover outstanding balance/ money, if any. At last, thanks the guest. Remember, server should never keep the balance amount without guest's permission.

COMMENT CARD/DIARY

After the settlement of bill, now it is the time to offer *comment card* and obtain the feedback of the guest. It may be in the form of comment card or diary. It works as an evaluation tool for the outlet and employee performance and also assists in *menu engineering* and *menu scoring* activity.

Task 1 Comment card is used to obtain the feedback (or response) of the guest on different parameters. It principally includes taste of the food, ambience of restaurant, standard of service, staff's code of conduct and so forth.

Task 2 It is presented after the settlement or payment of bill. It is given along with a pen from the right-hand side of the guest.

Note.

- The above-mentioned terms RHS and LHS are used for Right-Hand Side and Left-Hand Side of the guest. The table crumbing cloth can be handled by service gear as well as directly with hand also. It depends on comfort and outlet's policy.
- Before presenting the bill or after the clearance of dessert, the steward may also make an effort for up-selling by offering tea or coffee to the guest. At the time of offering bill, mostly mouth freshener along with the bill is offered to the guest.

CONDUCT DE-BRIEFING SESSION

Task 1 Call all the staff members and verify their presence/absence once again. Afterwards, take their feedback regarding the work that has been done by them or what problems they faced.

Task 2 Give appreciation to those who have performed well. On the other side determine the training requirement for those who did not perform up to the mark since last several days/weeks/months.

Task 3 Lastly, disperse the staff for the next shift or day. The captain may issue instructions (like modification in duty rota) for the next day/shift.

Comment Card

Date of visit ....

Dear Guests,

We request you to give us your valuable comments and suggestions in relation to meals, beverages and other related aspects, mentioned below, so that we can offer you improved services on your next visit.

What did you order? ....

Please Tick the Appropriate Box

Particulars	Excellent	Good	Fair	Poor
Food quality	☐	☐	☐	☐
Food portion	☐	☐	☐	☐

Service speed	☐	☐	☐	☐
Service quality	☐	☐	☐	☐
Friendliness	☐	☐	☐	☐
Outlet cleanliness	☐	☐	☐	☐
Menu choice	☐	☐	☐	☐
What prompted your visit?	Advertisement	☐	Prior Visit	☐
Do you plan to visit again?	Yes	☐	No	☐

Optional comments ....

Name of guest .... Address .... Contact No.............

KEY TERMS

Centre appointment	: Common-use items (like ABC) that are usually placed at the centre of the table.
Soft lunch	: Method of announcing the opening of a restaurant to limited guests with little fanfare.
Cover set-up	: A place set-up (or table layout) for an individual diner.
House water	: Regular filtered in-house drinking water.
Bar back	: Bar staff who works under the bartender/barman.
Dummy waiter	: Side station which is predominantly used to keep cutlery, crockery, glassware and so forth.
Pellet	: A preheated metal disk that is used to maintain the temperature of an individual portion of plated hot food.
Signature items	: A menu item/s that is prepared in a way that makes it unique and which the operation can then charge more for.
Meal solutions	: Menu items offered by restaurants that families can take home and eat together.
Order wheel	: Metal or wood wheel with clips used by stewards to track customer food orders.
Sous chef	: Second higher kitchen position that directly works under kitchen executive.
Room account	: Account of resident guest and most diners to transfer their bills into this account.
Dessert indicator	: Dessert cutlery and flatware, i.e., dessert spoon and dessert fork.
De-briefing	: Meeting session conducted after the completion of the operation

REVIEW QUESTIONS

1. Write a short note on the comment card and its role in guest's satisfaction.
2. Differentiate between mise en place and mise en scene.
3. Draw the layout of any high class restaurant and indicate stations/sections.
4. Explicate different stages of guest interaction with restaurant and enlist activities of each stage.

Room Service Operations

Objectives

Students will be able to:

- explicate room service and its types;
- understand the room service operational cycle; and
- comprehend that how a tray and trolley is laid down.

ROOM SERVICE

The provision of *room service* is also called "in-room dining" which means, service involving the delivering of food and beverage into a guest's room in any residential establishment. The room service menu is often a simplified version of what is available in the hotel, with slightly high price to compensate for the higher overheads in terms of staff and equipment.

Remember, the provision of room service is found in residential establishments, secondly this outlet works for 24 hours. Lastly, the provision is only for resident guests and for hotel's internal managerial level employees. Room service involves functions like:

- Serving of food and beverage in guest rooms of the hotel.
- Small orders are served in trays; major meals are taken on trolleys.
- Guests have to place their order through telephone to the room service order taker who further transmits this order to the kitchen.
- The bill goes along with the food order for the guest's signature or payment.
- Usually, clearance is done after half an hour or hour.

In residential hotels, room service is available in different forms. It may either be centralized, decentralized, mobile or combination of all. This particularly depends on the size of the organization, available space, number of rooms and floors, guest turnover ratio, available staff and so forth. Each room service provision has its own pros and cons.

Types of Room Service			
Room service	**Reporting**	**Duty starts from**	**Remark**
Centralized	Single point	Single point	Major as well as running orders processed from single point
Decentralized	Single point	Floor pantries	Running order processed from+clearance bring to floor pantry
Mobile pantry	Single point	Service elevator	Order processed for running items by switching elevator

OPERATIONAL ASPECTS OF ROOM SERVICE

Order Taking

Step 1 When guest calls the room service, order taker should pick up the phone within 3 rings and answer the telephone call promptly. Room service order taker should introduce him/her as well as the department with a greeting. Graciously ask for the guest's name and room number when caller ID does not display it.

Step 2 Order taker should obtain complete order by asking the guest about the appetizer, soup, main course, dessert, beverage and special preparation instructions, if any.

Step 3 Write the guest order in *room service order taking register*. Room service order taker should also do suggestive selling by encouraging guest to order something extra/expensive. If the guest has some doubt in choosing item/s from the menu, the order taker can suggest an appropriate dish but never force him to order it.

Step 4 Order taker should replicate the order that the guest has placed. Inform the guest about the time when the order will be delivered. If there is any delay, inform the guest immediately instead of avoiding him or her.

Step 5 Next, the order taker should thank the guest for calling and placing meal and beverage order with room service. Finally, it is preferred to allow the guest to disconnect the phone first.

Routing the Order

- It means transfer guest's order to the relevant section and department. The guest check/bill/KOT is printed and transferred to relevant sections. If property uses EPOS system then the guest order is automatically transferred to the relevant section. Most room service outlets use guest check/bill for routing order whereas some other outlets prefer KOT/BOT.

- The guest check could be prepared in triplicate (it means one original + two carbon copies). But most of outlets use five-pad guest check system, due to the complexity of the order which goes to different sections. The flow of triplicate as well as five-pad system is given below.

Situation 1 *Triplicate guest check system.* In it, 1st copy goes to kitchen section, 2nd copy goes to cashier (in most of hotels room service order taker also works as a cashier for room service section) and 3rd copy goes to the guest for obtaining authorization to charge in their room account or for instant cash payment.

Situation 2 *Five-pad guest check system.* In this system, 1st copy goes to hot kitchen, 2nd goes to cold kitchen, 3rd goes to bar, 4th goes to cashier and 5th goes to guest for signature or for cash payment.

Preparing the Order

Step 1 Make ready room service tray or trolley. It includes setting of service tray (for small and medium orders) or room service trolley (for large order) in accordance with laid down SOPs.

Step 2 For medium/heavy orders like American and English breakfast, steward should use medium or full size tray. Remember before placing any meal order, all trays must be covered with tray mats.

Step 3 From the perspective of mise en place, all trays are usually kept ready with obligatory cutlery, flatware, crockery and condiments. Tea trays are kept ready with tea cups, doily paper, saucer, tea spoon and accompanying cookies, usually in two and four portions.

Step 4 Place required condiments in accordance with the guest's order. Make sure all china, glassware and silverware should be clean and free from chips, cracks, water spots, etc. The steward should properly arrange all these items on the tray and ensure it must be well balanced before routing towards the room.

Step 5 Lastly, accumulate food and beverage order from different sections. First, collect and deliver beverage order from the bar then food order from kitchen (from appropriate section).

Note. In *split room service provision*, food orders are transferred one after another like send soup course first followed by main course, subsequently to dessert course.

Delivering the Order

Step 1 Select a pre-laid tray in accordance with the amount of menu items ordered by the guest then start placing meal order. After placement (either on tray or trolley), the steward should verify the order then show it to room service order taker or food checker to ensure its precision.

Step 2 Now, lift and carry the room service tray or move room service trolley. If steward is using tray then carry it lengthwise to balance it whereas room service trolley should always be pushed; never pulled.

Step 3 The steward should go directly to the guest room and knock the door. Only after getting the approval he should enter the room and place meals on the designated table/place.

Step 4 After placing the meals, the steward should ask for food service. If guest says yes, then give personalized food and beverage service. Now ask the in-house guest to call the room service department for any further requirement.

Step 5 Eventually, present the bill to the guest and collect payment or obtain his signature on the check. It depends on the guest that how he or she would like to settle down his/her account. If he pays in cash then do not obtain his signature on the guest check (or handover bill/check to guest).

Step 6 On the other side, if the guest wants to transfer the bill into his *room account* then the steward must obtain his signature on guest check and deposit it to the room service cashier. Lastly, thanks the guest for using room service.

Clearing the Order

Step 1 Approach to guest room, knock the door and announce "room service". If the guest does not give any response then again knock the door and announce "room service" once more. Repeat the same procedure for 3 times, afterwards report to captain.

Step 2 Only after getting permission, the steward should enter the guest room. But before entering, greet your guest in accordance with day time and request for the meal clearance. If guest says "Yes" then perform the clearance.

Step 3 In case of tray, place service ware, glasses, used linen and trash on the tray. If trolley is used then secure soiled items inside and in the centre of the trolley. Remember, push; do not pull the trolley into the hallway.

Step 4 Next thanks the guest and leave the room and return to room service area quickly. Finally, report to captain or order taker about the work done, so he/she can update the in-room meal clearance status.

After-Room Service

Task 1 Deposit guest's signed checks to the room service order taker or room service cashier. Now, it is the duty of order taker or cashier to transfer the due amount along with relevant bill details into *record register* or into point of sale system which will automatically update the respective guest's room account at front office.

Task 2 After recording, order taker will send all guest signed checks to the front office cashier. Subsequently, cashier will transfer the guest charges into respective room accounts (or guest accounts) before their departure.

Task 3 If room service staff forgets or delays delivering the guest checks to front desk cashier then room service staff will be responsible for this revenue loss. On the other side, if front desk cashier does not enter or forgets to enter the guest charges then the cashier is responsible for the revenue loss.

Task 4 In case of electronic point of sale system, all guest charges are automatically transferred through the computer terminal when entered in room service's computer system. In PMS (property management software) powered hotels, expenses occur at any electronic point of sale outlet can directly update into guest's room account.

Task 5 Finally, obtain "guest comment" on comment card regarding his/her satisfaction (in relation to food and beverage quality, temperature, service standards, etc.). Remember to obtain feedback on the expected date of departure (or after serving the last meal to the *due out* guest).

Note. In manual system, front desk agent intimates about the expected date of guest departure via sending *departure notification slip*. While in hotels where property management software (PMS) is used, room service employee can confirm the expected date of departure of any in-house guest as well as other relevant guest related information on his computer screen.

Room Service Tray Set-Up

Step 1 There are different sizes of trays available for room service. Generally, a few trays are kept ready with standard equipment. For instance, tea trays are kept ready with mat, tea cup, saucer, spoon, sugar sachet and complementary cookies. Similarly, meal trays are pre-laid with the tray mat, full plate, side plate, napkin, standard silverware (i.e., cutlery and flatware), condiments, cruet set and often accompanying salad.

Step 2 In meal tray pre-laying process, full plate/s (these trays are laid for those meal orders which are served in portion bowls) on LHS of the tray towards yourself. Usually, two to four full plates are placed in these trays. In pre-plated (in half plate) meal orders, unfilled trays are used. Here, meal plates should be covered with food cover.

Step 3 Now place side plate/s (as per the number of full plate/s) above the full plate/s then keep all the condiments on it or nearby. Nowadays, *portion-pack* of most of condiments is used in room service. Next place cloth napkin on the side plate.

Step 4 Place all the required cutlery (like knife, fork, spoon) in accordance with meal order on RHS of the full plate. Afterwards, place complementary salad on the side plate.

Process during placement of meal orders into tray

Step 5 Collect meal order/s from different sections then place them on pre-laid tray like place bread basket on full plate after placing napkin and other dishes (portion bowl) in the remaining empty space. Before delivering, the steward should take approval from concerned room service staff (like food checker).

Step 6 Finally, place guest folio in the bill folder. The steward can keep it on the tray, if space allows; otherwise carry it with right hand. And whenever the steward requires to operate anything like knocking door, pushing lift's button, etc., bill folder can be placed on the tray.

Room Service Trolley Set-Up

Step 1 Move trolley to the designated space then open or fold its supporting sides in accordance with the amount of menu items being ordered. Now lay tablecloth on the trolley.

Step 2 Next place all the required crockery, cutlery, flatware and glassware in conformity with the number of guests.

Step 3 Assemble all food and beverage order/s and place them on ready-to-move trolley. The pre-arrangement of trolley will make cold food cold and vice versa. Beverage orders like wine, beer, cocktail, mocktail or any other aperitif drink must be served immediately (or before delivering food) in tray.

Step 4 After placing all dishes on trolley, the steward should show it to room service order taker or food checker. Afterward, he should move towards guest room. Remember, the steward should push trolley because in case of pulling, the steward is not be able to see the passage which may cause accident. Do not forget to carry bill in the bill folder.

Step 5 The trolley should always be carried through service lift or slope-way (but never use staircase). The steward should use only service lift instead of guest lift to deliver the meal orders.

Note. Be careful at the time of moving trolley because its rolling wheels can rotate in 360 degree angle.

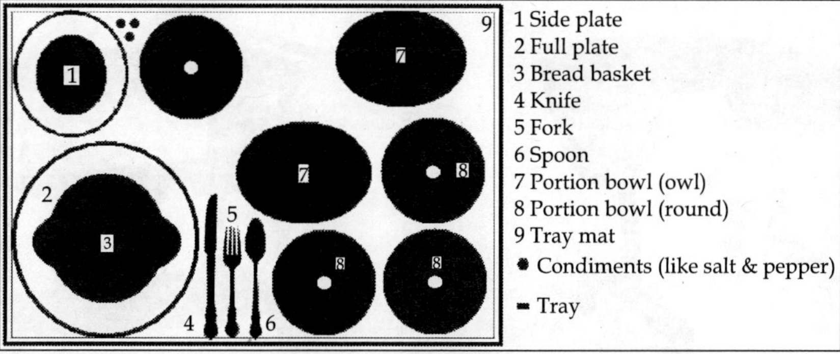

Full meal setup on tray

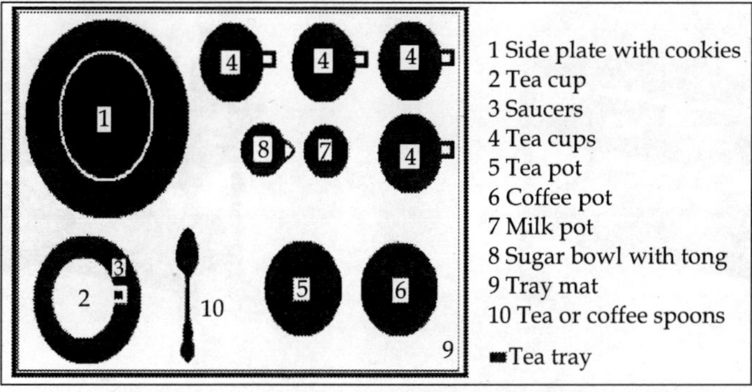

Tea tray setup with complementary cookies

Posture 1: Balance the tray with right hand.

Posture 2: Steward ready to move.

Trolley types

KEY TERMS

In-room dining	: Provision of room service. Remember, room service section usually works for 24 hours.
Floor pantry	: Decentralized room service facility whereby every floor has pantry for serving rooms on that floor.
Mobile pantry	: An elevator based room service provision.
Portion-pack	: Small individual-size portions of condiments like marmalade in disposable packaging.
Split room service	: In-room food delivery system whereby each dish is served in sequence/serial order.
Food checker	: The person who chiefly responsible to assure delivery of quality food.
PMS	: Single window software programme in which entire property can work.

REVIEW QUESTIONS

1. What is room service? Classify room service types and explain them briefly.
2. Draw a room service trolley and indicate its various sections/parts.
3. Expound any ten reasons that why room service provision adds value to the organization.
4. Explain room service operational cycle and enlist each stage activities.

Technical Proficiency

Objectives

Students will be able to:

- expound the role of technical proficiency at operational level;
- learn the rules for handling restaurant equipment; and
- comprehend the food service and beverage service sequentially.

TECHNICAL PROFICIENCY

The term *technical proficiency* means skill and expertise of an individual employee in applying technical knowledge into operational work to achieve the pre-determined target/objective/goal. Remember, this technical proficiency is the upshot of having great knowledge and experience of last so many years in a trade/profession. Proficient staff applies a comprehensive competence derived through regular training and practice.

In food and beverage service department, the staff must have technical proficiency about prevailing liquor laws; mixed drinks, their ingredients and preparation methods; accompanying sauces, wines and other liquors; knowledge of cigar and cigarette; food carving skill; food plating and presentation skills and so forth. Apart from standard *job description,* most organizations also demand technical proficiency (i.e., also known as *job specification*). These technical skills are also known as work handling skills. A brief description of certain major tasks and their standard handling skills (in the form of rules) are given below.

RULES FOR HANDLING TABLECLOTH

Laying and Relaying of Tablecloth

Step 1 Place folded tablecloth (or fresh tablecloth) on each table – double fold/hem (or closed fold/hem) should be on top side and remaining two single hems underside/beneath.

Step 2 Hold the tablecloth's top hem/double fold (between thumb and first finger) and first underside single hem (top one) between the first-finger and second finger.

Step 3 Now elevate the tablecloth and drop the bottom flap (or second underside single hem) over far edge of the table. Here, crease plays a crucial role in laying. Thus, the steward should take care of it.

Step 4 Now release the central fold and drag the tablecloth towards yourself. Finally, ensure that the tablecloth hangs equally on all four sides of the table.

Changing of Tablecloth

Task 1 If the guest table is unoccupied then it is easy to replace the tablecloth. But if table is occupied and tablecloth requires changing due to food/beverage spillage or any other similar kind of problem then the first preference is to shift the guest on another table, if available. Otherwise start changing tablecloth in front of the seated guest.

Task 2 Start tablecloth changing process, one by one fold/shift all four sides of the soiled tablecloth towards inside the tablecloth (one fold on each other). This shifting can be done either from all four corner sides of the tablecloth or from all straight edge sides of the tablecloth.

Task 3 Now lift the folded soiled tablecloth and transfer it to the appropriate place. Meanwhile, ensure that captured/arrested food particles/crumbs should not drop on the table/floor.

Task 4 Finally, lay fresh tablecloth on *make-up table* and allot this table to prospective guest instead of previously shifted guests. Because it is never preferred to repeatedly shift/disturb a guest while he/she enjoys the meal.

RULES FOR HANDLING CUTLERY AND GLASSWARE

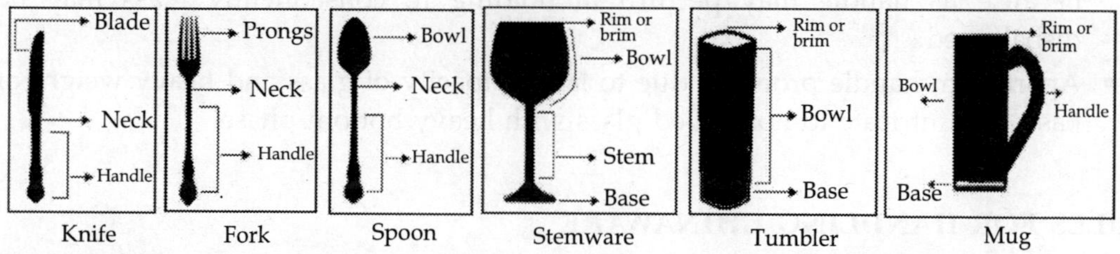

Fig. 7.1 Parts of cutlery, flatware and glassware.

Handling of Cutlery and Flatware (Spoons, Forks and Knives)

- All cutlery and flatware (forks, spoons and knives) should be handled with their neck only. These should not be handled with prong (fork), bowl (spoon) and blade (knives) because these are parts of dining. Thus, it is unhygienic to touch the prong, bowl or blade with bare hands.
- Simultaneously, handling these with bare hands will also create fingerprints on the flatware, cutlery and glassware. So, nowadays most of the properties use white gloves during the serving of dishes and handling of utensils.

Handling of Stemware/Stem Base Glasses

- Stemware should be handled with stem only. It is difficult to hold the stemware with base because it may perturb the balance of glass. Hence, the best way to handle stemware is by keeping the stem between the first two fingers and balance the glass with the thumb.
- Remember never handle stemware with their rim or brim because guests drink from this part. Stemware should also not be handled with their bowls because it will show your finger marks as well as it is unhygienic.

Handling of Tumbler Glasses

- Tumbler glasses should be handled (or carried) with their base; never with brim (because guest drinks from this part). Always try to avoid handling of tumbler glasses with bowl because it may have your finger marks.
- Consequently, tumbler glasses should always be handled with their base or just above the base. This will also not perturb the glass balance because of heavier weight or weighted base.

Handling of Mug Type Glasses

- Mug type glasses should always be held (or carried) with their handles. These glasses are also not handled with their brim and bowl. Besides, the problem of finger marks, these glasses are also difficult to handle with their bowls because its handle may perturb in holding it, consequently glass may be disbalanced.
- Apart from handle problem, due to large capacity of glass and heavy weight of base, it is intricate to hold filled glass with heavy bottom phase.

RULES FOR HANDLING CHINAWARE

(a)

(b)

(c)

Fig. 7.2 Handling of half plates in American or pre-plated service.

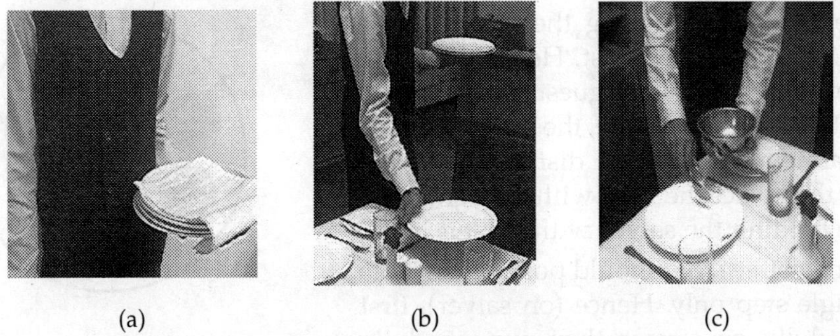

(a) (b) (c)

Fig. 7.3 Handling of full plates in platter to plate service.

Handling of Plates

- All plates should be gripped from the rim side only. While placing plates on the cover, all four fingers should position under the plate and keep the thumb on the outer side of the rim (or pile); thumb should never touch the inside of the plate.
- In case of American service, one can place thumb and last finger on the least corner of the plate pile in order to keep another plate on the same hand. But both, thumb as well as the last finger should not touch the food item.
- But in Russian service, plates are carried on the palm then placed on the cover by holding (or lifting) from the underside of the plate (with all fingers) and thumb on the outer circle/pile of the rim.

Fig. 7.4 Procedure for serving tea and coffee.

Handling of Tea and Coffee Cup and Soup Bowl with Saucer

- In case of tea and coffee service, the tea and coffee *set-up* (cup, saucer, doily paper and spoon) can be pre-placed on the cover (on RHS) for morning breakfast. But during lunch and dinner, it is in the centre of the cover (after taking guest's order).

- If the steward is placing the tea or coffee *setup* in front of the guest. He should place it from the RHS of the guest, in the centre or RHS of the cover. Here, the steward needs to maintain appropriate distance with the guest then place the *setup* with his right hand while holding the salver with his left hand.
- Tea and coffee *setup* should position on table in single step only. Hence (on salver), first place doily on saucer then cup on doily followed by spoon on the right side of the cup. The handle of the cup should be on the RHS of the cover.

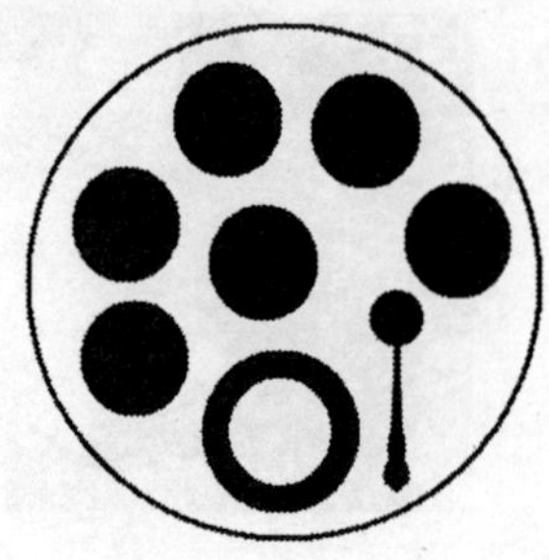

Fig. 7.5 Tray set-up for serving pre-plate

- When the steward places tea or coffee *setup* before the guest arrives as in case of morning breakfast, most of outlets prefer to place the *setup* in the night shift (or before the guest arrives). Here too, the steward has to follow the same procedure mentioned above.
- But in this *setup* the steward may not be too formal. For example, first the steward can place all tea or coffee cup (with saucer) at one step then place tea or coffee spoon in the next turn. But this style should never be followed while placing the *set-up* in front of the guests.

RULES FOR HANDLING TRAY AND SALVER

Handling of Tray

Tray is mostly used in room service and banqueting functions.

- The fundamental rule for tray handling is that it should never be carried with both the hands or by holding from right and left side corners, except in a few banqueting functions. For instance, in large conferences, meetings,. conventions and so forth trays can be carried with both the hands. Here, two persons are required—one person will carry the tray while another will serve the tea/coffee.
- Tray should always be held from the underneath by keeping on the left hand palm then position above the left hand shoulder. The right hand should be kept free for operating the lift, opening the door, knocking the door or ringing the door bell.

Fig. 7.6 Tray set-up and carrying technique

- Tray should always be carried above the shoulder level (in lengthwise direction). It should never be in front of steward's belly. If meal order is too large then use room service trolley instead of tray. There are different sizes of trays available for different purposes.

Handling of Salver

Salver is mostly used in restaurant, bar and in banqueting functions.

- Identical to tray, salver should also be handled with the left hand from the underneath by positioning the palm in the centre of the salver. A steward should never carry the salver above the shoulder level like tray.
- Salver should always carry just parallel to the shoulder (or may also keep in front of the belly) while transporting the meal/beverage order from the *hot plate*/kitchen/pantry/bar section to serving outlet. But at the time of service, salver should be on the left side of steward's body (when salver carries with left hand) and *vice versa*.
- In many restaurants, steward uses tray for fetching meal orders from the *hot plate*, kitchen or pantry section, whereas salver is used for delivering meals/beverages at the guest table.
- During guest serving, salver should never come in front of steward's body because it will perturb you (in serving food) as well as the guest. And in some situations, accident can also happen.

RULES FOR HANDLING WATER JUG AND PORTION BOWL

Handling of Water Jug (or Pitcher)

- First, at least two water jugs (one with cold water and other with normal water) filled with regular filtered in-house water should be kept ready at all times on the side station– on any corner of the side station. These water jugs should be covered with napkin, so as not to get contaminated with dirt or dust.
- At the time of serving water, steward can enfold the chilled water jug with his/her serviette in order to avoid spillage of water on cover, table or guest cloth.

Fig. 7.7 Serving Style

- Steward can also wipe out (with serviette) the water droplets formed on the outer due to chilled water before serving to guest.

Handling of Portion Bowl (or Serving Bowl or Entrée Dish)

- Portion bowls are always used in "platter to plate service". It is mostly used in restaurants and room service where *à la carte menu* is offered. Steward carries it in his left hand.
- These serving bowls are available in round shape (with lid) as well as in oval shape (without lid). It is used to portion (in kitchen section) the guest's food while serving in restaurant and for delivering a meal into resident guests' room (in case of room service order).

- During table service, portion bowls are kept on the left hand palm while service is given with the right hand. Before placing the portion bowl on left hand palm, steward needs to place serviette or napkin on his palm to avoid skin burn.

RULES FOR HANDLING SERVICE GEAR

Handling of Service Gear

- Service gear consists of service spoon and service fork. Sometime steward can also use two service forks in order to transfer few dishes into guest's plate like pancakes, omelettes, etc., when serving via Russian service.
- Service spoon should always be placed under the service fork because service spoon helps in transferring the gravy onto the guest plate whilst service fork helps in making a stiff grip around the food item. In table service, steward should hold service gear with right hand and portion bowl with left hand.
- Service gear is used only in "platter to plate service" and never found in American service. Its holding style may vary with the kind of dishes as in case of whole potato, it should be in round (like in Fig. 7.8 B); for boiled rice, service gear should be flat (like in Fig. 7.8 C) and so forth.

Fig. 7.8 A

Fig. 7.8 B

Fig. 7.8 C

Fig. 7.8 D

Note. If steward wants to make himself perfect in handling service gear then try to clatter (or rattle) the service gear after holding in a proper way by clanging the service fork over service spoon.

FOOD SERVICE GUIDELINES

Starters *(preferably offered in half plate accompanied with sauces/gravies)*

- Starters may be pre-plated or served via platter-to-plate service; it depends on the nature of dish. If offered pre-plated then serve in half plate. Starters may be finger foods like *vol-au-vent* as well as an elegant dish which requires cutlery (then place fish knife and fish fork). In case of finger food, generally no cutlery and flatware is placed on the cover.
- In English service, starters are offered in platter and steward directly places it in the centre of the table. This is self-help. Here, the steward changes side plate for next upcoming course (if side plate gets soiled).
- Starters are usually spicy in nature thus are offered with accompaniments. These accompaniments are offered in gravy or sauce boat (by placing on underliner with pre-serve spoon). Accompaniments must be offered first or both may be offered together. With most pre-plated starters, accompaniments are pre-portioned with main dish in the same half plate.

Soup

- Mostly soups are offered in a soup bowl but it may also be served in a soup cup or in a deep soup plate; it depends upon the type of soup. For example, all clear and consommé soups are offered in soup cups while broth soups are served in soup plate.
- Generally, soups are always pre-portioned (or rarely served via platter-to-plate service) in kitchen. Stewards just need to bring it and serve from the RHS of the guest. Steward places pre-portioned soup bowl/soup cup on underliner and then serves.
- Soup spoon is available in two forms – chinaware and stainless steel/EPNS. Stainless steel/EPNS soup spoon can be directly placed on the cover as well as offered separately with soup (by placing on underliner) whereas chinaware soup spoon should always be offered with soup and never be pre-placed on the cover.
- In case of using soup plate, stainless steel/EPNS soup spoon is mostly offered– it should be pre-placed on the guest cover. Instead of using underliner, soup plate is directly placed on the show plate/charger (as it works as an underliner). The clearance of all served soups should be done from the right side of the guest.

Main Course

- In restaurant and room service, main courses are offered in portion bowls and platters while in coffee shops meals are pre-plated (thus no portion bowls are required in pre-plated meals). In restaurant, steward can use *with lid* as well as *without lid* portion bowls but in room service, it is always enviable to use *with lid* portion bowls only.
- Platter-to-plate service is given from the left side of the guests with the help of *service gear*. Steward should forward the dish from his left hand (also forward his left leg to maintain an appropriate distance with guest) as to show the dish and announce the name then take approval for its service. Steward requires to place serviette on his palm before carrying portion bowl, as it prevents skin from burning.
- After serving, if dish remains in the bowl then steward may place it on the guest table (in the centre of the table, if space allows) or keep it on the side station (ready for second service). Steward should use separate service gear for all individual dishes.
- While clearing, all plates (full as well as side plates) and used cutlery should be removed from the right side of the guest, except side plate which will be picked up from the left. Remaining items like portion bowls (if placed on the table) and centre appointments should also be removed from the table but these can be removed from any side of the guest.
- On clearing a single guest cover, steward should first clear full plate then side plate. But when steward needs to clear the cover of more than two guests simultaneously, then he should clear all full plates in the first round and all side plates in the second round.

- If *dessert indicator* is already laid on the top of the cover then steward either directly shifts them on to their respective places on the cover or may shift them to the side station (if cover requires crumbing).

Dessert

- It can be hot as well as cold and usually pre-portioned in bowls, glasses, cups and in half plates.
- Before offering dessert, ensure that all previously served items are removed from the table (especially cruet set), except water glass and guest napkin.
- Dessert can be served either in dessert bowl, dessert cup, champagne saucer, sundae glass or dessert plate. It depends upon the nature of dessert as well as availability of equipment. Desserts are rarely served via platter-to-plate service, except when offered through dessert trolley.
- If dessert is offered in bowl, cup or champagne saucer (place doily paper between underliner and bowl/cup/saucer) the steward is required to place tea spoon on the right side of the saucer. Offer ice cream spoon with ice cream only. On the other side, if dessert is offered in dessert plate first place *dessert indicators* on their respective places on the cover then serve it.
- If *dessert indicator* is already placed on the top of the cover then transfer dessert spoon on right side and dessert fork on left side. Now offer dessert at the centre of the cover. Sundae ice cream is offered in sundae glass with sundae spoon.
- The service and clearance of dessert (when offered in bowl, cup or champagne saucer) is analogous to tea and coffee service and clearance. But if dessert is served in dessert plate then clearance will be as of full plate clearance.

AFTER MEAL BEVERAGE

- In beverages, generally tea, coffee, liquors and after dinner drinks are served to guest. A detailed description of these beverages (along with serving techniques) is given later in this book.

BEVERAGE SERVICE GUIDELINES

Service of Water

- Steward should carry water jug with his/her right hand and serve water and all other beverages from the right side of the guest. Never bring water directly in water glass; water tumbler/goblet should be placed first on the cover then pour water via jug or bottle.
- The outer surface of *chilled water* jug should be covered (or surrounded) with serviette in order to prevent water droplets from dropping on the plate or guest's clothes or valuables (like mobile).

- *Mineral water* bottles should first be shown (to verify temperature) to guest then takes approval to serve. Only after getting guest approval, steward should open the bottle cap. Cap of bottle should never split from the neck; tilt the cap during water service, and close the bottle with cap afterwards.

Menu Presentation

- After serving water, steward should present menu to each guest. Menu is mainly presented from the right side of the guest but in certain situations it may also be offered from the left side of the guest, for instance, when guest is busy with his/her right hand.
- Wine list or beverage menu should always be presented first followed by food menu thereafter dessert menu. Nowadays, most of the establishments offer common menu card. This menu card contains all meals, beverages and tobacco products which outlet offers to their guests.
- After giving menu card, a steward has to wait for at least five minutes, so that a guest can go through all the menu items. If guest faces any intricacy in selecting the food or beverage item then steward can do suggestive selling and show his/her salesmanship.

Order Taking

- In general, station head waiter is responsible for order taking. Order taker should stand at 45° angle (at corner of the table) on the right side of the host and must maintain an appropriate distance with guest.

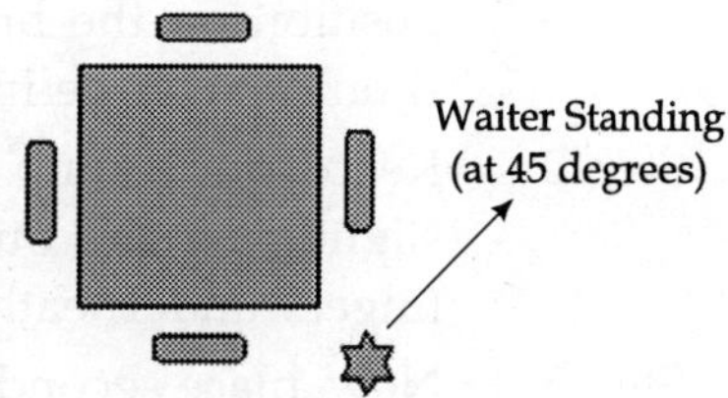

- Steward should try to take beverage order first as to do up-selling. Steward may take entire meal order at once or may also take order after the completion of first course/meal. It usually depends upon the type of meal guest wants to order, style of menu, time available with guest, etc.
- If outlet offers separate menu for separate courses such as beverage offered in one menu while main course offered in second menu followed by dessert in third menu and so forth. It will definitely be a time consuming process.
- The concept of separate menu for every course usually is offered in high class restaurants with the purpose to offer more variations in every individual course. Hence, in this case, steward usually takes order after the completion of previous meal.
- A single menu card contains all courses; from starter to beverage but it offers limited choice of meals and beverages. Here, the steward can take entire meal order at once then serve each course one after another. It is mostly offered in medium and small size restaurants.

Suggestive Selling or Salesmanship

- It means how a steward can augment the sale of food and beverage items in any restaurant, coffee shop, bar or any other outlet. At the time of suggestive selling steward should never compel a guest to choose any specific dish that he has suggested.
- Concurrently, steward should never give any wrong proclamation of any menu item to the guest. For example, if a guest wishes to take suggestion from the steward regarding what to order, simultaneously guest should also suggest something which he/she really wants to order. Here, a steward can reply either in one of these two ways:

Steward suggestion (or suggestive selling)	"Sir it's a very delicious preparation, you will definitely enjoy to it".
Steward reply towards guest suggestions	"Sir it is also a delicious preparation, you will definitely enjoy it".

Procedure for Carrying Plates (in Pre-Plated Service or American Service)

Step 1 Always hold a plate between the thumb and little/last finger (mid three fingers will be underneath the plate). Your thumb should be in horizontal position on the brim/rim of the plate, pointing towards the rim; finger should never be inside the plate pile.

Step 2 Keep your thumb and last finger (or little finger) above the first plate (or slightly on the outer pile/boundary of the plate) and rest of the three fingers underneath the plate as shown in Fig. 7.2 (a).

Step 3 Now, place second plate on/amongst upper part of the thumb, last finger and end part of palm like previously shown in Fig. 7.2 (b). Steward may also place one more plate on the same hand (on same forearm) but only when he/she is confident.

Step 4 Finally, steward will hold third/fourth plate by his right hand. This kind of serving style is called "American Service" in which pre-plated food is given from the right-hand side of the guest.

Note. In this kind of service, the food is always pre-plated/pre-portioned in the kitchen by kitchen staff. In this, food is usually offered in half plate (also known as blue plate or American plate). Examples include– pizza, burger, sandwich and so forth.

Procedure for Carrying Plates (in Platter-to-Plate Service)

First and foremost, steward should always carry limited number of plates which he/she can easily balance or handle. Enfold serviette (keep one hem on the palm then place plate/s and second hem on the top surface of the first plate) to cover top and bottom of the plate/s. Remember steward should not hold the plates against his/her body. A step-by-step procedure for carrying plates (suppose steward serves to four guests) is given below:

Step 1 Initially place one side of clean folded serviette on left hand palm then keep the required number of plate/s (full plates). Next place another folded side of serviette on the surface of the top plate (like in Fig. 7.3 (a)) to avoid any finger prints.

Step 2 Now approach the guest's table and remove folded side of serviette from top plate and start placing plates in front of each guest. Place plate one after another in the centre of the cover like in Fig. 7.3 (b). In this service, plates are placed from the right-hand side of the guest.

Step 3 While serving dishes, present food (in portion bowl) from left-hand side of the guest by taking your left leg and left hand forward.

Step 4 Afterwards, steward should announce the name of the presented dish and after getting guest's approval serve it (with the help of service gear) on the guest's plate. Steward should never place any food item in the centre of the plate (as this space is of guest) as well as on the pile of the plate.

Note. In this kind of service, dishes are pre-portioned in portion bowl or platter by the kitchen staff (as per the given meal order), afterwards served by the food and beverage serving staff. This service technique is also called *silver service*. Examples include – serving egg curry, mattar panner and several other gravy dishes. Remember, *bread croutons* and *bread sticks* (or soup sticks) is a standard accompaniment with cream soups. Croutons can be accompanied with soup as well as added as garnish. Apart from it, bread rolls plus other breads (like garlic bread) are also served with most of the soups. All types of bread products are offered in side plate from left side of the guest.

Procedure for Clearing Soiled Plates

Step 1 Steward approaches the guest's table then takes permission (from right-hand side) to clear the empty (or soiled) plates. If fork and spoon are positioned on each other or in criss-cross manner, it is an indication that guest has not finished his/her meal like in Fig. 7.9 (a).

Step 2 After obtaining permission for clearance, the steward takes away the plate from right side of the guest. He picks up plate with right hand and places it on the palm of his left hand (between thumb and last finger) in a similar fashion as plate seized in pre-plated food service.

Step 3 Now steward collects second plate with his right hand and places it on the upward thumb, last finger and end of the palm, in a similar fashion as plate held in pre-plated food service.

Step 4 Next transfer the food remains of second plate on to the first plate with the help of collected soiled knife, fork or spoon. Afterwards, steward should properly arrange the soiled cutlery on the first plate like in Fig. 7.9 (b).

Step 5 Now steward collects third plate and places (or stacks) it on the second plate then transfers all the food remains/particles and puts soiled flatware and cutlery on the first plate.

Step 6 Finally, the last cleared plate need not be emptied (placed on the previously stacked plates) as steward can easily carry it in his right hand.

Note. Steward should collect all soiled cover appointments from the right side of the guest. Do not carry too many plates, in order to avoid accident. Steward should always clear the cover only after obtaining guest permission even when positioned cutlery and flatware shows that meal has been finished.

If steward is clearing different sizes of plates at one time then full plate should be cleared first and placed in-between the left hand's thumb and last finger thereafter remaining full plates by placing on thumb, last finger and palm end side, like in Fig. 7.9 (b) (c). Finally, clear all side plates and place them on the top surface of last cleared full plate. Steward should never mount different sizes of plates on each other.

(a) (b) (c)

Fig. 7.9 Procedure for clearing of soiled plates

Basic Techniques of Soiled Plate Clearance

- After removing first plate, steward should arrange soiled *silverware* (cutlery and flatware) on it. The handle of firstly collected fork should be under the thumb. This will secure the remaining flatware. Then steward should slide the knife in at a right angle under the fork.
- Now clear the second plate with silverware and transfer the silverware on the first plate, fork beneath the thumb and knife below.
- The remaining plates are mounted on the second plate, while the flatware is arranged on the first plate.
- In an elegant service, no more than four plates are cleared at one time. Small food remnants on the plates can be pushed to the lower plate; be sure to turn away from the guest when doing this.

- When plates contain many leftovers, they must be scraped away from the table. Here, clear only two plates (preferable) at a time and directly bring it to the service pantry/dishwashing area.

Procedure for Offering Finger Bowl

Requirement	A steward requires finger bowl, saucer (or underliner), luke warm water with one lemon slice (rose petals may also be added) in each finger bowl.
Placement of finger bowl	Just before the clearance of full plate, a steward must keep ready the finger bowl on side station. After clearing the full plate/s, steward should immediately place finger bowl in the centre of the cover. It should be placed on the right-hand side of the guest.
Clearance of finger bowl	When guest rinses his/her fingers, remove the finger bowl from the cover/s. It is cleared from the right-hand side of the guest. The clearance procedure will be identical to soup bowl clearance.

Note.

- Lemon slices are round while lemon wedges are square in shape. In a finger bowl, steward needs to use lemon slices. In the absence of lemon slices steward may put rose petals but they do not have cleansing power.
- Finger bowl is mainly offered when guest has consumed finger foods such as breads; it may be roti, chapatti, bread rolls, French bread and so on.

Procedure for Crumbing Guest Table

Step 1 Approach the guest's table from the left side.

Step 2 Position a service plate just under the table lip.

Step 3 Start working from the centre of the cover position. Steward should use a folded service cloth or small brush to crumb down the debris onto the service plate.

Step 4 Now move to the right hand of the guests and repeat the same crumbing down procedure.

Note.

- In case of an *à la carte cover setup*, the cutlery for next course will be positioned on the cover only after the crumbing process. Whereas in *table d'hôte cover setup*, steward needs to crumb first then tumble down the dessert fork on left side and dessert spoon on right side.
- Crumbing can be done by holding service cloth directly with hand or by holding the service cloth with service gear. Often, brush is also used for crumbing. Steward starts crumbing either from right or left side of the guest.

Procedure for Clearing Ashtray from Guest Table

Step 1 Place a clean ashtray onto a cover plate or small salver.

Step 2 Approach the guest's table from the side nearest to the soiled ashtray.

Step 3 Pick up the clean ashtray from your cover plate or small salver, upside down in your hand.

Step 4 Ensure not to disturb the guests, lean forward and place a clean ashtray on the top of the soiled ashtray.

Step 5 Take hold of both ashtrays and lift them onto the salver or cover plate.

Step 6 Remove the clean ashtray from the soiled one and put it back on the table. Take the soiled ashtray to the scullery area.

Note.

- Ashtray should be changed every time the guest puts a cigarette out. Covering of soiled ashtray is necessary, so steward can prevent ash from falling out of the ashtray into the food.
- Nowadays, most outlets use two spare ashtrays on salver to exchange with the soiled one. First ashtray is used to cover the soiled ashtray on the guest table while second fresh ashtray is used directly to be placed on the table.

KEY TERMS

Technical proficiency	:	Practical/methodological skill of employees.
Make-up table	:	Process of table/cover laying.
Stemware	:	Collective term for all stem based glassware like champagne glasses, wine glasses and so forth.
English service	:	*Host service* whereby host serves food to all invitees.
American service	:	Pre-portioned and pre-plated service offered from right side of the guest.
Service gear	:	A set comprising of service spoon and service fork used jointly for serving food in silver service.
Vol-au-vent	:	A starter dish. It is a puff pastry case, usually eaten with fingers.
Silver service	:	Table serving technique whereby food is served from platter-to-plate by using service gear.
Crumbing	:	Process of removing leftovers/crumbs from guest table/cover before serving the next course.

REVIEW QUESTIONS

1. What is technical proficiency? Write any five desirable technical proficiencies of restaurant steward.
2. Write down step-by-step procedure for serving any dish through platter-to-plate service.
3. Enlist steps involved in pre-plated food service.
4. Suggest appropriate service types for the following outlets: restaurant, coffee shop, room service and kiosk.

Banquet

OBJECTIVES

Students will be able to:

- explicate banquet and type of banqueting functions;
- recognize different small and large group set-ups; and
- calculate the space required for different banquet set-ups.

BANQUET

Banquet is usually the highest revenue-generating outlet in the food and beverage service department. It serves food and beverage to a gathering of people under one roof for same kind of banqueting function. This function may be either- formal, semi-formal or informal. For instance, wedding, reception, ceremony, birthday party, exhibitions, concerts and so forth.

Conventionally, banquet halls are used for all kinds of functions but nowadays trend has absolutely changed. Today, banquet outlets are primarily catering to informal functions only. On the other side, conference centres and conventional halls are preferred for organizing large semi-formal functions.

Similarly, small business meetings, workshops, lectures, training classes and so forth are organized in hotel's *business centre*. Apart from hotels, nowadays independent banquet halls, convention centres, conference hall, etc., dominate the market. A brief description on banqueting function types and space requirement is given below:

Types of Banqueting Functions		
Formal Functions	**Semi-Formal Functions**	**Informal functions**
• State banquets	• Conferences and conventions	• Receptions and anniversaries
• Conclave luncheons	• Seminars and workshops	• Birthday and cocktail parties
• Wedding breakfasts	• Exhibitions and trade fairs	• Wedding receptions
• Diplomatic dinners	• Board meetings and lectures	• Christmas and theme parties

BANQUET SEATING ARRANGEMENT

✓ Seating along with related physical arrangements, which create the foundation for meetings, programmes, and training, are often called *room setups*. They encompass comfort, access and safety for the attendees, and when selected appropriately, extend a presenter's influence in the room, broadcast intention and eliminate distractions.

✓ Presenters, trainers, organizers and programme planners sometimes ignore physical arrangements and take whatever room setup is immediately available. But experienced presenters understand that a functional setup is essential and arranging for it is neither difficult nor expensive. It is just a matter of accurate planning and knowing the options.

✓ Banquet manager or banquet sales executive at hotels and conference centres must provide all relevant information to function organizer. Simultaneously, manager or sales executive should also ask the organizer about room setup requirements. Convention and visitor bureaus can also provide generic information about aisle widths and square feet per person.

✓ The type of seating arrangement usually depends upon various factors: number of attendees, nature of function, meal and beverage provision, wish of organizer, available banquet space and so forth. On these bases, seating arrangement can be classified into two broad groups — large group setups and small group setups.

Large Group Setups

The most commonly used, but not always, and the most appropriate style of seating for large groups is *theatre* style. Other alternatives are *classroom* and *fish bone or chevron* styles. Functions accompanied by meals have one choice- *banquet* style setup (large round tables). Banquet style setup has several limitations like difficulty to see orator (or presenter/toastmaster/master of ceremony) but attendees are accustomed to turn their chairs and heads to see the orator. This style of setup shows crowded tables and may also produce noise from the food service facility, thus not suitable for formal banqueting events. A brief description on preferable table setups for large groups along with ideal space requirement is given below.

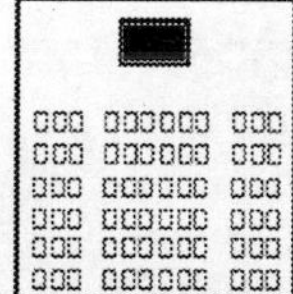
Theater Style

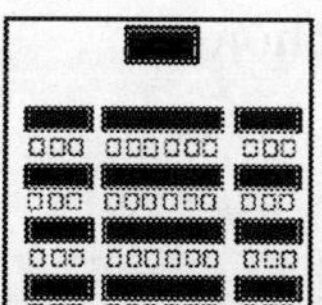
Classroom Style

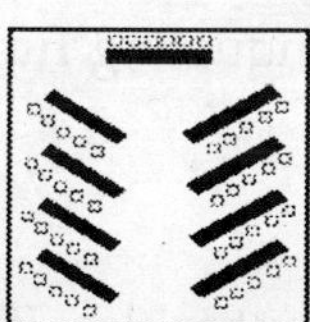
Chevron Style

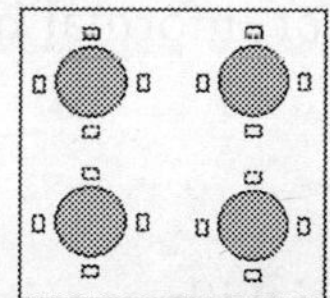
Round Style

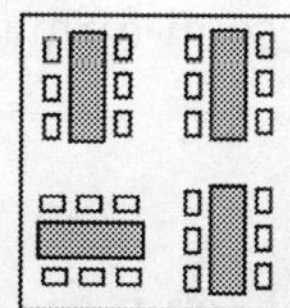
Oblong Style

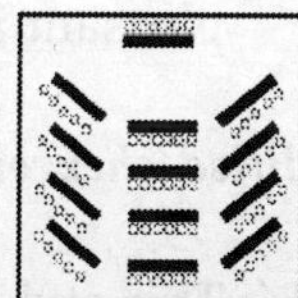
Modified Chevron

Theater style

- ✓ In this style of setup you can accommodate maximum people. It allows approximately 6-8 square feet space per person. This style of setup is usually appropriate for lectures and keynoters. But note taking is slightly cumbersome for attendees in this style of setup.

Classroom Style

- ✓ It is identical to theater style but with tables. It requires approximate area about 8-10 square feet per person. It has desk (or table) in front of chairs, so it supports note taking process and use of handout materials.

Chevron style

- ✓ It provides enough space for food and beverage service. This style of setup is more suitable for large groups of people because it promotes a sense of participation. It requires approximately 12-14 sq. ft of space per person. It can be set with or without tables.

Round style

- ✓ There should be approximately 60 inches (or 5 ft) distance between round tables (between the edges of the two tables) for placing chairs and providing service aisle. This 60 inches space comprises 24 inches (or 2 ft) service aisle and 36 inches (or 3 ft) for placing chairs on both round tables; every chair acquires around 18 inches space. It looks pleasant in formal banqueting functions.

Oblong style

- ✓ There should be approximately 60 inches (or 5 ft) distance between the oblong tables for placing chairs and providing service aisle. It also permits 24 inches (or 2 ft) distance for service aisle beside 36 inch dimension for placing two chairs on both oblong tables; every chair acquires around 18 inch space. But it looks pleasant in semi-formal or informal banqueting functions.

Modified chevron

- ✓ This style of setup can be with or without tables. It improves visibility of orator and visual aids (if used) can be seen from almost all sides. It is more interactive than theatre and classroom style table setup.

Small Group Setup

All small group setups (like– *Perpendicular, U-Shape, Semicircle, Hollow Square or Rectangle, Boardroom and Cluster*) should also provide enough space for movement and comfortable seating. In addition, setup should encourage attendees to take an active role in the presentation/meeting and to communicate with their peers and orator. Apart from main traffic aisles, almost all small group setup should allow 54 inches (4 ft 6 inches) space between round tables for placing chair and providing service aisle, similarly 60 inches (5 ft) between oblong tables where seating is back-to-back. This permits 24 inches (2 ft) service aisle beside 18 inches dimension for chair. Where food service is not required and seating is at one side of the table, small setup allows 36 inches (3 ft) space between tables. If table setup (especially square and round tables) is given in diamond fashion then same plinth area will typically permit to put one more row of tables.

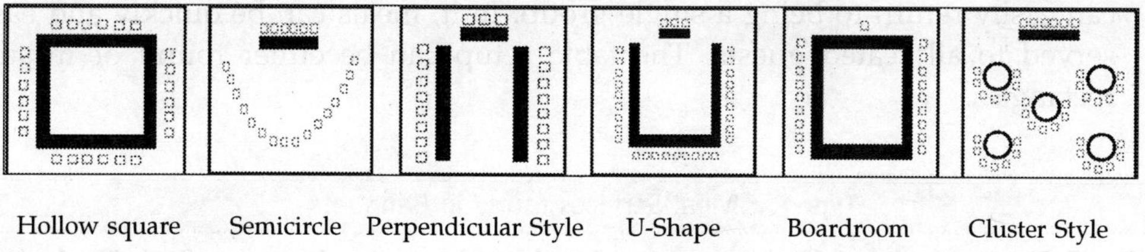

Hollow square Semicircle Perpendicular Style U-Shape Boardroom Cluster Style

Hollow square

✓ This style of setup is suitable for formal events like board meetings where formal pecking order is not an issue. It is an excellent setup for facilitator who leads meetings. The setup encourages the attendees' participation but does not use any visuals. This setup can easily convert into a rectangular shape.

Boardroom

✓ It is also called a "Rectangle Shape". This style of setup is good for group gathering of attendees between 6 to 15 pax. But this style of setup is usually preferred for those functions in which formality and pecking order is most important.

Perpendicular

✓ In it, seats can be on either outside or inside the tables. Orator or instructor can examine the attendees' work and can easily exchange the matter or any other material with attendees. The centre space can be used for exhibitions or for demonstrations.

U-Shape

✓ This style of setup encourages collaboration and centre space of the setup can be used for simulations and role plays (if any). U-shape setup can be used with or without speaker table.

Semicircle or circle

✓ This style of setup can also be set with or without tables. In it, the orator's/presenter's role is limited/minimum, thus it is excellent for emotional sessions such as sharing grief. It can encourage a sense of bonding.

Cluster

✓ This style of setup is good for presentations with breakout groups. The clusters can easily return to being a single group. In it, meals can be quickly and easily served to all seated guests. The table setup can be either round or in small rectangles.

Types of Meal Services found in Banquets

Service Type	Also called	Meal Portioning and Serving Style/Technique
American service	Pre-plated service	Food is pre-plated in half plate and served from right-hand side
French service	Cart/trolley service	Food is presented in trolley and served either pre-plated or platter-to-plate.
English service	Host service	Food is pre-portioned in serving bowls and host will serve to invitees.
Russian service	Platter-to-plate service	Food is pre-portioned in serving bowls and server serves from left side.
Buffet service	Self service	Food is displayed on buffet counter and guests serve to themselves.
Cafeteria service	Food control service	Food is displayed on buffet counter and serving staff will portion/serve.

BANQUET SPACE CALCULATION

Banquet space area consists of two aspects: aisle space and table arrangement space. **Aisle space** is needed for server and guest maneuverability and comprises service aisle and access aisle. Service side aisle is usually ranged from 4.5 feet (in case of Guéridon service) and varies with style of meal service. This service side aisle is made for the food serving staff, so they can easily (and without disturbance) prepare (in Guéridon service) and serve to their guests. Access side aisle allows the guests to get into and out of their chairs easily, in general 1.5 to 2 feet is sufficient. The type of guest, style of setup, number of attendees, size of chair and desired atmosphere also affect the banquet space calculation figure.

In **table arrangement**, there should be at least 6 ft distance among the placed sprigs (or table edges). This 6 ft distance comprises 3-4 ft passing space in between the two placed chairs and remaining 3-2 ft will be acquired by two adjacently placed chairs. Along wall side, edge of placed table should be at least 5 ft away from the wall. This 5 ft distance comprises 3 ft gangway space between chair's back side and wall and remaining 2 ft space will be acquired by the chair. This is an ideal space requirement which may alter in accordance with alterations in seating style, table's shape and size. An ideal space requirement for frequently laid seating arrangement is given below.

For Theatre Style Seating

✓ Divide *attendees* seating area (sq.ft) by 6. In theater style setup, try to avoid more than 12 people in one row of seats. The aisle space area will be 4 ft in a function of 100 pax while 6 ft aisle space is required in a function of 200 pax.

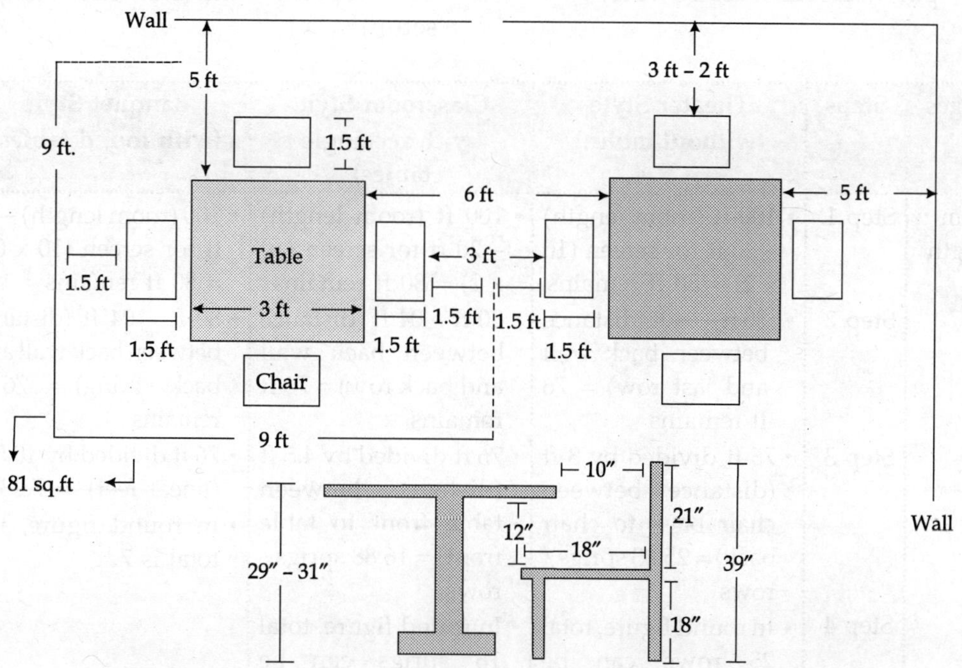

Fig. 8.1 Customary space dimension for square and round table setup

For Classroom Style Seating

✓ Divide the *attendees* seating area (sq.ft) by 8. In general, an aisle space of 30-36 inches should be left in between the tables; this may also vary. For example, in a function of 100 pax, provide 4 ft aisle space while in a function of 200 pax, provide 6 ft aisle space.

For Banquet Style Seating

✓ When using oblong tables, divide the room area (sq.ft) by 8 and when using round and square tables, divide the room area (sq.ft) by 10. These figures are for standard seating. If space is available for more comfortable seating, allow an additional 2 sq.ft per person.

Banquet Space Calculation Guidelines

Room size (assumed)	= 7500 sq.ft (100 ft × 75 ft)
Screen (on stage)	= 10 ft in height
Distance between rows/sprigs/chairs	= 3-6 ft (it may vary with setup style)
Distance between back row and back wall	= 4 ft
Aisle space (service + access aisle)	= 15 % of room width (for whole banquet setup)

Stages	Steps	Theater Style (without tables)	Classroom Style (with rectangle tables)	Banquet Style (with round tables)
Room Length (1)	Step 1	• 100 ft (room length) – 20 ft for screen (10 x 2) = 80 ft remains	• 100 ft (room length) – 20 ft for screen (10 x 2) = 80 ft remains	• 100 (room length) – 20 ft for screen (10 x 02) = 80 ft remains
	Step 2	• 80 ft – 04 ft (distance between back wall and last row) = 76 ft remains	• 80 ft – 04 ft (distance between back wall and back row) = 76 ft remains	• 80 ft – 04 ft (distance between back wall and back sitting) = 76 ft remains
	Step 3	• 76 ft divided by 3 ft (distance between chair back to chair back) = 25.33 sprigs/ rows	• 76 ft divided by 4.5 ft (distance between table front to table front) = 16.88 sprigs/ rows	• 76 ft divided by 10.5 ft (linear feet) = 7.23 • In round figure, the total is 7.
	Step 4	• In round figure, total 25 rows can be accommodated in the room.	• In round figure, total 16 sprigs can be accommodated in the room.	

Room Width (2)	Step 1	• 75 ft (room width) – 11.25 ft aisle space (15% of room width) = 63.75 ft remains	• 75 ft (room width) – 11.25 ft aisle space (15 % of room width) = 63.75 ft remains	• 75 ft (room width) – 11.25 ft aisle space (15% of room width) = 63.75 ft remains
	Step 2	• 63.75 ft divided by 3 ft (distance between chairs) = 21.25	• 63.75 ft divided by 3 ft (distance between tables) = 21.25	• 63.75 ft divided by 10.5 ft (linear feet) = 6.07
	Step 3	• In round figure, total 21 chairs can be accommodated in one row.	• In round figure, total 21 chairs can be accommodated in one row.	• In round figure, the total is 6.
Setup (3)	Step 1	• 25 sprigs multiplied by 21 chairs = 525 chairs.	• 16 sprigs multiplied by 21 chairs = 336 chairs.	• 7 multiplied by 6 = 42 tables
	Step 2			• 42 round tables multiplied by 8 chairs per table = 336 chairs.

Stage 1 Determine how many rows can be accommodated

Step 1 Subtract the space between screen and front row – it is usually two times the screen height (or 20% of the room length).

Step 2 Subtract the space between last row and back wall – it is usually 5/4 ft between back wall and back row.

Step 3 Resulted figure (or resulted room length) divided by the distance between rows – measured from chair back to chair back or table front to table front area.

Step 4 Now round off the resultant figure down to the nearest full row.

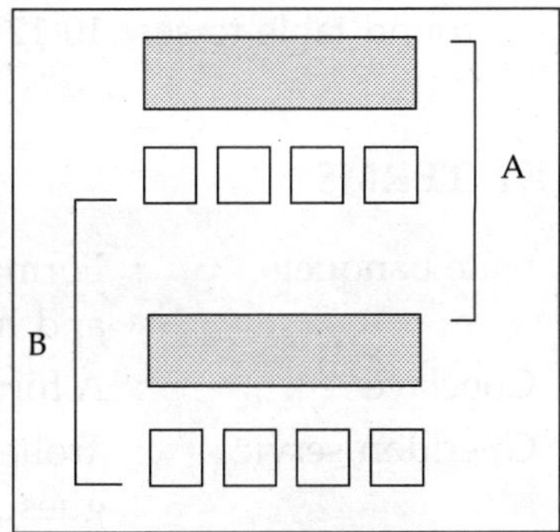

Fig. 8.2 (A) Table front to table front (B) Chair back to chair back

Stage 2 Determine how many chairs can be set in each row

Step 1 Now take the apparent room width and subtract space for service and access aisle (or normally about 15% of room width).

Step 2 Resulted figure (or resulted room width) to be divided by the distance between chairs/per chair – measured from chair centre to chair centre/table front to table front area.

Step 3 Now round off the resultant figure down to the nearest chair.

Stage 3 Multiply the number of rows by the number of chairs in each row

Note.

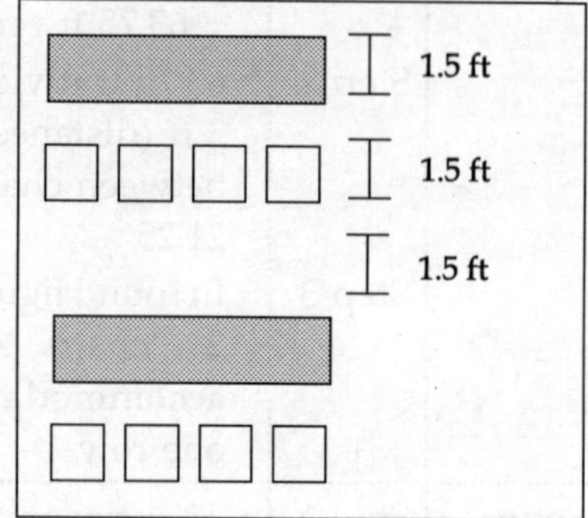

Fig. 8.3 Breakdown of 4.5 ft

- Nowadays, most banquets are equipped with *banquet space calculator* which automatically calculates the maximum number of possible seating in any functional room in accordance with different style of banquet layout.
- *This 3 ft distance comprises 1.5 ft chair dimension and 1.5 ft distance between chair back side (chair in first row) and chair front edge (chair in second row).
- **This 4.5 ft distance comprises 1.5 ft chair dimension, 1.5 ft table width (or bench width) and 1.5 ft distance between back side of placed chair and back table. These distances may also increase or decrease in accordance with room length and width.
- ***The linear feet for different sizes of round tables will be ideally around 10 linear feet for 60 inches (5 ft) round table to seat 6-9 pax; 10.5 linear feet for 66 inches (5 ft 6 inches) round table to seat 8-10 pax and 11 linear feet for 72 inches (6 ft) round table to seat 10-12 pax.

KEY TERMS

State banquets	: Formal and silent *state dinner* mostly settled by the government and hosted by head of state.
Conclave	: A formal, small and confidential meeting.
Guéridon service	: Trolley service whereby half done food is cooked in front of guest.
Service side aisle	: Guest table side space that requires to steward for serving meals and beverages.
Access side aisle	: Admittance space allows people to get into and out of the chairs easily.
Sprigs	: Number of rows, either or both sides of which chairs will be placed.
Linear feet	: It is often also called *lineal feet* and are the same as regular feet. For instance, if something is 6 linear feet long, it means it is 6 feet long.
Aisle space	: Collective term (service and access side aisle) used in lieu of space required around guest table/s.

REVIEW QUESTIONS

1. What is a state banquet? Classify banqueting functions, explain each briefly and support with function example.
2. Enlist different styles of banquet setups for organizing a small function of 75 pax and also suggest required per pax space for each.
3. Elucidate various suitable food service methods for organizing large banqueting functions.
4. Suggest layout, buffet counter style, apposite service type and required space for a formal banqueting function of 250 pax.

Meals and Menu

(With table appointments: centre and cover appointments/cover layout)

Objectives

Students will be able to:

- elucidate different meal occasions and their revenue impact;
- state major breakfast types along with choices of items/courses; and
- comprehend the role of menu as a selling tool and menu types.

MEAL AND MENU

The term *meal* indicates to extensive feast; it is also concerned with mealtime known as *meal period and dayparts*. Technically, *meal period* is relatively a fixed occasion at which food is consumed each day. As per the dictionary, meal means the act of serving of food or something to eat. The three major meals of the day are breakfast (in morning), lunch (in afternoon) and dinner (in night). But in food and beverage service industry (or in catering industry) *meal period* usually comprises several *meal occasions*.

On the other side, the term *menu* is a French word that indicates to a list of dishes that are available through the ordering process. Broadly, menu is classified into two categories, i.e., *à la carte* (separately priced menu) and *table d'hôte* (collectively priced menu). Menu shows prices of all available dishes along with standard portion, price, applicable taxes and other charges. In English, menu is known as *bill of fares* and it was presumed that menu originated in 1541 by Duke Henry in Brunswick. A brief description on meals and menus is given below.

MEAL OCCASIONS

Bed Tea or Coffee

- ✓ This early morning tea or coffee service is offered from the room service section. The ideal timing for serving bed tea/coffee is around 6:00 to 6:30 a.m., normally accompanied with cookies and often newspaper is also delivered.

Breakfast

- ✓ It is the first meal eaten within an hour or two after a person wakes up in the morning. The ideal timing for breakfast is between 7:00-10:00 a.m. Hotels which mainly cater to foreign guests offer breakfast between 6:30 a.m. and 9:30 a.m.

Elevenses (A Short Break During Morning for Light Refreshment)

- ✓ It is a tea or coffee preparation offered with light snack items. It is offered during late morning or after breakfast but before lunch. The ideal timing is between 10:30 to 11:00 a.m. In Spain, it is known as *la once*.

Brunch (A Second Breakfast)

- ✓ It is a late morning meal served between the typical time for breakfast and lunch, as a replacement for both meals. It is usually eaten by those guests who rise too late and thus miss their breakfast.
- ✓ In such situations, brunch serves as a specially planned meal. The term brunch is a portmanteau of *br*eakfast and *lunch*. The ideal timing is between 10:30 and 11:30 a.m.

TABLE APPOINTMENTS FOR AFTERNOON TEA

Centre	Cover
Ashtray (O)	Side plate
Bud vase	Side knife
Cruet set	Show plate
Table number	Tea cup on saucer with tea spoon
Sugar basin/bowl	Napkin
Sugar tong/spoon	Pastry fork
Preserve dish	Water glass
Preserve spoon	

TABLE APPOINTMENTS FOR EVENING TEA

Centre	Cover
Ashtray (O)	Side plate
Bud vase	Side knife
Cruet set	Show plate
Table number	Tea cup on saucer with tea spoon
Sugar basin	Napkin
Sugar tong	Joint fork
Preserve dish	Joint knife
Preserve spoon	Water glass

Lunch (de jeuner)

- ✓ It is a mid-day meal. It takes place in most of the available food serving outlets (often hotel based coffee shop outlet also serves lunch) and could include food from a variety of cuisines. It is served in the afternoon, usually between 1:00 and 3:00 p.m.

Afternoon/Low Tea

- ✓ This service of tea or/and coffee is offered with some light snacks such as sandwiches, scones, cakes, pastries, etc. It is normally served around 4:00 p.m. or between 4:00 and 4:30 p.m.

Evening/High Tea

- ✓ This tea is offered usually around 6:00 p.m. It involves the service of some substantial snacks (like cold meats, eggs or fish, sweets, buns, cakes and sandwiches) along with tea or coffee.

Dinner

✓ It is the main meal (or major meal) of the day served in almost all available food serving outlets. Menu consists of choice of beverages, tobacco products and food from several styles of cooking. Generally, dinner is served between 7:30 and 11:30 p.m.

Lupper

✓ It is a mid-afternoon full meal usually a substitute to both lunch and supper. It is well known by late risers and shift workers. It is served between 5:30 and 6:30 p.m.

Supper

✓ It is an evening meal usually served between 7:30 and 8:30 p.m. In general, guest demands supper when he/she does not wish to have dinner in the outlet, as he/she may be busy during evening meal time due to personal engagements.

Bed Lunch

✓ It is a light meal served during late evening. Bed lunch usually succeeds lupper. The service is mainly offered by room service section.

Midnight Snacks

✓ This food and beverage facility is offered to latecomers/late check-ins. In this, light meals are provided from midnight to 6:00 a.m. During night shift, food will be prepared by night kitchen chef and service will be given by night shift's food service staff.

BREAKFAST

The term *breakfast* is considered the combination of two words i.e. break + fast. *Break* means "to break" and *fast* means "period of starvation". In simple terms, to break the fast after the whole night is called "breakfast". Breakfast is usually eaten within an hour or two after a person wakes up in the morning. Hotel based food serving outlets mainly offer a variety of breakfasts via *à la carte* and *table d'hôte* menu. Following breakfast types are commonly offered in all hotel based food serving outlets.

Continental Breakfast (Three-course breakfast = Juice + bread + beverage)

If continental breakfast is offered along with tea then it is called "Thé Complet" and if served with coffee then it is called "Café Complet". If guest orders only tea or coffee then called "The simple (for only tea)" and "Café simple (for only coffee)". Continental breakfast is often also called "European breakfast". It comprises:

Juices	Fresh/canned – orange, mango, apple, pineapple, guava, tomato, etc.
Breads	Toasted/plain (brown/ white) with preserves (like jam, jelly, honey, marmalade, maple syrup or butter) and *soft breads* like Croissants, Brioche, Muffins, Doughnuts, Hot Danish pastry.
Beverages	Coffee/tea/milk (milk with Horlicks, Milo, Oval tine, Boost and so forth)

American Breakfast (Continental breakfast + two courses, i.e., choice of cereals + eggs)

A traditional breakfast in the United States and Canada is derived from the full English breakfast that features predominantly sweet or mild-flavoured foods, mostly hot. The American breakfast includes the following courses:

Juices	Fresh/canned – orange, mango, apple, pineapple, guava, tomato and so forth.
Cereals	Muesli, cornflakes and shredded wheat, porridge, oatmeal and so forth with hot or/and cold milk.
Breads	Toasted/plain (brown/ white) with preserves (like jam, jelly, honey, marmalade, maple syrup or butter) and soft rolls like Croissants, Brioche, Muffins, Doughnuts and Hot Danish pastry.
Eggs	Scrambled, poached, fried, boiled, choice of omelettes (omelettes accompanied with hash brown potatoes, grilled tomatoes and baked beans) and so forth.
Beverages	Coffee/tea/milk (Horlicks, Milo, Oval tine, Boost, etc., may also be offered with milk).

Table Appointments for English Breakfast

Center	Cover
Ash tray (O)	Side plate
Bud vase	Side knife
Cruet set	Show plate
Table number	Tea cup on saucer with tea spoon
Bread boat	Napkin
Butter dish	Dessert spoon
Preserve dish	Dessert fork
Preserve spoon	Joint knife
Sugar basin	Fish knife
Sugar tong	Fish fork
Joint fork	Water glass

Table Appointments for American Breakfast

Center	Cover
Ash tray (O)	Side plate
Bud vase	Side knife
Cruet set	Show plate
Table number	Tea cup on saucer with tea spoon
Bread boat	Napkin
Butter dish	Dessert spoon
Preserve dish	Dessert fork
Preserve spoon	All purpose knife
Sugar basin	Water glass
Sugar tong	

English Breakfast (American Breakfast + four courses, i.e., choice of fish, meat, fresh fruits and stewed fruits)

An English breakfast is an elaborate breakfast which is quite substantial in size and variety. The traditional or full English breakfast includes several courses. These courses are as follows:

Juices	Fresh/canned – orange, mango, apple, pineapple, guava, tomato and so forth.
Cereals	Muesli, cornflakes and shredded wheat, porridge, oatmeal, and so forth with hot or/and cold milk.
Stewed fruits	Prunes, grapefruit or mandarin segments that are cooked in sugar syrup and flavoured with cloves and cinnamon. It is offered in bird bath glass or champagne saucer.
Fresh Fruits	Apples, oranges, pears, grapefruit, bananas or compounded fruits.
Breads	Toasted/plain (brown/white) with preserves (like jam, jelly, honey, marmalade, maple syrup or butter) and *soft breads* like Croissants, Brioche, Muffins, Doughnuts and Hot Danish pastry.
Fish	Grilled, fried and poached fish (Herring, Sardines, Salmon, etc.)
Meats	Bacon, sausage, kidney, liver, ham, salami and so forth.
Eggs	Scrambled, poached, fried, boiled, choice of omelettes (omelettes accompanied with hash brown potatoes, grilled tomatoes and baked beans) and so forth.
Beverages	Coffee/tea/milk (Horlicks, Milo, Oval tine, Boost, etc., may also be offered with milk)

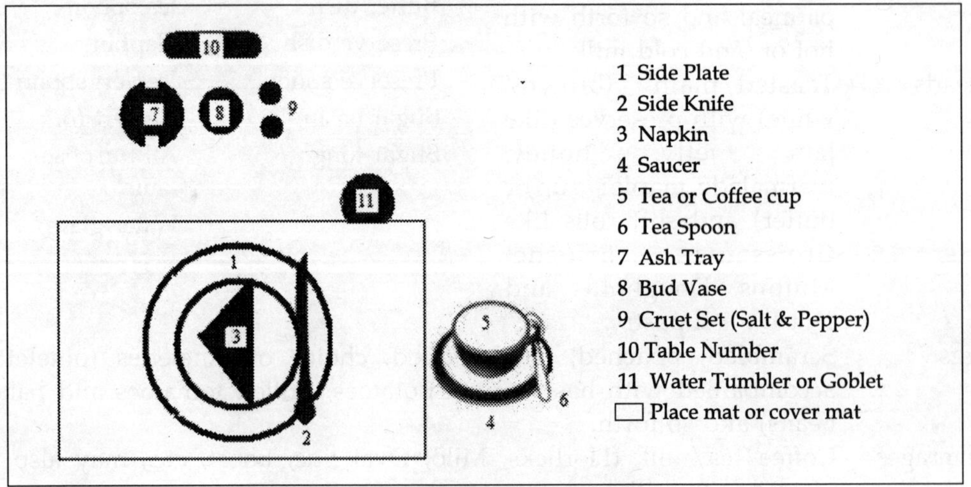

Fig. 9.1 Cover Layout for Continental breakfast

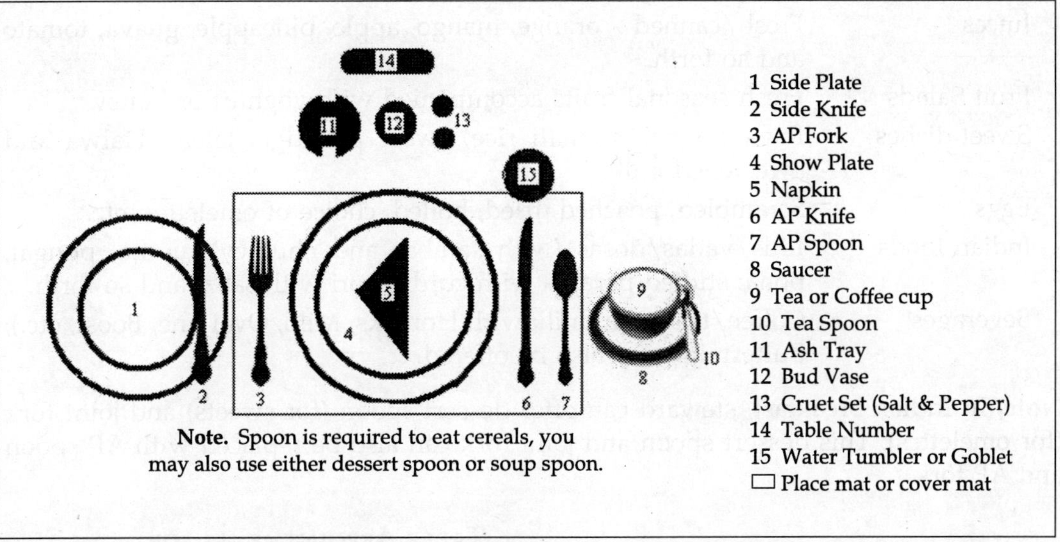

Note. Spoon is required to eat cereals, you may also use either dessert spoon or soup spoon.

Fig. 9.2 Cover Layout for American breakfast

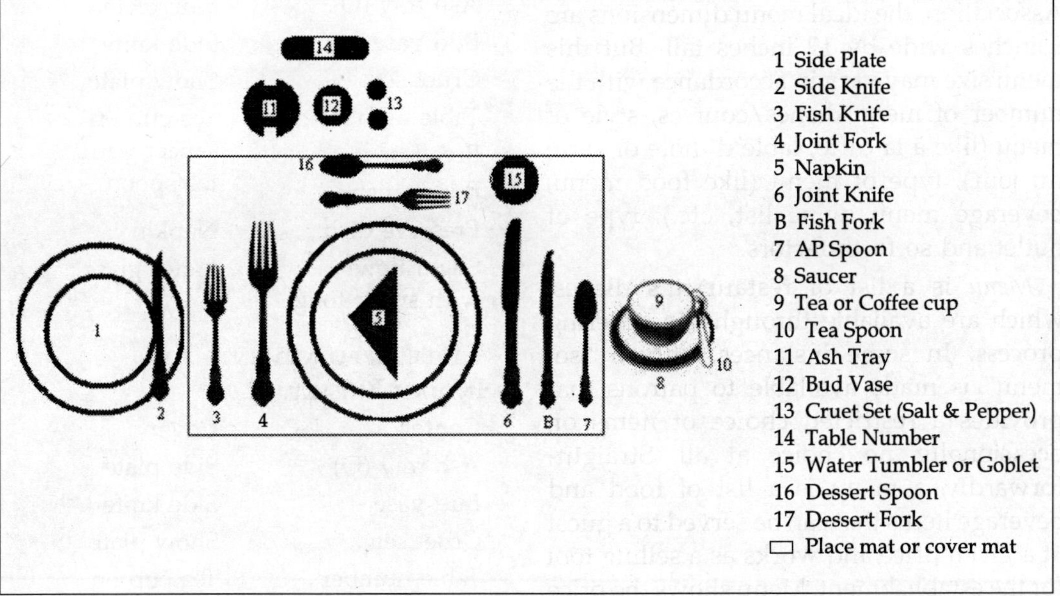

Fig. 9.3 Cover Layout for English breakfast

INDIAN BREAKFAST

An Indian breakfast varies from region to region and is mostly vegetarian in nature. The Indian breakfast comprises the following courses:

Juices	Fresh/canned – orange, mango, apple, pineapple, guava, tomato and so forth.
Fruit Salads	Fresh seasonal fruits accompanied with yoghurt or honey.
Sweet dishes	Rava Kesari, Basmati rice, sweet porridge, Jalebi, Halwa and Sweetened milk.
Eggs	Scrambled, poached, fried, boiled, choice of omelettes, etc.
Indian foods	Idlis/vadas/dosas (with sambar and chutney), upma, pongal, poha; stuffed paratha with curd; poori with sabzi and so forth.
Beverages	Coffee/tea/milk (milk with Horlicks, Milo, Oval tine, Boost, etc.), Buttermilk may also be offered.

Note. In Indian breakfast, steward can offer dessert spoon (for sweets) and joint fork (for omelettes). This dessert spoon and joint fork can also be replaced with AP spoon and AP fork.

AN INTRODUCTION TO MENU

According to the National Restaurant Association, the ideal menu dimensions are 9 inches wide by 12 inches tall. But this menu size may vary in accordance with the number of menu dishes/courses, style of menu (like à la carte, table d' hôte or carte du jour), type of menu (like food menu, beverage menu, wine list, etc.), type of outlet and so forth factors.

Menu is a list of restaurant's dishes, which are available through the ordering process. In some instances, only a "set menu" is made available to patrons that provides a restricted choice of items or, occasionally, no choice at all. Straightforwardly, a menu is a list of food and beverage items that can be served to a guest at a given price and works as a selling tool for the establishment. Menu shows the price of various food, beverage and tobacco items along with applicable service taxes and VAT and standard portion size. There are many types of menus; some of them are given ahead.

Table Appointments for Continental Breakfast

Center	Cover
Ash tray (O)	Side plate
Bud vase	Side knife
Cruet set	Show plate
Table number	Tea cup on saucer with tea spoon
Bread boat	
Butter dish	
Preserve dish	Napkin
Sugar bowl with sugar tong	Water glass

Table Appointments for Indian Breakfast

Center	Cover
Ash tray (O)	Side plate
Bud vase	Side knife
Cruet set	Show plate
Table number	Tea cup on saucer with tea spoon
Bread boat	
Butter dish	
Preserve dish	Napkin
Sugar bowl with sugar tong	Water glass

Meal Period Menus (occasional menus)

Breakfast menu

✓ The morning menu mainly includes – variety of breakfast rolls and breads with preserves; cereals with hot/cold milk; meat preparations (such as sausages, salami, bacon, etc.); fresh fruits; juices; tea and coffee.

> **HIGH TEA MENU**
> (@ 450 per person)
>
> **Sandwiches**
> Classic Cucumber
> Carrot, Ginger & Raisin
> Curried Roast Chicken
>
> **Savories in Puff Pastry**
> Fresh spinach, caramelized onion & feta palmier
>
> **Sweets**
> Orange chocolate truffle, Toasted hazelnut shortbread
>
> **Fresh Fruits**
> (In season)
>
> **One Large Pot of Tea**

Brunch menu

✓ Mid-to-late morning modest meal menu and the combo of breakfast and lunch items like Creole poached egg. It is commonly offered on weekends or catered events. Most of the on-site food service operations may serve brunch in lieu of both breakfast and lunch on weekends and for special occasions.

Lunch menu

✓ Mid-day meal menu, usually consisting of light as well as medium (but less preferred to heavy items) food items in the menu. The lunch menu is more complicated (or elaborate) than breakfast menu and mostly offers a variety of soups, main courses, desserts, tea or coffee preparations, etc.

Afternoon tea menu

✓ Menu offered after lunch, and usually consisting of range of tea and coffee preparations (English tea, Russian tea, lemon tea, cona coffee, Turkish coffee, espresso coffee, etc.) with some cookies and light snack items (such as sandwiches and small French pastries).

Evening tea menu

✓ This menu is usually offered during sunset similar to afternoon tea menu; it also contains assortment of tea and coffee preparations with choice of substantial snack items and cookies. This kind of menu is mostly offered in coffee shop outlets.

Supper menu

✓ This menu is offered in the late evening hours and usually consists of ready to cook food items like stuffed lobster tail broiled at last minute, prepared appetizers, quiche (as main course), polenta (with bacon) and so forth. But it is difficult to provide steak preparations in supper menu.

DINNER MENU (05 courses)

Salade de Viande

×

Consommé Celestine

×

Sole Veronique

Ou

Aspergus Flamande

×

Chocolate Soufflé

×

Café ou Tea

Dinner menu

✓ Dinner is a main or major meal menu of the day consisting of maximum number of food choices like steaks, roasts, chicken, seafoods and pasta choices mostly accompanied with wines, cocktails and other beverages.

Price Based Menus

À la carte menu

✓ It is a separately priced and an expensive menu that is primarily offered in haute cuisine restaurants. In this menu, the guest may select separately priced menu dishes to compose his/her own menu (to eat) and pays only for what he/she has ordered.

BREAKFAST MENU

Juice (Mango/Orange/Apple)

×

Cereal (Porridge/Cornflakes)

×

Bread (Toasted/Plain)

×

Egg (Omelette/Boiled/Fried)

×

Meat (Sausage/Bacon/Salami)

×

Beverage (Coffee/Tea)

Table d'hôte menu

✓ It is a collectively priced and an inexpensive menu (or low/fixed priced menu in comparison to *à la carte* menu) offered in casual as well as in high class restaurants. In this menu, guest pays for the full course whether he consumes all or certain dishes.

Combined menu

✓ This menu is the combination of *à la carte* and *table d'hôte* menu but with limited choices. In this menu, popular items are repeated each day and others changed on a cyclical or irregular basis. Sometimes it is also called Brasserie, coffee shop or popular catering menu.

Time Period/Duration Based Menus

Cyclic menu

✓ A menu that changes every day for a certain period of days before the cycle begins again. In simple terms, cyclic menu usually repeats after a particular period of time, it may be a week, fortnight or month. This menu is mainly found in institutional catering like hostel's mess.

Carte du jour menu

✓ It is literally called "card of the day". It is similar to fixed price menu which is usually a fixed meal with one or more courses for a set price. This menu highlights the special dishes/menu of the day. *Carte du jour menu* is actually a supporting menu to the main menu. It may also be attached as a clip-on menu on the main menu card.

Fixed menu

✓ A menu used for several months or longer before it is changed. *Daily specials* may be offered, but a set list of items forms the basic menu.

Cyclic Menu
(Of single course for a month with 8 days cycle or repeated after 8 days)

Weeks/Days	Day 1	Day 2	Day 3	Day 4	Day 5	Day 6
Week 1	Menu A	Menu B	Menu C	Menu D	Menu E	Menu F
Week 2	Menu G	Menu H	Menu A	Menu B	Menu C	Menu D
Week 3	Menu E	Menu F	Menu G	Menu H	Menu A	Menu B
Week 4	Menu C	Menu D	Menu E	Menu F	Menu G	Menu H

Menu A (Jacket potatoes with Tuna and sweet-corn), **Menu B** (Beans, sausages and buttered toast), **Menu C** (Scrambled egg with buttered toast and tomato sauce), **Menu D** (Sandwiches), **Menu E** (Pasta with mushroom sauce), **Menu F** (Meatballs on toast), **Menu G** (Hot Dog with tomato sauce) and **Menu H** (Chicken nuggets with spaghetti).

Clientele Based Menus

Children's menu

✓ Children's menu is usually designed to entertain kids; they may be folded into hats or masks, shaped like animals, or have word games, stories, or mazes printed on them. The offered dishes should not be heavy, simultaneously must provide a complete meal at one price (it means *table d' hôte* style menu).

Senior citizen's menu

✓ This menu seeks to accommodate senior citizens/aged people who have their special health needs. This menu is usually offered at low price. These are health conscious food and beverage items that are mainly low in calories, sodium, fat and cholesterol.

Course Based Menus

Dessert menu

✓ This menu is designed to remind the guest about the outlet's dessert items. It may list desserts which are not listed on the regular menu card or to include special desserts. Upscale restaurants may also include appropriate after dinner alcoholic drinks on their dessert menu.

Wine menu

✓ Often it is also known as *wine list* which enlists a range of wines. It is typically organized into sections, for example, white, red, rose, dessert, varietal wines, etc. of different countries of origin along with their prices, wine information (such as vintage year, grape name, producer name and vineyard name) and sometimes bin number also. Sommelier is responsible for making wine menu.

Beverage menu

✓ A menu that lists cocktails, wines and other alcoholic beverages which an outlet offers to its guest. It can be listed on a separate menu or included on the regular menu card. Many beverage menus also include no-or-low alcoholic drinks, for example, Bacardi Breezer.

Non-alcoholic menu

✓ This menu also contains a list of low/no-alcoholic beverages, for example, coffee, tea, milk based drinks (flavoured and shakes), soft drinks, *claytons*, alcohol free beers, low alcoholic beers, mineral water, etc. It may also include non-alcoholic cocktails, wines, beers and so on.

Specialty menu

✓ It may be an *à la carte* or *TDH style menu* targeted towards a specific market segment, as a result it contains dishes of a specific region. The offered dishes are not enormously accepted in the general market segment but targeted segment/s knows them splendidly. Consequently, not found in every food outlet. The specialty appears in everything including appetizers, soups, salads, sandwiches to entrée/main course.

Wine List					
B. No.	**Red wine**	**Price**	**B. No.**	**White wine**	**Price**
1011	Merlot, France	Rs. 10, 000	2011	Chardonnay, India	Rs. 15, 000
1012	Shiraz, America	Rs. 8,000	2012	Chennin Blanc, France	Rs. 12, 000
1014	Zinfandel, France	Rs. 12, 000	2014	Riesling, America	Rs. 14, 000
B. No.	**Vintage wine**	**Price**	**B. No.**	**Sparkling wine**	**Price**
3011	Sauvignon Blanc	Rs. 25, 000	5011	Dom Perignon, France	Rs. 20, 000
3012	Pinot Noir	Rs. 22, 000	5012	Krug, France	Rs. 22, 000
			5014	Mercier, France	Rs. 21, 000

Outlet Based Menus

Restaurant menu

- ✓ This menu is formal in nature and mainly offered in restaurants. In large establishments, there are separate menus for separate items like wine list, beverage menu, dessert menu, cocktail menu and so forth.
- ✓ But in smaller establishments, there is mainly single menu for all available food and beverage items. A typical fine dine restaurant offers an "*à la carte style*" menu but others may offer *à la carte menu*, TDH menu or their combination. Apart from it, these outlets also offer daily specials and may occasionally offer *carte du jour menu* too.

Menu Planning Principles

- Menu costing + pricing
- Menu controlling
- Menu sequence
- Signature dishes
- Menu balance
- Menu variety
- Menu design
- Menu language
- Font size & style
- Menu description
- Menu appearance
- Menu dimension
- Nutritional value
- Food group/pyramid

Room service menu

- ✓ A menu offered by lodging properties that serves food to guests in their rooms. Generally, this menu offers a limited number of preparations because it is difficult to maintain food quality while transporting the food to the room.
- ✓ This menu offers round-the-clock meals as well as also provides full course meals during major meal periods. It includes appetizers, soups, hot and cold main

dishes, sandwiches, sweets, fountain items, beverages, etc. The menu often contains dishes for all three major meals of the day.

Coffee shop menu

- ✓ The coffee shop menu is semi-formal or informal in nature due to the semi-formal or informal environment of the coffee shop. The coffee shop menu shares some of the features of a bar plus some of the features of a restaurant, but it is different from cafeteria.
- ✓ As the name suggests, coffee shops focus on providing range of coffee, tea and soft beverages with a wide variety of light/substantial food items (like sandwiches, pizza, burger, French fries, etc.).

Banquet menu

- ✓ It is usually a TDH menu, i.e., a set meal with few, if any, choices. Nowadays, the banquet menu mainly comprises five courses (i.e., starter, soup, main course, dessert and beverage).
- ✓ Generally, banquet menu comes in two varieties, i.e., without choices and with choices. Either or both menus mainly suggest and offer banqueting functions (like wedding, birthday, etc.). Hence, these are targeted to the invitees.

Bar menu

- ✓ Bar menu shows a wide array of hard and soft beverages and mixed drinks. For instance, whiskey, vodka, rum, gin, tequila, wine, beer, soft drinks, juices, cocktails, mocktails, etc., and tobacco products like cigars and cigarettes, are offered by the establishment.
- ✓ Nowadays, bar menu must also show the implemented taxes on the beverages and tobacco products (such as service charge, GST or any other taxes, etc.).

Fast food menu

- ✓ Fast food menu consists of convenience food items which are "easy-to-cook and ready-to-serve" in nature. For example, menu items like hamburger, fish burger, chicken, pizza, etc., can be consumed inside the fast food restaurant or guest can also take away in parcel boxes.
- ✓ Chain/franchised fast food outlets mostly offer western products like pitas, sandwiches, chicken nuggets, fried chicken, hamburgers, etc. Often it has been preferred that internationally recognized fast food outlets should offer famous national products of western countries such as fish and chips from Great Britain, Mexican tacos and Japanese sushi.

Other Menus

Doorknob menu (a component of room service menu)

✓ It is a type of room service menu that a housekeeper or some other staff member can leave in the room. A doorknob menu lists a limited number of breakfast items along with serving times, at which, the meal can be served. It aids to hotel's breakfast menu. It is even shorter than the normal breakfast menu, hence only some *à la carte* items are offered.

Doorknob Menu

(Please hang outside the room on doorknob before 12:30 midnight)

Room No. .... No. of Guests ....

Breakfast delivery time:- ☐ 05:00 to 05:30 a.m. ☐ 05:30 to 06:00 a.m. ☐ 06:00 to 06:30 a.m.

Juice	☐ Mango	☐ Orange	☐ Pineapple	☐ Apple	☐ Mixed
Breads	☐ Plain	☐ Toasted	☐ White	☐ Brown	
Soft rolls	☐ Muffins	☐ Doughnuts	☐ Brioche	☐ Croissant	
Beverage	☐ Tea	☐ Coffee	☐ Hot milk	☐ Cold milk	

Take out menu

✓ A menu that offers choices of food to guests who want to pick up their food at the restaurant and consume it elsewhere. Therefore, the items on the take out menu must be of such types that can be wrapped in some way, concurrently must have some hours of shelf-life.

✓ The most likely food items include sandwiches, hamburgers, pizza along with choice of beverages and shakes. Certain food items are often avoided to give via take out menus like pasta dishes such as spaghetti because it becomes hard and dry after a short period of cooking time.

Brasserie menu

✓ Generally, it is a limited *à la carte* style menu in which dishes are listed and priced separately. It usually offers light food items with choice of beverages, one plate item (instead of formal meals) or just a beverage. This type of menu is mainly popular in coffee shops.

Spoken menu

✓ The term *spoken menu* indicates that there is no written list (or menu card) of food and beverage items. These menus are usually orally presented or spoken by the server (in very small restaurant) or dietician (because it is mainly found in hospitals where dietetic technician announces to patient).

Static menu

- ✓ It means same menu items are offered every day. This menu is frequently used when restaurant's concept is built around the menu theme, including décor, advertising campaign and specific market segment identified as a target audience. Its example includes Red Lobster and Olive Garden restaurant offers static menu to their guests.

Californian menu

- ✓ This menu offers breakfast, lunch and dinner items on a single menu card. It is also called as "24 hours menu" and it can be offered in an *à la carte* or *semi à la carte* manner.
- ✓ This menu comprises breakfast items, appetizers, soups, salads, hot and cold sandwiches, entrees, desserts, beverages and fountain items. Californian menus often have laminated cover with extensive clip-on.

Menu Terminology			
À la	In the style of	À la broche	Roasted on a skewer
À la Creole	In the style of Louisiana	À la Florentine	With spinach base
À la mode	With ice cream	Au four	Baked in oven
Au jus	Natural juice or gravy	Au gratin	Baked/served in same dish
Au natural	Serve in its original state	Barquette	A boat shaped tartlet
Plat du jour	Dish of the day	Carte du jour	Menu card of the day
Brochette	On a skewer	Caviar	Egg or roe of fish
Châteaubriand	Double fillet steak	Farce	Stuffed
Foie gras	Flattened goose liver	Gateau/x	Cake/s
Medallion	Round slice of meat	Pilaf	Italian rice
Lard	Pork fat	Tournedos	Fillet steak
Vol-au-vent	Puff pastry case	Carte	Card
A l' Anglaise	In English style	A l' Americane	In American style
Rechaud	Warming unit on sidetable	Rechauffe	Reheat/warmed leftovers
Table d' hote	Fixed price menu (or from the card)	Fromage	Cheese
Entrée	Starting of main course	Entremets	Sweet course
Pot au feu	Meat broth with vegetable	Boisson	Beverage
Others - Citron (Lemon), Confiture (Jam), Champignons (Mushrooms), Glace (Ice cream), Frappe (Chilled), Flambé (flame), Bouillon/court (liquor for cooking fish), Béchamel (white sauce), Barquette (boat shaped tartlet case)			

Late snack menu

- ✓ This menu is also called "short order menu" but it is different from fast food menu. It mostly offers *cook-to-order* items (or prepared after getting the order from the server/guest, like in *à la carte* menu). The prices of offered dishes are usually low to moderate and service is offered in American style, hence guest turnover ratio will be fast and more.

All day menu (a variation of Californian menu)

- ✓ It is similar to coffee shop menu, but is used for short order operations. As the name suggests, there is only one menu (it means outlet offers only those items that appeal at all three main/major meals of the day) that are used all day.
- ✓ It generally offers breakfast items, salads, sandwiches, appetizers and/or soups, entrées, desserts and beverages. Straightforwardly, it offers only short-order items.

Function menu (a component of banqueting function menu)

- ✓ It is also known as "festive menu or occasional menu" which is especially printed for particular occasion or function. It contains foods and their garnishes in accordance with the nature of festival/occasion.
- ✓ Basic features of any function menu include sequence of dishes is fixed, and very few choices are available. Thus, this menu very much resembles *table d' hôte* style menu.

Ethnic menu (a component of specialty menu)

- ✓ Ethnic menu is similar to specialty menu and offers a wide range of dishes but from particular country or region only. Consequently, the name of offered dishes should be in their original language but their description should be in a standard or local language (or in English).

TDH MENU

Continental Breakfast
@ Rs. 1500 per pax
(Choice of Juice, Bread & Tea/Coffee)

×

American Breakfast
@ Rs. 2250 per pax
(Choice of Juice, Bread, Cereal, Egg & Tea/Coffee)

×

English Breakfast
@ Rs. 3700 per pax
(Choice of Juice, Stewed Fruits, Bread, Cereal, Egg, Fish, Meat, Fresh Fruits & Tea/Coffee)

×

Indian Breakfast
@ Rs. 1500 per pax
(Poori Bhaji or Stuffed Parantha with Curd; Idli/Dosa with Sambar & Chutney and Tea/Coffee)

À la Carte Menu

Starter Course	**Per Portion**
Smoked Salmon	Rs. xxx x
Florentine Artichoke Dips	Rs. xxxx
Jalapeno Peppers	Rs. xxxx
Green Olive Tempenade	Rs. xxxx
Soup Course	
Crème De Champignons	Rs. xxxx
Clam Chowder	Rs. xxx x
Carmen Veloute	Rs. xxx x
Potage Minestrone	Rs. xxxx
Main Course	
Boeuf Stroganoff	Rs. xxxx
Tournedos a l' Andalouse	Rs. xxxx
Veal Cordon Bleu	Rs. xxxx
Dessert Course	
Mango Soufflé	Rs. xxxx
Fruit Truffle Pudding	Rs. xxx x
Bavaroise Rubane	Rs. xxxx
Beverage Course	
Café Espresso	Rs. xxx
Thé	Rs. xxx

Pool side menu (a menu for recreational purpose)

- ✓ This menu features by its brevity and the absence of any hot entrée (excluding short-order items). It contains sandwiches, hamburgers, salads, desserts, fountain items, alcoholic and non-alcoholic beverages.

Promotional menu

- ✓ As the name suggests, this menu is used for promotional purpose. It can also be used on occasions featuring famous chefs, famous restaurants or famous recipes of the outlets. Promotional ideas can be used for short-term emphasis on certain food items like seafood week and game week.

Souvenir menu (a component of promotional menu)

- ✓ This menu is solely for advertising purposes; hence, the main prerequisite condition of this menu is to provide complete address of an outlet including a telephone number with area code. This menu is available in two fashions, i.e., miniature menu and normal sized menu.

Plat-du-jour menu

- ✓ Plat-du-jour is a French term which means "dish of the day or plate of the day" like today's chef special. But sometimes it is used in the sense of "menu of the day (or Carte du jour)", which can include more than one dish, i.e., entrée + main dish + dessert.

KEY TERMS

Expresso	:	Strong black coffee served in demi-tasse (or coffee cup).
Mexican tacos	:	Traditional Mexican dish composed of corn or wheat tortilla folded or rolled around a filling.
Japanese sushi	:	Dish that can be prepared either with brown or white rice. It may be prepared from raw or cooked ingredients which may be non-vegetarian (like seafood) as well as vegetarian in nature.
Carte du jour	:	Card of the day menu.
Wine list	:	Wine menu.
Doorknob menu	:	Disposable in-room breakfast menu.
Fountain items	:	Items that are served after dipping into fountain like chocolate fountain.
Miniature menu	:	Small size menu card that are used for promotional purpose, thus it may also be clipped on regular menu card.
Entrée	:	First main or meat course.
Claytons	:	Full-bodied non-alcoholic drink made from African cola nuts and citrus essence, complemented by the pure hop bitters. It is usually served with a mixture such as dry ginger or lemonade over ice.
Ashtray (O)	:	"O" indicates that ashtray is an optional centre appointment.

REVIEW QUESTIONS

1. What is menu? Classify meal based menus and briefly explain each classified menu.
2. Differentiate between *à la carte* and *table d'hôte* menu.
3. Plan a five-course continental menu and support each course with appropriate dish/beverage.
4. Define the term meal. Write down the meals (or courses) of Continental, English, American and Indian breakfasts.

French Classical Menu

OBJECTIVES

Students will be able to:

- explicate all 17 courses of French Classical Menu (FCM);
- suggest standard cover layout, accompaniments and service for different courses of FCM; and
- recognize how 17 courses of FCM work as a base for developing other menus.

FRENCH CLASSICAL MENU

The term *French classical menu* refers to the different courses of the classic menu for French cuisine. Conventionally, the classical French menu contains 17 courses. Today, a menu of this size is hardly ever offered. Although, shorter menus follow the structure of the classical French menus as far as succession of courses is concerned. They always start with something light to stimulate the appetite, build up to the main course, and then become lighter towards the end of the meal. The 17 courses of French Classical Menu are given below:

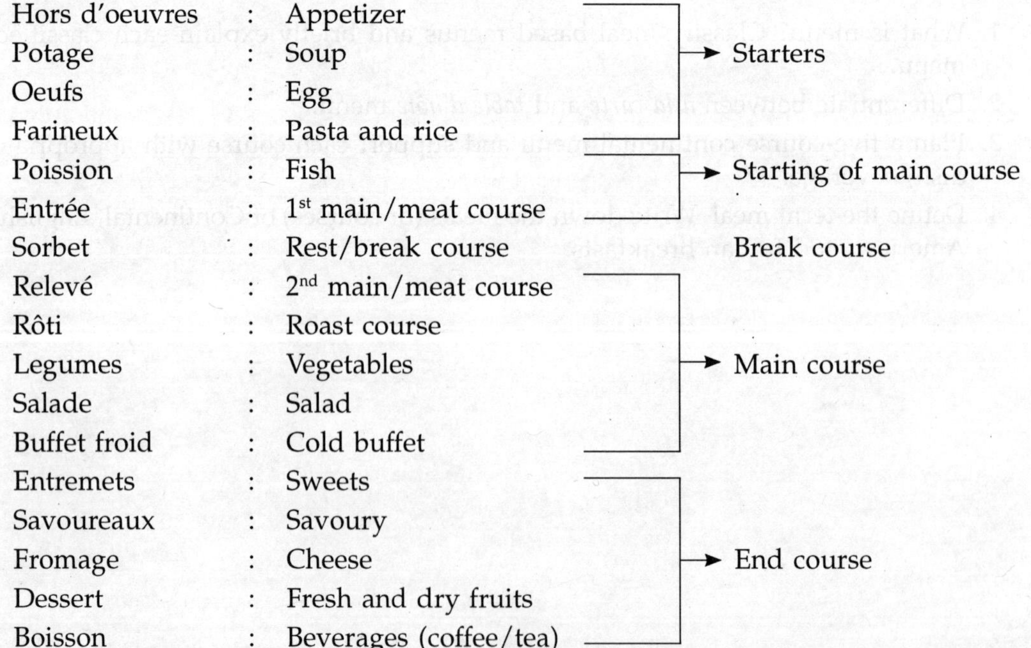

17 COURSES OF FRENCH CLASSICAL MENU (FCM)

Hors d'oeuvres

The name *hors d'oeuvres* comes from the French language and is literally translated as "out of the work", means little snack food that is served before or outside of (*hors*) the main dishes of a meal (the *oeuvres*). They are also commonly called "appetizers" which are basically meant to stimulate the appetite. They are traditionally served first, sometimes with a small cocktail called *aperitif*. Often, this course is classified into three broad groups, i.e., hot, cold and deluxe hors d'oeuvres. Many chefs also classify hors d'oeuvres as single and assorted starters. Some excellent examples of hors' d'oeuvre preparations are given below.

Dishes Names		Cover	Accom-paniment/s	Service
In English	In French			
Avocado with vinaigrette	Avocats vinaigrette	• Cold half plate • Teaspoon	• Vinaigrette sauce	• Place teaspoon on RHS (on cover) before serving avocado. • Serve vinaigrette in sauce boat on under-liner (on doily paper) with sauce spoon on RHS. • Offer pre-plated (in cold half plate) avocado from RHS of the guest.
Caviar	Caviare	• Cold half/ fish plate • Caviar knife/ gold plated fish knife	• Hot breakfast toast • *Blinis* (Russian pancakes) • Lemon wedges • Butter • Chopped shallots • Chopped parsley • Sieved hardboiled egg	• Place caviar knife or gold plated fish knife on RHS of the cover, before serving caviar. • Serve hot breakfast toast on side plate from RHS • Offer chopped shallots, chopped parsley, sieved egg white and egg yolk in four small bowls with separate tea spoon for each accompaniment.

				• Place all four above accompaniments on half plate with lemon wedge and *blinis* along side on the same plate. • Offer butter in butter dish with butter knife by placing on under-liner. • Offer pre-plated (in cold half plate) caviar from RHS of the guest.
Chilled melon	Melon Frappé	• Cold half plate • Dessert spoon • Dessert fork	• Castor sugar • Ground ginger	• Place dessert spoon on RHS and dessert fork on LHS of the cover, before serving melon frappe. • Serve castor sugar in dredger and ground ginger in coupe (with teaspoon) by placing both accompaniments on under-liner. • Offer pre-plated (in cold half plate) melon frappe from RHS of the guest.
Florida Cocktail	Cocktail de Florida	• Cold Paris goblet glass • Under-liner • Teaspoon	• Castor sugar • Maraschino cherry	• Place pre-portioned Florida cocktail (in Paris goblet glass) on under-liner. Put teaspoon on RHS of the Paris goblet on under-liner. • Offer castor sugar in dredger then place it on the

				under-liner and maraschino cherry in bowl. • Offer pre-portioned Florida cocktail from the RHS of the guest.
Goose liver paste	Paté de foie gras	• Cold half plate • Fish knife/ side knife • Fish fork/ dessert fork	• Hot toast • Butter	• Place fish knife/ side knife on RHS and fish fork/ dessert fork on LHS of the cover, before serving goose liver paste. • Serve hot toast in small bread basket and butter in butter dish (on under-liner with butter knife). • Offer pre-plated (in cold half plate) goose liver paste from RHS of the guest.
Assorted starters	Hors d'oeuvres assortis	• Cold half plate • Fish knife • Fish fork	• Oil • Vinegar	• Place fish knife on RHS and fish fork on LHS of the cover, before serving assorted starters. • Serve oil and vinegar in two small bottles by placing on under-liner. • Offer pre-plated (in cold half plate) assorted starters from RHS of the guest.

Oysters	Les huîtres	• Cold half plate/soup plate • Oyster fork • Fingerbowl • Spare napkin	• Oyster cruet set (it contains cayenne pepper, pepper mill, Tabasco sauce and chili vinegar) • Brown bread • Butter	• Place oyster fork on RHS of the cover, before serving oyster. • Place finger bowl (with lukewarm water + lemon slice) and napkin on under-liner on LHS of the cover (just above the side plate). • Offer oyster cruet set (after placing all four accompaniments) on under-liner. • Serve brown toast in small bread basket/side plate and butter in butter dish (on under-liner with butter knife). • Offer pre-plated (in cold half/soup plate) oyster from RHS of the guest.
Prawn cocktail	Cocktail de crevettes	• Cold Paris goblet glass • Under-liner • Teaspoon • Oyster fork	• Cayenne pepper • Pepper mill • Lemon segments • Brown bread • Butter	• Place oyster fork on LHS and teaspoon on RHS of the cover, before serving prawn cocktail. • Offer cayenne pepper, pepper mill and lemon segments on under-liner. • Serve brown bread in small bread basket/side plate and butter in butter dish (on under-liner with butter knife).

				• Place pre-portioned (in Paris goblet glass) prawn cocktail on under-liner and offer from the RHS of the guest.
Smoked salmon	Saumon fumé	• Cold fish/ half plate • Fish knife • Fish fork	• Cayenne pepper • Pepper mill • Lemon segments • Brown bread • Butter	• Place fish knife on RHS and fish fork on LHS of the cover, before serving smoked salmon. • Offer cayenne pepper, pepper mill and lemon segments on under-liner. • Serve brown bread in small bread basket/side plate and butter in butter dish (on under-liner with butter knife). • Offer pre-plated (in cold fish/half plate) smoked salmon from RHS of the guest.
Snails in garlic sauce	Escargots à la bourguignonne	• Cold fish/ half plate • Snail dish • Snail tong • Snail fork • Fingerbowl • Spare napkin	• Cubes of white bread in coupe.	• Place snail fork on RHS and snail tong on LHS of the cover, before serving snails in garlic butter. • Place finger bowl (with lukewarm water + lemon slice) and napkin on under-liner on LHS of the cover (just above side plate).

				• Offer cubes of white bread in coupe by placing on under-liner. • Offer pre-portioned (in snail dish) snails (after placing on cold half plate) from RHS of the guest.
Quails egg	Oeufs de caille	• Cold fish plate • Fish knife • Fish fork	• Oriental salt • Brown bread • Butter	• Place fish knife on RHS and fish fork on LHS of the cover, before serving quails egg. • Offer oriental salt in small bowl with tea spoon by placing on under-liner. • Serve brown bread in small bread basket/side plate and butter in butter dish (on under-liner with butter knife). • Offer pre-plated quails (in cold fish plate) egg from RHS of the guest.

Potage Course

The term *potage* refers to soup course. Soups can be defined as a liquid of varying consistency made from fish, poultry, meat or vegetable or a combination of these. In simple words, soups are wholesome and nutritious liquid food. Soups can be classified into a range of groups but broadly classified as thin and thick soups. *Thin soup* can be further classified as consommé and bouillon, whereas *thick soup* as passed and un-passed. Some excellent examples of soup preparations are given below.

Soup Names		Cover	Accom-paniment/s	Service
In English	In French			
Bortsch soup	Bortsch soup	• Hot soup plate • Dessert spoon	• Sour cream • Beetroot juice • Filled vol-au-vents	• Place dessert spoon on RHS of the cover, before serving bortsch soup. • Offer sour cream and beetroot juice in separate sauce boats/ gravy boats with two sauce ladles after placing on under-liner/ half plate. Offer filled vol-au-vents in other plate/dish. • Offer pre-plated (in hot soup plate) bortsch soup from RHS of the guest.
Bouillabaisse	Bouillabaisse	• Hot soup plate • Dessert spoon • Fish knife • Fish fork *(lay cover from inside to outside)*	• French bread slices • Garlic butter	• First place fish knife then dessert spoon on RHS and fish fork on LHS of the cover, before serving bouillabaisse soup. • Serve toasted French bread slices in small bread basket/ side plate and garlic mayonnaise in sauce boat by

				placing on under-liner with tea spoon. • Offer pre-plated (in hot soup plate) bouillabaisse soup from RHS of the guest.
Clear soups	Consommé soups	• Hot consommé cup • Dessert spoon	• As consommé name suggests	• Place dessert spoon on RHS of the cover, before serving consommé soup. • Offer pre-portioned consommé soup (in consommé cup) by placing on under-liner, from RHS of the guest.
Potage soups/thick consommé	Potage Germiny	• Hot soup plate • Soup spoon	• Cheese straw	• Place soup spoon on RHS of the cover, before serving potage soup. • Offer cheese straws in small glass/basket/ side plate. • Offer pre-plated (in hot soup plate) potage germiny from RHS of the guest.
French onion soup	Soupe a' l' oignon	• Consommé cup • Dessert spoon	• Grilled croute • Parmesan cheese	• Place dessert spoon on RHS of the cover, before serving French onion soup.

				• Offer grilled croute (filled with grated parmesan cheese) in side plate. • Offer pre-portioned (in consommé cup) French onion soup by placing on under-liner, from RHS of the guest.
Gazpacho soup	Potage gazpacho	• Cold consommé cup • Dessert spoon	• White bread crumbs	• Place dessert spoon on RHS of the cover, before serving Spanish gazpacho soup. • Offer white bread crumbs (with teaspoon) in small goblet shape glass or in bowl by placing on under-liner. • Offer pre-portioned (in cold consommé cup) gazpacho soup (by placing on under-liner) from RHS of the guest.
Puree potage	Puree soups	• Hot soup plate • Soup spoon	• Bread croutons	• Place soup spoon on RHS of the cover, before serving puree soup.

				• Offer bread croutons in sauce boat (with spoon) by placing on under-liner. • Offer pre-plated (in hot soup plate) puree soup from RHS of the guest.
Minestrone	Minestroni	• Hot soup plate • Soup spoon	• Grated parmesan cheese	• Place soup spoon on RHS of the cover, before serving minestrone soup. • Offer grated parmesan cheese in coup/bowl (by placing on under-liner) with teaspoon. • Offer pre-plated (in hot soup plate) minestrone soup from RHS of the guest.
Cream soups	Potage crème	• Hot soup plate • Soup spoon	• Cream (often garnished) • Bread croutons	• Place soup spoon on RHS of the cover, before serving cream soups. • Offer bread croutons in sauce boat with sauce ladle (by placing on underliner). • Offer pre-plated (in hot soup plate) cream soup from RHS of the guest.

Petite marmite	Petite marmite	• Petite marmite pot • Dessert spoon	• Poached bone marrow • Grilled croute • Parmesan cheese	• Place dessert spoon on RHS of the cover, before serving petite marmite soup. • Offer grilled croute (filled with grated parmesan cheese) in side plate. • Offer pre-portioned petite marmite soup (in petite marmite dish/ bowl) by placing on under-liner, from RHS of the guest.
Clear turtle soup	Tortue Claire	• Hot consommé cup • Dessert spoon	• Brown bread • Butter • Lemon segment • Cheese straw	• Place dessert spoon on RHS of the cover, before serving clear turtle soup. • Offer cheese straws in small glass/basket/ side plate and lemon segments on under-liner (along side of hot consommé cup). • Serve brown bread in small bread basket/ side plate and butter in butter dish (on

				under-liner with butter knife). • Place pre-portioned (in hot consommé cup) clear turtle soup on under-liner and offer from the RHS of the guest.
Shellfish soup	Bisque	• Soup bowl • Soup spoon	• Green salad with dressing • Garlic bread	• Place soup spoon on RHS of the cover, before serving shellfish soup. • Offer garlic bread in side plate and green salad in bowl/ plate (offer vinaigrette dressing in bowl on under-liner with tea spoon). • Offer pre-portioned shellfish soup (in soup bowl) by placing on under-liner, from RHS of the guest.
Clam chowder	Clam chowder	• Soup bowl • Soup spoon	• Oyster crackers or breakfast biscuits	• Place soup spoon on RHS of the cover, before serving clam chowder.

				• Offer oyster crackers/ breakfast biscuits in side plate or alongside clam chowder on under-liner. • Offer pre-portioned clam chowder (in soup bowl) by placing on under-liner, from RHS of the guest.
Mutton broth or Scotch broth	Mutton broth	• Soup bowl • Soup spoon	• Dices of vegetables (may also directly garnish on mutton broth) or *Skirlie* dumplings	• Place soup spoon on RHS of the cover, before serving mutton broth. • Serve dices of vegetables in small bowl with dessert spoon by placing on under-liner. Offer *Skirlie* dumplings (Mealie pudding) in side plate or in bowl by placing on under-liner. • Place pre-portioned (in hot soup bowl) mutton/ scotch broth on under-liner and offer from RHS of the guest.

Oxtail soup	Queue de boeuf	• Soup bowl • Soup spoon	• Bread and butter • Madeira wine	• Place soup spoon on RHS of the cover, before serving oxtail soup. • Serve bread in small bread basket/side plate and butter in butter dish (on under-liner with butter knife). Serve Madeira in wine glass. • Place pre-portioned (in hot soup bowl) oxtail soup on under-liner and offer from RHS of the guest.
Kidney soup	Soupe au rognons	• Soup bowl • Soup spoon	• Melba toast • Butter	• Place soup spoon on RHS of the cover, before serving kidney soup. • Serve Melba toast in small bread basket/ side plate and butter in butter dish (on under-liner with butter knife). • Place pre-portioned (in hot soup bowl) kidney soup on under-liner and offer from RHS of the guest.

Vichyssoise	Vichyssoise (famous as cold soup but may also be served hot)	• Soup cup • Dessert spoon	• Chopped chives (it may also be directly garnished on vichyssoise)	• Place dessert spoon on RHS of the cover, before serving vichyssoise soup. • Serve chopped chives in small bowl (alongside teaspoon) by placing on under-liner. • Place pre-portioned (in soup cup) vichyssoise soup on under-liner and offer from RHS of the guest.

Note. The above-mentioned word *Skirlie* dumpling is a Scottish dish, made with onions and oatmeal. It is most commonly used as a base for white puddings as well as also serves as a side dish, for example, with Scottish soup "mutton broth".

Oeufs

In general, *oeufs* usually refers to hen's egg although those from other birds can also be used. Egg provides protein, fat, calcium, iron and vitamins A, D, B_1 and B_2 in useful amount. Apart from their use as a main dish, eggs can be a part of any meal of the day, as an ingredient in entrée dishes, salads as well as used as a garnish. There are wide varieties of egg dishes beyond the usual omelettes but these have not retained their popularity on modern menus. Some excellent examples of egg preparations are given below.

Dishes Names		Cover	Accompa-niment/s	Service
In English	**In French**			
Egg in cocotte dish	Oeuf en cocotte	• Cocotte dish • Teaspoon	–	• Place pre-portioned *oeuf en cocotte* (in cocotte dish) on under-liner. Put teaspoon on RHS of the cocotte dish on under-liner.

				• Finally offer pre-portioned oeuf en cocotte from RHS of the guest.
Poached egg	Oeuf poché	• Dessert spoon • Dessert fork	–	• Place pre-portioned poached egg (in cocotte dish/bowl) on under-liner. • Finally offer pre-portioned poached egg from RHS of the guest.
Egg-in dish	Oeuf sur le plat	• Dessert spoon • Dessert fork	–	• Place pre-portioned egg-in dish (in cocotte dish/bowl) on under-liner. • Finally offer pre-portioned egg-in dish from RHS of the guest.
Omelette	Omelette	• Hot half plate • Joint fork	• Grilled tomatoes • Baked beans • Hash brown potatoes	• Place joint fork on RHS of the cover, before serving omelette. • Offer all three accompaniments alongside the omelette (in same hot half plate). • Place pre-plated (in hot half plate) omelette from RHS of the guest.
Scrambled egg	Oeuf brouille	• Hot half plate • Dessert spoon • Dessert fork	–	• Place dessert spoon on RHS and dessert fork on LHS of the cover, before serving scrambled egg. • Offer pre-plated scrambled egg (in hot half plate) from RHS of the guest.
Boiled egg	Oeuf à la coque	• Egg holder	–	• Serve in egg holder

Farineux/Farinaceous

Farinaceous are foodstuffs (usually pasta and rice) which consist very largely of starch based products like bread, oatmeal, flour, pasta and semolina. *Pasta* is an Italian preparation available in various shapes and designs. Pasta is made from durum wheat, semolina, water and often eggs. It is sold dried or ready-to-cook (in boiling water with salt). Pasta can be stuffed with a filling of minced meat, spinach, chicken liver, cheese, herbs, etc. In Italy, pasta is usually served as a main course, whereas in France, it is served as an accompaniment. Apart from pasta, rice preparations are also served in this course. *Risotto* and *pilaf* are excellent examples of rice. Some excellent examples of pasta based preparations are given below.

Dishes Names		Cover	Accom-paniment/s	Service
In English	In French			
Spaghetti with cheese	Spaghetti Italienne	• Hot soup plate • Dessert spoon • Joint fork	• Grated parmesan cheese • Pepper mill	• Place dessert spoon on LHS and joint fork on RHS of the cover, before serving spaghetti Italienne. • Offer grated parmesan cheese in coup/bowl (by placing on under-liner) with teaspoon. Separately offer pepper mill on under-liner. • Offer pre-plated spaghetti Italienne (in hot soup plate) from RHS of the guest.
Spaghetti with ox-tongue, ham and mushroom	Spaghetti Milanaise	• Hot soup plate • Dessert spoon • Joint fork	• Grated parmesan cheese • Pepper mill	• Place dessert spoon on LHS and joint fork on RHS of the cover, before serving spaghetti Milanaise. • Offer grated parmesan cheese in coup/bowl (by placing on under-liner) with teaspoon. Separately offer pepper mill on under-liner. • Offer pre-plated spaghetti Milanaise (in hot soup plate) from RHS of the guest.

Spaghetti in tomato sauce	Spaghetti Napolitaine	• Hot soup plate • Dessert spoon • Joint fork	• Grated parmesan cheese • Pepper mill	• Place dessert spoon on LHS and joint fork on RHS of the cover, before serving spaghetti Napolitaine. • Offer grated parmesan cheese in coup/bowl (by placing on under-liner) with teaspoon. Separately offer pepper mill on under-liner. • Offer pre-plated spaghetti Napolitaine (in hot soup plate) from RHS of the guest.
Spaghetti with minced beef in sauce	Spaghetti Bolognaise	• Hot soup plate • Dessert spoon • Joint fork	• Grated parmesan cheese • Pepper mill	• Place dessert spoon on LHS and joint fork on RHS of the cover, before serving spaghetti Bolognaise. • Offer grated parmesan cheese in coup/bowl (by placing on under-liner) with teaspoon. Separately offer pepper mill on under-liner. • Offer pre-plated spaghetti Bolognaise (in hot soup plate) from RHS of the guest.
Cannelloni	Cannelloni	• Hot half plate • Dessert spoon • Dessert fork	• Grated parmesan cheese	• Place dessert spoon on RHS and dessert fork on LHS of the cover, before serving cannelloni. • Offer grated parmesan cheese in coup/bowl (by placing on under-liner) with teaspoon. • Offer pre-plated cannelloni (in hot half plate) from RHS of the guest.

Gnocchi	Gnocchi	• Hot half plate • Dessert spoon • Dessert fork	• Grated parmesan cheese	• Place dessert spoon on RHS and dessert fork on LHS of the cover, before serving gnocchi. • Offer grated parmesan cheese in coup/bowl (by placing on under-liner) with teaspoon. • Offer pre-plated gnocchi (in hot half plate) from RHS of the guest.
Rice	Riz	• Hot half plate • Dessert spoon • Dessert fork	• Grated parmesan cheese	• Place dessert spoon on RHS and dessert fork on LHS of the cover, before serving rice. • Offer grated parmesan cheese in coup/bowl (by placing on under-liner) with teaspoon. • Offer pre-plated rice (in hot half plate) from RHS of the guest.
Butter noodles	Nouilles au Beurre	• Hot soup plate • Dessert spoon • Joint fork	• Grated parmesan cheese • Pepper mill	• Place dessert spoon on LHS and joint fork on RHS of the cover, before serving Nouilles au Beurre. • Offer grated parmesan cheese in coup/bowl (by placing on under-liner) with teaspoon. Separately offer pepper mill on under-liner. • Offer pre-plated Nouilles au Beurre (in hot soup plate) from RHS of the guest.

Spatzle	Spatzle	• Hot soup plate • Dessert spoon • Joint fork	• Grated parmesan cheese • Pepper mill	• Place dessert spoon on LHS and joint fork on RHS of the cover, before serving Spatzle. • Offer grated parmesan cheese in coup/bowl (by placing on under-liner) with teaspoon. Separately offer pepper mill on under-liner. • Offer pre-plated Spatzle (in hot soup plate) from RHS of the guest.
Fettuccine	Fettuccine	• Hot soup plate • Dessert spoon • Joint fork	• Grated parmesan cheese • Pepper mill	• Place dessert spoon on LHS and joint fork on RHS of the cover, before serving Fettuccine. • Offer grated parmesan cheese in coup/bowl (by placing on under-liner) with teaspoon. Separately offer pepper mill on under-liner. • Offer pre-plated Fettuccine (in hot soup plate) from RHS of the guest.

Poisson

It refers to fish course. A fish course garnished with vegetables sometimes comes in-between the starter and the meat course. Often, this course is followed by a small dish of lemon or lime sorbet to cleanse the palate and refresh the senses. Broadly, fish can be classified on three basis- habitat (it includes freshwater and saltwater fishes), shape (it includes round and flat fishes) and flesh (it includes white and dark flesh fishes). Apart from it, shellfish (including *mollusks* and *crustaceans*) also comes under the category of poisson. Some excellent examples of fish and shellfish preparations are given below.

Dishes Names		Cover	Accompa-niment/s	Service
In English	In French			
Frogs legs	Cuisses de grenouilles	• Hot half plate • Fish knife/side knife • Fish fork/ dessert fork • Fingerbowl • Spare napkin	–	• Place fish knife/side knife on RHS and fish fork/dessert fork on LHS of the cover, before serving frogs legs. • Place finger bowl (with lukewarm water + lemon slice) and napkin on under-liner on LHS of the cover (just above the side plate). • Offer pre-plated frogs legs (in hot half plate) from RHS of the guest.
Cold lobster	Demi homard	• Cold joint plate • Lobster pick • Fish knife • Fish fork • Lobster cracker • Finger bowl *(lay cover from inside to outside)*	• Mayonnaise sauce	• Place fish knife first, lobster pick next on RHS and fish fork on LHS of the cover, before serving cold lobster. Offer lobster cracker on under-liner (the same plate also works as a debris plate). • Place fingerbowl (with lukewarm water + lemon slice) and napkin on under-liner on LHS of the cover (just above the side plate). • Offer mayonnaise sauce in a sauce boat/ gravy boat with sauce ladle by placing on under-liner. • Offer pre-plated cold lobster (in cold joint plate) from RHS of the guest.

Flamed lobster	Homard flambé	• Hot half plate • Fish knife • Fish fork	–	• Place fish knife on RHS and fish fork on LHS of the cover, before serving flamed lobster. • Offer pre-plated hot lobster (in hot half plate) from RHS of the guest.
Lobster with white wine sauce	Homard thermidor	• Hot joint plate • Fish knife • Fish fork	–	• Place fish knife on RHS and fish fork on LHS of the cover, before serving lobster thermidor. • Offer pre-plated hot lobster (in hot joint plate) from RHS of the guest.
Lobster with cheese sauce	Homard mornay	• Hot joint plate • Fish knife • Fish fork	–	• Place fish knife on RHS and fish fork on LHS of the cover, before serving lobster Mornay. • Offer pre-plated hot lobster (in hot joint plate) from RHS of the guest.
Lobster with mushroom and lobster sauce	Homard cardinal	• Hot joint plate • Fish knife • Fish fork	–	• Place fish knife on RHS and fish fork on LHS of the cover, before serving lobster cardinal. • Offer pre-plated hot lobster (in hot joint plate) from RHS of the guest.

Mussels in white wine	Moules mariniere	• Hot soup plate • Fish knife • Fish fork • Dessert spoon *(lay cover from inside to outside)*	• Brown bread • Butter • Cayenne pepper • Pepper mill	• Place fish knife first, dessert spoon next on RHS and fish fork on LHS of the cover, before serving moules mariniere. • Offer cayenne pepper, pepper mill and lemon segments on under-liner. • Serve brown bread in small bread basket/side plate and butter in butter dish (on under-liner with butter knife). • Place pre-portioned (in hot soup plate) moules mariniere from RHS of the guest.
Poached salmon	Saumon poché	• Half plate (hot/cold) • Fish knife • Fish fork	• Lemon segments • Mayonnaise sauce or hollandaise sauce	• Place fish knife on RHS and fish fork on LHS of the cover, before serving poached salmon. • Offer mayonnaise/hollandaise sauce (sauce depends upon whether poached salmon is served hot or cold) in a sauce boat/gravy boat with sauce ladle after placing on under-liner • Place pre-plated (in hot/cold half plate) poached salmon from RHS of the guest.

Scampi with vermouth	Scampi boulevard	• Hot half plate • Fish knife • Fish fork	–	• Place fish knife on RHS and fish fork on LHS of the cover, before serving scampi. • Place pre-plated (in hot half plate) scampi with vermouth from RHS of the guest.
Deep fried sole fish	Sole Colbert	• Hot half plate • Fish knife • Fish fork	• Lemon segments • Parsley butter	• Place fish knife on RHS and fish fork on LHS of the cover, before serving Sole Colbert. • Offer parsley butter in butter dish or in side plate. Place lemon segments alongside the Sole Colbert. • Offer pre-plated (in hot half plate) Sole Colbert from RHS of the guest.
Grilled sole	Sole grille	• Hot half plate • Fish knife • Fish fork	• Lemon segments • Parsley butter • Anchovy butter	• Place fish knife on RHS and fish fork on LHS of the cover, before serving grilled sole fish. • Offer parsley butter and anchovy butter in two separate butter dishes or in two side plates/ bowls. Place lemon segments along the grilled sole fish. • Offer pre-plated (in hot half plate) grilled sole fish from RHS of the guest.

Whitebait	Blanchailles	• Hot half plate • Fish knife • Fish fork	• Lemon segments • Brown bread • Butter • Cayenne pepper • Pepper mill	• Place fish knife on RHS and fish fork on LHS of the cover, before serving whitebait. • Offer cayenne pepper, pepper mill and lemon segments on under-liner. • Serve brown bread in small bread basket/side plate and butter in butter dish (on under-liner with butter knife). • Place pre-portioned (in hot half plate) whitebait from RHS of the guest.

Note.

- Fish based preparations can be served as a starter course as well as main course. When it is served as a starter, serve in fish/half plate whereas when served as a main course, serve in full plate.
- Due to the hefty size of lobster, it is necessary to serve the lobster in large size joint plate (it is around 12 inches in diameter).

Entrée

Generally, these are small, well-garnished dishes that directly come from the kitchen to service point and usually accompanied with a rich gravy or sauce. If it is a main course then potatoes and vegetables can be served. Otherwise, it usually comprises a dish made up of steak, cutlets, casseroles or stews. Some excellent examples of entrée preparations are given below:

Dishes Names		Cover	Accompa-niment/s	Service
In English	In French			
Chicken in envelope	Volaille en papillotte	• Hot joint plate • Joint knife • Joint fork	• Not necessary	• Place joint knife on RHS and joint fork on LHS of the cover, before serving chicken in envelope.

				• Offer pre-plated (in hot joint plate) chicken in envelope from RHS of the guest.
Irish stew	Irish stew	• Hot soup plate • Joint knife • Joint fork • Dessert spoon *(lay cover from inside to outside)*	• Worcestershire sauce • Pickled red cabbage	• Place joint knife first, dessert spoon next on RHS and joint fork on LHS of the cover, before serving Irish stew. • Offer proprietary Worcestershire sauce and pickled red cabbage (with tea spoon) on two separate under-liners. • Offer pre-plated (in hot soup plate) Irish stew from RHS of the guest.
Kebabs	Kebabs	• Hot joint plate • Joint knife • Joint fork	–	• Place joint knife on RHS and joint fork on LHS of the cover, before serving kebab. • Offer pre-plated (in hot joint plate) kebab from RHS of the guest.
Flamed kidney (flamed in Armagnac)	Rognons flambé	• Hot joint plate • Joint knife • Joint fork	• Pilaf rice	• Place joint knife on RHS and joint fork on LHS of the cover, before serving flamed kidney.

				• Offer pilaf rice alongside the flamed kidney on hot joint plate or place flamed kidney on the bed of pilaf rice. • Offer pre-plated (in hot joint plate) flamed kidney from RHS of the guest.
Flamed steak (flamed in brandy)	Steak Diane	• Hot joint plate • Steak knife • Steak fork	• French mustard • English mustard	• Place steak knife on RHS and steak fork on LHS of the cover, before serving steak Diane. • Offer English mustard and French mustard in two separate bowls with two preserve spoons, place both on one under-liner. • Offer pre-plated (in hot joint plate) steak Diane from RHS of the guest.
Peppered steak (flamed in white wine)	Steak au poivre	• Hot joint plate • Steak knife • Steak fork	• French mustard • English mustard	• Place steak knife on RHS and steak fork on LHS of the cover, before serving peppered steak. • Offer English mustard and French mustard in two separate bowls with two preserve spoons, place both on one under-liner.

				• Offer pre-plated (in hot joint plate) peppered steak from RHS of the guest.
Steak tartare	Steak tartare	• Cold joint plate • Joint knife • Joint fork	• Pumpernickel (thinly sliced and buttered)	• Place joint knife on RHS and joint fork on LHS of the cover, before serving steak tartare. • Offer pumpernickel in side plate. • Offer pre-plated (in cold joint plate) steak tartare from RHS of the guest.
Flamed veal (flamed in Cognac)	Escalope de veau	• Hot joint plate • Joint knife • Joint fork	–	• Place joint knife on RHS and joint fork on LHS of the cover, before serving flamed veal. • Offer pre-plated (in hot joint plate) flamed veal from RHS of the guest.
Tournedos (grilled)	Tournedos grilles	• Hot joint plate • Steak knife • Steak fork	–	• Place steak knife on RHS and steak fork on LHS of the cover, before serving grilled tournedos. • Offer pre-plated (in hot joint plate) grilled tournedos from RHS of the guest.

Chops of lamb (grilled)	Cotelettes d' agneau grillee	• Hot joint plate • Joint knife • Joint fork	• Beurre Maître d' hôtel	• Place joint knife on RHS and joint fork on LHS of the cover, before serving grilled lamb cutlet. • Offer Beurre Maître d' hôtel in sauce boat with preserve spoon by placing on under-liner. • Offer pre-plated (in hot joint plate) grilled lamb cutlet from RHS of the guest.
Rump steak	Rump steak	• Hot joint plate • Steak knife • Steak fork	• French mustard • English mustard	• Place steak knife on RHS and steak fork on LHS of the cover, before serving rump steak. • Offer English mustard and French mustard in two separate bowls with two preserve spoons on one under-liner. • Offer pre-plated (in hot joint plate) rump steak from RHS of the guest.
Châteaubriand	Châteaubriand	• Hot joint plate • Steak knife • Steak fork	• French mustard • English mustard • Béarnaise sauce	• Place steak knife on RHS and steak fork on LHS of the cover, before serving Châteaubriand.

				• Offer English mustard and French mustard in two separate bowls with two preserve spoons on one under-liner. • Serve béarnaise sauce in sauce boat/gravy boat with sauce ladle after placing on under-liner • Offer pre-plated (in hot joint plate) Châteaubriand from RHS of the guest.

Sorbet

Traditionally, this course was also known as "Granita". It is a break between the meals; therefore sometimes it is also called "rest course". Sorbet or other palate cleansers are usually served between courses, especially in the mid of the 17 courses FCM. For instance, a bowl of mango sorbet (or sorbetto, sorbet) is a frozen dessert made from iced fruit (typically juice or puree) and other ingredients (like chocolate, wine, and/or liquor) can be served as a sorbet. In simple terms, sorbet is a light water ice with added Italian Meringue. Some excellent examples of sorbet preparations are given below:

Dishes Names		Cover	Accom-paniment/s	Service
In English	**In French**			
Russian cigarette	Russian cigarette	• Side plate • Doily paper	• Matchbox/ lighter	• Offer Black Russian Cigarette (with match box) in its sealed packet by placing on under-liner (after placing doily paper). • Offer Russian cigarette from RHS of the guest.

Champagne sorbet	Sorbet au Champagne	• Goblet glass • Teaspoon • Under-liner	• Black Russian Cigarette	• Place pre-portioned champagne sorbet (in goblet glass like tulip) on under-liner. Put teaspoon on RHS of the tulip glass on under-liner. • Offer Black Russian Cigarette (with match box) in its sealed packet by placing on under-liner. • Offer pre-portioned champagne sorbet from RHS of the guest.
Lemon sorbet	Sorbet au Citron	• Goblet glass • Teaspoon • Under-liner	• Black Russian Cigarette	• Place pre-portioned lemon sorbet (in goblet glass like tulip) on under-liner. Put teaspoon on RHS of the tulip glass on under-liner. • Offer Black Russian Cigarette (with match box) in its sealed packet by placing on under-liner. • Offer pre-portioned lemon sorbet from RHS of the guest.
Orange sorbet	Sorbet au Orange	• Goblet glass • Teaspoon • Under-liner	• Black Russian Cigarette	• Place pre-portioned orange sorbet (in goblet glass like tulip) on under-liner. Put teaspoon on RHS of the tulip glass on under-liner. • Offer Black Russian Cigarette (with match box) in its sealed packet by placing on under-liner. • Offer pre-portioned orange sorbet from RHS of the guest.

Blackcurrant sorbet	Sorbet au Cassis	• Goblet glass • Teaspoon • Under-liner	• Black Russian Cigarette	• Place pre-portioned blackcurrant sorbet (in goblet glass like tulip) on under-liner. Put teaspoon on RHS of the tulip glass on under-liner. • Offer Black Russian Cigarette (with match-box) in its sealed packet by placing on under-liner. • Offer pre-portioned blackcurrant sorbet from RHS of the guest.

Relevé

In English it means "remove course". It is also called as second main or meat course. This includes large joints of meat such as a rib of beef, a joint of lamb, mutton or pork, which have to be carved. A sauce or roast gravy, potato and green gravy are mostly accompanied with this course. Relevé course is classified in accordance with the type of meat or their cuts like *bovine* (beef and veal), *oviene* {lamb, sheep, mutton and hogget (yearling mutton)}, *porcine* (pork) and *caprine* (goat meat). Apart from it, few grilled poultry preparations may also be served in it. All these meat preparations (or meat cuts) can serve either as sauté, braised, grilled or boiled form. Some excellent examples of relevé preparations are given below.

Dishes Names		Cover	Accompa-niment/s	Service
In English	**In French**			
Double sirloin steak	Entrecote double grillee	• Hot joint plate • Steak knife • Steak fork	• French mustard • English mustard • Béarnaise sauce	• Place steak knife on RHS and steak fork on LHS of the cover, before serving double sirloin steak. • Offer English mustard and French mustard in two separate bowls with two preserve spoons on one under-liner.

				• Place béarnaise sauce in sauce boat/gravy boat with sauce ladle after placing on under-liner. • Offer pre-plated (in hot joint plate) double sirloin steak from RHS of the guest.
Porterhouse steak	Porterhouse steak	• Hot joint plate • Steak knife • Steak fork	• French mustard • English mustard	• Place steak knife on RHS and steak fork on LHS of the cover, before serving porterhouse steak. • Offer English mustard and French mustard in two separate bowls with two preserve spoons on one under-liner. • Offer pre-plated (in hot joint plate) porterhouse steak from RHS of the guest.
Grilled veal	Cote de veau grillee	• Hot joint plate • Joint knife • Joint fork	• French mustard • English mustard • Beurre Maître d' hôtel • Pommes pailles • Watercress	• Place joint knife on RHS and joint fork on LHS of the cover, before serving grilled veal. • Offer English mustard, French mustard and beurre Maître d' hôtel in three separate bowls with three preserve spoons on one under-liner. • Offer pre-plated (in hot joint plate) grilled veal from RHS of the guest. Place pommes pailles and watercress alongside the grilled veal.

Grilled lamb chop	Chop d'agneau grillee	• Hot joint plate • Joint knife • Joint fork	• Beurre Maître d' hôtel	• Place joint knife on RHS and joint fork on LHS of the cover, before serving grilled lamb chop. • Offer Beurre Maître d' hôtel in sauce boat with preserve spoon, after placing on under-liner. • Offer pre-plated (in hot joint plate) grilled lamb chop from RHS of the guest.
Grilled pork chop	Cotc dc porc grillee	• Hot joint plate • Joint knife • Joint fork	• English mustard • Beurre Maître d' hôtel/ sauce diable	• Place joint knife on RHS and joint fork on LHS of the cover, before serving grilled pork chop. • Offer English mustard and beurre Maître d' hôtel/sauce diable in two separate bowls with two preserve spoons on one under-liner. • Offer pre-plated (in hot joint plate) grilled pork chop from RHS of the guest.
Grilled chicken	Poulet grillee	• Hot joint plate • Joint knife • Joint fork	• Sauce diable	• Place joint knife on RHS and joint fork on LHS of the cover, before serving grilled chicken. • Offer sauce diable in sauce boat with preserve spoon, after placing on under-liner. • Offer pre-plated (in hot joint plate) grilled chicken from RHS of the guest.

Grilled spring chicken	Poussin grillee	• Hot joint plate • Joint knife • Joint fork	• Sauce diable	• Place joint knife on RHS and joint fork on LHS of the cover, before serving grilled spring chicken. • Offer sauce diable in sauce boat with preserve spoon, after placing on under-liner. • Offer pre-plated (in hot joint plate) grilled spring chicken from RHS of the guest.
Grilled spatchcock	Crapaudine grillee	• Hot joint plate • Joint knife • Joint fork	• Sauce diable	• Place joint knife on RHS and joint fork on LHS of the cover, before serving grilled spatchcock. • Offer sauce diable in sauce boat with preserve spoon, after placing on under-liner. • Offer pre-plated (in hot joint plate) grilled spatchcock from RHS of the guest.
Pork spareribs	Cotes de porc	• Hot joint plate • Joint knife • Joint fork	• English mustard • Beuree Maître d' hôtel/ sauce diable	• Place joint knife on RHS and joint fork on LHS of the cover, before serving grilled pork chop. • Offer English mustard and beuree Maître d' hôtel/sauce diable in two separate bowls with two preserve spoons, all on onc under-liner. • Offer pre-plated (in hot joint plate) grilled pork chop from RHS of the guest.

Veal spareribs	Cotes de veau	• Hot joint plate • Joint knife • Joint fork	• French mustard • English mustard • Beuree Maître d' hôtel • Pommes pailles • Watercress	• Place joint knife on RHS and joint fork on LHS of the cover, before serving grilled veal spareribs. • Offer English mustard, French mustard and beuree maître d' hôtel in three separate bowls with three preserve spoons, all on one under-liner. • Offer pre-plated (in hot joint plate) grilled veal spareribs from RHS of the guest. Place pommes pailles alongside the grilled veal.

Rôti

It refers to roast course. In it, each dish is accompanied by its own particular sauce and gravy with green salad. It mainly consists of roast games or poultry. Some excellent examples of rôti preparations are given below:

Dishes Names		Cover	Accom-paniment/s	Service
In English	In French			
Chicken	Poulet	• Hot joint plate • Joint knife • Joint fork	• Bread sauce • Game chips • Watercress • Roast gravy	• Place joint knife on RHS and joint fork on LHS of the cover, before serving roasted chicken. • Offer bread sauce and roast gravy in two separate bowls with two preserve spoons by placing on common under-liner. • Place game chips and watercress alongside the roasted chicken.

				• Offer pre-plated (in hot joint plate) roasted chicken from RHS of the guest.
Duck	Duck (canard) and duckling (caneton)	• Hot joint plate • Joint knife • Joint fork	• Apple sauce • Game chips • Watercress • Sage and onion stuffing • Roast gravy	• Place joint knife on RHS and joint fork on LHS of the cover, before serving roasted duck. • Offer apple sauce and roast gravy in two separate bowls with two preserve spoons, by placing on common under-liner. • Offer pre-plated (in hot joint plate) roasted duck from RHS of the guest. • Place game chips, watercress and sage and onion stuffing alongside the roasted duck.
Pheasant	Le faisan	• Hot joint plate • Joint knife • Joint fork	• Bread sauce • Game chips • Watercress • Fried breadcrumbs • Roast gravy	• Place joint knife on RHS and joint fork on LHS of the cover, before serving roasted pheasant. • Offer bread sauce, roast gravy and fried breadcrumbs in three separate bowls with three preserve spoons, by placing on an under-liner. • Place game chips and watercress alongside the roasted pheasant.

				• Offer pre-plated (in hot joint plate) roasted pheasant from RHS of the guest.
Turkey	Dindonneau	• Hot joint plate • Joint knife • Joint fork	• Cranberry sauce • Game chips • Watercress • Bread sauce • Chestnut stuffing • Bacon rolls • Roast gravy	• Place joint knife on RHS and joint fork on LHS of the cover, before serving roasted turkey. • Offer bread sauce, cranberry sauce and roast gravy in three separate bowls with three preserve spoons, by placing on an under-liner. • Place game chips, watercress, bacon rolls and chestnut stuffing alongside the roasted turkey. • Now offer pre-plated (in hot joint plate) roasted turkey from RHS of the guest.
Goose	Oie	• Hot joint plate • Joint knife • Joint fork	• Apple sauce • Sage and onion stuffing • Roast gravy	• Place joint knife on RHS and joint fork on LHS of the cover, before serving roasted goose. • Offer apple sauce and roast gravy in two separate bowls with two preserve spoons, by placing on an under-liner. .

				• Place sage and onion stuffing alongside the roasted turkey. Now offer pre-plated (in hot joint plate) roasted goose from RHS of the guest
Veal*	Veau	• Hot joint plate • Joint knife • Joint fork	• Parsley and thyme stuffing • Roast gravy	• Place joint knife on RHS and joint fork on LHS of the cover, before serving roasted veal. • Offer roast gravy in bowl with preserve spoon, by placing on an under-liner. • Place parsley and thyme stuffing alongside the roasted veal. Now offer pre-plated (in hot joint plate) roasted veal from RHS of the guest.
Wild duck	Canard sauvage	• Hot joint plate • Joint knife • Joint fork • Dessert fork (for orange salad)	• Orange salad • Game chips • Watercress • Acidulated cream • Roast gravy	• Place joint knife on RHS and joint fork on LHS of the cover, before serving roasted wild duck. • Offer acidulated cream (for orange salad) and roast gravy in two separate bowls with two preserve spoons, by placing on an under-liner.

				• Place game chips, watercress and orange salad alongside the roasted wild duck. • Now offer pre-plated (in hot joint plate) roasted wild duck from RHS of the guest.
Partridge	Le perdrix	• Hot joint plate • Joint knife • Joint fork	• Bread sauce • Fried breadcrumbs • Watercress • Game chips • Roast gravy	• Place joint knife on RHS and joint fork on LHS of the cover, before serving roasted partridge. • Offer bread sauce, roast gravy and fried breadcrumbs in three separate bowls with three preserve spoons, by placing on an under-liner. • Place game chips and watercress alongside the roasted partridge. • Offer pre-plated (in hot joint plate) roasted partridge from RHS of the guest.
Grouse	La grouse	• Hot joint plate • Joint knife • Joint fork	• Bread sauce • Fried breadcrumbs • Watercress • Game chips • Roast gravy	• Place joint knife on RHS and joint fork on LHS of the cover, before serving roasted grouse. • Offer bread sauce, roast gravy and fried breadcrumbs in three separate bowls with three preserve spoons, by placing on an under-liner.

				• Offer pre-plated (in hot joint plate) roasted grouse from RHS of the guest. Place game chips and watercress alongside the roasted grouse.
Quail	La caille	• Hot joint plate • Joint knife • Joint fork	• Bread sauce • Fried breadcrumbs • Watercress • Game chips • Roast gravy	• Place joint knife on RHS and joint fork on LHS of the cover, before serving roasted quail. • Offer bread sauce, roast gravy and fried breadcrumbs in three separate bowls with three preserve spoons, by placing on an under-liner. • Offer pre-plated (in hot joint plate) roasted quail from RHS of the guest. Place game chips and watercress alongside the roasted quail.
Woodcock	La becasse	• Hot joint plate • Joint knife • Joint fork	• Bread sauce • Fried breadcrumbs • Watercress • Game chips • Roast gravy	• Place joint knife on RHS and joint fork on LHS of the cover, before serving roasted woodcock. • Offer bread sauce, roast gravy and fried breadcrumbs in three separate bowls with three preserve spoons, by placing on an under-liner.

				• Offer pre-plated (in hot joint plate) roasted woodcock from RHS of the guest. Place game chips and watercress alongside the roasted woodcock.
Snipe	La becassine	• Hot joint plate • Joint knife • Joint fork	• Bread sauce • Fried breadcrumbs • Watercress • Game chips • Roast gravy	• Place joint knife on RHS and joint fork on LHS of the cover, before serving roasted snipe. • Offer bread sauce, roast gravy and fried breadcrumbs in three separate bowls with three preserve spoons, by placing on an under-liner. • Offer pre-plated (in hot joint plate) roasted snipe from RHS of the guest. Place game chips and watercress alongside the roasted snipe.
Venison*	Le venaison	• Hot joint plate • Joint knife • Joint fork	• Red currant jelly • Forcemeat balls • Croutons	• Place joint knife on RHS and joint fork on LHS of the cover, before serving roasted venison. • Offer red currant jelly (in jam shot/bowl) with teaspoon/ preserve spoon on under-liner and forcemeat balls in side plate.

				• Offer pre-plated (in hot joint plate) roasted venison from RHS of the guest. Place croutons alongside the roasted venison.
Wild rabbits*	Lapins Sauvages	• Hot joint plate • Joint knife • Joint fork	• Red currant jelly • Forcemeat balls • Croutons	• Place joint knife on RHS and joint fork on LHS of the cover, before serving roasted wild rabbit. • Offer red currant jelly (in jam shot/bowl) with teaspoon/ preserve spoon on under-liner and forcemeat balls in separate side plate. • Offer pre-plated (in hot joint plate) roasted wild rabbit from RHS of the guest. Place croutons alongside the roasted rabbit.
Hare*	Les Lievres	• Hot joint plate • Joint knife • Joint fork	• Red currant jelly • Forcemeat balls • Croutons	• Place joint knife on RHS and joint fork on LHS of the cover, before serving roasted hare. • Offer red currant jelly (in jam shot/bowl) with teaspoon/ preserve spoon on under-liner and forcemeat balls in separate side plate.

				• Offer pre-plated (in hot joint plate) roasted hare from RHS of the guest. Place croutons alongside the roasted hare.
Beef*	Boeuf	• Hot joint plate • Joint knife • Joint fork	• English mustard • French mustard • Horseradish sauce • Roast gravy • Yorkshire pudding	• Place joint knife on RHS and joint fork on LHS of the cover, before serving roasted beef. • Offer English mustard, French mustard, horseradish sauce in three separate bowls with three preserve spoons, on an under-liner. Place roast gravy in gravy boat with preserve spoon, after placing on under-liner. • Offer pre-plated (in hot joint plate) roasted beef from RHS of the guest. Do not forget to place Yorkshire pudding alongside the roasted beef.
Lamb*	Agneau	• Hot joint plate • Joint knife • Joint fork	• Mint sauce • Roast gravy	• Place joint knife on RHS and joint fork on LHS of the cover, before serving roasted lamb.

				• Offer mint sauce and roast gravy in two separate bowls with two preserve spoons, by placing on an under-liner. • Offer pre-plated (in hot joint plate) roasted lamb from RHS of the guest.
Pork*	Porc	• Hot joint plate • Joint knife • Joint fork	• Apple sauce • Sage and onion stuffing • Roast gravy • Game chips • Watercress	• Place joint knife on RHS and joint fork on LHS of the cover, before serving roasted pork. • Offer apple sauce and roast gravy in two separate bowls with two preserve spoons, by placing on an under-liner. • Offer pre-plated (in hot joint plate) roasted pork from RHS of the guest. • Place sage and onion stuffing, game chips and watercress alongside the roasted pork.

Note. *The above given examples of roasted game animals (such as hare, wild rabbits and venison) and red meats (such as beef, veal, pork and lamb) may also serve as a relevé course depending on preparation style.

Legumes

It refers to *vegetable course.* Vegetables, particularly the finer ones may be served as separate course after serving main course or quite commonly today, as an introductory course. In this stage, the balance of the course is gradually returning from heavy to light. In this course, vegetable dishes are served with their accompanying sauces. It includes vegetable preparations made (particularly continental vegetables) from cabbage family; stalk vegetables; leafy vegetables; salad greens; seeds, edible pods and shots; vegetable fruits; bulbs; edible fungi mushrooms; special vegetables, etc. Some excellent examples of legume preparations are given below:

Dishes Names		Cover	Accompa-niment/s	Service
In English	**In French**			
Artichoke (cold/hot)	Artichaut (Froid/ chaud)	• Cold/hot half plate • Joint fork • Fingerbowl • Spare napkin	• Cold (vinaigrette) • Hot (hollandaise)	• Place joint fork on RHS of the cover, before serving artichoke. Offer finger bowl (with lukewarm water + lemon slice) and napkin on under-liner on LHS of the cover (just above the side plate). • Offer vinaigrette sauce or hollandaise sauce (depends upon artichoke preparation) in sauce boat with sauce ladle, after placing on under-liner. • Present pre-plated artichoke (in hot/cold half plate) from RHS of the guest.
Asparagus (Cold/hot)	Asperges (Froid/ chaud)	• Cold/hot joint plate • Joint fork • Asparagus tong • Fingerbowl • Spare napkin	• Cold (vinaigrette) • Hot (hollandaise)	• Downturn joint fork then place diagonally across the cover and asparagus tong on RHS of the cover, before serving asparagus. Offer fingerbowl (with lukewarm water + lemon slice) and napkin on under-liner, on top LHS of the cover.

				• Offer vinaigrette sauce or hollandaise sauce (depending on asparagus preparation) in sauce boat with sauce ladle, after placing on under-liner. • Present pre-plated asparagus (in hot/ cold joint plate) on the surface of downturned joint fork (in order to tilt so that the points of asparagus can dip in the sauce) from RHS of the guest. Make sure points of asparagus should face the customer.
Corn on the cob	Mais naturel	• Hot half plate • Two corn on the cob holders • Fingerbowl • Spare napkin	• Melted butter	• Place fingerbowl (with lukewarm water + lemon slice) and napkin on under-liner, on top LHS of the cover. • Offer melted butter in sauce boat with sauce ladle after placing on under-liner. • Present pre-plated corn-on-the-cob (in hot half plate) from RHS of thc guest. Corn-on-the-cob holders should be inserted into each end of the cob by kitchen staff.

Flamed mushrooms	Cèpes flambé	• Hot half plate • Side knife • Dessert fork	–	• Place side knife on RHS of the cover and dessert fork on LHS of the cover, before serving flamed mushrooms. • Present pre-plated flamed mushroom (in hot half plate) from RHS of the guest.

Salade

Traditionally, simple green tossed salads with vinaigrette dressing were served as a means of cleansing the palate and aiding digestion. Modern French cuisine has brought about some very elaborate salads with diverse dressing flavours. Salads are also a kind of food, mainly accompanied with dressing; salads are made up of vegetables, fruits, piquant food, blend food, chopped food, potato, egg and meat. In 14 or 11 course menu, salads serve as a *hors d'oeuvres* or as an accompaniment to the entrée or other main course. A good salad food must possess a relish value. The flavour could be developed with marination of spices and herbs. Salads can be classified on the basis of ingredients (such as meat salad, fish salad, egg salad, fruit salad, pasta salad, vegetable salad, etc.); cooking medium (raw salad and cooked salad); and nature of preparation (such as simple salad and compound salad). As a nutritious food, it is very essential that the freshness should be preserved and delicacy must be maintained while preparing the salad. Some excellent examples of salad preparations are given ahead.

Dishes Names		Cover	Accom-paniment/s	Service
In English	In French			
Green salad (with vinaigrette)	Salade verte (avec vinaigrette)	• Cold half plate • Dessert fork	• Vinaigrette/ French dressing	• Place dessert fork on RHS of the cover, before serving green salad. • Offer vinaigrette sauce in sauce boat with sauce ladle, after placing on under-liner. • Offer pre-plated (in cold half plate) green salad from RHS of the guest.

Raw salad	Salade crue	• Cold half plate • Dessert fork	–	• Place dessert fork on RHS of the cover, before serving raw salad. • Offer pre-plated (in cold half plate) raw salad from RHS of the guest.
Compound salad	Salade composé	• Salad bowl or half plate • Dessert fork	• Salad dressing (may be directly added or offered separately)	• Place dessert fork on RHS of the cover, before serving compound salad. • Offer accompanied salad dressing in sauce boat with sauce ladle, after placing on under-liner. • Offer pre-plated (in salad bowl/half plate) compound salad from RHS of the guest.
Cooked salad	Salade cuite	• Salad bowl or half plate • Dessert fork	• Salad dressing (may be directly added or offered separately)	• Place dessert fork on RHS of the cover, before serving cooked salad. • Offer accompanied salad dressing in sauce boat with sauce ladle, after placing on under-liner. • Offer pre-plated (in salad bowl/half plate) cooked salad from RHS of the guest.

Chaud Froid

It includes a variety of cold meat and fish preparations together with a range of other preparations. It also includes those hot preparations which can be prepared hot but should be served only cold. These preparations may also be served as hors d'oeuvres and often found in buffet set-up. Some excellent examples of chaud froid preparations are given below:

Dishes Names		Cover	Accompaniment/s	Service
In English	In French			
Paté/paste (pork pie is paté)	Paté	• Cold half plate • Small knife • Small fork	• Crisp bread, baguette or crackers • Dill • Cumberland sauce • Redcurrant jelly	• Place small knife on RHS and small fork on LHS of the cover, before serving paté. • Offer bread/ baguette or cracker in side plate, dill and redcurrant jelly in small bowls with two teaspoons, by placing on under-liner. • Cumberland sauce is to be offered in its bottle only. • Offer pre-plated (in cold half plate) paté from RHS of the guest.
Country terrine (terrine is a meat loaf)	Terrine de champagne	• Cold half plate • Small knife • Small fork	• Cornichorns (small pickled gherkins) • Mustard • Bread/ crackers	• Place small knife on RHS and small fork on LHS of the cover, before serving country terrine. • Offer bread or cracker in side plate, mustard and cornichorns in small bowls with two tea spoons, by placing on under-liner. • Offer pre-plated (in cold half plate) country terrine from RHS of the guest.
Chicken galantine	Poulet galantine	• Cold half plate • Small knife • Small fork	• Boiled vegetables • Seasonal salad • Parsley	• Place small knife on RHS and small fork on LHS of the cover, before serving galantine.

				• Offer seasonal vegetables in side plate plus boiled vegetables and parsley alongside the chicken galantine. • Offer pre-plated (in cold half plate) chicken galantine from RHS of the guest.
Ballotine	Ballotine	• Cold half plate • Small knife • Small fork	• Riz pilaf • Nouilles au beuree • Jardinière/paysane	• Place small knife on RHS and small fork on LHS of the cover, before serving ballotine. • Offer nouilles au beuree and jardinière/paysane in two small bowls with two tea spoons. Offer riz pilaf alongside the ballotine. • Offer pre-plated (in cold half plate) ballotine from RHS of the guest.
Roulades (turkey roulade)	Roulades	• Cold half plate • Small knife • Small fork	• Bread sauce • Cranberry sauce/orange relish	• Place small knife on RHS and small fork on LHS of the cover, before serving roulade. • Offer bread sauce and cranberry sauce/orange relish in two small bowls/sauce boats with two teaspoons by placing on under-liner. • Offer pre-plated (in cold half plate) roulades from RHS of the guest.

Sausages	Sausages	• Cold half plate • Small knife • Small fork	• Mashed potatoes • Tossed green salad	• Place small knife on RHS and small fork on LHS of the cover, before serving sausages. • Offer tossed green salad in small bowl with teaspoon by placing on under-liner. Place mashed potatoes alongside the sausages. • Offer pre-plated (in cold half plate) sausages from RHS of the guest.
Jambon	Jambon à la crème or jambon au Madere	• Cold half plate • Small knife • Small fork	• Braised Belgian chicory • Puree of spinach (in early summer season, new potatoes may also be offered)	• Place small knife on RHS and small fork on LHS of the cover, before serving jambon. • Offer puree of spinach in small bowl with teaspoon by placing on under-liner. Place braised Belgian chicory alongside the jambon. • Offer pre-plated (in cold half plate) jambon from RHS of the guest.
Glazed ham	Glazed ham	• Cold half plate • Small knife • Small fork	• Piles of vegetables (it is made with carrots, tiny onions, mushrooms, peas and green beans) • Cream sauce	• Place small knife on RHS and small fork on LHS of the cover, before serving ham. • Offer cream sauce in small bowl/ sauce boat with tea spoon/sauce ladle by placing on under-liner.

				Place piles of vegetables alongside the ham. • Offer pre-plated (in cold half plate) ham from RHS of the guest.

Entremets

An entremet (it is an old French word, literally meaning "between servings") is a small sweet dish that is served between courses. Originally, it was an elaborate form of entertainment dish that is common in Europe. An entremet could be anything from a simple *frumenty* (a type of wheat porridge) to complex pancakes preparations. Broadly, entremets can be classified into two parts i.e. hot entremets and cold entremets. Some excellent examples of entremet preparations are given below.

Dishes Names		Cover	Accompa-niment/s	Service
In English	In French			
Baked Alaska	Baked Alaska	• Hot sweet/half plate • Dessert spoon • Dessert fork	–	• Place dessert spoon on RHS and dessert fork on LHS of the cover, before serving Baked Alaska. • Offer pre-plated (in hot half plate) Baked Alaska from RHS of the guest.
Flamed banana (in rum)	Banane flambé au rhum	• Hot sweet/half plate • Dessert spoon • Dessert fork	• Castor sugar	• Place dessert spoon on RHS and dessert fork on LHS of the cover, before serving Flamed banana. • Offer castor sugar in dredger by placing on the under-liner.

				• Offer pre-plated (in hot half plate) Flamed banana from RHS of the guest.
Flamed pancakes	Crepe suzette	• Hot sweet/half plate • Dessert spoon • Dessert fork	–	• Place dessert spoon on RHS and dessert fork on LHS of the cover, before serving Flamed pancakes. • Offer pre-plated (in hot half plate) Flamed pancakes from RHS of the guest.
Flamed peach	Peche Flambé	• Hot sweet/half plate • Dessert spoon • Dessert fork	• Castor sugar	• Place dessert spoon on RHS and dessert fork on LHS of the cover, before serving Flamed peach. • Offer castor sugar in dredger by placing on an under-liner. • Offer pre-plated (in hot half plate) flamed peach from RHS of the guest.
Flamed pineapple (with Kirsch)	Anaas Flambe au Kirsch	• Hot sweet/half plate • Dessert spoon • Dessert fork	–	• Place dessert spoon on RHS and dessert fork on LHS of the cover, before serving Flamed pineapple. • Offer pre-plated (in hot half plate) Flamed pineapple from RHS of the guest.

Strawberries Romanoff	Fraises Romanoff	• Coupe • Teaspoon • Under-liner	• Castor sugar	• Place pre-portioned Strawberries Romanoff (in coupe) on under-liner. Put teaspoon on RHS of the Strawberries Romanoff on under-liner. • Offer castor sugar in dredger, after placing it on the under-liner. • Offer pre-portioned Strawberries Romanoff from RHS of the guest.
Strawberries royal	Fraises Royale	• Coupe • Teaspoon • Under-liner	• Castor sugar	• Place pre-portioned Strawberries royal (in coupe) on under-liner. Put teaspoon on RHS of the Strawberries royal on under-liner. • Offer castor sugar in dredger, after placing it on the under-liner. • Offer pre-portioned Strawberries Royale from RHS of the guest.
Zabaglione	Zabaglione	• Goblet glass • Teaspoon • Under-liner	• Biscuit à la cuillere	• Place pre-portioned zabaglione (in goblet glass like tulip) on under-liner. Put teaspoon on RHS of the tulip glass on under-liner.

				• Offer Biscuit à la cuillere on the same under-liner. • Offer pre-portioned zabaglione from RHS of the guest.
Bombe	Bombe	• Cold dessert/ half plate • Dessert spoon • Dessert fork	–	• Place dessert spoon on RHS and dessert fork on LHS of the cover, before serving. • Offer pre-plated (in cold dessert/half plate) Bombe from RHS of the guest.
Peach Melba (a coupe dish)	Peche Melba	• Coupe • Ice cream spoon/Tea spoon • Under-liner	• Vanilla ice cream • Melba sauce (or raspberry sauce)	• Place pre-portioned Peche Melba (in coupe) on under-liner. Put ice cream spoon/teaspoon on RHS of the coupe on under-liner. • Offer vanilla ice cream in bowl with teaspoon, by placing on an under-liner or may also be directly poured in coupe. • Offer pre-portioned Peche Melba from RHS of the guest.

Savoureaux

It refers to savouries that are predominantly considered *on toast* course. The term savouries refers to the savoury items that are served hot on toast or as a savoury soufflé. Savouries can be based on either vegetable or non-vegetable preparations. Straightforwardly, savouries are small but spicy tit-bit preparations often considered finger foods. Some excellent examples of savoury preparations are given below.

Dishes Names		Cover	Accompa-niment/s	Service
In English	In French			
On toast (like canapés)	En croute	• Not necessary as it is a finger food	–	• Usually eaten with fingers but if guest desires then steward can offer side knife (on RHS) and dessert fork (on LHS). • En croute preparations are offered in hot half plates.
Quiche	Quiche	• Hot half plate • Side knife • Dessert fork	• Cayenne pepper • Pepper mill • Worcestershire sauce • Cruet set (already on table)	• Place side knife on RHS and dessert fork on LHS of the cover, before serving quiche. • Offer cayenne pepper, pepper mill and Worcestershire sauce on under-liner. • Offer pre-plated (in hot half plate) quiche from RHS of the guest.
Fritters	Fritters	• Hot half plate • Side knife • Dessert fork	• Cayenne pepper • Pepper mill • Worcestershire sauce • Cruet set (already on table)	• Place side knife on RHS and dessert fork on LHS of the cover, before serving fritters. • Offer cayenne pepper, pepper mill and Worcestershire sauce on under-liner.

				• Offer pre-plated (in hot half plate) fritters from RHS of the guest.
Soufflés	Soufflés	• Hot half plate • Side knife • Dessert fork	• Cayenne pepper • Pepper mill • Worcestershire sauce • Cruet set (already on table)	• Place side knife on RHS and dessert fork on LHS of the cover, before serving soufflés. • Offer cayenne pepper, pepper mill and Worcestershire sauce on under-liner. • Offer pre-plated (in hot half plate) soufflés from RHS of the guest.

Fromage

The French people eat more cheese than anyone else does in the world. After dinner, they appreciate a selection of cheese, it is served on a wooden board with assorted cut fruits. This signals the end of a casual, family-style meal. There are more than thousand varieties of cheese around the world which can broadly be classified into five groups, i.e., fresh, soft, hard, semi-hard (or semi-soft) and blue cheese. Nowadays, one more category, i.e., processed cheese is also available in the market. The guidelines for cover layout, accompaniment/s and service along with its imitative preparation *fondue* are given below:

Cheese and Fondue		Cover	Accompa-niment/s	Service
In English	In French			
Cheese (includes fresh/soft, semi-hard, hard, blue and processed cheese varieties)	Fromage (assorted cheeses are preferred to be served in a cheese basket or on cheese board)	• Side plate • Side knife	• Cruet set • Butter • Celery • Castor sugar • Assorted cheese crackers	• Place side plate with side knife in centre of the cover. • Offer accompaniments like cruet set, celery in tumbler glass (on ice) and assorted cheese crackers/biscuits in side plate.

				• Serve butter in butter dish with butter knife, after placing on under-liner. • Offer castor sugar (in bowl with teaspoon, after placing on under-liner) for cream cheeses. • Cheese can be served via pre-plated (served from RHS) as well as platter-to-plate service (served from LHS).
Fondue	Fondue	• Half plate • Fondue fork • Fondue lamp (or complete foundue set)	• Bread cubes • Kirsch	• Place fondue fork on RHS of the cover and fondue lamp on LHS (or in centre) on the guest's dining table. • Offer bread cubes in half plate (alongside the fondue) and Kirsch (a drink offered in glass) as an accompaniment. • After Guéridon cooking of fondue, transfer fondue pan to guest's table on fondue lamp. Lastly, guest will serve himself/herself.

Dessert

Dessert is a course that typically comes at the end of the meal. It indicates to both choice of fresh fruits and nuts. The word *dessert* has came from the old French word "Desservir", meaning 'to clear the table'. Broadly, dessert can be classified into two groups, i.e., fresh fruits and dry fruits. Some excellent examples of desserts are given below.

Dishes Names		Cover	Accompaniment/s	Service
In English	In French			
Fresh fruits	Fruits Frais	• Fruit plate/fruit basket • Fruit knife • Fruit fork • Grape scissor (for grapes) • Fingerbowl	• Castor sugar • Salt	• Place fruit knife on RHS and fruit fork on LHS of the cover, before serving pre-plated cut fruits. Offer grape scissor (on side plate) with grapes. • Offer castor sugar in dredger (on under-liner) and cruet set as an accompaniment. • Offer pre-plated cut fruits (in fruit/half plate) from RHS of the guest. Unprepared (or sliced) fruits are offered in fruit basket with finger bowl.
Dry fruits (especially nuts)	Fruits secs (en particulier les noix)	• Fruit basket • Nut cracker • Spare side plate	• Castor sugar • Salt	• Offer nut cracker on under-liner. Spare side plate will be used as a debris plate for nutshells. • Dry fruits like almonds, pistachios, etc., are offered in individual bowls by placing on under-liner.

Boissons

It refers to beverage course. Traditionally, it includes an array of tea and coffee preparations only. But nowadays, wide varieties are available like, tisanes, milk drinks, Horlicks, Milo, Oval tine, etc. Three excellent examples of beverage preparations are given below.

Dishes Names		Cover	Accompa-niment/s	Service
In English	**In French**			
Coffee	Café	• Coffee cup (demi tasse cup for espresso coffee) • Coffee spoon • Under-liner	• Brown sugar • Cigar • Liquor (offer cigar in cedar wood box and liquor in 02 fl. oz liquor glass in an encoded style)	• Now place *coffee set* (it comprises demi-tasse /coffee cup, saucer and coffee spoon) on RHS or centre of the cover. First place coffee cup on saucer (handle should be on RHS) then place coffee spoon (on RHS of saucer) in 90° position under the handle of coffee cup. • In *à la carte service,* place under-liner/s in the centre of the table (or within easy reach of guest) then put coffee liquor pot and milk pot on it. • Place accompaniments (like cookies in half plate and sugar cubes in sugar bowl) in the centre of the table or within easy reach of guest/s.
Tea	Thé	• Tea cup • Teaspoon • Under-liner (Place choice of tea bags in the centre of the table by placing in small rectangular shape bowl)	• Sugar cubes • Cold milk • Lemon slices {Offer lemon slices with lemon fork (to squeeze lemon juice) in lemon tea order- by placing on an under-liner}	• Place *tea set* (it comprises tea cup, saucer and teaspoon) on RHS or centre of the cover. First place tea cup on saucer (handle should be on RHS) then place teaspoon (on RHS of saucer) in 90° position under the handle of tea cup. • In *à la carte* service, place under-liner/s in the centre of the table (or within easy reach of

				guest) then put tea liquor pot and milk pot on it. • Place accompaniments (like cookies in half plate and sugar cubes in sugar bowl) in the centre of the table or within easy reach of guest/s.
Specialty coffee, like • Irish coffee • Café royale • Café brule • Monks coffee • Baileys • Calypso • Devilled	Speciality Café	• Goblet glass • Under-liner	• Cigars/ Cigarettes • Petit fours	• Pour sugar in goblet glass then add hot black coffee and stir with teaspoon until all sugar is dissolved. • Now add desired spirit and double cream (by pouring cream slowly on the back of teaspoon to run onto coffee). • Place goblet glass on under-liner and serve from RHS of the guest. • Place any accompaniments (like petit four on side plate) in the centre of the table or within easy reach of guest.

Note.

- For ordinary tea leaves, the tea strainer and slop basin (or drip bowl) is necessary. Steward may also place tea strainer beneath the teapot lid, reducing the need for a slop basin. But when tea bag is used, tea strainer is not required.
- Extra coffee may also be offered in small bowl with coffee spoon in the centre of the table after placing on an under-liner. Guests can add this extra coffee to make their coffee more strong.
- Example of specialty coffee includes Irish coffee, Turkish coffee, Devilled coffee, Spiced coffee, Café Brule, Flamed coffee and so forth.
- Cigars should be offered in their original wooden boxes (or humidor/cedar wood boxes) whereas cigarettes will be offered in their sealed packets with matchbox after placing on under-liner (place doily paper too).

Menu Adaptation Style	
13 + 1 course menu	Merge fromage with savoury course; *buffet froid and salade course* with hors d'oeuvres
11 + 1 course menu	Merge *salade, buffet froid* and *oeufs course* with hors d'oeuvres; *fromage* with savoury course and *farinaceous* with *entrée* course
07 + 1 course menu	Starter + Soup + Fish + Entrée + Relevé + Rôti + Entremet + Beverage
06 + 1 course menu	Starter + Fish + Entrée + Main Course + Entremet + Savoury + Beverage
05 + 1 course menu	Starter + Soup + Entrée + Main Course + Entremet + Beverage
04 + 1 course menu	Starter + Soup + Main Course + Entremet + Beverage
03 + 1 course menu	Starter + Main Course + Entremet + Beverage
02 + 1 course menu	Starter + Main course + Beverage

KEY TERMS

Blinis : Small round shaped Russian pancakes often served with caviar.

Skirlie : Scottish dish made with onions and oatmeal and commonly used for white puddings.

Bacon rolls : Thin slices of pork that are eaten fried or grilled, usually with eggs.

Watercress : Eurasian cress which grows in running water and whose pungent leaves are used in salad making.

Game chips : Thin crisp chips that are traditionally served with roast game birds.

Kirsch : French brandy made from cherry.

Petit fours : Small fancy pastry (or cake).

Devilled coffee : Liquor based spiced and heated coffee preparation.

Cedar wood : Wooden box used to keep mature cigars.

REVIEW QUESTIONS

1. Elucidate 17 course French classical menu along with three examples in each course.
2. Differentiate between dessert and entremets course.
3. What is soup? Classify soup into different groups and briefly explain each.
4. Define the term hors d'oeuvres? Classify hors d'oeuvres and support each category with five examples.

11 CHAPTER

Guéridon and Carving

Objectives

Students will be able to:

- impart the guéridon concept and its origin;
- prepare/suggest standard way to prepare dishes on Guéridon trolley; and
- learn standard carving skills to carve meat items.

GUÉRIDON

Major Guéridon Equipment

- Suzette pans
- Flare lamps
- Calor gas bottle
- Hot plats

The term *Guéridon* means a movable service or trolley on which food can be prepared, flambéd, carved then served to guest. In other words, it is a kind of movable sideboard that gives sufficient equipment for immediate cooking and serving beside guest table in restaurants; it should also carry special equipment that assists in preparing dishes. Nowadays, it is very difficult to trace *guéridon* service in Indian restaurants as it requires more space to move about, simultaneously very expensive in nature and demands showmanship in cooking, flambéing, carving and serving the prepared dishes. The concept of Guéridon service originated in France (in Paris) at Monte Carlo (region) in Café de Paris (restaurant) in 1894 by Henry Charpentier. The first dish made on it was "Crêpes Suzette".

The Japanese art of cooking a dish (like "Teryaki" Japanese dish) in front of guest is called "Tepanyaki". For instance, meat or fish that is grilled or broiled after being soaked in a seasoned soya sauce to marinade then it is prepared in front of the guest on "Tepon" table.

GUÉRIDON PREPARATIONS

Crêpes Suzette

A paper-like thin French dessert made of a *crêpes* (pancake) with beuree Suzette (orange sauce). Crêpes is usually rolled and folded into quarters then cooked in orange flavoured sauce and served flambéed. Its standard preparation process is given below.

Step 1 Make a *pancake* with batter (flour kneaded with egg, salt, mixture of water and milk and little hot melted butter). To make pancake, first heat Suzette pan over medium-high heat and brush the pan with a little melted butter.

Step 2 Slightly tilt the Suzette pan and pour in enough batter to just cover the base and cook for 1-2 minutes (or until the base of crêpes is not light brown). Afterwards, flip the crêpes to make the other side brown. Now thin pancake is ready.

Step 3 Prepare *orange sauce* by heating sugar with very little water over low heat and stir to dissolve sugar then add butter and cook for 4-5 minutes until golden brown.

Step 4 Now add orange juice and zest and simmer for a few minutes. Next pour in liquor (Orange Curacao) and brandy (for flambé) and stir to combine. Dip a crêpes into this *orange sauce* then fold it into quarters and place on a serving plate.

Step 5 The crêpes suzette can also be served through platter-to-plate method, i.e., directly serve from Suzette pan (in Guéridon service) into pre-placed hot dessert plate.

Banana au Rhum

A dessert made with banana then flambéed with rum. Bananas are first split then cut lengthwise and next cooked in orange juice. Finally season with brown sugar and cinnamon and serve flambéed. Its standard preparation process is given below:

Step 1 Melt butter in a frying pan and when heated, add peeled and lengthwise sliced banana in the pan. Now sprinkle with brown sugar and cinnamon (optional) and sauté until light brown.

Step 2 Now turn and sauté the other side and again sprinkle the second side with brown sugar and cinnamon. When bananas are soft enough but not mushy, pour two ounces of dark rum and ignite. Orange juice may also be added to make *pan juice*.

Step 3 Next place bananas directly in dessert plate and serve from right-hand side of the guest or offer through platter-to-plate (from pan to guest plate) service on the guest table.

Step 4 Before serving, pour the pan juice over bananas. Dish may also be accompanied with vanilla ice cream. During sauté, remember occasionally to pierce the banana with fork to allow the heat to penetrate into the banana halves.

Peach Flambé

A French dessert made with sliced ripened peaches then flambéed in rum. It can be accompanied with vanilla ice cream. Instead of rum, brandy or cognac can also be used for flambé. Its standard preparation process is given below.

Step 1 Select ripened peaches and prepare by cutting into half then into slices (4-5 slices). Take a pan and melt butter over medium heat.

Step 2 Add 2-3 tablespoons of brown sugar into it and stir. Now add sliced peaches and cook until fairly warm and starting to soften (for around 1 minute).

Step 3 Flip the peaches and allow to cook for an additional 30-45 seconds and then add rum (dark or light-dark rum has more flavour than light rum) for flambé.

Step 4 Swirl the pan and allow to flambé the dish. Finally remove it from the flame and serve either through platter-to-plate service or may be pre-plated in dessert plate.

Rhum Omelette

A French dessert made with omelette flambéed in rum. Simply, it is a kind of pudding omelette. Its standard preparation process is given below:

Step 1 Keep ready plain baveuse omelette (*baveuse* means cooked omelette, it should be firm from outside and runny from inside). Afterwards, trim the ends of the omelette.

Step 2 Now sprinkle the omelette with castor sugar and pass the pan under a pre-heated broiler for 30-45 seconds to caramelize the sugar.

Step 3 There are two styles of flambéing the omelette. First style, pour a measure of rum around the edge of the pan and heat. When sufficiently heated, it will ignite.

Step 4 Second style, heat the rum in a small pan until it bubbles then pour it over the omelette and ignite. Spoon the sauce (or burning rum) over the omelette until the flames die. Steward can use any of these styles.

Step 5 Fold the omelette into half and serve with prepared rum based sauce by pouring over the omelette. It can be served either via platter-to-plate or pre-plated (on dessert plate).

Steak Diane

It is an American dish made from thin slices of beef steaks (or sirloin steaks) and flambéed in cognac brandy. Its standard preparation process is given below:

Step 1 Melt butter in frying pan. Add *sirloin steaks*, sprinkle with salt and pepper and sauté for 2-3 minutes on both sides. Now sprinkle chives, lemon juice and Worcestershire sauce. Chopped parsley, shallots and mushrooms may also be added.

Step 2 For flambé, pour heated *cognac brandy* over the steak and ignite and when a flame goes out, transfer steak into a serving plate or platter.

Step 3 Prepared steak diane can be served either through platter-to-plate service (placed into hot joint plate) or directly placed on hot joint plate and served from right-hand side of the guest.

Step 4 Before serving, do not forget to pour pan juice over the steak.

Pepper Steak (Steak au Poivre)

It is a French dish made from the steaks, conventionally a fillet mignon, coated with loosely cracked peppercorns and then flambéed in cognac brandy. Its standard preparation process is given below:

Step 1 Take *tenderloin steaks* (no more than 1-½ inches thick) and sprinkle all its sides with salt. Coarsely crush the peppercorns and spread them evenly onto the plate.

Step 2 Now press the fillet, on both sides, over the crushed pepper until it coats the surface and set aside. Melt the butter and olive oil (in pan) over medium heat and when it turns golden brown, gently place the steak in the pan.

Step 3 Once done, remove (from pan) the steak on a plate then wrap with silver foil and keep aside. Pour out the excess fat of fry pan but it does not mean completely wipe the pan.

Step 4 Now take Cognac brandy, ignite in the used pan and gently shake pan; then add cream and bring the mixture to boil. Whisk until the sauce coats.

Step 5 Season it and add the steaks back to the pan, spoon the sauce over and serve. It can also be served either via platter-to-plate or pre-plated (offered in joint plate).

CARVING TECHNIQUE

Carving Equipment

- Carving knife
- Carving fork
- Carving board
- Carving trolley

In food service industry, *carving* is an art of cutting the item into specified form and shape. In culinary, there are basically two types of carving, i.e., edible carving and non-edible carving. Edible carving means, carving of items like fruit carving, cooked meat carving (like joint carving), vegetable carving, etc., while non-edible carving includes – ice carving, thermocal carving, salt dough, tallow carving, etc. In this chapter, we will discuss the carving of several meats/joints, poultry and fish items.

Carving is a skill as well as an art that comes with practice. Carver or *trancheur* should keep the following points in mind while carving the prepared dish: use sharp carving knife and hold tightly the carving fork over the food item. The preparation of meats/ joints before cooking is most important at table side carving. The knowledge of bone structure also plays a crucial role in successful carving of joints. Carving of some famous table side preparations are given below.

Beef Fore-rib

✓ Loosen the meat from the narrow ribs then carve from the thick end of the joint. In English style carving, cut into thin slices whereas in American style carving, cut into thicker slices.

Beef Sirloin

✓ Loosen the meat from the bone and then start carving from the wing end and cutting down to the bone. Thereafter, remove the bone and carve the remaining meat.

Saddle of Lamb

✓ Carve from either side of the backbone and across the base of the chump and release the flesh from the ribs underneath. In accordance to English style of carving, cut slice thickly slice across each loin.

Leg of Lamb

✓ Hold firmly from knuckle end and turn meatiest side upwards and carve out two slightly thick slices from the centre of the leg, cutting down to the bone. Keep on cutting from both sides of the first cut, gradually slanting the knife to obtain longer slices. Now turn the joint over and carve horizontal slices together with a slice of the thick bottom of the leg.

Loin of Pork

✓ The crackling can be left on the pork joint. Otherwise it can be removed in sections from the joint to make the carving task easier. Cut the loin at a slight angle to enlarge the slices. Carve pork thicker than beef.

Leg of Pork

✓ First, eradicate the outside shell of crackling then start carving by removing a triangular section next to the knuckle end. Carve a V formation along the bone then obtain slices from both sides. Gradually, move the knife (into oblique angle) along the bone. Cut long thin slices from either side until all meat has been removed.

Carving of Roasted Chicken

✓ Place roasted chicken on the carving board with breast side up then remove legs from both sides by cutting through the joint. Next separate the thigh from the drumsticks and remove the breast meat. Finally, remove the wings from the chicken and serve to guest.

Carving of Roasted Turkey

✓ Place roasted turkey on the carving board, remove string and start carving by separating legs and thighs by cutting through the joint. Next separate the drumsticks and wishbone and remove the breast meat. Do not forget to slice the breast and thigh meat after separating from joints. Finally, remove wings and serve.

Carving of Roasted Duck

✓ Place roasted duck on the carving board with breast side up, remove legs from both sides by cutting between the leg and breast. Next separate the breast by cutting on the side of the breast bone from front to back then alongside the wishbone. Finally, cut the breast in halves or thirds and serve.

Carving of whole Cooked Fish

✓ Place cooked fish on carving board and remove fin bones then separate top fillet from head and collar bone. Next separate top fillet from tail then separate dorsal and belly fillet halves from the top fillet. Finally, remove bone cage and clean bottom fillet halves and serve.

Table Side Carving Guidelines			
Beef	Carved into slightly thick slices	Pork	Carved into slightly thick slices
Lamb saddle	Carved into long thick slices	Leg of lamb	Carved into slightly thick slices
Loin of pork	Carved thicker than beef	Leg of pork	Carved into slightly thin slices
Chicken	Carved into six portions	Turkey	Thinly carved into six portions
Duck	Thickly carved into six portions	Smoked salmon	Carved into slightly thin slices
Tongue	Carved into double thicker than beef and pork		

KEY TERMS

Guéridon	:	Trolley service on which half done food items are fully prepared in front of guests.
Crêpes suzette	:	Thin dessert pancake flamed and served in orange sauce.
Orange sauce	:	Liquid solution in which crêpes suzette is prepared.
Baveuse	:	Cooked omelette that is firm from outside and runny from inside.
Salt dough	:	Molding material made from a mixture of flour, salt and water (colouring agents may also be added).
Tallow carving	:	Carved sculptures that are specifically used for the purpose of *piece montee* (centre piece) on buffet.
Guinea fowl	:	Large African game bird of slate-colour, white spotted plumage.

REVIEW QUESTIONS

1. Define the term guéridon service? Enlist major equipment required on guéridon trolley.
2. Write a short note on poultry carving.
3. What is carving? Describe the basic carving skills that are required for table side carving.
4. Describe the step-by-step procedure for preparing banana au rhum.

12 CHAPTER

Types of Service

Objectives

Students will be able to:

- demonstrate serving skills, styles and measure its impact;
- compare and explain the idiosyncrasies of service methods; and
- recognize why different outlets use different serving patterns.

SERVICE

When someone (or group) offers something to someone (or group) and takes something in return then it is known as *service*. Often the term service is associated with product but in reality it is totally different from product. Although, service can be a part of product or both can be in combination, for instance formal dining hall like restaurant requires focusing equally on meal/product as well as its service. Four common characteristics of service include-

- Perishability — Service has limited shelf-life of specified time period.
- Inseparability — Service cannot be separate from server/provider.
- Intangibility — Service cannot be touched; guests can only experience it.
- Invariability — Every time service experience will differ.

In hotel industry, the term service refers to the exchange of food, beverage, accommodation or combination of two or all against cash payment or any other negotiable instrument. The payment is collected in the form of food and beverage charges, room rent, service tax, service charge, luxury tax, GST and so forth. The mode of payment may vary. For instance cash, plastic money (or *charge card*) or third party billing like use of traveller's cheque, travel agent vouchers, etc.

Hotel industry offers combination of both service and product but their proportion varies with the type of establishment. For instance, Quick Service Restaurant (QSR) is 75% product oriented and 25% service oriented whereas Fine Dine Hall (FDH) is 50% product and 50% service oriented. Similarly, in front office guest relation desk has 75% service component and 25% product component. For eating establishments, the meal preparation method depends upon standard recipe which also affects its service patterns. A brief description on different patterns (or forms/methods) of food and beverage service is given here.

FORMS AND METHODS OF SERVICES

Meal service is the way in which food is served to the guest. Meal time should be enjoyed and any method used for serving meals should be as simple as possible. There are various styles of meal and drink services which are given below in detail.

Table Service: A type of service in which guest is seated at a table and food servers attend to them. Menu lists are given or displayed for orders. The orders are taken by waiter/waitress. There are four basic styles of table service: plate (American), family style (English), cart (French) and platter (Russian). A brief description of each style of table service is given below.

American Service (Pre-plated Service of Food)

- ✓ A table service style in which menu items are individually produced, portioned, plated and garnished in kitchen by chefs. Food is primarily portioned in half plate (American plate) then served to each seated guest directly.
- ✓ Pre-plated foods are served by the server from the right-hand side of the guest. This type of service is prominently offered in coffee shops, banquets and group events. The serving technique is also known as "plate service, blue plate service or pre-plated service".

English Service (Host Service or Family Style Service)

- ✓ A table service style in which server takes food on large platters or in large bowls from the kitchen and delivers to guest tables. Next, host seated at each guest table will either serve to every seated guest or pass the food around the table for self service.
- ✓ In simple terms, dishes are brought by server then guests serve themselves. It is also called "host service" or "family style service" because frequently hosts serve to their guests.
- ✓ *Canadian service* is a variation of English service in which the host or hostess portions the food on a plate and passes it to all the guests around the table.

French Service (Trolley Service or Cart Service)

- ✓ A table service style in which specially trained staff members prepare menu items beside the guest table using a cart. The placed food order will prepare, portion, plate on the cart then serve to the guest.
- ✓ All types of trolley services come under the concept of French service. If food requires carving then this is also done on the trolley itself. Remember, carving is done if recipe demands or only on the request of the guest.

✓ It is also called a "cart service". *Guéridon service* is a famous variation of it. In this style of service, foods are usually pre-portioned then served from the right-hand side of the guest.

Russian Service (Platter-to-plate Service, Platter Service or Silver Service)

✓ It is a table service style in which the server carries platters of fully cooked food from kitchen to the dining room and keeps them on side stations. Thereafter, the steward will take permission to start meal service. After getting permission, steward starts placing hot plate/s in front of each seated guest.

✓ Now steward will present each portioned dish to guest and take approval to serve it. The steward starts serving dishes from left-hand side of the guest. Food will be served with the help of *service gear* (service spoon + service fork).

✓ This style of food service is found in expensive haute cuisine restaurants. The service style is also called "platter-to-plate service" or "platter service".

Features of Table Service Type	American Service	English Service	French Service (Especially in Guéridon)	Russian Service
Price	Less expensive	Moderate	More expensive	Expensive
Guest turnover rate in outlet	High	Moderate	Limited	Limited
DPM on per menu item	Limited	Moderate	Extremely high	High
RevPOT opportunity	High from high sale	High from moderate sale	High from limited sale	High from moderate sale
Revenue from each dish	Limited	Moderate	Extremely high	High
Outlets where offered	Coffee shops	Multi-cuisine restaurant	Specialty restaurant	Haute cuisine restaurant

Self-Service: When guests "help themselves" at a service counter, it is called *self-service* or *assisted service* as often counter staff assists guests in serving displayed food items. Up to some extent, this service style reduces the workload of food and beverage serving staff. In this style of service, the guest enters the dining area and assists himself/herself for getting the food from the *buffet counter*. For second service, either guests may be served partly at their table by steward/stewardess or they can come to the display counter and serve themselves. There may or may not be the provision of table cover layout. The service can be provided either in banquet hall, lounge, nearby swimming pool or in garden area. The variation of self service includes the following options:

Buffet Service

- ✓ Buffet is a type of food service where guest pays a set amount and selects from a range of food items which are often displayed on table for self-service. In buffet service, offered dishes are displayed on a long array of table (in *chafing dishes*) from where guest will select and serve to themselves.
- ✓ Buffet setup can be scrambled style (or *scrambled buffet* or *shopping centre style*) or single station type. Scrambled style buffet provision is offered in large banqueting functions where all individual courses like salad counter, soup counter, plate counter, water counter, dessert counter and so on are located separately.
- ✓ On the other side, *single station* style buffet provision is offered in small and medium banqueting functions where guest turnover rate is limited. In it, all offered courses are displayed on a single counter.
- ✓ Guest collects plate from buffet/display counter or steward standing behind the buffet/counter can also offer plate to guest. This steward assistance (in distribution of plates) is necessary where per plate price system is offered. Thus, here steward is required to count plates or collect token/coupons from each guest.
- ✓ All these conditions usually depend upon certain factors, significantly on choice of host, available space, number of dishes in the menu, number of attendees and so forth.
- ✓ Buffet arrangement can be offered in a range of fashions, for instance, restaurant buffet, meal period buffet, brunch buffet, fork buffet/stand up buffet, finger buffet, sit-down buffet, formal buffet, regional buffet and ethnic buffet. Meal period buffet includes breakfast, lunch and dinner buffet.

Major Buffet Arrangements	
Meal period buffet	It indicates to meal hour/meal occasion buffet arrangements like breakfast, brunch, lunch, evening tea, high tea and dinner buffet arrangement.
Fork buffet	It is also known as *stand-up buffet* because there are no seating arrangements/table layouts for guests, consequently either fork or spoon is only offered; knives are not offered.
Finger buffet	Mistakenly also known as *display buffet*. Actually, it is buffet where finger foods/bite size food items such as sandwiches, rolls, canapés, bouchees and open sandwiches are offered.
Sit-down buffet	Also known as *full buffet* because there are full seating arrangements/ table layouts, consequently spoons, forks and knives could be offered on buffet counter or directly laid on the guest table.
Other buffets	Display buffet (usually a promotional effort), ethnic buffet (specialty cuisine based buffet), *Smorgasbord* (Swedish buffet), action station buffet (live counter buffet) and so forth.

Cafeteria Service

- ✓ A type of meal service provision in which guest passes through serving lines and receives food items from waiting staff. "Scrambled" cafeteria layouts reduce long serving lines by providing separate serving stations for different types of meal items. Cafeteria service is similar to buffet service because sometimes guests can also serve themselves the items on display. This service is mainly found in industrial and institutional establishments.
- ✓ Principally, *portion control* is a major concern behind offering cafeteria service. Consequently, waiting staff portions food items and serves to guest.
- ✓ In case of institutional catering (like in schools, colleges, universities, etc.) often *counter service* is also found where a display board is hung on the wall that shows available dishes with their prices. Most of the food items are also displayed in "hot or cold display cabinet" with their names and price. These display cabinets work as an upselling tool.
- ✓ Here, guest needs to purchase the token from cash counter then hand it over to food server to get desired food and beverage item of specific amount.
- ✓ There is no table service provision and only one or two table clearers are available in cafeteria to clean the soiled plates and glasses from the standing counter or table. Meals offered through pre-plated service and required cutlery (usually disposable) are directly handed over to the guest. Thereafter, guests may sit at provided facility and consume meals.

Specialized Services (In Situ): Table service, buffet service and cafeteria are just a few of the most common approaches to food service today. *In situ* service is the service provided at the place, which is primarily not only meant for service. There are also some highly prized *in situ* (or specialized services) prevailing in the market. Some of them are as follows:

Guéridon Service (A Variation of Trolley Service)

- ✓ It is a specialized cart or trolley service. The cart carries raw or semi-prepared foods that are fully prepared (or fully cooked) in front of the guest at their table side. The cooking is done on Guéridon trolley, a mobile trolley with gas cylinder (it contains calor gas), burners and other serving and cooking utensils and equipment.
- ✓ Dishes prepared on Guéridon trolley require elaborate service and more personal attention. The chef/steward plays a prominent part, as he is required to perform fillet, carve, flambé and prepare the food with showmanship. Thus, the preparation is done by Maitre-de-hôte who is further assisted by Chef-de-rang or/and Commis-de-rang.

- ✓ Restaurants offering guéridon service will have low guest turnover rate because of high price menu. Basic features of gueridon service include: it requires highly skilled staff, more space to move trolley, offer high price menu, require more time to prepare a dish, limited dishes are offered, etc. The style of serving food may be pre-plated or platter-to-plate.

Tray Service

- ✓ In it, meals are portioned, plated and put on trays then steward carries it with his left hand or can also use special transport cart (in case of large orders) to deliver food items. Generally, tray service is found in airlines, hospitals, fast food outlets and in residential hotels (which offer in-room dining provision).
- ✓ There are a handful of differences among all these outlets (in reference to tray service) like airline offers pre-packed meals on trays, hospitals offer balanced diet in their tray (in accordance with doctor's recommendation), fast food outlets offer pre-placed fast foods along with accompaniments on their trays whereas hotel's room service outlets offer their meals on trays, particularly light meal orders.
- ✓ Most outlets offer disposable cutlery and crockery in their tray service while several others like hotel's room service and hospital catering offers chinaware and flatware. The tray can be made up of stainless steel, EPNS or fiber. Nowadays generally anti-skit fibre made trays are used in most of the outlets.

Trolley Service

- ✓ The basic purpose of using trolley is to transport or display a number of dishes simultaneously. There are various types of trolleys used in catering industry, some of them are as follows – hors d'oeuvres trolley, carving trolley, dessert trolley, room service trolley and wagon service.
- ✓ Each of the above-mentioned trolley types offers different food items to their guest, hence every trolley setup requires different utensils and equipment like hors d'oeuvres trolley requires half plate, cutlery and accompaniments to offer variety of hors d'oeuvres while carving trolley mainly requires carving board, carving knife and fork with joint plates, joint knives and forks.
- ✓ Similarly, a wine trolley or liquor trolley carries enormous range of wines and spirits along with range of glassware and other necessary equipment like jigger, pourer, waiter's friend, rimmer, straw and so forth.

Lounge Service

- ✓ It indicates to the service of variety of food and beverage items in lounge area by appointed food and beverage service personnel. The lounge staff may be appointed either permanently or temporarily. In large hotels, they are separately hired for lounge section while in small hotels they are deployed on rota basis.

✓ Lounge staff works from the lounge pantry section which is built in back office area. This pantry has provision of making and serving tea and coffee, welcome drink, house water as well as also support lounge staff in serving running meals (like range of ready to serve meals such as hamburger, pizza, French fries, etc.) throughout the day.

Room Service (A Provision of In-room Dining)

✓ It means serving food and beverage items to guests in their rooms, by stewards, who pick meal orders from the kitchen; hence it is also called "in-room dining".

✓ Generally, room service order taker receives the guest's meal order over the telephone. Afterwards, these meal orders are processed into respective kitchens.

✓ Orders are taken into guest room either via tray (for small orders) or trolley (for large orders) service. Star hotels provide round-the-clock (or 24 hours) room service facility. Therefore, room service menu is limited.

✓ Room service menu is a simplified version of a coffee shop menu but prices of dishes are slightly higher because room service needs extra efforts, manpower and equipment. Clearance is another important aspect of room service. All trolleys and trays should be cleared at assigned time.

The Carousel

✓ It is also called as *roundabout server* which consists of a number of rotating shelves (usually three) at different heights, all of which are approximately six feet in diameter and rotate at one revolution per minute.

✓ Dishes are filled then passed from the kitchen to a plating table still on the servery side of the carousel, from which the carousel is fed with hot and cold plated food.

✓ In simple terms, carousel is a circular counter that revolves and displays the food items. The carousel should fit in such a way so that one side is always inside the kitchen and other side in service area.

Parcel Service

✓ This kind of service is mostly found in take-away outlets, home delivery outlets, railways and airlines catering units. In case of railways, the food orders are pre-packaged in the "pantry car" then served on tray to passengers in accordance with their placed meal orders. In airline catering, food items are pre-packed on the airports (in flight catering units) then transferred to airplanes. After takeoff, flight steward and air-hostess serve the meal orders on tray to passengers.

- ✓ Generally, table d' hôte menu with limited choice is offered. For instance, there are different pre-fixed packages of meals offered at different pre-fixed prices to travelling commuters. Guest has choice to choose any particular package of meal but do not have further choice to select from the chosen meal. Nowadays, parcel boxes are made or insulated with material which keeps the food hot for long.

Drive-in and Drive Through

- ✓ Guests place meal and beverage orders from the vehicles parked at designated area/s. The service of meal and beverage will be done at the vehicle. Sometime this service is also called as "Drive-through" but it is different from "drive-in" service in several ways.
- ✓ For instance- the cars create a line and move in one direction in drive-throughs, and do not need to park, whereas drive-ins allow cars to park next to each other, the food is generally brought to the window by a server, called *carhop*, and the guest remains in the parked car to enjoy his feast.
- ✓ In drive-through service, outlet allows guests to purchase food and beverage items without leaving their cars. This concept was first pioneered in the US in 1930.

Synchronized Service

- ✓ It is a type of banquet service in which servers enter the function room through one set of doors to serve each course; they serve all tables in unison, using precise movements.
- ✓ Often wine service is also synchronized; obviously, this style of banquet service requires a great deal of training, rehearsal, skill and additional staff to work.

Single Point Service: It means the provision of food and beverage service to the guest at single point– guest can consume meals on the premises or may take away with him. In simple terms, in single-point service guests pay for their orders and get served at a single point. They may or may not have the provision of any dining area or sitting arrangements. Different types of single-point service includes the following options.

Take away (a close component of parcel service)

- ✓ This style of service is usually given by the fast food outlets. In it, food orders are required to be packed which will be taken away by the guest to consume outside the premises. Take away service is also called as *carry out* or *take out service*.
- ✓ Its basic features include: it is a kind of quick service which requires limited serving staff. This kind of service provision is mostly demanded by very busy working employees like call centre workers.

Vending Machine

- ✓ In it, the provision of food service and beverage service is offered by means of automatic retailing machines. Its commercial utilization was seen in 1960 when fresh brewed coffee was sold through vending machines. At the same time, post mix soda machine, complete with flaked ice, came into the market. They work like an ATM machine, after inserting money; guest justs need to follow the instructions given by the machine.
- ✓ In simple terms, vending machines are those machines which dispense the foods (pre-packed) and beverages. Nowadays, these machines are often found at airports and railway terminals. The main advantage of vending machine is: it is very convenient and does not require any staff to operate, whereas its main disadvantage is that it offers limited choice.

Other Types of Services

Kiosks

- ✓ These are stalls on roadsides for serving snacks and are open from all sides. Nowadays, hotels also use this concept for the purpose of promotional selling and upselling. Kiosks are not used to sell only food and beverage items but may also be used to sell newspaper, magazines and so forth. In hotels, often self-service kiosks are available for guests.
- ✓ For instance, many hotels provide a live counter, under the canopy, near the swimming pool or some other chosen location for selling savouries.
- ✓ Similarly, when any hotel wants to introduce new items into its regular menu then also it uses kiosk provision in the lobby. Kiosks were common in Persia, India, Pakistan, and in the Ottoman Empire from the 13th century onwards.

Food court

- ✓ It refers to an open area, often a part of shopping facility, where a number of restaurants or food outlets are located in close proximity.
- ✓ It involves the preparation of food in different kitchens, each representing a different cuisine. The food is chosen then picked up from individual section and eaten at a common dining area. There is no waiting staff for table service, thus cover layouts are not available.

Bar service (or a permit room or licensed outlet)

- ✓ It is similar to counter service and is predominantly used in cocktail bars where guests sit on bar stools at the counter and ranges of beverages are prepared, then served by the bartender.

- ✓ Generally, there are two kinds of bar, i.e., the *public/display bar* and *service/dispense/restaurant bar*. The term *bar service* is particularly used in reference to public bar.

Carvery

- ✓ Carvery is a type of assisted service. This service method includes both table service and self service. In it, some parts of service are made by waiter at the guest table while remaining services are made by guests themselves.

Snack-bar service

- ✓ In snack-bar service, tall stools are placed along a counter so that guest may eat the food at the counter itself. In better establishments, the covers are laid-out on the counters.
- ✓ Food may be either displayed behind the counter for the prospective guests to choose from, or may be listed on a menu card. Sometimes, white or blackboard may also be used to write the available menu items.

Echelon

- ✓ In echelon service, the counters are arranged in such a way that it provides better view of the food, at the same time it can be arranged in an angular way.

Dumb waiter

- ✓ It is a small specialized service elevator that carries food between the floors of a hotel. Nowadays, it is also used in many fast food outlets in order to bring food order from kitchen to service point.

KEY TERMS

Canadian service : English service in which host portions the food on a plate then passes it to all guests.

Scrambled cafeteria : Shopping service/satellite style buffet counter whereby separate serving stations are offered.

Ethnic buffet : Specialty cuisine based buffet counter or buffet counter of any specific regional cuisine.

In situ : Collective term for all kinds of specialized services.

Portion control : Yield control of offered or planned menu item. A crucial constituent of a standard recipe.

Counter service : Cafeteria service whereby buffet staff is responsible for serving items in pre-determined portion.

Roundabout server	:	Carousel service in which revolving circular counter is used for self service.
Smorgasbord	:	Danish buffet/Swedish buffet in which variety of breads are offered.
Action station buffet	:	Live counter whereby standing patrons get served by food preparing staff.
Carhop	:	Stewards who brings food to people in their cars at drive-in restaurants.

REVIEW QUESTIONS

1. Describe the characteristics of service and explain each one briefly.
2. Differentiate between buffet service and cafeteria service.
3. What is table service? Classify table service in broad types and enlist any five merits and demerits of each service type.
4. Define the term buffet and briefly explain fork, finger and sit-down buffet.

13 CHAPTER

Introduction to Beverages

Objectives

Students will be able to:

- explicate the term alcohol and beverage and classify its types;
- categorize alcoholic beverages and distinguish with examples; and
- recognize different non-alcoholic beverages on different foundations.

ALCOHOL

Alcohol can be defined as the hydro-oxide-organic-radicals which are naturally occurring and easily synthesized compounds that induce intoxication in body when consumed. All potable beverages which contain these hydro-oxide-organic-radicals are collectively called *alcoholic beverages*. It includes strong beverages like whiskey, brandy, gin and milder ones like beer and wine. In simple terms, an alcoholic beverage is a drink containing ethanol (or ethyl alcohol). Ethanol (CH_3CH_2OH) is a psychoactive drug, a depressant, thus many societies regulate or restrict its sale and consumption.

All potable alcoholic beverages usually contain alcohol content between the ranges 1% to 76% by volume. Alcohol above this level will be considered a medicine like anesthesia and chloroform. But neutral alcohol contains up to 96% of alcohol. Apart from strong and milder beverages, there are also low/reduced alcoholic beverages for *teetotalers*. Broadly, alcoholic beverages can be classified into three groups', i.e., *fermented* (such as wine), *brewed* (such as beer and sake) and *distilled beverages* (such as rum, gin, vodka, brandy, tequila, etc.). A classification with brief description of these stated alcoholic beverages and their derivative products is given below.

ALCOHOLIC BEVERAGES

Fermented and Brewed Beverages

Fermentation is a biological process of converting sugar into alcohol with the help of either natural or cultured yeast whereas *brewing* is a hot treatment (like boiling and infusion) used to produce brewed beverages like beer and sake. Both methods are used to produce low alcoholic beverages. Whereas, brewing technique is also used to brew tea and coffee. Any fruit or grain (wheat, rice, barley, etc.) which contains sugar can be used to make fermented alcoholic beverages like:

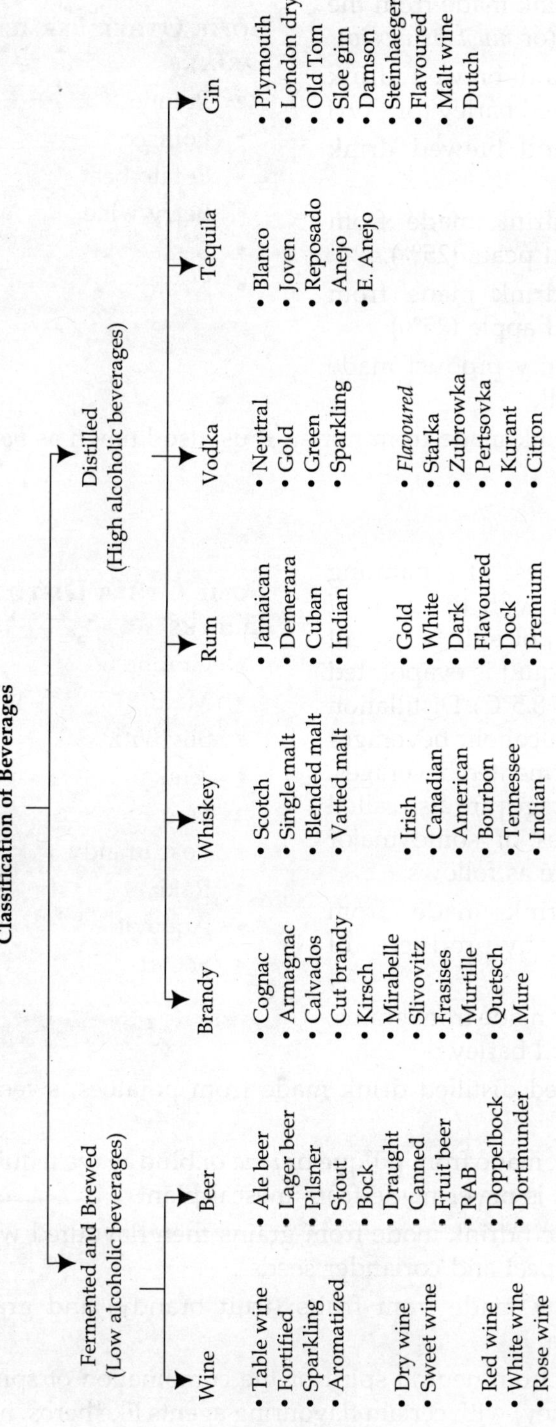
Classification of Beverages
Fermented and Brewed
(Low alcoholic beverages)
Distilled
(High alcoholic beverages)
Wine
• Table wine
• Fortified
• Sparkling
• Aromatized
• Dry wine
• Sweet wine
• Red wine
• White wine
• Rose wine
Beer
• Ale beer
• Lager beer
• Pilsner
• Stout
• Bock
• Draught
• Canned
• Fruit beer
• RAB
• Doppelbock
• Dortmunder
Brandy
• Cognac
• Armagnac
• Calvados
• Cut brandy
• Kirsch
• Mirabelle
• Slivovitz
• Frasises
• Murtille
• Quetsch
• Mure
Whiskey
• Scotch
• Single malt
• Blended malt
• Vatted malt
• Irish
• Canadian
• American
• Bourbon
• Tennessee
• Indian
Rum
• Jamaican
• Demerara
• Cuban
• Indian
• Gold
• White
• Dark
• Flavoured
• Dock
• Premium
Vodka
• Neutral
• Gold
• Green
• Sparkling
• *Flavoured*
• Starka
• Zubrowka
• Pertsovka
• Kurant
• Citron
Tequila
• Blanco
• Joven
• Reposado
• Anejo
• E. Anejo
Gin
• Plymouth
• London dry
• Old Tom
• Sloe gim
• Damson
• Steinhaeger
• Flavoured
• Malt wine
• Dutch

Wine — A fermented drink made from the juice of grapes (or *must* or *mosto*)

Beer — A fermented and brewed drink made from malted barley (or *wort*)

Sake — A fermented and brewed drink made from rice

Cider — A fermented drink made from apple (75%) and pears (25%)

Perry — A fermented drink made from pears (75%) and apple (25%)

Kumis — A fermented dairy product made from mare's milk

Mead — A fermented drink made from honey, thus also known as *honey wine.*

Some Other Fermented Drinks

- Pulque
- Pomace
- Potato beer
- Berry wine
- Basi
- Neero

Distilled Beverages

Distillation is a refinement process of separating alcohol from the water/liquid with the help of distillation process, either by pot still or patent still method. In it, the water/liquid is evaporated at 100°C and alcohol at 78°C (or 78.5°C). Distillation process is run to produce high alcoholic beverages which are mostly made from fermented beverages. Often these high alcoholic beverages are also called *hard liquor* or *spirit*. Examples of some major distilled alcoholic beverages are as follows:

Rum — A distilled drink made from molasses, a by-product of sugarcane.

Whiskey — A distilled drink made from grains, especially malted barley.

Vodka — A highly rectified distilled drink made from potatoes, sweet potatoes, grains or fruits.

Tequila — A distilled drink made from pulque or *pina* of blue agave tequilana plant. Original tequila is never made from mescal plant.

Gin — A neutral distilled drink made from grains then flavoured with juniper berries, orange peel and coriander seeds.

Brandy — A distilled drink made from fruits (fruit brandy) and grains (grain brandy) or wine.

Liquor — A cordial made from neutral spirit or the combination of spirit (usually brandy or whiskey) with certain flavouring agents like herbs, nutmeg, etc.

Calvados — A distilled drink made from cider or fermented apple juice.

Some Other Distilled Drinks

- Grappa
- Marc
- Slivovitz
- Araka
- Feni
- Pear brandy
- Raki
- Aquavit
- Sochu

NON-ALCOHOLIC BEVERAGES

Stimulating

✓ A kind of energy drink which stimulates the appetite like tea and coffee, it raises the level of physiological or nervous activity in the body.

Water

✓ In food service industry, it is a potable drink which is available in different forms like mineral water, spring water, well water, artesian water, distilled water, demineralized water and so forth.

Nourishing

✓ A kind of drink which nurtures the human body; hence these are heavy in body and consistency. Milk based drinks like variety of milk shakes are example of nourishing beverages.

Refreshing

✓ A kind of rejuvenating drinks which cool down the individual's appetite. Generally, aerated drinks with some non-aerated drinks come under this category.

KEY TERMS

Must/mosto : Unfermented grape juice. It contains grape skin, pulp and other grape particles.

Honey wine : Another term for *mead*, i.e., a fermented beverage with alcohol content between 8-18%.

Wort : Unfermented brewed beverages like *wort is beer before it becomes beer*.

Malted barley : Basic raw material (i.e., roasted barley) used for making beer.

Pina : Centre core (or the heart) of blue agave tequilana plant.

Neutral drink : Clear, colourless, flammable, distilled liquid with very high ethanol content (96%).

Ethanol : Drinking alcohol.

Grappa : Italian brandy alike the term *marc* used for local French brandy.

Aerated drink : Carbonated drinks like soft drinks, soda water and so forth.

REVIEW QUESTIONS

1. What is beverage? Classify beverages and support each category with suitable examples.
2. Differentiate between fermented and brewed beverages.
3. Enlist any ten differences between fermented and distilled beverages.
4. Classify non-alcoholic beverages and explain each briefly.

14
CHAPTER

Non-Alcoholic Beverages

Objectives

Students will be able to:

- expound different non-alcoholic beverages;
- prepare and serve different styles of tea and coffee preparations; and
- eloquent internationally famous tea and coffee brands.

NON-ALCOHOLIC BEVERAGES

Non-alcoholic beverages are those drinks which do not contain any sign of alcohol but nowadays, most beverages with very little amount of alcohol (0.5% ABV) are also considered a part of non-alcoholic beverages. This category includes low-alcohol beer, non-alcoholic wine and apple cider. In this unit we will discuss only stimulating, nourishing and refreshing beverages along with water and its types.

There are many ways for classifying non-alcoholic beverages, for instance on the basis of temperature (hot vs. cold beverages), carbonation (aerated vs. non-aerated beverages) and nature (stimulating, nourishing and refreshing beverages). But among these, nature based classification is widely accepted as well as covers majority of non-alcoholic drinks. A classification and brief description is given below.

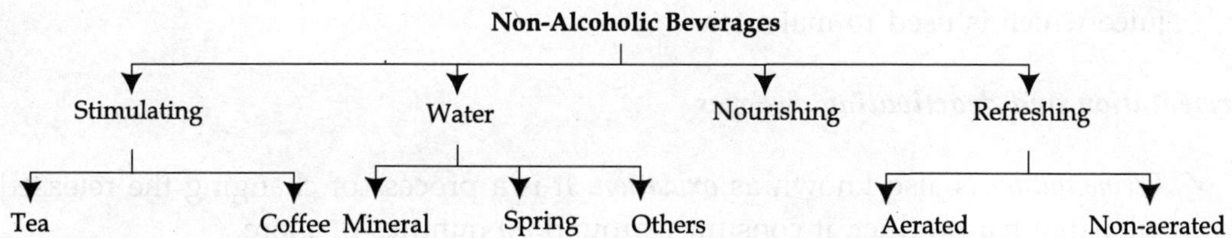

TEA (AN AVERAGE CUP OF TEA CONTAINS ABOUT 0.75 GRAINS OF CAFFEINE)

Tea is a non-alcoholic fermented beverage made from leaf buds of a plant called "Camellia sinensis". Tea contains *caffeine* as well as *tannin* which help in stimulating the appetite. It is considered a healthy beverage because it aids in muscle relaxation and stimulates the CNS (central nervous system). The word "tea" also refers to the leaves, leaf buds, and internodes of the plant, which have been prepared and cured for the market by several recognized methods (like rolling of tea either by CTC or orthodox method). Tea contains half the caffeine of coffee.

Types of Tea		
Green tea	Light	Non-fermented
Oolong tea	Medium	Semi-fermented
Black tea	Strong	Fully-fermented

Manufacturing Process of Tea

Raw material and plucking of leaves plus buds

- ✓ Tea is made from the leaves of Camellia sinensis, a plant which produces tea leaves. The upper leaves and buds of this plant are harvested for tea. When tea leaves and buds attain maturity, they are plucked either manually or through mechanical harvesters.

Withering process and drying of tea leaves

- ✓ *Withering process* means sorting out of tea leaves; unsuitable tea leaves and buds are removed. It is mostly required when tea leaves and buds are plucked mechanically.
- ✓ After withering, the selected tea leaves are spread out on long, enclosed troughs and air is blown through them in order to dry them. This process releases the juice which is used to make tea.

Fermentation and deactivating enzymes

- ✓ *Fermentation* is also known as *oxidation.* It is a process of changing the released juice into tea product, it consumes around 90 minutes or more.
- ✓ The fermentation process is stopped at a predetermined stage by heating, which *deactivates the enzymes* and produces almost a finished product.

Sorting and packing

- ✓ At final stage, the tea leaves are separated according to the colour and particle size and then packed in accordance with requirement or grades (or *tea grades*).

Tea Grades (or Leafy Tea Grades and Broken Tea Grades)			
Leafy Tea Grades		*Broken Tea Grades*	
- FP	Flowery pekoe	- BOP	Broken Orange Pekoe
- OP	Orange pekoe	- FOP	Flowery Orange Pekoe
- P	Pekoe	- TGFOP	Tippy Golden Flowery Orange Pekoe
- PS	Pekoe Souchong	- FTGFOP	Finest Tippy Golden Flowery Orange Pekoe
- S	Souchong		

Golden Rules of Tea Making

To make a perfect cup of tea, the steward should follow the below given steps. Remember, an ideal capacity of a tea cup is approximately 06 fl. oz. A standard process for making a tea is given below-

Tea ingredients ↓	Use 2 grams (or 1 teaspoon) of loose tea or one tea bag for making a cup of tea. For one portion (it comprises two cups of tea) , use 4 to 5 grams (or 2 to 2 ½ teaspoons) of loose tea or two tea bags.
Tea preparation ↓	Boil water. The ideal brewing temperature for tea is the boiling point (means 100°C). Now pour (in tea cup/tea pot) the boiling water over placed loose tea or tea bags.
Tea brewing ↓	After pouring boiled water, now tea must be infused (or brewed) for 3-5 minutes in the hot water. The best flavour develops after three to five minutes of brewing.
Tea service	Tea prepared with tea bags is directly served whereas tea prepared from loose tea will go through filtration process then served.

Service of Tea

Place a tea cup (handle on RHS) with saucer and teaspoon (place it on the saucer at RHS in 90° angle vertical position under the handle of cup) on the RHS or centre of the cover. Remember, plain tea, flavoured tea as well as all kinds of other beverages are served from the RHS of the guest. Some standard guidelines for various tea preparations and their services are given below.

English tea (or separate tea)- In *English tea* preparation steward offers separate tea liquor (in tea pot), milk (in milk pot) and sugar (in sugar bowl with sugar tong or as separate sugar sachet). Its preparation stage involves: first place sugar/sugar free (as per guest request) in tea cup then pour tea liquor (75% of the cup) and finally top-up with milk (15%).

Readymade tea: In readymade tea preparation, steward is required to prepare (but without sugar) tea inside the pantry room or still room. Thereafter, offer this ready-to-serve (it indicates tea liquor + milk) tea directly to the guest. Offer sugar cubes (or sugar sachet) separately in sugar pot/sugar basin with sugar tong.

Leaves tea: Steward offers cured tea leaves (or the *Camellia sinensis* plant) in container, hot/boiling water in tea pot, tea strainer with drip bowl and sugar/sugar free in sugar basin. Serve in an English tea style and do not forget to strain tea thereafter to keep strainer on the drip bowl.

Lemon tea: Offer separate tea liquor in tea pot accompanied by lemon wedges in side plate with lemon fork (or AP fork). A lemon fork is used to squeeze the lemon juice from lemon over the poured black tea. Either guest may directly serve himself/herself or steward can also assist in squeezing lemon. Remember, milk is never preferred to be added in lemon tea but sugar/sugar free may be added.

Cream tea: It means separate tea liquor in a tea pot accompanied by cream (in creamer) and sugar cubes (or sugar sachet) in sugar pot with sugar tong. It is served like a separate tea.

Ice tea: It is also called *cold tea* or *Russian tea*. In it, ice, lemon slice and sugar are combined in a tall tumbler-shaped glass which is served by placing on a saucer with tea spoon and straw.

Herbal teas: For good service, herbal teas (such as *peppermint, rose hip, lime blossom* and *chamomile teas*) are almost always in tea bags. They are brewed like black tea – placed in a tea cup then brewed in boiling water. Lastly, served on a saucer with a tea spoon and sugar.

MISE EN PLACE

- Tray or salver
- Tray mat/salver mat
- Tea or coffee pot
- Jug of cold or hot milk
- Sugar pot with tong/spoon
- Tea strainer (for tea leaves)
- Tea cup, saucer, tea spoon
- Jug of hot water (for tea leaves)

Flavoured Teas

Name of tea	*Country*	*Aroma strength*
Ceylon tea	Sri Lanka	Perfumed aroma
Darjeeling tea	India	Strong full aroma
Lap sang tea	China	Strong and smokey aroma
Jasmine tea	China	Perfumed and flowery

COFFEE (AN AVERAGE CUP OF COFFEE CONTAINS ABOUT 1.5 GRAINS OF CAFFEINE)

Coffee is made from coffee beans. Coffee beans are the seeds inside the red fruit from coffee trees. The flesh of the coffee fruit is removed and the coffee beans are dried and sorted by their quality. Coffee trees are indigenous to Africa, and can still be found growing wild in the hills of Ethiopia. Today coffee is cultivated in some eighty countries in South and Central America, the Caribbean, Africa and Asia, generally in areas found between the Tropics of Cancer and Capricorn. The two biggest producers by far are Brazil and Colombia, followed by Indonesia, Vietnam and Mexico.

Types of Coffee		
Coffea Arabica	From Latin America	90 %
Coffea Robusta	From Africa and Asia	09 %
Coffea Liberica	From Africa	01 %

Manufacturing Process of Coffee

Raw material: Coffee is made from the fruit (it is 1.5 cm in length and oblong in shape) of evergreen shrub, known as *Genus coffea* that belongs to the Rubiaceae family.

Drying: It is a method of separating the seeds from the pulp/coffee fruit either by fermentation (dried under sun) or frying method (manual method).

DEGREE/TYPE OF ROASTING

Type	Coffee produced
Light	Mild
Medium	Strong
Dark	Very strong

Roasting: It is a process of heating to obtain the coffee seeds. Coffee seeds are roasted at 150-250°C by hot dry air to give required colour and strength to seeds. The degree of roasting (or type of roasting) determines the ultimate aroma/bouquet of coffee as well as its potency.

Quenching: When desired colour is achieved during the roasting process, a calculated amount of cold water is added to stop any further roasting. This entire process is called *quenching*.

Grinding: Now roasted as well as unroasted coffee seeds are ground to form coffee powder. The degree of grinding ranges from fine to medium followed by coarse powder; it depends upon the requirement of customer/market.

Service of Coffee

> **GOLDEN RULE OF COFFEE MAKING**
> Hot water (approx. 95°C) is poured over coffee grounds with or without pressure; one serving of coffee requires between one quarter & one half ounce of coffee. Usually, coffee quantity depends on the desired strength.

Regular coffee

✓ Steward offers separate coffee liquor accompanied by sugar and coffee cream or milk. Often, it is also known as *English coffee.*

Espresso coffee

✓ It is a concentrated coffee brewed under pressure. The amount of coffee grounds used is the same as for regular coffee but the amount of water is reduced by half. Espresso is served in special small *espresso cup* (or *demi tasse*) with saucer. It is accompanied by granulated sugar as well as coffee cream, if guest requests.

Black coffee

✓ Steward offers separate coffee liquor in coffee pot accompanied by sugar and artificial sweetener. In simple terms, it means English coffee minus milk.

Decaffeinated coffee (regular coffee powder minus caffeine)

✓ Instead of caffeine based coffee powder, decaffeinated coffee grounds are used to prepare this coffee and remaining things are same as in the case of regular coffee.

Devilled coffee

✓ It is a liquor based spiced and heated coffee preparation. Generally, a measure of liquor is poured in the cup. Remember, these are usually offered at tables in restaurants, and not bars.

Cappuccino coffee

✓ In order to prepare a cappuccino, a coffee cup is filled two-thirds with black coffee liquor; hot and steamed milk foam is added to fill the remaining cup. A pinch of cocoa powder is sprinkled on top. It is served like black coffee with separate sugar.

ALCOHOLIC COFFEES

Café royale	Cognac
Irish coffee	Whiskey
Café Brule	Brandy
Monks	Liqueur
Baileys	Liqueur
Calypso	Liqueur
Devilled	Liqueur

Café au lait (coffee with milk)

- ✓ A coffee cup is filled with two parts of coffee and one part of milk. Offer sugar or sugar free separately. In simple terms, it is called "milk coffee".

Café mélange (coffee with whipped cream)

- ✓ A cup of coffee topped up with whipped cream. Offer sugar separately. The serving style will be similar to regular coffee.

Frappé coffee

- ✓ Frappé coffee is a Greek foam-covered iced coffee drink made from instant coffee.

Irish coffee

- ✓ Take a pre-warmed Irish coffee glass then combine 1.5 fl. oz of Irish whisky with 2 to 3 bar spoons of sugar. Now, stir well and fill the glass with hot, strong coffee to about three quarters inch below the rim.
- ✓ Pour lightly whipped cream over the back of a spoon into the glass onto the surface of the drink. It should float on top but not be mixed with the coffee.

Brand Names of Tea and Coffee	
Tea	Fauchon (France), Tata Tea (India), Lyons Tea (Ireland), Twinings (UK), Nestea (bottled tea from America), Dilmah (Sri Lanka), Billy Tea (Australia) and so forth.
Coffee	Nescafe (America), Starbucks (Global), Nabob (Canada), Jacob (Germany), Kenco (UK), Maccona (Dutch), Coop Kaffe (Norwegian), Bravo coffee (Greece), Marcilla (Spain) and so forth.

WATER

Water is available in different forms like mineral water, spring water, well water, artesian water, distilled water, demineralized water and so forth. A brief description of most commonly used water is given below.

Mineral Water

- ✓ Mineral water is often effervescent (but not always) and commonly used as a refreshing beverage, either alone or mixed with flavouring. As the name suggests, it contains minerals. It can but need not contain carbon dioxide, which makes it fizzy or bubbly.

- ✓ Mineral water can be classified as natural, artificial and sparkling mineral water. *Ginger beer, tonic water* and *ginger ale* are perfect examples of artificial mineral water whereas *soda water, seltzer water* and *club soda* are perfect examples of sparkling mineral water.

Brand Names of Mineral and Spring Water	
Mineral water	Badoit, Isabelle, Fontel, Corail Bulles, Volvic, Vichy Celestines, Vittel, Contrex (France); Glen Orrin, Gower Spring (UK); NOVA (Saudi Arabia); Himalayan and Golden Valley (India); Grand Springs and English Mountain (USA); Golden Circle and Fraser Blue (Australia); Golden Tulip (South Africa); Fuji (Japan); Alphina (Switzerland); Appollinaris (Germany); San Pellegrino (Italy).
Spring water	Evian, Perrier and Badoit (France); Ashboure, Buxton and Malvern (England); Poland Spring (Poland); Zephyrhills Water (Florida); Nestlé Waters, Evans Natural Spring Water (USA); Glacier Water (Australia); Snowcap Waters (Canada); Highland Spring (Belgium), etc.

NOURISHING BEVERAGES

The term *nourishing* beverage refers to all those drinks which foster or nurture the human body, for instance milk based drinks. These milk based refreshing drinks can be prepared either hot or cold. A brief description of each is given below.

Hot Milk Based Drinks

- ✓ Hot chocolate beverage is an excellent example of hot nourishing drink. In order to prepare it, warm the milk and pour in a coffee cup then place on saucer and put coffee spoon on right-hand side of the cup (on saucer). Finally serve.
- ✓ Provide the packet of chocolate, Oval tine, Bournvita, Milo, Horlicks powder, etc. on the side (in saucer). Apart from hot chocolate, variety of tea and coffee preparations are also perfect examples of hot milk based beverages but these are stimulating drinks.

Cold Milk Based Drinks

- ✓ Milk shakes and milk frappés are two perfect examples of cold milk based drinks. *Milk shakes* are popular thirst quenchers on hot days. In order to prepare it, take five ounces of milk with 1½ ounces of fruit syrup or fruit juices or other flavourings (such as vanilla, strawberry, chocolate, etc.), sugar and 2-3 ice cubes (or crushed ice). Mix well all these ingredients in shaker (or blend) then serve in Tom Collin glass or milk glass.

- ✓ *Milk frappé* consists of milk with ice cream. In order to make one portion, combine 5 fl. oz of milk, 1 scoop of ice cream and fruit (optional) for flavour. Mix well in blender then serve in Collin glass. Its few examples include vanilla frappé, banana frappé and chocolate frappé.

REFRESHING BEVERAGES

The term refreshing beverage refers to a kind of rejuvenating drink which cools down the individual's appetite. Generally, aerated drinks with some non-aerated drinks come under this category. A brief description of each is given below.

Aerated Drink (carbonated beverages)

- ✓ It is concerned with carbonated drinks which may be plain or flavoured. In simple terms, these drinks/water are charged with carbon dioxide. It can be bottled or canned.
- ✓ Few famous aerated water examples include lemonade, ginger ale, tonic water, coke, soda water, Pepsi, etc. Remember, aerated drinks can be consumed on their own as well as mixed with other drinks. *Gimlet* (gin with carbonated citrus drink like Limca) is a perfect example of mixed aerated drink.

Non-aerated Drink (non-carbonated beverages)

- ✓ It refers to all those beverages which do not have supersaturated carbon dioxide in solution. But often these drinks are flavoured in nature.
- ✓ Fruit juices (these are fruit drinks or *Ades*), squashes (these are concentrated drinks), cordials (these are modifying agents) and syrups (these are thick, sweet, sticky and flavoured sugar based liquids) are few perfect examples of non-aerated drinks.

KEY TERMS

Oxidation	:	Fermentation process or result of oxidizing or being oxidized (or oxygen is adapted to a compound).
Ades	:	Plural form of ade; a sweetened beverage of diluted fruit juice.
Cordials	:	Sweet fruit-flavoured drink such as wine cups and fruit cordials.
Tonic water	:	Carbonated soft drink with a bitter flavour, used as a mixer with gin or other spirits. *Canada dry* is an excellent example of tonic water.
Ginger ale	:	Clear effervescent non-alcoholic drink flavoured with ginger extract.

Lemonade : Sweet, colourless and carbonated drink containing lemon flavouring.

Frappé : Iced or chilled, also a drink served with ice or frozen to a slushy consistency.

Seltzer water : Carbonated water into which carbon dioxide gas has been dissolved under pressure.

Club soda : North American term for soda.

Devilled coffee : Coffee that is spiced, heated, thereafter a measure of liquor is poured into the cup.

REVIEW QUESTIONS

1. Classify non-alcoholic beverages and explain each type briefly.
2. Define the term tea. Explain its types and describe the golden rules of tea making.
3. What is coffee? Enlist any eight coffee preparations and write in short about their ingredients and preparation method.
4. Give ten brand names of mineral water and sparkling water.

15 CHAPTER

Fermented Beverage – Wine

OBJECTIVES

Students will be able to:

- explicate wine basics, its classification, manufacturing process and grapes;
- expound wine serving techniques for table and sparkling wines;
- suggest wine with food and find out wine faults; and
- explain factors affecting wine and different vine diseases.

WINE

Wine is an alcoholic beverage which is principally made from the fermented juice of grapes. Wine may also be made from various other fruits like *cider* made from apple, *perry* made from pears, etc. Apart from grapes, if any other fruit is used to produce wine then the name of that fruit must appear on the wine label. This category of fruit based wine is collectively termed "fruit wine". The alcoholic content of wine ranges from less than 14 per cent and up to 22 per cent.

Some grains are also used to make wine, such as *barley* used to produce *barley wine* and *rice* used to produce *rice wine* (for example *sake*). These wines are made from starch based materials, thus collectively termed "grain wine" and resemble more with beer than wine.

Ginger wine is a fortified wine made from a fermented blend of ground ginger root and raisins then fortified with the addition of brandy. Wine serving rules are also in accordance with the ingredients used to produce it. For instance, fruit based wines are always preferred to be served first followed by grain based wines.

WINE TAXONOMY

The term *wine taxonomy* is related to wine classification. Wines can be classified on a range of bases like nature, colour, dryness/sweetness, specialty and so forth. Wine can also be classified as generic, varietal and proprietary wines. A brief description of different classes of wine is given below.

Nature based wine taxonomy (table, fortified, sparkling and aromatized wines)

Table Wine (country wine with low alcoholic content)

- ✓ These wines are also called *still wines, natural wines* or *vin de table* which are mostly consumed with food; they tend to compliment the meal.
- ✓ This is the largest category of wine. The alcoholic strength may range between 10 to 14% by volume. These table wines are available in three forms: *red, white* and *rose wines.*

Fortified Wine (table wine fortified with brandy)

- ✓ It refers to the high alcoholic wine in which distilled spirit, usually brandy, is added. The process of addition of brandy into wine in order to halt the fermentation process is known as *fortification*. Often, these fortified wines are also termed "Vin de liqueur". But it is different from *liquor brandy*.
- ✓ In fortified wine, brandy is added in order to stop the fermentation process simultaneously to enhance the alcoholic strength of wine. Thus, their alcoholic strength usually ranges between 15-22% by volume. Fortified wines are available in two forms: dry and sweet fortified wines.

THERAPEUTIC VALUE OF WINE

- Light wine has vitamins A, B & C.
- Wine also contains minerals like calcium, phosphorous, iron, sodium, magnesium, potassium, chlorine, sulphur, copper, manganese, iodine, cobalt.
- Aperitif wine stimulates appetite.
- Psychologically, wine raises fortitude.
- Wine acts as a tonic, in convalescence
- Red wine is richer than white wine.
- 750 mL of wine contains 850 calories.

Sparkling Wine (table wine with carbon dioxide)

- ✓ It is a simple table wine with the addition of carbon dioxide (CO_2), in order to make it "fizzy or effervescent". The carbon dioxide may result from natural fermentation or impregnated, either directly in bottle or in tank. Champagne is an excellent example of sparkling wine.
- ✓ These wines are drunk for the most part on festive occasions such as weddings, birthdays or during holidays. Sparkling wine made outside the Champagne region is known as Vin Mousseux (in France), Spritzig (in Germany) and Espumante (in Portugal).

Aromatized Wine (fortified wine marred with aromatic agents/botanicals)

✓ It refers to the fortified wine (or *mistelle*) that has been flavoured with various aromatic agents like herbs, spices, fruits or other natural flavourings. The alcoholic content in aromatized wine usually ranges from 10 to 20% by volume. Remember, aromatized wines are generally served as an *aperitif* and usually not offered more than 60 mL.

✓ Vermouths and Dubonnets are excellent examples of aromatized wine. There are four main types of vermouths dry vermouth, sweet vermouth, rose vermouth and red vermouth.

Different Flavours of Wine for Interest	
Mistelle	Slightly fermented white wine to which brandy is added to mute fermentation. It is used in production of wines like vermouth.
Vermouth	It is an aromatized fortified wine flavoured with various botanicals. The term is derived from German word *wermut*— meaning wormwood.
Bitters	It refers to an alcoholic beverage which is often based on *neutral spirits* and can be flavoured with various herbs, roots and other aromatic ingredients.
Ginger wine	It is a fortified wine made from a fermented blend of ground ginger root and raisins which was first produced in England.

Colour based wine taxonomy (red, white and rose wines)

Red Wines

✓ These wines are made from red/ black/dark grapes. They are fermented in contact with the grape skins. The *tannin* in the skins gives the colour to the wine. These wines are normally dry in nature (also called dry wines).

Wine Accompanying Food	
Red wine	Red meat
White wine	White meat
Rose wine	Both red or white meat

White Wines

✓ These wines may be made from white (or green) grapes, dark grapes or combination of both, but with white wine the grape skins and pressed juice do not come into contact contrasting to red wine.

Rose Wines (or blush wines)

Wine Accompanying Food	
Sweet wine	Dessert
Dry wine	Starter

- ✓ These wines are the products of dark grapes; their skins remain in contact with the juice only until it has turned into a pale pink colour. Remember during grape skin contact, minimal amount of tannins should enter the wine. Rose wine can also be made by blending red wines with white wines. Rose wines are sweet as well as dry in nature.

Dryness/sweetness based wine taxonomy (sweet and dry fortified wines)

Sweet Fortified Wines (brandy or spirit added during fermentation)

- ✓ Sweet wines have had their fermentation muted by the addition of alcohol so that they retain their natural sweetness. Muting takes place when the alcohol level reaches 5-8 % by volume. They have a final alcoholic strength between 9 and 17% by volume.

Dry Fortified Wines (brandy or spirit added after fermentation)

- ✓ These are made by the addition of brandy or any other spirit after the completion of fermentation process. These dry wines are preferred to be served with appetizer and soup courses.

Specialty based wine taxonomy (vintage, non-vintage and other wine)

Vintage Wines (special wine of any year)

- ✓ The wine made during a particular year in which all wine affecting factors (rain, sun, temperature, etc.) were in the favour of the producer is known as *vintage wine*. It always costs higher in comparison to non-vintage wines.

Non-vintage Wines (regular wines of all years)

- ✓ The production of wine in any year for sale is termed as *non-vintage wine*.

Others

- ✓ It indicates to enormous wine types which are usually not popular as above stated wines. For example, *organic wines* (or green wines), vin doux naturels, modest alcoholic wines, *resinated wine*, young wines, old wines and so forth.

WINE MAKING PROCESS

Raw Material

✓ Plucked, screened (remove rotten, damaged and non-ripened grapes) and de-stalked grapes are used to produce wine or grape wine.

✓ Conventionally, grapes were plucked with the help of special scissors (or grape shears) then put into conical shaped *wire baskets* (which pluckers hang on their backside). Nowadays, machines are used for grape harvesting.

> **SUGAR IN WINE**
>
> - Sugar in grapes are formed by sunlight. 100 grams grapes contain 16 grams of sugar.
> - In grapes, sugar is available in two forms - glucose and fructose.
> - Tartaric, tannin and citric acid in *must* work as a preservative agent in wine.
> - When wine acids come in contact with alcohol – *esters* are formed.
> - Formed *esters* give wine its aroma or bouquet.

Must Making

✓ Collected grapes are crushed in order to extract the juice, known as *must*. These collected grapes can be crushed with several methods like-hydraulic pressure, balloon, roller or traditional treading style.

✓ Now, sugar content of *must* (or grape juice) is measured by a scale, called "Baume" reading scale.

Chaptalisation (process of sugar balancing)

✓ If *must* contain less than desired amount of sugar then extra sugar is added. The process of adding extra sugar into the *must* (or grape juice) before fermentation is known as *chaptalization*.

✓ The resulted wine will be high in alcohol content but should never be considered great neither marketed by the vintage wine.

Fermentation (process where *wine tannins* are generated)

✓ Now it is the time to start the fermentation process. This fermentation process activates with the help of either natural or cultured yeast (*Saccharomyces ellipsoids*). Remember, most of the wines also face *malolactic fermentation*.

✓ During fermentation, yeast transforms sugars present in the *must* into alcohol (ethanol) and generate *wine tannins* and carbon dioxide (as a byproduct). The fermentation takes place between the temperature range from 18 to 20°C.

Racking and Fining (process of wine clarification)

✓ *Racking* is the process of transferring wine from one cask to another in order to remove the visible sediments whereas *fining* is the process of removing of invisible/suspended sediments (with the help of egg albumen or *icing glass*). Yet if wine does not clear enough then it is passed through the filtration process.

Maturation (refers to wine aging period)

✓ Red wines are matured for a short period of time, usually one year whereas white wines are usually matured for six months. Remember, sparkling wines are never matured (after secondary fermentation).

Bottling/Corking (refers to wine packaging stage)

✓ Now matured wines are filled in appropriate bottles and finally corked in order to protect them from the air, which can oxidize the wine prematurely. There are different varieties of corks used for corking different kinds of wine.

GRAPES

Grapes are the fruit of the vine (plant), which grows in bunches on a stalk. The skin may be green, yellow or purple that enclose a sweet pulp with one to four seeds. Both white and red grapes are used to make wine. Grapes comprise four elements – skin (20%), pulp (76%), pips/seeds (4%) and stalk (an external part).

VINE FAMILIES

- *Vitis vinifera*
- *Vitis riporia*
- *Vitis rupestris*
- *Vitis labrusca*
- *Vitis berlanieri*

Red Grapes (used to produce red wines only)

✓ These grapes are used to make red and rose wines. Examples include: Cabernet Sauvignon, Merlot, Shiraz, Zinfandel, Pinot Noir, Barbera, Bonarda, Cinsaut, Dolcetto, Aleatico, Brunello, Cabernet Franc, Carignan, Gamay, Grenache, Grignolino, Lambrusco, Malbec, Nebbiolo, Petit Verdot, Sangiovese, Syrah, Tempranillo, Zinfandel, Mourvedre and Pinotage.

White Grapes (used to produce red as well as white wines)

✓ These grapes are used to make red as well as white wines. Examples include: Chardonnay, Chennin Blanc, Sauvignon Blanc, Bual, Furmint, Palomino, Riesling, Seyval Blanc, Silvaner/Sylvaner, Aligote, Blanc Fume, Chasselas, Fendant, Folle Blanche, Greco, Gewürztraminer, Kerner, Malvesia, Marsanne, Muller-Thurgau, Muscadet, Muscat, Pedro Ximenez, Pinot Blanc, Pinot Gris, Semillon, Sercial, Steen, Tokay, Traminer, Trebbiano, Ugni Blanc, Verdejo, Verdelho, Vermentino, Vernaccia, Viognier and Tocai Friulano.

WINE SERVICE

Steps	Particulars	Red Wine	White Wine	Sparkling Wine	Remarks
1	Take wine order from host	On BOT	On BOT	On BOT	Completely fill to BOT
2	Transfer first copy of BOT	To bar	To bar	To bar	To public bar or service bar
3	Check wine temperature	15-18°C	10-12°C	04-10°C	Check wine bottle temperature before accepting from bar.
4	Collect wine from bar along with glasses	In cradle	In bucket	In chiller*	Glasses from bar is optional
5	Present wine bottle to host and take approval for opening the bottle	In baby fold	In baby fold	In baby fold	Present from right-hand side of the host
6	Open wine bottle (use *waiter's friend* to open red and white wine).	Insert screw	Insert screw	By turning *agrafe*	Ensure champagne cork does not hit anybody.
7	Offer wine cork in side plate for smelling	On side plate	On side plate	Champagne/any sparkling wine should never be offered to host for tasting. All carbonic drinks must be served instantly, else CO_2 will escape.	Insert first prong of fork in cork then place on side plate.
8	Place appropriate wine glass for wine tasting	Red wine glass	White wine glass		Place red/white wine glass below water glass – in 45 degree angle.
9	Serve wine for tasting and take approval	To host	To host		If guest does not like red/white wine, then replace it.
10	Change wine tasting glass after getting guest approval in order to finally serve	In red wine glass	In white wine glass		Place fresh glass for red and white wine service

11	Serve wine in fresh glass	In red wine glass	In white wine glass	In Champagne glass	From right-hand side of the host and guest.
12	Place remaining wine (or bottled wine)	In cradle	In bucket	In chiller	On guest table or wine stand
13	Check for second service, else take clearance	Repeat	Repeat	Repeat	Repeat same procedure for second service of new wine.
14	Bill presentation and payment collection (either via cash or through charge card)	In cash or credit	In cash or credit	In cash or credit	Present bill in bill folder from right-hand side.
15	Return any change and do not solicit for tips				In bill folder

*Wine steward may also use an ice bucket with plenty of ice and cold water to form an *ice bath* in order to place Champagne or any other sparkling wine in it.

WINE LABEL READING

Wine label provides enormous information about the wine to *wine sommelier* which helps him/her in order taking process, serving wine as well as in suggestive selling. It provides information like- brand name of wine, its origin, quality, vintage year, grape used to produce wine, country/region of production and so forth.

French wine label reading	
Cru Bourgeois	Official classification of Bordeaux
Château Lamothe Bergeron	Brand name of the wine
1998	Vintage year/year of production
12% Alc	Alcoholic percentage
Haute Médoc	Sub-region of Bordeaux
37.5 cl	Quantity of bottled wine
Appellation Haute Médoc Contrôlée	Quantity designation
Produce of France	Country of origin
Mis en Bouteille en Château	Estate of bottled wine

German Wine Lable Reading	
Mosel-Saar-Ruwer	Specified wine region
1989er	Vintage year/year of production
Avelsbacher Avelsbach	The village where grapes are grown
Hammerstein	Name of vineyard
Riesling	Grape variety
Kabinett	Degree of quality within Qmp
Qualitätswein mit Prädikat	Germany's highest quality category
Produce of Germany	Country of origin
A.P. Number - 3 562 107 765 90	Certification number
Alc 7.5% by volume	Alcohol percentage
750 mL	Quantity of bottled wine
Erzeugerabfullung	Address of vineyard

Note. In German wine label, the acronym A.P. (Number) stands for "Amtliche Prüfung" Number. It shows on the label of QmP and QbA German wines. It is an official test number.

FOOD AND WINE MATCHING

Food and wine matching is a process of pairing a food with complementary flavours, aromas, and textures found in wine. There are six basic principles of food and wine matching, these are: *good wine before great wine, fruit wine before grain wine, young wine before old wine, light wine before full bodied wine, white wine before red wine, dry wine before sweet wine, low tannin wine before high tannin wine* and *national food with national wine*. In the below given table, few menu examples of food with appropriate wine names are given.

Courses (In French)	In English	Preparation	Matching wine
Hors d' oeuvres	Appetizer		Fino or Manzanilla Sherry, Sancerre or Gewürztraminer
Potage	Soup course	Cream Stock	Dry Oloroso Sherry Dry Riesling
Oeufs	Egg course		Cote du Rhone, Alsatian /Riesling or Sylvaner
Poisson	Fish course	Grilled Poached Sautéed Pan fried	Sauvignon Blanc, Chardonnay, Sparkling wine Dry Riesling, Champagne. Chennin Blanc, off-dry Riesling, Sparkling wine Sauvignon Blanc, Chablis, Sémillon, Sancerre
Farinaceous	Pasta course		Chianti, Barolo, Barbara, Zinfandel, Sauvignon Blanc
Entrée	The 1st meat course		Moselle, Bordeaux, Burgundy
Relevé	The 2nd meat/ main course		Claret, Burgundy, Chianti, Champagne
Rôti	Roast course		Pinot Noir, Cabernet Sauvignon, Chardonnay
Legumes	Vegetable course		Merlot and light style white wines, Chardonnay and dry Riesling wines
Salade	Salad course		Mostly Champagne wines
Buffet froid	Cold buffet		Hocks and Rose wine
Entremets	Sweet course		Champagne and Sauternes

Fromage	Cheese course	Mild Medium Ripe	Chardonnay, Riesling Young Pinot Noir Burgundy, Cabernet Sauvignon, Syrah, Port
Dessert	Fruits		Muscat, Sweet Riesling, Botrytis wines
Boisson	Beverage		Brandy (Cognac, Armagnac), Liquors, Ports, Calvados.

Mexican Menu	Continental Menu	Italian Menu
Tortilla (Navarra)	Caesar Salad (Dry Sauvignon Blanc)	Bresaola (Valpolicella Red)
Pozole (Fidello)	Crème de Tomate (Dry Riesling)	Minestrone (Chianti)
Tacos (Chardonnay)	Poulet Sauté Chasseur (Cote du Rhone)	Pancetta (Cabernet)
Ou Burrito (Mas de Bazan Rosado)	Ou Pommes Châteaux (Light and White Merlot)	Ou Fettuccine Alfredo (White Zinfandel)
Churros (Verdejo)	Gateaux Moka (Sweet Champagne)	Biscotti (Asti Spumante)
Cafe (Liquor)	Café (Liquor)	Café (Liquor)

WINE FAULTS

The term *wine fault* refers to all those wine tribulations which may spoil the taste of wine, consequently affecting its sale. These faults occasionally develop in the wines when they mature in the bottles. Nowadays, through improved techniques and attention faulty wine is a rarity but faults can never be fully eliminated. These faults can be easily detected directly in wine bottles or during wine decanting and wine tasting process. Given below are some faults/common causes, which make the wine faulty:

Cloudiness

- ✓ It is concerned with the suspended matter in the wine disguising its true colour and making the wine cloudy. Wine may also cloud due to extreme storage temperature.

Sulphur Dioxide

- ✓ This is used for sterilizing the wine barrels and for killing yeast, hence helping in maintaining the freshness of a wine once bottled. It is often found in white wines, especially those sealed with screw-caps or other synthetic closures. Its smell will disappear after opening the bottle.

Tainted/Corked

- ✓ This happens when wine is continuously in touch with faulty cork. This fault is caused by a chemical compound (TCA, i.e., Trichloroanisole) that can occur naturally in cork bark.
- ✓ A wine which has become *corked* will have smell of a damp basement, wet cardboard/newspaper/mushrooms.

WINE TASTING TECHNIQUE

(Features of good wine)

Swirl	Pleasing aroma/bouquet
Sniff	Pleasurable smell
Sight	Clear and bright colour
Sip	Wine taste - sweet/dry

Oxidation

- ✓ This is caused by faulty storage or when wine has been allowed to react with oxygen, possibly due to faulty cork or cork getting dried in storage conditions.
- ✓ A wine that has *oxidized* will have the smell of cooked fruit and walnuts and may also develop a brownish appearance. This fault is also known as *maderization*.

Acetification

- ✓ This is caused when wine is overexposed to air, the resultant wine will have smell of vinegar. A small percentage of acetic acid is nearly always present in wine, as it is a byproduct of fermentation. A wine which has been acidified (or contains acetic acid) will have a sour taste like vinegar.

Other Wine Faults

- ✓ These faults are sediments/lees available in wines (it can be removed by decanting), inclusion of foreign contamination, tartare flake, any faulty smell (like smell of vinegar or rotten eggs) and so forth.

Note.

- Remember, all wines breathe like humans, thus they need constant air supply (but not more air, as it could convert wine into vinegar) for their maturity. They breathe through the pores of the cork, therefore it is very important for the cork to be in touch with the wines (therefore wine bottles must be stored in 180° angle)

- A small degree of maderization/oxidation is to be expected for many older wines (such as aged red **Bordeaux** or **Rioja**), but it is undesirable in young wines, in which fresh fruit flavours and vibrant colours are required.
- The smell/appearance of sulphur dioxide will not be called a wine fault; actually sulphur dioxide is used to preserve the wine and make it healthy for consumption. It will disappear after opening the bottle.

FACTORS AFFECTING VINE/WINE

It is associated with all those aspects which directly or indirectly affect viticulture and vinification. In general, most of these aspects are external components which a vine grower can never control or change. Internal components also play a significant role in wine making like vinification process. Some of these factors are listed below along with a brief description.

Soil

- ✓ Soil rich in mineral components is always considered best for vine growing, as it provides nutrients such as phosphate, iron, potassium, magnesium and calcium.
- ✓ The vine could grow in any type of soil but *flavoured soils* (such as chalky soil, slate, limestone, sandy soils, gravel or volcanic) are often preferable choices as they have good drainage and moisture retention capacity which keeps the vine roots healthy.
- ✓ It is good to analyze the soil annually (before planting vine) and if any chemical deficiency is found, it must be compensated.

Wine Storage Guidelines	
Cellar temperature	11-13°C
Cellar room	Underground
Angle of bottle	180°
Humidity level	13-18°C
Heat source	Keep away
Light	No direct rays
Vibration	No vibration

Climate

- ✓ Like soil, climatic conditions also play a crucial role in vine growing. A preferable climatic condition is a good balance of moisture with heat.
- ✓ The lowest annual average temperature necessary for the vine to flourish is 10°C; the ideal average temperature is 14 to 16°C.
- ✓ Most vine growers estimate that the vines need about 68 cm of rain per year-mainly in winter and spring, along with at least 1400 hours of sunshine.

Vineyard Location

- ✓ Ideally, vines should be planted (in France) on south facing slopes where they point at the sun, thus receive the maximum benefit of sunshine with good drainage. Vineyard location is of prime importance to capture the sunlight for photosynthesis and good ripening.
- ✓ Some vineyards are sited up to 243 m (266 yards) or even more on mountain sides whereas many of the great vineyards are located in river valleys and along lakeside benefiting from humidity and reflected heat.

Wine Bottle Openers

- Lever Opener
- Angle Winged
- Waiter's Friend
- Two-pronged

Grape

- ✓ The grape variety and its quality play a decisive role in making a good quality wine. Ideally, grape must harmonise with soil, prevailing climatic conditions and location of vineyard. It must be reasonably disease-resistant to produce a good wine.
- ✓ Wine can be produced either from *varietal grapes* usually a classic single grape like Riesling or from *hybrid* (such as Riesling x Silvaner = Muller Thurgau).
- ✓ Lastly, remember that different varieties of grapes react differently in different soil and climatic conditions. For example, *pinot noir* is a classic grape in Burgundy but a disaster in Bordeaux.

Others

- ✓ It includes factors like viticulture (harvesting method, amount of rainfall, skill and ability of vine grower, etc.) and vinification (such as *must* making process, fermentation process, prevailing laws, maturation period, bottling style, crowning/corking style and so forth).

Champagne Bottle Sizes

Bottle Name	Capacity	Capacity (Bot.)	Bibliography/Meaning/Associated with
Magnum	1.5 litres	2 bottles	Originated from the Latin word *magnus* – meaning large
Jeroboam	3 litres	4 bottles	Named after first king of Israel (931–910 BC)
Rehoboam	4.5 litres	6 bottles	Named after son of Solomon {King of Judag (22–908 BC)}
Methuselah	6 litres	8 bottles	Named after biblical patriarch (969 BC)
Salmanazar	9 litres	12 bottles	Named after king of Assyria (859–824 BC)
Balthazar	12 litres	16 bottles	Named after regent of Babylon (539 BC)

Nebuchadnezzar	15 litres	20 bottles	Named after king of Babylon (605–562 BC)
Solomon	20 litres	28 bottles	Named after Solomon, King of Judag
Primat	27 litres	36 bottles	

Vine Diseases

The term *vine disease* refers to all those infections or syndromes which may affect the growth of vine, consequently its flowers/grapes. Thus, it is important for vine grower to heal vine from all such possible diseases. Few vine diseases along with their treatment are given below.

Diseases	Description	Treatments
Mildew	• Develops in damp areas. • Very common vine disease. • It is noticed when yellow patches appear on the leaves. • When leaves wither	Spray vine creeps with copper sulphate
Grey root	• It can be malevolent or benevolent. • It is produced in humid conditions. • It is a grey mould which destroys colour pigments in black grapes.	Spray anti-rot vine.
Coulure	• It happens when soil has deficiency or there is too much rain or uneven temperature. • Flowers of vine are infertile resulting in a disappointing yield of grapes.	Use good fertilizers
Cholrosis	• Too much limestone in soil causes yellowing or even death of the plant.	Spray iron sulphate
Pyralis, endemis and cochylis	• These tiny butterfly moths pierce the grapes and destroy the crops within hours.	Spray vine creeps with insecticides
Frost	• Especially in spring, frost stunts the formation of the buds which greatly reduces yield.	Fire heat and spray with water
Hail	• It is a particular danger especially just before the vintage when the grapes' skins are very thin and hence, the grapes are very vulnerable. • Hail can easily puncture the skin and ruin the crops.	Spray with sulphur dioxide

KEY TERMS

Fortification	:	Process of addition of brandy into table wine to produce fortified dry/sweet wine.
Liquor brandy	:	Brandy of great age and excellence.
Fining	:	Wine clarification process in order to remove suspended particles.
Esters	:	Chemical compounds formed by the reaction of alcohol and acids during fermentation.
Agrafe	:	Wire cage (or camp) tied around champagne cork to hold pressure.
Ice bath	:	Ice bucket with plenty of ice and cold water to immerse sparkling wine.
Maderization	:	Oxidation of some types of wines.
Chaptalization	:	Addition of extra sugar into *must* due to lack of sugar in grapes.
Noble rot	:	Fungus *botrytis cinerea* that grows on white grapes which increases sweetness and flavour.
Varietal grapes	:	Wine whose brand name is based on the name of grape used to produce it.

REVIEW QUESTIONS

1. What is grape wine? Classify wine on the basis of nature and explain each one briefly.
2. Describe the factors that affect vine and wine.
3. Give a step-by-step procedure for serving red wine.
4. Prepare a five-course continental menu and suggest appropriate wines with each course/dish.

Old Wine World

(Wine of France, Germany, Italy, Spain and Portugal)

Objectives

Students will be able to:

- expound old wine producing countries of the world;
- elucidate prevailing wine laws, famous communes and wine brands; and
- gain knowledge about major grapes used to produce wines and their imitations.

OLD WINE WORLD

The term *old wine world* refers all those wine producing countries which are in wine trade from last many decades. But remember, the term *old wine world* does not refer to a homogeneous type with "old world wine regions" like France, Germany, Italy, Portugal and Spain each making immensely different styles of wine even within their own legal boundaries. Rather, the term old wine world is used to describe the general differences in viticulture and vinification philosophies in terms of tradition, customs and the role of *terroir*.

In simple terms, old world wine refers to all those wines that are produced in Europe but can also include other regions of the Mediterranean basin with long histories of wine making such as North Africa and the Near East. Wines in the old world are *terroir driven* and are often labelled based on the region of origin (or *generic wines*). Here, wine makers primarily use wild yeast for fermentation process. Wine makers refer to extended *maceration* period and higher fermentation temperature. It creates more tannic and austere wines with more layers of complexity that entails bottle aging to mature.

WINE OF FRANCE

France is the most prominent wine producing country in the world and has developed superfine *natural still wines* and the finest sparkling wine like *champagne*. A brief profile of major French wine growing regions/communes is given below.

Alsace	Famous for producing dry wines, both red and white
Bordeaux	Famous for producing dry red wines and some sweet wines
Burgundy	Famous for producing dry white wines and some red wines
Champagne	Famous for producing sparkling wines like champagne
Loire valley	Famous for producing dry white and rose wines
Rhone valley	Famous for producing dry red, white and rose wines.

Wine Laws/Quality Control of France

VDT	It stands for "Vin de Table" – these are ordinary and cheapest table wines not recognized under any quality control standards.
VDP	It stands for "Vin de Pay" – these are medium quality and low priced wines. These are further classified into following parts- Vin de pays du zone, Vin de pays Regioneaux, Vin de pays Departmentalux.
VDQS	It stands for "Vin Délimite de Qualité Supérieure" – these are quality wines of normal price range and just below the appellation-controlled standard.
AOC/AC	It stands for "Appellation de Origine Contrôlée" – these are quality wines from approved areas and are usually higher in price.

Wine Producing Regions/Communes of France

Alsace

Alsace is situated in the northern corner of France bordering the German territory. Alsace includes Strasburg and River Rhine. Alsatian vineyards produce the pleasant luncheon wines. Alsace is famous for producing *dry white wine*. Other types of wines are rarely found. This is the only major French wine region that identifies its wine by the name of the grape. The grapes mainly used to produce Alsatian wine include:

Riesling	A white grape variety used to produce best Alsatian wines. Alsatian wines made from Riesling grapes are best to offer with fish based preparations.
Gewürztraminer	A white grape variety with rich spicy flavour and overpowering fruitiness. It is best to offer with highly seasoned food and strong cheeses.
Muscat	A white grape variety used to produce good sweet wines (especially in Europe). It is best to serve as an aperitif.
Tokay d' Alsace	An alternative name of *Pinot Gris* grape used to produce full bodied, subdued flavoured wine. It mellows as time passes. This variety of wine is mostly used for the purpose of blending.
Sylvaner	A white grape variety mostly used to produce everyday drinking wine. It is predominantly grown in Northern Alsace.

Brand names (or wine shippers) of wine from Alsace region

Red wines	Domaine Des Marroniers Gewürztraminer, Domaine Des Marroniers Riesling Kastelberg, Domaine Albert Mnn Muscat, Domaine Allimant, Domaine Kirmann Sylvaner, etc.

White wines	Domaine Hering Pinot, Domaine Rene Mure Pinot Noir Clos Saint, Domaine Roll Gassmann Pinot Noir, Pinot Noir Cuvee Frederic, Pinot Noir Rouge d' Alsace, etc.

Bordeaux

The Bordeaux region situated in South Western France is famous in wine trade for centuries. Bordeaux is most noted for its red wines of exceptional quality. Many consider Bordeaux as one of the most important wine producing regions in the world. Predominantly, only five grape varieties are used to produce red Bordeaux wines—cabernet sauvignon, merlot, cabernet franc, malbec and petit verdot. In England, red Bordeaux wines are known as *claret*. The wine can be named as Bordeaux wine when produced within the legal boundaries of Gironde valley that is formed when the Garonne and Dordogne rivers converge. Some major wine producing communes of Bordeaux include:

Médoc

- ✓ This wine commune is situated in the northwest of the city of Bordeaux, on the left bank of the Garonne River. It is famous for producing wines made with a high proportion of *cabernet sauvignon grapes*.
- ✓ Most of the wines for the basic appellation "Médoc" come from the north while wine from the southern part is entitled to be labeled as "Haute Médoc/Upper Médoc". In 1855, Médoc wines were classified into five grand crus:

Médoc's Five Grand Cru Classes (*with limited wine names/wine communes)		
Premiers	1st Great Growths	*Château Lafite-Rothschild (Pauillac), Château Margaux (Margaux), etc.
Deuxiemes	2nd Great Growths	*Château Cos-d'Estournel (St. Estephe), Château Durfort-Viviens (Margaux), etc.
Troisiemes	3rd Great Growths	*Château Ferriere (Margaux), Château Calon-Segur (St. Estephe), etc.
Quatriemes	4th Great Growths	*Château Beychevelle (St. Julien), Château Lafon-Rochet (St. Estephe), etc.
Cinquiemes	5th Great Growths	*Château Batailley (Pauillac), Château Belgrave (Saint-Laurent), etc.

Graves

- ✓ This wine commune is situated in the south of Médoc on the left bank of the River Garonne. It is famous for producing finest claret and good dry white wines.

The well-known Classification of 1855 did not include the Graves except Château Haut-Brion. The Châteaux of the Graves region were finally classified in 1953; it was made official in 1959.

✓ The Châteaux were qualified separately based on their white wines and red wines. Few Châteaux were also recognized for producing both red as well as white wines. The classified growth of Graves wine is given below.

Classified Growths of the Graves (*with limited wine names/wine communes)	
Red wines	*Château de Fieuzal, Ch. Haut-Bailly, Ch. Haut-Brion, Ch. La Tour Haut-Brion, Ch. Pape Clement
White wines	*Château Couhins, Château Couhins-Lurton, Château Laville Haut-Brion
Red and white wines	*Château Bouscaut, Ch. Carbonnieux, Domaine de Chevalier, Ch. La Tour-Martillac, Ch. Olivier

Sauternes and Barsac

✓ These wine communes are neighbours situated on a portion of land within the Graves area. Sauternes and Barsac wines can be classified into different classes, i.e., Premier grand cru, Premier cru classes and Deuxieme/Second cru classes.

Sauternes and Barsac Wine Classes (*with limited wine names/wine communes)		
Premier grand cru	1st Great Growth	Château D'Yqueem
Premier cru	Best/First Growth	*Château Climens, Château Guiraud, Ch. Coutet, Ch. Latour Blanche, etc.
Deuxieme cru	Second Growth	*Château Caillou, Ch. d' Arche, Ch. de Myrat, Ch. Romer, Ch. Suau, etc.

Note. Cru– it means a grade or class of wine (traditionally translated as growth).

St. Estephe and Pauillac

✓ *St. Estephe* wine commune is situated in the Gironde department in Aquitaine, southwestern France which produces robust full-bodied red wines with plenty of tannin so they need time to develop fully.

✓ *Pauillac* wine commune is situated in the département of the Poitou-Charentes region, south-western France. It is famous for producing red wine of powerful fruity bouquet and rich velvety texture when mature.

St. Julien and Margaux

- ✓ *St. Julien* wine commune is situated in the Médoc region of Bordeaux and is famous for producing gentle and supple wine (after maturation).
- ✓ *Margaux* wine commune is also situated in the Médoc region. It is famous for producing red wines, in good years these wines are excellent but in poor years – it produces thin wines.

Entre deux mers

- ✓ The largest wine commune lies in the area of Gironde – between the river Dordogne and Garonne in Southern France. Only white wines are authorized to carry the designation AC "Entre-deux-Mers" while red wines from this region are sold under the AC "Bordeaux".

St. Emilion and Pomerol

- ✓ *St. Emilion* is the oldest wine commune which lies on the north bank of the Dordogne River. It is famous for producing less tannin, soft and full flavour wines (mostly made from merlot grape variety).
- ✓ *Pomerol* wine commune adjoins St. Emilion on the north bank of the Dordogne River. It is famous for producing well known, gentle and rich red wines (or clarets) which are predominantly made from Merlot grapes.

Other regions

- ✓ Other regions include – Moulis and Listrac, Cerons, St. Croix du Mont, Loupiac, Premieres Cotes de Bordeaux, Fronsac, Bourge and Blaye, etc.

Brand names (or wine shippers) of wine from Bordeaux region

Graves	Famous red wine includes – Château Lehoul, Château Magneau, Château Rahoul, Château Renon and famous white wine includes – Château Brillette, Château De Chantegrive, Château Le Bonnat, Château St. Robert
Médoc	Famous red wine includes – Château Beaumont, Château Belair, Château Camensac, Château Charmail, Château La Cardonne, etc.
St. Estephe	Famous red wine includes – Château Calon Segur, Château Cos D' Estournel, Château Cos Labory, Château Haute Beausejour, Château Marbuzer, etc.
Pauillac	Famous red wine includes – Château Batailly, Château Clerc Milon, Château D' Armailhac, Château Duhart, Milon, Fondadet, etc.

St. Julien	Famous red wine includes Château Beychevelle, Château Branaire, Château Gloria, Château Gruaud, Larose, Château Langoa Barton, etc.
Margaux	Famous red wine includes Château Bel Air Marquis D' Aligre, Château Cantenac Brown, Château De Angludet, Château d' Isson, Château Dauzac, etc.
Entre Deux Mers	Famous red wine includes Château Bel Air, Château Bonnet, Château Castelneau, Château Castenet Graffier, Château de Fontenille, etc.
St. Emilion	Famous red wine includes Château Angelus, Château Ausone, Château Beausejour, Château Belair, Château Calon, etc.
Pomerol	Famous red wine includes Château Beauregard, Château Certan de May, Château Clinet, Château de Sales, Château Gazin, etc.

Burgundy

Burgundy is located in the central part of eastern France. The Burgundy region is home of some of the finest Chardonnay and Pinot Noir wines in the world. At the southern end of the region is the area of Beaujolais which is known for its Gamay based wines. The Chablis area is a sub-region of Burgundy that makes wonderful Chardonnay based wines from a poor chalky soil. The wines from the vineyard 'Le Montrachet' and from the adjoining vineyards of Chassagne Montrachet and Puligny Montrachet are prized around the world for their fine quality. *Fixin* is a commune known for its red wines. Some major wine producing communes of Burgundy include:

Burgundy Wine Appellations (*with limited wine names)

Appellations	Feature of Wine and Vine	Wine Name Based on	Example
General App.	Wine made anywhere in Burgundy region	Wine named under Burgundy	*Bourgogne Aligote
Village App.	Wine made within the particular vineyard	Wine named under vineyard	*App. Beaune Contrôlée

Chablis

✓ This wine commune is situated in the north-west of Dijon and famous for producing fine dry white wines (known as Chablis and also classified as a *white Burgundy*) made from chardonnay grape variety. Chablis wine carries one of the following appellations – Petite Chablis, Chablis, Chablis Premier Cru or Chablis Grand Cru.

Chablis Wine Appellations (*with limited vineyard names)			
Appellations	**Alcohol Content**	**Feature of Wine**	**Area/Vineyard**
Petite Chablis	9.5% above	Lowest AC quality wine	Basic wine of the area
Chablis	10% above	Good AC quality wine	Blended wines from the several vineyards
Chablis Premier Cru	10.5% above	Best AC quality wines	*Mont de Milieu, Vaillons, Fourchaume
Chablis Grand Cru	11% above	Excellent AC wines	*Vaudesir, Bougros, Preuses, Clos, Valmur

Côte de nuits and beaune

- ✓ *Côte de nuits* wine commune is situated on either side of the Route National 74 from Dijon to Nuits-St-Georges and is famous for producing highly priced and well matured fruity red wines.
- ✓ *Côte de beaune* wine commune is situated in the centre of the Burgundy and is famous for producing world class finest wines as well as good red wines.

Côte chalonnaise and côte mâconnais

- ✓ *Côte Chalonnaise* wine commune is situated on the south of both – Côte de beaune and Mâconnais and famous for producing both light bodied red wines (from Givery and Mercury) and white wines (from Rully and Montagny).
- ✓ *Côte Mâconnais* is situated on the left bank of the River Caone and famous for producing both red wines (made from gamay grapes) and white wines (made from chardonnay grapes).

Beaujolais

- ✓ This wine commune is situated on the south of both – Mâconnais and city of Lyon. It is famous for producing fresh fruity red wines made from *gamay grapes.* It is also best known for producing *Beaujolais Nouveau,* a new year's vintage wine.

Gevrey and chambertin

- ✓ The largest wine appellation in Côte de Nuits, *Gevrey* is famous for producing red wines whereas *Chambertin* is famous for range of wines from average to supreme. The best Gevrey-Chambertin grand crus are Chambertin and Clos de Bèze. They are among the finest French red wines.

Meursault

- ✓ *Meursault* is a name of wine commune as well as a famous finest white wine from Meursault (in côte-de-beaune), a sub-region of Burgundy.
- ✓ *Meursault* wine has a Premier Cru label and is considered a great quality wine. The best of the best are Les Perrières, Les Charmes, Les Gouttes d'Or.

Pommard

- ✓ Pommard is a wine commune in the Côte-d'Or department in Bourgogne (Burgundy) in eastern France. It is famous for producing red wines which are robust and contain more tannin and are much stronger than Beaune and Volnay wines.

Nuit- St. George

- ✓ It is a name of famous fine red wine from Nuits-Saint-George, a sub-region of Burgundy. It is famous for producing red wines.

Brand Names (or *wine shippers*) of Wine from Burgundy Region

Red wines

Côte Chalonnaise	Château de Chaimery Mercurey, Givery (F. Lump), Joblot Givery, Mercuery (M. Juillot), etc.
Beaujolais	Georges du Boeuf Morgon, Georges du Boeuf Moulin A Vent, Jean Foillard Morgon, Paul Janin Et Fils Moulin A Vent, etc.
Gevrey and Chambertin	Burguet Gevrey Chambertin Vilely Vignes, Chassagne Montrachet Girardin, Faiveley Mazis Chambertin, Gevrey Chambertin (C. Dugat), Ponsot Griotte Chambertin, etc.
Pommard	De Courcel Pommard Rugiens, De Montille Pommard Pezerolles, Pommard Clos De Epeneaux, Pommard Saussilles, etc.
Nuit- St. George	Faively Nuit St. George Clos De La Marechale, Gouges NSG Les St. Georges, Grivot Clos De Vougeot, Meo Camuzet NSG Aux Murgers, NSG Le Cailles, etc.

White wines

Chablis	Chablis (A. Boudin), Grossot Chablis, Raveneau C. Les Clos, Raveneau C. Montee De Tonnerre, Chablis Les Preuses, etc.

Mâconnais	Bonhomme Macon Vire, Château Du Fuisse Pouilly Fuisse, Forest Pouilly Fuisse, Guffens Heynen Pouilly Fuisse, Pouilly Fuisse (Madame Ferret), etc.
Meursault	Boyer Martenot Meursault, Coche Dury Meursault, Coche Dury Meursault Perrieres, Ente Meursault, Fichet Meursault, Javillier Meursault, Roullot Meursault Perrieres, etc.

Fortified and sweet wines (or wine shippers)

Fortified Wines	Banyuls Dom La Tour Vieille Vin De Meditation, Campadieu Mavry Dom La Pleidade Vintage, Campadieu Banyuls L' Etroile Grand Reserve, Campadieu Banyuls Blanc Vial Magneres (Monique Saperas), Campadieu Rivesaltes Domaine Cazes Cuvee (Alime Cazes), etc.
Sweet Wines	Château La Rame, Château La Tour Blanche, Château Loubens, Château Memoires, Château Raboud Promis, Château Rayne Vigneau, Clos Jean, Château Sigalas Rabaud, Cru Barrijats, Domaine De Petite Quarte Bonnezeaux, etc.

Loire Valley

The Loire River is the longest in France. In the span of its valley are produced some of the finest white wines. Near the coast, Chenin Blanc is the preferred grape and Vouvray is the wine produced. Further, up the river, Sauvignon Blanc is the grape of choice with Sancerre and Pouilly Fume as the wines that are produced. Rose d'Anjou is a popular semi-dry rose wine that is also made in the Loire Valley. Four famous wine communes of Loire valley are:

Nantes district

- ✓ This wine commune surrounds the city of Nantes in Brittany. It is famous for producing Muscadet wines which are made from Muscadet grapes. The best wine is entitled to the Appellation "Muscadet de Sevre-et-Maine". It is best to offer with seafood preparations.

Anjou and Saumur

- ✓ Both wine communes are collectively known as the "Middle Loire". These communes are famous for producing red, white and rosé wines, still and sparkling wines, which range from dry to very sweet. *Saumur* is especially famous for producing fine sparkling wines.

Touraine district

- ✓ This wine commune surrounds the city of Tour. It is famous for producing soft, light-bodied red wine made from Cabernet franc grape variety.

Central vineyards

- ✓ This wine commune is situated in the centre of France. It is famous for producing wine made from white grapes, especially from Sauvignon Blanc grapes.

Brand Names (or *wine shippers*) of Wine from Loire Valley

Anjou Saumur	Cabernet d Anjou Rose (Rose wine), Cremant de la Loire (still wine made from Chenin Blanc grape variety).
Touraine district	Vauvray (white wine)
Central vineyards	Sancerre and Pouilly Fume (white wines from Sauvignon Blanc grape variety)

Rhône Valley

This wine region is situated in southeastern France and is famous for producing red wines. The region is just under 150 miles long (north to south) and located between the cities of Lyon in the north and Avignon in the south. All qualities of wine are produced here, from Appellation Contrôlée to Vin de Table. Rhône valley produces around 2% white wines with 98% red and rose wines. Châteauneuf-du-Pape and Côtes-du-Rhône (means 'Slopes of the Rhône') are the two best-known wines that come from this region. A wide variety of grapes are grown and blended in this region but the two most commonly used are Syrah and Grenache. There are several wine communes in Rhône valley, some of them are as follows:

Côte Rôtie

- ✓ This wine commune is situated (on hills) on the west bank of the Rhône Valley. It is famous for producing perfumed red wine of great elegance and somewhat softer than the wine of Hermitage. Syrah and Viognier are the two main grape varieties used to make wine in Côte-Rôtie.

Condrieu and châteaux grillet

- ✓ Both wine communes are situated in the Northern Rhône Valley, *Condrieu* is in upper area whereas *Châteaux Grillet* is nearby the Vienne. Here, the Viognier grape is used to produce dry white wine of a delicate flowery bouquet.

✓ *Condrieu* is the only homeland in the world for growing Viognier grapes whereas *Château grillet* has the only distinction of being the single estate to have its own appellation. It is also the smallest commune in France.

Hermitage

✓ This wine commune is situated (on hills) on the right bank of the Rhône river, in Drome department. It is famous for producing strong finest rich red wines made from Syrah grape variety. It is also well known for oldest dry white Hermitage wine for its longevity.

Crozes hermitage and St. Joseph

✓ Both are small AOC wine communes, situated in the Northern Rhône, France (on the foot of the hill of Hermitage, around the Tournon).

✓ These are famous for producing light red wines made from the Syrah grapes, sometimes blended with small quantities of white Roussanne or Marsanne grapes. Some white wines are only made with Marsanne and/or Roussanne.

Cornas

✓ This small AOC wine commune is situated in the Northern Rhône, France (south of Lyon). It is famous for producing red wines made from Syrah grape variety.

✓ Any wine designated as Cornas AOC will be made from 100% Syrah and no addition of white grapes is permitted, thus no white wines are produced here.

St. Péray

✓ This small AOC wine commune is situated in the Northern Rhône, France. It is famous for producing best sparkling wines, especially made from the *Méthode Champenoise.*

✓ Marsanne grapes are used to produce these full-bodied wines. 90% of the planting is Marsanne, the remainder being made up of Rousanne and the lesser known Roussette.

Châteauneuf du pape

✓ This AOC wine commune is situated in the Vaucluse department in the Provence-Alpes-Côte d'Azur region in southeastern France.

✓ It permits around 13 grape varieties to produce wines, i.e. Cinsault, Counoise, Mourvedre, Muscardin, Syrah, Terret noir and Vaccarese (all these seven are red grapes) and Grenache blanc, Bourboulenc, Clairette, Picardan, Roussanne and Picpou (all these remaining six grapes are white). The blend is usually predominantly of Grenache grape variety.

Gigondas and lirac

✓ Both wine communes are situated on the southern Rhône and famous for producing good red wine of similar style to Châteauneuf. *Gigondas* is primarily a red wine region, with a very small amount of rosé wine production whereas *Lirac* is famous for producing rose wines.

Tavel

✓ This wine commune is situated in the southern Rhône and famous for producing strong fruit flavoured, dry rose wines. These wines must have a minimum alcohol content of 11% by volume. Grenache and Cinsault are the main grapes used in the appellation's wines, along with Syrah and Mourvedre.

Beaumes de venise

✓ This wine commune is situated in Vaucluse, next to Vacqueyras and Gigondas and was upgraded to AOC status in 2005. It is famous for producing sweet fortified wines, made from Muscatel grape variety. It is also known as "Vin doux naturel". These wines are best to be drunk when young and served with desserts.

Famous Wines (*or wine shippers*) from Rhône

Red wines	Alain Graillot Crozes Hermitage, Auguste Clape Comas, Chapoutier Château Neuf Du Pape La Bernadine, Chapoutier Côte Du Rhône Belleruche, Château Beaucastel Châteauneuf Du Pape, etc.
White wines	Auguste Clape St. Peray, Chapoutier Côte Du Rhône, Château Beaucastel Côte Du Rhône Coudoulet, Château Beaucastel Côte Du Rhône Perrin Reserve, etc.

Champagne

The Champagne region is located in northeastern France and is the home of sparkling wine. Champagne is one of the best known wine regions in France. Legally, only three grape varieties are used to produce Champagne, i.e. 30% Chardonnay (for delicacy), 38% Pinot Noir (for power) and 32% Pinot Meunier (for fine bouquet). Champagne comes in a range of sweetness levels like brut, extra sec, sec, demi sec and doux. There are other sparkling wines produced in many countries around the world but none of them is entitled to be called *Champagne*. The name is reserved only for sparkling wines that are produced in the Champagne region of France and that have been produced in line with very specific and strict practices (AOC regulations). Apart from AOC, CIVC (*Comité Interprofessionnel du vin de Champagne*) is the governing body for Champagne that enforces all AOC regulations. The wine producing region covers around 80,000 acres of land, it comprises 120 communes, which are divided into three areas – montagne de reims, vallée de la marne and côte des blancs. Apart from these three, there are two more famous vine growing communes in Champagne region, i.e., aube and côte de sezanne.

Styles of Champagne		
Style	**Type**	**Sweetness**
Brut	Very very dry	0.5-1.5%
Extra sec	Extra dry	1.5-3%
Sec	Dry	3-5%
Demi sec	Medium dry	5-7%
Doux	Very sweet	Above 7%
Rich	Very very sweet	Exception

Montagne de reims

- ✓ This wine commune is situated nearby the slopes of Reims and famous for planting Pinot noir vines/grape variety.

Vallée de la marne

- ✓ This wine commune is situated on the either side of the river Mame and famous for planting Pinot meunier grape variety which is said to contribute a particularly fine bouquet.

Côte des blancs

- ✓ This wine commune is situated in south of the river Mame and famous for planting Chardonnay vines/grape variety.

Manufacturing Process of Champagne

Raw material

- ✓ Only three grape varieties are used to produce champagne – Chardonnay (white grape), Pinot noir and Pinot meunier (both red grapes). After plucking, rotten and damaged grapes are removed to improve the quality of wine – this process is known as *eplughage*.

1st juice extraction

- ✓ Now selected grapes are put into Marc (it holds 4000 kilos of grapes and produces 3000 kilos of juice) to extract grape juice. Juice from 1st extraction (law allows only the first 2666 litres of grape juice to make good Champagne) known as "Vin de Cuvée or Premier taille" (all best champagnes are made from it).

2nd juice extraction

✓ Juice from 2nd extraction (or remaining 266 litres) is known as "Vin de Taille or Deuxie Taille" (it is used to make less fine or regular champagne). The remainder is known as "Rebéche" which is distilled to make brandy (like Marc de Champagne) for the local market.

Le Débourbage

✓ It is essential that all impurities in the *must* be given time to fall at the bottom of the cask, so that the clean *must* may be drawn off. In very hot weather, *must* is passed through refrigerated columns to prevent any kind of premature fermentation.

1st fermentation

✓ First or primary fermentation takes place between the temperature ranges of 18 to 20°C for about two weeks so as to convert the grape juice sugar into alcohol. During this fermentation, casks must be regularly topped up to prevent bacterial attack on wine.

Racking and fining

✓ Perform *racking* two to three times to remove visible sediments and *fining* (with Bentonite or Isinglass) to remove suspended particles. Now this wine is added with *liqueur de tirage* (combination of sugar, old wine and yeast) to start second fermentation in bottle. Lastly the bottle is sealed.

2nd fermentation

✓ To start second fermentation, sealed bottles are kept in *pupitre*. The secondary fermentation (here champagne becomes effervescent) is carried out at 10 to 12°C for about three to six months. The bottle will be standing vertically with neck downwards, so that remaining sediments could be derived on the cork. This whole process is known as *remuage*.

Degorgement

✓ Sediments deposited on the neck of the bottle are removed through a process known as *degorgement/ disgorgement*. In it, neck of bottle is dipped in a freezing brine solution (-25°C) which freezes the bottom wine and locks the sediments.

When cork is removed, a pressure builds up inside the bottle which expels the ice block that contains sediments.

Dosage

- ✓ The space appearing after removing the ice block is filled up/top-up with *liqueur d' expédition* (liquor made of sugar to obtain a demi-sec, brut or extra brut champagne). Finally, champagne is bottled, corked, wired (with Agrafe clip) and sealed.

Methods of Manufacturing of Champagne

Champagne method

- ✓ An English term for "Méthode Champenoise", it is a labour-intensive process by which the second fermentation is created in the bottle itself, resulting in carbonation. The sediments are removed by the process of *remuage* or *degorgement*.

Méthode cuvée close

- ✓ It is an inexpensive process for producing huge amounts of sparkling wine. It is also called "Bulk method or Charmat method". Contrasting the Champagne method, the second fermentation takes place in a vat or tank and the resulting product is filtered under pressure into bottles.

Transfer method

- ✓ In transfer method, the champagne is fermented and matured in bottles itself. The sediments are removed by transferring into vat under high pressure and then filtered.

Carbonation method

- ✓ Sometimes it is also referred to as "impregnation" where CO_2 (carbon dioxide) is injected into a vat of still wine which has been chilled and then bottled under pressure. It is an economical method.

Types of Champagne

Non vintage (N.V.)

- ✓ These are blended wines of several years (in house style) and require at least 15 months or more to mature before selling. After purchasing and keeping in cellar room, as the bottle ages, the Champagne becomes softer on the palate and richer in taste.

Vintage champagne

✓ These are blends of wines from a particular year, when the quality of the harvest was sufficient to declare it a "vintage". Remember every year is not a vintage year. These champagnes require maturing for at least 36 to 39 months before selling.

Rosé champagne

✓ These champagnes can be made either by adding a small proportion of red wine from champagne region or by macerating the black grapes during juice extraction. The true rosé wines are made with *de saignée method;* it is more expensive and produces a better Champagne. An excellent Rosé is Laurent-Perrier, produced de saignée.

Prestige/deluxe cuvées

✓ These champagne wines are most prestigious than others produced in vintage year. They cost around three times more than a Non-Vintage, and around double the price of a Vintage Champagne. Moët's Cuvée Dom Pérignon (DP) is an excellent example of it. In fact, Moët invented the Cuvée Prestige with D.P. in 1921.

Blanc de blancs

✓ These champagnes are made exclusively from the Chardonnay grapes (white grapes) and are always preferred to be served as an aperitif wine. It is of a lighter style than normal blends of champagne. It comes from the Côte de Blancs region and marketed as premium champagne.

Crémant

✓ It is a term used to denote semi-sparkling wine and more winy in taste. When applied to champagne wine, it means that less amount of yeast and sugar is added to the *liqueur de tirage*, the resultant champagne has half the normal gas pressure, i.e., 35 pounds PSI (not to be confused with *crémants* from other regions).

Millésime and brut sans millésime

✓ Millésime refers to the vintage champagnes that come only from years in which conditions have been particularly good. They are aged for three and often six years and have more volume, body and mature well for many years in the bottle. On the other side, Brut Sans Millésime refers to bone-dry, non-vintage that represents 80 per cent of total turnover.

Blanc de noirs

✓ Made exclusively from Pinot noir or Pinot meunier grapes (both are black grapes); this has powerful structure and fruitiness. It is mainly produced for local consumption.

Still champagne

✓ It is available in two forms – red and white still champagne wines. This type of champagne is also known as *coteaux champenois*. The red still champagne wines come from Bouzy and Sillery town of France.

The Saignée Method

The *saignée* (a French term means *bleed*) method is the practice of removing (or bleeding off) some of the juice from the *must* in order to more deeply concentrate the phenolics, colour and flavour of the red wine. A *rosé de saignée* is made by directly macerating Pinot noirs. This method of vinification is more demanding and requires grapes with an excellent degree of maturity. This is the real rosé.

Brand Names of Champagne

Abelé, Ayala, Dom Perignon, Besserat De Bellefon, Billecart-Salmon, Bollinger, Lanson, Laurent-Perrier, Mercier, Charles Heidsieck, Moët et Chandon, G.H. Mumm and Cie, Perrier Jouet, Piper-Heidsieck, Louis Roederer, etc.

WINE OF ITALY

Italy is the largest and one of the oldest wine producing countries in the world. Italian wines are frequently named after the grape rather than the region of origin; hence a wine excellent in one locality may be inferior in another. The best of the wines in Italy qualify for the designation as DOC or DOCG quality. Italy produces more wine and more variety of wine than any other country in the world and about 60% of Italian wines are red, the remaining white. Italian wines are classified (or its name based on) as *generic wines, varietal wines* and *proprietary wines*. Major Italian wine producing regions/communes are given below:

Style of Italian Wine

Abboccato	Semi sweet
Blanco	Sweet
Doce	White
Rosata	Rose
Rosso	Red
Spumante	Sparkling

Tuscany

- ✓ This wine commune is situated around Florence and Siena in the home of Chianti, the most famous of all Italian wines. The best known is *Chianti*, red or white, and properly a Tuscan wine (from Tuscany).
- ✓ Tuscany also produces the esteemed red blends known as *Super-Tuscans*. The wine makers classify Chianti wines into two major consorzio – *Chianti Classico* (from heart of the town) and *Chianti Putto* (from other vineyards).

Piedmont

- ✓ It is situated in the northwest of Italy and borders France. It is famous for producing table wines and sparkling wines. Most of the table wines are made from Nebbiolo grapes and are named after place of origin while Barbera grapes are used to produce sparkling wine. "Asti" is the centre of Italy's sparkling wines industry, which uses the Muscat grapes.

Campania

- ✓ Campania and its nearby wine communes Basilicata, Apulia and Calabria, all situated in southern Italy, are famous for producing vast quantity of highly alcoholic red wines. Campania is famous for well-known *Lacrima Christi* and *Falerno*, descendant of Horace's Falernian.

Veneto and Trentino

- ✓ *Veneto* wine commune is situated in southern Italy and is famous for *Valpolicella wine* which is dark red in colour with a rich texture.
- ✓ *Trentino* (Alto Adige) wine commune is situated on the border of Austria and famous for producing wines made from Cabernet, Merlot, Riesling, Traminer and Moscato grapes.

Sicily

- ✓ This wine commune is itself an Island where vines are grown on the slopes of Mount Era. It is famous for producing Marsala wine which is available in both dry and sweet form and produced in different styles – Marsala fine, Marsala superior, Marsala Speciale and Marsala Vergine. Sweet Marsalas are best to serve as a digestive and used in cookery, whereas dry Marsalas are suitable as an aperitif.

Styles of Marsalas	
Fine	It varies in styles from dry to sweet and requires minimum four months of ageing and must have no less than 17% alcohol by volume.
Superior	It varies in styles from dry to sweet. It must be aged for minimum of two years with no less than 18% alcohol by volume.
Speciale	The name Marsala Speciale is given to Marsala with added flavours such as almonds, coffee, or fruits.
Vergine	It is much drier than others and is normally served lightly chilled as an aperitif. It is aged for a minimum of five years and must contain at least 18% alcohol by volume.

Emilia-Romagna and Latium

- ✓ Emilia-Romagna is situated around the Bologna, Parma and Modena. It is famous for quantity wine production.
- ✓ Latium wine commune is situated around the hills of Rome and famous for producing the clear, golden *Frascati* wines. It is made in three different styles, i.e., *secco, amabile* and *aboccato*. Est! Est! Est! is a more notable wine from here (marketed in a flat flask-shaped bottle).

Lombardy and Friuli-Venezia

- ✓ Lombardy wine commune is situated in the far north of Italy and famous for producing red wines like Sassellas, Grumello, and Inferno.
- ✓ Friuli-Venezia wine commune is situated near the Yugoslavia border and famous for producing wines made from Pinot, Cabernet and Riesling grape varieties (wines are also named after grape varieties). Tocai is the best-known wine from Friuli-Venezia.

The Marches and Umbria

- ✓ The Marches wine commune is situated on the Adriatic coast and famous for producing wine made from Verdicchio grape.
- ✓ Umbria wine commune is situated in the central of Italy and famous for producing light delicate white wines named after the town Orvieto (available in flask-shaped bottle). Umbria wines are usually made from Trebbiano grape variety.

Wine Laws/Quality control of Italy

Vino da tavola	These are unclassified and ordinary table wines.
IGT	It stands for "Vino tavola con Indicazione Geografica Tipica" – it means the wines from a defined area.

DOC	It stands for "Denominazione di Origine Controllata". These are quality wines from an approved area.
DOCG	It stands for "Denominazione di Origine Controllata e Garantita". These are guaranteed quality wines from an approved area.

Brand Names (*or wine shippers*) of Wine

Red wines	Allegrini La Poja IGT, Amino Primitive IGT (Mark Shannon), Bartolo Mascarello Bardo DOCG, La Pupille Morellino Di Scansano DOC, Caldaro and Santa Maddalena, Valpolicella, Sangiovese, Bardolino, etc.
White wines	Kante Carso Malvasia DOC, Planeta Chardonnay IGT, Villarussiz Collio Tocai Friulano DOC, Vinnaioli Jermann Vintage Tunina IGT, Soave, Recioto, Gamellara, Trebbiano, Albana dia Romagna, etc.
Sparkling wine	Lambrusco

WINE OF GERMANY

Fine German wines are generally light and dry in nature. German white wines are made from the Riesling grape and characterized by a fresh, flowery bouquet. Nearly all of the grape varieties that are successfully grown in Germany are white. The Riesling grape variety produces the finest wines in Germany, but the variety that is most planted is the Müller-Thurgau. Müller-Thurgau is a hybrid between Riesling and Sylvaner. Müller-Thurgau ripens earlier than Riesling. There are 13 significant wine producing regions/communes (among these major 11 wine regions are given below) in Germany, the best are found along the Rhine River and Mosel River. Earlier wine produced was red, today entirely white. Beer is the national drink of Germany.

Style of German Wine

Landwein	Country wine
Trocken	Dry
Halbtrocken	Half dry
Rosewein	Rose wine
Keller	Wine cellar
Kellerei	Winery

Moselle River Area

- ✓ It is one of the most northerly viticulture areas in the world, situated along the Moselle (Mosel) River and tributaries the Saar and the Ruwer, and furnishes extremely light and delicate wines.
- ✓ Moselle wines are drawn off into green bottles, Rhine wines into brown. Other good wines are made in Baden, and in Franconia in Bavaria, noted for Stein wine. Pies porter is a well-known wine from Moselle.

Rheingau and Nahe

- ✓ Rheingau wine commune, situated on the right bank of the Rhine River, is famous for producing high quality wines made from Riesling grape varieties.
- ✓ Nahe wine commune, situated around the Bad Kreuznach on the river Nahe, is famous for producing crisp, clean, fruity and delicate wines made from Riesling, Sylvaner and Müller Thurgau grape varieties.

Rheinhessen and Rheinpfalz

- ✓ Rheinhessen wine commune, situated in between the Nahe and Rhine rivers, is famous for growing Sylvaner and Müller-Thurgau grapes. Most of the wines from here exported are called *Liebfraumilch.*
- ✓ Rheinpfalz wine commune, situated just north of Alsace, is famous for producing full-bodied grapey wines. This wine commune is also referred to as Palatinate.

Hessische-Bergstrasse and Baden

- ✓ Hessische-Bergstrasse wine commune, situated near the Worms, is famous for producing blend wines meant for immediate consumption.
- ✓ Baden wine commune stretches along the Rhine facing Alsace and famous for growing Müller-Thurgau grapes (for producing fruity white wines) and Spatburgunder grapes (for producing good red wines).

Ahr and Württemberg

- ✓ The Ahr wine commune, situated in northern Germany, is famous for producing light red wines which are low in alcohol content and are made from Spatburgunder grape.
- ✓ Württemberg wine commune is situated around the city of Stuttgart, is famous for producing more red wines than white wine. They are mixed together to make the pink Schillerwein, which the locals consume in great quantity.

Mittelrhein and würzburg

- ✓ Mittelrhein wine commune, situated around the Bonn and Koblenz, is famous for much of the wines of Sekt style. Here, it is difficult to cultivate vine because of steep slope and high winds.
- ✓ Würzburg wine commune, situated in the centre of the Franken region, is famous for fine dry white wines which are mostly made from the Sylvaner grapes. Famous Franconian wine from here is marketed in the squat Bocksbeutel and can be referred to as Steinwein.

Wine Laws/Quality Control of Germany

Deutscher Tafelwein	These are often blended and cheaper wines made in one of the four wine regions designated for table wine (Rhein, Mosel, Neckar and Overrhein)
Deutscher Landwein	These are quality wines and it can be trocken (dry) or halb-trocken (medium dry)
QbA	It stands for "Qualitätswein Bestimmter Ànbaugebiete" – these are also quality wines but of medium price range.
QmP	It stands for "Qualitätswein Mit Prädikat (Distinction)" – these are quality wines of distinction and special features. There are six categories of it: Kabinett (specific growing area), Spätlese (late harvest), Auslese (selected grapes), Beerenauslese (grapes selected from the harvest), Eiswein (ice wine) and Trockenbearnauslese (selected dry grapes).

Famous Wines (*or wine shippers*) from Germany

Red wines	Schwegler Granat, Schwegler Saphir, Meyer Nakel Spatburgunder Trocken, Nelles Spatburgunder Trocken 52, Hubber Spatburgunder Trocken Reserve, etc.
White wines	Schales Rieslaner Auslese, Weins Prum Erdener Pralat Riesling Auslese, Weil Kiedricher Grafenberg Riesling Auslese, Selbach Oster Zeltinger Sonnenuhr Riesling TBA, Von Kanitz Lorcher Krone Riesling Spätlese, etc.

WINE OF SPAIN

Spain is best known for its sherry wine. Until recently, sherry was the major Spanish wine sold; sherry is available in various styles. Today, Rioja, a leading table wine, is Spain's most widely exported wine. Ribera Del Duero, Priorato and Navarre are some famous wine regions/communes for producing fine Spanish wines. The word sherry is the anglicized version of "Jerez", the name of the town in Sherry district, Spain. All other sherry-like wines must include on their labels the name of the place of origin. These sherry-like wines are also produced in South Africa and Australia. The type of soil has a great impact on the attribute of sherry wines.

Types of Soil in Spain			
Albariza	Absorbent soil	Contain 50% chalk	Good to produce superior sherries
Barros	Soil with clay	Contain 10% chalk	Produce coarser and heavier sherries
Arenas	Sandy soil	Contain 10% clay/chalk	Produce lower quality sherries

Wine Laws/Quality Control of Spain

Vino de Mesa	These are ordinary table wines from no particular region and may be a blend of wines.
DO	It stands for "Denominación de Origen". It is a designation of geographic origin and quality of Spanish wines as laid out by the Spanish wine law.
Gran Reserva	Designation limited to wine from an excellent vintage that has been well aged before release.
Reserva	Spanish as well as Portuguese designation are used for a wine from a good vintage. In Spain the term also denotes longer ageing, while in Portugal it means that the wine has a higher than normal alcohol content.
DOC	It stands for "Denominación de Origen Calificada". The highest category of Spanish wines and intended to recognize the country's finest wine regions.

Wine Producing Regions/Communes of Spain

Rioja and Navarre

- ✓ Rioja wine commune is situated in the town of Haro and borders southern Navarre. It is famous for producing table wines, generally with 75% red wine {Tempranillo (a premier red grape), Graciano, Mazuelo and Garnacha}, 13% white wine (Viura, Garnacha and Malvasia are major white grapes) and 12% rose wine.
- ✓ The Rioja region is planted with 80% red grape varieties and 20% white grape varieties. Navarre, situated just north of Rioja, is also famous for producing table wines, like of Rioja.

Catalonia

- ✓ This wine commune is situated along the Mediterranean coast in northeastern Spain. The Alella area (just north of Barcelona) produces pale, light bodied white wine and Penedes area, south of the city, makes good quality red and white wines.
- ✓ This wine commune is famous for producing sparkling wines labelled as Espumoso (made by Méthode Champenoise).

Valencia and Alicante

- ✓ Valencia wine commune is situated in province of Valencia and Alicante wine commune is situated in the province of Alicante. These wine communes are famous for producing ordinary blended red, white and rośe table wines in bulk quantities.

La mancha and Málaga

- ✓ La Mancha wine commune, situated in Castile-La Mancha in central Spain, is famous for producing blended wines of high alcohol content.
- ✓ Mâlaga wine commune, situated in the South of Spain, is famous for producing rich, dark, sweet wines, known as *Lagrima*. It is made from Pedro Ximénez and Moscatel grapes and matured in solera system.

Galicia

- ✓ This wine commune is situated in the extreme northwest of Spain just across the border from Minhao. It is famous for producing best "Vinho Verdes" wines, green tasting wines similar to those of Portugal.

Sherry Manufacturing Process

Raw material

- ✓ The Palomino de Jerez grape is the principal grape used to make sherry. The other two used are the Pedro Ximénez (PX) and Moscatel grapes (both are white grapes), especially to produce dessert sherry and for the purpose of blending for colouring and sweetening.

Harvest

- ✓ Both white grapes are widely planted in the "Albariza" soil. Harvest takes place in the mid September. The grapes are plucked and transferred to the press houses. Harvested grapes are placed on *Esparto Mats* to dry in the sun, making these grapes very high in sugar.

Pressing

- ✓ Now grapes are placed on asbestos sheets covered with tents of polythene sheets which draw the moisture from the grapes and finally grapes are pressed, to produce the must. Remember, grapes are not destalked before actual pressing. Traditionally, *yeso* is added to the pressing, to make wine drier and acidic in nature.

Fermentation

- ✓ The must is pumped into traditional wood butts open to the air or stainless steel fermenting containers/casks. After three days of fermentation, when most of the sugar is converted into alcohol, the wine is drawn off into another cask. The wine cask should never be filled to the top, so that new wine can come in contact with air.

Fortification

- ✓ Now the wine is ready for fortification process where grape spirit like brandy is used for this purpose but the quantity used varies according to the required sherry. Due to fortification, several wines turn to vinegar and will have to be distilled whereas some others get oxidized, while several others affected by the *flor*.

Flor and its types	
At the stage of fortification, a strange scum called "flor" (flower) develops on the top surface of the sherry wine. In most wines other than sherry, this would be considered as a disaster and the wine would soon turn to vinegar. It is the result of the natural yeast peculiar to Jerez and vine grower does not have choice to deal with this *flor*. Its development produces different style of sherries, like:	
Fino	If flor develops, it produces fino style of sherries. In fino sherries, flor forms a very thick white blanket or white layer.
Amontillado	If flor develops slightly, it produces Amontillado style of sherries. In Amontillado sherries, a flor forms a thinner film or layer.
Oloroso	If flor does not develop, it produces Oloroso style of Sherries. In Oloroso sherries, there is no such flor film or layer.

Classification

- ✓ Obtained wines are classified into four basic types, i.e., *palma* (used for fino and Amontillado sherries), *raya* (used for fino and oloroso), *dos rayas* (also used for fino and oloroso) and *palo cartado* (used for the sweeter version of sherries).

Blending

- ✓ Now for the purpose of blending and maturation, new sherry is put into solera system. *Solera system* is like an inverted pyramid of wine barrels known as *butts*. In this system, old wine is constantly refreshed by the addition of younger wine of the same type.

Note.

- *Yeso* is gypsum; nowadays tartaric acid is used to make the sherry drier and acidic in nature. At the same time, it also aids in sherry clarification process.
- *Palomino must* is fermented right out but PX and Moscatel *must* have to add wine spirit as to stop the fermentation and retain the sugar content.
- The wines with flor are fortified up to 15-16 per cent alcohol by volume, whereas other wines will be fortified up to 18% alcohol by volume. The developed flor is passed through the wine to the bottom of the cask after racking, fining (sherry is fined with egg white and white Spanish earth) and filtration.

Solera System

The word *solera* refers to the butts nearest the ground, which contain fine old wine. As we have already studied that solera system is like an inverted pyramid of wine barrels (or butts). Each row of butts contains wine and are arranged in continuous tiers/stages, each tier/stage is known as *criadera* which contains progressively younger wine; the new wine goes into the last/top *criadera*. The number of criaderas in a solera system varies from producer to producer and from style to style. Wine is withdrawn from the bottom level of the solera, as per law no more than one-third wine is taken from the butt. After a few months, the wine in the solera butt is indistinguishable from what it was before. The systematic replacement (or refilling) of the *criadera* is known as the *solera system*. Remember that solera system is never used to produce a vintage sherry.

Note.

- A brand of sherry can be a mixture of several solera. In order to produce darker sherry – *vino de color* (a boiled and concentrated mixture of *must/mosto*) may be added; to produce sweeter sherry – *vino dulce* (made by adding brandy to *must/ mosto* at an early stage of fermentation) may be added.
- To sweeten and darken the brown sherries, the *mosto* of grapes dried on asbestos sheets may be added. Nowadays, *dulce apagado* (extra-sweet sherry used in blending cream sherry) is used to sweeten the sherries. Many producers also use caramel for the purpose of colouring sherries.
- *Venencia* (a soup ladle-like equipment or a cup with long handle) is used to take the sherry from butt through the bung hole in order to taste sherry before bottling.

Styles of Sherry

Fino

✓ It is a very pale light dry style of sherry made entirely from Palomino grapes. Fino sherries have a delicate aroma with a clear taste. It is less dry than Manzanilla sherries.

Amontillado

✓ It is an aged *fino* with amber colour and dry nutty flavour. These are also known as *cocktail* or *dry sherry* because it is good for making cocktails. It is also excellent for cooking purpose.

Manzanilla

✓ It is a *fino* which is pale, very dry and very crisp with slightly bitter taste. It is produced in the town of Sanlucar de Barrameda, a town nearby the sea coast (sea air affects the flavour of wine).

Oloroso

- ✓ It is a semi-sweet, full-bodied, dark gold wine (in comparison to fino and amontillado) with plenty of body and distinctly nutty flavour. *Pure oloroso* are dry but most are sweetened for international market.

Cream

- ✓ These are rich sherries with deep amber to golden brown colour. It is a totally sweet cream sherry made entirely from Pedro ximénze grapes and frequently also termed *brown sherry*.

Palo cortado

- ✓ A rare *oloroso* is not produced every year. Its body and colour is very similar to *oloroso* but the nose and dryness is similar to *amontillado*.

Montilla

- ✓ The regions of Montilla have the same *albariza soil* and it produces a style of wine similar to sherry. Fermentation takes place in traditional large earthenware jars and modern cement-lined vats. There is little need for fortification as the wines have naturally high alcohol content.

British sherry

- ✓ It is the cheapest form of sherry made from dehydrated grape juice. Water and yeast are added to the concentrates, which then ferment in the usual manner until it is fortified and sweetened.

Famous Wines (*or wine shippers*) from Spain

Red Wine	Farina Primero, Emilio Moro, Contino, Guelbenzu Evo, Lopez Cristobal, Huertas Rodrejo, Luberri, Rimarte, Mauro, Montecillo, etc.
White Wine	La Val, Jean Lean Chardonnay, Ostatu, Miguel Torres Framsola, Macia Battle, Martin Codax Burgans, Raimal Casal, Roura Chardonnay, Terras Gauda, Valdamor, etc.
Sparkling Wine	Torreblanca, Signat, Rovellars Brut, Mas Florit, Gramona Cellar Batle, etc.
Fortified Wine	Sandeman Coprimar Armada, Valdespino Solera 1842, Robles Cream Seleccion, Osborney Y Cia Bailen, Pedro Domecq Botania, etc.

WINE OF PORTUGAL

Portugal is the fifth largest wine producing country in the world. It is best known for port wines with some excellent table wines. Portugal grows a wide selection of grape varieties including – Touriga Nacional and Touriga Francesa. Other than Port, the most notable export successes for Portuguese wines have been Vinho Verde *(a high acid white wine that goes well with seafood)* and the Portuguese Rose (Mateus and Lancers). Most of the Portugese wines come from north of the river called "Tagus". There are seven regions authorized by the government to produce wine.

Wine Laws/Quality control of Portugal

Vinho de Mesa	Table wine
Vinho Regional	This is the lowest official classification of Portuguese wine, equivalent to France's *Vin De Pays.*
DC	It stands for "Denominação de Origem Controlada". The designation of geographic origin and quality of Portuguese wines is laid down by the Portuguese wine law.

Wine Producing Regions/Communes of Portugal

From seven authorized wine producing regions, four are as follows:

Minho

- ✓ This wine commune is situated in the northeast of Portugal in an area between the rivers of the Douro (to the south) and the Minho on the Spanish border (to the north).
- ✓ It is famous for producing green wines, well-known as "Vinhos verdes". White "Vinhos verdes" is very pale with a flowery bouquet and delicate lemony flavour wine whereas red Vinhos verdes is quite a hard dry wine.

Dão

- ✓ This wine commune, situated in the Região Demarcada do Dão, is famous for producing quality blended and matured wines, known as *Vinho Maduro*. Some firms do market with a well aged wine as a "Dão Reserva".

Douro river

- ✓ This wine commune/river, situated between Porto (right) and Vila Nova de Gaia (left), is famous for best known port wines but it also produces red, white and rose wines. *Mateus Rose* is a famous sparkling wine from here which is made from black grapes.

Lisbon

✓ This wine commune, situated between the foothills of Sintra and Roca Cape, is famous for *Colares wine*. The red grapes produce dark tannic wines which need many years to mature fully. *Bucelas* and *Carcavelos* are the straw coloured fresh dry white wines from here.

Port Wine Manufacturing Process

Viticulture

✓ Vines are planted at the temperature range around 50°C. Port wines could be made from forty varieties of grapes (red as well as white) but most commonly used include Codega, Verdelho, Viosinho, Rabigato and Malvasia (all red grapes) and Bastardo, Tinta Barroca and Roriz, Touriga nacional and Francesa (all white grapes).

Harvest

✓ The harvest takes place in the month of September. At the ideal moment for each state, known as "Quinta", the grapes are picked up by hands with the help of scissors and put into conical shape baskets. Each basket usually holds 75 kilos of grapes. Nowadays, machines are also used for grape harvesting.

Pressing

✓ Now grapes are crushed to produce *must*. This *must* is transferred into "Cuba" which is fitted with *autovinificator*, where a short fermentation takes place and the maximum colour of grape skin is extracted in minimum time.

Fermentation

✓ *Cuba* is a fermenting vessel which could be made up of stainless steel or concrete. The fermentation usually takes place for around 36 hours. The short fermented *must*, low in alcohol content but high in sugar content, is strained off into another vessel for fortification.

Fortification

✓ Brandy (77% alcohol by volume) is added in wine in the ratio of 20:80 for the purpose of fortification. At this point, fermentation is muted, thus producing a wine with a higher sugar level and alcohol content between 18 and 20 per cent by volume.

Note.

- On behalf of early characteristics, the new wine will be put into either blend, rare or vintage category. The blends are put into enormous wooden casks in order to prevent oxidization and too rapid evaporation.

Different Types of Port Wines

Vintage port

✓ It is a quality blend but only with wines of the same year. Vintage year is declared by the individual shippers in accordance to their experience. Vintage port is sweet, full-bodied and deep purple in colour with an alcoholic content of 20–22% by volume.

Late bottled port

✓ It is a port of a single year that has been in wood from four to six years before bottling. It is dark garnet in colour with slightly less body and bouquet than vintage port. It is ready for consumption immediately after bottling. The label must carry the vintage date and the year of bottling.

Crusted port

✓ It is a blended port that has been bottled after five or six years of maturation and then cellared until it throws a crust. Crusted port requires at least seven years of bottle aging in cellar room. This style is not sold in Portugal.

Tawny port

✓ As port ages in oaks, its colour changes from purple through ruby to a light tawny; a fine tawny port has usually been in wood for about ten years and has a velvety consistency. It can also be made by blending red and white port.

Ruby port

✓ It is ruby red in colour with sweet flavour. It is a blend of old and young wine and is usually bottled and sold after around four years of maturation. The old wine contributes softness and character, whereas the young wine incorporates fresh fruitiness. It is chilled before bottling to precipitate any sediment, so lengthens its shelf-life.

White port

✓ It is made from white grapes. *Taylor's fine white port* is a perfect example of white port wine. It is available in various forms from dry to sweet and light straw to golden in colour. It is drunk as an aperitif, especially its drier version.

Vintage character

✓ It is a quality blended port of different quality ports of more than one year and is matured in wood. It is less expensive than vintage or late bottled vintage port. It is ready for immediate drinking after bottling. It is not necessary to carry vintage date on these ports.

Note.

- Vintage port throws sediments, thus it must be handled (or decanted) carefully so that sediments do not get disturbed. Whereas late bottled port does not require decanting.
- Port that has been in wood for at least seven years then bottled, must carry the vintage date, year of bottling, designation (like *reserve*) and also state that the port has been aged in cask.
- Tawnies that have been aged for 10, 20, 30, or over 40 years must carry an indication of age, the year of bottling and also state that the port has been aged in cask or not.

Famous Wines (*or wine shippers*) from Portugal

Red Wine	Some famous red wines include Casa Burmester, Caves Alianca Garrafeira, Faluatercius, Luis Pato Vinha Pan, Niepoort Passadouro, etc.
White Wine	Some famous white wines include Dona Paterna, JP Vinhos Catarina, Murganheira Cerceal, Niepoort Redoma Reserva, Quinta De Murta, etc.

MADEIRA

It is a name of fortified wine which comes from the island of Madeira in the Atlantic Ocean. In this island, the vines are grown on terraced hillsides on Trellis, similar to those for *vinho verde*. The term *terrace* is used for small plots for growing grapes. It is known as *poios* in Madeira Island.

Madeira Manufacturing Process

Viticulture

- ✓ The grapes are harvested on overhead pergolas (*pergolas* means garden) in order to protect it from the scorching sunrays which could bluntly affect the ripening of grapes. An optimum ripening temperature for grapes is around 20°C or slightly higher.

Pressing

- ✓ Grapes are plucked and pressed to obtain the *mosto* (or grape juice/*must*). This *mosto* is transported to Funchal (the capital of island) for the purpose of fermentation. Afterwards, the fermented *mosto* is termed as "Vino Claro" (or fermented juice).

Fortification

- ✓ The obtained Vino Claro is fortified with the addition of locally made grape brandy (of 96 proof) in order to bring its alcoholic content between 17 – 20 per cent by volume.
- ✓ The sweet Madeiras are fortified before being put into the Estufa whereas dry Madeiras are put into Estufa after the completion of fermentation but prior to fortification. *Estufa* is a large central heated hall, also known as hot room/chamber.

Estufagem

- ✓ *Estufagem* is a process which develops the same caramel-like flavour into wine that the long sea voyages used to produce. In Estufa room, the casks of Madeira (also known as *pipe*) are very gradually heated to a maximum of 50°C.
- ✓ Wines are held at this temperature up to three months and then very slowly cooled to normal temperature. This process makes the Madeira to withstand extremes of temperature and resist oxidation.

Blending

- ✓ Now Madeira is blended before bottling; usually by *solera system*.

Styles of Madeira

Generally, there are four main styles of Madeira wines and each takes its name from the grape variety, i.e., Sercial, Verdelho, Bual and Malmsey. All these Madeira wines are fortified in nature and blended by *solera system*. A brief description of each is given below.

Sercial

✓ It is a pale-dry white Madeira wine with a slight almond flavour. It has a very dry finish that makes it an excellent aperitif wine which is served chilled or with consommé soup. It is quite harsh when young and takes a long time to mature.

Verdelho

✓ It is a darker, golden wine with a smoky flavour. It is soft and sweet and benefited from even a few months bottle aging. This can be the most elegant of the Madeira's and considered a classic wine to serve as an aperitif or served with consommé soup and other soups.

Bual

✓ A velvety brown coloured Madeira wine with a rich flavour. It is slightly darker in colour and sweet in nature in comparison to Verdelho Madeira wine and often found suitable to be drunk as a digestive drink or at the end of the meal or on its own.

Malmsey

✓ A dark rich wine with soft sweet flavour. It takes its name from the grape, Malvazia. The sharp tangy finish balances the sweetness and many people consider it one of the world's supreme wine. It is best suited to serve as digestive or after dinner drink.

Note.

- There is also vintage Madeira wines available in the market but found rarely. A few Madeiras are blended and marketed under the shipper's trade name. Example, *Rainwater* and *London*.

KEY TERMS

Terroir driven	:	Wine making techniques that are completely based on local area/ local practices.
Generic wines	:	Wine name based on the place of origin like *Château la tour*.
Maceration	:	Like infusion but in it mashed fruits are soaked directly into pure alcohol to extract flavour.
Claret	:	An English term used in England for red Bordeaux wines.
Cru	:	French term that literally means growth. It may also refer to a winery or vineyard.

Château	:	French term (used in Bordeaux) for a piece of land like Château Latour.
Domaine	:	French term (used in Burgundy) for a piece of land/vineyard like *Domaine de Chevalier.*
Saignée	:	French term (for bleed) associated with the practice of removing some of the juice from *must* in order to more deeply concentrate the phenolics, colour and flavour compounds of the red wine
Eiswein	:	German term for dessert wine (also known as *ice wine*) — a wine made from frozen grapes.
Flor	:	Yeast sometimes seen during the fermentation period on the surface of sherry wine.
Vinho verde	:	Portugese term for green wine.
Venencia	:	Soup ladle-like equipment used to take out sherry from barrel in order to taste it.
Estufa	:	Large central heated chamber for Madeira wines.

REVIEW QUESTIONS

1. Elucidate French wine laws that implement to control wine quality.
2. What is solera system? Classify style of sherry wines, explain each briefly.
3. Differentiate between sparkling and champagne wine. Enlist any ten famous brands of champagne.
4. What is port wine? Classify style of port wines and explain each briefly.

New Wine World

Objectives

Students will be able to:

- explicate new wine producing countries of the world; and
- elucidate famous wine communes and wine brands of the new wine world.

NEW WINE WORLD

The term *new wine world* refers to all those wine producing countries which have been recently recognized: USA, Chile, Argentina, South Africa, New Zealand, India, Australia, Bulgaria, Greece, Hungary, Romania, England, Switzerland, Brazil and so forth.

Straightforwardly, new world wines refer to all those wines that are produced outside the conventional wine growing areas of Europe and the Middle East, in particular from Argentina, Australia, Chile, New Zealand, South Africa and the United States.

Wines in the new world are *fruit driven*, thus often label based on the *varietal wines*. Here, wine makers primarily refer to cultured yeast during the fermentation process. In the new wine world, wine makers transfer *must* into oak barrels during fermentation and induce *malolactic fermentation*.

WINE OF USA

Traditionally, American wine makers were satisfied with quantity production and imitations—largely in name only—of foreign wines. But since the mid-1960s the quality of domestic wine industry has grown, and many excellent and some superb wines have been made in the United States. Low alcoholic wines of America are known as *soft wines*. The most famous wine producing regions are given below.

California

- ✓ It is the nation's richest wine producing state, followed by New York and the Pacific Northwest states. In California and the Northwest, grapes of the Old World species, *Vitis vinifera,* are grown, and some of the varieties produced from these grapes have come to rival the finest French wines.

San Francisco

- ✓ Some of the best wines come from the Napa Valley, north of San Francisco. Distinguished wines from this region include *Cabernet Sauvignon, Chardonnay* and *Zinfandel*.

New York

- ✓ Most of the eastern American wines are from New York State, especially from the Finger Lakes region. Traditionally, most of New York's wines were made mainly from native grapes such as Concords, Catawbas, and the southern Scuppernong, but nowadays these wines are produced from the Old World species and hybrids.

Chile and Argentina

- ✓ The best wines from South America come from Chile which produces both fortified and table wines. Argentina is another significant producer of wine. For more detail on wine of Chile and Argentina, please refer to wine of South America.

Quick Scroll	
Napa Valley	This wine commune, situated in Napa County (California), is famous for producing finest red wine which is mostly made from Cabernet and Brunache grape varieties.
Sonoma Valley	This wine commune, situated in Sonoma County (California), is famous for producing Italian style wines because it has strong Italian connection due to its location.

Famous Wines (*or wine shippers*) from USA

Red Wine	Bedell Cellars Merlot, Boyer Pinot Noir, Case Pinot Noir, Château Julien Sangiovese, Clayton Lodi Zinfandel, Kenwood Lodi Old Vine Zinfandel, Boyer Arroyo Seco Syrah, etc.
White Wine	Argyile Reserve Riesling, Amity Pinot Noir, Bernardus Chardonnay, Bernardus Sauvignon Blanc, Château Julien Chardonnay, Caramel Road Chardonnay, Lucas Lodi Chardonnay, etc.
Sparkling Wine	Lenz Winery Sparkling Wine, Oasis Vineyard Cuvee D' Or, Pindar Vineyard Cuvee Rare, Sakonnet Vineyard Samson Brut, Westport Vineyard Blanc De Noirs, etc.
Fortified Wine	Taylor California Cellars Reserve Marsala, Stony Ridge Sangiovese Robusto Dessert Wine, Savannah Chanel Amador Muscat Canelli, St. Amant Lodi LBV Port, Renaissance North Yuba Muscat, etc.

Rose Wine	Vino Noceto Rosato Di Sangiovese, Ventana Vineyard Monterey Rose, Sonora Sierra Foothills Vintage Port, Carmela Vineyard Blush, etc.
Sweet Wine	White Hall Vineyard Soliterre, Story Vinery Amador Sweet Mission, Naylor Vineyard and Wine Cellar Vidal Ice Wine, Château Grand Traverse Ice Wine, Camas Winery Tej Hopped Mead, etc.

WINE OF SOUTH AMERICA

South America is a continent located in the western hemisphere. It is a counterpart of new wine world but the flavour of South American wines contains the characteristics of both new wine world and old wine world that makes it distinctive and special from other wine producing countries. Chile and Argentina are two significant wine communes of South America; a brief description of each is given below.

Chile

Chilean wines are made in the South America. It is famous for producing fortified and table wines. The most common grapes grown in Chile include Cabernet Sauvignon, Merlot and Carmenère. So far, Chile has remained free of *Phylloxera louse* which means that the country's grapevines do not need to be *grafted*. Few famous red and white Chilean wines are given below:

Famous wines (or wine shippers) from Chile

Red Wine	Some famous red wines include Montes Alpha M, Calitera Merlot, Carmen Petite Sirah, Clos Robert Merlot, La Palma Merlot, etc.
White Wine	Some famous white wines include Santa Monica Chardonnay, Caliterrs Chardonnay, Casa Donoso Reserve Chardonnay, Veramonte Chardonnay, Pionero Sauvignon Blanc, etc.

Argentina

Argentina is more famous for producing red varietal wines than white varietal wines. The primary wine production area is in the Mendoza Valley. Few famous red and white Argentinean wines are given below:

Famous wines (or wine shippers) from Argentina

Red Wine	Some famous red wines include Norton Barbera, Putini Malbec, Q Merlot, San Telmo Merlot , Santa Silva Barbera, etc.

White Wine	Some famous white wines include Provia Chardonnay, Santa Julia Torrontes, Vinterra Chardonnay, Valentine Bianchi Sauvignon Blanc, Trapiche Medalla Chardonnay, etc.

WINE OF SOUTH AFRICA

South Africa is a country on the southernmost tip of the African continent. It is one of the prominent wine producing countries in the Southern Hemisphere with more than 300 years of wine making history. Wines of Constantia vineyard, near Cape Town, are considered one of the greatest wines in the world. South Africa is considered counterpart of new wine world and its famous wine communes are given below.

Constantia

- ✓ This wine commune, situated close to Cape Town, is famous for producing matured fine quality wines made from Chenin Blanc (it is locally known as *Steen-Pinotage), Cabernet Sauvignon* and *Shiraz grapes*.

Durbanville

- ✓ This wine commune, situated in the hills to the north of Cape Town, is famous for producing quality red wines and liquors. Here, two properties are defined as wine estate, i.e. Meerendal and Diemersdal.

Stellenbosch

- ✓ This wine commune, situated around the town of Stellenbosch and Strand, is famous for producing quality white wines (come from west) as well as red wines (come from east).

Paarl and Piquet-berg

- ✓ Paarl wine commune, situated in the Berg river valley, is famous for producing white wines. Piquet-berg wine commune, situated on the west coast, is famous for producing dry white and dessert wines.

Little Karoo and Overberg

- ✓ Little Karoo wine commune, stretching from the town of Montagu in west, is famous for producing muscatel wines. Overberg wine commune surrounds the town of Caledon and is famous for producing white table wines and dessert wines made from Muscat grapes locally known as *Hanepoot*.

Robertson and Swatland

✓ Robertson wine commune, situated in the Breede river valley, is famous for producing Muscat dessert wines. Swatland wine commune, centred on the town of the Malmesbury is famous for producing dry white wines and distilling wine.

Tulbagh and Worcester

✓ Tulbagh wine commune, a small area surrounding the town of Tulbagh, is famous for producing high quality white wines and sherry style wines. Worcester wine commune, situated around the town of Worcester, is famous for producing dry white wines and dessert wines.

Famous Wines (*or wine shippers*) from South Africa

Red Wine	Backsberg Merlot Shiraz, Boschendal Merlot, Delheim Merlot (it is also made from Shiraz), Fairveiw Shiraz, Genesis Shiraz, etc.
White Wine	Glen Carlou, Konu Chardonnay, Longridge Chardonnay, Jordan Chardonnay, Hartenberg Chardonnay, etc.
Sparkling wines	Boschendal Brut Mcc, Graham Beck Blanc De Blanc Mcc, Jc Le Roux Chardonnay Mcc, Jc Le Roux Pinot Noir Mcc, Pongracz Mcc, etc.

WINE OF NEW ZEALAND

New Zealand is especially noted for its Sauvignon Blanc; along with this, Pinotage and Pinot noir grape varieties are also planted to produce wines. Vines were introduced in 1819 by Europeans. New Zealand's wines are sold by the name of the grape variety (or grapes used to produce wine) and the name of the producer. New Zealand comprises two islands, North Island and South Island. Both islands offer a wide variety of generally cool climates that are influenced by the ocean. A brief description of each island is given below.

North Island

✓ It includes Auckland, Hamilton, Gisborne, Napier, Hastings and Wellington. This Island (or all these wine communes) situated on the same latitude as Tasmania and is famous for producing white wines.

✓ Due to heavy rainfall and cyclonic damage, North Island has high humidity level causing grape rot problem. Here, wine production was started around Auckland and nowadays has spread to Gisborne, Hawkes Bay and Tolaga Bay on the eastern coast.

South Island

- ✓ It includes Nelson, Blenheim, Christchurch and Dunedin. This island has two well known wine communes – Marlborough and Canterbury. Marlborough is the largest exporter of New Zealand's wine.
- ✓ In general, Marlborough has cooler climatic conditions with plenty of sunshine and a lighter rainfall. The grape varieties which produce best wines here include Müller– Thurgau, Chardonnay, Sauvignon Blanc, Sémillon, Cabernet Sauvignon and Chenin Blanc.

WINES OF INDIA

The popularity of wine in India has started growing rapidly. Along with it, India is also experiencing a boom in *wine tourism.* There are more than 30 vineyards in India, among these Château D'Ori ; Château de Banyan; Costa and Company; Grover Vineyards; Château Indage Group; ND Vineyards; Riona Wines Pvt. Ltd.; Shaw Wallace; Sula Vineyards; Terroir India Wineries; Vinbros and Co; Zampa Vineyards; Good Earth; Indian Ambience; Vinsura; York; Mountain View; Soul Tree are several famous wineries. Most famous Indian wine producing regions/communes are given below.

Maharashtra and Karnataka

- ✓ Well known wine producing areas in Maharashtra include Nasik, Sangli, Sholapur, Satara, Ahmednagar and Pune. On the other side Nandi Hills nearby Bangalore is well known wine producing area in Karnataka. Famous wineries include Grover Vineyard, Naka Wines and Nandi Wine Valley.

Mizoram and Deccan Plateau

- ✓ In Mizoram, the well known wine producing area is Champhai wine region. The Champhai and Hnahlan Grape Winery Ltd. is a famous winery from here with its famous brand, Zawlaidi.
- ✓ Deccan plateau is one of the major wine producing region of India which is divided into three sub-regions – northern part (Nasik – Sula Vineyard is famous from here); central part (around Narayangaon – Château Indage and Four Season vineyards are famous here) and southern part (centered around Sangli and Bijapur– Krishna Valley Wine Park and Nasik Wine Park are famous).

Goa and Others

- ✓ Goa is famous for producing port-like fortified wines using Vitis labrusca grape varieties such as Bangalore Blue is a famous brand. Famous wineries include Big Banyan Wines, Tonia Liquor Industries, and Vinicola.

✓ Apart from the above regions, several other well known grape growing areas are found in the states of Himachal Pradesh, Tamil Nadu, Punjab, Jammu and Kashmir and Andhra Pradesh (around Hyderabad).

Famous Wine Growers of India			
Grover Vineyard	Doddaballapur	Nandi Hills	Karnataka
Nandi Valley	Bangalore	Nandi Hills	Karnataka
Naka Wines	Bangalore	Nandi Hills	Karnataka
Château Indage	Narayangaon	Central Deccan Plateau	Maharashtra
Deccan Plateau Winery	Haveli (Near Pune)	Central Deccan Plateau	Maharashtra
Four Seasons	Baramati	Central Deccan Plateau	Maharashtra
Château d' Ori	Dindori	Northern Deccan Plateau	Maharashtra
Indus Wines	Igatpuri	Northern Deccan Plateau	Maharashtra
Mercury Winery	Ozar	Northern Deccan Plateau	Maharashtra
Mountain View Wines	Nashik	Northern Deccan Plateau	Maharashtra
York Winery	Gangavarhe	Northern Deccan Plateau	Maharashtra
ND Wines	Dindori	Northern Deccan Plateau	Maharashtra
Sula Vineyard	Govardhan	Northern Deccan Plateau	Maharashtra
Vallee-de-vin	Igatpuri	Northern Deccan Plateau	Maharashtra
Hampi Heritage	Bijapur	Southern Deccan Plateau	Maharashtra
Nandi Valley	Near Sangli	Southern Deccan Plateau	Maharashtra
Krishna Valley Wine	Bijapur	Southern Deccan Plateau	Maharashtra
Alpine Wineries	Kaveri valley	Southern Deccan Plateau	Maharashtra

Famous Wines from India

Red Wine	Some famous Indian red wines include Anarkali, Tantra-Baramati, Sula Cabernet/Shiraz, Le Vino, Riviera, Fouray, La Reserve, etc.
White Wine	Some famous Indian white wines include Chhabri, Soma, Sauvignon Blanc, Princess, Riviera, Aurum, Chenin Blanc, Madeira, 28 Carats, Casal white, etc.
Sparkling Wine	Some famous Indian sparkling wines include Joie (cuvée close non-vintage), Marquis de Pompadour or MDP (Brut), Omar Khayam (Brut), Sula Brut, Sula Seco, Apple Champagne, etc.

WINE OF AUSTRALIA

Australia is the seventh largest wine producing country in the world. There are over 1100 wineries in Australia and wine is produced in many regions that are widely spread across the southern half of the country. Each of these wine regions/communes has different climate and soil and should be considered distinctly different as Bordeaux and Burgundy in France; and California and Washington in the United States. Australia is in the southern hemisphere and its growing season is the reverse of the United States and the European countries. Harvest begins in March and continues into April. Some famous Australian wine regions/communes are given below.

Hunter Valley and Mudgee

- ✓ Hunter Valley is situated in the north of Sydney and famous for its quality table wines. Generally, Cabernet sauvignon and Shiraz grape varieties are used here to produce colour-rich red wines.
- ✓ Mudgee is also located on the same latitude as the Hunter Valley but about 130 kilometres further west. It is famous for producing rich fruity and longevity wines.

Riverina and Goulburn Valley

- ✓ Riverina is situated in the south of New South Wales. It is famous for producing good quality (because wines are made from premium quality grapes) everyday drinking wines.
- ✓ Goulburn Valley, situated around the town of Hag, is famous for producing quality red and white table wines of distinctive character.

Great Western and Ruther Glen

- ✓ The name Great Western already suggests the location of this wine region. It is famous for producing fine quality sparkling wine.
- ✓ Ruther Glen, situated in the northeast of Melbourne, is famous for producing dessert wines. The liquor Muscatel and Tokay of Baileys and Morris are luscious sweet wines.

Barossa Valley and Great Southern

- ✓ Barossa Valley, situated in New South Wales, is famous for producing table wines in bulk quantity along with sparkling wines and brandy.
- ✓ Great Southern, situated in Western Australia, is famous for producing fine quality wines primarily made from Cabernet and Shiraz grape varieties.

Margaret River and Others

- ✓ Margaret River, situated in Western Australia, is famous for producing top quality wines made from Cabernet Sauvignon, Riesling, Sémillon and Chardonnay grape varieties.
- ✓ The above listed wine regions (listed before great southern) are located in New South Wales. In other wine regions one can include Victoria, Riverland, Clare, Coonawarra, McLaren vale, etc.

Famous Wines (*or wine shippers*) from Australia

Red Wine	Some famous red wines include Glenguim Merlot, Barwang Shiraz, Brown Brothers Barber, Giaconda Pinot Noir, Wignalls Pinot Noir, Plantagener Shiraz, Salitage Pinot Noir, etc.
White Wine	Some famous white wines include Bimbadgen Semillon, Bloodwood Chardonnay, Cafield Chenin Blanc, Voyage Chardonnay, Westfield Chardonnay, Paul Conti Chardonnay, etc.
GSM Blends	It is a name commonly used in Australia for a red wine consisting of a blend of Grenache (it contributes alcohol, warmth and fruitiness), Shiraz (or Syrah contributes colour and body) and Mourvèdre (contributes elegance, structure and acidity).

WINES OF EAST EUROPE

East Europe (or Eastern Europe) is the eastern part of the European continent. Predominantly, Bulgaria, Greece, Hungary and Romania are four major wine producing countries from East Europe. Eastern Central Europe produces a huge variety of wine from powerful reds to the famous dessert wines of Tokaji. A brief description of major wine producing regions of East Europe is given below.

Bulgaria

- ✓ It is one of the world's largest wine producing country famous for Gumza, Dimiat, Pamid, Muscat, Misket, Mavrud and Melnik wines.
- ✓ South Bulgaria is well known for producing red wines while north Bulgaria is famous for white wines. The Black Sea area, Bourgas, Pomorie and Verna are a few famous wine growing regions here.

Greece

- ✓ It is one of the oldest wine growing regions in the world. Greek white wines may be more consistent but the Greek red wines are considered the best.

Hungary

- ✓ It is also a world famous wine growing region best known for white dessert wine Tokay (Tokaji) and Bull's Blood (Egri Bikaver), a full-bodied red wine.

Romania

- ✓ It is situated in South Eastern Europe (nearby the Black Sea) and best known as *vine homeland* of Europe. Famous grape/vine varieties include – Zghihara de Husi, Cramposia de Dragasani, Galbena de Odobesti, Feteasca alba, Feteasca neagra, Babeasca, and Tamâioasa româneasca.

Famous Wines (or wine shippers) from East Europe

Bulgaria	Famous wines include Assenovgrad Merlot Reserve, Damianiza Melnik, Russe Azbuka Merlot, Russe Chardonnay, Sakar Azbuka Merlot, etc.
Greece	Famous wines include Sigalas Mezzo, Semeli Château Semeli, Oenoforos Asprolithi, Antonopunos Adoli Ghis, Château Carras Cotes De Meliton, etc.
Hungary	Famous wines include Aliscavin Boraszati Rt. Cabernet Franc, Bock Pince Villanyi Cabernet Sauvignon, GIA Kft Egri Bikaver, Zwack Kft Egri Bikaver, Takler Pince Szekszasdi Merlot, etc.
Romania	Famous wines include Dealul-Mare Premiat Merlot, Dealul-Mare Premiat Pinot Noir, Murfatlar Pinot Gris, Rovit Special Reserve Pinot Noir, Tirnave Vlajmuscat Attonel, etc.

OTHER WINE PRODUCING COUNTRIES

Apart from the countries of old wine world, new wine world and East European continent, still there are many countries that are producing range of wines from the last so many decades. Some of these are given below with their wine communes and famous brands of wine.

England

The Romans introduced wine making to the United Kingdom. England is a major customer of *clarets* (i.e. red wines) from Bordeaux, France. Here, the blended white and red sweet wines are known as *cream wines.* The famous wine regions of England include Hampshire, Sussex, Kent, Essex, Suffolk, Berkshire, Cambridge shire, Wiltshire, Dorset, Devon, Somerset, Cornwall, Yorkshire, Shropshire, Derbyshire, Leicestershire and Lancashire.

Famous red wines	Biddenden Ortega, Chapel Down Bacchus, Chiltern Valley Dry, Wooldings Vintage Port, Nutborne and so forth.

Switzerland

It is famous for producing several white wines and a few red wines (especially Merlot). The famous wine regions of Switzerland include Lake, Geneva, Valais, Ticino and Neuchâtel.

Famous wines (or wine shippers) from Switzerland

Red Wine	Provins Cobassieres Rouge, Bon Pere Germanier Syrah Cayas, Les Perrieres Peissy Gamay, Simon Maye Et Fils Chamoson Syrah, Duprez Et Fils Coteau Du Lully Gamaret, etc.
White Wine	Imesch Petite Arvine, Yvorne Château Maiso Blanche, Provins Vieilles Vignes Blanc, Les Perrieres Peissy Chasselas, Fendant Le Murettes (Robert Gilliard), etc.

Brazil

Majority of Brazilian wine comes from the mountainous regions of the most southern state of the Brazilian Federation, called *Rio Grande do Sul*. Currently, local winemakers supply the market with wines of outstanding quality.

Typical Wine Terms	
Edelzwicker	A German term *Edelzwicker* is used to denote a dry light wine that is a blend of several white grape varieties (mostly used are Tokay D' Alsace, Sylvaner and Chasselas) from the Alsace region.
Reserve	Reserve or *cuvée exceptionelle* is a term used at the discretion of the maker to indicate top quality wines.
Vendange tardive	A term used for grapes that have been harvested late in the season so that the wine will have a more concentrated sweetness. It is equivalent to the German term "Spatlese".
Eaux de vie	It means orchard fruits and wild berries from the mountain forests and used to produce many famous "Alcools Blancs" in Alsace.
Sur lie	This term is used for wine which is directly transferred from the cask to bottle without being filtered. Thus, it possesses freshness and slight effervescence. It is usually made from Muscadet grapes.

KEY TERMS

Fruit driven	:	Wine making techniques whereby emphasis is placed on extracting flavour from fruit.
Varietal wines	:	Wine name based on the name of grape/s used.
Malolactic fermentation	:	Secondary fermentation.
Catawbas	:	Grape of New York.
Phylloxera louse	:	Vine disease.
Graft/grafting	:	Horticultural technique in which tissue of one plant is inserted into the tissue of another plant so that they may join together.
Wine tourism	:	Tourism type (or attraction type) whereby people move to see viticulture and vinification.
Vitis Labrusca	:	Vine family from old world species.
Bull's Blood	:	Egri Bikaver, a full-bodied red wine from Hungary.
GSM blends	:	An Australian term for a red wine consisting of a blend of Grenache, Shiraz and Mourvédre.
Cream wines	:	In England, the blended white and red sweet wines.

REVIEW QUESTIONS

1. Write a short note on Chilean wines.
2. Enlist major grapes used to produce Indian wines.
3. Enlist any ten internationally famous wines from New Zealand.
4. What is GSM blend?

18 CHAPTER

Brewed Beverage: Beer

Objectives

Students will be able to:

- explicate major brewed beverages, i.e., beer and sake; and
- enlighten major beer and sake types with brand names.

BREWED BEVERAGE

The term *brewed beverage* refers to beer, sake and other similar beverages. In reality, the term *brew* is concerned with manufacturing process whereby cereal/s or grain/s is processed either via boiling, infusion, steeping and lastly passes through fermentation process. Unlike malt for beer, rice for sake does not contain *amylase* that is necessary for converting starch to sugar and so it must undergo multiple fermentations. Remember, tea and coffee are also prepared by brewing process but it is not an alcoholic product.

Primary brewed product is *beer* produced from malted barley whereas *sake* (a rice beer or rice wine) is made from rice. Remember, beer is a national drink of Germany, on the other side sake is a national drink of Japan. Both these beverages are available in different varieties.

BEER

Beer is a low alcoholic beverage made from malted barley, hops, sugar, yeast and liquor (brewery/brewer's water). Remember, some waters are suitable for ale but not for beer, and vice versa. For example, hard water is not suitable for making certain kinds of beers. Because the pH level between 5.0 and 5.8 is good for beer making. Apart from it, mineral contents are also significant in beer making, as it contributes taste to beer.

Beer Composition

Water	85-90%
Carbohydrates	03-04%
Proteins	0.4-0.5%
Alcohol	03-05%
CO_2	0.4-0.5%
Minerals	0.1-0.2%

Other starchy cereals such as corn and rice may also be used to produce beer. Beer is considered a refreshing and stimulating beverage. It is available in different forms: ale (top fermented), lager (bottom fermented), draught (or draft beer), stout, porter, bock, pilsner and so forth.

Beer Manufacturing Process

Beer Hops

- Cairt
- Sussex
- Worcester shirk
- Saaz
- Spalt
- Tettnang
- Hallertau
- Amarillo
- Cascade
- Willamette
- Galena
- Vanguard
- Simcoe
- Perle

Raw material — The basic raw materials required for beer making are barley, sugar, brewer's yeast, hops and liquor treated water, used often after taking permission from Local Corporation. In US, *malt adjunct* or *grain adjunct* is also added in addition to malt.

Green malting — Collected, sorted and screened barley is soaked in water which cause *germination*, thus converting the starch into sugar. The resultant malt is termed *green malt*.

Malting — The collected green malt is then heated in the kiln to stop further germination; this heating process is known as *malting*. The resultant product is termed *malted barley*.

Brewing — Now, the malted barley is ground into *grist* and then sent with water for second time heating. Afterwards, the resultant product *wort* (or unfermented beer) is sent with hops for third time heating into brewing kettle.

Fermentation — At this moment, the collected wort goes for fermentation by "pitching the wort" (it means adding brewer's yeast to the wort). Ale or top fermented beers are fermented at 18-25°C with *Saccharomyces cerevisiae* yeast *(or brewer's yeast)*, whereas *lager* or bottom fermented beers are fermented at 7-12°C with *Saccharomyces uvarum* yeast. The resultant fermented product will be green beer.

Lagering — It is concerned with storing and conditioning of beer. This step matures or ripens the *green beer* and mellows its flavour. Both lager and ale beers are matured in stainless-steel tanks. *Ale beers* are usually matured (between 40-55°F) for more than a few weeks whereas *lager beers* (between 32-45°F) may be kept for a few months for maturation, usually four to five weeks.

Filtration — *Ale beers* may be filtered before use but many *draught ales* are not, so it must be left to settle before being consumed. Whereas *lager beers* are carbonated, filtered and directly bottled.

Bottling — Generally, *ale beers* are filled into bottles, *lager beers* are filled into kegs, bottles or cans and *draught beers* are mostly filled into large size barrels.

Pasteurization — After packing/bottling, most canned and bottled beers are stabilized by *pasteurizing* process. This pasteurization process takes place between the temperature ranges of 140-150°F for about 20-25 minutes. This heating process kills bacteria plus any remaining yeast cells.

Note. The manufacturing process for ale and lager beer starts to differentiate after brewing stage. After brewing, the hops are strained out and the *wort* is cooled. For *ales* the wort is cooled to a range of 10°C to 21°C whereas for lager beers, the wort is chilled to a range of 3°C to 10°C.

Types of Beer

Ale

✓ These are top fermented beers which are sweet in nature with full body and fruity taste. These beers are brewed with top fermenting yeast (*Saccharomyces Cerevisiae).* Famous ales include bitters, pale ales, porters, stouts, barley wines, Trappist, alt, etc. Most of the English beers are ale beers.

Lager (it means to store or stock)

✓ These are bottom fermented beers which are thinner in body with dry and subtle flavours. These beers are brewed with bottom fermenting yeast (*Saccharomyces uvarum*). Lagers include bocks, doppelbocks, Munich, Vienna, Märzen, Pilsners, etc. Most of Australian and Indian beers are lager beers.

Draught

✓ These are freshly gassed beers and also known as *draft beers*. These beers are filled in sterilized kegs and are allowed to mature in the cellar room before it is sold for consumption. Sometimes *priming* is added, in order to encourage the secondary fermentation in the cask itself. Cobra gun is mostly used to serve draught beer in bars.

Others

✓ Others include canned beer, fruit beer, pilsner beer, reduced alcohol beer, *Hefeweizen* (it is made with the addition of malted barley), Witbier (it is a *white beer* made from herbs or fruits instead of or in addition to hops) and so forth.

SERVICE OF BEER

At the time of serving *ale* and *lager beer* (bottled beer), take beer goblet, tilt it to 45 degree angle thereafter pour beer slowly without creating froth. *Draught beers* are usually kept in store room in the casks then pumped; after passing through the chilling unit it comes into beer bar from where stewards serve it with the help of "Cobra Gun". It can also be served directly through the casks with the help of pitcher or jug. Draught beer can create more froth in the glass than that of bottled beer. *Canned beer* is always sold chilled in their own original containers. People mostly prefer to take canned beers with themselves and drink directly from the cans. The standard beer serving guideline is given below.

Serving glass — Beer can be served in a range of beer glasses like beer goblet, beer mug, beer tanker and in pilsner glass. Beer goblet is mainly used in formal restaurants. Beer mug and beer tanker is mostly used in pubs and beer bars. The holding capacity of both glasses is high in comparison to beer goblet. Pilsner glass is used to serve pilsner beer. Paris Goblet is used for brown, pale and strong ales. Ensure glasses should be free from cracks, chips, smudge, etc., and must be handled by base or stem; but never with brim.

Serving temperature — All kinds of beer like ale, lager and draught are served chilled. The ideal temperature for serving beer is 12-14°C. Steward should never add crushed ice or ice cubes in the beer glass because it will spoil the taste of beer by absorbing CO_2 (carbon dioxide).

Brand Names of Beer		
Country	**Bottom Fermented Beers**	**Top Fermented Beers**
Australia	Foster's, Hahn premium and Victoria	Cooper's export, James Boag's and Redback
Germany	Beck's, Berliner, Hansa and Dunkelgold	Boten ale, Dom Kolsch and Gleumes
Canada	Labatt ice, Molson dry and Moosehead	Le cheval blanc (rousse and amber) and Maudite
Belgium	Heartog jan pilsner, Loburg and Maes cool	Aubel, Bacchus, Hapkin and Campus gold
US	Brooklyn, Blue ice and Budweiser	Red Seal ale, Celis grand cru and Widmer

SAKE

It is a slightly sweet Japanese wine that is brewed from fermented rice. It is made from rice and usually served hot or warm. It is also called rice wine or rice beer. Rice wine is a potent wine which resembles the flavour and appearance of sherry. Sake is classified on the basis of degree of *rice polishing* and addition of *brewer's alcohol* content. But broadly, it can be classified into two groups:

Standard Sakes (or Pure Rice Sake)

✓ This term refers to all those sake types that are produced from the fermentation of rice and no sign of brewer's alcohol is added. Standard sakes contain two main elements, i.e., extended milled and polished rice and distilled alcohol (it is added after brewing the sake).

✓ Standard sake types include Junmai, Junmai Ginjo and Junmai Daiginjo.

Processed Sakes (or Fortified Sake)

✓ The standard sake can be post-processed in many different ways. The final processing of the sake is just as important as the quality of rice used and the amount of brewer's alcohol added because it determines the final characteristics of the sake.

✓ Processed sake types include Honjozo, Ginjo, Daiginjo.

Classification of Sakes		
Degree of rice polishing	**Standard sakes/Pure rice sakes (no brewer's alcohol)**	**Processed sakes/Fortified sakes (with addition of brewer's alcohol)**
50% polish	Junmai Daiginjo	Daiginjo
60% polish	Junmai Ginjo	Ginjo
70% polish	Junmai	Honjozo

Service of Sake

Service glass	Sake is usually served in tiny porcelain cups or bowls called as "Sakazuki or Ochoko" which hold a little more than one ounce. Sakes are preferred to be filled up to the brim. Traditionally, sakes are usually drunk from small cups called *choko*. These are poured into this choko from the ceramic flasks called *tokkuri* but nowadays, footed glasses made specifically for premium sakes are preferred.
Service temperature	Sake is usually served warm (between the range 100-110°F) because at this temperature, sake's heady bouquet is released. Sake is a versatile beverage therefore, it can be served chilled, or on the rocks with a twist of lemon. It can also be an alternative to dry vermouth in a martini, called "Sakini".
Serving style	To warm sake, place the opened bottle into a pot of boiling water and remove it when temperature reaches around 100-110°F. According to Japanese tradition, warm sake is decanted into a small ceramic pitcher, called as Tokkuri or Ochosi, later served to guests from the pitcher.

KEY TERMS

Brewery water	:	Liquor (or treated water) that is used to add into beer.
Wort	:	It means beer before it becomes beer. After boiling the ingredients together that mixture is called wort.
Malt adjunct	:	Any cereal grain that is added to malted barley in making of beer.
pH	:	Acidity level of water. The range goes from 0-14, with 7 being neutral.
Green malt	:	The resultant product of germination or fully germinated barley is known as green malt.
Malt	:	After kilning, the green malt becomes *malt*.
Hop	:	A beer preservative agent.
Draft beer	:	Freshly gassed draught beer that is directly served from sterilized kegs with the help of cobra gun.
Priming	:	Solution of sugar and hop that are added into beer to promote secondary fermentation.
Sake	:	A Japanese rice wine that is mostly served warm in footed glasses.
White beer	:	Bear made with herbs or fruit instead of or in addition to hops.
Cobra gun	:	Hand-held device (or control unit) used to pour draught beer.

REVIEW QUESTIONS

1. Define the term beer. Explain step-by-step process of beer making.
2. Write a short note on draught beer and its serving procedure.
3. Differentiate between ale and lager beer. Enlist any five famous brand names of each ale and lager beer.
4. What is sake? Classify different types of sake and support each with brand name.

19 CHAPTER

Distilled Beverages: Spirits

OBJECTIVES

Students will be able to:

- expound spirit (its classes/types) and proof calculation;
- explain the role of pot and patent still method; and
- elucidate the kinds of spirits made via pot still and patent still method.

SPIRIT

Spirit is a general/collective term given to all alcoholic beverages, which have high content of alcohol. *Alcohol* is a colourless, volatile and flammable liquid obtained through the fermentation of sugar or sugar containing liquid (it may be fruit based as well as grain based) which is thereafter distilled to enhance alcoholic percentage up to 96%. All spirits contain alcohol but alcoholic strength differs from spirit to spirit. The alcoholic strength of beverage is measured via *proof* system. Mainly Sikes scale, Gay Lussac (or OIML) and American scale is used.

The term *proof* is a measure of how much alcohol (ethanol) is contained in an alcoholic beverage. The term was originally used in the United Kingdom and was defined as 7/4 times the alcohol by volume (ABV). The UK now uses the *abv* standard instead of alcohol proof. Every country has its own legal regulations to determine the level/percentage of alcohol in any beverage, for instance in India most of high alcoholic beverages (or spirits) contain 42.8% alcohol by volume.

Proof Calculation			
Gay Lussac/OIML	France	100 degree French proof is equal to	100 % abv
Sikes Scale	UK	175 degree UK proof is equal to	100 % abv
American	US	200 degree US proof is equal to	100 % abv

STANDARD MANUFACTURING PROCESS OF SPIRITS

Raw Material

✓ It includes range of fruits and grains. These fruits/grains are mashed first then fermented; thereafter the resultant product (often termed *base wine*) is used to make spirit. For instance:

• Grape	Produce ⟶	Wine ⟶	Produce ⟶	Brandy
• Apple	⟶	Cider	⟶	Calvados
• Malted barley	⟶	Beer	⟶	Whiskey
• Any grain	⟶	Base wine	⟶	Gin and vodka
• Sugar cane	⟶	Basi	⟶	Rum
• Blue agave tequilana	⟶	Pulque	⟶	Tequila
• Mezcal	⟶	Pulque	⟶	Mescal/duplicate tequila

✓ Traditionally, potato and sweet potato were used to make vodka but nowadays any grain even grapes are used to manufacture vodka, for example, French Ciroc vodka is made from grapes.

Making of *Mash*

✓ After the collection of required raw material, the second most important step is to convert the collected raw material into *mash* (like *wort* or *must*). The mash is made by grinding up one of three things (from given below) and mixing it with water:

- Whole grains — For example, corn or rye
- Malts (produce *wort*) — For example, dried sprouted grains (malted barley).
- Other plants — For example, sugar cane, agave, potatoes, etc.
- Fruits (produce *must*) — Squeezing fruits like grape, apple, pears for its juice

Fermentation

✓ The next step is fermentation. This converts the natural plant sugars to alcohol. Fruit juice/grain mash will ferment naturally over time when left exposed to the yeast or bacteria found in the open air, or, as is usually the case, the yeast is artificially introduced (or cultured yeast).

✓ Artificial yeast (*cultured yeast*) is introduced into the *mash*. Yeast breaks down the sugar or starch molecules, consequently producing alcohol and byproduct, carbon dioxide. This is, incidentally, the same thing that happens to bread during its rising process.

Fermentation	Temperature
White wine	8 – 19°C
Red wine	25 – 32°C
Ale beer	18 – 25°C
Lager beer	7 – 12°C
Cider	4 – 16°C
Sake	8 – 10°C
Rum	20 – 24°C
Gin	27 – 32°C
Vodka	18 – 22°C
Whiskey	20 – 32°C
Tequila	20 – 22°C
Brandy	18 – 24°C

✓ Mashing and fermenting are two common steps with beverages like beer and wine, but making hard liquor or spirits requires one more step, i.e., distillation. The resultant fermented beverage contains alcohol, particles and *congeners*, or the elements which create flavours.

Distillation

✓ It is a method used to capture and concentrate the alcohol developed in fermentation stage. The fermented *mash* or fruit juice solution (or *fermented must*) is brought to a boiling point in an apparatus called "still". This *still* is usually either a hollow vertical column or a pot with a long, very narrow spout; both are designed to capture and condense the vapours coming from the boiling liquid.

✓ Alcohol has a lower boiling point than the other components of *fermented must* (or fermented juice) or *mash*, particularly water. In distillation process, this water is evaporated at 100°C whereas alcohol at around 78.5°C. The liquid collected in the first phase of distillation is low in alcohol (25-30%) thus known as *low wine* whereas alcohol collected in the second phase of distillation (or in repeat distillation) is high in alcohol content (60-65%) thus known as *high wine*. It is later adjusted to produce the desired alcoholic beverage/hard liquor/spirit. Neutral spirit contains up to 96% alcohol.

METHODS OF MAKING SPIRIT (DISTILLATION METHODS)

Pot Still Method

✓ It is also known as *batch still* method and is used to produce quality spirits of high price, for example cognac brandy, Irish whisky and dark rums.

✓ In pot still, the *kiln* (or apparatus) is fire/coil heated from below which makes heated liquid to condense, evapourate and vaporize. This process is very slow because less quantity is distilled at one time. First phase of distillation produces *low wine* (it contains heads and tails) and second phase produces *high wine*.

Patent Still Method

✓ It is also known as *continuous* or *coffey still* method and is used to produce regular low priced spirits. It comprises two columns: *analyzer* (to start distillation) and *rectifier* (to make spirit neutral).

✓ This process is very fast, least expensive and less time consuming. It is particularly used for producing Armagnac brandy, gin and other regular spirits.

TYPES OF SPIRIT

Brown Spirits

- ✓ The term *brown spirit* refers to all those hard beverages which are dark in colour (or brown in appearance) with heavier body and strong taste sensation in comparison to white spirits. Often brown spirits (as compared to white spirits) are higher in alcohol content also (it is around 180 to 190 proof) but not always.
- ✓ Whiskey and brandy are two excellent examples of brown spirits. These spirits are brown due to barrel aging (or oak aging); brown spirits obtain colour as well as flavours, aromas and textures from the wooden barrels. Sometimes, these spirits are also coloured by adding caramel.

White Spirits (further classified into neutral and rectified)

- ✓ The term *white spirit* refers to all those hard beverages which are colourless and lighter in body and taste in comparison to brown spirits. Simultaneously, white spirits are also lighter in alcohol content (it is around 80 proof) than brown spirits.
- ✓ Vodka, gin, tequila and white rum are examples of white spirits because they are almost similar in colour and appearance. These spirits are white because they have usually not been aged in colour inducing wooden barrel. Although, some of them are aged in barrels but afterwards they are filtered clear, for instance most white rums.

Neutral Spirits (byproduct of silent spirits)

- ✓ Originally, it means colourless, flavourless and tasteless spirit but after distillation flavours, may be added, for example, vodka and gin. Gin is a white neutral spirit that can be made from any grain.
- ✓ After distillation process, gin has no flavour except for the taste of alcohol it contains. At this stage, flavouring agents like juniper berries (it has medicinal value) and coriander seeds are added to give gin its distinctive character.

Rectified Spirits (purified spirits)

- ✓ These spirits have high concentrated ethanol (drinking alcohol). These spirits are purified by repeated distillation, a process known as *rectification*. Vodka is an example of highly rectified spirit.
- ✓ Gin is also a kind of flavoured vodka. Rectified spirits are used in mixed drinks, in the production of liqueurs, for medicinal purposes, and as a household solvent.

Flavoured Spirits

- ✓ It means spirits which have their own intrinsic flavour. For example, brandy is derived from fermented juice of grapes or other fruits. This basic wine has multitude of flavours, many of which remain in the spirit after distillation.
- ✓ Spirits infused with different flavouring agents or botanicals are also considered as a diversity of flavoured spirits. For instance, flavoured gin, vodka, rum and so forth.

KEY TERMS

Rectified spirit	: Highly purified spirit. Afterwards flavouring agents can be incorporated like juniper berries in gin.
Neutral spirit	: An odourless, colourless and usually tasteless spirit.
Proof	: Alcohol content available in any spirit.
Brown spirit	: Group of brown coloured spirits, primarily includes whiskey and brandy.
White spirit	: Group of white coloured spirits, primarily includes gin, vodka, tequila and white rum.
Rectifier	: Columns in patent still which rectify or purify the spirits.
Analyzer	: Columns in patent still, which is used for distillation of spirits.
Kiln	: A technical term for container or apparatus used in pot still in order to distillate the spirits.
Batch still	: Pot still method of distillation which is mainly considered best for producing quality spirits.
Coffey still	: Patent still method of distillation is considered best for producing regular spirits.
Still	: An apparatus or alembic that is used for pot distilling the spirit.
Congeners	: Particles present in minute amount in beverage which provides distinctive flavour and aroma.

REVIEW QUESTIONS

1. What do you mean by the term spirit? Give the step-by-step standard procedure for making spirit.
2. Differentiate between pot still and patent still method.
3. Classify different types of spirit. Explain each one in brief along with appropriate examples.
4. Write a short note on proof. Explain different proofing systems that are used to determine the alcoholic percentage of any beverage.

Brown Spirits

Objectives

Students will be able to:

- explicate brandy (Cognac, Armagnac and Calvados) and whisky/whiskey; and
- elucidate brandy and whiskey types, brand names and serving standards.

BROWN SPIRIT

The term *brown spirit* is a collective term for all those groups of hard beverages which are dark/brown in colour, heavier in body and strong in taste in comparison to white spirits. Often brown spirits are higher in alcohol content too (it is around 180 to 190 proof) but it is not always.

Whiskey and brandy are brown spirits. These spirits are brown due to barrel aging (or oak aging). Spirits obtain colour as well as flavour, aroma and texture from the wooden barrels. Sometimes, these spirits are also coloured by adding *caramel.*

BRANDY

The term brandy is a "generic term", therefore it can be made anywhere in the world. It is also called "fruit brandy, Eaux-de-vie, delightful soul of wine or water of life". It is a distilled spirit made from the fermented juice, mash or wine of fruit. Originally, it is made from wine; therefore, it is also termed "burnt wine". In simple terms, brandy (it is derived from Dutch word *brandewijn,* means "burnt-wine") is a spirit produced by distilling wine, the wine having first been produced by fermenting grapes. Remember, grape is a primary raw material for wine making. Therefore, simply the term *wine* indicates to grape wine. But brandy can also be produced from fermented fruits other than grapes; these products are called *eaux-de-vie.*

Manufacturing Process of Brandy

Raw material	Base wine is used to make brandy – *Cognac and Armagnac* are made from three grape varieties – St. Emilion (or ugni blanch), Folle Blanche (or Picpoul) and Colombard.

Fermentation	Both go through primary fermentation and then the secondary fermentation process. This fermentation takes place between the temperature range of 18 to 24°C.
Distillation	*Cognac* is pot distilled (as it is a fine brandy) whereas *Armagnac* is patent distilled (as it is a regular brandy). Cognac goes through double distillation whereas Armagnac goes through single distillation.
Maturing	*Cognac* is matured in Limousin or Troncais oak cask whereas *Armagnac* is aged in Monlezun oak. The maturation period differs for Cognac and Armagnac and is indicated by different symbols/stars.
Blending	It means mixing of old brandies with new ones to improve the quality and taste of newly produced brandies. The cellar master is responsible for this task.
Bottling	*Armagnac* is bottled in flat faced bottle, known as a *basquaise* in French. Whereas *Cognac* is added with distilled water before bottling in order to reduce its alcoholic strength.

Famous Brandies

Cognac

✓ It is the best brandy of the world produced by double distillation process through pot still method. The Cognac region is divided into six sub-regions, these are Grande Champagne, Petite Champagne, Borderies, Fins Bois, Bons Bois and Bois Ordinaries.

Label Designation

VS	3 star
VSO	3 star
VSOP	4 star
XO	5 star

Armagnac

✓ It is the oldest brandy of the world made by single distillation process through patent still method. The Armagnac region is divided into three sub-regions: Bas Armagnac (or *black Armagnac*/lower Armagnac), Tenareze and Haut Armagnac (or *white Armagnac*/upper Armagnac).

Calvados

✓ It is made from fermented apple juice, i.e., *cider*. In England, it is also known as *Applejack*. Calvados is a double distilled brandy produced in the Normandy region in north-west France as well as in other regions such as Brittany.

Other brandies

✓ It includes Cut brandy, Marc (French brandy), Grappa (Italian brandy) and Fine brandy. Apart from it, range of stone fruits and soft fruits can also be used to make brandy. Some of them are listed below.

Classification of Brandy

Stone Fruit Brandies (It refers to a group of brandies made from fruits which contain stones or seeds with soft fleshy exterior surrounding)			**Soft Fruit Brandies** (It indicates to group of brandies made from fruits that grow on bushes, such as berries, strawberries, currants, etc.)		
Name	**Made from**	**Country**	**Name**	**Made from**	**Country**
Barack Palinka	Apricot	Hungary	Brombeergeist	Blackberry	Germany/ Swiss
Kirsch (it may also be included)	Cherry	France	Myrtille	Blueberry	France
Prunelle	Pears	France/ Austria	Mure	Blackberry	France
Mirabelle	Plums	France	Himbeergeist	Raspberry	Germany/ Swiss
Prune	Plums	Switzerland	Fraises	Strawberry	France
Kirschwasser	Cherry	Germany	Fraises de bois	Strawberry	France
Quetsch	Blue plums	France	Erdbeergeist	Strawberry	Germany/ Swiss
Slivovitz	Plums	Hungary	Houx	Houx	France
Coing	Quince	France			

Service of Brandy

Brandy can be served neat or on the rocks as well as also added to other beverages to make mixed drinks (or cocktails) like Brandy Alexander, Sidecar, Brandy Sour, etc. The standard brandy serving guidelines are given below.

Serving glass	Brandy can be drunk *neat* at room temperature (in Western countries) in *brandy snifter* or in champagne tulip glass. In Asia, it is usually consumed *on the rocks.*
Serving temperature	Brandy has a more pleasant aroma at a lower temperature (16°C). In winter, brandy is also served with lukewarm water.

Brand Names of Brandy	
Indian	Doctor's, Beehive, Aristocrat, Golconda, Hayward's and so forth
Cognac	Remy Martin (VSOP), Martell, Hennessey, Camus, Bisquit and so forth
Armagnac	Janneau, Laressingle, Napoleon, Baron de Sigognac, Château de Laubade and so forth.
Calvados	Boulard, Busnel, Montgommery, Morice, Norois, Père Magliore, Chevalier de Brevil.

WHISKY/WHISKEY

Whiskey is a brown spirit obtained by the distillation of fermented mash of grain (usually barley, maize, rice or all together), thereafter aged in oakwood casks. The spelling of whiskey also differs in different regions. Like in Scotch, Canadian, Tennessee and Japanese terminology, the spelling is "Whisky" (without "e") but in Irish and Bourbon (US), the spelling would be "Whiskey" (with "e").

Manufacturing Process of Whiskey

Raw material	Whiskey is made from *malted barley* or fermented mash of grains (like maize, barley, rye or all together). Therefore, beer (or *base* product in place of beer) can also be used as a base product to make whiskies because it is also made from malted barley or from other similar grains.
Fermentation	Now it is the time to start the fermentation process. *Sweet mash* (fresh yeast) or *sour mash* (used yeast/batch) is added to start the fermentation process. The fermentation takes place between the temperatures ranges 20 to 32°C. The resultant product will be called *base beer*.
Distillation	*Base beer* is used to make all whiskies. Whiskies must be distilled out at less than 190 degree proof so that the distillate possesses the character of whiskey. Afterwards, distilled water is added to this *high wine* to bring its proof down at least to 110 degree proof but not less than 80 degree proof.
Maturation	Distilled liquid is matured in oak barrels. Longer maturation can incorporate the flavour of oakwood into whiskey whereas too short matured whiskies will be called *green whiskies*. All Scotch whiskies must be aged in oak barrels for at least three years.
Blending	Whiskies are blends in order to get required bouquet, colour and flavour. Most of the whiskies are made by combination of whiskies from different distilleries as well as with the combination of malt and grain whiskies.

Bottling — *Caramel* is added to give a tawny tinge to the colour and *soft water* is added to reduce the alcoholic strength of whiskies. Finally, whiskey is filtered and bottled.

Classification of Whiskey

Whiskey can be either classified on the basis of their region of origin (Scotch, Irish, Canadian, American, Japanese whiskies, etc.), method of manufacturing (pot still and patent still whiskies), type of yeast (sour mash and sweet mash whiskies), combination of grains/cereals (malt whiskies, grain whiskies and their variation) and duration of aging (green whiskies and matured whiskies). A brief description of region based whiskies is given below.

Scotch whiskey

✓ These are twice distilled (in pot still) whiskies which must be distilled in Scotland and matured for a minimum of three years in oak casks. Scotch whiskies are made from malted barley. Blended scotches are made from malt and grains.

Scotch Malt Whiskies

Highland Malt

- The Belvenie
- Cardu

Lowland Malt

- Auchentoshan
- Rosebank

Islay & Campbell Malt

- Bowmore
- Lagavulin

Irish whiskey

✓ These are thrice distilled whiskies which must be aged for a period of no less than three years, thus its taste and flavour is smooth. Most Irish whiskies are made via patent still method. It is made from the combination of grains – barley, wheat, oats and rye.

Canadian whiskey

✓ It is made from corn with rye and barley through patent still method. It is aged in wooden casks for at least three years, thus its flavour is smoother and colour is lighter. Little rye with caramel is added to give extra colour, before bottling.

American whiskey

✓ It is made from various cereals/grains like rye, barley, corn, maize, wheat or combination of all. It is made through patent still method and no colouring or flavouring is allowed to be incorporated. It is aged in charred new oak barrels or uncharred oak barrels.

Bourbon whiskey

✓ The United States produces *Bourbon Whiskey*. These whiskies are made from corn and are aged for at least four years before bottling. These whiskies generally come from Kentucky in America.

Tennessee whiskey

✓ Most of Tennessee whiskies are made from *sour mash*; it means that special yeast is used in making the original beer, which goes for distillation into whiskey. Sour mash gives the whiskey certain tartness. The best example is 'Jack Daniels'.

Japanese whiskey

✓ Pot still method is used for producing full-bodied Japanese whiskies whereas patent still method is used for lighter bodied whiskies. Most of the blended Japanese whiskies are made from a combination of millet, corn and rice. It is aged in used charred oak wood cask.

Australian whiskey

✓ Australia produces single malt whiskies. These are produced on the island state of Tasmania.

Brand Names of Single and Blended Malt Whiskies		
Scotch	Single	Ardmore, Port Ellen, Glenlivet, Glenfiddich, Highland, Bell's and Sons, etc.
	Blended	Cutty Sark, The Antiquary, Passport, Dimple, VAT 69, Chivas Regal, etc.
Irish	Single	Tyrconnell, Merry's, Locke's, Shanahans, Michael Collin, Connemara, Clonmel, etc.
	Blended	Clontarf, Golden Irish, Jameson gold, Millar's, Paddy, Tullamore, Strangford, etc.
Canadian	Single	Glen Breton (Rare, 10 year old and 15 year old)
	Blended	Canadian Mist, Canadian Club, Rich and Rare, Black Velvet, Windsor, Gibson's Finest.
American	Single	Notch, Old Overholt, Old Potrero, St. George, Woodstone Creek, etc.
	Corn	Old Gristmill, Old Oak, Platte Valley, Georgia Moon, Virginia Lightening, etc.
	Rye	Red Hook, Templeton Rye, Rittenhouse, Jim Beam Rye, Jack Daniel's Rye, etc.

Note. *Single malt* whiskey uses only one strain of malt in fermentation whereas *blended malt* whiskey uses many types of malts in fermentation.

WHISKEY SERVING STANDARD

It can be served neat and on the rocks (means firstly decant ice into glass then whiskey). After making the peg, now steward may add (or fill up) water, soda (or to both water and soda) or cold drink. It can also be used as a base in making cocktails like "Rusty Nail". The standard serving glass and temperature is given below.

Serving glass	Whiskey is mostly served in "old fashion glass". The ideal capacity of old fashion glass is approx. 8 – 10 fl. oz. The repeat drinks can be served in small peg glasses or juice glasses.
Serving temperature	Whiskey is preferred to be served at room temperature (means 65°F or 18°C).

Brand Names of Whiskies		
Country	**Delux brands of whiskies**	**Regular brands of whiskies**
Indian	Peter Scot, Royal Challenge, Bagpiper and Aristocrat	Royal Reserve, Officer's choice
Scottish	Johnny Walker, Chivas Regal, Glenlivet and Glenfiddich	VAT69, Ballantine, Teacher's and Dewar's.
Irish	Slaney Malt, Clonmel, Knappogue and Connemara	Clontarf, Old Dublin and Bushmills
Canadian	Canadian Club, Seagram's, Wiser's and G&W.	Canadian Host, Hiram walker
Bourbon	Notch, Old Forester, Old Potrero and Woodstone Creek	GW Bourbon, Southern Comfort
Japanese	Yamazaki, Hibiki, Hakushu and Miyagikyo	Karuizawa, Shirakawa, Kagoshima
Tennessee	Jack Daniels and George Dickel	Partichard's

KEY TERMS

Sour mash	: Spent yeast/mash that adds to start fermentation process into new batch.
Caramel	: Burnt sugar which is often used to give tawny tinge to brown spirits like whiskey.
Soft water	: Pure water added into distilled beverage to bring down its high alcohol content.
Base beer	: Base product used to produce whiskies.
On-the-rocks	: Drinks over crushed ice/ice cubes.
Brandy snifter	: Brandy balloon, also known as brandy inhaler glass.

Cider : Fermented beverage made from apple juice thereafter used to produce calvados.

White Armagnac : Sub-region of Armagnac, i.e., Haut Armagnac.

Eaux-de-vie : French term referring to fruit brandy. It can be made from any fruit.

Basquaise : French term for a flat faced bottle used to fill Armagnac brandy.

High wine : Distilled beverage with higher alcohol in which distilled water is added to bring down its alcohol content.

REVIEW QUESTIONS

1. What do you mean by the term brown spirit? Classify brown spirits and explain each one briefly.
2. Differentiate between Cognac and Armagnac.
3. Classify different types of whiskies and enlist at least three brands in each type.
4. Describe the standard serving procedures for whiskey and brandy.

White Spirits

Objectives

Students will be able to:

- elucidate white spirits, their making process and types; and
- expound major brands and serving standards of white spirits.

WHITE SPIRIT

The term *white spirit* is a collective word for all those hard beverages which are clear or colourless in appearance and are lighter in body and taste in comparison to brown spirits. Simultaneously, white spirits may also be lighter in alcohol content (it is around 80 proof) than brown spirits.

Vodka, gin, tequila and white rum are white spirits because they are almost similar in appearance and colour. These spirits are white because they are not aged in colour inducing wooden barrels. Although, some of them are aged in barrels but afterwards they are filtered, for instance, most of the white rum brands.

RUM (REGULAR USE MEDICINE)

Rum is an alcoholic beverage made by fermenting sugarcane juice, particularly its byproduct, molasses. The resultant fermented product is known as *basi* which further moves for distillation. *Molasses* is dark sticky substance left behind after the sugar crystals have been extracted from the sugarcane juice. The distillate, a clear liquid, is then aged in oak barrels. Rum is also called as *cane spirit* as it is made from sugarcane. Majority of the world's rum production occurs in Caribbean and Latin American countries and territories.

Rum Manufacturing Process

Raw material	*Molasses* is used as a raw material to produce the rums. Molasses is a byproduct of sugarcane which is a thick black liquid that remains after all of the commercially producible sugar has been recovered from sugarcane juice.

Extraction of juice	After sufficient granulation, the granulated product needs to go through double extraction. First extraction gives molasses and second extraction (from molasses) is used for making rum.
Fermentation	Now it is the time to start the fermentation process. The yeast is added to start the fermentation process (the resultant product will be known as *basi*). The fermentation takes place between the temperature range of 20 to 24°C.
Distillation	The fermented liquid (*basi*) is distilled. For producing *dry white rums* patent still method is followed whereas for producing *quality rums* and *dark rums* pot still method of distillation is allowed.
Maturation	*White rums* are matured in pure oak cask whereas *dark rums* are matured in charred oak barrels. The spirit spends at least three years in the barrels before bottling.
Bottling	Bottling is the last stage in rum making process but before bottling it might be blended with water to bring the alcoholic content down to the required strength level.

Classification of Rum

Alike whiskey or rum can also be classified on the basis of their region of origin (Jamaican, Cuban, Demeraran, etc.), period of maturation (Ron Viejo, Ron Añejo, etc.), body (light, medium and heavy rum) and colour (dark, golden and white rum). A brief description of region based rums is given below.

Jamaican rum

- ✓ These are rich, full-bodied and usually dark colour rums from Jamaica. These rums are aged in oak for approximately five to seven years. They are given colour by adding *caramel*.

Demeraran rum

- ✓ These are also rich and full-bodied rums from Guyana (nearby Demerara river) but not as pungent or flavourful as Jamaican rums. They are darker in colour than the Jamaican rums.

Cuban rum

- ✓ These are dry and light-bodied rums from Cuba. These rums are made through patent still method and then aged in oak barrels for one to four years. Its best example is white Bacardi rum.

Other rums

✓ It includes Indian rum, Augardiente de café, Batavia rum and so forth. Rum can also be classified on the basis of colour like white rum, golden rum and dark rum.

Rum Serving Standards

It can be served neat (mostly dark rum), or on the rocks (means firstly decant crushed ice/ice cubes into glass then pour rum). After making the peg, guest may demand to add water, soda, water + soda or cold drink (like Cuba Libre). It can also be used in making of cocktails like "Grasshopper". Mostly white rum like Bacardi is used in mixed drinks. The standard serving glass and temperature is given below.

Serving glass	Rum can be served in a variety of glasses but mostly served in "old fashion glass or also in High ball glass (both are 8-10 fl. oz)". The repeat drinks can be served in small peg glasses or juice glasses.
Serving temperature	Rum is preferred to be served at room temperature (means 65°F or 18°C). In winters, it can be served with lukewarm water.

Brand Names of Rum	
Indian	Old Monk, McDowell's No. 1, Contessa, Hercules, Royal Choice, Old Port, Old Cascade, Black Fort, Six Shooter, Original Choice.
International	Lemon Hart and Appellation White (Jamaica), Santiago White and El Dorado (Demerara), Cabot Tower and London Dock (Canada), Crustal and Cajun (US), Bacardi and Ron Rico (Cuba).

VODKA

Original vodka is a highly *rectified spirit* (means it is an odourless, colourless and usually tasteless spirit). Vodka can be made from any substance, which contains starch or sugar. Traditionally, it was made from potato and sweet potato but nowadays, it is also made from grains (such as corn, rye and wheat) and fruits, like *ciroc vodka* (made from grapes). The finest vodka is needed to pass through the layers of sand, vegetable charcoal, coal and quarts to make it pure. Being a flavourless spirit, it is also an easy ingredient for the cocktails and cups. Vodka is good to accompany with nibbles of food, caviar and smoked salmon. Nowadays, vodka is available in various flavours, from chocolate to cayenne pepper.

Vodka Manufacturing Process

Raw material	Originally, it was made from potatoes and sweet potatoes but nowadays it can be made from grain (like rye and wheat) or anything that contains starch or sugar including molasses, corn and grapes.
Mash preparation	The used raw materials are pressure cooked and then ground. Unfermented liquid is known as *wort*. Malt or special enzymes are added to the *wort* to start the fermentation.
Fermentation	Now, it is the time to ferment the *wort*. Yeast is added to start the fermentation process. The fermentation takes place between the temperature range of 18-22°C.
Distillation	The fermented liquid is distilled at very high proof through patent still method. High degree of distillation extracts all flavouring elements, thus it makes vodka a highly rectified/purified spirit.
Purification	Patent stills have two columns –one for distillation and the other for rectification. A third column may also be added when the vodka has to be more purified.
Bottling	Now the purified/rectified spirit is diluted with water to decrease its alcoholic strength. No ageing is required for vodkas. Consequently, they can be bottled the same day.

Types of Vodka

Neutral Vodka	It is rectified, diluted and filtered (through vegetable charcoal) vodka. The water and used grain can have an effect on the quality. Polish vodka, for instance, is always made from rye.
Gold Vodka	This vodka has been cask maturated, sometimes as long as 10 years. Smirnoff gold cinnamon vodka is a perfect example of gold vodka.
Green Vodka	This vodka is made by steeping Zubrowka grass in Polish vodka, and has a delicate aromatic bouquet. The bottle frequently contains a stem of the grass.
Flavoured Vodka	Vodka is often flavoured with various herbs, chilies, fruits, peppercorns, etc. Flavouring can also be created by adding varying aromatic agents. The process of adding flavour into vodka is often called "Vodka infusion".
Sparkling Vodka	It is carbonated vodka (or vodka charged with carbon dioxide). CO_2, Le Grand Saint, Camitz, Voz (a cassis flavoured vodka), Pink V (vodka with gold particles), Absolute Botanik are some famous brands of sparkling vodka.

Vodka Serving Standard

It can be served neat, chilled and can be drunk in one gulp. After making the peg, guest may demand to add water, soda, water + soda or cold drink like Limca. Vodka is also used as a base in making cocktails like "Bloody Mary "and Screw Driver". The standard serving glass and temperature is given below.

Serving glass	Vodka can be served in variety of glasses but preferred to be served in "Paris Goblet (6-8 fl. oz) or Old fashioned glass (8-10 fl. oz). The repeat drinks can be served in small peg glasses or juice glasses. Both glasses are very much similar to tequila shot glasses but may differ in capacity.
Serving temperature	Vodka is preferred to be served at room temperature (meaning 65°F or 18°C) as well as chilled or directly from refrigerator.

Brand Names of Vodka	
Flavoured	Starka (vanilla), Zubrowka (zubrowka grass), Citron (lemon/lime), Kurant (black currants) and Cytrynowka (Polish lemon).
International	Cooranbong (Australia), Iceberg and Fuel (Canada), Finlandia (Finland), Ciroc and Grey Goose (France), Absolute (Sweden), Xellent (Switzerland), Smirnoff (UK), Belvedere (Poland), Nikolai (USA).
Indian	Romanov, Czar Alexander, Magic Moments, White Mischief.

TEQUILA

Tequila is a Mexican spirit made by fermenting then distilling the juice of the blue "Agave Tequilana" plant. The spirit gets its name from the town of Tequila, situated in west central Mexico. Mexican laws state that tequila can be produced only in the state of Jalisco and limited regions in the states. Tequila is most often made at a 38–40% alcohol content (76–80 proof), but can also be produced between 35–55% alcohol content (70–110 proof). *Mezcal* is a close cousin of tequila but it is not real tequila, because it can be produced from any tequilana plant as well as can be produced in any state of Mexico.

Tequila Manufacturing Process

Raw material	Original tequila is made from *piña* of blue Agave Tequilana plant whereas substitute tequilas (like its close cousin, Mezcal) can be produced from any agave plants. *Pina* is heart of agave plant.
Chop and cook	Roughly chopped *piña* is steamed in an oven for 24 hours thereafter cooled. After cooling, *piñas* are washed, shredded and pressed between rollers to extract the juice. It turns the starch into sugar.

Fermentation	The extracted juice is fermented between the temperature range of 20° to 22°C for two days. A little of the fermented material is always added to the fresh batch.
Distillation	The fermented liquid (or *pulque*) is distilled twice in pot still. After distillation, it comes out at a powerful proof of 90-95°.
Maturation	*White tequila* is aged for a few months, *gold tequila* is aged for nine months, *añejo tequila* for three years and *extra aged tequila* for more than three years.
Bottling	The last step in tequila manufacturing process (after the completion of maturation) is bottling of the matured liquid.

Types of Tequila

Blanco tequila

✓ Blanco is *white* or *silver tequila*. It is clear, un-aged tequila, that is, normally bottled right after being distilled.

Joven/Gold tequila

✓ Also known as *suave tequila,* it means young or smooth tequila. Colourants and flavourings are incorporated before bottling.

Reposado tequila

✓ An *aged* or *rested tequila,* it means that tequila remains in wood for a period of two months but no longer than 12 months.

Añejo tequila

✓ It is *extra aged* or *vintage tequila*. The term vintage can only appear on bottles that contain tequila which is aged in oak barrels for a minimum period of one year.

Extra Añejo tequila

✓ These are Añejo tequilas that have been aged for a period of at least three years, without specifying the aging time in the label.

Tequila Serving Standards

Tequila is mainly served neat and accompanied by salt and a lemon (or lime) wedge. First lick the salt then swallow the drink quickly and immediately bite the lemon or lime wedge because tequila is harsh in nature. It is believed that salt lessens the burn of the tequila and the sour fruit balances and enhances the flavour. This style of drinking tequila is called *tequila cruda* and is sometimes referred to as *training wheels, lick-sip-suck* or *lick-shoot-suck* (referring to the way in which the combination of ingredients is imbibed). The standard serving glass and temperature is given below.

Serving glass	Tequila (neat tequila) is mostly served in "Tequila shot" glass or "Caballito glass", the ideal capacity of this glass is up to 2 fl oz.
Serving temperature	Tequila is preferred to be served at room temperature (meaning 65°F or 18°C).

Brand Names of Tequila	
Blanco	Cabo Wabo, Cabrito, Espolon, El Tesoro, Corralejo, Don Fernando, Sol Dios.
Joven	1800, Two fingers, Pepe Lopez (Gold), Jose Cuervo, Citrico, Herradura.
Reposado	Casa Noble, Corzo, El Diamante Cielo, Partida, Trago, Siete Legus.
Añejo	Don Eduardo, Patron, 15 Corzo, Corazon, Ocho.
Extra Añejo	Don Julio 1942, Sauza Tres, Chinaco Negro, Patron Burdeos.

GIN

Before infusion, *gin* is a *neutral spirit*. The term gin is taken from the French word "Geniévre" which means "juniper". *Juniper* is a kind of berry which acts as a main flavouring agent in making of gin. Apart from it, coriander seeds, orange peel, cinnamon, angelica, lemon liquorice and bitter almonds are also used to incorporate the flavour into gin. The minimum bottled alcoholic strength for gin is 37.5% ABV in the E.U., and 40% ABV in the U.S.

Gin Manufacturing Process

Raw material	It can be made from many grains like malted barley, rye or maize. Nowadays, it is also made from the combination with corn. First, raw material is cooked then sent for fermentation.
Fermentation	Cooked *mash* is fermented between the temperature ranges from 27° to 32°C; afterwards the resultant product will pass for distillation and purification.
Distillation	Collected fermented liquid is distilled in patent still with at least three columns. The aim is to purify the spirit and leave it flavourless and make it strong at about 160° proof.

Adding botanicals	Gin is a flavoured spirit. It consists of more than 108 botanicals: the predominant flavours are of juniper berries, coriander seeds and orange peels.
Ageing	Gin does not require ageing; you can drink it the day it is made. But some companies age their gins in wooden casks to give a pale gold colour. This type of gin is called "golden gin".
Bottling	Before bottling, de-mineralized water may be added to gin to reduce the alcoholic strength. It may be filtered also to remove trace of any botanicals. Finally, bottle the spirit.

Types of Gin

Plymouth gin

✓ It is a pungent and aromatic gin with around 41.2% alcohol by volume. These are made by the Devonshire of Coates and Compound in Plymouth, England.

London dry gin

✓ It is an unsweetened and classic gin made from grain mixture – more barley and less corn. These are distilled at high proof and then redistilled with juniper berries and citrus botanicals.

Sloe gin

✓ It is a red colour gin made by steeping sloe berries and the addition of sugar syrup and bitter almonds. Its alcohol content is around 15% to 30% by volume.

Old Tom gin

✓ It is slightly sweeter than London dry gin and slightly drier than Dutch gin. It is produced in Scotland for export in international market.

Dutch gin

✓ It is a slightly sweet gin also known as *Holland gin* and made from barley, malt, corn and rye. It is distilled at a lower proof and then redistilled with juniper berries in another still at low proof.

Flavoured gin

✓ It is basically a gin to which natural flavourings have been added (like lime, lemon, orange and so on). The name of flavourings must always appear on the bottle. These are also called "fruit gins".

Malt wine

✓ Malt wine is a type of gin made in the Netherlands by four distillations in a pot still. These are cold compounded gins. These are made from cheap neutral spirit flavoured with essence.

Damson gin

✓ It is a British gin or liquor made from damson plums; it is macerated in a sugar and gin syrup for eight weeks or more. The proof will vary somewhat but generally is around 44 proof.

Infused gin

✓ It refers to those gins which are infused by various agents. For example, Ferdinand's Saar Dry Gin (it is a German gin that infuses with wine made from Riesling grapes).

Gin Serving Standards

It can be served neat or on the rocks (means firstly decant crushed ice or ice cubes then pour gin). After making the peg, guest may demand to add water, soda, both soda and water (in 1:1), tonic water or cold drink (especially Limca or Citra). It can also be used in making cocktails like "Gimlet". It can replace vodka in many cocktails like Bloody Mary and Screw Driver. The standard serving glass and temperature is given below.

Serving glass — Gin is mostly served in "old fashioned glass". The ideal capacity of old fashioned glass is approx. 8 to 10 fl. oz. The repeat drinks can be served in small peg glasses or juice glasses.

Serving temperature — Gin is preferred to be served at room temperature (meaning 65°F or 18°C).

Brand Names of Gin	
Indian	Mikado, Whitefield, Blue Riband, Booths, Mansion House, Silver Anchor, Forbes, High Society, Dunhill, Aristocrat, Blue Angle.
International	Ginebra San Miguel (Philippines), Seagram's and Bluecoat (USA), Larios (Spain), Cork Dry (Ireland), Tanqueray and Blackwood (Scotland), Steinhager (Germany), Citadelle (France), Beefeater, Booth's and Gordon's (UK).

KEY TERMS

Golden gin : A gin that has been aged in wood which contributes a light golden colour.

Mash	: A process of releasing sugar from grains into water. The mixture resulting from mashing.
Tequila cruda	: A drinking style of tequila which is simply known as lick-sip-suck. It is also termed 'training wheels'.
Demineralized water	: Pure water (or water without any minerals and impurities) used for diluting beverages.
Piña	: Heart of blue agave tequilana plant. It is called piña due to its strong resemblance to pineapple.
Wort	: Boiled thick mixture of grains (or ingredients) used for making beer thereafter spirits.
Sparkling vodka	: Carbonated vodka, O2 is famous brand of sparkling vodka.
Caviar	: Roe (or egg) of fish, considered good to serve with vodka.

REVIEW QUESTIONS

1. What is rum? Classify different types of rum and enlist at least five brand names of rum in each type.
2. Differentiate between gin and vodka.
3. What is tequila? Classify different types of tequila and enlist at least three brands in each type.
4. Describe standard serving procedure for gin, vodka and tequila.

Liqueurs, Aperitifs, Vermouths, Bitters and Other Spirits

Objectives

Students will be able to:

- elucidate the types of liqueur, aperitif, vermouth and bitters; and
- enlist major brands of liqueurs, vermouths, bitters and other spirits.

LIQUEURS

The word *liqueur* comes from the Latin word "liquifacere" ("to dissolve") and refers to the dissolving of flavourings in the spirits. Artificial flavourings are strictly regulated in most countries, and where allowed, it must be prominently labelled as such. These are made from any spirit or simply a base spirit with no flavour of its own (or *neutral spirit*).

The alcohol content of liqueurs varies from 15 to 55 per cent. Flavourings added may range from peppermint, apricot, honey, herbs and even tea and coffee, thereafter it is redistilled. In general, liqueur is divided into two broad categories, i.e., generics and proprietary. *Generic liqueurs* are the liqueurs that many manufacturers can make, such as crème de menthe whereas *proprietary liqueurs* are with unique brand names, such as Kahlúa and Grand Marnier. Liqueurs are also known as *cordials*. A brief description on liqueur manufacturing process and its types is given below.

LIQUEUR MANUFACTURING PROCESS

Extraction	Juice/flavour extraction is performed through either infusion (of any fruit), percolation (used for hard fruits), maceration (used for soft fruits) or hydraulic pressure (used for peels).
Distillation	Collect middle fraction, it is colourless and with high alcohol content. This liquid is then redistilled in order to remove impurities which may change the flavour of spirit.
Blending	Assembled ingredients are marred together by the cellar man in accordance with required taste and flavour.
Maturing	All liqueurs are matured but the finest liqueurs are matured in oak wood cask, thus produce mellow (it is a flavour received from oakwood) flavour and amber colour.

Fining — Vegetable matter may still be suspended in the liquid, thus it must be removed by fining process. The procedure of fining is similar to the fining of wine and finally the liqueur is bottled.

TYPES OF LIQUEUR

Particulars	Alc.P. %	Base	Flavour	Colour	Country	Remark
Tia Maria	53	Cane spirit	Coffee	Brown	Jamaica	Sweet in taste
Kahlúa	53	Cane spirit	Coffee	White	Mexico	Sweet in taste
Evil Monk	48	Brandy	Coffee	Brown	Kansas	Contains 12 mg caffeine
Kamora	20	Neutral spirit	Coffee	Brown	Mexico	Slightly sweet with 20% abv.
Sheridan's	30-40	Whiskey	Coffee	Black/dark brown	Irish	Filled in two-section bottle
Grenadine	34-50	Neutral spirit	Fruit	Red	Global	Pomegranate flavoured
Maraschino	50-60	Neutral spirit	Fruit	Colourless	Yugoslavia	Made from cherries.
Rock and rye	48-80	Rye whiskey	Fruit	Gold	U.S.A	Fruit juice, rock candy and fruit slices.
Peter herring	49	Brandy	Fruit	Red colour	Denmark	Sweet and cherry flavoured
Pucker	15	Neutral spirit	Fruit	Artificial	Dutch	Sour apple flavoured
Midori	46	Clear grain spirit	Fruit	Green	Japan/ Mexico/ France /US	Muskmelon flavoured
Amer Picon	78	Brandy	Orange	Dark	France	Bitter in taste and made from quinine and spices
Curaçao	27-40	Grape spirit	Orange	Clear/ Blue/ Orange	Dutch	Made from dried orange peels
Triple Sec	38-40	Grape spirit	Orange	Colourless	Dutch	Sweet white Curaçao
Cointreau	40	Brandy	Orange	White	France	After dinner liquor
Grand Marnier	40	Cognac	Orange	Brown	France	Sweet liquor

Anisette	25-30	Brandy	Licorice	Clear	Global	Anise seed flavoured liqueur
Pernod		Brandy	Licorice	Yellowish	France	Anise seed flavoured liqueur
Absinthe	120	Brandy	Licorice	Yellow/ Green	France	Unsweetened and wormwood and aniseeds flavoured
Raki	80-90	Brandy	Licorice	White	Turkey	Sweet liqueur
Ouzo		Brandy	Licorice	Cloudy white	Greece	Sweet, anise flavoured
Crème De Noyaux	50-60	Brandy	Nut	Creamy/ light yellow	France	Bitterish sweet liqueur
Crème De Noisette		Neutral spirit	Nut	Golden	France	Made with hazelnut syrup
Nocino		Grappa	Nut	Green	Italy	Made by infusing nut (i.e. green walnut) husk in spirit
Amaretto	24-28	Brandy	Nut	Dark brown (like rum)	Italy	Made of almond/ hazelnut and coloured with caramel.
Frangelico	24	Neutral spirit	Nut	Golden	Italy	Sweet and made from hazelnut
Chartreuse	55	Brandy	Herb	Yellow/ Green	France/ Spain	Angelica herb flavoured liqueur
Kümmel	54-70	Brandy	Herb	Clear	Global	Caraway and anise seed flavoured liqueur
Drambuie	40	Scotch malt	Herb	Golden	Scotland	Sweet liqueur
Izarra	86-100	Armagnac	Herb	Yellow/ Green	France	Available in two forms – green and yellow version
Vana Tallinn	80-100	Rum	Spices	Dark brown	Estonia	Cinnamon, and vanilla flavoured
Crème De Cacao	25-27	Brandy	Cream	White/ clear or dark/ brown	France	Made from Cacao and Vanilla beans
Crème De Cassis	18-30	Brandy	Cream	Black	France	Made from Black Currants

Crème De Menthe	20-30	Grain spirit	Cream	White/ clear or dark/green	France	Made from mint
Crème De Yvette	50-60	Neutral spirit	Cream	Pink/ purple	France	Made from violets
Advocaat	15-18	Brandy	Egg yolk	Yellow	Dutch	Sweet in nature
Cherry liqueur	50-60	Brandy	Black Cherries	Black	France	Fruit brandy and differ from cherry brandy
Bénédictine	40-43	Brandy	Herbs and Peels	Golden	France	Spicy and sweet
Glen mist	70	Irish whiskey	Honey	Golden	Ireland	Honey flavoured
Goldwasser	38	Brandy	Aniseed/ Orange	Golden	Poland/ Germany	It has gold flakes.
Kirsch	90-100	Brandy	Bitter almond	Clear colour	Alsace	Unsweetened
Ocha		Brandy	Tea	Mild green	Japan	Fresh green tea
Slivovitz	80-112	Brandy	Plum	Clear/light brown	Yugoslavia/ Romania	Colour and flavour of plums
Nuvo	30	French Vodka	Passion fruit (Nectar)	Pink	USA	World's first *sparkling liqueur*
VINIQ	40	Vodka	Moscato or other fruit	Purple	USA	Made by infusing premium vodka.

Service of Liqueurs

Liqueurs can be drunk on their own (or with ice, called as *frappé*) as well as used in making cocktails like Grasshopper (it contains crème de menthe and crème de cacao). These are also served as an accompaniment with coffee or as after dinner drinks or digestives. The standard serving glass and temperature is given below.

Service glass	The service of liqueur differs from country to country but in majority of cases, these are served in "Liqueur Glass" (capacity of upto 2 fl. oz). In many cases, these are also served in *brandy snifter*.
Service temperature	Like any other spirits, liqueurs are also served at room temperature (usually at 65°F or 18°C).

APERITIFS

- ✓ These are the drinks, especially wines, with not less than alcoholic content of 15-25%. These are made from grape wine containing any distilled spirits but most preferably brandy.
- ✓ Aperitifs are flavoured with various herbs and other natural aromatic agents, thus possess a good aroma and taste characteristics. Aperitifs are primarily served as before-dinner drink or in the form of beverage appetizer/starter.

Serving Standards

Serving glass	Aperitifs are served in Sherry taster glass (or *copita glass*) but nowadays these can be served in small versions of the classic "Champagne Tulip".
Serving temperature	Aperitifs are preferred to be served at room temperature (65° F) as well as chilled.
Serving style	It can be directly served from the refrigerator (it is the best way of serving) or with plenty of fresh ice.

VERMOUTHS

- ✓ *Vermouth* is an aromatized wine that has been altered by the infusion of number of botanicals. It is made with a base of dry fortified white wine (except for the rose variety) and flavoured with herbs. The alcohol content of vermouth is between 16 and 18 per cent.
- ✓ The best known vermouths were produced on both the French and Italian sides of the Alps. The French traditionally produced the lighter and drier vermouths whereas the Italians produced the sweeter and heavier vermouths. The term *French vermouth* is used for dry vermouths while *Italian vermouth* is used for sweet vermouths.

STYLES OF VERMOUTH

- Red
- Bianco
- Rose
- Fruit-flavoured

Types of Vermouth

Vermouths can be classified on the basis of country of origin (prominently French, Italian and Chambery), colour (like white, red and rose), nature (like sweet and dry) and so forth. A brief description of country based vermouths is given below.

French vermouth

- ✓ It is also known as *dry vermouths* and takes almost four years to be made. The centre of its production is Marseille. It is made from the dry white wine that is flavoured and fortified. Its colour varies from water white to light gold.

Italian vermouth

- ✓ It is also known as *sweet vermouth* and takes almost two years to be made. The centre of its production is Turin. All styles of Italian vermouths have much broader flavour than their French counterparts.

Chambéry

- ✓ It is particularly a fine example of dry vermouth. The centre of its production is Chambéry town. Herbs found only in the Chambéry region are used as flavouring agents and pure sugar is used for sweetening.

Other vermouths

- ✓ Virtually every country that produces wine also makes vermouth, most of which is consumed locally. Most vermouths are served over ice or with soda and dash of bitters.

Serving Standards

Serving glass	Vermouths are mainly preferred to be served in "old fashioned glass". But if vermouths are used as a base or modifying agent in cocktails then mixed drink is mostly offered in cocktail or martini glass.
Serving temperature	Vermouth can be served chilled "straight up" or over the ice with a twist of lemon or orange.
Serving style	When serving vermouth, use plenty of ice and fresh citrus fruits, particularly with dry vermouth. Vermouth is also an important ingredient of gin or vodka martini.

Brand Names of Vermouth			
Dry	Cinzanao, Dubonnet, Martini and Rosso	French	Noilly Prat, Dubonnet, Lillet
Italian	Riccadonna, Boissiere, Gallo and Gancia	Sweet	Cinzano, Bianco, Rosso
Rose	Chambéryzette	Red	Punte Mes, Antica Formula

BITTERS

- ✓ One family of distilled spirit is known as *bitters*, these are alcoholic beverages flavoured with herbal essences. These essences are extracted from plants, stems, barks, fruits and roots of various binds (these herbal essences have a bitter or bittersweet flavour).
- ✓ Bitters can be used in many ways such as "pick-me-ups" or consumed with soda (or as digestive drinks). They can also serve as aperitifs or used to flavour other drinks/cocktails. Bitters commonly have an alcoholic strength between 28 and 45% and are often also known as *digestifs*. French alcoholic beverages that have the letter "D" stamped on their labels are also *digestives*.

Types of Bitters

Aperitif bitters (or cocktail bitters)

- ✓ Aperitif bitters are also called *cocktail bitters* and refer to all those bitters used for flavouring cocktails. These are used as drops or dashes, thus often also known as *concentrated bitters*. In the United States, many cocktail bitters are classified as alcoholic non-beverage products.
- ✓ As such, they are often available from retailers who do not sell liquor, such as supermarkets in many US states. Some notable examples of cocktail bitters include: Angostura (Venezuela), Dubonnet (France), Fee Brothers (New York), Bittermens (New Orleans), The Bitter Truth (Germany), etc.

Digestive bitters (or drinking bitters)

- ✓ Digestive bitters refer to all those bitters consumed either neat or with ice at the end of a meal. Thus, often these bitters are also known as *drinking bitters*.
- ✓ Many of these bitters are also used in making cocktails. Some notable examples of digestive bitters include Amer Picon (France), Aperol (Italy), Fernet Branca (Italy), Campari (Italy), Cynar (Italy), Underberg (Germany), etc.

Non-alcoholic bitters (alcohol free bitters)

- ✓ There are a few non-alcoholic drinking bitters such as *San Pelligrino* and *Crodino* (ditto Fanta), and a few such as Aperol that are low in alcohol. Most Italian bitters are dark brown; *Campari* is an exception.

Service of Bitters

- ✓ Bitters are not usually served neat or on their own. In majority of cases, bitters are used as a modifying or flavouring agent in a mixed drink. For example, Campari with soda (pour Campari bitters into a highball glass until half-full then top up the glass with soda water and then serve).

Brand Names of Bitters	
Aperitif bitters	Dubonnet (France), St. Raphael (France), Ratafia (France), Peychauds (New Orleans) and so forth.
Digestif bitters	Amer Picon (France), Aperol (Italy), Jeppson's (US), Suze (France), Fernet Branca (Italy) and so forth.
Non-alcoholic bitters	San Pelligrino and Crodino (ditto Fanta) and few Aperol and most Italian bitters are non-alcoholic.

OTHER FERMENTED AND DISTILLED BEVERAGES

Fermented Beverages	Major Ingredients	Flavoured with (Optional)	Country	Remarks
Schnaps	Potato (or neutral grain spirit)	Caraway seeds	Germany	American term is *Schnapps*
Sake	Fermented then brewed from rice	Any fruit	Japan	Serve Luke warm
Cider (1.2-8.5% alcohol content)	75% apple + 25% pears	Usually not	US/Global	Often also known as *apple wine*
Perry	75% pears + 25% apples	Usually not	England/ France	Often also called *pear cider*
Pulque	Agave plants	Any fruit	Mexico	Also known as *Mexican beer*
Pomace	Solid remains of grapes/other fruits after pressing/juice extraction	Usually not	Global	Contain skins, pulps, seeds and stems of the fruits
Mead (8-20% alcohol content)	Honey	Spices/fruits/ hops	Europe/ Africa/ Asia	May be still or carbonated
Pastis	Traditionally from whole herbs	Anise/liquorice	France	Its alcohol free varieties also exist
Tequiza	A brand-name of beverage that is a blend of beer, tequila, and lime	Lime touted	Mexico	Also described as *blue agave nectar*
Cauim	Made by fermenting *manioc* (a large starchy root) or maize	Fruit juices	Brazil	It is a beer of Brazil, also known as *Manioc beer* in English.

Distilled Beverages	Major Ingredients	Flavoured with (Optional)	Country	Remarks
Aquavit	Potato and grain mash	Caraway seeds	Scandinavia	Strong and clear
Arrack	Sap of palm tree	Aniseed/ liquorice	South Asia	Also made from rice, molasses
Marc	Grape pomace	Usually not	France	Local French brandy
Grappa	Grape pomace	Any fruit	Italy	Local Italian brandy
Calvados	Cider (or apple)	Usually not	Normandy	In UK, it is called *apple jack*
Slivovitz	Juice of plums	Fruits and herbs	Balkan	Also called *plum brandy*
Raki	Grapes	Aniseed	Turkey	Similar to *Italian grappa*
Feni	Coconut/juice of cashew apple	Usually not	India	Country liquor of India
Zivania	Grape pomace and local dry wines	Cinnamon	Cyprus	Distilled in *kazani* (an apparatus)
Punsch	Neutral spirit/ arrack	Various fruits	Sweden	It can be served hot as well as cold
Poire Williams	Made from pears (or William pears)	Usually not	France/ Switzerland	A colourless brandy
Tiquira	Made from Cassava	Usually not	Brazil	It is usually drunk on special occasions
Poitin/Poteen	Malted barley, grain or potatoes	Usually not	Ireland	Strongest alcoholic beverage in the world
Raicilla	Made from agave plant	Usually not	Mexico	Very much similar to tequila and mescal
Singani	Made from white muscatel grapes	Usually not	Bolivia	A clear alcoholic spirit/brandy
Pisco	Grape brandy	Usually not	Peru/Chile	Yellowish to amber in colour spirit/brandy

KEY TERMS

Frappé	:	Service of liqueur on crushed ice.
Cordial	:	Liqueurs which are a sweet alcoholic drink normally served after a meal.
Grasshopper	:	A rum based cocktail. The green colour hue is due to crème de menthe liqueur.
Grappa	:	Italian brandy that is produced for local consumption.
Apple jack	:	A term used in United Kingdom for calvados (or distilled apple juice).
Neutral spirit	:	Clear, colourless and flammable liquid/spirit that has very high ethanol content.
Grain spirit	:	Collective term for all grain made spirits.
Molasses	:	A byproduct of sugarcane used to produce rum, rum is often known as *cane spirit*.
Copita	:	Wine glass that is used to taste sherry wine.
Sparkling liqueur	:	A carbonated liqueur like French Nuvo liqueur.

REVIEW QUESTIONS

1. What is liqueur? Enlist ten neutral spirit liqueurs on following parameters: name, base, flavour, brand, country and remark (if any).
2. Define the term vermouth. Classify major types of vermouths and explain each briefly along with brand names/examples.
3. What is bitters? Classify major types of bitters and explain each briefly along with brand names/examples.
4. Write a short note on aperitif.

23
CHAPTER

Introduction to Bar

OBJECTIVES

Students will be able to:

- identify bar sections and placed equipment; and
- explain bar dimension and major bar types.

BAR

A bar (or *permit room*) is an outlet that serves alcoholic drinks — mostly beer, wine, spirit, liquor and cocktails — for consumption on the premises (it may be *public bar* or *service bar*). Exactly, bar is the part of the front bar where customers sit on bar stools or stand around the front counter and consume their beverages. Front bars also serve as a serving station for drinks and frequently as a platform for mixing drinks. Some bars have entertainment on a stage, such as a live band, comedians, go-go dancers, or strippers. Remember, *profit percentage* of beverage is higher than food. Simultaneously, efficiency of beverages is based on pour/cost percentage; it is usually 16-24% pour/cost percentage.

Bar Equipment and Supplies	
Small	Blenders, Shakers, Bar glasses, Peg measures (or *jiggers*), Spirit pourers, Service trays, Glass racks, Drip trays, Cutting boards, Knives, Ice buckets, Ice crusher, Juicers, Stirrers, Ashtrays, Rubbish bins, Bottle openers (like *waiter's friend*), Bitters bottle, Ice tong/scoop, Cork extractor, Decanter, Water pitcher, Funnel, Strainer, Optic measure, Muddler, Squeezer, Wine cradle, Rimmer, etc.
Heavy	Bar counter, Bar stools, *Speed rack*, Sinks, Beer taps, Cobra guns (used to serve draught beer), Refrigerator, Glass chillers, Ice machine, Bulk beer cooling system, Glass washer, Cash register, Electronic spirit dispenser, Express machine, Shelves, Cigar and Cigarette display cabinet, Television (most important in sports bar) and so forth.
Supplies	It includes *food supplies* like Castor sugar, Lemon, lime, Orange, Olives, Tiny/pearl onions, Maraschino cherries, Salt and pepper and Snack foods like wafers and peanuts; and *liquor supplies* like- Lemon juice, lime juice, Tomato juice, Egg white, Angostura bitters, Grenadine syrup, Worcestershire sauce, Tabasco sauce, Cream and Ice cream, etc.

PARTS OF BAR

BRAND IDENTITY

House brand	Associate brands
Call brand	Well known
Premium brand	Luxury brands

Front bar

- ✓ It is a fixed counter for beverage services, from where guests (as well as server) have direct access to place order as well as to consume/enjoy drink. It is open for business on scheduled basis. Front bars are permanently fixed in locations within the establishment.
- ✓ It comprises drip/glass rail, counter to place drink, armrest, *bar die*, footrest and *masonry curb*. Nowadays, the ceiling of front bar section is used to hang bar glasses (upside down) in hanging racks.

Back bar

- ✓ It is the back part of a bar counter– the *under part* of back bar is used to keep dry grocery and other food and liquor supplies in cabinets whereas *top part* is used as a display cabinet (or known as *speed rack*).
- ✓ Generally, call brands, house brands and premium brands are placed in speed rack; beer and soft drinks are never displayed. The back bar speaks volumes about a bar operation. It conveys the image of the establishment and displays the kinds of beverage collections.

Under bar

- ✓ It is usually the last section of the bar where most of the bar requirements and supplies are compactly and efficiently arranged, to facilitate speed of service. It comprises pouring station or working station where bartender prepares all drinks to serve both guests and stewards (who will serve to seated guests).
- ✓ Another area of underbar contains glass washing equipment – a three or four compartment sink with drain boards on both sides – or, in some cases, a mechanical dishwasher. Together, the underbar and back bar must provide enough storage for the day's reserve supplies of liquors, mixes, wines, beers, ice, garnishes, etc.

Bar Dimensions

Bar Section	Height	Width	Remarks
Front bar	42-48 inches	16-18 inches	Bar die, footrest, armrest and spill/drip/glass rail are important parts.
Under bar	28-32 inches	20-22 inches	Speed rail requires around 4-6 inches space gap from under bar top.
Back bar	30-42 inches	22-26 inches	Around 34-36 inch gap is required between back bar and under bar.

Note. Width of speed rack's shelves should be 10 to 14 inches, distance between under bar to bar top should be 12 inches, height of bar die should be 40 inches from the ground, distance between edge of speed rack and bar rail should be 14 inches, distance between the bar stool seat and bar top should be 12 inches.

MAJOR TYPES OF BARS

Beverage aided revenue; bar is an authorized place where alcoholic, non-alcoholic drinks and often mixed drinks along with snacks are served. In bars, bartender along with his team of *bar back* performs all tasks. There are various types of bar available in the food service industry. Among these, two major forms of bar are given below.

Bar Concepts

- Saloon bar
- Banquet bar
- Pool bar
- Night club
- Sports bar
- Cocktail bar
- Ice bar
- Island bar
- Sunken bar

Public Bar (Display bar)

- ✓ It is a bar where bartender prepares alcoholic, non-alcoholic and mixed drinks and serves them directly to guests. Guests either directly stand in front or are seated on bar stools. In simple terms, guests can order and pick up their own beverages at public bars. These bars have no or limited provision of food orders but must have bar snacks like peanuts, wafers, etc. It is also called "display bar".

Service Bar (Dispense bar)

- ✓ It is a bar where bartender prepares alcoholic, non-alcoholic and mixed drinks for server only, who then takes the drinks to the table seated guests.
- ✓ This bar is also called "dispense bar or restaurant bar". Service bar is located inside the restaurant and mainly caters to restaurant diners. Hence, serving staff of restaurant must have the knowledge of pairing of food and drink.

KEY TERMS

Permit room	:	A bar or any room that holds required licence/s for serving/offering alcoholic beverages.
Jigger	:	Peg measure that is used to measure the drink/hard beverages.
Bar die	:	Front part of the bar that creates distance between the bartender and guests.
Masonry curb	:	Bottom part of the front bar made up of stone or brick of ideally four inches.

Saloon bar	:	Lounge bar.
Call brand	:	Most famous liquor brands.
Speed rack	:	Display rack to keep call, premium and house brands.
Speed rail	:	Glass rail or drip rail found in manually operated bars.
Bar back	:	Bar staff who works under a bartender.

REVIEW QUESTIONS

1. Enlist the emerging trends of bar.
2. Differentiate between bar back and back bar.
3. Explain the different parts of bar. Enlist the standard figures or bar dimensions.
4. Differentiate between service bar and public bar.

24 CHAPTER

Tobacco Products (Cigar and Cigarette)

Objectives

Students will be able to:

- elucidate tobacco making process and its major products; and
- explain shape, components and storage of cigar.

TOBACCO

Tobacco is an agricultural product processed from the fresh leaves of plants in the genus *Nicotiana*. It is most commonly smoked in the form of cigarettes and cigars. Tobacco is one of the most widely used addictive substances in the world. Tobacco, a plant native to the America, was grown and used by the Mayans. These were the indigenous people of Mexico and parts of Central America. There are different types of tobaccos that are used for making different tobacco products like:

Tobacco	*Uses*	*Tobacco*	*Uses*
• Virginia	Pipe tobacco	• Burley	Cigarettes
• Oriental	Cigarettes	• Latakia	Cigarettes
• Perique	Pipe tobacco	• Kentucky	Pipe tobacco
• Cavendish	Cigars and pipe	• Criollo	Cigars
• Dokha	Pipe tobacco		

TOBACCO MANUFACTURING PROCESS

Cultivation

✓ Scatter seeds into the soil and when tobacco plants reach relative maturity, they are transplanted into the field.

Harvesting

✓ Tobacco is annually cultivated and harvested either by traditional method (cutting entire plant from the ground) or modern method (plucking of leaves by hand).

Curing

✓ It means drying tobacco leaves either by natural heat (sunlight) or artificial heat (in forced air chambers). The ideal curing time is two to six weeks between the temperature ranges of 21-77°C.

Fermentation

✓ Tobacco leaves are fermented by storing them for six weeks to two years with about 18% moisture content at 27-43°C.

Final tobacco

✓ Finally, ground the fermented tobacco leaves. The flat product made from ground tobacco and binding agents is often blended with tobacco leaves.

CIGAR

A *cigar* is a tightly rolled bundle of dried and fermented tobacco which is ignited so that its smoke may be drawn into the smoker's mouth. They come in different shapes and sizes. Cigar tobacco is grown in significant quantities in Brazil, Cameroon, Cuba, Dominican Republic, Honduras, Indonesia, Mexico, Nicaragua, the Philippines and the United States.

Storage of Cigar

Quality cigars	Cedar wood box
Green cigars	Humidor box
Single cigar	Aluminum pipe

Manufacturing Process of Cigar

Preparing tobacco leaves

✓ Tobacco leaves are harvested and aged using a process that combines use of heat and shade to reduce sugar and water content without causing the large leaves to rot.

Shapes of Cigar

Parejo

Torpedo

Pyramid

Perfecto

Presidente

Curing and fermentation

✓ Curing process takes place for 25 to 45 days. Afterwards fermentation is carried out between the temperature zones of 50-55°C.

Sorting

✓ Now tobacco leaves are sorted for use as filler or wrapper, based upon their appearance and overall quality. Next sorted out leaves are kept for maturation. When the leaves matures (as per the requirement) it will be used to make cigar.

Making of cigar

✓ Quality cigars are handmade whereas regular cigars are machine made. An experienced cigar-roller can produce hundreds of very good, nearly identical cigars per day.

Storage

✓ Once rolled, both handmade and machine made cigars are stored in wooden boxes (*green cigars* stored in humidor box whereas matured cigars are stored in cedar wood box), in which their uncapped ends are cut to a uniform size.

Components of Cigar	
Wrapper	It is cigar's outermost leaves that come from the widest part of the plant. It may be Claro (light yellow), Colorado (reddish brown), Colorado Claro (mid-brown), Colorado Maduro (dark brown), Maduro (very dark brown) and Double Claro (slightly greenish).
Filler	It refers to stuffing that is usually crushed leaves (it contains oil that affects cigar's strength and flavour). It can be Volado (medium flavoured – taken from bottom part of the plant), Seco (light flavoured – taken from middle part of the plant), ligero (strong flavoured – taken from upper part of the plant).
Binder	Binders are elastic leaves used to hold together bunches of fillers. In simple terms, these are the leaves which are smaller in size and are bound around the filler.

CIGARETTE

A cigarette (combination of two words- cigar + ette, *ette* means small, hence cigarette is also known as *small cigar*) is a product consumed through smoking and manufactured out of cured and finely cut tobacco leaves and reconstituted tobacco, combined with other additives then rolled or stuffed into a paper wrapped cylinder (generally less than 120 mm in length and 10 mm in diameter or *ring gauge*).

Manufacturing Process of Cigarette

Raw material

COMPONENTS OF CIGARETTE	
Raw material	Reconstituted tobacco
Filter	Cellulose acetate
Flavouring	Sweetening agent – *casing*
Rolling paper	Fire safe paper
Binder	Polyvinyl acetate (PVA) glue

- ✓ Cigarette is made with three components, i.e., crushed reconstituted tobacco, rolling paper, filter and glue to bind.
- ✓ *Tobacco* is available in two varieties – cultivated tobacco (*Nicotiana tabacum*) and wild tobacco (*Nicotiana rustica*). *Rolling paper* is made with seed flax mixed with paper pulp and *filters* are made of synthetic, cotton-like fibre.

Harvesting

- ✓ Hand planted or machine planted tobacco plants are harvested either by *priming* or by stalk cutting method.
- ✓ Under *priming method*, the tobacco leaves are barn cured as they ripen whereas in *stalk cutting method*, the entire plant is cut and allowed to wilt in open fields before taking to curing barn.

Curing

- ✓ Obtained tobacco leaves are carefully and gradually dried in a barn by *air curing* (curing under sunlight), *flue curing* (curing by artificial heating) or *fire curing* (curing over burning woods). Now cured tobacco leaves must be conditioned (moist) so they do not break when handled.

Sorting and blending

- ✓ Tobacco leaves are sorted into grades based on size, colour and quality. Afterwards they are completely dried and a uniform amount of moisture is added and kept in *hogsheads* for one to three years of aging (it develops flavour and aroma). After ageing, leaves from different types of tobacco are mixed to create a particular flavour.

Making of cigarettes

- ✓ Now blended tobacco leaves are pressed into cakes and mechanically shredded. Flavouring agents like fruit juices or menthol and *casing* is added at this stage. Finally, shredded tobacco leaves are dispersed over a continuous roll of cigarette paper.

✓ A machine rolls the shredded tobacco into the paper and cuts into required length and fastens a filter at one end. Modern machines can make 25-30 cigarettes in a second.

Packaging

✓ The finished cigarettes are packaged in hard or soft cardboard boxes and wrapped in protective cellophane. The hard or soft packs are mechanically sealed in cellophane and hand-placed in cartons. Cigarettes can also be made by hands but it will take more time.

SERVICE OF CIGAR AND CIGARETTES

Steps	Tasks	Cigarette	Cigar	Remarks
1	Take order from guest/host	On BOT	On BOT	*Sommelier* takes order for both
2	Process order	To bar	To bar	Either at service bar or public bar
3	Collect cigar/ cigarette from bar	In packet	In cigar box	Also collect gas lighter or matchbox
4	Approach the guest for service	On side plate	In cigar box	From right-hand side of the guest/host
5	Perform service of cigar (in cedar wood or humidor box)/ cigarette	Place side plate on cover	Offer cigar box to guest	Guest can purchase one cigar but cannot purchase one cigarette for smoking.
6	Remove band and cut the end	Not necessary	Necessary	Cigar cutter is used to cut the cigar end
7	Offer lighter to light the cigar/cigarette	Any lighter	Gas lighter only	Petrol lighter may affect the flavour/aroma of cigar. Match box can be used for both.

Brand Names of Cigar and Cigarette			
Cigars		**Cigarettes**	
Bengal Tiger	Indian	Pallmall	American
Corona Deluxe	Dutch	555	English
Diplomat Deluxe	Jamaican	Benson and Hedges	English
Ambapsado	Holland	Dunhill	English
Ducados	Danish	Phillip Morris	USA (New York)

Romeo Juliet	Cuba	Gold Flake	Indian
Robert Burns	America	Camel	American
Veracruz	Mexico	Winfield	Australia
White Owl	America	520	Taiwan
Vegueros	Cuba	Export A	Japan
Swisher Sweet	Florida	Gauloises	France
Vegafina	Spain	Du Maurier	Canada
El Siglo	Venezuela	Davidoff	Switzerland
Quintero	Cuba	Djarum	Indonesia
Plasencia	Spain	Lambert and Butler	UK

KEY TERMS

Casing	:	Sweetening agent used in cigarette.
Sommelier	:	Position of wine steward/waiter who is also responsible for serving cigar and cigarette.
Cedar wood	:	Box used to store mature cigars like Havana cigars.
Humidor box	:	Cigar box used to keep cigar but green cigars (or fresh cigars).
Green cigar	:	Fresh cigar.
Ring gauge	:	Cigar dimension/measurement which is always measured in 64^{ths} of an inch.
Nicotiana	:	Genus plant of tobacco.
PVA	:	Polyvinyl acetate (PVA), a kind of glue to bind cigarettes.
Nicotiana tabacum	:	Cultivated tobacco.
Nicotiana rustica	:	Wild tobacco.

REVIEW QUESTIONS

1. What is tobacco? Elucidate various tobacco based products, explain each briefly.
2. Define the term cigar. Describe the components of cigar and explain the terms used to denote cigar's strength.
3. What is cigarette? Describe the step-by-step procedure for serving cigar and cigarette.
4. Enlist any five famous brands of cigar and cigarette.

25 CHAPTER

Sales/Revenue Control

OBJECTIVES

Students will be able to:

- explicate different checking systems and their flow;
- explain different payment modes; and
- reveal formulas used to calculate outlet cost.

CONTROL

Control means checking the ongoing work that it is being performed in accordance with plan or not, simultaneously ensuring that the stated target is achieved in given time-frame. In simple terms, *controlling* is a process of verifying the actual performance in comparison with the planned standards, ascertaining deviations and suggesting remedial measures to stop recurrence of such deviations. These deviations can be minor as well as major. *Minor deviations* (or adjustable deviations) can be avoided but *major* (or non-adjustable deviations) ones should always be addressed properly. Every effective control process comprises the following four steps/functions:

- Establishment of standards
- Appraisal of performance, measurement of actual performance
- Ascertaining degree of deviations (major or minor) and their causes
- Take corrective or remedial measures

MAJOR CONTROLLING/CHECKING SYSTEM

Duplicate Checking System

- ✓ Sometimes this system is also called "single carbon system or dupe system". In this system of controlling, there are two copies of KOT or BOT. The 1st copy is original whereas 2nd copy is carbon or duplicate copy.
- ✓ Both copies should be transferred to the concerned section and department. For example, 1st copy goes to kitchen/bar to make the order ready and 2nd copy will remain with steward on station or sent to the cashier to make the bill ready. This type of system may be used for both types of menu; *á la carte* as well as TDH.

Triplicate Checking System

- ✓ This system is also known as "double carbon system". In this checking system, there are three copies of KOT or BOT to control/track the food/drink orders. The 1st copy is original while 2nd and 3rd copy (often indicated by different colours) is carbon or duplicate copy.
- ✓ All copies should be sent to relevant sections and departments like 1st copy goes to kitchen/bar to make the order ready, 2nd copy goes to the cashier to make/update the bill and 3rd copy remains with steward on side station (for further reference). This system is exclusively for a full *á la carte* restaurant.

Special KOT's/BOT's

- Retour (return)
- En place (in place)
- Supplement (extra)
- En suit/Suivant
- No charge (FOC)
- Cancellation
- Duplicate
- Extra charge

Triple carbon copy

- ✓ In this system, there is one transparent sheet or paper (often called *flimsy copy*), so the steward has an original copy. The *flimsy* copy remains on the side station with waiter.
- ✓ The flow of remaining two copies is same as above-mentioned *triplicate checking system*. This system is usually followed in very busy and high-class *á la carte* restaurant.

Room service guest check

- ✓ The guest check in room service section may consist of three copies or five copies. If it is three copies system then 1st copy goes to kitchen section, 2nd (it may remain with cashier/order taker) and 3rd copy goes to guest for payment or for signature.
- ✓ In case of five pad system, 1st copy goes to hot kitchen, 2nd copy goes to cold kitchen, 3rd copy to bar section, 4th copy may remain with cashier/order taker and 5th copy goes to guest.

FLOWCHART OF KOT/BOT (IN RESTAURANT)

A KOT/BOT is an internal control document used to take and write guest order in any available food and beverage point of sales outlet, thereafter steward routes it to the concerned person. After writing the guest order on KOT or BOT, steward will transmit to generated KOT/BOT through *bus person* to the relevant person of the sections/departments like 1st or top copy goes to *sous chef* in kitchen section (or to *aboyeur* in hot plate area, if there is any), 2nd copy goes to cashier of that outlet and 3rd copy will remain with steward for further reference.

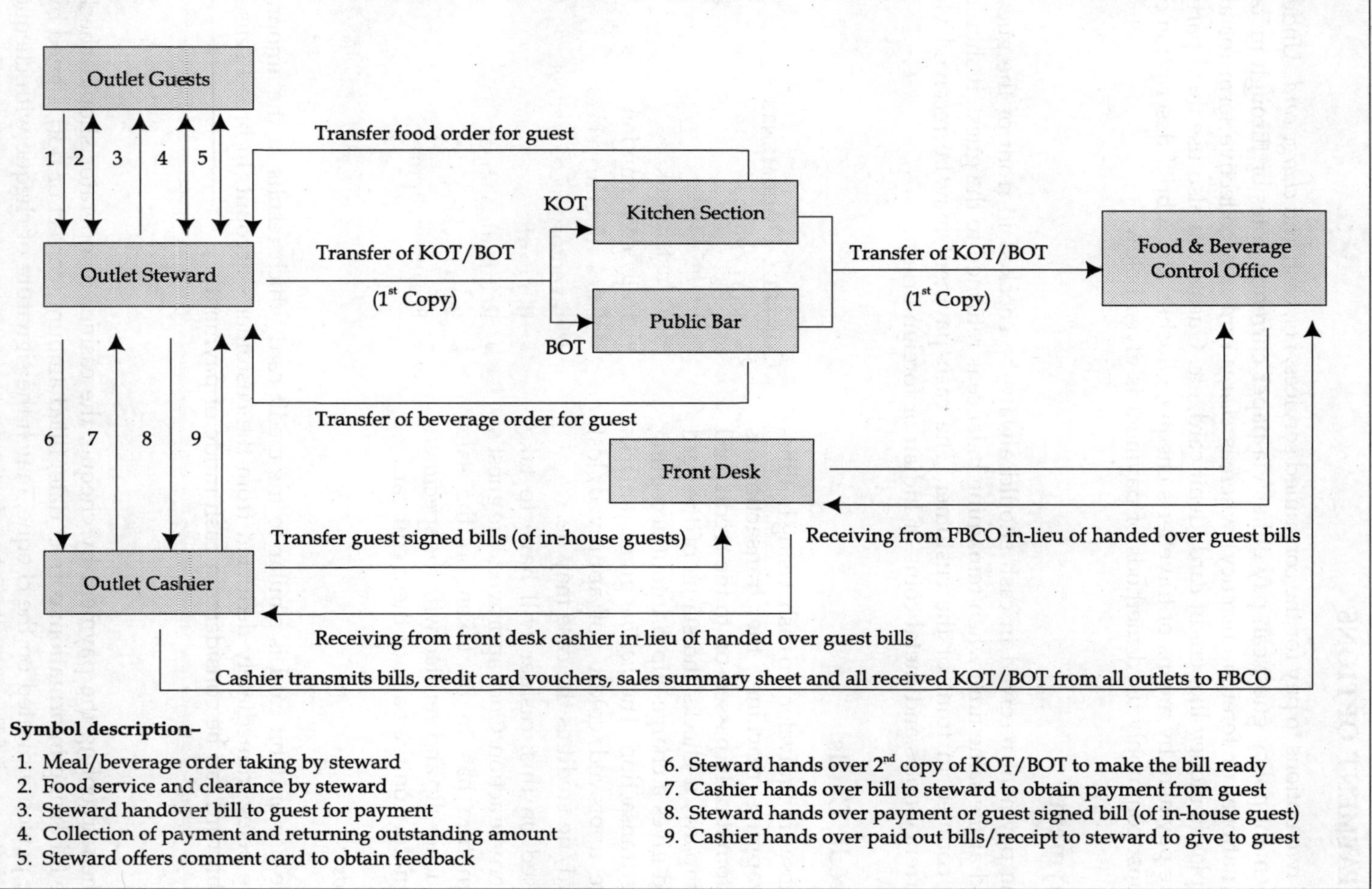

Fig.25.1 Flow Chart of KOT under Triplicate Checking System

GUEST PAYMENT OPTIONS

There are two options to pay for the consumed services, i.e., cash and *charge card*. Under cash settlement policy guest can pay either via paper currency notes or through metal coins (of national or foreign currency) whereas *charge card* is a collective term for all forms of plastic money like credit card, debit card, etc. Guests can also use third party billing like payment by means of traveller's cheque, voucher, etc. A brief description of several most commonly used methods of payment is given below.

Cash Payment

✓ The payment received in cash should always be checked in front of the guest and at the same time when remaining balance is returned to the guest, it should be counted in front of the customer. The cash payment may be received via currency notes and metal coins of Indian or foreign origin.

Bank Credit Cards

✓ These are equivalent to cash. Using hotline-swapping machine, the transaction is automatically passed on to the credit card company; it checks the status of the card and gives a charge-slip printout accepting the transaction. The *hotline* gives remarks like approved/credit not approved/lost card/no credit as the case may be.

✓ Based on this, cashier will have to take alternate action. Once approved, the guest's signature has to be taken on the sale voucher slip and verified with the specimen signature on the back of the credit card.

Control Documents

- KOT/BOT
- Cellar book
- Transfer book
- Daily consumption sheet
- Sales summary sheet
- Inventory record/sheet
- Bin card
- Requisition sheet
- Bar checklist
- Breakage report

Debit cards

✓ The use of debit card is similar to the credit card which results in the amount due being immediately deducted from the customer's account. In broad sense, debit card can be considered a cash mode of payment.

Cheque

✓ When accepting the payment by cheque, the cashier or operator should check the following information: correct date, filled amount (correct or not), signed by the person indicated on the cheque, match the signature of cheque with cheque card (in case of Euro card) and so forth.

✓ Remember, cheque should always be accompanied by the *cheque card*. Generally, Euro cheques and traveller's cheques are widely acceptable whereas personal cheque's, acceptability is limited.

Traveller's cheques

✓ These cheques are issued by financial institutions like American Express and are very much similar to *bankers' cheque*. The traveller's cheque must be signed once when issued and again (second sign in front of cashier) when used to pay.

✓ Travellers' cheque of alien countries (or foreign countries) is exchanged in a similar fashion as foreign currency. But property must have all required RLM series of license/s to exchange foreign currency and travellers' cheque.

Personal cheques

✓ It is up to the policy of a hotel that whether it accepts guests' personal cheques or not. If yes then, check the date, name of the hotel (or in favour of payee), amount (in figure as well as in words), finally the signature of the guest. Ensure crossing on the cheques for safety. Personal cheques of foreign banks and third party should not be accepted.

COSTING FORMULAS

Particulars	Formula	In ratio	In percentage
Food cost	$\frac{\text{Cost of sale (of foods)}}{\text{Total revenue (of foods)}}$	Formula as it is	Multiplied by 100
Beverage cost	$\frac{\text{Cost of sale (of beverages)}}{\text{Total revenue (of beverages)}}$	Formula as it is	Multiplied by 100
Labour cost	$\frac{\text{Cost of labour}}{\text{Total revenue (of food and beverage)}}$	Formula as it is	Multiplied by 100
Average rate per guest or Average per cover (APC)	$\frac{\text{Total revenue (of food and beverage)}}{\text{Number of guests served}}$	Formula as it is	Multiplied by 100
Average spending power	$\frac{\text{Total revenue (of food and beverage)}}{\text{Number of covers}}$	Formula as it is	Multiplied by 100
Seat turnover rate	$\frac{\text{Number of guests served}}{\text{Number of available seats/covers}}$	Formula as it is	Multiplied by 100
Average per steward	$\frac{\text{Total revenue (of food and beverage)}}{\text{Number of stewards}}$	Formula as it is	Multiplied by 100

Restaurant occupancy	$\frac{\text{Total number of covers served}}{\text{Total number of covers offered}}$	Formula as it is	Multiplied by 100
Departmental profit	$\frac{\text{Departmental profit}}{\text{Total revenue (of food and beverage)}}$	Formula as it is	Multiplied by 100

Guest Bill

Date .... Serial No............
Table no. ....
No. of pax ....

S.No.	Particulars	Item code	Price	Qty.	Total

Total
Add: Service Charge
Add: SGST/CGST
Less: Discount

Grand total amount

Guest Signature

Note. If paid in cash then don't sign this slip

Sales Summary Sheet

Meal ....
Date.....................

Bill No.	Table No.	No. of Covers	Room No.	Amount paid			Foods	Beverages	Tobacco	Flowers	Extras	Sundry expenses	Total	Remarks
				Cash	Credit	Others								

Consumption Control Sheet

Meal ....
Date.....................

Particulars	Portion issued	Portion returned	Portion consumed	Billed portions	Discrepancy		Remarks
					Plus	Minus	

Kitchen Order Ticket	
Date _____ Day _____ Time _____	
No. of Pax _____ Table No. _____ Steward No. _____	
Quantity	**Items**
	Sig. of waiter
Note. Guests please do not pay against this check	

KEY TERMS

Control	: Crucial functions of management by which executed work is compared with planned work.
Dupe system	: Duplicate checking system of KOT/BOT.
Flimsy copy	: Transparent sheet or paper under triple carbon checking system.
APC	: Average per cover, i.e., average revenue generated from each cover sold.
Bin card	: Stock control tool that shows daily receipts, issues and closing balance.
Hot line	: Fully automatic credit card approval machine which works online.
Cheque card	: Card that is accompanied with cheques like Euro cheques with euro cards.
En suit/Suivant	: Special kind of KOT used for placing running meals.

REVIEW QUESTIONS

1. What different modes of payment a property can offer to their guests for settling accounts?
2. Give the formulas of the following: APC, food cost, beverage cost, department profit and average per steward
3. Draw the format of KOT. Elucidate special types of KOTs and explain each briefly.
4. Draw the flow of KOT under triplicate checking system.

26
CHAPTER

Alcoholic and Non-Alcoholic Cocktails

OBJECTIVES

Students will be able to:

- expound golden rules of cocktail making; and
- explain different methods used to make cocktails.

COCKTAIL

A *cocktail* is a style of mixed drink (but at least contains one alcoholic beverage). A cocktail usually contains one or more types of liquor (or spirits like gin, vodka, brandy, rum, etc.) + flavouring agents + smoothing agents and modifying agents. It may also contain fruit juices, sauces, sugar, spices, honey, milk, egg and so forth ingredients. The cocktail became popular during prohibition in the United States primarily to mask the taste of bootlegged alcohol.

Various bar mixtures, or so-called *cocktails,* can be divided into several groups in accordance with the number of criteria/bases. In general, these bases are nature of mixture, sugar content, quantity of drink, time of consumption. A brief description of each type of cocktails is given below.

CLASSIFICATION OF COCKTAILS

On the Basis of Nature of Mixture

Alcoholic cocktails

✓ The mixture of two or more alcoholic beverages with other alcoholic or non-alcoholic beverages (like fruit juices, squashes, cold drinks, bitters, etc.) is called "cocktail" or "alcoholic cocktail".

Non-alcoholic cocktails

✓ The mixture of two or more non-alcoholic beverages with soft drinks, juices, syrups, squashes, etc. But mixture should contain only non-alcoholic beverages; these may be termed "mocktail" or "non-alcoholic cocktail".

On the Basis of Sugar Content

Sweet cocktails

✓ Sweet cocktails are those cocktails in which extra sweetening agents like sweet vermouths, sugar syrup, grenadine syrup, castor sugar, etc., are added, for example, smash, sours, sungaree, flips, etc.

Medium cocktails

✓ These cocktails are neither sweet nor dry in taste. They are medium, therefore called medium cocktails, for example, Rolls Royce, Bamboo, etc.

Dry cocktails

✓ These cocktails are dry in nature (not sweet), a famous ingredient which creates dryness, i.e., dry vermouth, is often added, for example, Gibson, dry martini, dry Manhattan, etc.

On the Basis of Quantity of Drink

Short drinks

✓ These drinks are served in small quantity, thus mainly served in cocktail or martini or short glass. These cocktails may also be known as "small cocktails", for example, daiquiri, B and B, Margarita, Gimlet, etc.

Long drinks

✓ These drinks are served in large quantity, thus usually served in long glasses such as High ball and Collin glass are called "Long drinks", for example, John Collin, Gin fizz, Pimms' cup, Horse's neck, etc.

✓ These drinks are often served on ice and are frequently fruity and softened with a generous proportion of fruit juices, soft drinks and milk.

On the Basis of Time of Consumption

Aperitifs

✓ These drinks are usually consumed before the meals; therefore, sometimes are also called "pre-dinner drinks", for example, White lady, Gibson, Screwdriver, Manhattan, Bloody Mary, etc.

✓ These cocktails are usually acidic or dry in nature when mixed with tart ingredients like lemon juice to refresh the palate and act as an aperitif before meal.

Digestives

- ✓ These drinks are usually consumed after the meals; therefore, these are also called "after dinner drinks". For example, Sidecar, Black Russian, Grasshopper, Rusty Nail, Frappes, etc.
- ✓ These cocktails are made by using more creamy ingredients. They tend to be richer in texture and are frequently quite sweet.

Methods of Making Cocktails

Blend cocktails

- ✓ It means putting the ingredients into the electric blender. Add crushed ice if required by the recipe and blend until the required consistency is obtained. Pour unstrained into a suitable glass.

Build cocktails

- ✓ Pour the necessary ingredients directly into a suitable glass without any premixing. Add ice only if required by the recipe. Mixed drinks made in this way are usually served with a stirrer.

Mixed cocktails

- ✓ Put the ingredients into the cone of the electric drink mixer and add crushed ice if specified. Mix until the drink reaches the required consistency, then pour or strain into a glass.

Parts of cocktail

Agent	Role	Ratio
Base agent	Major	40-50%
Flavouring	Flavour	15-25%
Modifying	Revamp	25-35%
Garnish	Décor	05-10%

Shake cocktails

- ✓ Put ice into the cocktail shaker and pour in the necessary ingredients. Shake shortly and sharply unless mixed well (never add soda) and then strain into the required glass.

Stir cocktails

- ✓ Put ice into the chilled mixing glass and pour in the necessary ingredients. Stir until cold and strain into the required glass.

Stir-in cocktails

✓ When topping with the final ingredient then the steward needs to use the bar spoon to stir in, as it is added. These types of cocktails are also called "stir-in cocktails".

Golden Rules of Making Cocktails

Use correct method

✓ It is most important to use the right method for the making of cocktail in order to get a good result and to avoid any mis-happening. For example, soda based cocktails should never be shaken.

Use correct shaker

✓ There are two types of shakers (*cocktail* and *Boston shaker*). Both shakers can be used for making cocktails. But in some cases they have their own importance like when egg white or yolk is used in cocktail, it is preferred to use Boston shaker while cocktail shaker is used in fruit juices, cream, sugar, etc., based mixed drinks.

Clean cocktail shaker

✓ One may use either cocktail shaker or Boston shaker, but make sure that the shaker should be perfectly cleaned before starting cocktail operation as well as at every time before making new cocktails (hence, keep a large size punch bowl with lukewarm water in your under bar section in order to clean shaker before making every new mixed drink).

Serve in chilled glass

✓ Cocktails are usually served chilled. So, it is good to chill the cocktail glasses in advance, by keeping in chillers before starting the operation as well as during the operation (after receiving clean glasses from dishwashing).

Glass Capacity

Glasses	Fl. oz
Water glasses	08 – 10
Beer glasses	12 – 14
Brandy balloon	08 – 10
Wine glasses	06 – 08
Champ. glasses	06 – 08
Cocktail glass	03 – 05
Paris goblet	06 – 08
Margarita glass	06 – 08
Collin glass	10 – 12
Whiskey glass	08 – 10
Parfait glass	10 – 12
Tequila shot	01 – 02
Roly poly glass	08 – 10
Juice glass	04 – 06
Irish coffee glass	08 – 10
Pool glass	10 – 12
Decanter	Varies

Use clean ice

- ✓ Ice is an important ingredient in the making of cocktails. The ice should always be clean or free from any type of particles like dust, grass, paper, etc.

Sequence of pouring

- ✓ The sequence of adding ingredients is also an important rule like – firstly put ice in mixing glass followed by non-alcoholic beverage and then alcoholic beverage. Lastly add garnish.

Use branded product

- ✓ In order to make a good cocktail, barman needs to use only the best known proprietary brand of spirits. Good spirits create a fabulous taste.

Garnishing

- ✓ If barman adds any kind of garnish like lemon slice, orange peel, cherry, etc. into the cocktail, then this garnish should always be added after the cocktail has been made. Garnish should not be too large, as it can cover the face of cocktail.

Correct measurement

- ✓ Alike to kitchen preparation, cocktail should also have *standard recipe*, in order to achieve an excellent taste. Therefore, a bartender should always measure the amount of ingredients accurately.

Don't overfill

- ✓ It is also a golden rule to never overfill the shaker because it will create difficulty during shaking or drink may not mix properly. It is also important from the point of view to avoid spillage or wastage of drink.

Don't repeat ingredients

- ✓ To create a perfect taste in cocktail, bartender should never use the same ice for preparing second drink (even if he/she is making the same cocktail). As observed the taste and flavour of ingredients could destroy the taste and flavour of new drinks when the same ice is used.

EXAMPLES OF COCKTAILS AND MOCKTAILS

Vodka Based Cocktails

Cocktail Name	Ingredients		Method	Glass	Garnish
	Qty.	Ingredients			
Black Russian	30 mL 30 mL	Vodka Kahlúa	Build over ice	Old Fashioned	Cherry
Bloody Mary	30 mL 120 mL 2 drops 5 mL 5 mL	Vodka Tomato Juice Lemon Juice Tabasco Worcestershire (an optional)	Build over ice	Highball	Stick of celery and lemon slice
Harvey Wallbanger	30 mL 30 mL 150 mL	Vodka Galliano Orange juice	Stir and strain	Collin	Orange slice and cherry
Blue Lagoon	60 mL 30 mL 60 mL 30 mL	Vodka Blue Curaçao Lemonade Double cream	Shake and strain	Collin	Twist or slice of lemon
Screwdriver	30 mL 120 mL	Vodka Orange juice	Shake and strain	Highball	Twist or slice of lemon

Gin Based Cocktails

Cocktail Name	Ingredients		Method	Glass	Garnish
	Qty.	Ingredients			
Pink Lady	60 mL 10 mL 10 mL 1 dash	Gin Cream Curaçao Grenadine	Stir and strain	Cocktail	No garnish
Tom Collin	30 mL 5 mL 1 tspn. Cubes	Gin Lemon Juice Fine Sugar Ice	Build up	Highball	Lemon slice
Gimlet	60 mL 15 mL	Gin Lime juice/ Lemon cordial	Stir and strain	Cocktail/ Champagne Saucer	Lemon slice/Cherry on stick
Martini-Dry	60 mL 10 mL Cubes	London Dry Dry Vermouth Ice	Stir and strain	Cocktail	Olive or Twist lemon

White Lady	30 mL 15 mL 15 mL	Gin Cointreau Lemon Juice	Shake and Strain	Cocktail	Cherry
Gin fizz	30 mL 30 mL 2 tsp Top-up	Gin Lemon juice Castor sugar Soda siphon	Shake and strain	Old Fashioned	Lemon slice
Gibson	60 mL 30 mL 1 dash 30 mL	Gin Dry vermouth Angostura bitter Orange juice	Shake and strain	Cocktail	Cocktail onion and twist of lemon
Bronx	45 mL 15 mL 15 mL 30 mL	Gin Dry vermouth Sweet vermouth Orange juice	Stir and strain	Champagne saucer	Orange slice
Gin sling	60 mL 15 mL 1 dash Cubes	Gin Fresh lime juice Grenadine syrup Ice and soda to top-up	Build up	Highball	Lime slice and cherry
Singapore sling	45 mL 15 mL 15 mL 15 mL Top-up	Gin Cherry brandy Sugar syrup Fresh lime Soda to top-up	Build up	Highball	Slice of orange and cherry

Tequila Based Cocktails

Cocktail Name	Ingredients		Method	Glass	Garnish
	Qty.	Ingredients			
Sunrise	30 mL 2 dash 120 mL	Tequila Grenadine Orange juice	Stir and strain	Collin	Twist of orange peel
Margarita	30 mL 30 mL 15 mL	Tequila Cointreau Lemon Juice	Shake and strain	Cocktail	Frost rim of glass with salt and put lemon slice

Matador	45 mL 75 mL Half lime	Silver or Blanco tequila Pineapple juice Juice of half a lime	Shake and strain	Cocktail	Lime slice or twist
Tequila Slammer	30 mL 30 mL	Tequila 7 Up or ginger ale	Straight	Rock glass	Not necessary
Brave Bull	15 mL 15 mL	Tequila Kahlúa	Build-up	Old Fashioned	Not necessary

Rum Based Cocktails

Cocktail name	Ingredients		Method	Glass	Garnish
	Qty.	Ingredients			
Between the Sheets	15 mL 15 mL 15 mL 1 dash	Bacardi rum Brandy Cointreau Lemon juice	Shake and strain	Cocktail	Lemon slice
Piña colada	30 mL 30 mL 90 mL	White Rum Coconut cream/ coconut milk Pineapple Juice	Blend	Calada	Wedge of pineapple with leaves and maraschino cherry
Cuba Libre	30 mL 30 mL Top-up	White rum Fresh lime juice Cola	Shake and strain	Collin	Slice of lime or lemon.
Planters punch	60 mL 5 mL 30 mL 60 mL	Orange juice Fresh lime juice Pineapple juice Dark rum to float	Build-up	Highball	Pineapple slice
Daiquiri	30 mL 10 mL 3 dashes	White Rum Fresh lime juice Gomme syrup	Shake	Cocktail	Appropriate fruit segment or lemon
Bacardi	30 mL 30 mL 01 tsp	Bacardi rum Fresh lime juice Castor sugar	Shake and strain	Cocktail	Twist lemon

Whisky Based Cocktails

Cocktail Name	Ingredients		Method	Glass	Garnish
	Qty.	Ingredients			
Whisky sour	60 mL 1 tsp ½ nos.	Whiskey Sugar Lemon juice	Shake and strain	Medium size	Slice of orange and cherry
Manhattan (dry/sweet)	45 mL 20 mL 1 dash	Bourbon whisky Dry/sweet vermouth Angostura bitter	Stir and strain	Cocktail	Cherry in the bottom of glass
Old Fashioned	60 mL 1 dash 1 tspn.	Rye whiskey Angostura bitter Sugar	Mix together and muddle	Old Fashioned	Slice of orange and cherry
Rob Roy	30 mL 30 mL	Scotch Whisky Vermouth	Shake and strain	Cocktail	Not necessary
Churchill	90 mL 30 mL 30 mL 30 mL	Scotch whisky Lime Juice Sweet Vermouth Cointreau	Shake and strain	Cocktail	Not necessary
Rusty nail	30 mL 30 mL Cubes	Scotch whiskey Drambuie Lots of ice	Build and stir	Roly poly	No garnish

Brandy Based Cocktails

Cocktail Name	Ingredients		Method	Glass	Garnish
	Qty.	Ingredients			
Alexander	30 mL 45 mL 30 mL	Brandy Brown crème de cacao Single cream	Shake and strain	Cocktail	Sprinkle with nutmeg
Side car	60 mL 15 mL 15 mL	Brandy Cointreau Fresh lime juice	Shake and strain	Champagne saucer	Lemon slice
The Blenheim	90 mL 60 mL 30 mL 30 mL 30 mL	Brandy Yellow chartreuse Lillet Orange Juice Dubonnet	Shake and strain	Cocktail	Not necessary

Four Score	90 mL 60 mL 30 mL	Brandy Lillet Yellow Chartreuse	Stir and strain	Cocktail	Garnish with a twisted lemon rind
Brandy Crusta	60 mL 15 mL 15 mL 1 dash	Brandy Lemon juice Maraschino liqueur Angostura bitter	Shake and pour	Brandy ballon	Garnish with Maraschino cherry

Wine Based Cocktails

Cocktail Name	Ingredients		Method	Glass	Garnish
	Qty.	Ingredients			
Champagne cocktail	15 mL 100 mL 60 mL 1 4 drops	Brandy Grand Marnier Champagne Sugar Cube soaked in bitter Bitter	Build	Champagne flute	Float strawberry
Kir	15 mL 150 mL	Crème de cassis Dry white wine	Build and stir	Wine glass	Not necessary
Bellini	15 mL 30 mL	Peach juice Champagne	Build and stir	Champagne flute	Wedge of peach
Black velvet	15 mL 15 mL	Chilled Guinness Champagne	Build-up	Beer glass	Not necessary
Buck's fizz	15 mL 30 mL	Fresh orange juice Champagne	Build-up	Champagne flute	Not necessary

Mocktails

Mocktini — Tonic water + Fresh lime juice + Fresh lemon juice = Stir and strain in cocktail glass and garnish with twist of lemon or lemon slice.

Nutty cola — Hazelnut syrup + Fresh lime juice + Top up with cola = Shake and strain (Hazelnut syrup + Fresh lime juice) in Collin glass and garnish with twist of lemon or lemon slice.

Pomegranate julep — Pomegranate juice + Grapefruit juice + Fresh lime juice + Honey syrup + Mint sprigs = Shake and strain in old fashioned glass and garnish with mint sprigs.

Virgin Piña Colada — Fresh pineapple juice + Sprite or any lime soft drink + Vanilla ice cream + Coconut milk + Ice + Fresh pineapple = Blend and serve in Collin glass and garnish (optional) with slice of pineapple.

Sparkling punch	Ginger ale + Pineapple juice + Lime juice + Lemon juice + Orange juice = Mix all juices and serve in punch bowl. Garnish with twist or slice of lemon or pineapple or lime.
Cinderella	Lemon juice + Orange juice + Pineapple juice = Shake and strain in medium size glass and garnish with slice of lemon, orange or pineapple.
Pussy Foot	Lemon juice + Orange juice + Lime juice + Grenadine + Egg yolk = Shake and serve in cocktail glass. Garnish with slice of lemon, orange or lime.
Shirley Temple	Ginger ale + Grenadine = Build and stir in Highball glass and garnish with cherries.
Virgin Mary	Tomato juice + Lemon juice + Worcestershire sauce + Celery salt = Shake and strain in highball glass and garnish with a slice of tomato or lemon.

KEY TERMS

Boston shaker	: Cocktail shaker that consists of two glasses.
B&B	: Brandy and Bénédictine and indicates to cocktail.
Curaçao	: Liqueur flavoured with dried peel of the laraha (similar to orange fruit) citrus fruit, grown on the island of Curaçao.
Vermouth	: Aromatized wine like cinzanao, martini, campari, dubonnet, lillet, etc. It is available in both dry and sweet versions. Dry indicates French vermouth and sweet indicates to Italian vermouth.
Bitter	: Spirit family or alcoholic beverages flavoured with herbal essences.
Virgin Mary	: Mocktail, i.e., Bloody Mary minus vodka.
Grenadine syrup	: French term for sugar syrup.
Lime cordial	: Mixture of concentrated lime and sugar, sometimes used as a mixer for cocktail.

REVIEW QUESTIONS

1. Define the term cocktail. Give five cocktails (along with recipe) under each base: whiskey, gin, tequila, vodka and rum.
2. Define the term mocktail. Give five mocktails along with their standard recipes.

PART B

Food and Beverage Production Operations

27 CHAPTER

Introduction to Cuisine

Objectives

Students will be able to:

- expound cuisine classes and required equipment to prepare cuisine;
- explain different sections of Continental, Larder, Bakery, Chinese and Indian kitchen; and
- understand layout of different kitchen sections.

CUISINE

Cuisine is a French word, that means style or method of cooking like *haute cuisine* means high level cuisine. Since, French food is very popular, and most modern cooking has persued French food, thus the word "cuisine" was more often used. In other words, a *cuisine* is a specific set of cooking traditions and practices, often associated with a place of origin. Religious food laws also put a strong influence on cuisine, for example, Jewish food laws permit only foods that are *kosher*. A cuisine is principally influenced by the ingredients that are available locally or through trade. It is often named after the region or place where its underlining culture is present.

As cuisine means *style of cooking* so it can be used with any traditional cooking style, like Indian, Chinese, etc. But fast food cannot be termed a cuisine. Simply, the term cuisine is used in reference to elaborate kitchen preparations. The kitchen is the central point of all activities for all food and beverage outlets; therefore, kitchen can be termed *heart of organization.* This kitchen can be centralized (a single food production unit for all food and beverage outlets) or decentralized (several food production units for separate or major food and beverage outlets). In kitchen, food preparation methods (such as one off, batch, mass, just-in-time) depend upon the time required to serve, type of customer, place of consumption, etc.

Quick Scroll on Cuisine Classes	
Haute	It is a *grande/high level* cuisine featured by French cuisine in elaborate preparations and presentations.
Bourgeois	It is a *mid-level cuisine* characterized by good quality raw materials to prepare good preparations.
Classic	It is a style of *French cuisine* based on Chef Auguste Escoffier; it is refinement of the early cuisines.

Fusion	It is an innovative cuisine that combines the elements or different culinary traditions in an offered menu.
Creole	Cooking style from southern USA (combining Caribbean, French, Spanish and African traditions), based on shellfish, rice, okra and *filé powder* (or gumbo filé).
TexMex	It refers to Texan and Mexican style of American cooking, based on steaks and barbecued meats.
Nouvelle	It is a *new cuisine* characterized by lighter, more delicate dishes with an increased emphasis on presentation.

MAJOR SECTIONS OF FOOD PRODUCTION DEPARTMENT (OR KITCHEN)

Continental Section

The term *continental food* is used for a range of dishes that are eaten particularly in European countries, thus often also termed western cuisine. The continental kitchen explores exotic continental delights prepared by skilled continental chefs. The *chef de partie* (CDP) is responsible for the smooth functioning of the kitchen or its respective sections. He ensures that each chef working under him should follow the laid standards in the kitchen. The continental kitchen prepares numerous dishes starting from appetizers to end on desserts.

Few Famous Continental Preparations	
Main courses	Chicken stroganoff, Vegetable au gratin, Chicken Maryland, Beef Wellington, Chicken à la Kiev, Chicken Marengo, Lasagna, Sole Dieppoise, Sole Normande, Oeuf Rossini, Fish steak, etc.
Desserts	Chocolate mousse, Cheesecakes, Baked Alaska, Diplomat pudding, Tarts and brownies, Gateaux and muffins, etc.
Sandwiches	Club sandwiches, Banh MI, BLT sandwich (Bread, Lettuce and Tomato), Uncle Jam's burger, Buttwich, Tea sandwiches, Open/Plain/Closed sandwiches, Breakfast sandwiches, Hot dog, Pizza, etc.

The continental chef prepares delicacies such as soups, salads, roast items and desserts. Often *kitchen pantry* is found next to continental kitchen. It gives ice cream, fresh juices, fruit plates, milk shakes, cold coffees, buttermilk, etc. Next to this is *restaurant pantry* (or *still room*) which provides hot beverages such as tea, coffee, milk based drinks like milk shakes, milk stirred with Bournvita, Horlicks, Milo, Ovaltine, and hot chocolate, etc. The continental section can be broadly classified into three parts, i.e. *stock and soup section, roast section* and *vegetable section.*

Stock and Soup Section

Within a kitchen brigade, a stock and soup section is responsible for making variety of stocks which eventually work as a foundation in creation of various sauces, soups, gravy based dishes and so forth. Due to the multifaceted work profile of this section, its staff requires to work in close coordination with other kitchen section's station chefs. The classical title for a person who is making soup is *potager*. The soup cook and his team may be responsible for a range of duties but it doesn't mean that all soup cooks have to make soup only. For instance, in a small kitchen, the section may be responsible for peeling vegetables and cooking pasta, as well as preparing soups and stocks. Some major duties of soup section are given below.

Continental Kitchen Equipment

- Griddle
- Convection oven
- Microwave oven
- Steam kettle
- Tilting frying pan
- Potato peeler
- Stock pot
- Deep fat fryer
- Griller
- Sink unit
- Cooking ranges
- Slicer
- Sauce pan
- Roast pan
- Food mixer
- Salamander
- Bain Marie
- Microwave

Mise en place

✓ It means placing everything in its right place before starting food preparation work, so that during actual cooking process chef does not need to move here and there to seek the required items. Thus, soup kitchen makes ready mise en place before making stocks and soups.

Preparing Stocks

✓ As the title *stock* suggests that this section is responsible for preparing various types of stocks like fish, chicken, veal, game, beef, mutton, lamb stock, remouillage, glace, broth/bouillon, essence, fish fumet and so forth.

Preparing Soups

✓ This section also prepares basic and special soups like *basic soups* that include consommé, cream, puree and broth, and *special soups* that incorporate bisque, French onion, and others featured on the menu. Cold soups are prepared and passed to larder section for service.

Preparing Garnishes

✓ Apart from soup preparation, its garnishes which enhance soup appearance and sometimes its flavour/bouquet are also prepared by the soup section.

Roast, Sauce and Vegetable Section

Roast section is responsible for the preparation of roasted items, particularly those based on meat, poultry and game. Roast chef is in-charge for all roasted, grilled, broiled and braised preparations. Apart from roasting, chef or *rotisseur* chef (roast chef) also performs the task of carving; also ensures that it is presented on the plate in a visually appealing manner. He or she also prepares gravies, and may prepare some deep fried meat or fish based preparations.

The *sauce section* is responsible for preparing sauces (like five basic grand sauces and their derivatives), sautés, stews and possibly even hot hors d'oeuvres, all to *à la carte* order. It never deals with grilled or roasted preparations. Generally, *saucier* is the highest ranking of all the station chef positions. In small establishments, besides sauce preparations sauce section is also held responsible for preparing various vegetable based dishes, all to *à la carte* order. But in large establishment, there is a separate sub-section or station in continental kitchen for preparing guest's ordered vegetable based dishes. To prepare the entremets is also the responsibility of vegetable section. Some major tasks of *vegetable section* are mentioned below.

For mise en place

- ✓ In order to prepare and provide everything (or dishes) timely without creating any trouble, it is vital to have everything ready and must be kept at its designated place (or mise en place), so during the actual cooking process chef should not chop, peel or search for the items.

For dishes

- ✓ The major responsibility of vegetable section is to prepare various hot hors d'oeuvres, salads, pasta dishes, rice based dishes, vegetable based dishes (such as asparagus, artichoke, mushrooms, turnips, etc.) and special vegetarian delicacies, as ordered by a guest.

For garnishes

- ✓ As in continental kitchen, vegetable section prepares various vegetable based continental dishes, so the responsibility of its garnish is also of vegetable section (both simple and compound garnishes).

For side dishes

- ✓ Side dishes or accompaniments like boiled or glazed vegetables, baked or hash brown potatoes, grilled tomatoes, baked beans, etc., which are offered with the main course is also prepared by vegetable section.

For meat and fish

- ✓ In small establishments, there is a common kitchen for preparing various vegetarian and non-vegetarian continental dishes (meat or fish based). This section prepares meat, poultry and game in various styles (as and when required) like grilled, roasted, fried and stewed.
- ✓ Besides, it also prepares all fish and shellfish based items in various styles like grilled, fried, poached and baked. It also prepares various accompaniments and garnishes for meat and fish.

GARDE MANGER/LARDER/COLD KITCHEN

Garde manger is the cold section or kitchen in the classical kitchen brigade system. This section focuses on the cold salads, patés and cold buffet items. In many kitchens, the garde manger and pastry cooks assist each other during the plate-up process because they serve the first and last course to the guest. For the effectual work performance, garde manger section is further subdivided into three categories: butchery, hors d' oeuvres and cold salad sections. Garde manger section is headed by either larder chef or butcher chef who works in close liaison with other relevant sections. A brief work profile of garde manger section is given below.

Cold Sauces

- ✓ It includes various cold sauces and their derivatives like Vinaigrette, Mayonnaise, Horseradish, Gribiche, Mint sauce, Cocktail sauce, Cumberland sauce, Andalouse sauce, Green sauce, etc.

COLD KITCHEN EQUIPMENT

Major Equipment

- Steel tables
- Butchers block
- Griller/toaster
- Grinding machine
- Weighing scales
- Weighing machine
- Slicing machine
- Sauce pans & lids
- Wooden spatula
- Wooden spoons
- Frying kettles
- Frying pans
- Gas boiler
- Boiling plates
- Gas rings

Butcher's Equipment

- Butcher's chopping knives
- Tranchelard knife
- Palette knife
- Potato peeler
- Mandoline vegetables slicer

Other Equipment

- Cutlet or meat bat
- Trussing needles
- Larding needles
- Larding pin
- Lemon zester
- Lemon decorator
- Vegetable scoop
- Butcher's hook
- Skewers

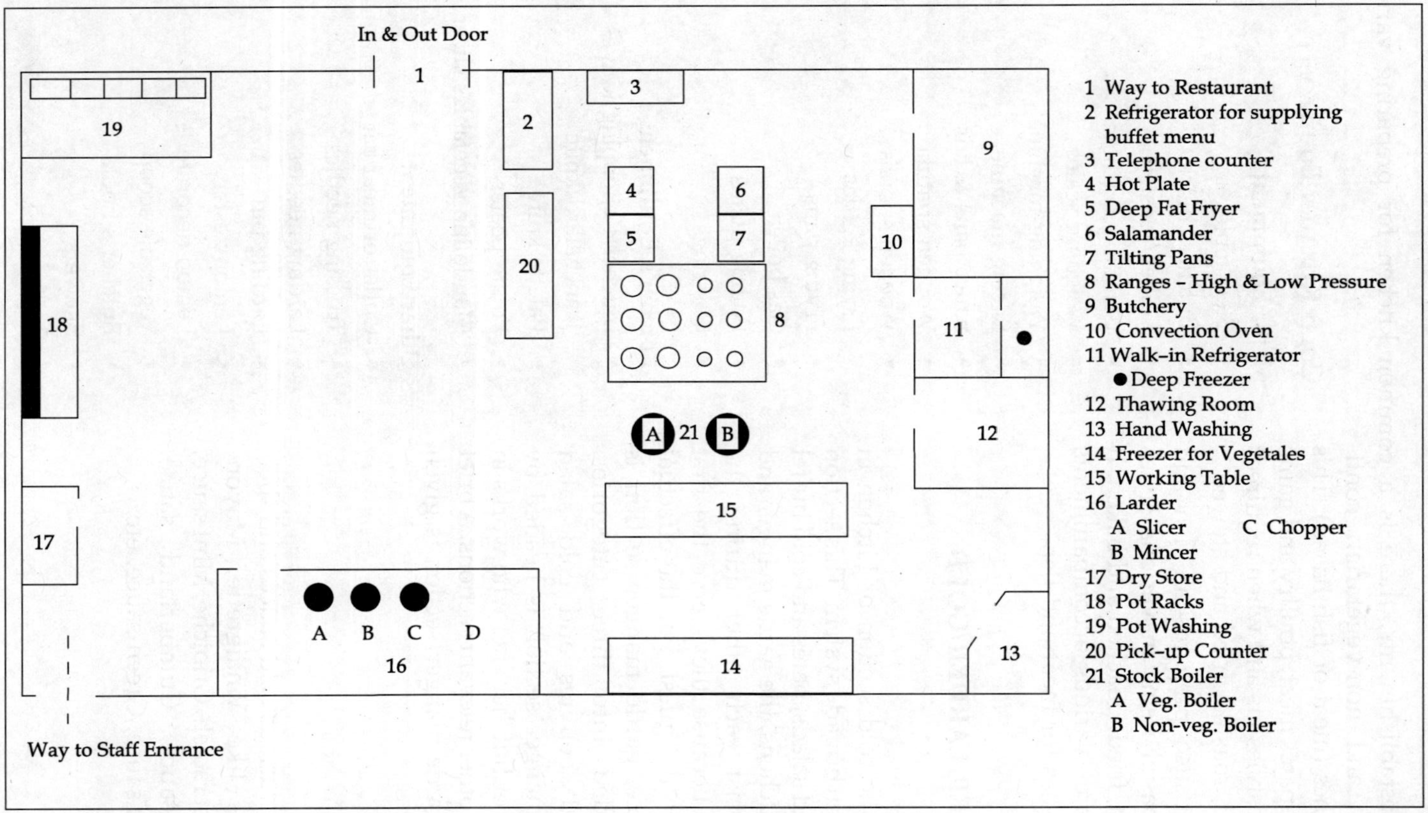

In & Out Door

1 Way to Restaurant
2 Refrigerator for supplying buffet menu
3 Telephone counter
4 Hot Plate
5 Deep Fat Fryer
6 Salamander
7 Tilting Pans
8 Ranges – High & Low Pressure
9 Butchery
10 Convection Oven
11 Walk-in Refrigerator
● Deep Freezer
12 Thawing Room
13 Hand Washing
14 Freezer for Vegetales
15 Working Table
16 Larder
A Slicer C Chopper
B Mincer
17 Dry Store
18 Pot Racks
19 Pot Washing
20 Pick-up Counter
21 Stock Boiler
A Veg. Boiler
B Non-veg. Boiler

Way to Staff Entrance

Fig. 27.1 Layout of continental kitchen

Dressings

- ✓ It includes salad dressings like Vinaigrette, Thousand Island, Mayonnaise, Acidulated cream, Lemon, French, English, American, Escoffier, Roquefort, etc.

Cold Meats

- ✓ It prepares and arranges cold meat platters, for example, paté, terrine, galantine, ballotine, roulades, mousse, mousseline, timbales, Wellington and cold roasts for the buffet.

Carving

- ✓ Garde manger is also responsible to prepare non-edible showpieces like butter carvings, ice carving, salt dough, etc. Besides this, it also prepares/carves cold decorative centrepieces (for placing in buffet counter) like whole turkey, sirloin and paté.

Cold Sandwiches

- ✓ It includes numerous cold sandwiches like fancy tea sandwiches, open sandwiches, submarine sandwiches, finger sandwiches, wraps, cold canapés and so forth.

Cold Appetizers

- ✓ Garde manger assembles and prepares various cold salads, antipasti and hors d'oeuvres for the buffet, restaurants, etc. Famous cold appetizers include relishes, seafood cocktails, cold canapés, savoury jellies, finger foods, crudités, petit choux, carolines, spreads, dips and so forth.

Cold Savouries

- ✓ Garde manager section also prepares a range of required cold savoury items mentioned on the menu card.

Other Preparations

- ✓ Besides the above-mentioned preparations, garde manger is also responsible to carve fruits and vegetables for the buffet counter, to prepare sausages, to pickle and smoke fish and meats, etc.

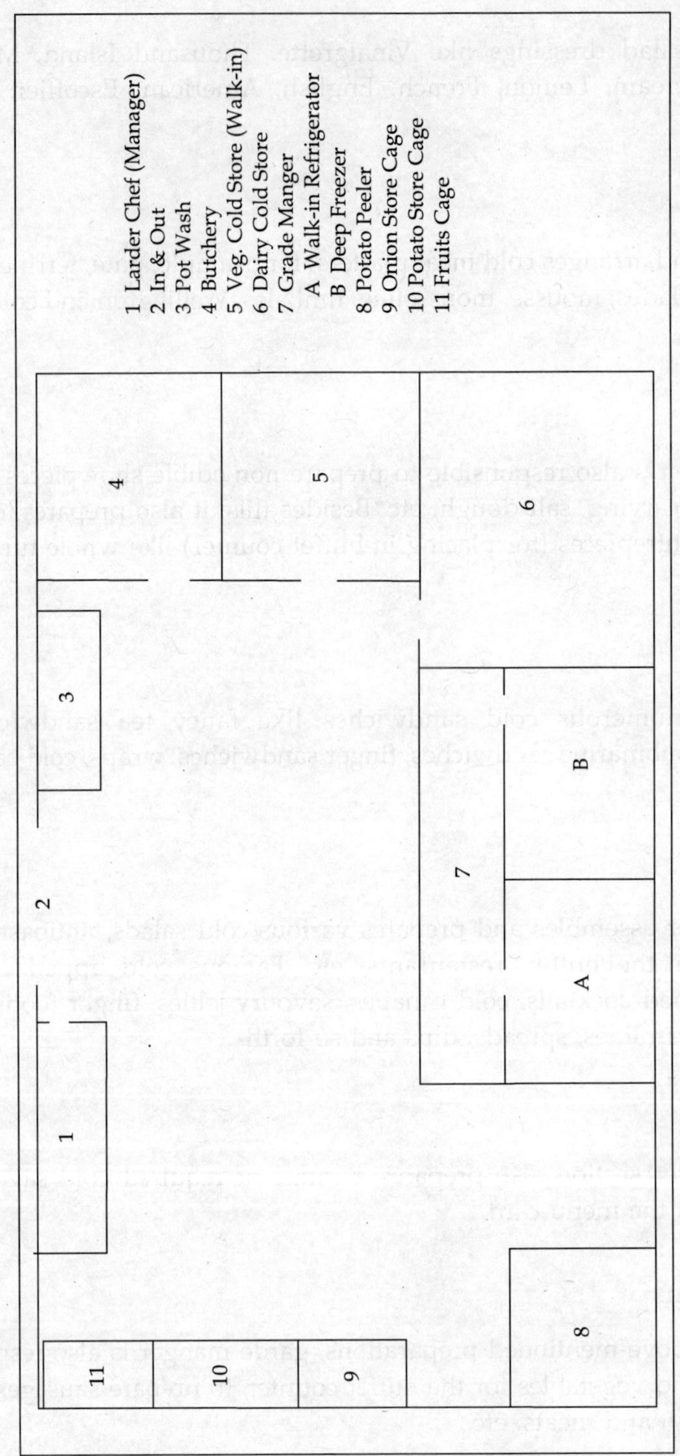

Fig. 27.2 Layout of larder section

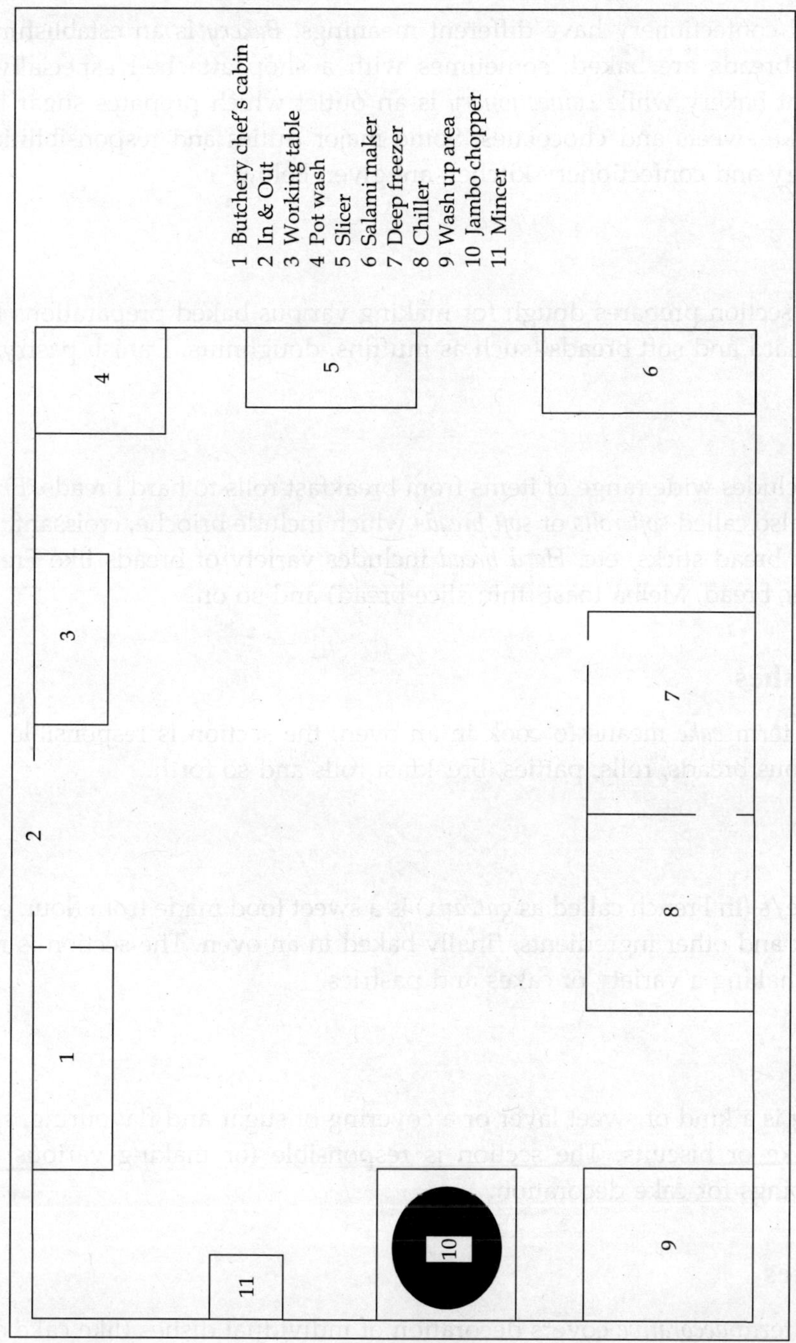

Fig. 27.3 Layout of butchery

BAKERY AND CONFECTIONERY

Bakery and confectionery have different meanings. *Bakery* is an establishment where cakes and breads are baked; sometimes with a shop attached especially when an independent bakery while *confectionery* is an outlet which prepares sugar based food products like sweets and chocolates. Some major duties and responsibilities of hotel based bakery and confectionery kitchen are given below.

Dough

- ✓ The section prepares dough for making various baked preparations like dough for hard and soft breads (such as muffins, doughnuts, Danish pastry, etc.).

Breads

- ✓ It includes wide range of items from breakfast rolls to hard breads. *Breakfast rolls* are also called *soft rolls* or *soft breads* which include brioche, croissant, bread rolls with bread sticks, etc. *Hard bread* includes variety of breads like French bread, garlic bread, Melba toast (thin slice bread) and so on.

Baked Dishes

- ✓ The term *bake* means to cook in an oven; the section is responsible for baking various breads, rolls, patties, breakfast rolls and so forth.

Cakes

- ✓ Cake/s (in French called as *gateaux*) is a sweet food made from flour, eggs, sugar, milk and other ingredients, finally baked in an oven. The section is responsible for making a variety of cakes and pastries.

Icing

- ✓ *Icing* is a kind of sweet layer or a covering of sugar and flavouring, spread over a cake or biscuits. The section is responsible for making various icings and toppings for cake decoration.

Decoratives

- ✓ The term *decorative* covers decoration of individual dishes (like cake decoration) as well as making of centre decorative pieces like pulled sugar basket and gum paste.

Entremets

- ✓ In 17-course French classical menu, the term entremets cover various hot and cold sweet preparations. It is the bakery and confectionary department (as *pastry section* is part of bakery) which is mainly responsible for making these sweet preparations like baked Alaska, diplomat pudding, chocolates, mousse, apple strudel and so on.

Other Tasks

- ✓ There are countless preparations for which bakery and confectionary is responsible like preparing pastes (such as for puff, short crust, choux, etc.), petit fours, cookies, prepare sponge for cakes and so forth.

Note. *Petit four* is a small sweetmeat, chocolate or tiny decorated cake served with coffee at the end of a meal.

CHINESE AND INDIAN SECTION

Chinese Section

- ✓ Chinese cuisine is the oldest continuous cuisine in the world; the adversity forced the Chinese to always seek new sources of food.
- ✓ They put everything edible to use, finding wonderful ways to utilize strange plants and roots, lily bulbs, bamboo shoots, jasmine flower, etc.
- ✓ Chinese cooking calls for the maximum preparation of raw ingredients and minimum cooking 'fan and cai'. The dishes have a balance, combination and blend of colour, flavour, texture, shape and size.
- ✓ In Chinese cuisine, a special kind of stock, i.e., *master stock* (it is flavoured with various ingredients, mainly soya sauce, sugar, garlic, ginger and other aromatic agents) is primarily used for poaching meats.

Chinese Kitchen Equipment

- High pressure range
- Dimsum steamer
- Food chopper
- Frying pan
- Chinese wok
- Flat spoons
- Round ladles
- Chopping board
- Strainer
- Round spoon
- Pickle pot
- Chopping block
- Hand held chopper

Indian Kitchen Equipment

- Tandoor
- Dough kneader
- Sigri
- Chappati puffer
- Range with tawa

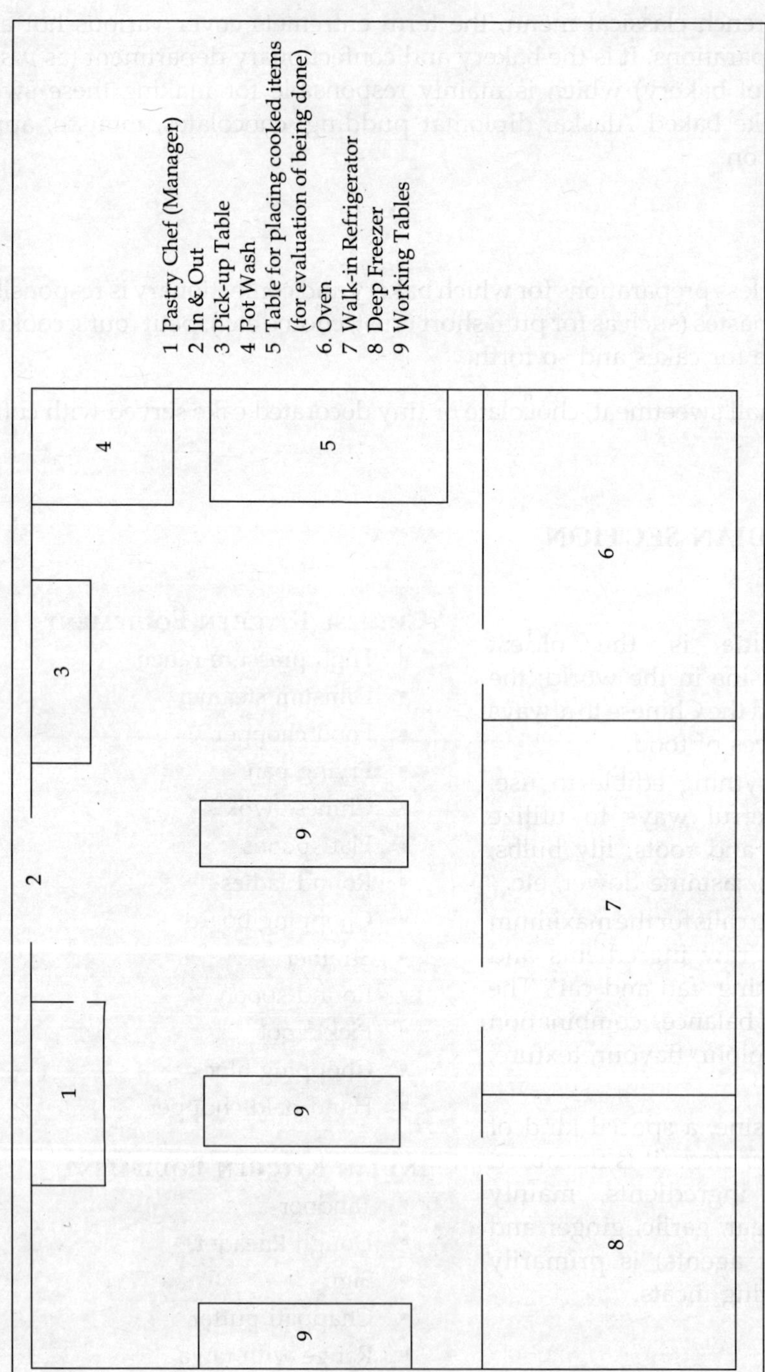

Fig. 27.4 Layout of bakery

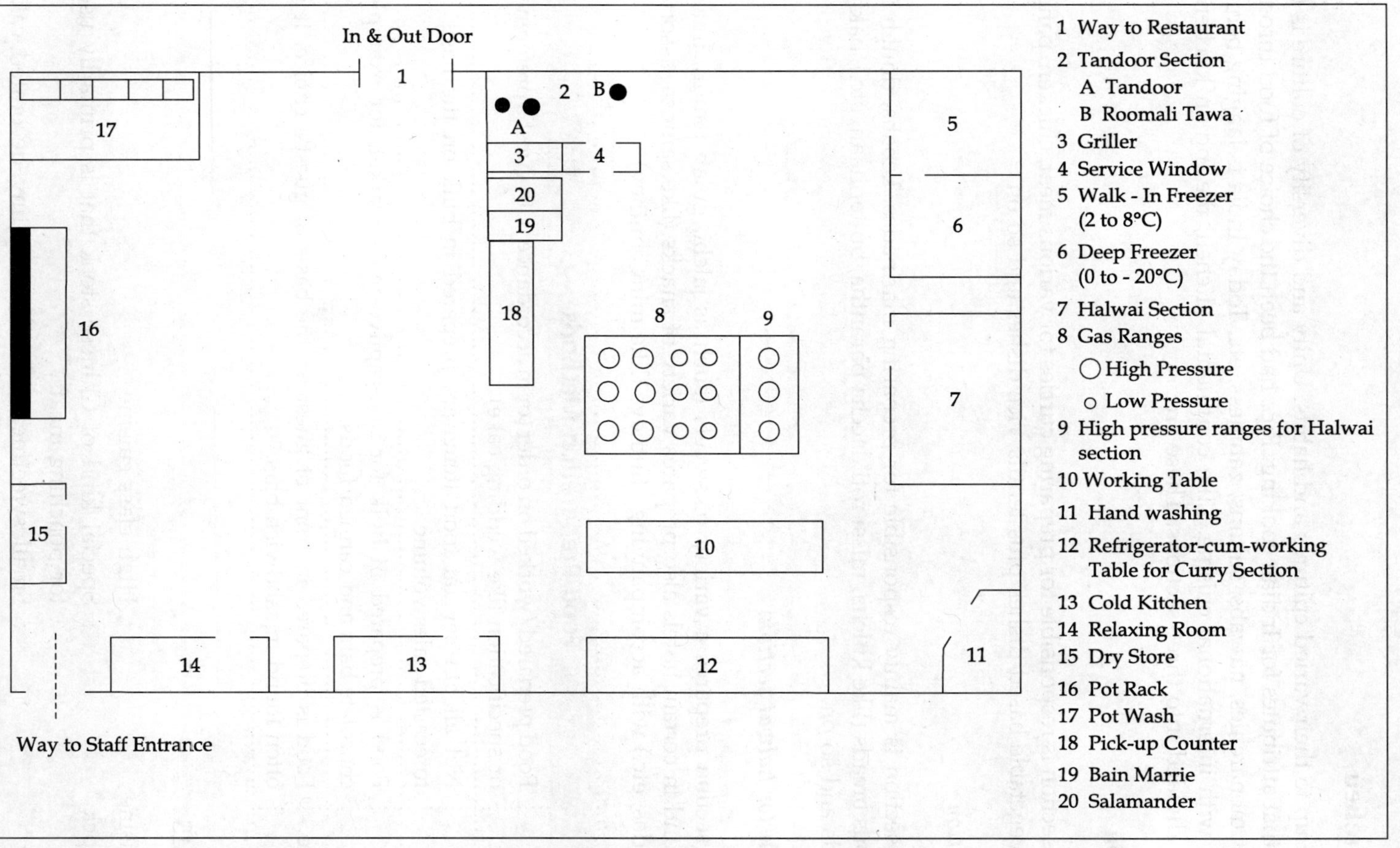

Fig. 27.5 Layout of Indian kitchen

Indian Kitchen

Indians live up to their varied cultures and habits. Unity and diversity of culture is the main thing that attributes for Indian cooking. Rice had been the choice of food through the different monarchies, nawabs, sultans, zaniness, etc. Today India is lagging behind to catch up with international cuisine. Like continental kitchen, the Indian kitchen is particularly divided into three sections. These are:

Curry section

- ✓ This section is responsible for preparing curries for various meat, chicken, paneer and vegetable based dishes plus lentils, rice dishes and so on.

Tandoor section

- ✓ This section is mainly responsible for preparing marinades, kebabs, dough for various breads (like kulcha, missi roti, laccha parantha, butter naan, etc.), baking breads and so on.

Sweet section (or halwai section)

- ✓ This section prepares a variety of sweets (such as jalebi, gulab jamun, imarti, etc.) and in certain hotels also prepares variety of snacks (like samosa, assorted pakodas, etc.) with accompanying chutneys (like mint chutney).

Food Preparation Methods	
One off	Food prepared/worked on order (or in accordance with guest's preference or specification like wedding cake)
Batch	Not all but several food items are prepared in bulk on the basis of forecasted sales volume.
Mass	Food is prepared in bulk for non-captive mass market, for example, chocolate bars and canned foods.
Just in time	Food is prepared in front of guest on the basis of guest's choice. It is often found in sandwich bars.

KEY TERMS

Haute cuisine : High class cuisine.

Master stock : Special kind of Chinese stock that is primarily used for poaching meats.

Petit four : Small sweetmeat, chocolate or tiny decorated cakes served with coffee at the end of a meal.

Gateaux : French term for cakes; Gateaux is plural of gateau.

Breakfast roll : Collective term for all breakfast breads, i.e., soft breads as well as hard breads.

Melba toast : Thin slice of bread.

Crudités : Group of crisp vegetables suitable for eating raw with a dipping sauce like mayonnaise.

Petit choux : Small and filled crusts that are made from unsweetened choux paste.

Carolines : Small éclair made from choux pastry, often filled with a savoury stuffing as a hors d'oeuvres

Relishes : Appetizer that consists of raw or pickled vegetables.

REVIEW QUESTIONS

1. Define the term cuisine. Describe the different classes of cuisine that prevail in the international market.
2. Draw the layout of standard continental kitchen and indicate different sections and major equipment.
3. Differentiate between bakery and confectionary. Enlist different equipment required in any standard bakery.
4. Draw the layout of Indian kitchen and indicate the major sections of Indian kitchen.

28 CHAPTER

Introduction to Kitchen Organization

OBJECTIVES

Students will be able to:

- explicate the kitchen staff and their job profiles;
- reveal different styles of kitchen layout and kitchen areas; and
- enlighten fuel types and their pros and cons.

KITCHEN ORGANIZATION

The term *kitchen organization* (or often termed *kitchen brigade*) is concerned with organizational structure of kitchen department. In order to perform all kitchen tasks efficiently and effectively, hotel needs to design structured span of control system, so that authority and responsibility among all chefs, CDPs, DCDPs, commis, cooks and helpers can flow and be delegated properly. This systematic relation among all involved members and chain or flow of command is collectively known as *organizational structure* or *hierarchy*.

In large hotels, executive chef is head of food production (or kitchen) department who is responsible and accountable for all activities and functions of kitchen. *Sous chef* (assistant to executive chef) and CDPs (incharge of respective kitchen sections/kitchen areas), DCDPs (works under CDPs) and commis all work under the supervision of kitchen executive.

The classical *kitchen brigade* is suitable for large or luxury establishments where each section has its own manager and staff members. Remember, organizational structure always varies with the size of establishment, for instance organizational structure of large hotels always carries more job positions than medium and small establishments. An ideal organizational structure (along with staff duties and responsibilities) of kitchen department of small, medium and large hotel is discussed below.

DUTIES AND RESPONSIBILITIES OF FOOD PRODUCTION STAFF

Executive Chef

- ✓ In kitchen, all sectional heads carry full responsibility of their section/kitchen. Executive chef works as a chief officer above all these sections heads. So, executive chef must have a strict sense of economy and efficiency. He should be fully aware of the prices, market trends, commodities, seasons and prospective guests' requirements.

✓ Executive chef is also known as "Chef de cuisine". His foremost function is to plan, organize, supervise and control the work of kitchen. He is responsible for staffing, selection and dismissal in coordination with the HRD/ personnel department.

✓ Modern experts favour keeping the chef away from the details of purchasing so that he can concentrate on more important aspects of manning his kitchen and attending to the actual food production unit. The executive chef is also responsible for organizing the duty roster.

MAJOR ROLE OF EXECUTIVE CHEF

- To organize kitchen
- To compile menu
- To supervise staff
- To train staff
- To motivate staff
- To order supplies
- To manage kitchen

Sous Chef

He is assistant executive chef who understudies the executive chef in all his duties. He is mainly responsible for the efficient day-to-day functioning of the kitchen. The sous chef supervises the practical kitchen activities. When the executive chef is busy, he can make necessary staff changes during the working day to relieve pressure. His basic duties and responsibilities include:

- To take charge in the absence of executive chef.
- Plan and organize pre-preparation lists and workflows.
- Assist executive chef in developing menu and standard recipes.
- Produce all special items related to the designated part of the menu to the establishment's standards in order to satisfy guest's expectations.
- Impart knowledge, train cooks and to encourage high standards.
- Announce received food order from outlets.
- Ensure equipment and work environment are operational.
- Control quality and costs and ensure proper execution of standard operating procedures in kitchen.
- Manage staff roster in conjunction with executive chef/head chef.

Chef de Partie

There is separate chef de partie (CDP) for different sections in the kitchen. Each chef de partie is assisted according to the production load by one or more commies (first, second and third commies) and, of course, by trainees too. Chef de partie may be regarded as a supervisor or fireman of their section as well as skilled craftsman. Generally, the following activities are performed by the chef de partie:

- Take charge in the absence of the sous chef and perform all his duties.
- Work unsupervised as per laid standard by establishment.
- Prepare and deliver ordered food items when required.
- Communicate with other sections or outlets and support peers.
- Train new staff.
- Maximize quality whilst maintaining food and labour costs.

Commis-Chef

Most of the duties of the kitchen posts require little skill and usually commis are responsible for this work. Their duties include mise en place, keep work area neat and clean, pick-up indented items from stores, care and maintenance of equipment and finally commis 1 is also responsible for supervising commis 2 and commis 3. By good training, they become most valuable members of the kitchen brigade.

Chef Saucier

✓ The *sauce cook* is usually the focal point because his work profile is more complex than others. The chef saucier will be chief in the making of various basic and international sauces and will eventually rise to the post of chef de cuisine. It is here where all sauces, meat, poultry; entrée dishes are prepared together with necessary garnishes.

Chef Uniform

- Chef coat
- Chef pant
- Chef scarf
- Apron
- Chef cap
- Shoes
- Socks
- Trochon

Chef Poissonnier

✓ The *fish cook* prepares majority of fish based preparations. The fish in semi-prepared form comes from the larder section and the chef poissonnier does the cooking, garnishing, saucing and the dishing of fish.

Chef Rotisseur

✓ Like chef poissonnier, the *roast chef* is responsible for most fish and other roasted meat preparations. The roast cook (or chef rotisseur) deals with all roasts and deep fried foods.

Chef Potager

✓ The *soup chef* prepares all basic and special types of soups and is also responsible for the garnishes accompanying the prepared soup.

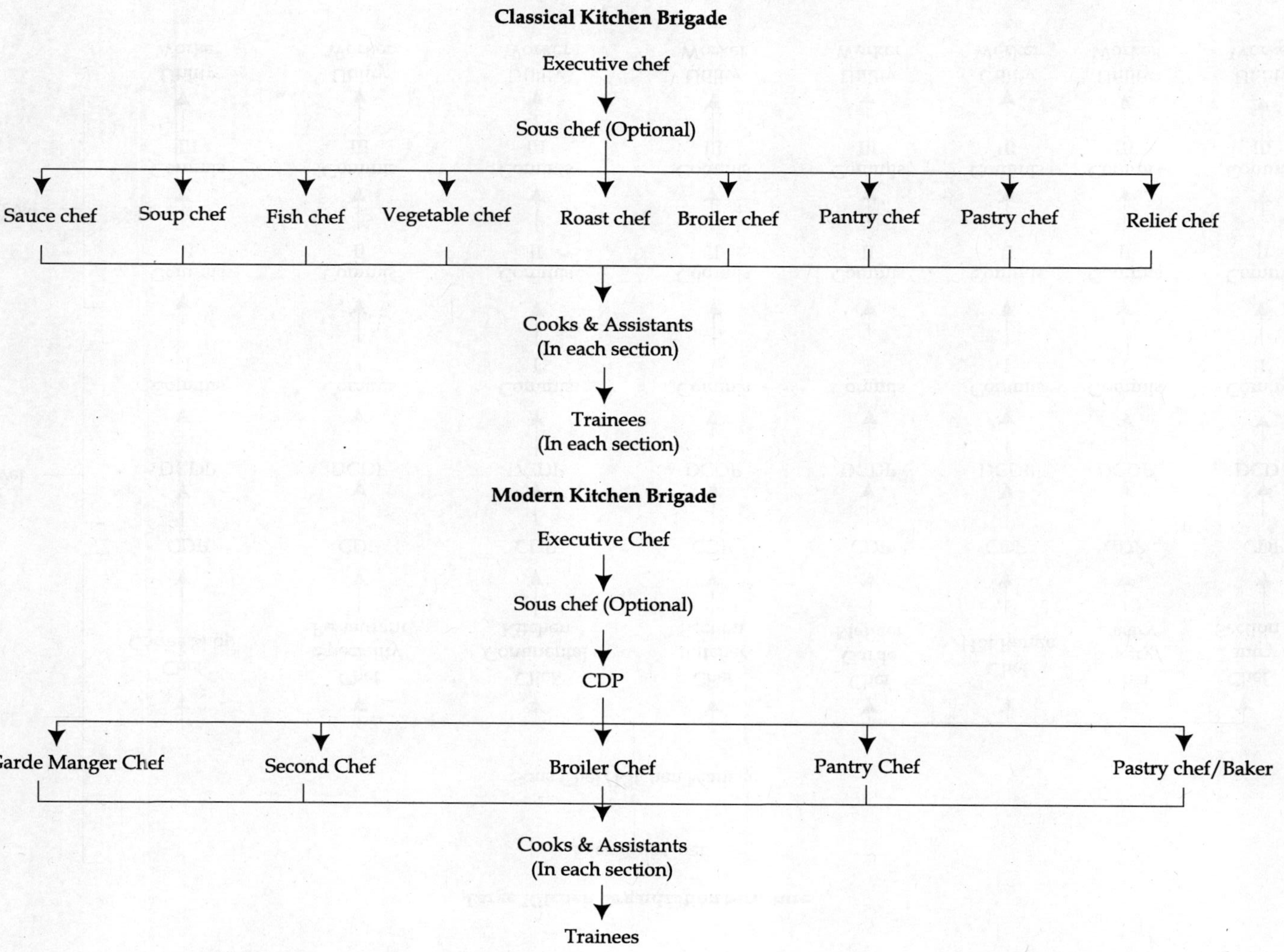
Classical Kitchen Brigade
Executive chef
Sous chef (Optional)
Sauce chef
Soup chef
Fish chef
Vegetable chef
Roast chef
Broiler chef
Pantry chef
Pastry chef
Relief chef
Cooks & Assistants
(In each section)
Trainees
(In each section)
Modern Kitchen Brigade
Executive Chef
Sous chef (Optional)
CDP
Garde Manger Chef
Second Chef
Broiler Chef
Pantry Chef
Pastry chef/Baker
Cooks & Assistants
(In each section)
Trainees

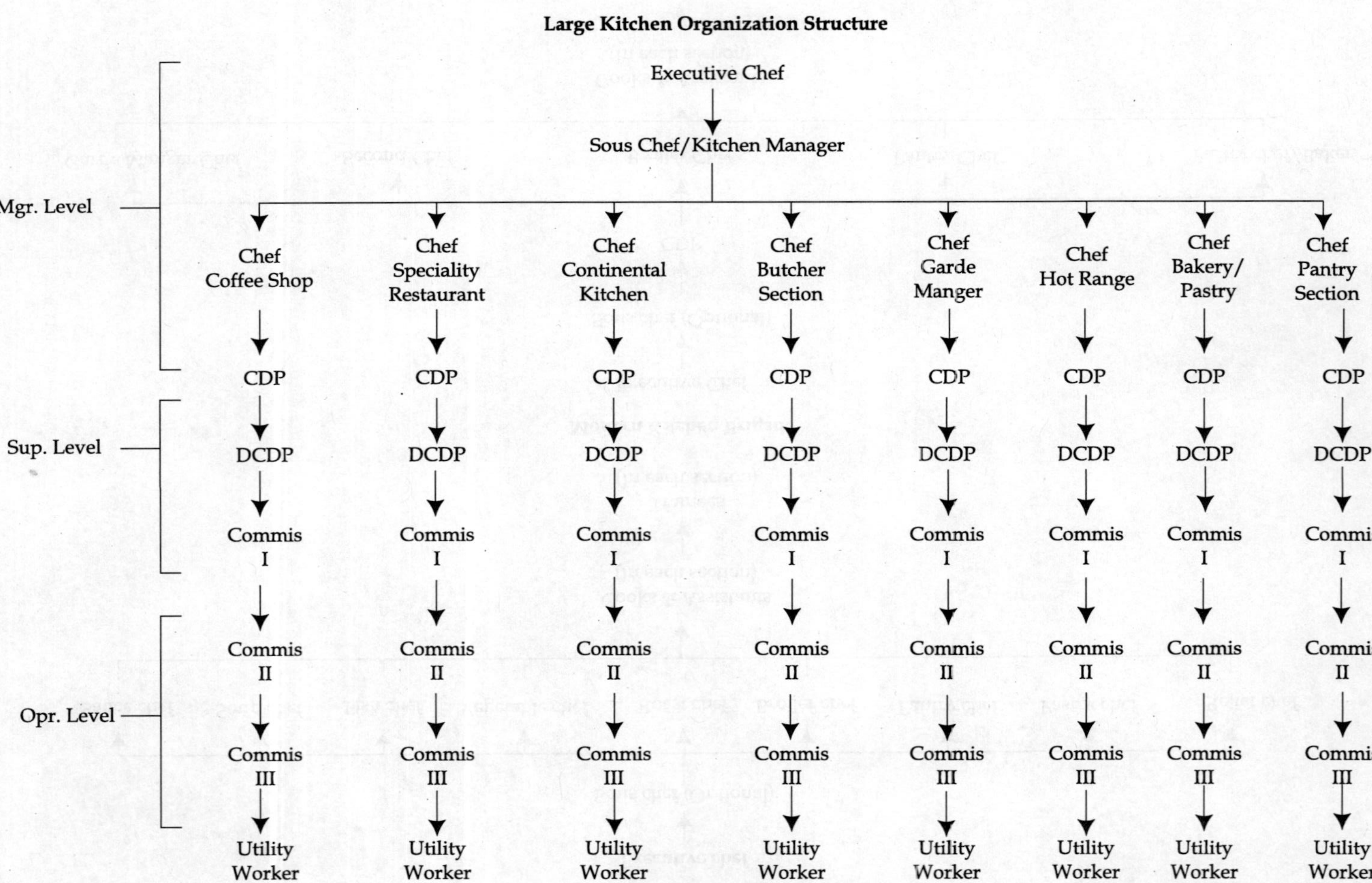
Large Kitchen Organization Structure
Executive Chef
Sous Chef/Kitchen Manager
Mgr. Level
Sup. Level
Opr. Level
Chef Coffee Shop
Chef Speciality Restaurant
Chef Continental Kitchen
Chef Butcher Section
Chef Garde Manger
Chef Hot Range
Chef Bakery/Pastry
Chef Pantry Section
CDP
DCDP
Commis I
Commis II
Commis III
Utility Worker

Chef Entremetier

✓ The *vegetable chef* is responsible for producing vegetable and potato based preparations.

Chef Patisserie

✓ The *pastry chef* has different status but certainly not less than the sauce chef or the larder chef. His work is specialized: preparing hot and cold puddings, cakes, pastries, bread and many other preparations.

Chef De Banquet

✓ The *banquet chef* specializes in making formal dinners. He is also responsible for organizing the services in coordination with the chef de parties. The banquet chefs will coordinate with the banqueting manager regarding service numbers, special dishes required and special instructions.

Chef Tournant

✓ He is a chef (also known as line, floater, swing, relief or station chef) who is available to work in any of the sections of a kitchen, helping out when other chefs are on their weekly off's or on holiday.

Chef Cohhanar

✓ In small establishments, the staff food is prepared by different chef de partie. In large establishments, a separate section in a separate kitchen prepares this staff meal. Chef cohhanar is responsible for preparing staff meal.

Chef Traiteur

✓ He is the chef who is in-charge of outside functions (or off-shore catering or ODCs), such as buffets or meals which are prepared in the kitchen but served at a different venue.

Kitchen Commis

✓ There are numerous duties in the kitchen department which require little skill; kitchen commis are responsible for performing all these supportive duties. By good training, they become most valuable members of the kitchen brigade.

Note.

- The room/unit of cooks (or kitchen staff) and their assistants under the partie system are commonly called kitchen brigade or *Brigade de cuisine* in French. Remember, it is different from *battterie de cuisine.*
- Generally, CDP is specialized in his/her area thus he/she leads/heads each party along with their assistants and helps in producing complex dishes with great care and efficiency.
- All heads of the parties come under the direct supervision and control of the chef de cuisine/executive chef, aided by one or more sous chefs.
- In large properties, every chef requires some people to assist him (i.e., cooks and assistants) during the working hours. For example, assistant vegetable chef may be involved in washing, peeling and trimming the vegetables.

Difference between Batterie de Cuisine and Brigade de Cuisine	
Batterie de cuisine	It is a French term for a range of kitchen tools needed to create complete meal courses. This includes basic cooking items like bowls, knives, cutting boards, small appliances, etc., and specialized tools like baking pans, mandolines and pastry utensils. But it never includes large appliances such as cooking ranges and refrigerators.
Brigade de cuisine	It is a French term for a system of hierarchy found in food outlets (like in restaurants, especially in kitchen) and hotels in France that employ extensive staff and are commonly referred to as kitchen staff in English speaking countries. The concept was developed by **Georges Auguste Escoffier**. This structured team system delegates responsibilities to different individuals who specialize in certain tasks.

KITCHEN LAYOUT

In hotels, kitchen can be centralized or decentralized. It depends upon the number of serving outlets, size of organization, available space, work flow, guest turnover rate and so forth. Kitchen is one of the most active work areas of a hotel, thus it is important to select the right layout in order to speed up the work, keep it clean/hygienic and attractive. There are seven primary kitchen layouts/shapes, these are *Corridor, L-Shaped, U-Shaped, Island, G-Shaped, Gallery/ Single wall* and *Comb shapes*. A brief description of each is given ahead.

Kitchen Designing Aspects

- Humidity
- Ventilation
- Lightening
- Temperature
- Space
- Noise
- Equipments

Corridor Layout

It is also known as *parallel layout*. This is meant for a narrow kitchen, where there are two rows – these rows may be face-to-face or back-to-back. In face-to-face layout, one row is for storage and the other for cleaning and cooking. Back-to-back layout, centralizes the utility lines required for equipment (when a partition wall is created between two rows). The separation of major groups of equipment is easily accomplished in face-to-face layout. Its features include:

- ✓ Great layout for smaller establishments
- ✓ Appliances are close to one another
- ✓ Easy for one cook to maneuver
- ✓ This layout can easily be converted to a U-shape by closing off one end.

L-shaped Layout

This is a layout, where the rows are diagonal to one another, thus forming an L-shape or also written as Ell shape. It is a modified version of single wall layout to accommodate more equipment and workplace; it is sometimes used where linear space is limited. This layout provides the kitchen working space into the corner, thus giving a lot of free space to move about. Its features include:

- ✓ It is a flexible kitchen layout and often preferable in smaller establishments.
- ✓ Major appliances can be placed in a variety of areas or can be separated into two major groups.
- ✓ Work areas are close to each other.
- ✓ This layout can also easily be converted into a U-shape with a cabinet leg addition.

U-shaped Layout

This is the best choice for small kitchens and very convenient too. The major drawback of this layout is that straight-line flow through the area is not possible. The U-shaped kitchen is popular in medium and small establishments. Its features include:

- ✓ Perfect for those establishments which use their kitchens frequently
- ✓ Provides plenty of counter space
- ✓ Efficient work triangle
- ✓ One can convert one cabinet leg into a breakfast bar (when built in homes)

Island Layout

This is meant for large kitchens. Here the cooking hob is altogether into a different box unit, while the L-shaped row is meant for the sink and storage purposes. Its features include:

- ✓ Islands kitchen cannot only keep work areas traffic-free, but also creates a wealth of extra counters and storage space.
- ✓ An island style kitchen prepares and offers food from all four directions.
- ✓ The island is also an ideal place to add an extra sink or an island grill.

G-shaped Kitchen

It is built very much identical to the U-shaped kitchen with the addition of an elongated partial wall; the G-shaped kitchen offers a great deal of space. Its features include:

- ✓ Ideal for large cooking (thus suitable for medium and large establishments)
- ✓ Plenty of counter and cabinet space
- ✓ Multiple cooks can function well in this layout
- ✓ In it, one cabinet leg can be converted into a breakfast bar or entertaining area (when built in homes).

Single Wall

It is also called "pullman kitchen" which is designed for homes or apartments or resort cottages or small establishments. The single wall kitchen offers great movement space. It is the simplest of all designs, at the same time it is limited for the placement of kitchen equipment. In this style of kitchen layout, equipment may be placed along the wall or take the form of an island. Its features include:

- ✓ Ideal for apartments and resort cottages
- ✓ Provides limited space for placing equipment
- ✓ Lacks control over access
- ✓ Can be enhanced with the addition of extra working stations/tables.

Comb Style

Nowadays, this is the most common layout of kitchen that almost every large hotel follows. In this layout, kitchen is divided into several sections which are managed and organized by respective station chefs (or CDPs). Due to its structural design, scores of kitchen equipment can be placed in it which principally depends upon *menu explosion*. Its features include:

✓ Suitable for large establishments.
✓ Every section is situated nearby each other.
✓ Ease to directly offer dishes to serving personnel.
✓ Executive chef can directly inspect every station, hence good control over staff.

These are the different ways in which a hotel management can plan their kitchens, and also make changes and alterations as and when required. In today's scenario, one can also see the concept of "Open Kitchen" where the guests can watch the chefs at work. Generally, a continental restaurant has an open-view built around a rôtisserie. Simply, it's a kind of live kitchen concept.

KITCHEN AREAS (RECEIVING, SERVING AND WASH-UP AREAS)

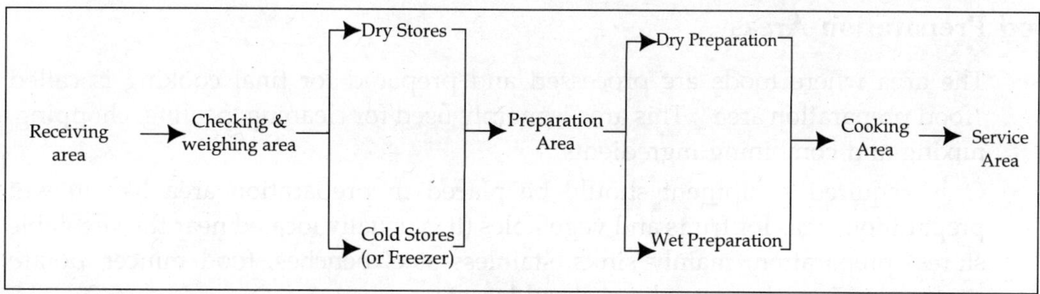

Receiving Areas

✓ It is the first and foremost point for the food and other commodities to be received from the supplier, thus planned carefully. The receiving dock should be located at the back of the premises, but with easy access from the street. Visibility of the receiving area from manager's office is always desirable.
✓ The outer platform of the receiving area is usually found elevated. The depth of the dock must provide enough space to easily unload the vehicle. The dock should be protected from excessive temperature and rain – thus often dock should have a roof or be enclosed.
✓ The receiving area for checking, weighing and counting should be located inside the facility. This area must be equipped with scales, hand trucks, utensils to open the cases, a desk and a computer system (with printer) to record products status.

Storing Areas

✓ It is concerned with store room– store room must have sufficient space for storing commodities. Storage section for storing bulk commodities should be located within easy access of the receiving and production areas.

STORAGE TEMPERATURE	
Dry	50-70°F
Wet	40-42°F
Freeze	0-(-10)°F

- ✓ The actual amount of storage space required for different commodities usually depends upon the number of meals served per day, the variety of menu items, the frequency of deliveries and the management policies.
- ✓ Some managers prefer to maintain a large *par stock* level whereas many others prefer to minimize the cash investment in maintaining huge stock. Generally, three kinds of storage areas are required to keep most of the commodities, i.e. dry storage, wet storage and freezer storage. Each of these storage areas serves different purposes.

Food Preparation Areas

- ✓ The area where foods are processed and prepared for final cooking is called "food preparation area". This area is mainly used for cleaning, peeling, chopping, mixing and combining ingredients.
- ✓ Only required equipment should be placed in preparation area like in wet preparation areas for fruits and vegetables (it is usually located near the vegetable stores) preparation, mainly sinks, stainless steel benches, food mincer, potato peeler machine, chopper, slicer, shredder, etc.
- ✓ A well-designed food preparation area should allow you to make changes to the menu without having to reorganize the equipment. When menu consists of items that are bought already prepared, this area is relatively small in size.

Cooking Areas

- ✓ It is an area where foods are finally cooked and made ready to serve guests. This cooking area should be located between storage area and service point. Food preparation area is usually situated adjacent to cooking range/area.
- ✓ Each cooking area, such as hot food area, cold food area and final food preparation area should be properly designed in accordance to the menu items requirements.
- ✓ Equipment in cooking area are usually grouped into island sites with benches between or on each side. For example, equipment like pressure steamers, tilt pans and stockpots are grouped together near the floor drains while equipment like griddle, fry pans and char-grills are positioned together near ventilation in order to exhaust heat and fumes.

Service Areas

- ✓ Service areas (like *hot plate area*) are platform or place where foods are kept after final cooking, so that stewards receive the prepared food then serve to the waiting guest. Service area's design and dimension is usually based on style of service which is already planned for a facility during the *concept development* phase.

- ✓ A heating or cooling provision or facilities is necessary in service area, so that food can be kept hot or cold until it is not picked up by the waiting staff. Major equipment in service areas include bain marie, hot press or refrigerated case, plate warmer, hot plate counter (to keep prepared dishes hot), etc. are positioned near the dining room entrance.
- ✓ Beverage and toast making facilities are also located near the service section for quick and easy access by steward. In hotels, usually these provisions are found in *still room* (pantry section) and hot plate area.

Wash-up Areas

- ✓ Kitchen wash-up area is also called "pot washing area". This area is used to wash the soiled kitchen equipment and utensils, especially pots, for example sauce pot, stock pot, etc. In small establishments, usually pot washing is done nearby the kitchen stewarding (or in dish washing area).
- ✓ But in large establishments, it is separate from kitchen stewarding (as kitchen stewarding is mainly responsible for dishwashing of utensils of food and beverage department) because pots and pans are washed in separate area or in area near to their use as they can damage the restaurant's cutlery, crockery and glassware; it also depends on the size of the kitchen.
- ✓ Equipment found in wash-up area include dishwasher, large sinks, stainless steel benches, food disposal unit, rubbish bins and other cleaning equipment.

FUELS

There are three major alternatives of fuel and the selection of best one or their combination depends upon the policy of management. These three fuel types are liquid, solid and gaseous. All these are available for firing in boilers, furnaces and other combustion equipment. The selection of right type of fuel depends on various factors such as type of cuisine, fuel availability, storage, handling, pollution and landed cost of fuel and prevailing laws. The knowledge of the fuel properties helps in selecting the right fuel for the right purpose and efficient use of the fuel. The associated characteristics are generally used for assessing the nature and quality of fuels. A brief description of each fuel type is given below.

Types of Fuel

Solid fuels

- ✓ These are cheap sources of fire but they are dirty and more expensive in nature. The control of heat in solid fuels is difficult in comparison to others. It also requires more space for storage and huge duct panels (or chimney's) for proper functioning. Property will also face problem with the ash handling after burning of materials. Its example includes coal, firewood, etc.

Liquid fuels

- ✓ Main application of liquid fuel is required in boilers. It also requires space for storage and is found noisier than gas. It requires a motor or pump to spray the oil into the combustion chamber. For example, furnace oil, kerosene, etc.

Gaseous form

- ✓ Gas is efficient, clean, silent and controllable, simultaneously found cheaper to install than oil heating. Its example includes LPG (liquefied petroleum gas) and CNG (compressed natural gas).
- ✓ LPG is propane or butane or a combination of both produced by refining crude petroleum oil. While natural gas (CNG) is an alternative, environment friendly fuel (mainly methane) can be stored under pressure in the boot as compressed natural gas (CNG).

Electricity

- ✓ It is the cleanest of all fuels. It can easily control and does not require space for storage. Nowadays, you will find that majority of equipment are operated via electricity.

Comparative Study of Different Types of Fuels

Properties	Liquid (Like Fuel Oil)	Solid Fuel (Like Coal)	Gas (Like Natural Gas)
Carbon	84	41.11	74
Hydrogen	12	02.76	25
Sulphur	03	0.41	–
Oxygen	01	09.89	Trace
Nitrogen	Trace	01.22	0.75
Ash	Trace	38.63	–
Water	Trace	05.98	–

Advantages and Disadvantages of Different Fuels		
Solid fuels	• It is easy to clean	• It has low fuel value and is also scarce
	• Gives cheerful fire	• Requires large storage space
	• It can be stored for future use	• Requires more labour for preparation
	• Cheap in certain localities	• Gives unsteady fire/does not hold fire for long time
Electricity	• Easy to clean and less maintenance	• Time consuming (time taken to heat up)
	• Easy to control and labour saving	• Requires specified or particular utensils
	• Little heat loss during operation	• More expensive than gas (initial investment)
	• No extra storage space required	• Not possible to operate in absence of electricity
	• Low ventilation required	• May affect workflow during electricity breakdown
Gas	• Labour saving and no smoke and dirt	• Loss of some heat during operation
	• No extra space required for fuel storage	• Requires regular cleaning and maintenance
	• No special/particular utensils are required	• Requires adequate ventilation
	• Easy to operate and control	• Requires government concern during laying pipeline
	• Cheaper than electricity	• Heavy installation expenses

Features of Liquefied Petroleum Gas (LPG)

- It gives an instant cooking flame.
- It is easy and instantaneous to light.
- It is easy to control. The blue flame is visible and its size is easily controlled over a wide range so that the required rate of heating can be obtained.
- It is non-poisonous and safe to use.
- It burns cleanly and does not produce any soot, smoke or smell during combustion, therefore leaving the kitchen clean.

- It is pure and very consistent in quality.
- It adds comfort because cooking is quick and the kitchen does not get heated as with other fuels like wood or charcoal.
- It is easily available in the market and also compatible with many appliances plus easy to maintain.

KEY TERMS

Kitchen brigade : Team of kitchen staff who works in different sections of kitchen.

Par stock : Minimum level of back-up-stock for emergency cases.

Open kitchen : Live counters where chefs prepare food in front of guests.

Pullman kitchen : A single wall kitchen which is often preferred in apartments or in resort cottages.

Hot plate area : Meeting point between kitchen and serving staff. *Aboyeur* is the incharge of this area.

Aboyeur : The head position in hot plate area and also termed barker or announcer.

Receiving areas : Space provided for unloading of food and non-food items.

Menu explosion : Process by which management determines kitchen equipment needs in a new or remoulded kitchen. It is a process that calculates the amount of food prepared for each menu item in a specific kitchen.

Chef de cuisine : French term for a position title of kitchen executive.

Batterie de cuisine : French term for a range of kitchen tools needed to create complete meal courses.

REVIEW QUESTIONS

1. Explain the kitchen brigade and enlist the duties and responsibilities of kitchen executive/executive chef.
2. Write a short note on different styles of kitchen layout and enlist pros and cons of each layout over one another.
3. With the help of diagram/flow chart explain the role of different kitchen areas in food preparation.
4. Write down the advantages and disadvantages of LPG.

29

CHAPTER

Fundamentals of Food Production

Objectives

Students will be able to:

- elucidate principles of food production;
- enlist different food preparation techniques;
- reveal different food textures; and
- expound different cooking mediums and their further types.

BASIC PRINCIPLES OF FOOD PRODUCTION

The term *basic principle of food production* is directly concerned with the fundamentals of kitchen operation without which it is very difficult to work in kitchen. Few basic principles are given below.

Before the Cooking

- Purchase quality products at right price.
- Do a market survey before purchasing in order to choose right supplier.
- Purchase non-perishable items in bulk and perishable items at regular intervals.
- Thoroughly wash and clean the food items before cooking.

During the Cooking

- Add proper seasoning in food items according to the requirements.
- Use right or preferable cooking method to cook the food items.
- Use right cooking technique to cook the food item.
- Follow the standard recipe and produce pre-determined portion yield.
- Cook only in required quantity.

After the Cooking

- Serve the prepared food item as soon as possible after cooking.
- Use right garnishing and accompaniments in right quantity.

- Check for excess wastage.
- Always try to put some new idea in the prepared food items.

Aims and Objectives of Cooking	
• To kill bacteria	Cooking destroys harmful microorganisms and parasites, making the food safe for consumption.
• To help in digestion	Digestibility of starchy foods is enhanced through release of starch from cereal grains after cooking.
• Increase palatability	Cooking enhances the deliciousness of the food items which ultimately affect the apetite of humans.
• Improve appearance	Cooking makes the food more attractive in appearance and therefore more appetizing.
• Improve flavour	Apart from appearance improvement; cooking also enhances the flavour of cooked food items.
• Make food eatable	All foods are not possible to be consumed without cooking like pulses, beans, etc.
• Provide balanced diet	Scientific knowledge in cooking fulfil/balance the nutritional requirements of every menu/dish.
• Create variations	Different cooking methods offer variations in taste, flavour, aroma and texture even with same item.

FOOD PREPARATION TECHNIQUES

The term *food preparation technique* refers to the activities that are required to be performed from the very beginning stage of mise en place till the finished product. It primarily covers following tasks.

Pre-Preparation Techniques: The term pre-preparation techniques is associated with all types of pre mise en place errands. It is the activity or process of making food ingredients ready to cook. It comprises:

Blanching	Removing skin by putting food in boiling water and then in cold water.
Washing	Cleaning food with water.
Mincing	Food ingredients are finely ground.
Cutting	Passing a knife through the food in order to produce pieces.
Peeling	To remove skin by using a knife/peeler. Often peeling is also called as *scraping*.
Mashing	Turning a soft food into a paste form.
Grating	Breaking food into fine pieces using a grater.
Pressing	To separate the liquid portions from solids by weights or mechanical pressure.

Shredding	Cutting food into very fine pieces.
Grinding	Breaking food into powder/paste form by using grinder.
Steeping	Soaking food in liquid.
Sieving	Separating/removing larger pieces from small ones.
Slitting	To give a cut (or slit) usually in the middle and lengthwise, for example, slitting green chillies or ladyfinger.
Mixing	Putting different foods together then blending or combining.
Filtering	Removing of unwanted particles (like dirt) or moisture (like whey water from cheese).
Coating	To cover a food with a layer of crumbs, flour or other fine substances before cooking.
Marinating	To soak a food (before cooking) in a marinade.
Soaking	To saturate in water either plain or salted with sodium chloride or sodium bicarbonate.
Refining	Purifying or freeing the ingredient from the impurities, as in refining cane sugar.
Skimming	To remove scum from the boiling liquid like *raft* is removed from tomato soup.
Rendering	Separating fat from connective tissues by heating such as rendering of lard.
Flavouring	To impart flavour into the food like herbs and *bouquet garni* used to flavour stock and sauce.
Sprouting	Soaking, draining and then moistening seeds at regular intervals until they germinate.
Flotation	To separate, generally, on the basis of certain differences usually gravity.

Additional Pre-Preparation Techniques

Each food item requires different pre-preparation activities depending upon its end-use. For example, coriander leaves and potatoes undergo different activities for different end uses like:

Coriander leaves	For green garnish	Plucked → Cleaned → Washed → Chopped finely
Coriander leaves	For chutney	Plucked → Washed → Ground to a fine paste
Potatoes	For making chips	Washed → Peeled → Thinly sliced
Potatoes	For making tikki	Washed → Boiled → Peeled → Mashed

Cutting Techniques: *Cutting* is dividing a food into smaller parts by using a sharp knife. Safety plays an important role in cutting techniques. A chopping board is also essential for safe and efficient cutting. It protects the countertop of working station as well as the chef who chops. There are various techniques to cut the food into different ways. A brief description of some accustomed cutting techniques is given below:

Mirepoix    Julienne    Brunoise    Batons    Turned Vegetable

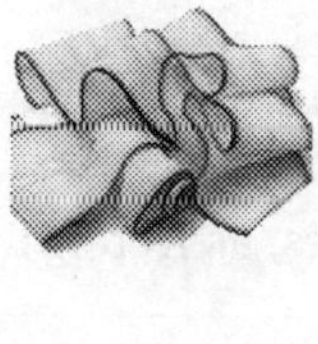

Rubans 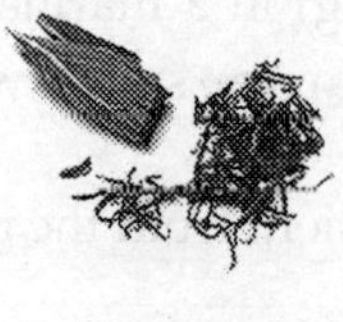   Chiffonade 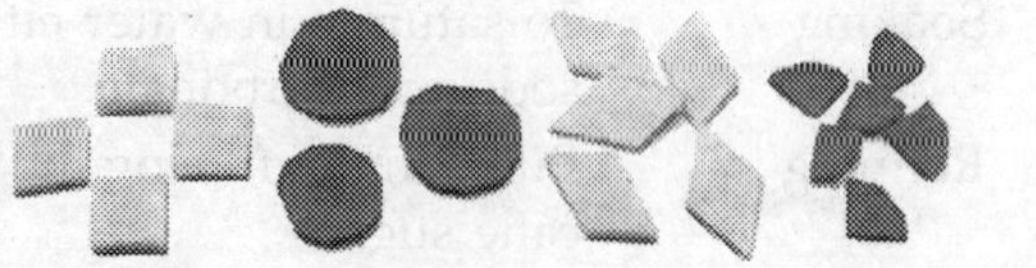   Paysanne

Pare	To cut/peel (like to rind) into very thin layers with a paring knife/peeler, for example paring an apple.
Score	To make straight shallow cuts with a slicing knife on the surface of food. *Scoring* is often done to tenderize the meat like ham, so that sauces can sink in.
Slice	To cut into large and thin pieces (often round or oval shape) by using sawing motion while pressing the knife down gently.
Sliver	To cut into very thin strips like almonds into very thin strips. The cutting styles described are only a few ways to change the size and shape of food.
Crush	To pulverize the food into crumbs, powder or paste form. It is usually done with a rolling pin, blender or food processor.
Emincer	To cut fruit into thin slices, shorter than for juliennes. This term is most often used when referring to meats, but it also applies to fruits and vegetables.
Flake	To break or tear off the small layers of food items, often cooked fish with a fork.
Grate and shred	To incise into small pieces or shreds by pressing and rubbing the food (like cheese and carrots) against the rough surface of a grater.

Grind	To mill the food items but before grinding, food items are broken into coarse, medium or fine particles. For example, meat or coffee beans are often ground.
Mash	To crush the food item with a masher or beater in order to achieve a smooth mixture.
Puree	To mash or grind cooked foods until they are smooth (usually a blender/food processor/food mill and sieve is used to mash the food).
Quarter	To divide the food items into four equal sections or parts. For example, boiled egg is generally cut into quarters.
Snip	To cut food into small pieces with kitchen cutters or shears. Usually, fresh herbs and dried fruits are used to snip.
Vandyke	To cut fruits and vegetables into various fancy shapes like diamond, star or rose. This food cut is mostly used as a garnish or to decorate a dish.
Mirepoix	To roughly cut vegetables (like carrots, celery and onions); shape and size is not important. Often mirepoix is used in making of stock.
Matignon	To mince or finely chop aromatic vegetables and use in the same way as a *mirepoix*. But there is difference between matignon and mirepoix.
Julienne	To cut into long thin strips, similar to matchsticks. Often this cut is also known as *shoe string*.
Brunoise	To cut into exact and fine pieces. The food item is first julienned and then cut into a fine cube/dice by slicing the lengths.
Batons/Jardinières	To cut into matchstick lengths (these are thicker versions of the julienne). The batons can be cut with a chef's knife or with a French mandoline equipped with the cutting blade.
Rubans	To cut into thin, long and broad slices like ribbons. It is often used to add a decorative, elegant look to any salad or dish.
Chiffonade	To cut into thin strips often made from herbs or any leafy vegetables. Stack the leaves and roll tightly then slice across the roll to create fine ribbons. It makes a nice decorative garnish.
Paysanne	To cut into thin slices at the cross section. These can be cut into triangular, square or round or diamond shapes. Root vegetables such as carrots are perfect for this style of cutting.

Note. The main difference between a mirepoix and a matignon is that a *mirepoix* is rough cut and strained out, unlike a *matignon*, that is, carefully cut and served as a part of the garnish of a dish.

Mixing Techniques: Mixing means blending of two or more ingredients altogether. Most of the standard recipes require some kind of mixing or combining of two or more ingredients together, so they blend. Usually, spoon, whisker, food processor or blenders are used for this purpose. Few mixing techniques are given below with a brief description:

Beating	To mix thoroughly by incorporating air into foods. Usually, whisker or spoon is used for this purpose. One can also use a mixer or food processor to beat.
Cream	To beat ingredients such as shortening and sugar, combining until soft and creamy consistency is obtained.
Folding	To mix a light, fluffy mixture into a heavier one. For example, egg whites are often folded into a cake batter.
Stiring	It often applies to food that is cooking. Mix with a spoon or wire whisk in a circular motion. It distributes the heat and keeps food away from sticking to a pan.
Tossing	To mix ingredients such as salad greens and dressing by tumbling them with tongs or a large spoon or fork.
Whipping	To beat quickly and vigorously to incorporate air into a mixture, thus making it light and fluffy.
Shaking	To move to and fro with jerky movements like shaking cocktails.
Blending	To mix an ingredient into another ingredient/s so that they combine together as a mass, usually through blender.
Cutting in	To mix cold fat (like margarine or butter) into dry ingredients (like flour). This technique is mostly used in pastry making.
Kneading	To mix by rubbing process often used in making of bread and pastries (or dough). This can be done by hand, using the press-fold-turn action or through food processor/mixer.
Whisking	To rapidly whip or beat as much air (or volume) as possible, for example, whisking of heavy cream or egg white.

Coating Techniques: It is another common food preparation technique. In it, food is coated with a thin layer of another food. Coating gives flavour and texture to the main food. It also helps in making the food brown better and retain moisture. A coating may be in dry or wet (liquid) form. In *dry coating,* ingredients like flour or cornmeal are used to coat meat, poultry and seafood. A convenient way to apply it is to place it in a large plastic bag and add the food to be coated. Coating can also be liquid as well. Foods may be brushed with a sauce or dipped in a batter, which is a dry coating mixture with liquid added. Few coating techniques are given below with their brief description:

Baste	To add moisture, flavour and colour to foods by brushing, drizzling or spooning pan juices or other liquids over the food during cooking.
Breaded	To coat a food with three different layers; first with flour (to make surface dry) then with liquid (like milk or beaten egg) and finally with seasoned crumbs or corn meal.
Brush	To coat a food surface (like meat or bread) with melted butter or glaze. Usually pastry brush is used for this purpose.
Dot	To place random bits of food (like butter) on the surface of another food.
Dredge	To coat food surface with dry ingredients such as flour, corn meal, or bread crumbs before cooking. For example, desserts are dredged with sugar after baking or frying.
Dust	To sprinkle food lightly with food materials like spices, sugar, or flour.
Flour	To dry coat a food like fish or chicken with flour.
Glaze	To liquid coat a food surface in order to give shiny coating. It can be a savoury glaze on meats or a sweet glaze on pastry and baked goods.
Napé	To completely coat a food surface with a light, thin, even layer of sauce.

Other Techniques: The above mentioned food preparation techniques are mainly used while cooking the food. But it doesn't mean that, these are the only techniques, one may also require many other techniques in different or particular situations. Few of them are given below with a brief description:

Blanch	To pour boiling liquid over food or vice versa (to loosen skins) then plunging into cold water (to set colour and stop any further cooking)
Candy	To cook food into sugar syrup, for example, stewed fruits (in it cut fruits are cooked in sugar syrup then add cinnamon and cardamom to enhance the flavour).
Caramelize	To heat sugar until it liquefies and darkens in colour. Other foods may be caramelized to release their sugar content.
Clarify	To make a liquid clear by removing solid particles. For example, a *broth* is clarified by removing fat and straining or stock by heating the liquid, then straining or skimming it.
Core	To remove the central part of a fruit such as an apple or pineapple.
Deglaze	To reduce the meat sediments in pan (after sautéing or frying) in order to make a *jus* lié/pan juice/gravy or sauce (wine may also be added for this purpose). This mixture is used as a base in sauces and gravies.

Drain	To remove liquid from/pour off (strainer or colander may be used for draining). In simple terms, it means to remove water from solid foods like vegetables or cooked pasta.
Marinate	To incorporate flavour into food by soaking in a cold and seasoned liquid. This seasoned liquid usually contains an acid, in which foods such as meat or vegetables are soaked (marinated) before cooking.
Mold	To shape food, usually by pouring the liquefied food into a mould. When the liquid is cooled, it will retain the shape of the mould.
Pit	To remove the seed from a piece of fruit usually by cutting around the sides of the fruit and pulling the seed away from the flesh.
Reduce	To boil a liquid until a portion of it has evaporated. This reduction process intensifies the flavour which results in a thicker liquid. The process is also known as *evaporation*.
Scald	To heat milk or cream to a temperature just below the boiling point. It may also be used to blanch the vegetables/food.
Season	To add such flavourings as salt, pepper, herbs and spices to a food in order to enhance the flavour of food.
Shell	To remove the tough outer skin or coating of food. For example, removing of shell from nuts and boiled eggs.
Steep	To soak a food in water just below the boiling point in order to extract its flavour and colour. Dry ingredients like tea or herbs are soaked in hot water to extract the flavour or soften the texture.
Strain	To separate the solid particles from a liquid, such as broth by pouring the mixture through a strainer or sieve.
Vent	To leave an opening space in a container so that steam can escape during the cooking process.
Masking	To cover or coat cooked meat or a similar dish with aspic, glaze or sauce. It is also used to coat the inside of a mould with jelly.
Bruise	To partially crush an ingredient in order to release its full flavour, such as bruising of garlic clove.
Homogenization	The act of converting the immiscible liquid into an emulsion. Simply, it is the process of making something homogeneous or uniform in composition such as homogenization of milk.
Emulsification	Dispersing one liquid into another in which it is insoluble such as water and oil with the addition of an emulsifier.

FOOD TEXTURES AND CONSISTENCIES

The term *food texture* refers to the properties of the food/beverage that can be sensed by touch and felt inside the mouth. On the other side, the term *consistency* refers to the physical nature of a food/beverage that can be defined in terms of degree of density, firmness or viscosity. There are many words to describe the food textures and consistencies such as crunchy, soft, crispy, hard, lumpy and so forth. A brief description of several of these terms is given below.

Solid	This state of texture is mainly related to *cheese products* because it has different textures and consistency like soft cheese, hard cheese and semi-hard cheese. Its stages can be further classified elasticity, crumbly and creamy.
Melted	This state of texture is mainly related with "butter and margarine". It can also be further divided into two parts, liquid and viscous.
Thick	This texture is mainly related with the gravies, soups and sauces. It shows the consistency of any product. In order to make a thicker product one needs to use variety of thickening agents like roux (equal mixture of flour and butter), starch (corn-flour and arrowroot), potato starch and so forth.
Thin	This term is again related with the consistency of soups, sauces and gravies. But it is just opposite of the above mentioned "thick" texture. Its best example include "series of consommé soups".
Lumpy	Its best example includes Béchamel sauce because if chefs do not stir it continuously, the sauce will get lumpy.
Crisp & crunchy	This state is mainly found in roasted food items like tandoori chicken. It happens due to the direct exposition of food to fire. It can also form with the help of various alcoholic beverages in flambé dishes.

METHODS OF COOKING

These are different sets of heat based food preparation techniques. The selection of appropriate method to cook a food depends upon many factors, prominently nature of incorporated dish, time required to prepare a dish, requirement of nutritional balance, time required to serve the end-user and so forth. Cooking methods can be broadly classified into two groups: moist heat and dry heat methods. Apart from it, fat heat is another way of cooking a food. A brief description of each cooking method and its sub-category is given below.

Methods of cooking

- Moist heat method
  - High Heat
    - Blanching
    - Boiling
    - Par boiling
  - Low heat
    - Poaching
    - Simmering
    - Steeping
    - Stewing
  - Indirect heat
    - Bain Marie
    - Sous vide
    - Steaming
- Dry heat method
  - Conduction
    - Roasting
    - Searing
  - Convection
    - Baking
    - Smoking
  - Radiation
    - Grilling
    - Rotisserie
- Fat
  - Frying
  - Sauté
  - Sweating

Moist Heat Methods: In moist heat method, food is cooked in hot liquid (like water, stock, milk, etc.), steam or a combination of the both. Moisture allows heat to transfer by both conduction and convection. This method is generally used for the less tender cuts of meats, fruits and vegetables, and exclusively for those items that require a softening process. Moist heat cooking helps in tenderizing the food and also blends flavours. Food can be cooked through moist heat in a pan with or without a tight fitting lid. A lid prevents the liquid from evaporating, so foods do not get burnt. Moist heat can be produced through a variety of techniques. Few of them are given below.

Boiling (food boils at 100°C)

- ✓ It means cooking food in a liquid at the boiling point of water. At this temperature, water/liquid is suitable for blanching and parboiling of those food items which require partial cooking. For example potato, kidney beans, egg, chicken, mutton, beef, etc., are required to be partially cooked before the starting of operation. This method cooks food more quickly than poaching and simmering.
- ✓ The final finishing of above-mentioned food items are performed after receiving the guest order from the restaurant but must be kept in fully cooked form at the time of banqueting operation or when an outlet offers TDH menu.

Poaching (food poaches between 80-90°C)

- ✓ It means cooking food in liquid below the boiling point of water. At this temperature water/liquid will remain at constant temperature and there is no movement in water, which undeniably happens in the boiling method.
- ✓ In this method, food items are cooked in stable hot water. Foods prepared via this method include poached fish, poached egg, etc. This method is primarily used for delicately flavoured foods that do not require lengthy cooking time to tenderize them. The boiling temperature is not preferable for poached preparations because boiling can break the food (or flesh) into two or more parts.

Simmering (food simmers between 85-96°C)

- ✓ It means cooking food in liquid below the boiling point (or to boil gently) of liquid. It is a time consuming process of cooking because after reaching the boiling point the gas needs to be brought to low flame. This method is primarily used for foods that need to be tenderized through a long, slow and moist cooking medium such as less tender cuts of meat.
- ✓ The food item take long time to get partially or fully cooked through simmering method but it helps in extracting the maximum flavour from the used herbs, spices and other condiments.

Steaming (food starts steaming when water reaches 100°C)

- ✓ It is a more gradual process of cooking which allows the natural juices to be retained more completely. In steaming, the water used to cook the food item will vaporize by heating (it occurs at boiling point), for example, cooking of idli in steamer, cooking of rice in pressure cooker, etc. This method is primarily used for food items that do not require long cooking time. Cooking of food items with this method helps in retaining the nutrients of a food plus enhances its natural flavor.
- ✓ Excess of steam or pressure can damage the food item. Therefore, a special mechanism is equipped in the utensil to maintain the pressure level like "pressure release gauge". Steaming is a satisfactory and economical means of cooking for puddings and potatoes.

Stewing (combination of dry + moist heat)

- ✓ It means cooking the food items in minimum amount of liquid (but food must be covered completely) - it may be water, stock or sauce. It is a slow cooking process; therefore it will take more time in comparison to other cooking methods except braising.
- ✓ In it, food items are firstly cut into *small pieces*, so it can simmer into the water at a constant temperature until tender. For example, hard root vegetables, fruits, tough meats like joints, etc. are preferred for this method of cooking. The cooked food is served with its own gravy/pan juice/*jus* lié.

Braising (combination of dry + moist heat)

- ✓ It is a simple method of cooking in which meats or vegetables are cooked in a covered pot with very little water/liquid (½ or ⅓). It is similar to simmering, and is a combination of roasting and stewing; it is used mainly for cooking *large pieces* of meat such as inferior joints, poultry, offal and certain vegetables.

✓ Meat or poultry should be sealed quickly in a hot oven on a bed of roots. It should then be half covered with brown stock, covered with a lid and put back into the oven at a lower temperature about 180°C to raise. Meat cooked in this way retains its own juices and also absorbs the flavour of the vegetables with which it is cooked.

Important Terms

Blanching: It means cooking food just long enough to set colour or make them easy to peel. It is performed by pouring the boiling water over food to loosen the skins (e.g., tomatoes or peaches). Food may also be blanched by boiling for a specified time, then plunging the food into cold water to set the colour and stop any further cooking.

Par-cooking/boiling: It means food is partially cooked or cooked to partial doneness (like par-boiling) as might be appropriate for vegetables and grains to be finished by sautéing or stewing.

Bain Marie: It is a French term which means water bath. In it, food container is placed in a large, shallow pan of warm water, which surrounds the food with gentle heat. This technique is good for cooking sauces, custards, savoury mousse (with breaking or curdling) and often also used to keep cooked foods warm.

Sous vide: It is a French term which means under vacuum. Actually it is a food packaging technique in which fresh ingredients are combined into various dishes then vacuum packed, next cooked under a vacuum and finally chilled.

Dry Heat Methods: Dry heat means cooking food in an uncovered container without adding any liquid or fat. This method makes the food dry and gives soft and chewy texture to food. Food preparations using any of the dry method/s have a rich flavour due to caramelization and browning of the foods. Dry and radiant heat gives food a crispy brown crust with a distinctive flavour while the inside remains moist and tender. It also helps in retaining water soluble vitamins. Dry heat method includes roasting or baking, broiling and grilling. Few most commonly used dry methods of cooking are given below.

Baking

✓ It is the dry heat method (without the addition of fat or basting) of cooking food items in an oven. Oven may be domestic (for cooking less quantity of food) or heavy commercial oven for large quantities of cooking.

✓ Food products like muffins, brioche, croissant, buns, bread, pies, tarts, cakes, cookies, etc., are baked in an oven. Baking is almost analogous to roasting but this term is most commonly used in bakery for fruit, vegetable, pastry and bread items whereas roasting is usually applied to meat and poultry preparations.

Roasting (Rotisserie)

- ✓ It is almost similar to baking principles but especially applicable to meat and poultry items. Roasted foods are cooked by radiant heat in a heated air in a closed environment like in oven. An important part of roasting is that during cooking process a small amount of fat, oil or cooking juices are used to coat the food item.
- ✓ This coating is called *basting* and it seals the pores of the flesh and prevents the loss of nutritious juices during the cooking process plus also keeps the food moist, gives the food colour and enhances the flavour.

TYPES OF ROASTING

- Pot roasting
- Pan roasting
- Spit roasting
- Oven roasting

Broiling

- ✓ It means cooking of food items at a high temperature on a rack that is located above, below or between the heat sources. The food to be broiled is placed on a preheated metal grate.
- ✓ Radiant heat from top cooks the food while preheated metal grate marks it with attractive cross hatch marks. The example of cooking equipment include griller, salamander, etc. The preferable food items for broiling include steak, fish, seafoods, etc.

Barbecuing

- ✓ Barbecue is a grill, pit, or outdoor fireplace for cooking meat over direct heat. It is usually done outdoors by cooking and smoking the meat over wood or charcoal. *Barbecue Nation* is perfect example of an outlet that specializes in an on-table barbecuing preparation.
- ✓ In barbecuing, food items are cooked either by broiling, grilling or roasting while continuing basting with a required sauces.

GRILLING MODES

- Under heat
- Over heat
- Between heat
- Infrared

Grilling

- ✓ Similar to broiling, except that grilling uses heat from beneath the cooking surface. Simply, it means cooking food on an open grid over the gas, charcoal, or electric heat. Grilled foods are usually identified by cross-hatch markings. The equipment required for grilling includes a small grill on which food items are placed and then directly placed above the heat.

- ✓ The food items cooked by grilling method include steak, fish, seafoods, vegetables, etc. In grilling, the heat cooks the meat while the grill below marks it.

Ovenizing and Food Smoking

- ✓ Ovenizing means cooking of food on greased pans in ovens at high temperature whereas food smoking is concerned with incorporating flavor into the food by smoking.
- ✓ Smoking is the process of flavouring, cooking, or preserving food by exposing it to the smoke from burning or smoldering plant materials, most often wood. Meats and fishes are the most common smoked foods (such as smoked salmon, smoked trout, smoked ham, etc.)

ADDITIONAL COOKING MODES

- Pan searing
- *Vacuum flask*
- Steeping
- Bain Marie

Note. *Searing* or *pan searing* is a technique in which the surface of the food (usually meat, poultry or fish) cooks at high temperature so a caramelized crust could form. Its excellent example includes food cooked through grilling, baking, braising, roasting or sautéing.

Cooking with Fat: As the title suggests, food items are cooked with fat. It can be a part of dry heat cooking mode or moist heat cooking method. Some most commonly used cooking-with-fat methods are explained below.

Poeleing (or butter roasting)

- ✓ It is a dry heat method of cooking and often associated with white meats and game birds. Conventionally, it was famous by the name *butter roasting*. In this method, meat items are allowed to cook in their own gravy or juices in a covered vessel (casserole) on a bed of aromatic vegetables known as "matignon".
- ✓ The matignon then becomes a garnish and is served as a part of the sauce. *Jus* is often used to prepare a sauce from the pan dripping.

Sweating

- ✓ Sweating is a process of cooking where ingredients are added in a very small amount of oil or butter and cooked for a short period of time. It takes the moisture out from the ingredients.
- ✓ It is a well known medium of cooking as it brings out the flavours of the vegetables, while sautéing seals them within.

Frying

Types of Frying

- Pan frying
- Stir frying
- Sauté
- Deep frying
- Shallow frying

✓ Frying means quick cooking of food in fat and/or oil. All frying requires fat and/or oil but deep frying demands more oil than any other method of frying.

✓ Frying techniques vary in the amount of fat required, the cooking direction of the food and the type of vessel required to cook also differs with frying type.

Solar Cooking

✓ Solar cooking is based on the principle that black surface and background absorb solar rays and get heated. Foods kept in the black boxes are cooked with this heat.

✓ It is used for making lentils, boiled rice and vegetables, breads and biscuits. The maximum temperature it attains is around 100°F, thus cannot be used to make chapattis and for roasting dishes. It cannot be a good choice for professional cooking.

Griddling

✓ It means cooking of food on a solid heated surface, usually with a small amount of fat. A *griddle* is a piece of cooking equipment. In the industrial world usually, it is a flat plate of metal (aluminums, stainless steel or cast iron).

✓ Griddled foods include pancakes, oatcakes, crepes, grilled cheese, unleavened breads (roti or chapati), dosa, Irish boxty and Welsh cakes.

Methods of Heat Transfer

Method	Heat Transfer Mode	Speed of Heating	Types
Conduction	Through direct contact (via pan)	Slow heat movement	Usually mechanical
Convection	Through fluid - liquid/gas	Fast heat movement	Natural and mechanical
Radiation	Through waves/light striking	Fast heat movement	Infrared and microwave

KEY TERMS

Standard recipe	: Set of instructions describing the way a particular establishment prepares a particular dish.
Scraping	: Removing skin by using a knife/peeler. Often peeling is also called *scraping.*
Scoring	: Straight shallow cut with a slicing knife in the surface of food to tenderize it.
Raft	: Skimming/removing of scum from the boiling liquid like *raft* removed from tomato soup.
Sautéing	: Rapid cooking in small amount of fat over relatively high heat.
Vacuum flask	: Cooking mode in which food cooks inside a vacuum flask under high temperature.
Sous vide	: French term for *under vacuum* cooking. Food is cooked in sealed airtight plastic bags in a water bath for a long time.
Water bath	: French term for *bain marie* often described as double boiler.
Poeleing	: Dry heat method and traditionally also known as *butter roasting.*
Shoe stirring	: Another name of juliennes. It means to cut into long thin strips, similar to matchsticks.

REVIEW QUESTIONS

1. Describe the fundamental rules of food preparation before, during and after cooking processes.
2. Describe the different food textures/consistencies and explain them briefly.
3. Differentiate between the following—mirepoix and matignon, coating and marinating, brushing and basting, cutting-in and kneading, Vandyke and batons, shaking and stirring and juliennes and brunoise.
4. What are the different methods of cooking? Explain each method briefly.

30 CHAPTER

Stocks, Soups and Sauces

OBJECTIVES

Students will be able to:

- explicate stock types, their ingredients and cooking process;
- explain soup types, their garnishing and thickeners;
- expound grand sauces and their derivatives; and
- express the culinary uses of sauces and roux.

STOCK

Stock can be defined as a clear and thin liquid flavoured by soluble substances extracted from meat, poultry, fish, bones, vegetables, aromatic ingredients and seasonings. Stocks are almost like sauces but never served by themselves; it is usually formed as components of many other preparations like base for sauces, stews, braised dish, glazes, soups, jellies, and many other dishes. Simply, stocks are very tasty and nutritious liquid, made by gently simmering selected ingredients. This liquid can then be used in cookery to add flavour and to provide a nutritious value to the cooking food. Stock can be used in thickened or unthickened form. The type of stock one makes, and its use, will depend on the offered menu items.

Stocks can be made from an array of different ingredients including meat bones and trimmings, vegetables, herbs and spices. In certain cases, readymade or manufactured stocks are purchased and used. The advent of readymade stocks and stock cubes reduce the use of traditional stocks. The best ingredients and correct techniques make good quality stocks. It is an art as well as science to prepare a good stock because good stock depends on an individual's skill as well as on some scientific principles.

Note. In French, stock is called as "fond (it means foundation)" which means it is a foundation or base for other preparations. Stock is the foundation of cookery because a series of food preparations are prepared around it or are based on stock.

CLASSIFICATION OF STOCK

Major Stock Types

White stock

✓ For white stock preparation, ingredients are directly placed into the cooking liquor. It is made from chicken, beef and veal with the addition of aromatic vegetables. An additional ingredient is the *mirepoix* (it is a flavouring agent based on diced vegetables) and occasionally pork fat.

✓ These stocks are light in colour and are used to make white sauces, blanquettes and poached chicken dishes. Sauces made from white stock are always called white sauces. Often, a white beef stock is also known as neutral stock.

INGREDIENTS OF MIREPOIX

- Onion
- Carrot
- Celery
- Leeks

Brown stock (Estouffade)

✓ For brown stock preparation, ingredients are first browned in fat then added to the cooking liquor. It is made from browned chicken or beef bones and browned mirepoix. Roasting the ingredients to light brown causes them to undergo the *maillard reaction*.

✓ This is when the natural sugars in the ingredients get caramelized and produce complex brown colour. This reaction is the reason that boiled meat tastes different than roasted meat. This stock is used for brown sauces and gravies; braised dishes and meat glazes. Sauces made from brown stock are called *brown sauces*.

Vegetarian stock

✓ For vegetarian stock preparation, ingredients are first gently fried in butter. Any pleasantly flavoured combination of vegetables and aromatic herbs simmered together may produce a vegetable stock. As with meat-based stocks, the mirepoix can still provide a substantial flavour base, especially in combination with a suitable bouquet-garni.

✓ For preparing vegetable stock, clean vegetable trimmings are to be used. For best results choose cuts according to uses of stock. Vegetable stock is also called "neutral vegetarian stock".

Basic Elements of a Stock	
Nourishing agents	It includes meat, bone, offal, trimmings, vegetables and so forth
Flavouring agents	It includes mirepoix, bouquet garni, roots, herbs and so forth
Liquid agents	It includes wine, water, remouillage, consommé and so forth
Seasoning agents	It includes salt and pepper

Supportive Stocks

Beef stock/veal stock

✓ Beef stock can be prepared as white or brown beef stock. *White beef stock* is made with beef bones plus fat and minus bone marrow, blanched and refreshed, simmered with aromatic vegetables and a bouquet garni.

✓ *Brown beef stock* is made with chopped beef bones, it is roasted in the oven until brown and the fat poured over. The bones, deglazed pan juices, chopped aromatic vegetables browned in fat and a bouquet garni are added to water, simmered for 6-8 hours, skimmed continuously and strained.

✓ Veal stock is also prepared in a similar fashion as beef stock, i.e., by roasting the veal bones and meat until they are deeply golden in colour before simmering. Veal stock is good to use for rich soups like *à l'oigon* (French onion soup) as well as for making different sauces.

Ingredients of Bouquet Garni

- Celery
- Thyme
- Parsley
- Bayleaf
- Leeks

Lamb/mutton stock

✓ Lamb/mutton stock, made either white or brown, provides a resonant flavour base for lamb preparations particularly in braised lamb dishes. It is prepared by using lamb bones and cuts such as lamb forequarter chops or lamb shanks. Simmer the bones and meats for about 2-½ hours.

✓ *Lamb stock* is made as for brown beef stock, but with mutton or lamb bones substituted for beef bones and vice versa (for brown lamb/mutton stock). A little white wine may also be added to enhance the flavour of the stock. Lamb/mutton stock has distinct flavour, thus it is suitable to combine well with dishes of other meats.

Pork stock

✓ Pork stock is sweet and rich with a high extraction of gelatin. Pork bones, skin, trotter, or extremities can be added to stocks and stews to add richness and body, but the flavour can dominate the principle ingredients.

Chicken stock

✓ It is the most important stock in Chinese cooking made by simmering chicken carcasses and giblets with onions and ginger. The stage of adding salt in chicken stock plays a crucial role. This stock is used for a range of chicken based preparations such as chicken vol-au-vent, creamed chicken, etc.

✓ Salt is added to this stock to flavour the chicken especially when using whole birds; otherwise the meat has a tendency to get bland.

Game Stock

✓ Game stocks can be made with specified game to accompany dishes of that variety. It is made with game bones and trimmings with vegetables to add flavour. It is prepared in a similar way as brown beef stock but substituting game bones in place of beef bones.

- ✓ A combination of game enriched with an appropriate stock, white or brown, will produce good results. It is used for making game soups and prepared sauces are offered with cold game preparations.

Major Ingredients of Stock

- Bones/vegetables
- Mirepoix/matignon
- Bouquet garni
- Acid products (like wine, tomatoes)
- Seasoning
- Spices
- Leftovers and scraps
- Liquid/water

Essence

- ✓ It is also called *extract*, and is used for flavouring (like coffee essence). Essences are stocks made in a reduced form which create a concentrated flavour. It is very similar to *fumet* but contains highly aromatic ingredients like mushrooms, truffles, celery and morels.
- ✓ It is a concentrated aromatic liquid used either to enhance the flavour of certain culinary preparations (such as stocks, sauces and soups) or to flavour certain foods. They may be plant extracts.

Fish Stock/Fumet

- ✓ The term *fish fumet* is used for highly flavoured and concentrated *fish stock*. Fish stock is made from fish trimmings including bones, skin, fins and head of fish but avoid using scales, gills and internal organs. Fish bones are generally full of flavour and require little additional flavourings so that adding leeks, onions and parsley stalks may be enough.
- ✓ Fish stock is made with bones (0.4 kg bones for making 1 litre stock) of fish sweated with onions, parsley stalk and lemon juice in butter then simmered for 30 minutes (do not forget to continuously skim). Lastly, strain the prepared fish stock.
- ✓ This stock requires very little cooking time as the bones are generally quite fine and easily broken down. Overcooking spoils the flavour of fish stock as it gives the stock a bitter taste and cloudy appearance.

Court Bouillon

- ✓ Court bouillon is also called "short stock or short broth"; it is a flavourful poaching liquid. In order to make it, an acid ingredient such as vinegar, lemon juice, white or red wine is added to water with other aromatic vegetables and herbs (for the purpose of flavour) such as onion, carrots, bay leaf, thyme, peppercorns and parsley stalks.

Court Bouillon

Water	15 liters
Carrot	900 gram
Onion	900 gram
B. Garni	Same as other
Seasoning	To taste
Vinegar	750 mL

Method- Place all ingredients in stockpot, bring to boil (for 1 hour), finally strain and refrigerate.

✓ The ingredients are simmered together, and then the liquid is passed and refrigerated for future use. It can be used for fish (like salmon and trout), shellfish and some other preparations like sweetbreads.

Fish Stock			
Ingredients	**Quantity**	**Ingredients**	**Quantity**
Bone and head	15 kg	Water	22 litres
Onion	2 kg	B. Garni	Same as other
Seasoning	To taste	Lemon juice	15 lemons
White wine	Chablis	Margarine	75 grams
Method- Sauté mirepoix (in margarine) and fish bones in stockpot then cook until the essence has been extracted (or for 5 minutes). Now add other ingredients and bring to boil (for 20 minutes), finally strain and refrigerate.			

Glace

✓ It is a highly reduced stock or remouillage. Simply glace (French for "glaze") is a stock that is reduced until it coats the back of a spoon and concentrated by ¾ or more, so stocks become solid and rubbery when chilled because they have been reduced to the consistency of jelly or syrup. This consistency feature distinguishes it from the essence.

> **Glaze**
>
> (Yield 2.5 liters)
>
> Stock 10 litres
>
> *Method*- Reduce stock by boiling until it coats the back of spoon. Afterwards allow to cool and refrigerate for future use.

✓ But its flavour is highly concentrated. Glazes do not taste like the stocks because of long cooking hours. It is available as glace de viande (meat glaze), glace de volaille (chicken glaze) and glace de poisson (fish glaze).

Remouillage

✓ It is a weak stock made from bones already being used. Thus, it is also known as "second stock, second wetting or rewetting". It is less strong thus usually reduced and used to make a glace, often used as a liquid for broth preparation.

✓ In order to make second stock, after draining away the first stock, more water with mirepoix is added to the base ingredients and simmered again. This yields a weak stock but richer than water. The remouillage is often used as the liquid for making a new stock, thereby yielding a richer stock.

Broth/Bouillon

- ✓ Broth is a stock (or derivative of a stock) that is made from simmering meats. The term *broth* is used for both stock as well as soup. Broth itself can be served as soup. Bouillon is a French term for broth.
- ✓ *Bouillon* is a stock especially for soup (particularly for consommé soup made by clarified beef broth). These are also used in making of some other preparations like for stews and braise preparations.

Major Uses of Stock	
As a base	Stock is used as a base for making sauces, soups, stews and braises.
Cooking mode	Stock is also used as a cooking medium for vegetables, grains and meats.

Ingredients/Indents for Making Stock

(Yield – 15 Litre Stock)

Ingredients	Quantity	Stocks					
		Brown	White	Chicken	Game	Veal	Beef
Bones	10 kg	Roast bones	Bones	Carcass	Roast bones	Bones*	Bones*
Liquid	25 litre	Water	Water	Water	Water	Water	Water
Mirepoix	500 gram	Carrot	Carrot	Carrot	Carrot	Carrot	Carrot
	500 gram	Onion	Studded onion	Studded onion	Onion	Onion	Onion
Bouquet garni	250 gram	Leeks	Leeks	Leeks	Leeks	Leeks	Leeks
	250 gram	Celery	Celery	Celery	Celery	Celery	Celery
	50 gram	Parsley	Parsley	Parsley	Parsley	Parsley	Parsley
	3 sprigs	Thyme	Thyme	Thyme	Thyme	Thyme	Thyme
	3 leaves	Bay leaf	Bay leaf	Bay leaf	Bay leaf	Bay leaf	Bay leaf
Seasoning	To taste	Salt	Salt	Salt	Salt	Salt	Salt
	To taste	Black pepper	White pepper	White pepper	Black pepper	Black pepper	Black pepper
Fat/Oil	As needed	Oil			Oil	Oil*	Oil*

Note. * Veal/beef stock can be white veal/beef stock or brown veal/beef stock. To make brown veal/beef stock, roasted veal/beef bones (in oil) are used.

Method of Cooking

Steps	Particulars	Brown	White	Chicken	Game	Veal	Beef
Step 1	Mise en place (for bones)	Saw the bones	Saw the bones	Saw the bones	Saw the bones	Saw the bones	Saw the bones
Step 2	Pre-cooking bones (roast or brown)	Brown in oven			Brown in oven	Plain or roast*	Plain or roast*
Step 3	Place bones in stockpot and cook	In cold water	In cold water	In cold water	In cold water	In cold water	In cold water
Step 4	Bring water to boil and skim	Remove raft	Remove raft	Remove raft	Remove raft	Remove raft	Remove raft
Step 5	Simmer for particular hour/s	For 2 hours	For 4 hours	For 1 hour	For 1 hour	For 4 hours	For 4 hours
Step 6	Add vegetables (or mirepoix) to stock	Sautéd mirepoix	Diced mirepoix	Diced mirepoix	Sautéd mirepoix	Diced mirepoix	Diced mirepoix
Step 7	Add aromatics (or *bouquet garni* - leeks, celery, parsley, thyme and bay leaf) to stock	Bouquet garni	Bouquet garni	Bouquet garni	Bouquet garni	Bouquet garni	Bouquet garni
Step 8	Again simmer	For 4 hours	For 2 hours	For 2 hours	For 2 hours	For 2 hours	For 2 hours
Step 9	Finally, skim and fine strain	Skim and strain	Skim and strain	Skim and strain	Skim and strain	Skim and strain	Skim and strain
Step 10	Refrigerate for future use	Cool and refrigerate	Cool and refrigerate	Cool and refrigerate	Cool and refrigerate	Cool and refrigerate	Cool and refrigerate

Note. *Veal/beef bones would be plain or roasted, it depends upon the type of stock required like to make brown veal/beef stock - veal/beef bones are required to brown/ roast in oven.

SOUP

Parts of Soup
- Base
- Body
- Thickening agent
- Garnish
- Seasoning

Soup/s can be defined as a liquid of varying consistency made from fish, poultry, meat or vegetables or a combination of these. In simple words, soups are wholesome and nutritious liquid food. Conventionally, the term *soupe* (a French term) was used for a slice of bread with addon cooking pot (*potage*). But nowadays, both terms are synonymous. Soup is most often served as a starter/as the first part of dinner, depending on the type of soup. It can also be the focal point of a dinner, being supplemented with bread or toast. Soup is also used for medicinal purposes, as a way to provide a nutritional meal that is easy to digest (ideally its serving portion is around 250 mL).

Classification of Soup

Consommé

Standard Soup Garnishing
- Croutons
- Crème
- Bay leaf
- Boiled rice
- Pasta
- Crisp bacon
- Popcorn
- Grated cheese
- Mushrooms
- Onion and leeks
- Parsley and chives
- Frankfurters
- Chopped herbs

- ✓ The word consommé originated from *consummate* which means to bring to completion or perfection. Consommés are one of the subcategories of clear soup. It is always clarified and sometimes thickened with little tapioca. They normally include a light garnish in keeping with the character of the consommé.
- ✓ Hence, in simple terms, consommé is a beef broth, flavoured with raw chopped meat and vegetables clarified with egg whites and then strained. Consommés get their names from the garnishes used.

Puree-based soups

- ✓ These are thick soups made from fresh or dried vegetables (like dried beans, kidney beans, lentils, split peas, etc.), cooked with stock and sometimes with the addition of meat, poultry or cereals. The vegetable based puree soups are thickened with the starch contained in the pureed vegetables; hence, these soups usually do not need any additional thickening agent.
- ✓ The degree of consistency of a pureed soup varies with the ingredients used and the way in which they are processed. A food mill produces a more coarsely

textured puree than does a food processor. The finest consistency is achieved by straining the pureed soup through a fine sieve prior to *serving*.

Veloutés

- ✓ These soups are prepared from a base of roux diluted with the appropriate flavoured stock and cooked with the addition of blanched vegetables, meat, poultry, game or fish.
- ✓ They are passed, finished with a liaison of egg yolks and cream and are invariably garnished. In simple terms, velouté soup is a mixture of vegetable puree, meat and velouté sauce.

Soup Thickening Agents

- Liaison
- Roux
- Slurry
- Vegetable puree
- Beurre manié

Crèmes/Cream soups

- ✓ These soups must be of a smooth consistency and it is essential that they are finished with cream. These soups are thickened with béchamel sauce. Cream soup can be made from nearly all vegetables, especially those which are lighter, more delicately flavoured.
- ✓ There are three acceptable methods of preparation. The classical method using Béchamel, secondly puree of the appropriate cooked ingredients and thirdly puree of the appropriate stock finished with cream.

Bisques

- ✓ These soups are made specifically from raw shellfish, vegetables, fish stock, wines, herbs and seasonings, thickened with rice, passed and finished with wine and cream. Bisque is a creamy puree that concentrates the essence of a single ingredient into a rich perfumed soup.
- ✓ Bisque is usually prepared with pureed shellfish such as lobster, prawns or oysters plus fresh cream. These soups are usually thickened with liaison of egg yolk and cream (earlier it was thickened with rice or crust of butter fried bread).

Chowder

- ✓ These are thick heavy soups owing their own consistency due to potatoes. In general, chowder is the name for fish soups generally based on a mixture of fish stock and milk with sweated chopped vegetables usually including potatoes and sweet corn.

✓ Generally, the pieces of fish and/or shellfish are added towards the end so as not to overcook and occasionally thickened with corn flour, a similar starch or beurre manié. In the USA, meat, salt pork and bread or crackers may be included.

Broth

✓ It is a brunoise of various kinds of vegetables cooked in, chicken or game stock, with the addition of cereal then garnished with meat or poultry, in accordance to the type of broth. Normally, broth gets its flavour from long simmering of a variety of ingredients together in one pot.

✓ Instead of water, the white stock or plain, unclarified broth from boiling meat, fish or vegetables is often used for cooking certain dishes and for preparing soups and sauces. The type of stock used is indicated by the name of the broth being made.

Potage

✓ These soups are usually farinaceous in nature and do not require any thickening agent. Sometimes potage soups are also called "vegetable soups" because they contain one or more vegetables—diced, brunoise, julienne, Chiffonade or paysanne and eaten with liquid they have flavoured.

✓ However, vegetable soup is usually made of clear broth of potatoes and other ingredients like tomatoes, as it gives the broth a certain thickness. Vegetables with strong flavour must be used in smaller quantities than others because they can dominate the flavour of other ingredients.

Cold Soups

✓ This includes specially prepared cold soups as well as those, which can be successfully prepared cold as well as hot but served only cold, for example, cream of watercress, lobster bisque and borscht. Cold soups should be served well chilled in chilled cups or bowls.

Examples of Soups

Consommé	Puree soups	Veloute	Crème	Bisque	Chowder	Broth
Brunoise	Conty	Chicken	De riz	D' ecrevisses	Oyster	Beef
Celestine	Crécy	Celery	De tomates	D' homard	Clam	Mutton
Mikado	Victoria	Almond	D' asperges		Seafood	Chicken
Dubarry	St. Germain	Carmen	À la reine			Barley
Royale	Florentine		D' avoine			Scotch

SAUCE

PARTS OF SAUCE

- Base of sauce
- Thickening agent
- Flavouring agents
- Seasoning agents

Sauce is a French word taken from the Latin word *salsus*, meaning salted. Nowadays, sauce is a term used in cookery to describe a wide range of flavoured liquids that are served as part of the meal, or dish. The addition of a sauce to a dish can be used to transform the overall presentation of a dish by adding flavour, moisture, richness and visual appeal. Sauces come in a variety of different styles and consistencies. They can be thick or thin, strained or unstrained, rich and creamy, or light and delicate; sauces can also be strongly flavoured, hot and spicy, or even sweet to be served with a dessert, depending on the intended purpose. The eventual and elementary purpose/function of every sauce is to add a flavour to a dish that is compatible with the ingredients. The way in which a sauce is presented depends on the dish being served. The sauce may be used to coat some other preparations and served partially over the food, under the food, or in a separate dish or gravy boat (ideally its serving portion is around 50 mL).

Sauces are considered an orchestration and accompaniment of the fine meal. They were designed to mask the harsh flavours of poorly prepared, slightly spoiled food. Each sauce, either hot or cold, has its own well defined special distinctive taste and flavour. This taste and flavour is the result of the combined flavours of all incorporated ingredients. When used with or in another dish, the sauce becomes a complement to the dish, not a distinct addition to it.

Note. A sauce works like a seasoning. It enhances and accents the flavour of the food but remember it should not dominate or hide the original flavour and taste of the food.

Classification of Sauces

Conventionally, sauces are categorized in five grand sauces which are also known as five mother sauces. These grand sauces were introduced in 19th century by a French Chef Marie Carême Antoine. Thus, he is also known as father of basic mother sauces. Apart from it, there are three fundamental bases to classify sauces into broad categories. These are explained below.

Hot Sauces: The term *hot sauce* does not indicate to spicy sauce but it reflects to those sauces which are prepared hot and may be served hot as well as cold. Generally, all five mother sauces are considered under this category. According to Carême, hot sauces can be classified as *brown sauces* (espagnole, demi-glace and tomato sauce) and *white sauces* (béchamel and veloute). Remember, the term mother sauce is used because each category is like the head sauce of its own unique family of sauces. It includes:

Béchamel (white)

- ✓ It is also called "white cream sauce". The basic principle of making béchamel sauce is to first make a *white roux* without adding anything to it. A *roux* is an equal combination of butter and flour (normally one tablespoon of each), simmered over low heat until it bubbles; milk (one cup) is then added. The flour/butter roux thickens the milk and creating a rich sauce.
- ✓ Béchamel sauce is a mother sauce for making plentiful other derivative sauces like Mornay sauce, and it is widely used for egg, vegetable and gratin dishes. It also forms the foundation for many savory soufflés. In Italy, béchamel sauce is known as *balsamella*.

SAUCE THICKENERS

- Roux (white/blond/brown)
- Beurre manié
- White wash & tapioca
- Corn-flour/Arrowroot
- Modified starch/waxy maize
- Pre-gelatinized starches
- Breadcrumbs & nuts
- Whole grains (rice/barley/oats)
- Protein (egg yolk)
- Emulsion
- Reduction

Velouté (blond)

- ✓ Velouté is a light brown or golden colour sauce. The term veloute means velvet, which describes the smooth velvety texture that these sauces should have. A *light brown* (*or blonde colour*) roux is used to make veloute sauce. Bringing together a *blond roux* and a white stock such as veal, chicken or fish makes these sauces.
- ✓ It is very similar to béchamel sauce; although instead of adding milk to the roux, white chicken or veal stock (and sometimes *fish fumet*) is added. It works as a mother sauce for making variations like Allemande, Nantua and Aurore sauces. Velouté is often made even richer by adding egg yolks or cream.

Espagnole (brown)

- ✓ Espagnole is a basic brown sauce made from brown stock plus *brown roux*. Traditionally, it was made from beef/brown stock, brown roux, mirepoix (aromatics + herbs) and, sometimes, tomato paste. Brown sauce consists of a liquid thickened with a cooked mixture of butter and flour called *roux/brown roux*. This roux differs from white roux (i.e., used in béchamel sauce).
- ✓ The difference is that for a brown sauce, the roux is cooked much longer; it must be stirred over low heat until it acquires a nut-brown shed that intensifies the colour and flavour of the sauce. During cooking, the sauce needs to be skimmed, stirred and lastly strained. The lengthier cooking diminishes the thickening power of the starch.

✓ This brown roux also works as a base for preparing other main/entrée dishes and for preparing many other sauces (or derivative sauces like demi-glaze) like Bordelaise, Bercy and Madeira sauce.

DEMI GLAZE

(Yield 2.5 Litres)

Brown stock 2.5 litres

Brown sauce 2.5 litres

Method- Mix brown stock with brown sauce and reduce it to half (by boiling). Add sherry (optional), finally refrigerate for future use.

Hollandaise (butter)

✓ Hollandaise is a hot emulsified sauce based on egg yolks and clarified butter. It is flavoured with a reduction of white vinegar and peppercorns in sabayon, which is essentially a flavoured liquid base with egg yolks continuously whisked over heat (in Bain Marie) to form a thick creamy liquid.

✓ After removing from heat, molten clarified butter is poured in slowly with vigorous whisking to form a stable emulsion. It is finished with a little lemon juice. In case, sauce gets curdled then it can be re-emulsified with a spoonful of water; use hot water if the sauce is cold and vice versa. Finally, season with salt and cayenne in very small amounts.

✓ This sauce is served warm with hot fish preparations (such as fish cooked in court-bouillon) and with some vegetable preparations. Hollandaise sauce is the foundation of several other sauces like Béarnaise sauce which is most often served with steak dishes.

Tomato (red)

✓ Tomato sauce is based on tomato puree with flavourings and seasonings, plus liquid added. Accurately, it is made with mirepoix of onion, carrot, celery, bay leaf and thyme browned with bacon scraps in butter, flour added and cooked to a slight colour, tomato puree and white stock added.

✓ Finally, boiled and simmered with garlic and lastly strained then seasoned. This sauce has a deep, rich tomato flavour. The tomato sauce is slightly coarser than any other grand sauces because of the degree of texture that remains even after pureeing and straining tomatoes.

Five Basic Grand/Mother Sauces and their Making Guidelines

Sauce	Roux	Liquid	Time	Colour and remarks
Béchamel	White	Milk	35-40 min	White (add onion studded with cloves in milk)
Velouté	Blond	Stock	40-45 min	Blond (usually made with chicken/ fish stock)

Espagnole	Brown	Stock	4-6 hours	Brown (usually made with beef bones/stock)
Hollandaise	-	Butter	-	Yellow (usually made with fat and butter)
Tomato	Red	Stock	35-45 min	Red (made with tomato puree, bones and vegetables)

Cold sauces: Generally cold sauces are prepared in *garde manger* section because they are most often associated with salads, sandwiches and cold hors d'oeuvres which are produced by the garde manger/cold kitchen. Sometimes these cold sauces are perceived as sauce dressing. Cold sauces are usually based on mayonnaise or vinaigrette sauce and they too have many derivatives. Many cold sauces have become so commonly available to the average guest in a ready-to-use form whereas others are prepared in kitchen. A brief description of several famous cold sauces is given below.

Mayonnaise

- ✓ It is made by combining egg yolk, vinegar, French mustard and seasoning then poured in oil slowly with vigorous whisking until the desired consistency is achieved.
- ✓ Strongly flavoured oil may dominate the dish, thus it may be better to use a good quality lightly flavoured salad oil. It can be used as a basic sauce or as an accompaniment to a dish or can be used to make extended sauces like Tartar sauce. This sauce must be stored below 5°C.

Vinaigrette

- ✓ The basic recipe includes three parts oil to one part vinegar plus various herbs and spices, usually salt, pepper, possibly with mustard and sugar then shaken together but not so as to make a stable emulsion. This may be used to serve separately as well as to dress a salad or as a dip. Often, it is also termed *French dressing*.

Horseradish (Horseradish is a perennial plant of the Brassicaceae family)

- ✓ This is a mayonnaise based sauce which is made by combining *horseradish* (peeled and grated) mixed with mustard, sugar, salt, vinegar, whipped cream and a stabilizer of either breadcrumb or flour. Horseradish is a sauce traditionally served with roasted beef; it can be served with chicken maryland or smoked trout too.

Gribiche

✓ A famous French sauce made with oil and vinegar (or lemon juice) beaten into hard boiled egg's yolks and flavoured with mustard, chopped gherkins, chopped capers and herbs. Finally finished with a julienne of egg white and served with fish and cold meats.

CULINARY USES/ROLE OF SAUCE

- Enhances flavour
- Gives moistness
- Aids in digestion
- Incorporates colour
- Accompaniment
- Enhances nutritional balance
- Makes food more palatable
- Gives tartness and colour contrast
- Balances a bland dish

Mint sauce

✓ A famous British sauce made or prepared with chopped mint leaves, macerated with boiling water and sugar and combined with an equal amount of vinegar. Mint sauce is traditionally served with cold or hot roasted lamb or mutton and also goes well with pork and certain game dishes.

Cocktail sauce

✓ It is the most common mayonnaise based cold sauce preparation. It is a piquant and slightly acidic sauce, containing tomato puree, horseradish sauce, Worcestershire sauce and Tabasco sauce. It is used extensively with seafood preparations like prawns, crabs and lobsters.

Cumberland sauce

✓ A famous English sauce, this piquant sauce is a cooked mixture of red currant jelly, port wine, shallots (blanched, refreshed and chopped), orange and lemon zest, with a little dry mustard (or English mustard) and cayenne. It goes well with pork, venison and cold ham.

Andalouse sauce

✓ It is a famous sauce from England and France. The base of this sauce is mayonnaise sauce which is mixed with tomato puree and garnished with julienned red sweet peppers.

Green sauce

✓ This sauce is made with blanched and refreshed leaves of spinach, tarragon, chives, chervil and watercress, squeezed dry, passed through a fine sieve and combined with mayonnaise.

Note. Fat and cholesterol content are major nutritional concerns in the production of cold sauces. One can use substitute stocks lightly thickened with arrowroot instead of using egg yolk as an emulsifier.

Sweet sauces: The term *sweet sauce* itself reflects the definition and characteristics plus indicates about its variations/derivative sauces. Sweet sauces are mainly offered with entremets or sweet preparations.

Chocolate

- ✓ A chocolate sauce is made with unsweetened chocolate or cocoa, sugar and water. It may also be made with cornstarch, cocoa, sugar, milk and lumps of butter. It is mainly used with baked or steamed puddings.

Coulis

- ✓ Coulis are small sauces made from fruits and vegetables, sometimes sweetened or flavoured with herbs, but not thickened. Simply, it is a thin puree of fruits and vegetables used as a garnish.

Fruit sauce

- ✓ Fruit sauce is made from stewed fruit, usually strained to remove skin and fibres and often sweetened. For example, apple sauce, plum sauce, cranberry sauce, etc.

Anglaise

- ✓ It is also called as "Crème Anglaise"; it is light pouring custard used as a dessert cream or sauce. It is a mixture of sugar, egg yolk, and hot milk and often found flavoured with vanilla.

Butter-scotch

- ✓ Its primary ingredients are brown sugar and butter, although other ingredients such as corn syrup, cream, vanilla and salt may be used. Butterscotch sauce is often made into a syrup consistency, which is used as a topping for ice cream (particularly sundaes).

Caramel sauce

- ✓ An English hot sauce made by whisking together three parts caramel with two parts butter and two parts water (3:2:2).

SAUCE DERIVATIVES

A sauce which is derived from one of the mother sauces/grand sauces is called *derivative sauce, small sauce, extended sauce* or *secondary sauce*. Most sauces commonly used in classical cuisine are small sauces, or derivatives of the basic mother sauces. Mother sauces are not commonly served as they are; instead they are augmented with additional ingredients to make small (derivative) sauces. For example, béchamel can be made into Mornay by the addition of Gruyère or any cheese one may like, and Espagnole becomes Bordelaise with the addition and reduction of red wine, shallots, and poached beef marrow. A brief profile of several derivative sauces is given below.

Béchamel Sauce Derivatives

Homard à l'Anglaise	Béchamel sauce + Anchovy + Cayenne + Lobster
Cardinal	Béchamel sauce + Fish Stock + Truffle + Cream + Lobster Butter
Crème	Béchamel sauce + Cream + Lemon Juice
Mornay	Béchamel sauce + Butter + Gruyère or Parmesan Cheese
Soubise	Béchamel sauce + Chopped Onion
Oeufs à l'Anglaise	Béchamel sauce + Diced Hard Boiled Egg + Nutmeg

Velouté Sauce Derivatives

Allemande	Velouté sauce + Veal Stock + Mushrooms
Curry	Veal Stock + Onions + Apple + Curry + Coconut Milk
Normande	Fish Stock + Mushrooms + Oysters + Egg Yolk + Butter + Cream
Diplomat	Sauce Normande + Lobster Butter + Lobster + Truffle
Suprême	Chicken Stock + Reduced Heavy Cream
Ivoire	Sauce Suprême + Meat glaze
Aurore	Sauce Suprême + Tomato
Hongroise	Sauce Suprême (Veal Base) + Onion + Paprika + White Wine
Vin Blanc	Fish Stock + Shallot + Butter + Fine Herbs

Brown Sauce Derivatives (Demi-Glace)

Bordelaise	Brown sauce + Reduced Red Wine + Shallot + Poached Marrow
Chasseur	Brown sauce + Mushroom + Shallot + White Wine + Tomato concassé
Lyonnaise	Brown sauce + Butter fried onions
Madere	Brown sauce + Madeira Wine
Périgueux	Brown sauce + Chopped Truffles + Madeira
Robert	Brown sauce + White Wine + Onions + Mustard + Butter

Hollandaise Sauce Derivatives

Bavaroise	Hollandaise sauce + Reduced Pepper + Horseradish + Thyme + Bay Leaves + Parsley + Vinegar + Crayfish + Garnished with Crayfish Tails
Béarnaise	Hollandaise sauce + Chopped Tarragon + Chopped Chervil
Choron	Sauce Béarnaise + Tomato puree
Foyot	Sauce Béarnaise + Meat Glaze
Maltaise	Hollandaise sauce + Blood of Orange Juice
Mousseline	Hollandaise sauce + Stiffly Whipped Cream
Noisette	Hollandaise sauce + Brown Butter
Paloise	Hollandaise sauce + Mint

Tomato Sauce Derivatives

Chaufroid	Tomato sauce + Aspic Jelly
Meat	Tomato sauce + Cooked Ground Meat
Nantua	Tomato sauce + Mirepoix (Onion, Celery, and Carrot) fried in Crayfish Butter + White Wine + Cognac + Tomatoes + Fish Velouté + Cayenne
Portugaise	Tomato sauce + Fried Onions + Tomato Concassé {*tomato concasse* means peeled, seeded (seeds and skins removed), and chopped specified sized tomatoes} + Meat Glaze + Garlic + Parsley
Provençale	Tomato sauce + Sliced Mushrooms + Sugar + Garlic + Parsley + Oil

Mayonnaise Sauce Derivatives

Cocktail sauce	Mayonnaise sauce + Ketchup + Worcestershire sauce + Horseradish + Tabasco sauce + Lemon juice
Remoulade	Mayonnaise sauce + Chopped gherkins + Capers + Parsley + Anchovies
Tartar	Mayonnaise sauce + Chopped gherkins + Hard boiled eggs + Capers + Parsley + Onions
Tyrolienne	Mayonnaise sauce + Tomato puree
Verte	Mayonnaise sauce + Puree of spinach + Parsley + Tarragon
Véron	Tyrolienne sauce + Normande + Finish with meat glaze and anchovy essence.

KEY TERMS

Fumet	:	Fumet or fish fumet indicates to fish stock.
Glace	:	Glace or glaze indicates to a reduced stock.
Maillard reaction	:	Reaction of heat or roasting the ingredients to light brown.
Mirepoix	:	Roughly cut vegetables.
Derivative sauces	:	Auxiliary sauces made from basic mother sauces.
Balsamella	:	Italian term for béchamel sauce.
Bouquet garni	:	Group of five herbs, i.e., parsley, thyme, bay leaf, celery and leek.
Bouillon	:	French term for broth as well as for stock (especially for preparing consommé soup).
Short stock	:	Court bouillon.
Tapioca	:	Starch that is extracted from cassava root.
Garde manger	:	Cold kitchen or larder section where cold preparations are done.
Concasse	:	French term meaning to crush or grind, usually vegetables.

REVIEW QUESTIONS

1. What are the five basic mother sauces? Explain each one briefly.
2. Write down the different uses of stock in cookery.
3. Define the term soup. Classify different types of soup and support each category with at least five examples.
4. Define the term sauce and elucidate the derivative sauces of Béchamel, Velouté, Espagnole, Hollandaise and Mayonnaise sauce.

31 CHAPTER

Fruit and Vegetable Cookery

Objectives

Students will be able to:

- expound fruit composition, fruit classes and effect of heat on fruit;
- explicate vegetable classes and their colouring pigments; and
- plan a menu based on fruits and vegetables.

FRUIT

The term *fruit* refers to the matured ovary of a plant including the seeds and adjacent parts. It is the reproductive body of the seed plant. In cookery it refers to edible parts of a plant which are usually served at the dessert course of a meal. Fruit contains fructose and is a good source of vitamins (such as vitamin C), minerals, carbohydrates, water and some dietary fiber. Dried fruit has higher sugar content but less Vitamin C than fresh fruit. Generally, ripe fruits are used for food production because they are full in size; good in colour, texture and taste; and have soft and tender tissues. It is due to transformation of fruit starch into sugar, resulting in the development of aroma. Broadly, fruits can be classified into two groups, i.e., fleshy fruits and dry fruits.

Fruit Composition	
Water	85%
Carbohydrates	5-10%
Cellulose	2-05%
Minerals	0.5%
Vitamins	C

FLESHY FRUITS

The term *fleshy fruit* refers to a group of fruits that have fleshy part as its main constituent. This group can be broadly divided into two sub-groups, i.e., fleshy fruits with *high water content* (up to 90%) and *high sugar content* (20-30 cal per 10 gm). It can be further classified as simple, aggregate or multiple fleshy fruits in which they come out from ovary. A brief description of each is given below.

Fleshy Simple Fruits: These are those fruits which contain more or less a soft *pericarp*. In other words, fleshy fruits offer "fleshy material" around the stone. Besides, they are all derived from a single ovary, so they can be considered simple fruits. The following are types of simple fleshy fruits.

Berries	For example, Grapes, Tomatoes, Bananas, Raspberry, Avocados, Eggplants, Currants and Persimmons.
Hesperidiums	For example, Orange, Lemon, Grapefruit, Limes, Citron, Mandarin, Clementine and Ugli fruit.
Pepo	For example, Cucumber, Watermelon, Squash, Pumpkin, Honeydew melon and Sunberry.
Drupe	For example, Cherry, Peach, Plum, Almond, Apricot, Olive, Lychee, Pin cherry and Coconut.
Pome	For example, Apples, Pears, Quince, Chokeberry, Haw, Juneberry, Medlar, Rowan and Sorb apple.

Fleshy Aggregate Fruits: These fleshy aggregate fruits also contain a soft pericarp but they do not come from flowers containing a single ovary, but from single flowers with many carpels or ovaries. Some examples of fleshy aggregate fruits are given below.

Polydrupes	For example, Strawberry, Blackberry, Raspberry, Boysenberry, Loganberry, Cloudberry and Wineberry.

Melon Types
- Honeydew
- Charentais
- Cantaloupe
- Ogen
- Kiwano

Apple Types
- Ambrosia
- Bramley
- Baldwin
- Cameo
- Haralson
- Macoun

Mango Types
- Langara
- Alphonso
- Kent
- Carrie

Fleshy Multiple Fruits: The individual ovaries from different flowers get clustered together forming a fruit. The example of fruits under the type of fleshy multiple fruits are Mulberry, Pineapple, Fig, Pomegranate and Date fruit.

DRY FRUITS

Dry fruits refer to a group of fruits from which majority of the original water content has been removed either naturally, through sun drying, or through specialized techniques. Thus, these fruits contain *high fat with low water contents* (around 65 cal per 10 gm). Dry fruit category can be differentiated as *dry dehiscent* and *dry indehiscent*.

Dry Dehiscent Fruits: Fruit types that contain seeds in a seedpod that opens up and releases the seeds are known as *dry dehiscent fruits*. These seedpods are open when they grow up and let their seeds go away. Several fruits under this category include:

Follicle	For example, Columbine and Milkweed
Legume	For example, Sweet pea, Beans, Peanut and Runner Bean
Silique	For example, fruits under the Cruciferae family
Capsule	For example, Cotton, Poppy and Primrose.

Dry Indehiscent Fruits: The *dry indehiscent* fruits do not have seedpods that open. Hence, these fruits do not open when becoming ripe thus leaving their seeds inside them. Most important fruits under this category include:

Achene	For example, fruits of buckwheat and sunflower family.
Samara	For example, fruits such as elms, ash and maple.
Caryopsis	For example, fruits include grains like, wheat, oats, rice, corn, barley and rye.
Nuts	For example, fruits under this type include Walnut, Hazelnut, Chestnut and Acorn.

Effect of Heat on Fruits and Vegetables	
Anthocyanins	It is a water-soluble pigment– vegetable colour may be leached if it is cut and then cooked. So, it is good to cook vegetable first and then cut to avoid colour loss. The red colour is intensified by adding acids like lemon juice or vinegar as a dressing. In the presence of alkalis, the anthocyanins turn blue green.
Chlorophyll	It is an olive green coloured compound and when vegetables (like spinach or beans) are cooked with lid on, the volatile plant acids are released and dissolved in steam (in cooking pan) where they react with chlorophyll to form phaeophytin. If the cooking water is alkaline, the green colour of chlorophyll becomes intense.
Carotenoids	These are soluble pigments which may cause change/darken the food colour during prolonged cooking.
Flavours	The flavour will definitely change due to change in components like acid, salts and sugar present in food.
Flavones	Crystalline compounds (water soluble) from which yellow pigments are derived during prolonged cooking.

VEGETABLES

The term *vegetable* refers to any plant grown for an edible part other than the ovary. Generally, vegetables have less sugar and more starch in comparison to fruits. Vegetables are good source of minerals and vitamins. It is always desirable to use seasonal vegetables because during season vegetables are fresh, more nutritious and less costly. Remember, as time passes vegetables shrink and wilt. The structure of vegetables is formed by cellulose and it can be maintained only when water remains in the cell. Vegetables can be classified in numerous categories. In French classical menu, the main course is served with a selection of courses, simultaneously FCM also contains an individual course for serving vegetables, i.e., legume course. Vegetable family includes the following:

COLOURING PIGMENTS IN FRUITS & VEGETABLES

- Carotenoid
- Chlorophyll
- Flavonoid
- Anthoxanthan
- Anthocyanin
- Tannins

Cabbage Family

- ✓ Cabbage is a green and round heart style vegetable. This family is a group of crisp, pungent vegetables which come from different parts of the plant species.
- ✓ It is known by the Latin name "Brassica Oleracea". The varieties of this plant include cabbage, brussels sprouts, cauliflower, broccoli, kohlrabi, etc.

Stalk Vegetables

- ✓ These are plant stems that are high in cellulose fibres. These fibres are the strings that hold the stalks erect under the weight of the leaves and buds. As the plant ages, the fibres toughen.
- ✓ In order to use in cooking, the stalk vegetables should be young because tough fibers will not soften with cooking and should be trimmed before being used. Stalk vegetables include asparagus, celery, Swiss chard, bok choy, etc.

Leafy Vegetables

- ✓ These are the plants grown specifically due to their edible leaves. Leafy vegetables include spinach, kale, collards, sorrel, etc.

Salad Greens

- ✓ The term *salad green* is related with various green leaves that can be used in salads while a term *green salad* is related with a salad of mixed raw green leaves.
- ✓ Salad greens are also termed "lettuce". They are family members of the daisy family. A salad green includes endive and lettuce.

Seeds, Edible Pods and Shots

- ✓ As the long title suggests it covers a wide range of vegetables from seed base vegetables to shots like vegetables plus edible pods. It includes peas, bean sprouts, beans, corn, snow peas, etc.

Vegetable Fruits

✓ Botanically, vegetable fruits are considered fruits; however, they are used in the kitchen as vegetables. It includes cucumbers, okra, eggplant, tomatoes, peppers, squash, etc.

Bulbs

✓ As the title bulb itself suggests, these vegetables look like a tuber shape. These are stems holding a food reserve in the fleshy, overlapping leaves. It includes onions, scallion, green onions, shallots, leeks, chives, garlic, etc.

Edible Fungi Mushrooms

✓ These are not actually vegetables but can be eaten like any other vegetable. These are edible fungus like mushroom. It includes truffles and variety of mushrooms.

Specialty Vegetables

✓ These are vegetables which do not fit in any other category of vegetables, for example artichoke and rhubarb.

Note.

- Traditionally tomato is also called "love apple". Cabbage like *green cabbage* is usually eaten boiled; *red cabbage* may be eaten cooked or pickled in vinegar; *white cabbage* can be shredded to make coleslaw.
- Fruits and vegetables may be fresh or canned but fresh are preferable than canned, therefore, use fresh fruits and vegetables as much as possible. Canned fruits and vegetables are stored in jar/can in brine solution (preservative used).
- In French, apple is called *pomme* whereas potato is called *pomme de terre* (it means apple of the soil). Remember, potato is a favourite vegetable of Germans.

Examples of Vegetable Based Dishes

Truffles	Haricot	Eggplant	Boiled Potatoes
• À La Créme	• À la Bretonne	• À la Creme	• À l anglaise
• Sous à la Cendre	• À l Americaine	• Frites	• Paysanne
• Au Champagne	• À la Lyonnaise	• À la Napolitaine	• Maitre d' hotel
• À la Serviette (with champagne)	• Panaches	• A l' egyptienne	• Mousseline
• Leberwurst	• À la Tourangelle	• Au gratin	• Aux fines herbs

Poise (Peas)	Carrot	Cardons	Fried Potatoes
• A l' Anglaise	• À la Créme	• Au Jus	• Allumettes
• À la francaise	• Au Flan	• Au Parmesan	• Berny
• À la Flamande	• À la Vichy	• Mornay	• Frites
• Bonne Femme	• Marianne	• À la Moelle	• Dauphine
• Bonne Femme			• Croquettes
Chou-fleur) (Cauliflower)	**Mushroom**	**Asparagus**	**Roasted Potatoes**
• A l' Anglaise	• Grilles	• À la Flamande	• Boulangere
• À la Creme	• Farcis	• Au Gratin	• Château
• Au gratin	• Aux fine herbs	• À la Milanaise	• Fondants
• À la Polonaise	Morrels	• Mornay	• Parisienne
• À la Milanaise	• À la Poulette	• À la Polonaise	• Noisettes
	• Sautees		
Epinards (Spinach)	**Cabbage**	**Artichoke**	**Sauté Potatoes**
• A l' Anglaise		• À la Provencale	• Sautees
• À la Creme	• À la limousine	• Clamart	• Bearnoise
• Au Gratin	• A l' Anglaise	• Stanley	• Lyonnaise
• Mere Louisette		• Grand Duc	
• Aux Crepes		• Cavour	
	Lettuce		**Baked Potatoes**
	• À la Moelle		• Duchesse
	• À la Serbe		• Au four

KEY TERMS

Love apple	:	Traditional American term for tomato.
À l' anglaise	:	Dish prepared in English style.
Salad green	:	Green leaves that can be used in salads.
Dehiscent fruits	:	Fruits containing seeds in a seedpod that opens up and releases the seeds.
Fleshy fruits	:	Fruits containing more or less soft pericarp/fleshy material.
Bonne femme	:	In lieu of vegetable preparation; *petit pois bonne femme* preparation.
Marianne	:	French dish made from carrots.

Leberwurst	:	German word which in English is spelled as liverwurst, meaning liver sausages.
Pomme	:	Apple, whereas the term pomme de terre means, the potato.

REVIEW QUESTIONS

1. Differentiate between pomme and pomme de terre.
2. Enlist dishes for a continental menu based on different vegetable preparations.
3. Classify vegetables into different categories and support each category with at least five vegetables.
4. Elucidate the various functions of fruits in cookery.

32 CHAPTER

Egg Cookery

OBJECTIVES

Students will be able to:

- expound egg types/sources and egg composition;
- explicate culinary uses of egg in cookery; and
- plan a menu, based on different kinds of egg preparations.

EGG

In general when we use the term *egg*, it usually refers to hen's egg but in cookery it covers a wide range of species or it includes eggs from other birds also. Eggs are good source of vitamins and minerals. Egg preparation can be served as an accompaniment, as a main course like egg curry and omelettes, as a salad, as a dessert meal, as a garnish and under entrée.

In cookery, the term *egg* refers to oval, thin shelled ovum of a bird, used as food. There are many sources of egg (or types of eggs) like goose, hen, quail, guinea fowl, duck, turkey and so forth. Except hen's egg, all other eggs must be labelled accordingly. Due to egg's versatility, it is considered a primary ingredient in cookery because it provides moisture, structure and richness to dishes. In many preparations, it also works as an emulsifier and aerator when properly handled and used. A basic rule for eggs in breakfast cookery is freshness. Remember that, as an egg ages, the egg white begins to thin and the yolk begins to flatten, so always try to use fresh egg, especially in breakfast cookery.

STRUCTURE OF EGG

Eggs have a hard shell made of calcium carbonate, an inner membrane, an air pocket at one end between the membrane and the shell, a central yellow to orange yolk supported by two filaments and a surrounding transparent white. On an average, the weight of a hen's egg is around 60 grams. Broadly speaking, egg is the combination of egg yolk and egg white with egg shell. In cookery, we only use egg yolk and egg white but never use egg shell.

Egg Yolk

Egg Composition

- Air cell
- Egg yolk
- Yolk membrane
- Chalazae
- Shell
- Shell membrane
- Germinal dish
- Albumen

- ✓ It is the central part of the egg usually light yellow to orange, semi-liquid and held separate within a fragile membrane. The "egg yolk" is made up of about 1/3 of an egg which provides 3/4 of egg's calories and almost half of the protein and riboflavin.
- ✓ Egg is a major source of vitamins, minerals, fat and cholesterol. Egg yolk comprises 87% water, 10% protein, 0.5% minerals with sufficient amount of vitamins.

Egg White

- ✓ It is a transparent gel surrounding the yolk of an egg. It is made up of about 2/3 of an egg which provides more than half of egg's protein and riboflavin.
- ✓ A fresh egg white is viscous but as it ages it becomes thinner and is better for whisking. Egg white comprises 47% water, 15% protein, 33% fat, 2% minerals with sufficient amount of vitamins.

Note. In egg composition, a whole egg contains 73% water, 12% protein, 11% fat, 1% minerals and remaining 3% contains sufficient amount of vitamins.

FUNCTIONS OF EGG IN COOKERY

Egg is one of the most versatile and nutritious food source. They are easy to digest and one can serve them to people at nearly all stages of the life cycle. The various uses of egg in cookery are given below:

Emulsifying Agent

- ✓ An *emulsion* is a mixture formed when you combine liquids that don't usually mix such as oil and water. Emulsifying agents keep the liquids from separating. In cookery, eggs are often used as an emulsifying agent in sauces and mixtures like mayonnaise.

Foaming Agent

- ✓ Foams are used to add air to foods. Eggs are good source of foaming agent. When beating egg whites, it creates air in cells. The more you beat, the more cells you make and the thicker the foam becomes. But you need to avoid under- or over-beating foams.

Thickening Agent

✓ Egg also works as a thickening agent because heat causes the egg proteins to coagulate. It can be used to thicken sauces, custards, and puddings.

EGG PREPARATIONS

- En cocotte
- À la coque
- Fried egg
- Boiled egg
- Omelettes
- Poached
- Scrambled
- Coddled
- Shirred/baked

Binding Agent

✓ Eggs also work as a binding and interfering agent. It binds in things like meat loaf and croquettes. In frozen desserts egg works as an interfering agent like in ice creams, eggs inhibit the formation of large ice crystals.

Clarifying Agent

✓ When egg protein coagulates, it helps in clarifying the unwanted materials like raft/scum (dirty foam) from various dishes. For example, eggs clarify soups and coffee and retard crystallization in boiled candies and frostings.

Coating

✓ Egg is also used as a coating agent. Coating batters use whole eggs and breadcrumbs to provide a coating or protection for the food item prior to cooking. For example, fried or deep fried foods, such as fish, meats, chicken and vegetables.

Main Dish

✓ Although eggs are widely known as *breakfast entrees*, they are also served in many other ways. For instance, egg is used in making pancakes, custards, soufflé, frittata, quiche, stuffed preparations, etc.

Leavening Agent

✓ Eggs also act as a leavening agent for pancakes, muffins, and omelettes or cakes. A leavening agent increases the volume of a food product and lightens its texture.

As a Salad

✓ One can also prepare salad with the help of egg. Usually, boiled egg is used to produce egg based salads or egg salads.

Garnishing

- ✓ In most of the dishes, an egg (boiled egg) can be used as a garnishing agent (in the form of sliced, sieved/chopped hard boiled egg). For example, Consommé Xavier, in it threads of egg are used to garnish the soup.

Glazing

- ✓ In most bakery products, beaten whole egg or yolk is brushed onto food items before baking because it gives a gloss or glazed finish. For example, bread and bread rolls, Duchesse potatoes, etc.

Other Uses

- ✓ In other uses, egg works as a nutritive, flavouring and colouring agent. As a *nutritive agent* (like in egg nog drinks, pasta and puddings) it provides proteins, vitamins and minerals.
- ✓ As *flavouring* and *colouring agent,* it adds flavour and colour to puddings and custards and helps to add colour in baked product. Often egg (like slices, sieved and quarters) are also used as a *decorating agent*.

Note. Besides cooking, an egg is also used to propagate viruses for various vaccines and also used in animal feed, shampoos, and cosmetics.

Examples of Egg Based Dishes

Boiled Eggs	Poached Eggs	Sur le plate	Fried Eggs
• Oeufs Soubise	• Oeufs Cardinal	• Oeufs Bercy	• Oeufs Montargis
• Oeufs Sevigne	• Oeufs Mignon	• Oeufs à la Florentine	• Oeufs a l' Anglaise
• Oeufs Stanley	• Oeufs Princesse	• Oeufs au Parmesan	• Oeufs à la Diable
• Oeufs Viroflay	• Oeufs Chivery	• Oeufs aux Anchois	• Oeufs a l' Espagnole
• Oeufs Victoria	• Oeufs Chantilly	• Oeufs à la Normande	• Oeufs a l' Americaine
Omelettees	**Scrambled Eggs**	**En cocotte**	**Cold Eggs**
• Oeufs Crecy	• Oeufs Chantillon	• Oeufs Diane	• Oeufs Alexandra
• Oeufs Clamart	• Oeufs Orloff	• Oeufs Colbert	• Oeufs Argenteuil
• Oeufs Bretonne	• Oeufs Magda	• Oeufs à la Crème	• Oeufs Mosaique
• Oeufs Chasseur	• Oeufs Balzac	• Oeufs au Jus	• Oeufs à la Moscorite
• Oeufs Lorraine	• Oeufs Marinette	• Oeufs à la Parisienne	• Oeufs à la Ravigote

KEY TERMS

Emulsion	: Mixture of oil and liquid in which tiny globules of one are suspended in the other.
Breakfast entrée	: Slightly heavy menu items like egg preparations mainly served in breakfast.
Crystallization	: Formation of sugar crystals (like lumpy or grainy) in sugar syrup.
Poached egg	: Egg prepared in simmer water.
Scrambled egg	: Egg mixed with milk and prepared over low heat.
Consommé Xavier	: Consommé (or clarified beef broth) soup garnished with egg drops.
Croquettes	: Small savoury or sweet preparation.
Albumen	: Egg white or protein contained in it. There are two layers, thick and thin albumen.
Chalazae	: A pair of spiral bands that anchor the yolk in the centre of the thick albumen.

REVIEW QUESTIONS

1. Classify the different components of egg and their contribution into cookery.
2. Enlist dishes for a continental menu based on different egg preparations.
3. Enlist the different sources of egg.
4. Elucidate the various functions of eggs in cookery.

33 CHAPTER

Seafood Cookery

Objectives

Students will be able to:

- categorize fish on different basis;
- explicate seaweed, fish cuts and roe; and
- plan a menu based on different fish types.

SEAFOOD

Seafood consists of an extensive variety of seawater based *flora* and *fauna* (sea animals and sea weeds) which are served as a delicacy or is regarded as suitable for the purpose of eating. Seafood usually comprises mostly of seawater *fauna* (or animals), such as fish and shellfish (including mollusks and crustaceans). But in many parts, the term seafood is also used collectively to refer to animals from fresh water and also any other kind of edible aquatic animals. This category makes up the bulk of the human food that comes from the water world. Under this classification, *edible seaweed* is also included, though it is specifically termed *sea vegetables*. Fish and seafood may be grouped into categories by both their structure and preparation techniques and methods used for cooking them.

Edible seaweed (or *flora* or edible sea vegetables) is consumed in many parts of the world, especially where fresh vegetables are scarce during the winter season. Its examples include wakame and knobu, red dulse, laver, algae, agar agar, rock, sloke, etc. and these have a good amount of mineral content. Seaweed can be eaten raw in salads, stir-fried or dried and used as a seasoning. These can be purchased fresh or processed but are mostly preferred processed.

Fish Cuts

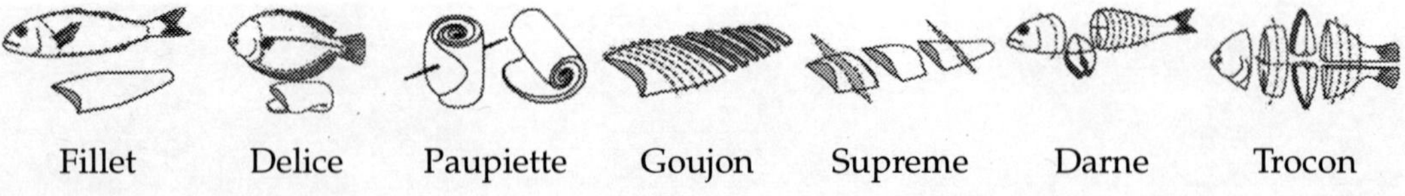

Fillet Delice Paupiette Goujon Supreme Darne Trocon

Fillet	Flesh from the bone in long flat pieces. A flat fish yields 4 fillets whereas round fish yield 2 fillets.
Delice	Folded fillets – usually of a small flat fish like sole. It is trimmed and neatly folded into half.

Paupiette	Rolled and stiffed fillet, usually of a small flat fish. It is spread with fish stuffing and rolled up (farce).
Goujon	Fish finger/baton (around 80 × 10 × 10 mm), a *Goujonette* is smaller and may be used as a garnish.
Supreme	Fish cut on the slant from the fillet of a large round or flat fish like turbot, brill, halibut or cod fish.
Darne	Darne/steak (around 25 mm thick) is a section/cut across the backbone of round fish like cod and salmon.
Troncon	Alike darne (around 45 mm thick) is a section of a large flat fish after being split down the backbone.

CLASSIFICATION OF SEAFOOD

Fish

A fish without shells and which could generally be separated into two groups: freshwater fish and saltwater fish. These are also called "finfish". These fishes having bony skeleton and considered edible fish. On broad basis, fish classification can be done on the basis of habitat, shape and flesh.

Habitat: The term *habitat* refers to the natural home or where fishes get what they need to survive.

Freshwater fish

✓ These fishes are usually mild and delicate in flavour. The structures of these fishes are based on hundreds of minuscule bones instead of heavy skelton framework. Examples of freshwater fish include Trout, Redfin, Carp, Murray Cod, Eel and so forth.

Salt water fish

✓ Salt water provides more buoyancy than freshwater fish, hence salt water fish like Tuna, Shark, Herring, Snapper, Mackerel, Mulloway, Cod, etc. have stronger or thicker bone structure.

Note. In recent years freshwater fishes are continuously getting contaminated by polluted water. This has created problems in obtaining good yield. Thus, be careful while choosing fish for preparing a menu.

Shape: It refers to the general shape and appearance of the fish. There are two broad categories of fish in accordance with shape structure, i.e., round and flat. A brief description of both is given below.

Round fish

- ✓ Round fishes have a rounder body, with eyes on both sides of the head. Its examples include Carp, Coley, Gudgeon, Gurnard, Monkfish, Pike, Pollack, Rockfish, Snapper, Swordfish, Whiting, Wrasse, Cod, Haddock, Mackerel, Mullet, Herring, Taylor, Atlantic salmon, Bass, Hake, Ling, etc.

Flat fish

- ✓ These fishes can swim horizontally along the bottom of the sea and are shaped like an oval platter, the top side being dark and the bottom white. Both eyes are on the side of the body facing upward. Its examples include Skate, Megrim, Witch, Flounder, Sole, Halibut, Brill, Plaice, Turbot, Dab, etc.

Flesh: It refers to the colour and texture of flesh of the fish. There are two categories: white and dark.

White fish

- ✓ These white fishes can be flat or round. Its example include Cod, Turbot, Flounder, Sole, Snapper, Whiting, etc.

Dark fish

- ✓ This category includes fishes like Herring, Sardine, Salmon, Tuna, Mullet, Skate, etc.

Fishes on the basis of fat content		
Fat Quantity	**Fat Proportion**	**Examples**
Lean fat	2.5%	Cod, Herring, Halibut, Flounder, Hack and so forth
Moderate	6%	Swordfish, Bonito, Tuna, Whiting and so forth
High fat	12%	Herring, Mackerel, Sturgeon and so forth. Fat may also go up to 30%.

SHELLFISH

The main difference between fish and shellfish is their skeleton structure. Shellfishes have an external skeleton or shell. There are two main categories of shellfish – crustaceans and mollusks.

PRAWN PREPARATIONS

- Crevettes Frites
- Coquilles de Crevettes Garnies
- Crevettes au curie
- Coquilles de Crevettes Glaces

Crustaceans

✓ These shellfishes have elongated bodies and segmented soft shells like a brush with a covered body. Its examples include Lobsters, Shrimps, Crabs, Moreton Bay Bugs, Crayfishes, Marrons, Yabbies, Prawns and Scampies.

Mollusks

✓ It can also be spelt as "molluscs". These shellfishes have hard hinged shells with soft bodies and partially or fully enclosed in shells. Its examples include Sea-urchin, Winkles, Oysters, Clams, Scallops, Mussels, Pipis, Abalones and Cockles.

ROE OF FISH

Roe is a fully ripe egg mass of fish including certain marine animals, such as sea urchin, shrimp and scallop. As seafood it is used both as a cooked and as a raw ingredient in many dishes. *Caviar* is a name for processed and salted roe which is consumed as a delicacy. Other forms include Ikura (Salmon Roe), Kazunoko (Herring Roe), Lumpfish Roe, Masago (Capelin Roe), Shad Roe, Tobiko (Flying-Fish Roe), etc. The four world famous caviar include Beluga, Sterlet, Ossetra, and Sevruga. Roe of sturgeon fish is black while roe of salmon fish is red in colour.

Note.

- There is one more class of shellfish i.e. *cephalopods*. Technically cephalopods (like squid and octopus) are classed as mollusks, these animals have a reduced internal shell called pen or cuttlebone.
- *Cephalopods* or often termed *invertebrates* (come under the category of mollusks) are spineless marine animals (with soft and unsegmented bodies) with no outer shell. They include the squid and octopus family. For instance, Squid, Octopus, Snails, Cuttlefish, etc.
- Crustaceans can be further classified into: *univalved* (it means single shell like snail, conch and abalone) and *bivalved* (it means double shell like clams, oyster and mussels). These shells expand as the animal grows.

Menu Examples of Seafood Based Dishes

Shrimp	Clam	Sauté fish	Grilled fish
• Camaron rebosado	• Clams casino	• A' l' anglaise	• Kippers
• Har gow	• Clams Oreganata	• Colbert	• Sole à la Nicoise
• Potted shrimps	• Clam chowder	• Grenobloise	• Fillet de Sole St. Germain

• Shrimp DeJonghe	• Stuffed clams	• Murat	• Anguille à la Menagere
• Drunken shrimp	• Fried clams	• Meuniere	• Brocheton à la Martiniere
Crab	**Lobster**	**Poached fish**	**Fried fish**
• Crab Rangoon	• Homard Cardinal	• Bonne femme	• A' l' Orly
• Gejang	• Lobster stew	• Sole cubat	• Sole Colbert
• Bisque	• Lobster roll	• Au bleu	• Sole Meuniere
• Chili crabs	• Lobster Thermidor	• Duglere	• Fillet de Sole Belle
• Deviled crab	• Homard Newburg	• Sole à la Florentine	• Anguille frite

KEY TERMS

Seaweed : Sea vegetables.
Univalved : Single shell based shellfishes like, snail, conch and abalone.
Bivalved : Double shell shellfishes like, clams, oyster and mussels.
Caviar : Roe (or egg) of fishes.
Cephalopods : Shellfishes like squid and octopus classed as mollusks.
Deviled crab : Crab meat croquette preparation.
Flora and fauna : Plants and animals.
Finfish : Fish with fins, other than flatfish and shellfish.

REVIEW QUESTIONS

1. What is seaweed? Enlist any five seaweeds.
2. Enlist dishes for a continental menu based on seafood preparations.
3. Write a short note on *roe*.
4. Classify fishes into different groups and support to each group with five fish names/examples.

34 CHAPTER

Poultry Cookery

Objectives

Students will be able to:

- expound standard check and species;
- explicate parameters to identify specific poultry; and
- plan a menu based on different poultry species.

POULTRY

The term *poultry* covers any domestic bird that has been bred for the table/cooking. The poultry family generally includes chicken, turkey, duck and geese. In simple terms, the term poultry refers to barnyard fowl, most of which have been domesticated for centuries and are now mass-produced. Therefore, the term 'poultry (or volaille)" applies to all domesticated birds, whether bred for table purposes or for their eggs. This broadly includes the following groups.

- Duck
- Goose
- Turkey
- Capon
- Chicken

Duck

✓ They are force-fed to produce foie gras; the magret, or breast meat; it can be roasted, fried or smoked. *Magret* is the breast meat from a mallard or Barbary duck. These ducks are specially raised for foie gras. Their breasts are large and have a much thinner layer of fat than do the Peking or Long Island duckling.

Goose

✓ Often force-fed to produce foie gras, it is delicious and often stuffed or served with a fruit sauce; goose stuffed with chestnuts is a classic European dish. The female species is simply known as a *goose*, a male as a *gander*, and a young goose of whichever sex, as a *gosling*.

Turkey

✓ Prepared like chicken although its meat is drier; in North America, turkey with stuffing is the traditional Thanksgiving and Christmas meal.

Capon

✓ Young rooster which is castrated and fattened for slaughter; it grows to twice the size of a chicken (or capons have a higher fat content thus yield more meat than roosters) yet has tender juicy meat.

Chicken

✓ The most popular poultry produced is chicken. The offspring hen 4 to 12 months old is cheap, tasty and can be prepared in numerous ways, thus it is the most popular type of poultry. The *Cornish hen* is a crossbreed of the White Rock and the Cornish chicken.

Poultry and their Species fed for Eggs	
Chicken	Sussex, Old English Game, Indian Game, Dorking, Bresse, Courtes Pattes, Crève Coeur, La Flèche
Turkeys	Different types originate from Norfolk, Cambridgeshire, Devon, Scotland, Ireland and America
Ducks	Aylesbury, Peking, White Campbell, Stanbridge White, Rouen, Nantes, Huttegem, Blue Swedish
Geese	Emden, Toulouse, Roman, Chinese-White, Strasbourg

CLASSIFICATION OF POULTRY

P*oultry* is a category of domesticated fowl, such as chicken, turkey, duck, geese, etc. especially those fowls/birds which are valued for their eggs or meats. Within each poultry variety, there are number of types and sizes of bird. Each poultry variety can be classified on several bases like age, weight, family and so forth. Some of them are classified as below:

Chicken (Scientific name *Gallus domesticus*)

✓ The term *chicken* is used for a domesticated fowl which belongs to the family or sub-species of Red Junglefowl. Chicken is one of the most popular, common and widespread domestic fowl with plentiful breeds/names.

✓ For example, Broiler, Silkie, Bantam, Plymouth rock, Orpington, Australorp, Black shumen, Cubalaya, Crevecoeur, Faverolles, Phoenix, Onagadori, Aseel, Orloff, Sumatra, Leghorn, Barnevelder, Minorca, etc. A brief description of most commonly used chicken for cookery purpose is given below.

Name	French Term	Age (in weeks)	Weight	Characteristics
Squab chicken	Le poussin	4 – 5	250 – 350 gm	Baby chicken (also known as *poussin*) - one bird gives one portion. It is best to roast and grill.
Spatchcock	Le crapaudine	6 – 8	650 – 800 gm	Young birds (also known as *double poussin*) - one bird gives two portions. It is best to cook as poussin.
Spring chicken	Le poussin	7 – 8	850 gm – 01 kg	In size, it is larger than spatchcock and one bird gives three portions. It is mostly roasted.
Broiler		6 – 8	750 gm – 1.5 kg	Also known as *fryer* and considered good to roast. In size, it is smaller than rooster.
Rooster chicken	La poularde	12 – 20	2.5 kg - 3.5 kg	Mature hen (also known as *rooster*) – one bird gives four to six portions. These are best to cook as roast, grill, fry, bake or casserole.
Boiling fowl	La poule	About 8 months	2 – 3 kg	Older hens – it is meaty but fatty and is best for stews or casseroles, thus considered cheap meat. One bird yields six to eight portions.

Turkey (Scientific name *Meleagris*)

- ✓ The term *turkey* is used for a game bird structured with fan-shaped tail and wattled neck. The turkey species can be classified into three categories: domesticated (for example, Poult, Bronze, Midget white, Norfol black, Blue Slate, etc.), wild (for example, Jocelyn, Ontario, M.G. Silvestris, Goulds, etc.) and ocellated turkeys.
- ✓ Turkeys are prepared like chicken although its meat is drier. In North America, turkey with stuffing is a famous meal for several occasions like during Christmas. A brief description of most commonly used turkeys for cookery purpose is given below.

Name	In French	Age (in weeks)	Weight	Characteristics
Young turkey	Le dindonneau	Up to 14	3 – 4 kg	Young birds – one young turkey yields eight to ten portions.
Tom/Cock turkey	Le dindon	Up to 14	8 – 10 kg	Young male birds – one male turkey yields eighteen to twenty four portions.
Hen turkey	La dinde	Up to 14	4 – 7 kg	Young, female birds – one female turkey yields twelve to sixteen portions.
Large turkey		22 – 24	Upto 18 kg	Older birds

Duck (Scientific name *Anatidae anseriformes*)

- ✓ The term *duck* is commonly used for a large number of species that belong to Anatidae family of birds, including swans and geese. Ducks are mostly aquatic birds and mostly smaller than the swans and geese and may be found in seawater and freshwater bodies.
- ✓ Its examples include Bufflehead duck, Mandarin duck, Pecten, Red crested Pochard, Mallard, Widgeon, Wood duck, Ringed Teal and so forth. Often ducks are force-fed to produce foie gras or to make various paté based preparations. The magret or breast meat of duck can be roasted, fried or smoked. A brief description of most commonly uses ducks for cookery purpose is given in the table.

Name	In French	Age (in weeks)	Weight	Characteristics
Duckling	Le caneton	8 – 9	1.5 – 2 kg	Young birds – if roasted, then yield two to four portions.
Duck	Le canard	4 – 16	1 – 2 kg	Mature birds – they are fat, so best to roast but can also be braised or casseroled. One duck yields four to six portions.
Green duck		8 – 9	1.5 – 2.5 kg	Young duck

Goose (Scientific name *Anseriniformes*)

✓ The term goose/geese commonly used for waterfowl, belongs to the tribe Anserini of the family Anatidae. The term *goose* applies to the female in particular while *gander* to the male. Young birds before fledging are called *goslings.* Its examples include Cape Barren, Greylag goose, Branta Canadensis, Orinoco, Nettapus, Magpie, Northern Gannet, Sheldgeese and so forth.

✓ Like ducks, gooses/geeses are also force-fed to produce foie gras. It is a delicious stuffed preparation (like chestnut stuffing goose is a famous European delicacy) served with a fruit sauce. A brief description of most commonly used goose for cookery purpose is given below.

Name	In French	Age (in weeks)	Weight	Characteristics
Gosling	L'oison	Up to 10	2 – 3 kg	Young birds – one gosling yields six to eight portions.
Goose	L'oie	Up to 26	4 – 7 kg	A mature and fatty bird with creamy white flesh cooked to light brown and has a distinctive flavour. One goose yields ten to twelve portions.
Green geese		Up to 10	4 – 6 kg	Young geese

Others

✓ There are enormous species under the heading poultry which are difficult to cover in one unit. For example, pigeon, guinea fowl, capon, snipe, spatchcock, pheasant, partridge, quail and so forth. Some of these also come under the category of game birds.

Name	In French	Age (in weeks)	Weight	Characteristics
Pigeon	Le pigeon	06 – 10	300 – 500 gm	One pigeon yields only one portion. *Tame pigeons* are smaller than *wood pigeons.*
Guinea fowl	La pintade	18 – 28	750 gm – 1.5 kg	One guinea fowl yields two to four portions.
Capon	La chapon	10 – 12	2.5 – 3.5 kg	Castrated, fattened cock birds. These are full breasted with tender, juicy, flavourful meat that is usually suited for roasting.

Poultry Offals/Fancy Meats/Giblets	
Poultry offals are also known as giblets, which include- livers, heart, kidney, neck and feet. Practically gizzard, heart and liver are commonly called *giblets*. Brief profile of poultry offal is given below:	
Liver	Livers are usually used for flavouring of soups and stocks. Goose liver is frequently used in paté preparations.
Heart	Poultry hearts are either grilled on skewers, used in terrines, incorporated in mixed salads or merely seized in butter.
Kidney	Kidneys are usually grilled or sautéed, but may also be stewed with a sauce that will improve their flavour. In many preparations, kidneys are combined with pieces of meat or liver, like in mixed grill.
Neck	In poultry, the neck forms part of the giblets. Goose neck may be eaten stuffed. Neck is also known as "Scrag".
Feet	Chicken feet are considered a delicacy in certain Asian dishes.

Menu Examples of Poultry Based Dishes

Grilled Chicken	Sauté chicken	Turkey
Chicken Yassa	Chicken à la Creole	Turkey schnitzels
Chicken à la Tyrolienne	Sauté chicken Alexandra	Mole Poblano
Fried Chicken	Sauté Chicken Chasseur	**Goose**
Chicken à la Viennoise	Sauté chicken Stanley	Pate de foie gras
Chicken Maryland	Supereme of chicken a l' Anglaise	
Braised Chicken	**Roasted chicken**	**Duck**
Poulet doria	Bonne femme	Canard de Maison
Poulet chasseur	Bigarade	Roasted duck

Poached and Steamed	Demidov	
Chicken a las Chivry	Grand mere	
Chicken à la d' Albufera	Roast chicken Rossini	
Chicken au Blanc	**Boiled chicken**	
Chicken à la Reine	Cominee de gelines	

KEY TERMS

Rooster : Mature chicken or roosting chicken.
Fryer : Broiler chicken.
Poussin : Baby chicken or squab chicken.
Pate : Rich poultry preparation cooked in pastry and served cold.
Terrine : Poultry preparations that are poached and cooled in a mould, called *terrine*.
Gander : Male goose.
Magret : Breast meat from a mallard or Barbary duck.

REVIEW QUESTIONS

1. What is poultry? Classify poultry into different groups and explain their breeds.
2. Enlist dishes for a continental menu based on different poultry breeds.
3. Write a short note on poultry offals.

35 CHAPTER

Meat Cookery

Objectives

Students will be able to:

- classify bovine, ovine, porcine and caprine;
- explicate meat cuts, offals and their culinary uses; and
- plan a menu based on different meat types.

MEAT

Meat is generally processed in butchery and prepared in the cold larder/garde manger kitchen (especially cold preparations) and in hot kitchen. Meat used in kitchen operations is principally derived from farmed sheep, beef cattle, pigs, or goats that have been raised on a farm. Most of the meat industry is strictly controlled to ensure the quality of meat products as well as the benevolent treatment of livestock.

Commercially produced meat arrives at the butchers or kitchen is already dressed. This means the skin, extremities and internal organs have been removed and the carcass is ready to be broken down into smaller pieces or cuts. The younger the animal the more tender the meat is. Therefore, lamb is more tender than mutton, and veal is more tender than beef. Gender, breeding, feeding, lifestyle and handling all affect tenderness and flavour. Meat can be classified as bovine, ovine, porcine and caprine.

BOVINE MEAT

The term *bovine* is related to or resembling a ruminant mammal of the genus *Bos,* such as an ox, cow, or buffalo. According to UNECE (United Nations Economic Commission for Europe) code specification (species code), there are mainly beef and veal that come under the category bovine. A brief description of both is given below.

Meat Offal's

Red offals - bone-marrow, testicles, brain, mesentery, feet, sweetbreads, stomach and head.

White offals - heart, liver, tongue, lungs, spleen, kidneys.

Beef (le boeuf)

- ✓ It means the meat of an adult (over one year) bovine/beef. It is principally derived from young *steers* which are castrated males over three months of age. Many factors influence the appearance and tenderness of beef, such as breed, feed, age, and lifestyle.

✓ In general, beef should be bright red with firm white fat (fat should be brittle in texture) and light marbling. Beef from some cattle varieties, older animals, and dairy cattle may have yellower and softer fat. There are different categories of beef depending on the age of the cattle at the time of processing. Therefore, beef can be further categorized as:

Name	Age (in months)	Characteristics
Steer	12–36	Also known as "young prime beef".
Baby beef	15–18	Its flesh is coarser, strong flavoured and from pink to light red in colour. These are ready to be slaughtered.
Beefling	18–24	Young beef – its bones are soft, porus and red.
Mature beef	Above 24 years	Beef tenderness and flavour are improved with aging.
Aged steer	Up to 42	Also known as "prime beef".
Heifers	Under 24	Females that have never borne a calf.
Others	Above 42	It includes ox, cow, steer, etc.

Note.

- *Steers* are male castrated (when very young) bovine. While *cows* are those females that have borne at least one calf. *Bulls* are usually under two years of age. Its pubic bone will be large, the pelvic cavity narrow and cod fat almost non-existent.
- A well-matured beef (which is above 2.5 years old) will be full-flavoured, as beef ages the meat begins to toughen and darken to a purplish red.
- Famous breeds of beef include Aberdeen Angus, Welsh Black, Highland, Lincoln Red, South Devon, Sussex (red breed) and Hereford, Irish Moiled, Beef Shorthorn, Belted and Black Galloways, Red Poll, White Park, British White, Longhorn, Gloucester and Dexter.

Uses of Different Cuts of Beef

Cut (English Name)	Cut (French Name)	Use in Cookery	Name of Dish
Neck	Le cou de boeuf	Braising, stewing or boiling	Meat balls
Chuck		Stewing and braising	Steak and kidney pie
Fore rib	Les cotes de boeuf	Roasting, grilling or frying	Roast beef
Sirloin	L'aloyau de boeuf	Roasting, grilling or frying	Entrecote grille
Rump	La culotte de boeuf	Grilling, frying or braising	Grilled rump steak

Topside	La tranche tender	Braising, stewing or roasting	Bitok and braised beef with noodles
Silverside	La gite à la noix	Pickled in brine then boiled	Spiced silverside
Flank (thick)	La tranche Grasse	Braising and stewing	Ragout de boeuf aux legumes
Flank (thin)	La bavette	Stewing, boiling	Sausages, Boeuf bouilli à la francaise
Brisket	La poitrine	Pot roasting	Ale brisket and *corned beef*
Ribs*	Les cotes de boeuf	Roasting, grilling or frying	Cote de boeuf roti a' l' anglais
Shin	La jambe	Consommé, stewing	Consommé Royale
Blade		Braising and roasting	Beef ragout
Fillet	Le fillet de boeuf	Roasting, grilling or frying	Filet de boeuf bouquetiere
Leg	Le cuissot de boeuf	Braising, boiling or stewing	Stocks, soups and sauces
Shank (fore)	La jambe	Braising, boiling or stewing	Stocks, soups and sauces
Shank (hind)	La jambe	Braising, boiling or stewing	Stocks, soups and sauces

Note.

- Broadly beef cuts can be divided into two parts, i.e., hind quarter and forequarter. *Hindquarter* includes shank, topside, silverside, flanks, rump, sirloin, wing ribs, fillet while rest of the beef cuts come under *forequarter*.
- *Ribs are received from both quarters (hind as well as fore). From *hindquarter*, wing ribs while from *forequarter*, fore ribs, middle ribs and chuck ribs are received.

Veal (le veau)

✓ Veal is the meat of a calf of a one-year old. Veal has white, tender and very lean meat thus many chefs treat veal meat as a delicacy.

✓ For *haute cuisine*, good quality veal is required which often comes from Holland and its weight should be around 100 kg (it is produced from calves slaughtered at 12-24 weeks). Veal can be classified as shown in the table below.

Name	Age (in months)	Weight	Characteristics
Slink	Unborn	Up to 70 kg	It is unborn or still born veal.
Milk fed veal	2–3 months	Up to 210 kg	Its flesh is firm and creamy white with a pale greyish pink tinge.
Formula fed veal	3–4 months	Up to 210 kg	Fed with special diet of milk solids, fats, various nutrients and water. Its meat is not as rich or delicate as milk fed veal.
Calf	Below 6 months	Above 200 kg	Young cattle that are allowed to eat grass and grain.
Others			It includes *bobby calves* (these are slaughtered within 10 days of birth), *stirk* (weaning calf both male + female upto six months),

Note.

- Often, the term *veal* is used for meat from beef cattle less than three months of age which has only been milk fed. After three months of age, cattle start on a full grass fed diet which darkens the flesh and the flavour becomes more distinct.
- *Stirk calves* are also known as "vealers". Calf or young cattle is also known as "heavyweight veal". The dressed carcass of veal will weigh around 40 kg.

Uses of Different Cuts of Veal			
Cut (English Name)	Cut (French Name)	Use in cookery	Name of Dish
Scrag	Le cou de veau	Stewing, stock	Fond de veau
Neck End	Le cou de veau	Stewing, sauté	Fricassee de veau a l' ancienne
Best End	La carre de veau	Roasting, frying and grilling	Cote de veau milanese
Saddle	La selle de veau	Roasting, frying and braising	Veal chops with spaghetti
Loin	La longe de veau	Roasting, frying and braising	Same as above
Chump/rump	Le quasi de veau	Roasting, braising and grilling	Sauté de veau
Leg	Le cuissot de veau	Roasting, braising, sauté	Roast leg of veal
Breast	La poitrine de veau	Stewing, roasting	Blanquette de veau aux nouilles
Shoulder	L'epaule de veau	Braising, stewing	Goulash de veau
Knuckle	Le jarret de veau	Sauté, stock	Osso Buco

OVINE AND CAPRINE MEATS

The term *ovine* is related to or resembling sheep like meats. Broadly it includes lamb, sheep, mutton and hogget (yearling mutton). On the other side the term *caprine* is related with the goat.

Sheep

- ✓ Sheep (or lamb as it is often sold) is a popular and versatile meat that can be used in a variety of dishes. It is particularly well suited to Mediterranean and Middle Eastern dishes.

Lamb

- ✓ These are sheep under one year and mostly castrated males. For identification the carcass is marked with bright red stripes labelled *lamb*. Lamb flesh should be light reddish pink, with white firm fat. Lamb flesh has a delicate texture and flavour. It is suited for roasting, frying or grilling.

Hogget

- ✓ These are mostly castrated male lambs between 10–18 months old. For identification the carcass is marked with purple stripes and labelled *hogget*. Hogget is suited to the same methods of cookery as lamb, but may be a little tougher and stronger in flavour and slightly less tender flesh. The meat is a little darker than lamb. It is also known as "yearling mutton".

Mutton

- ✓ Mutton is sheep over two years. For identification the carcass has dark brown markings labelled *mutton*. Mutton has darker flesh than hogget and a stronger sheep flavour and smell than hogget or lamb. Mutton is generally suited to stewing and full flavoured dishes.

Goat (caprine)

- ✓ All goat meat is very lean and requires some care in cooking so that it doesn't dry out. Goat is flavoursome meat, which is gaining popularity. Goat is mostly sold as kids or capretto.

Note. Domestic lamb between 3–5 months old is often called "spring, summer or early lamb".

Name	Age	Characteristics
Kids	Up to 3 months	Castrated male kids
Capretto	Up to 18 months	These are also castrated male kids but older than kids.
Baby lamb	1-2 months	These are not weaned; put out to graze. Also known as *easter lamb.*
Sheep	Below 12 months	Sheep known for its tender meat.
Lamb	Up to 12 months	Lamb is young animal but below the age of one year
Mutton	Above 24 months	Mutton is larger, darker and fatter than lamb.
Others		It includes spring/early/summer lamb (3–5 months), yearling (lamb of above one year), goat (above one year).

Note.

- Older goats begin to have strong smelling and tasting meat, which is suited to well flavoured dishes. A regular lamb is slaughtered under a year of age.
- Several famous *breeds of mutton* include – Dishley, Dorset and Southdown. Famous *lamb breeds* include – Pouillac (France), Welsh and Devon (Britain), etc.
- Other breeds include - Boreray, Castlemilk Moorit, Hebridean, Manx Loghtan, North Ronaldsay, Soay, Balwen Welsh Mountain, Cotswold, Devon and Cornwall Longwool, Dorset Down, Dorset Horn, Greyface Dartmoor, Hill Radnor, Leicester Longwool, Lincoln Longwool, Llanwenog, Norfolk Horn, Oxford Down, Portland, Ryeland, Shropshire, Southdown, Teeswater, Wensleydale, Whitefaced Woodland, Whiteface Dartmoor.

Uses of Different Cuts of Mutton and Lamb			
Cut (English Name)	**Cut (French Name)**	**Use in cookery**	**Name of Dish**
Scrag end	Le cou	Stewing, broth	Mutton broth
Middle neck	Le cou	Stewing	Navarin d'agneau printanier
Shoulder (both)	L'epaule d'agneau	Roasting and stewing	Epaule d' agneau boulangere
Best end (both)	Le carre d'agneau	Roasting, grilling and frying	Carre d'agneau persille
Breast (both)	Le poitrine	Roasting and stewing	Irish stew
Saddle/Loin	La selle d'agneau	Roasting, grilling and frying	Selle d'agneau nicoise
Chump (bones)		Boiling, stewing, braising	Stock and sauces
Leg (both)	Le gigot d'agneau	Roasting (mutton boiled)	Roast leg of lamb

Note. Saddle and chump are quite close to each other. A long saddle incorporates the chump, so be careful while cutting it.

PORCINE MEAT

According to UNECE code specification (species code), the term *porcine* is related to pork. The word porcine is derived from the French term *porcin* or directly from the Latin word *porcinus* which means pig. A brief description of pork and its further categorized genus is given below.

Pork (le porc)

- ✓ Pork is the most popular meat in Scandinavia, Germany, and France. Pork is valued as a lean, pale-pink meat with a distinct and delicate flavour. Pork, unlike lamb and beef is often sold skin-on, as the skin is nutritious and also valued for its flavour and texture.
- ✓ Commercially available pork falls into one of the following four categories, i.e., suckling pigs, porkers, baconers and choppers.

Name	Age (in months)	Weight	Characteristics
Suckling pigs	Up to 4 months	Up to 10 kg (dressed)	They are usually prepared whole after dressing and are generally bred for commercial industry and for festive occasions.
Porkers	4–6 months	Up to 50 kg (dressed)	These are bred for consumption as fresh pork meat. Most of these are castrated males.
Baconers	6–9 months	60–70 kg	They are used for the manufacturing of pork based meats such as ham and bacon.
Choppers	Above 6 months	Around 100 kg	These are derived from pigs above six months and principally used for small goods manufacturing. Most of these are females.
Others			It includes piglet, figs or stags. Fig is a castrated pig.

Note.

- In the past, you could find a big size pig that ranged between 200–250 kg. Today, the average weight of any pig can range between 50–60 kg per side.
- The term *pork* is used for pig only after slaughtering (or killing). Though pork generally refers to young swine less than a year old. There are certain pigs which are specifically reared for bacon.

- Famous pig breeds include Saddlebacks, Gloucestershire Old Spots, Berkshire, British Lops, Yorkshire, Tamworth, Ulster, Wessex, Cumberland, Welsh, Large black, Middle White, etc.

Uses of Different Cuts of Pork

Cut (English Name)	Use in cookery	Name of Dish
Head	Headcheese, boiling, baking	Pork brawn and salad
Collar	Boiling, grilling	Boiled bacon
Loin	Roasting, grilling and frying	Roast loin of pork
Chump	Frying, grilling and roasting	Honey pork chops
Leg	Roasting and boiling	Roast leg of pork
Feet	Grilling	Crubeens
Belly	Braising and stewing	Salted pork
Ribs	Chops, roasting	Barbecued ribs
Spare ribs	Roasting, boiling	Pork pie
Shoulder	Steaks, roasting, curing, smoking.	Saucisse de porc grille
Hocks	Boiling, making jelly	Boiled bacon

Menu Examples of Meat Based Dishes

Sauté mutton/lamb	Sauté Pork	Sauté Veal	Sauté Beef
• A l' Argenteuil	• Zingara	• Cote de veau	• Clamart
• Marechal	• Charcuterie	• Holstein	• Provencal
• Nelson	• Milanaise	• Viennoise	• Forestiere
• Bergere	• Robert	• À la crème	• Stroganoff
Roasted mutton/lamb	• Bruxelloise	• Aux morilles	• A l' americaine
• Boulangere			
• Bretonne			
Other Mutton/Lamb Dishes	**Roasted Pork**	**Other Veal Dishes**	**Other Beef Dishes**
• Lamb Shashlik	• A l' allemande	• Weiner schnitzel	• A l' andalouse
• Noisette d' agneau	• Florentine	• Veal cordon bleu	• Nivernaise
• Navarin de mouton	• Flamande	• Marengo	• Tivoli
• Irish stew	• A l' Argenteuil	• Printaniere	• Bourgeoise
			• Bourguignonne

KEY TERMS

Offal	:	Giblets/variety meats/fancy meats like kidney, liver, head and so forth.
Bovine	:	Beef.
Ovine	:	Sheep-like meats.
Porcine	:	Pork meats.
Caprine	:	Goat meats.
Fig	:	Castrated pig.
Porkers	:	Castrated male pork.
Baconers	:	Pig that weighs between 83 and 101 kg, from which bacon is cut.
Choppers	:	Pigs above six months.
Easter lamb	:	Baby lamb.

REVIEW QUESTIONS

1. What is bovine? Enlist any five dishes made with bovine meats.
2. Write a short note on offal.
3. Enlist the cuts of pork and describe their best cooking medium.
4. Differentiate between porcine and caprine.

36 CHAPTER

Game Cookery

OBJECTIVES

Students will be able to:

- classify furred and feathered games; and
- explicate game offals.

GAME

Game is a meat which comes from wild animals and birds that are hunted for food or sport. In French, all games are collectively called "Gibier" (this word is derived from "Gibercier" which means *to hunt*). The gourmet considers game as an excellent food, healthy and fit for the most delicate palates. Games can be divided into two parts:

- Furred games — It refers to game animals.
- Feathered games — It refers to game birds.

GAME OFFALS

- Brain
- Heart
- Kidney
- Liver
- Tongue

CLASSIFICATION OF GAME

Game is generally classified as either feathered or furred. In addition, some reptiles, such as crocodiles, lizards and snakes, are also classified as game. The reason behind calling them "game" is that because these are hunted for the purpose of various sports. The tables below outlines the most common species of game.

Furred Game

✓ These are also called "game animals", in French furred games are called "Le gibier a poil". These animals have fur and are hunted for sports and food, e.g., deer and rabbit.

✓ The furred games are varied in kind and large in numbers like red deer, chamois, Roebuck, etc. But on broad basis it can be classified as large size (venison, buffalo, wild boar and bear) and small size (rabbit, squirrel, etc.) games.

Various Furred Games			
Name	**French**	**Weight**	**Characteristics**
Deer/venison	La chevrette	14–16 kg	The term *venison* is used for flesh of deer. It is usually preferred to roast or braised in joints.
Roebuck	Le chevreuil	Around 20 kg	Roebuck up to six months is called *fawn up*; up to 18 months *yearling* and then *brocket*.
Hare	Le lievre	3–5 kg	Its red wine based preparation known as "stew" is famous as *jugged hare*.
Rabbit	Le lapin	1.5–2.5 kg	Rabbit is distinguished (from hare) by shorter ears, feet and body.
Chamois	Le chamois	30–60 kg	It is a goat antelope species – male chamois are larger than females (females are 25–45 kg).
Reindeer	Le renne	160–180 kg	It is a species of deer and also known as the *caribou* in North America. Females weighed between 80–120 kg.
Hind	La biche	Upto 20 kg	A female deer, especially a red deer.
Boar/bear	Le verrat	50–90 kg	An un-castrated domestic male *hog*. Wild boar is not as heavy as domestic hog.

Feathered Game

✓ These are also called "game birds"; in French feathered games are called "Le gibier a plumage". The game birds can be further divided on the basis of size like large (wild turkey and goose), medium (pheasant and wild duck) and small (grouse, hazel hen, partridge, pigeon, plover, snipe, quail and woodcock).

Various Feathered Games			
Name	**French**	**Weight**	**Characteristics**
Pheasant	Le faisan	1.5–2 kg	Its genus includes, Ithaginis, Pucrasia, Syrmaticus and Rheinardia.
Partridge	La perdrix	200–400 gm	In market, there are two forms of partridge, i.e., young and rock partridge.
Woodcock	La becasse	200–300 gm	Its genus includes, Eurasian, American, Sulawesi, Dusky and Moluccan.

Snipe	La becassine	100–125 gm	Its species can be classified into three genres, Gallinago, Coenocorypha and Lymnocryptes.
Hazel hen	La gelinotte	250–350 gm	Also known as *hazel grouse, wood grouse* or *ruffled grouse.* It is cooked in a similar way as partridge.
Grouse	La grouse	250–300 gm	Its famous species is *red grouse* which is usually preferred to be roasted.
Quail	La caille	50–100 gm	It may be roasted, grilled, sautéed, braised or stuffed and served as a canapé.
Teal	La sarcelle	200–400 gm	It is a small duck which yields one per portion.
Plover	Le pluvier	50–110 gm	This weight specification is given of golden plover. It is usually preferred to be roasted.
Guinea fowl	La pintade	1–1.5 kg	It resembles chicken with darker flesh. The young guinea fowl is known as *squabs.*
Pigeon	Le pigeon	300–400 gm	It is usually roasted. The *rock dove* is the ancestor of all domestic pigeons.
Turkey	Le dinde	3–15 kg	Both old as well as young turkey yield 250 gram per portion
Ostrich	Autruche	50–130 kg	Its flesh/meat is very much like beef, thus preferred to be cooked in the same way as tender beef.

Note. Guinea fowl which used to be classed as game bird is now raised on farms and is classed as poultry.

Games	
Furred/animal	It includes boar and bear, rabbit, hare, deer, chamois, roebuck (a male roe deer), hind (a female deer), stag (a young deer), reindeer (a large deer from Arctic and North America), camel, water buffalo, crocodile, kangaroo, etc.
Feathered/bird	It includes pheasant, pigeon, partridge, woodcock, snipe, grouse, goose, duck, teal, plover, hazel hen, quail, turkey, ostrich, guinea fowl, mountain cock, dove, coot, lark, rail, thrush, fieldfare, lapwing, corncake, etc.

KEY TERMS

Caribou : North American term for a species of deer.
Fawn up : Roebuck of up to six months.
Yearling : Roebuck of up to 18 months.

Brocket : Roebuck above 18 months.

Jugged hare : Red wine stew preparation made from hare.

Hog : Term is often associated with pork but also with uncastrated domestic male boar.

Squabs : Young guinea fowl.

Rock dove : Ancestor of all domestic pigeons.

REVIEW QUESTIONS

1. What is Le gibier a poil? Enlist any eight le gibier a poil and describe their parameters for quality selections.
2. What is Le gibier a plumage? Enlist any eight le gibier a plumage and describe their parameters for quality selections.
3. Enlist dishes for a continental menu based on game animal and game bird.

37 CHAPTER

Dairy Products

Objectives

Students will be able to:

- explain dairy products and further classify dairy products and their uses;
- explicate milk, its types and explain its culinary uses; and
- expound milk, cheese and butter composition.

DAIRY PRODUCT

The term *dairy product* is a collective term for all kinds of milk based products. These are usually high energy yielding food products. A production unit for the processing of milk is called *dairy factory*. Dairy products of all types whether simple or processed are among the most widely used ingredients in cooking and baking. Dairy products include milk, cheese, cream, butter and yogurt. Whether acting as a primary or secondary component in a dish, dairy products contribute in many ways to the final character of the finished products. Dairy products are an excellent source of calcium and proteins. They are also rich in Vitamins A, B and D. Most milk products are high in fats, which help to build up the body and provide energy.

But remember, most foods in this category do not consist of vitamins and minerals. Therefore, they are also known as *empty calorie* foods. A detailed description of various raw as well as processed dairy products is discussed below.

MILK

Milk Composition

Water	87 %
Proteins	3-4%
Fats	3-4%
Sugars	4-5%
Minerals	0.7%
Vitamins	A,B,D

Milk is a complete food. It is white, opaque liquid which is slightly sweet and nutritious produced by the mammary glands of mammals. Milk has been used for human consumption for thousands and thousands of years, as proven by cave drawings showing cows being milked. Today cow's milk is still one of the most popular (especially in the United States) animal milks consumed by humans. In a mixed diet it is particularly significant as a source of protein, calcium and riboflavin. Fresh whole milk contains a minimum of 3.25% butter fat (also known as *milk fat*), 8.5% non-fat milk solids and remaining 88% water. Milk is one of the most nutritious and wholesome natural product. Generally, milk is classified into two types (after processing), as given below.

(i) Pasteurized Milk

Pasteurization is a process of destroying bacteria (it may cause diseases like salmonella and hepatitis) with the help of controlled heating (at 145°F for 30 minutes), then quick cooling (to 40°F), in order to make the milk safe for consumption. It eliminates the possibility of diseases and gives milk a longer shelf life. Most commercial milk and cream products are pasteurized. The pasteurized milk can be further classified as skimmed milk and semi-skimmed milk.

Skimmed Milk

- ✓ It is pasteurized milk from which nearly all the fat has been removed (or contains less than ½ per cent milk fat). This milk is also known as "non-fat milk". As a result, the vitamin and mineral content is also reduced.

Semi-Skimmed Milk

- ✓ It is also pasteurized milk from which some of the fat has been removed, with a subsequent reduction in vitamin and mineral content. This milk is also known as "low-fat milk". It comes in two forms, i.e., with 2 per cent fat and with 1 per cent fat.

(ii) Homogenized Milk

Homogenization is a process by which the fat globules of milk are broken down mechanically until they are evenly and imperceptibly distributed throughout the milk. It helps in preventing milk from separating into fat and liquid parts. The end result is that the cream does not separate from the milk and the liquid is uniformly smooth. The homogenized milk can be further classified as sterilized milk, UHT milk and evaporated milk.

Sterilized Milk

- ✓ It is homogenized milk that is heated to about 150°C (or 276°F) for several seconds. Sterilization destroys all germs and increases the shelf life in an unopened bottle, which can be kept at room temperature for several weeks. After opening, it should be stored in refrigerator. Its flavour resembles that of caramel.

Other Milk Classes

- Condensed milk
- Untreated milk
- Fortified milk
- Flavoured milk
- Powdered milk

UHT Milk

✓ In it, homogenized milk is given an ultra heat treatment (heated at 132°C or 270°F for one second), then rapidly cooled. Nutritionally, it is similar to pasteurized milk although some vitamin B 12 may be lost during storage. When unopened, it has a shelf life of six months but once opened it should be kept in the refrigerator. Its flavour is different from pasteurized milk.

Evaporated milk

✓ It is concentrated homogenized milk, which is sterilized in the container and which, if unopened, will keep almost indefinitely. The water has been removed up to 60 per cent from this milk by the process of evaporation before canning/packing.

Note. Pasteurization is a process of heat treatment used to destroy bacteria in certain food products, particularly milk; it is invented by the French chemist Louis Pasteur.

Culinary Uses of Milk	
Soup and sauce	Milk can be used in preparing enormous range of soups (like in court bouillons) and sauces (like in béchamel sauce). Milk can be used to thicken sauces and to give flavour to various desserts.
Main dish	Milk is also used in *au gratin* dish and in most of the situations even used in meat cookery. Cream (a byproduct of milk) is used for garnishing many soups, especially cream soups.
Entremets	There are majority of hot and cold entremets which are made either directly from milk or indirectly from the milk based products like puddings, cakes, ice creams, pastries, etc.
Beverage	Milk plays a crucial role in making certain drinks like milk shakes, malted drinks, English tea, coffee, cocoa and chocolate. It is also used in making of various cocktails.
Others	Milk is used to produce various processed products like butter, cheese, yogurt, buttermilk, etc. It can also be consumed on its own or flavoured with vanilla, chocolate, etc.

PROCESSED AND FERMENTED MILK PRODUCTS

Cream

✓ *Cream* is produced from whole milk by separation and can be described as the fat of the milk with varying milk nutrients and water. The fat globules are more concentrated in cream than in the whole milk. It provides richness and body in items containing cream.

- ✓ Cream is separated from the milk and heat treated. Cream is separated from the milk by the process of *centrifugal force*. Unhomogenized milk naturally separates into two layers – a *milk fat* (rich cream on top) and almost *fat-free* (or skimmed) *milk* on the bottom.
- ✓ Many beverages, cereals, creamy casseroles, soups, sauces, ice creams, baked goods and sweet syrups contain creams.

Types of Pastry Cream

- Chantilly cream
- Confectionary
- French butter
- Almond cream

- ✓ When using cream in any dish add a thickening agent in order to replace the body that the cream would have given to the dish. A thickening agent will help to replace the texture but cannot normally replace the rich flavour. Cream is available in different forms like pastry cream, single cream, light cream and so forth.

TYPES OF CREAMS

Half Cream

- ✓ It is a thin cream with a minimum butterfat content of around 12%. This cream is mainly used as a pouring cream because it cannot be whipped. This cream is suitable for low fat diets. It is also known as *coffee cream* or *top of the milk* cream.

Half and Half Cream

- ✓ It is lighter than other creams and has a mixture of equal parts of milk and cream with butterfat content between 10.5–18%. Like half cream, this cream cannot be whipped, but it is good to serve with coffee, or on cereal.

Single Cream

- ✓ A cream or single cream has a minimum butterfat content of 18%. This cream is suitable for pouring but not for whipping. It is suitable to accompany desserts and also poured in cereals, coffee, soups, fruits plus a valuable addition to various cooked dishes.

Light Cream

- ✓ It is also called "coffee cream or table cream" and often single cream, it is richer with 18-30% butterfat (but commonly contains 20% butterfat), but still it cannot be whipped. It is a pasteurized cream made from cow's milk and mainly added in coffee preparations.

Double Cream

- ✓ Double cream is the name in Britain for a very rich cream, containing 48% butterfat. It is so rich and easy to over-whip which may cause it too thicken.
- ✓ Thus, some chefs add a tablespoon of milk to 8–10 ounces of double cream before whipping it to keep it loose enough. It is suitable to pour or float on coffee or soup preparations.

Whipping Cream

- ✓ Whipping cream or light whipping cream (with a butterfat content of 30–36%) is lighter than heavy cream, but it does whip. It develops a stable form when whipped. Its butterfat content creates a supporting structure, encapsulating air and holding it.
- ✓ Whipping cream will double in volume when whipped. It is suitable for topping, piping, cake and other entremets decoration and an ingredient for several other preparations (like pastry filling).

Heavier Cream

- ✓ Heavier cream or heavy whipping cream (with at least 36% fat) is heavy enough to whip, and is not as prone as lower-fat creams to curdling in sauces.
- ✓ The higher the butterfat content, the less beating is required to get whipped cream. It is suitable for cake decoration and enriching sauces and soups.

Crème Fraiche

- ✓ Crème Fraiche (contains 28% fat content) is a matured and thickened cream with a slightly tangy, nutty flavour and velvety rich texture. The thickness of crème fraiche can range from that of commercial sour cream to almost as solid as room-temperature margarine.
- ✓ It is suitable for sauce and soup preparations because it can boil without curdling. It is also delicious over fresh fruits or desserts like warm cobblers or puddings.

Clotted Cream

- ✓ Clotted cream (contains 55% fat content) is made by gently heating to rich un-pasteurized milk until a semi-solid layer of cream forms on the surface. After cooling, the thickened cream is removed.
- ✓ It is suitable for spreading on bread or spooned atop fresh fruits or desserts (such as with scones, fruit and fruit pies) and in traditional English *cream tea*. It is also known as "Devonshire or Devon Cream".

Sour Cream

- ✓ Sour cream (contains 18% butterfat content) is a fermented milk product cultured or fermented by the addition of lactic acid bacteria to cream. The bacteria grow in the cream and make acid a byproduct, giving the cream a tangy flavour and thick texture. It often contains gelatin, rennin and vegetable enzymes. It is suitable for cooking and baking.
- ✓ *Smetana* is one of the names for a range of sour creams which is very much similar to Crème Fraiche. Smetana (containing 10–30% milk fat content) is cross between soured cream and yogurt. It is suitable for baking and cooking.

Note.

- A chef can substitute the cream by evaporated milk (it is lower in fat, and hard to whip plus it also has a slight burnt milk taste) or yogurt (it tends to curdle in hot sauces or soups, but it works well in cold soups.)
- Europeans go for even heavier creams, like double cream (with a butterfat content from 42% to 48%), extra-thick double cream, and clotted cream or Devonshire cream, which is often spread like butter over scones.
- Sour cream is not soured cream. *Sour cream* is sweet cream blended with a culture and allowed to ripen to a tart flavour whereas *soured cream* is suitable for savoury dishes and also widely used in salad dressing.

CHEESE

- ✓ The term *cheese* refers to a dairy product made from the pressed curds of milk. It is available in different textures usually soft, semi-soft, hard and fresh cheese.
- ✓ The expensive cheeses do not necessarily contain higher food value. The extra expense is due to the cost of popular flavouring techniques and the supply and demand status of market. Cheese takes approximately nine parts of milk to produce one pound of cheese.

CHEESE COMPOSITION	
Fat	35%
Water	30%
Proteins	30%
Minerals	4.3%
Vitamins	A & D

- ✓ Cheese is produced by separating milk solids (or curds) from *whey* by curdling process (by selected bacteria or *rennet*), causing the proteins (*casein*) to coagulate. The curds are then drained, processed and cured or aged in a variety of ways. The milk can be of cow, goat, ewe, camel or buffalo.
- ✓ Cheese is eaten raw and is also cooked (or used) in large number of dishes, from cocktail snacks to main meals. Cheese can become tough and rubbery when it is heated for too long hours or at a very high temperature. Remember that protein coagulates with heat.

✓ Fat in cheese is solid at room temperature and when warmed it softens, therefore when cheese is heated, it melts. Cream cheeses are mostly used in cooking like "Cheddar". A brief description on different varieties of cheese is given below.

Soft Cheese

Usually cow's, goat's and sheep's milk is used for making soft cheese. Soft cheese owes its soft texture to high moisture content as *whey* is only partially drained from the curd. Cheese is then ripened and hence derived its name from the mould or bacteria used during their ripening process. The majority of soft cheeses is foreign in origin and is sold either in the fresh state or when fully ripe and mature, when the flavour is strongest. Its examples include Lymeswold, Camembert, Brie (also known as *queen of cheese*), etc. Few famous soft cheese names are given below.

Brie	It is a French cheese which is made from cow's milk and round in shape like a small disc.
Camembert	It is also a French cheese which is made from cow's, goat's and sheep's milk and is round in shape.
Feta	It is a Greek cheese which is made from goat's and sheep's milk.
Munster	It is a French cheese which is made from cow's, goat's and sheep's milk.
Demi sel	It is also a French cheese which is made from sour milk.

Hard Cheese

The texture of these cheeses ranges from semi-hard to hard. Harder cheeses have lower moisture content than softer cheese. They are generally packed into molds under more pressure and aged for a longer period. Parmesan and Gruyere cheese are excellent examples of hard cheese. Few famous hard cheese names are given below.

Cheddar	It is an English (England) cheese which is nutty in flavour, relatively hard in texture and creamy in colour.
Cheshire	It is also an English (England) cheese which is slightly crumbly and soft in texture.
Derby	It is again an English cheese which is sage flavoured.
Parmesan	It is an Italian cheese which is dry in nature and exclusively used for cooking purpose.
Gruyere	It is a Swiss cheese made of cow's milk. It is darker in colour with more dense texture.

Semi-Hard Cheese

These cheeses range from semi-soft to fine in texture; the same bacteria that gives such cheeses their holes also contribute to their aromatic and sharp flavours. Cheeses of this type are ideal for melting and are mainly used on toast for quick snacks. Its examples include Port Salut and Edam. Few famous semi-hard cheese names are given below.

Caerphilly	It is an English cheese which is buttermilk flavoured.
Port Salut	It is a French cheese which has hard rind.
Lancashire	It is an English cheese which is similar to Cheshire cheese.
Leicester	It is an English cheese which is mild in flavour and orange in colour.
Wensleydale	It is a Yorkshire cheese which is made from sheep's, goat's or cow's milk.
Edam	It is a cheese from Holland which is pale yellow in colour and has a waxy texture.

Blue Cheese

It is made when the cheese is still in the form of loosely pressed curds, and may be further enhanced by piercing a ripening block of cheese with skewers in an atmosphere in which the mould is prevalent. The mold grows within the cheese as it ages. The cheese moulds may range from pale green to dark blue, and may be accompanied by white and crusty brown moulds. These cheeses have distinct blue veins which gives them their name, and, often, assertive flavours. This veining is caused by bacteria in the cheese which may occur naturally or be introduced. Blue cheese includes:

Danish Blue	It is a cheese from Denmark which is made from cow's milk and wrapped in foils.
Gorgonzola	It is an Italian cheese in which white curd is intersected by blue veins.
Roquefort	It is a French cheese which is made from cow's milk and has creamy and crumbly texture.
Stilton	It is an English cheese which has wrinkled surface and brownish grey in colour.
Dorset blue	It is an English cheese which is made from skimmed milk and closed in texture.

BUTTER

Butter is a natural dairy product made by churning fresh cream. During the churning process, the butter globules in the cream combine to form butter and the excess liquid known as *buttermilk* is drained off. Butter must have at least 80% milk fat and remaining 20% water and milk solids. Butter hardens at low temperature and melts when heated. Butter is valued as lubricant and flavouring agent

BUTTER COMPOSITION

Fat	83%
Water	13%
Salt	1%
Vitamins	A & D

for culinary preparations; butter gives richness and flavour to foods which are difficult to duplicate. But butter is not recommended for baking because it can add air due to whipping process which changes the density. Butter can be coloured (artificially) with *annatto*. Its colour may vary from creamy white to golden yellow. Butter is available in different forms; some of them are listed below.

TYPES OF BUTTER

Brown Butter

- ✓ It is also called "Beurre Noisette" in French. Brown butter is a whole melted butter that has been heated until it turns light brown or hazelnut (or noisette) in colour and gives off a nutty aroma.
- ✓ It is used for cooking poisson (fish) cooked *à la meuniere* in this butter. It is also used as an accompaniment for fish, sweetbreads, eggs and with certain vegetable based preparations.

Black Butter

- ✓ It is also called "Beurre Noir in French. It is made like brown butter but heated until it is little darker (but not absolutely black) in colour and then flavoured with a few drops of vinegar or lemon juice, capers and parsley.
- ✓ This butter has a strong flavour and often used to heighten the flavour of the item. It should accompany a dish but not over-power it. For instance, it usually accompanies eggs, fish, offal (like brains) and some vegetables.

Light Brown Butter (or Lemon Butter)

- ✓ It is also called "Beurre Meuniere" in French; it is a butter heated gently to a light brown colour. The cooking is finished with a dash of lemon juice and a pinch of chopped fresh parsley. This is mostly served with fish cooked *à la Meuniere.*

USES OF BUTTER

- As spreader
- Accompaniment
- As filling
- As base
- As frying agent
- As foundation
- As basting agent
- As glaze
- Preservative agent
- In bakery items

Lactic Butter

- ✓ It is made by ripening the cream under special conditions by bacterial culture that produces lactic acid and giving the butter its distinctive flavour and smooth texture.
- ✓ Thus, it is mildly acidic which enhances the keeping properties. This type of butter can be purchased unsalted or slightly salted where 1–1.5% salt is added.

Pasteurized Butter

✓ It is a commercial/factory produced and officially monitored butter. It has a fresh uniform taste (the milk is re-cultured with commercial fermenting agents). It can be kept for up-to-a-month in the refrigerator.

Cooking Butter

✓ It is a type of pasteurized butter which is mainly used in day-to-day cooking. Therefore, it is also called "table butter or dairy butter". It cannot be kept for a long time as in the case of pasteurized butter.

Restored Butter

✓ This type of butter is produced from poor quality of creams, re-blended with bicarbonate of soda for de-acidification.

Concentrated Butter

✓ It is an ordinary butter with water, salt and non-fat milk solids. It has a firm texture due to low moisture content. It is excellent for shallow frying, braising, and sautéing because it does not decompose at high temperature.

COMPOUND BUTTERS

- Garlic butter
- Anchovy butter
- Lobster butter
- Maitre d' hotel
- Shellfish butter

Flavoured Butter

✓ These are the butters to which various herbs and other ingredients have been added, creating different colours and flavours. Thus, they are also known as *compound butter*.

✓ These are served cold with grilled meat, fish and with boiled vegetables. Its examples include garlic butter, anchovy butter, prawn butter, parsley butter, lemon butter, mustard butter, sardine butter, tarragon butter, and watercress butter.

Plain Butter

✓ Its examples include black butter, clarified butter, creamed butter, kneaded butter, melted butter, *noisette butter*, landaise butter, and so forth.

Melted Butter

✓ It is also known as "drawn butter". It is the simplest butter preparation of all, and one of the most widely used, especially as a dressing for legumes like asparagus, corn-on-the-cob, globe artichoke and so forth.

Sweet Cream Butter

✓ Sweet cream butters are most commonly used butters. These are made by using pasteurized cream to which salt is added to give a long life. The salt content is usually between 1–1.5%. They have a mild and delicate flavour and can be stored for six weeks (in refrigerator).

Other Butters

✓ These include butters like salted, unsalted, clarified, whipped butter, kneaded butter, white butter, beurre maitre d'hotel (or parsley flavoured butter) and so forth.

Note.

- *Kneaded butter* or beurre manié (a French term) is a paste made of softened butter and flour (usually in equal parts) used to thicken the sauces.
- *White butter* or beurre blanc (a French term) is a classic French sauce made of wine, vinegar and shallot reduction into which chunks of cold butter are whisked until the sauce becomes thick and smooth. It is excellent with poultry, seafood, vegetables and eggs.

YOGURT (HUNG CURD)

Classes of Yogurt

- Plain yogurt
- Frozen yogurt
- Flavoured
- Fat free yogurt
- Low fat yogurt
- Jameed yogurt
- Matsoni

Yogurt is made by adding special harmless bacteria to milk. The result is a thick, creamy product that is like custard and has a tangy flavour. Nowadays, yogurt is made in carefully controlled environments and by the requisite bacteria (usually *Lactobacillus bulgaricus* and *Streptococcus thermophilus*). Though yogurt can be made from the milk of many animals but among all cow's milk is most commonly used. Yogurt contains similar nutrients as milk because it is more concentrated, however, yogurt has more nutrients than similar amount of milk. It may be fortified with vitamins A and D. Generally, yogurt comes in several forms, plain, frozen, flavoured, fat free (0.5%) and low fat (1.5%). Remember curd is different from yogurt. Particularly curd is prepared by curdling milk with an edible acidic substance like vinegar and lemon juice. Now curd has lactic acid bacteria or *Lactobacillus.*

KEY TERMS

Homogenized milk	: Milk that has been processed so that the cream does not separate out.

Au gratin	:	Dish baked and served in same container.
Centrifugal force	:	Process by which cream is separated from the milk.
Devonshire cream	:	Devon cream or cream used in tea preparation.
Whey	:	Mixture of water, salt and other solids present in the milk.
Queen of cheese	:	Brie cheese.
Annatto	:	Artificial colouring agent used to colour butter.
Compound butter	:	Term for all types of flavoured butter.
Hung curd	:	Yogurt; but not curd.
Smetana	:	Low fat byproduct; it is a cross between soured cream and yogurt.

REVIEW QUESTIONS

1. What is milk? Enlist any ten different products made from milk and explain them briefly.
2. Differentiate between curd and yogurt.
3. What is cheese? Classify cheese into different groups and explain each one with examples.
4. Elucidate different types of butter and describe their uses in different food preparations.

38 CHAPTER

Rice, Cereals, Pulses and Pasta Cookery

Objectives

Students will be able to:

- classify cereal, rice, pulses and pasta products;
- explicate culinary uses of cereals; and
- plan a menu based on different cereals.

CEREAL

Cereals are the products of the widely cultivated grasses (for their edible seeds called *grain*) which provide a staple food for humans. Different cereals are grown in different regions of the country. The most popular grains are – barley, corn, millet, oats, rice, wheat, etc. As cereals are inexpensive, thus they are readily available source of protein; simultaneously they have more carbohydrates than any other food. Nowadays, cereals are a staple food commodity throughout the world.

Note. Generally, cereal is composed of 60-80% carbohydrates, 7-13% protein and 1-8% fat.

Commonly Eaten Breakfast Cereals

- Granola
- Groats
- Porridge
- Flakes
- Grits
- Oatmeal
- Muesli

CLASSIFICATION OF CEREALS

Wheat

✓ It grows in dry and temperate climates; it is the most common cereal in the Western world. Wheat is the world's largest cereal grass crop and position as a staple commodity after rice. Unlike other cereals, wheat contains a relatively high amount of gluten – the protein that provides the elasticity which is necessary for bread making.

✓ It is ground into flour which is used in making numerous preparations. Wheat varieties include wheat berries (or hard wheat berries), soft wheat berries (or pastry berries), cracked wheat, rolled wheat (or wheat flakes) and so forth. Most of the wheat based products are eaten as *breakfast cereals*.

Rice

- ✓ It grows in damp, tropical climates; it is chiefly grown in India, South America and Italy. Today, rice is a staple diet for almost half the world's population, particularly in parts of China, India, Indonesia, Japan and Southeast Asia. Currently, there are more than 7000 varieties of rice cultivated.
- ✓ Rice is generally eaten whole (apart from the husk) but it can also be eaten in other forms like as rice flour, fermented drink (or *sake*); also served as a side dish, and as base for entrées or desserts.

Corn

- ✓ It is also known as "maize, sweet corn or corn-on-the-cob". It is mainly grown in parts of America, Africa and India. Corn is not only a popular commodity, but the foundation of many byproducts including corn flour and corn whiskey.
- ✓ Besides being served as a vegetable, it is processed into cornflakes and cornflour. Its oil is also suitable for cooking purpose. Cornstarch (ground corn flour) is used for making puddings and cakes or eaten as whole kernels or on the cob.
- ✓ Corn flour is also used as a thickening agent in several dishes. Corn's varieties include *baby corn, popcorn, purple corn, Indian corn, nixtamal*, etc.

USES OF CEREALS

- Thickening agent
- Coating agent
- Beverage making
- Dessert making
- Side dishes
- Fermented cereals

Oat

- ✓ It is mainly grown in Scotland and the north of England. It is ground particularly into three grades, i.e., fine, medium and coarse. It is used in several forms like oatmeal for porridge (or rolled oats), cookies, scones; rolled oats are also used.
- ✓ Oatmeal is also used for thickening soups, coating foods, in cakes and *haggis*. Oats are high in vitamin B_1 and contain a good amount of vitamins B_2 and E. Its varieties include *instant oats, quick oats, oat groats, rolled oats, steel cut oats*, etc.

Others

- ✓ Cereals like bran (the outer layer of grains), rye, barley, buckwheat, triticale, black quinoa, millet/pearl millet, sago (made from pith of the sago palm), arrowroot (made from maranta, a West Indian plant), tapioca (made from cassava plant) and so on.

✓ In barley, the whole grain of barley is called "pot or scotch barley". *Pearl barley* has most of the bran and germ removed and then polished. *Sprouting barley* (or unrefined barley) and *hulled barley* (or processed barley) are other famous varieties of barley.

Note. In cereal cookery, often a term *whole cereal* is used which means cereals with only the husk removed; these are too hard for human consumption. But it is high in nutrition; refined cereals have less flavour and provide less fibre and vitamins than whole cereals.

Processed Cereals	
Bran based	Raisin Bran, Fiber One, Bran Flakes, etc. are some excellent examples.
Oat groat	Oatmeal and Cheerios are excellent examples of oat based breakfast cereals.
Corn based	Corn Flakes and Frosted Flakes are two excellent brands of corn based cereals.
Rice based	Cerelac and Rice Krispies are excellent brands of rice based cereals.
Wheat based	Raisin Wheat, Wheatena, Wheat Flakes, Wheaties, Weetabix, Shredded Wheat, etc.

PULSES

According to FAO (Food and Agriculture Organization of the United Nations), *pulses* are defined as annual leguminous crops yielding from one to twelve grains or seeds of variable size, shape and colour within a pod. Pulses are important food crops due to their high protein and essential amino acid content. Like many leguminous crops, pulses play a key role in crop rotation due to their ability to fix nitrogen. Pulses are available in enormous range.

Classification of Pulses

There are incalculable ways to classify pulses, for example in India pulses are usually classified into three categories, whole pulses, split pulses with skin and split pulses with skin removed. But broadly, pulses can be classified as given below.

Uses of Pulses

- In soups
- In stews
- As a salad
- As a side dish
- As a main dish

Dry beans

✓ These beans include pulses like Kidney bean, Haricot bean, Pinto bean, Navy bean, Lima bean, Butter bean, Azuki bean/Adzuki bean, Mung bean, Golden gram, Green gram, Black gram, Urd, Scarlet runner bean, Moth bean, Tepary bean, etc.

Dry broad beans and peas

✓ Dry broad beans include Horse bean, Broad bean, Field bean, etc., and dry peas include Garden pea, Protein pea, etc.

Minor pulses

✓ These include pluses like Lablab, Hyacinth bean, Jack bean, Sword bean, Winged bean, Velvet bean, Cowitch, Yam bean, etc.

Others pulses

✓ These include pluses like Chickpea, Garbanzo, Bengal gram, Dry cowpea, Black-eyed pea, Blackeye bean, Pigeon pea, Cajan pea, Congo bean, Lentil, Bambara groundnut, Earth pea, Vetch, Common vetch, Lupins, etc.

RICE

Rice is the seed of the grass species *Oryza sativa* (Asian rice) or *Oryza glaberrima* (African rice). As a cereal grain, rice is a staple food mostly growing in tropical and temperate zones and it is cultivated in more than 100 countries. There are more than 7000 varieties of rice produced throughout the world. Rice is always eaten cooked either hot or cold, as a sweet or savoury dish.

CLASSES OF RICE

- Long rice
- Medium rice
- Short rice

Classification of Rice

Everyone knows that there are many different types of rice. There are more than 7000 rice varieties throughout the world therefore it is very difficult to define every variety. The below given rice classification is based on the type of processing rice receives after harvesting:

USES OF RICE

- As stuffing
- As main dish
- As thickener
- As sweet dish
- As side dish

Paddy rice

✓ It is also called "aquatic rice" as it is cultivated in flooded areas. It is un-husked rice in its raw position, with no further treatment after threshing. It contains approx. 20-25% moisture content.

Brown rice

✓ It is also called "husked or whole rice". It is unprocessed rice from which the outer husk is removed. Thus, it takes more time to cook. It is light brown in colour and more flavourful and chewy than polished rice. This rice variety has some of the B complex vitamins, phosphorous and starch.

White rice

✓ It is also called "un-polished rice". The white rice has the husk, bran and germ removed by passing the grains through the machines that scrape the grains. It takes less time to cook in comparison to brown rice.

Polished rice

✓ Regular white rice is sometimes referred to as "polished rice". It is white rice that has been passed through machines that remove any flour still adhering to the grain.

Glaced rice

✓ It is polished rice which is covered but with a fine layer of French chalk suspended in a glucose solution and specially processed to give it an attractive sheen.

Steamed rice

✓ It is also called "pre-treated rice". This is paddy rice that has been meticulously cleaned, soaked in hot water, steamed at a low pressure and then dehusked, finally blanched.

✓ *Pre-cooked rice* is also known as "instant rice" but it is different from steamed rice. It is completely cooked then dehydrated and can be made ready to eat just after five minutes of boiling.

EXAMPLES OF RICE DISHES

- Risotto Maigre
- Riz à la Creole
- Riz Pilaf
- Riz à la Grecque
- Riz a l' Indienne
- Riz Portugaise
- Riz au Blanc
- Riz au Gras
- Risotto a l' Italienne
- Riz à la Turque

Parboiled rice

✓ It is also called "converted rice or processed rice" as the rice that has been husked or blanched, soaked afterwards boiled for 1-3 minutes then dried at 200°C.

✓ This treatment gelatinizes the starch in the grain and also infuses some of the nutrients of the bran and germ into the kernel's heart. It will be fluffy, plump and separate when cooked.

Wild rice

- ✓ The seed (black and white seed) of this rice is from aquatic grass (type of rice plant). It is grown mainly in China, Japan and USA and grown one by one up the stalk.
- ✓ It is more expensive and sometimes added with brown rice. It is cooked like other rice but requires around 45 minutes of boiling.

Basmati rice

- ✓ Basmati is long-grain rice from India, considered one of the best quality white rice. It has a distinctive aroma and, when cooked, each grain should remain separate, giving a light, fluffy result.
- ✓ It is a perfect accompaniment to Indian curries and is used in biryani and pilaf dishes. Basmati rice should be rinsed thoroughly twice or thrice, with clean water everytime before cooking.

Ways of Cooking Rice

- In water
- In milk
- Au gras
- In steam

Aromatic rice

- ✓ A general term used for rice with a perfumy, nutlike flavour and aroma. It is a broad category of rice in itself and the category is also known as "perfumed rice".
- ✓ Among the category, the most popular aromatic rice is Indian Basmati rice, Thai Jasmine rice, Texas Texmati rice, etc.

Arborio

- ✓ It is medium, superfine, pearly rice (or the classic *risotto rice*) from the north Italian region of Piedmont. It is probably the best all-rounder for cooking.
- ✓ It is a medium to long grain rice that can absorb a lot of cooking liquid yet retain a good 'bite' when fully cooked (it takes 20 minutes to cook). Starch releases during the cooking process that makes the grains creamy.

Other rices

- ✓ These include rice like *popped rice* (resemble popcorns), *camolino rice* (polished and oil coated rice), *Surinam rice* (long and thin sized rice), *sticky rice* (long rice with high starch content), *puffed rice* (Indian style rice, roasted and fried on hot sand), *Mochi* (a short rice from Japan), etc.

Note.

- Rice can also be prepared as a breakfast cereal like *rice flakes*. This is the rice that is steamed, husked then flattened into thin flakes; it is mostly eaten during breakfast hours with milk and sugar.
- *Rice semolina* also called "rice flour" is another famous cereal product. It is made by grinding fragments of very white rice; it is used in making cakes and pastries and to thicken sauces.
- *Rice paper* is a thin edible paper produced from rice and used in the preparation of nougat and macaroons.

PASTA COOKERY

It is an Italian preparation available in various shapes and designs. In Italy, the word *pasta* means "paste" and refers to the dough used for making pasta. The pasta is made from durum wheat, semolina, water and often eggs. It is sold dried or ready to cook (in boiling water with salt) form. Pasta can be stuffed with a filling of minced meat, spinach, chicken liver, cheese, herbs, etc., and may also be prepared plain with appropriate sauce. Broadly, it can be classified into two groups—long and short pastas.

Classification of Pasta

The term pasta is used broadly and generically to describe a wide variety of noodles made from this type of dough. Some dough has a little egg added, though doughs made with only flour and eggs are generally referred to as noodles. There are hundreds of shapes, sizes, thicknesses and colours of pasta. But broadly it can be classified as long and short pasta.

Long pasta

- ✓ Long pasta shapes differ only by the section, length is approximately ten inches. For this reason, eating requires some practice. Do not let pasta stick together while cooking, so as soon as chef dips the pasta into water, he stirs with a wooden spoon.
- ✓ Some famous long pastas include fettuccine (like ribbon and flat spaghetti), spaghetti (like strings), spaghettini (thinner strings than spaghetti), vermicelli (very thin), linguine (wider), tagliatelle (like ribbon and flat spaghetti but thin), angel hair (extremely thin), capellini (thin and round pasta, substitute of vermicelli but slightly thicker than angel hair) and so on.

Other Pastas

- Alfabeto
- Stelle
- Ravioli
- Cannelloni
- Gnocchi
- Lasagne
- Retelle
- Tortellini
- Ziti rigati
- Gemelli
- Acomo pepe

Short pasta

✓ Short pastas can have a variety of shapes and are easier to eat than long pasta. Some famous short pastas include farfalle (like bow ties), conchiglie (like sea shell), conchigliette (like small sea shell), conchiglioni, lumache, radiotore, fusilli (like spiral), gemelli, penne, macaroni, rigatoni, ruote, cavatelli, mostaccioli (shorter and wider tubes), ziti (break if too long), perciatelli (broken), tubetti (little tubes), tripoline (bow tie shaped but with round edges) and so forth.

Note. In Italy, pasta is usually served as a main course, whereas in France, it is served as an accompaniment. Like Italians enjoy their pasta, Germany has *spaetzle*, Poles have *pierogi* and Orient enjoy varieties of noodles.

Examples of Pasta Based Dishes

Spaghetti Based	Gnocchi Based	Macaroni Based
• Alla Bolognese	• Piemontaise	• Au gratin
• Italienne	• Romaine	• Au Jus
• Alla Napoletana	• Parisienne	• Nantua
• Au Parmesan	• Au gratin	• Aux Truffes
• Alla Carbonara	• Alla bava	• A' l' anglaise
• Alla Carrettiera	• Venitienne	• A' l' italienne
• Alla zappatora		• En croquettes
• All' amatriciana		**Other Pastas**
• Al dente		• Lasagne al forno
• Milanaise		• Cannoli
		• Vongole

KEY TERMS

Nixtamal	:	Maize kernels which have undergone nixtamalization, i.e., hulling, soaking and cooking in an alkaline solution.
Sake	:	Japanese brewed drink usually serves warm.
Pearl barley	:	Barley that has most of the bran and germ removed and then polished.
Hulled barley	:	Processed barley.
Risotto	:	Italian rice (as well as rice preparation) like Arborio rice.

Rice flakes : Rice that is steamed, husked then flattened into thin flakes; mainly eaten during breakfast hours with milk and sugar.

Rice paper : A thin edible paper produced from rice and used in the preparation of nougat and macaroons.

Pierogi : Polish specialty which looks like half-moon-shaped noodles.

Spaetzle : Literally means *little sparrow,* a mixture of flour, eggs, cream/milk, salt and sometimes nutmeg which is formed into small dumplings. These are poached in boiling water.

REVIEW QUESTIONS

1. What is cereal? Enlist any ten processed cereals.
2. Define the term pasta. Classify pasta and support each category with ten pasta examples.
3. Elucidate different types of rice and briefly explain each type.
4. Write down the different uses of cereals in cookery.

39

CHAPTER

Introduction to Basic Ingredients

Objectives

Students will be able to:

- classify flour, salt, pepper and sugar;
- explicate wheat structure and type; and
- expound functions and culinary uses of basic ingredients.

BASIC INGREDIENTS

The term *basic ingredient* refers to all those essential materials without which no one/ any products (or dish) can be prepared in any kitchen department. In simple terms, basic ingredient is related with all those fundamental kitchen ingredients used in majority of preparations. It is very difficult to surmise and describe every basic ingredient in one chapter because these are countless. But some of them which are constantly found in every kitchen are listed here, for instance, flour, salt, pepper, sugar, mustard, vinegar, colourants, essence, nuts and so forth.

Remember, these basic ingredients are often used in almost every kitchen unit and in majority of dishes (from hot kitchen to cold kitchen preparations). A brief description of each of these given ingredients is given below.

FLOUR

The finely ground and sifted meal of any of the various edible grains is called *flour*. It can range in texture from coarse to extremely soft and powdery, depending on the degree of bolting (sifting) it receives at the mill. Wheat is the most common source of the multitude of flours used in cooking. It contains gluten, a protein that forms an elastic network which helps to retain the gases and make mixtures (such as batters and doughs) rise as they are baked.

Wheat Structure

- Endosperm
- Bran
- Scutellum
- Germ

Types of Flour

Flour can be classified on the basis of ingredients used to mill, intended purpose of use in cookery, gluten content/protein content and so forth properties. Different types of flour are suited to different products, thus one cannot switch flour type with another particularly while making bakery products. Broadly, flour can be classified as given below.

Wheat based flour: It is the most commonly used flour in catering industry and is available in two forms — white wheat flour and whole wheat flour. *White wheat flour* is made after removing the bran (outer covering layer) and germs from kernels. It contains approximately 63-73% starch with 7-12% protein. The rest is moisture, fat, sugar and minerals. On the other hand, *whole wheat flour* is coarser than white wheat flour and contains the bran, germ and endosperm of the wheat kernel, which give the flour a high fibre, nutrition and fat content. Some common wheat based flours are given below.

Bread flour (12-14% protein)

- ✓ It contains high gluten and is made from mixing of milled wheat grains. As it has high gluten content, thus suitable for making breads with good volume. It is usually bleached, which results in flour being stripped off the bran and germ, so it needs to be enriched for nutritional reasons.
- ✓ It is usually milled using steel rollers instead of stone grinding, the higher temperature from the steel rollers destroys more of the delicate nutrients, which then also need to be replaced.

> **WHITE WHEAT**
> Includes bread flour, AP flour, cake flour, etc.

Cake (5-8% protein) and pastry flour (8-9% protein)

- ✓ *Cake flour* contains low gluten and comes from soft wheat, thus it has a fine texture with high starch content like a powder and is suitable to make cakes and other delicate tender baked goods.
- ✓ *Pastry flour* is very similar to cake flour (in texture) and suitable to make pastries and other delicate baked goods. But it contains medium gluten while cake flour has low gluten.

All-purpose flour (10-12% protein)

- ✓ It contains medium gluten (with moderate amount of protein) and it is a very versatile flour made with blends of hard and soft wheat flours, usually bleached and enriched.
- ✓ Dough made with all-purpose flour should be kneaded shorter than dough made from bread flour to fully develop the gluten. It is suitable for making bread and pastry. All-purpose flour comes in two basic forms, bleached and unbleached.

Types of All-Purpose Flour	
Bleached flour	It is artificially aged flour, aged with bleaching agent (it affects carotenoids), maturing agent (it affects gluten formation) or both.
Unbleached flour	It is simple flour that has not been treated with any bleaching agent, thus the resultant flour differs in colour and is not pure white in colour like graham flour.

Patent flour

✓ It contains high gluten and it is a super blend of hard and soft wheat flours, usually bleached and enriched. It is suitable for making high quality baked bread products.

Self rising flour

✓ It contains medium gluten and it is simply an ordinary all-purpose flour to which baking powder has been added. It should not be used with yeast fermented products, and is generally suitable for making cakes and muffins.

Other forms of flours: As we have discussed above that flour is made by grinding and sifting wheat but along with wheat it can also be made from some other grains, for instance, rye, barley, corn, rice, potato or soya products. A brief description of several flours except wheat based are given below.

Uses of Flour

- As binding agent
- As main item
- Thickening agent
- Texture
- Yeast grower
- Nutritive agent

Corn flour

✓ It is a finely ground cornmeal based flour. It is white or yellow in colour and is mainly suitable to use as a breading or in combination with other flours.

Durum flour

✓ It contains high protein and is made from durum wheat. Durum wheat is used to make semolina, which is combined with water to make pasta dough. It is also known for its high amount of gluten.

Rice-flour

✓ An extremely thin noodle, resembling translucent white hair, made from rice flour. They explode upon contact with hot oil, becoming a tangle of light, crunchy strands. They are a traditional ingredient in Chinese chicken salad and can be pre-soaked and used in soups and stir-fries.

Rye flour

- ✓ It contains very low gluten and it is a finely ground flour made from rye grain. It is usually blended with white or whole wheat flours to increase its gluten content. It may be white, medium or dark in colour, among which medium being the one used for rye bread making. It is the most important bread flour after wheat flour.

Masa harina

- ✓ It is traditional Mexican flour. *Masa* is a paste made by soaking maize in lime and then grinding it up. Masa Harina is the flour made by drying and powdering masa. It is used in Mexican cooking for items such as *corn tortillas.* The literal meaning is "dough flour".

Others

- ✓ It includes flours like bolted flour (unbleached flour), semolina flour, instantized flour, seasoned flour, pumpernickel flour, instant flour, gluten flour, etc.
- ✓ *Seasoned flour* is made by adding seasoning (it may include salt, pepper, paprika, herbs, spices, etc.) to any flour. *Pumpernickel flour* contains very low gluten and is a coarsely ground rye flour with bran particles left in. *Instantized flour* is pre-sifted, specially prepared to dissolve smoothly into gravies and sauces.

Note. Whole wheat flour contains medium gluten and it is usually stone grounded which results in a higher level of natural nutrients, it is due to lower milling temperature. It contains the germ or fat portion of the wheat kernel and if to be stored for any length of time then it should be refrigerated. The highest amount of protein content is found in *durum wheat* which is used to make macaroni.

Hard and Soft Wheat	
Wheat and its processed product flour is classified on the basis of its consistency (or hardness), therefore wheat can also be classified as	
Hard wheat	A wheat which is high in protein and well suited for bread making, pasta, semolina because it produces flour that is rich in gluten, is known as *hard wheat.* The flour made from this wheat is called *hard flour* and produces a large volume and fine texture in bread products. It contains 10–14% protein.
Soft wheat	It is ground for flour and available in varying degrees of whiteness, depending on how much of the husk is removed. The flour made from this wheat has lower protein content, hence called *soft flour* and is mainly used to make cakes, pastries, cookies, etc. It contains 5–10% protein.

SALT

Forms of Salt

- Coarse salt
- Cooking salt
- Table salt

Salt (sodium chloride) is a mineral deposit found in different parts of the earth. It is a white crystallized odourless sharp tasting substance which is used as a condiment and preservative agent. In its pure state, salt consists of sodium chloride and is abundant in nature. The term *salt* is derived from the Latin word "salary" which means money for the purchase of salt. Commercially solid salt comes from two major sources i.e. – sea (sea salt) and mine (rock salt).

Types of Salt

Salt is an essential condiment and remains an essential raw material in the food industry (for canned foods, salted meat and fish, charcuterie, cheese, etc.). In the market, salt is available in several types.

Functions of Salt

- Enhance flavour
- Nutritive agent
- Leavening agent
- Binding agent
- Colour control
- Curing agent
- Preservative agent
- Maintain body
- Control fermentation
- Flavouring agent
- Freezing agent
- For skinning
- For filleting

Iodized salt

✓ It is a mixture of table salt with added iodine (sodium iodine), thus sold as table salt. It is an important preventative for hypothyroidism.

Celery salt

✓ It is a mixture of salt and celery root and is purchased as ready-made product. It is used for seasoning and flavouring certain dishes as well as stocks and consommés and soups as an alternative to fresh celery or celery seed. It is also used in tomato juice based cocktails.

Lovage salt

✓ It is a table salt flavoured with dried ground *lovage root* (from plant *Levisticum officinale*). It has more body than celery salt. It is mainly used in soups and sauces, particularly in German culinary.

Kosher salt

✓ It is an additive-free, coarse salt used in preparing meat based dishes in accordance to orthodox Jew's religious law. Many non-orthodox cooks also prefer it to cling to the food.

Spiced salt

- ✓ It is a mixture of ordinary table salt with white ground pepper and mixed spices in the ratio of 10:1:1. It is used to season forcemeats, pies and terrines.

Pickling salt

- ✓ It is a fine-grained salt used to make brines for pickles, sauerkraut, etc. It contains no additives, which would cloud the brine.

Seasoned salt

- ✓ It is a regular salt but with the combination of other flavouring ingredients, for instance, onion salt, garlic salt and celery salt.

Curing salt

- ✓ It is also called "nitrite salt" and mainly used to cure meats and retain the red colour of the meat product. It is a preservative salt which is used in the delicatessen and food preservation industry. It is a blend of 94% salt and 6% sodium nitrite.

Hickory salt

- ✓ It is a smoky flavoured American condiment; consists of sea salt mixed with smoked finely pounded hickory wood. It has slightly nutty taste and is mainly used in barbecue preparations. It is good for seasoning traditional southern-style barbecue preparations particularly ham or pork roast.

Other salts

- ✓ These include salts like *Sel Chinois* (a Chinese salt called Monosodium Glutamate–MSG in France), *Diet salt* (a substitute salt- salt minus sodium chloride), *Tenderizing salt* (an ordinary salt with 2–3% papain), etc.

Important Fact

To make the salt less hydroscopic, various products are added to it (like magnesium carbonate, sodium silicoaluminate, etc.), the quantity of which must never exceed 2%.

PEPPER

Pepper is one of the most important spices derived from the genus *Piper nigrum.* It is used in a variety of dishes around the world to enhance the flavour of both savoury and sweet preparations. Besides, the term pepper is also used for several other seasonings and condiments particularly paprika and cayenne. As pepper stimulates the gastric juices, it delivers a digestive bonus and gentle warmth (to food) as well. As we know, pepper is a condiment that has been salt's associate on every guest table. It adds a flavour of its own to dishes, as well as enhancing the taste of other ingredients.

USES OF PEPPER

- As seasoning
- In sauces
- As condiment

Types of Pepper

Pepper is the world's most popular spice and it is a berry that grows in grape-like clusters on the pepper plant (*Piper nigrum*), a climbing vine native to India and Indonesia. The berry is processed to produce three basic types of peppercorn, black, white and green peppers. In the market, pepper is available in several types.

Black pepper

✓ It is the most commonly used peppercorn, which is picked when the berry is not quite ripe, then dried until it shrivels and the skin turns red/dark brown to black.

✓ It is very strong and pungent in flavour, slightly hot with a hint of sweetness. Among the best black peppers are the *Tellicherry* and the *Lampong*.

White pepper

✓ It is less pungent than black pepper and has been allowed to ripen, after which the outer husk is removed by rubbing in salt water (or remove skin from black peppercorn) and the berry is dried.

✓ The result is a smaller, smoother-skinned, lighten berry with a milder flavour. White pepper is used to a great extent for appearance, usually in white sauces and light-coloured foods where dark specks of black pepper would stand out.

Green pepper

✓ The green peppercorn is the soft, under-ripe berry that is usually preserved in vinegar or brine. It has a fresh flavour thus less pungent and fruitier than the berry in its other forms. These peppercorns are mostly used in broiled meat or poultry. They can also be mashed and added to sauces.

Paprika

✓ It is produced from capsicums grown in Hungary. It is a bright red mild pepper mostly used in *goulash* and for decorating hors d'oeuvres, for example, egg mayonnaise. It has a fine aromatic taste and it is also not as hot as other peppers.

Szechuan pepper

- ✓ Truly, it is not a kind of pepper but resembles black peppercorns with a tiny seed. Simply, one can say that these are dried red brown berries that come from prickly ash tree that have a peppery and lemony aroma.
- ✓ It is also one of the spices used in Chinese five-spice powder. It is also known as *anise* pepper, *Chinese* pepper, fagara, flower pepper, *sansho* and *Sichuan* pepper.

Cayenne pepper

- ✓ A hot, pungent powder made from several of various tropical chilies that originated in cayenne region of French Guiana. Cayenne pepper is also called *red pepper*.

Pink pepper

- ✓ Along with the above-mentioned peppercorn variety, there is one more type of peppercorn known as "pink peppercorn". But this is not a true peppercorn. It gives a rosy hue and peppery touch to the prepared food.

Note. Black and white peppercorns are available whole, cracked and coarsely or finely ground. It is always preferable that whole peppercorns should be freshly ground with a pepper mill - in order to deliver more flavour than does pre-ground pepper, which loses its flavour somewhat quickly.

SUGAR

Sugar is also known as "white gold". The term sugar usually denotes cane sugar or beet sugar, obtained from various plants. The scientific name of sugar is "sucrose"; it consists of a molecule of glucose combined with a molecule of fructose. The two main commercial sugar sources are sugar cane in tropical regions and sugar beet in temperate regions. The sugar type that is mainly used in the home is *sucrose*.

SUGAR TYPES

Glucose	Fruits
Fructose	Fruits
Sucrose	Beet
Lactose	Milk
Maltose	Grain

Note.

- Sugar starts caramelizing at 170°C and starts burning at about 190°C. Melting sugar in a sauce pan creates *caramel*.
- Crystallization of sugar is the technique of dissolving and boiling sugar and it requires great care, as the syrup has a tendency to re-crystallize, if not handled correctly.
- *Fructose* (sugar of *hexose class*) is a kind of sugar found in honey, fruit and castor sugar; *glucose* is found in animal's blood and honey; and *sucrose* is found in cane sugar.

Classification of Sugar

There are varieties of commercially prepared cane and beet sugar which are all the same in structure. Some of them are mentioned below.

FUNCTIONS OF SUGAR

- Enhance flavour
- Smooth flavour
- Modify texture
- Impart colour
- Preservative agent
- Prevent lumping
- Impart sweetness
- As a condiment
- Nutritive agent
- Used in syrup
- Start fermentation
- Maintain body
- Leavening agent

Refined sugar

✓ It is a white crystalline carbohydrate used as a sweetener and preservative agent. It is made from beet or cane sugar containing at least 99.9% sucrose with less than 0.06% moisture (dried in oven at 105°C) and less than 0.04% invert sugar. It is a highly purified sugar that may be sold as *granulated, castor* (superfine), or *lump sugar*.

White sugar

✓ It is a refined sugar with no or very limited impurities. It is purified by dissolving the sugar in water and then evaporating this treated water until it crystallizes. It contains at least 99.7% sucrose. It can be flavoured in a number of ways like with vanilla, orange peel, rose petals, ginger, etc. It is sold as fully refined sugar in the form of *granulated, castor* or *lump sugar.*

Brown sugar

✓ It is an unrefined (or partially refined) sugar which contains 85–99.5% sucrose. It is available in light and dark colour. Brown sugar gets its colour from some impurities or from just adding molasses back to white sugar to colour it. Lighter versions are mostly used in baking and making butterscotch, condiments and glazes whereas dark versions are good for gingerbread. True brown sugar is crystallized from the syrup remaining at the end of the refining process. Like the above both sugar types, it is also marketed as *granulated, castor* or *lump sugar*.

Granulated sugar

✓ It is white coloured refined sugar with coarse granules. In simple terms, it is a standard refined white sugar (with 99.9% sucrose) with crystals from 0.5 mm to 1 mm. This sugar is mainly used in bakery products (like to make *meringue*) because it easily dissolves in cake mixtures and other batters.

Castor sugar

✓ It is also known as "superfine or refined white sugar (or sucrose)" which can be made from crushed and sieved granulated sugar. Its sugar crystals are smaller than granulated sugar thus it can quickly and easily dissolve without forming lumps. Thus, it is mainly used in making desserts, pastries, cakes, meringues and other dairy products and drinks.

Lump sugar

✓ Refined sugar moulded into rectangular shape, thus found in packed cartons. This is a quick dissolving sugar that is compressed only, to give an open texture and quicker dissolution. It is good for all hot drinks and also for preparing sugar syrup and caramel.

Powder sugar

✓ It is also called "icing sugar, confectioner's sugar or sucre glace". It is a granulated sugar that has been crushed into a very fine powder with no particles larger than 0.1 mm (100 microns). It may also contain around 3% cornstarch to prevent caking. This sugar is mainly used to make icing, to dredge desserts and cakes, in whipping cream, etc., for decoration, and to make some confectionery items.

LIQUID SWEETENERS

- Barley malt syrup
- Blackstrap molasses
- Coconut syrup
- Corn syrup
- Orgeat syrup
- Maple syrup
- Simple sugar syrup

Maple sugar

✓ It is a solid sugar (saccharose) with a characteristic flavour crystallized from the sap of the sugar maple tree, i.e., *Acer saccharum.* It is also known as *stirred sugar* or *Indian sugar*. In sweetening powder, it is similar to cane and beet sugar. It also comes in syrup form, Maple Syrup.

Coloured sugar

✓ It is a tinted granulated sugar mainly used for decoration purpose. This sugar may be found in several crystal sizes.

Flavoured sugar

✓ It is a granulated sugar but with the combination of various flavouring ingredients. It may include seeds, roots, barks, stalks, etc. For instance, vanilla flavoured and cinnamon flavoured sugar.

Coarse sugar

✓ It is also known as "decorating sugar, crystal sugar or sanding sugar", as it contains granules about four times larger than those of regular granulated sugar. Like colour sugar, it is also used for decorating purpose mainly baked goods such as fondants and confections. It reflects light and gives the product sparkling appearance.

Stages of Sugar Cooking							
S. No.	Stages of Sugar	Degree of Cooking	Intended Purpose or Uses for	S. No.	Stages of Sugar	Degree of Cooking	Intended Purpose or Uses for
1.	Coated	100-101°C	Fruit syrups	2.	Small thread	101-102°C	Almond paste
3.	Large thread	102-103°C	Icing and frosting	4.	Small pearl	103-105°C	Jams and *torrone*
5.	Large pearl	107-109°C	Jams, sugar coated fruits, icings and frostings	6.	Soft ball	116-118°C	Jams, soft caramels, jellies nougats and Italian meringue
7.	Hard ball	121-124°C	Jams, sugar decorations, Italian meringue, fondant and caramels	8.	Soft crack	129-135°C	To make toffees
9.	Hard crack	149-150°C	Boiled sweets, candies, sugar flowers, icings, candy floss	10.	Light caramel	151-160°C	Caramelization (crème caramel) and flavouring sweets like puddings and cakes
11	Brown caramel	161-170° C	Colouring sauces, cakes and stocks				

OTHER INGREDIENTS

Mustard

- ✓ Mustard is obtained from the seeds of the mustard plant. It is usually available in whole, paste and powdered form. A pungent powder or paste prepared from mustard seeds is used as a food seasoning or condiment.
- ✓ In kitchen, mustard is used for sauces (like mayonnaise, mustard and vinaigrette sauces) and for making devilled dishes like grilled leg of chicken and *Welsh rarebit*.

Vinegar

- ✓ A sour-tasting liquid containing acetic acid, obtained by fermenting dilute alcoholic liquids, typically wine, cider or beer. Malt vinegar is made from malt, which is produced from barley.
- ✓ In market, vinegar is available in four forms – *imitated* (artificial vinegar), *wine based* (made from red or white wine), *spirit based* (made from potatoes, grain or starchy vegetables) and *flavoured* vinegar (like tarragon flavoured). All vinegars can be distilled in order to remove the colour present.

Colourants

- ✓ Colouring agents are available in dry as well as liquid form which could be artificial as well as naturally available in fruits and vegetables.
- ✓ *Natural colouring agents* include cochineal (for red), spinach (for green), turmeric (for yellow), caramel (for brown and dark brown) and coffee beans (for brown). On the other hand, there is a large range of *artificial colouring agents* produced from *coal tar*.

Essence

- ✓ In general, it is produced from a solution of essential oils with the addition of alcohol and is often used in bakery and confectionary products and other regular menu dishes.
- ✓ Essence is available in three forms – *natural* (like in fruits, spices, herbs, roots, nuts, etc.); *artificial* (like imitated from vanilla, coconut, rum, pineapple, etc.) and *compound* (blend of natural and artificial).

Nuts

- ✓ A nut is a fruit composed of a seed and a hard shell. These are reproductive kernels of the plant from which they are obtained. Nuts are mainly used in pastry, confectionery and vegetarian cookery and often used for decorating and flavouring purposes.
- ✓ Its variety includes almond, chestnut, pine nuts, acorn, pistachio nut, hazel nut, pecans, walnuts, pea nuts, cashew nuts, etc. Nuts can be used whole or halves and remember almonds could be used ground, nibbed or flaked.

KEY TERMS

Corn tortillas : Thin disk of unleavened bread made from masa or wheat flour and baked on a hot surface.

Durum wheat	:	High protein (and high gluten) wheat used to make semolina, which combines with water to make pasta dough.
Sucrose	:	Sugar type obtained from sweet fruits, roots, sugarcane and beetroot.
Imitated	:	Artificial ingredients.
Devilled dishes	:	Spicy preparations coated with a mixture of highly seasoned ingredients like mustard or hot spices.
Bran	:	Pericarp, outer layer of grain wheat.
Scutellum	:	Part of the structure of a grass seed such as barley and rice seed. In simple terms, it is a modified cotyledon in the embryo of a grass seed (or a modified seed leaf).
Candy floss	:	Also known as *cotton candy*. Simply, a mass of pink or white fluffy spun sugar wrapped around a stick.
Fondant	:	Smooth, creamy white icing or candy consisting of very finely crystallized sugar syrup.
Meringue	:	Light patisserie made from stiffly whisked egg whites and sugar.
Torrone	:	Candy made of honey and almonds.

REVIEW QUESTIONS

1. Define the term flour. Enlist different types of flour and briefly explain their uses in cookery.
2. Define the term pepper. Enlist and explain any eight types of pepper.
3. What is white gold? Classify white gold and explain each one.
4. Write a short note on liquid sweeteners.

40 CHAPTER

Shortening (Fats and Oils)

Objectives

Students will be able to:

- classify fats and oils and their sources; and
- understand culinary uses of fats and oils.

SHORTENING

Any fat used in baking is termed *shortening* because it shortens gluten strands. It does this by surrounding the particles and lubricating them so they do not stick together. Shortening fat has additives that enhance its usage in baked goods or as a frying fat. Shortening can be

- Compound shortening
- All-purpose shortening
- Emulsified shortening
- Frying shortening

Uses of Shortening

- In frying
- In folding
- In basting
- In roasting

Role of Shortening

- Add flavour
- Add nutritive value
- Enhance appearance
- Increase volume
- As ingredient
- Keeping qualities

Frying Shortening

✓ It is a hydrogenated vegetable oil or winterized fat to which an anti-foaming agent (methyl silicone) is added.

✓ It is often a mixture of fats like all vegetable shortening. It may or may not contain antioxidants.

All-Purpose Shortening

✓ It is a vegetable oil that has been hydrogenated to the point of plasticity so that it can be spread or will cream smoothly when beaten. It contains too many antioxidants.

Emulsified Shortening

- ✓ It is also called *baker's shortening* which is hydrogenated to the point of plasticity and contains emulsifiers.
- ✓ These allow more liquid and sugar to be incorporated into baked goods. Due to emulsification, it is bad shortening for frying foods because it breaks down faster.

Compound Shortening

- ✓ It is made from the combination of vegetable and animal fats.

Saturated fat

On broad basis, fats and oils are either saturated or unsaturated, the later classification being broken down into monounsaturated and polyunsaturated fats.

- ✓ Generally, saturated fats come from animal sources and are solid enough to hold their shape at room temperature (65°F). Except coconut oil and palm oil (highly saturated), these come from plant sources and are semi-solid at room temperature.

Unsaturated fat

- ✓ These are primarily received from the plants and are liquid (in the form of an oil) at room temperature. In general, oils are composed (in varying percentages) of both *monounsaturated* and *polyunsaturated* fats.

Monounsaturated fat

- ✓ In short it is known as "MUFA" and these fats do not have hydrogen atoms at every available bonding site on the molecule. Monounsaturated fats are usually liquid at room temperature, but can turn solid in the refrigerator. The three widely used oils with high monounsaturated fats are olive oil, canola oil and peanut oil.

Polyunsaturated fat

- ✓ These fats have more than one hydrogen atom. Polyunsaturated fats/oils (such as safflower oil, soybean oil, corn oil and sesame oil) are liquid even in refrigerator. It is available in two forms – *omega 3* and *omega 6* fats which are essential fatty acids (EFA).

Important Fact

Fats are solid at room temperature while *oils* are liquid at room temperature. Fats and oils do not dissolve in water but they may emulsify with water (like margarine and butter making).

FAT

Fat is a basic nutrient that provides energy by furnishing calories. Fats are compounds of fatty acids and glycerol like many organic compounds; they contain carbon, hydrogen and oxygen. They are valuable *fuel foods,* as they supply more than twice as many calories for heat and energy than either protein and/or carbohydrates. If more fat is taken than required, it is stored in body. Some fats also supply vitamins A & D. The key sources of fats are animal foods (like meat, dairy products and oily fish) and vegetable foods such as nuts from which oil is extracted.

Animal originated fats: It refers to a fat received from various animals like *direct fat* (such as suet, lard, bacon, meat fat, oily fish, etc) and *indirect fat* (such as cheese, cream, butter, etc). All foods, before they are absorbed by the intestines, must be first brought into a fluid form. This rule holds good for the fats, therefore, such fats are not soluble and do not melt at the temperature of our bodies and are digested with difficulty. For example, lamb fat melts around 55°C (very indigestible), beef fat melts around 45°C (indigestible), pork fat melts around 40°C (digestible), and goose fat melts around 30°C (easily digestible). A brief description of some major animal fats is given below.

Types of Lard and Suet	
Lard	Leaf, pork and supplement fat
Suet	Leaf, carcass and shop

Lard

- ✓ Lard is obtained from pork fat mostly used in cooking variety of dishes especially in European preparations. *Beef suet* is also used but particularly in English dishes.
- ✓ Lard is the fat from clean, fresh and sound fatty tissue of *hogs* in good condition. There are three basic types of lard – leaf lard, pork fat and other supplement fat.

Suet

- ✓ It is a hard and solid fat which is deposited in the kidney region of animals. Beef suet is the best that is used for suet paste and mince meat. The processing of beef fat is similar to lard processing. Beef fat can also be divided into three parts – leaf fat, carcass fat and shop fat.

Dripping

- ✓ Dripping is obtained from clarified animal fats and used for deep or shallow frying.

Meat Fats

- ✓ As we already know that meat is an animal flesh that is often used as a food. But along with this, it is also used as a fat. It includes fat from various animal sources like poultry fat, goose fat, lamb fat, veal fat and so on.

Other Fats

- ✓ In other fats, one may include fats like butter, cream, cheese, bacon and oily fish because these fats are also obtained from the animals/animal originated products.

Vegetable originated fats: Fat received from various plants (or vegetables), it includes margarine, cooking fat, nuts, soya beans, etc. Vegetable fats are sometimes referred to as butters or tropical oils, as these are derived from tropical plants or fruits such as cocoa, coconut and palm. These contain high amounts of saturated fats. These butters are unusual in that at least one of the fatty acids in the triglycerides is unsaturated. This causes all of the fat to melt within a very narrow temperature range but it is valuable in confectionery work. A brief description of some major vegetable originated fat is given below.

Margarine

- ✓ It is a solid fat invented in 1869 by a Frenchman, Meges Mouries, to replace butter in cooking and baking. Originally, it was composed entirely of beef fat. But today, margarine is made with a variety of fats (usually vegetable), water, whey, yellow colouring and nutritional additives.

Note. Besides beef fat, fat can also be received from other animals like veal and poultry. *Veal kidney fat* is the leaf fat from the veal carcass and is highly prized and mild in flavour. *Poultry fats* have distinctive flavour and aroma. *Goose* and *chicken fat* is sometimes used in paté to enhance the flavour of the ingredients.

OIL

Oils are chemical combination of three molecules of fatty acids and one molecule of glycerol. The fatty acids may be of different types and this leads to the difference in features between, say, a *firm fat* such as beef fat and a *liquid* one such as olive oil. Oils have preponderance or unsaturated fatty acids which make them liquid instead of solid.

Oils are used for frying, baking, roasting and in cake, bread and pastry making. Sources of oil are as follows.

Animal originated oils: Oil extracted or received from different animals like sea fishes such as Halibut and Cod liver oil. The extracted fish oils are valuable sources of Vitamin A & D.

Vegetable originated oils: Vegetable oil received from the plants or vegetables or from the seeds and nuts. It includes peanut oil, almond oil, avocado oil, canola oil, olive oil, hazelnut oil, grape-seed oil, cottonseed oil, coconut oil, walnut oil and so forth. A brief description of some major vegetable based oil is given below.

Peanut Oil (smoking point 232°C)

- ✓ It is a clear oil received from pressed peanuts; it is very useful in frying, cooking and as a salad oil. It contains monounsaturated fatty acids. Peanut oil has a delicate and bland flavour (hence good for cooking because it doesn't absorb or transfer flavour) and high smoke point, making it perfect for deep frying. Its smoking point is slightly lower than corn or safflower oil.

Almond Oil (smoking point 216°C)

- ✓ This oil is obtained by pressing sweet almonds and contains monounsaturated fat. Generally, nut oils are best used in cold dishes instead of almond oil because heat destroys the delicate flavour of almond oil. Almond oil is best suited for sauces and stir frying in Asian foods. French almond oil (*huile d'amande*) is more expensive than other almond oils, as it has delicate flavour and aroma of lightly toasted almonds.

Avocado Oil (smoking point 271°C)

- ✓ It is vibrant green in colour with soft nutty taste and mild avocado flavour. It also contains monounsaturated fat. This oil is often made from damaged and cosmetically inferior avocados. It is low in saturated fatty acids and high in polyunsaturated acids. It is slightly nutty in flavour and best for stir frying, searing and salad dressing.

Canola Oil (smoking point 204°C)

- ✓ It is light, golden colour oil, similar to safflower oil and found low in saturated fat. In simple terms, it is bland oil made from rapeseeds; contains omega-3 fatty acids and less saturated fat than other vegetable oils.
- ✓ It is often blended with other oils to make *margarine*, and because of its neutral taste it is considered a good all-purpose oil. It is most suitable for salad dressings

and cooking. It is also known as *rapeseed oil*. It has a mild flavour and aroma and mostly used in Indian and Mediterranean food (in salads and cooking) preparations.

Olive Oil (smoking point 160°C to 242°C, depends upon grade)

- ✓ It is monounsaturated oil obtained by pressing tree-ripened olives. It has a distinctive fruity, olive flavour and is graded according to its degree of acidity. It is used as a medium of cooking, and flavouring. It is good for salad dressing, sautéing, pan frying, deep frying, broiling, grilling and baking.
- ✓ Olive oils range from light amber to green in colour and bland to extremely strong in flavour. Colour of olive oil depends upon the fruit used and its processing. It is available as virgin oil, extra virgin and pure olive oils.

Hazelnut Oil (smoking point 221°C)

- ✓ Extremely expensive, but very delicately nutty flavoured oil extracted from hazelnuts. It contains monounsaturated fatty acids. As it is highly concentrated, it is often combined with lighter oils before using. It is an excellent ingredient for salad dressing and may also be used to flavour sauces, marinades, main dishes and baked goods.

Grape seed Oil (smoking point 200°C)

- ✓ It is an oil of delicate flavour which is good for cooking foods at very high temperature. It contains polyunsaturated fatty acids. This light, medium yellow, aromatic oil is a byproduct in wine making. It is used in salads and some cooking (as sautéing and frying) and in the manufacturing of margarine.

Cottonseed Oil (smoking point 216°C)

- ✓ Extracted from the seeds of the cotton plant. It contains polyunsaturated fatty acids. Most of the cottonseed oil produced is used in combination with other oils to create vegetable oil products and often as blend in margarine. This oil is much used in the United States, particularly to prepare fried products, salad dressing and shortening.

Coconut Oil (smoking point 177°C)

- ✓ The nut from the coconut plant. The dried coconut meat (called as *copra*) is pressed and used to make coconut oil. It contains high proportion of saturated fatty acids. It is a heavy and almost colourless oil. It yields a variety of oils with a strong flavour; these require a lot of refining before they can be used for culinary purpose. It is best suited for coatings, confectionery and shortening.

Walnut Oil (smoking point 204°C)

✓ It is a medium yellow oil with nutty flavour and aroma. This oil is extracted from the walnut. It contains monounsaturated fat. It can be quite expensive and goes rancid quicker than most oils. On the other hand, it gives most foods a wonderful nutty flavour whether chef cooks with it or drizzles it. It is suitable for sautéing, broiling, grilling and deep frying but best suitable to cook with greens, pastas or vegetables.

Sunflower Oil (smoking point 230°C)

✓ This is taken from the *Helianthus annuus*. It has a pleasant rather than neutral taste and can be used for all culinary purposes from cooking to salad dressings. It has a relatively low smoking point, as the sunflower seeds contain a very high amount of polyunsaturated fat with low saturated fat.

Safflower Oil (smoking point 232°C)

✓ It is a golden colour light textured oil made from the seeds of safflowers. It contains polyunsaturated fat which helps in keeping cholesterol level down. It is tasteless with a high smoking point and used in margarine making, cooking, mayonnaise and salad dressing. It is, however, not recommended to use this oil exclusively, as it lacks vitamin E.

Corn Oil (smoking point 232°C)

✓ It is pale yellow oil obtained from corn endosperms. It contains polyunsaturated fatty acids. It is odourless, almost flavourless and has a high polyunsaturated fat with a high smoking point. It is suitable for frying and also used in shortening, baking, salad dressings and to make margarine.

Sesame Oil (smoking point 232°C)

✓ It is made from sesame seeds. Light sesame oil has a nutty flavour and may be used in a variety of ways. It comes in two varieties—middle eastern type (light and very mild oil) and Asian type (dark and strong flavoured oil). The stronger flavoured dark sesame oil is most often used as a flavouring agent in *Oriental dishes*. It is best suited for cooking and salad dressing. But both varieties are high in polyunsaturated fat.

Soybean Oil (smoking point 232°C)

✓ It is a heavy oil that comes from the seeds of the soybean. It contains polyunsaturated fat. This is one of the most produced oils and has a fairly pronounced flavour and aroma and is considered a medium to heavy oil. It is fairly suitable for shortening, dressing, frying and in cold kitchen work. It is considered a good all-purpose oil that is also used in cakes and pastries.

Other Oils

✓ These include oils from mustards, pumpkin seeds and so forth. *Mustard seeds* based oil is extremely hot and pungent and suitable for stir frying, marinades and salad dressings. *Pumpkin seeds* based oil is made from roasted pumpkin seeds and is robustly flavoured. Due to its strong flavour it is combined with other oils and is suitable for cooking, salad dressings and other preparations.

Grading of Olive Oil

Virgin (smoking point 216°C) These are those olive oils which have been obtained from the first pressing of the olive without further refinement. It has slightly higher level of acidity; it is between 1 – 4%.

Extra virgin (smoking point 160°C) Finest, fruitiest and expensive olive oil with an acid content of 1% (the acidity level of superfine olive oil is around 1 to 1.5%).

Fino (smoking point 242°C) It is an Italian term which means *fine*. It is a blend of extra virgin and virgin oils. Its acidity level will be around 3%.

Pure (smoking point 240°C) These olive oils are extracted by heat. These are 100% olive oils, but their flavour can result in a harsh and bitter after-taste. The label may also simply call it as *olive oil*.

Pomace (smoking point 238°C) It is refined from the final pressings under heat and pressure. Its taste is inferior than other olive oils; hence it should never be substituted for them.

KEY TERMS

Shortening : Any fat that is used in baking because it shortens gluten strands.

MUFA : Mono Unsaturated Fatty Acids.

Suet : Hard solid fat deposits in the kidney region of animals.

Lard : Pork fat or lard is the fat from clean, fresh and sound fatty tissue of hogs.

Fuel food : Foods supplying more than twice as many calories for heat and energy than either protein or carbohydrates.

Leaf fat : True fat (or quality fat) received from the fat that surrounds the kidneys.

Margarine : A processed solid fat that replaces butter. Originally, it was composed of beef fat but nowadays is also obtained from refined oils.

Copra	:	Dried coconut meat (called as *copra*) that is pressed and used to make coconut oil.
Oriental dish	:	Asian foods or food prepared in a style resembling to East Asia, including Chinese, Japanese, Thai, Korean, etc., style of cooking practices.
Endosperm	:	Tissue produced in the seeds of most flowering plants during fertilization, mainly consists of starch and proteins.

REVIEW QUESTIONS

1. Differentiate between fat and oil.
2. Describe shortening and the medium of shortening.
3. Define oil. Enlist any ten sources of vegetable oils and their brief description.
4. Write a short note on margarine.

41

CHAPTER

Supporting Agents

OBJECTIVES

Students will be able to:

- understand taxonomy of leavening agents;
- explicate different garnishes and sauces; and
- expound culinary uses of garnishes and sauces.

LEAVENING

The term *leavening* means production or incorporation of gasses in a baked product in order to increase its volume and produce the desired shape and texture. A leavening agent or leavener is a substance that generates a chemical reaction and makes a baked product grow larger or rise such as breads, cakes and cookies. Baking powder, baking soda and yeast are the most common leaveners. When mixed with a liquid they form carbon dioxide gas bubbles, which cause the batter or dough to rise during (and sometimes before) the baking process.

A brief description of various supporting agents like leavening agents, famous garnishes and additional sauces is given below.

Classification of Leavening Agents

Chemical agents

- ✓ The chemical leavening agents work in the presence of liquid like milk, egg and warmth (the oven). In it, a chemical reaction occurs producing CO_2 gas which causes the product to rise.

Mechanical techniques

- ✓ In mechanical leavening, air is incorporated into the mixture. During the baking process, this air expands which causes the product to rise.

Biological agents

- ✓ Yeast is a biological leavening agent. It is a fungus that multiplies rapidly in suitable conditions, thus used as a raising agent in various kinds of dough. It feeds on simple sugar present in the flour and added sweeteners (if any). As it grows, yeast gives off carbon dioxide while other byproducts lend a distinctive flavour and aroma.

Examples of Leavening Agents	
Chemical agents	Baking powder, baking soda (sodium bicarbonate), ammonium bicarbonate, potassium bicarbonate (potash), potassium bitartrate (cream of tartar), monocalcium phosphate, self raising flour, etc.
Mechanical techniques	Sifting, whisking, creaming, docking, beating, foaming, rolling, folding, rubbing-in. Steaming and airing technique also work as leavening agents.
Biological agents	Dry yeast, activated dry yeast, compressed yeast, quick raising yeast, brewer's yeast, butter milk, yogurt, sour dough starter, etc.

Note. Baking soda is different from baking powder. *Baking soda* (or bicarbonate of soda) is alkaline and it reacts when it comes in contact with acidic ingredients like yogurt and curd whereas *baking powder* is a mixture of baking soda and cream of tartar (a dry acid) and reacts when it is exposed to moisture or heat.

COATING/BATTER/MARINATING

When preparing any delicate crispy and crunchy food item especially with meat cuts like tender cuts of meat, poultry, or fish, it is a common practice to coat or batter the outside of the ingredients first then fry/deep fry. This coating creates crunchiness and crispiness in the prepared item as well as also prevents the loss of moisture and oil that may be absorbed by the flesh. Coatings can be divided into two categories, i.e., dry coating and wet coating.

Dry Coating

- ✓ Dry coatings include coating with flour, corn-flour, bread crumbs, semolina, oatmeal, etc. The two most common types of dry coatings are *seasoned flour* and *crumbing*.
- ✓ Flour with added seasoning, which may include salt, pepper, herbs, paprika, spices, or a combination, such flour is called *seasoned flour*. On the other hand, *crumbing* is the process of making a thin layer of crumbs (white or brown) to the outside of a commodity before cooking.

Wet Coating

- ✓ Wet coatings/batters are suitable for those commodities that are suited for shallow or deep frying or for quick cooking on a flat top grill. Some examples of wet coatings include flour followed by egg-wash and velvet coating, in which corn-flour is mixed with beaten egg white.

Marination

- ✓ Like wet coating, *marination* is also a wet technique of coating. In it, commodities like meat, poultry, fish and vegetables are soaked (or marinade) in seasoned liquid in order to absorb flavour and, in some instances, to be tenderized. Most marinade mixtures contain an acid (lemon juice, vinegar or wine) and herbs or spices.
- ✓ The acid ingredient is especially important for tough cuts of meat because it serves as a tenderizer. Due to presence of acid ingredients, the marination should be done in a glass, ceramic or stainless steel container but never in aluminium.

FAMOUS GARNISHES

A l' Alsacienne: It consists of tartlet cases (filled with braised Choucroute and sliced lean ham) and is used to garnish joints of meat, fillet of beef and tornedos. Serve Jus de veau lie separately.

A l' Americaine: It consists of sliced lobster tail (prepared in a l' Americaine style) and used to garnish special fish preparations. Serve Lobster sauce separately.

A l' Andalouse: It consists of grilled pimentos (filled with riz à la Grecque) and used to garnish joints or cuts of meat and poultry. Serve Jus lie separately.

A l' Arlesienne: It consists of eggplant slices (seasoned, flavoured and fried in oil), peeled tomatoes (sliced and sautéed in butter), bouquet of onion rings (deep fried). It is used to garnish tornedos and Noisette. Serve tomato flavoured demi-glace sauce separately.

A l' Hongroise: It consists of cauliflower florets coated with paprika flavoured Mornay sauce. Arranged in Duchess potato cases or browned in oven. It is used to garnish various dishes. Serve paprika flavoured sauce separately.

A l' Indienne: It consists of Indian rice preparation in a l' Indienne style and used to garnish cuts and joints of meat and poultry. Serve Sauce a l' Indienne separately.

A l' Italienne: It consists of artichoke hearts (prepared in a l' Italienne style), macaroni croquettes (bound with cheese). It is used to garnish cuts and joints of meat and poultry. Serve sauce Italienne separately.

A l' Orientale: It consists of small tomatoes (stuffed with rice pilaf) together with okra and peppers, braised in butter. It is used to garnish poultry preparations. Serve tomato flavoured demi-glace sauce separately.

A l' Orleanaise: It consists of chopped braised endive bound with egg and butter; with Maitre d' Hotel potatoes. It is used to garnish joints of meat and served with cooking liquor separately.

Brehan: It consists of artichoke bottoms separately (filled with broad beans puree), cauliflower bouquet (coated with Hollandaise sauce), butter cooked potatoes and sprinkled with chopped parsley. It is used to garnish joints of veal and beef. Serve with braised liquor from veal or beef separately.

Bretonne: It consists of cooked Haricot beans (mixed with bretonne sauce) and sprinkled with chopped parsley. It is used to garnish mutton preparations. Serve with cooking liquor from mutton separately.

Bristol: It consists of croquettes of braised rice, haricot beans (bound with veloute sauce) and butter cooked potatoes. It is used to garnish joints of meat and serve braised liquor from joints separately.

Choisy: It consists of braised lettuce and Château potatoes and used to garnish Tournedos and Noisette. Serve buttered meat glaze separately.

Choron: It consists of artichoke bottoms (garnished with buttered asparagus tips) and Noisette potatoes. It is used to garnish Tournedos and Noisette. Serve Choron sauce separately.

Conti: It consists of lentil puree and salted belly of pork. It is used to garnish braised joints of meat. Serve sauce braised liquor from joints separately.

Daumont: It consists of butter cooked mushroom, fish quenelles, creamed forcemeat (decorated with truffles) and thick slices of roe (egg, bread crumbed and deep fried). It is used to garnish fish preparations. Serve sauce Nantua separately.

Dauphine: It consists of Croquettes (prepared from Dauphine mixture) and used to garnish joints of meat, Noisette and Tournedos. Serve Madeira flavoured demi-glace sauce separately.

Doria: It consists of pieces of cucumber cooked in butter. It is used to garnish fish preparations.

Dubbary: It consists of Château Potatoes and small florets of blanched cauliflower, coated with Mornay sauce, sprinkled with grated cheese and browned on grill. It is used to garnish joints of meat, Noisette and Tournedos and served with cooked liquor separately.

Florian: It consists of braised lettuce, small glazed onions, shaped glazed carrots and small potato croquettes. It is used to garnish joints of lamb preparations and served with gravy from joints separately.

Jardinière: It consists of vegetable mixture (essentially carrot, turnip and French beans). The vegetables are cooked separately then mixed with garden peas and bound with butter. It is used to garnish joints of meat and served with gravy from joints separately.

Judic: It consists of braised lettuce, cock's kidney and slices of truffles. It is used to garnish Noisettes, Tournedos and poultry and sauce demi-glace is served separately.

Lorette: It consists of chicken croquettes, small bunches of asparagus tips and sliced truffles. It is used to garnish Noisettes and Tournedos. Serve Jus lie separately.

Louisiane: It consists of sweet-corn in cream (sometimes in tartlet), rice molded in Darioles and fried thick slices of banana. It is used to garnish poultry and served in reduced gravy (prepared from cooking of poultry) separately.

Macedoine: It consists of vegetable mixture like carrot and turnips (one may also make it with fruits) – cut into small pieces. Vegetables are cooked separately then mixed with peas and other vegetables then bound with butter. It is used to garnish joints of meat.

Madeleine: It consists of artichoke bottoms (filled with thick Soubise), puree of Haricot beans (mixed with egg) and finish with butter. It is used to garnish cuts and joints of meat and poultry. Serve sauce demi-glace separately.

Marechal: It consists of bundles of asparagus tips and a slice of truffle. Serve in a ring of thickened Châteaubriand sauce. It is used to garnish chicken supremes, escalops of calves sweetbread, Noisette and cutlets of lamb.

Massena: It consists of artichoke hearts (filled with Béarnaise sauce) and slices of poached beef bone marrow. It is used to garnish Noisettes and Tournedos. Serve tomato sauce separately.

Parmentiere: It consists of dices of potatoes (cooked in butter) as for Château potatoes and sprinkled with chopped parsley. It is used to garnish joints of meat and poultry and served in its own gravy separately.

Rachel: It consists of artichoke bottoms (garnished with slices of poached bone marrow and chopped parsley). It is used to garnish Noisettes and Tournedos and sauce Bordelaise is served separately.

Ravioli: It consists of small pasta (ravioli is name of pasta) filled according to the kind of preparing food or dish. It is used to garnish cuts and joints of meat and poultry.

Rossini: It consists of foie gras, truffles and demi-glace (flavoured with truffle essence). It is used to garnish Noisettes and Tournedos. Serve demi-glace sauce (flavoured with truffle essence) separately.

Saint Germain: It consists of puree of green peas which is fairly thick and bound with egg yolk and Béarnaise sauce. It is used to garnish joints of meat and served with Bordelaise sauce.

Talleyrand: It consists of buttered macaroni flavoured with cheese and serve with juliennes of truffles, dices of foie gras and Perigueux sauce. It is used to garnish cuts and joints of meat and poultry. Serve sauce Perigueux separately.

Vegetable puree: It consists of puree of vegetables and used in accordance with the preparing dish. It is used to garnish a variety of vegetarian preparations.

À la Berny: It consists of Pomme Croquette and tartlet case (filled with buttered chestnut puree with glazed truffle slices). It is used to garnish game and marinated joints of meat. Serve sauce Poivrade separately.

À la Boulangere: It consists of butter cooked sliced onion, sliced potatoes with seasoning. It is used to garnish mutton, lamb and poultry preparations. Serve braised liquor separately.

À la Bouquetiere: It consists of carrot, turnip, Châteaux potatoes, peas, French beans, cauliflower bouquet (coated with hollandaise sauce). It is used to garnish large joints of meat. Serve cooked liquor separately.

À la Bourgeoise: It consists of carrot, glazed button onion and salted belly of pork (diced, blanched and fried in butter). It is used to garnish cuts or joints of meat.

À la Bourguignonne: It consists of glazed butter onion, butter sauté mushroom and salted belly of pork. It is used to garnish joints of beef. Serve braised liquor separately.

À la Cardinal: It consists of slices of lobster tail and slices of blanch spinach. It is used to garnish fish preparations. Serve Cardinal sauce separately.

À la Chipolata: It consists of glazed button onions, grilled chipolata sausages, chestnut (butter cooked), salted belly of pork (fried) and carrot. It is used to garnish joints of meat and poultry. Serve braised cooking liquor separately.

À la Clamart: It consists of tartlet cases (filled with peas puree and shredded lettuce) and *Macaire potatoes*. It is used to garnish cuts or joints of meat. Serve Jus lie separately.

À la Commodore: It consists of Cassolettes (garnished with crayfish tails), Quenelles of crayfish, mussels à la villeroy. It is used to garnish whole or large cuts of fish. Serve sauce Normande (finished with crayfish butter) separately.

À la Duchess: It consists of Duchess Potatoes mixture, egg washed then cooked in oven (at last moment). It is used to garnish joints of meat, Noisette and Tournedos. Serve sauce Madere separately.

À la favourite: It consists of slices of foie gras, seasoned, flavoured and sauté in butter with slices of truffles; bouquet of asparagus tips. It is used to garnish Noisette and Tournedos. Serve Jus lie separately.

À la Fermiere: It consists of buttered cooked vegetables (like carrot and turnip) with onion and celery, add salt and little sugar. It is used to garnish poultry preparations.

À la Financiere: It consists of a Ragout of cockscomb, chicken quenelles, finely sliced mushroom and shredded truffles flavoured with Madeira. All bound with a sauce containing Madeira wine and truffle essence. It is used to garnish cuts of joints of meat and poultry. Serve *sauce Financiere* separately.

À la Flamande: It consists of stuffed braised balls of green cabbage, shaped pieces of glazed carrot and turnip, potato a l' anglaise, dices of belly of pork (salt pork) and sausage slices cooked with cabbage. It is used to garnish joints of meat and served with gravy from joints separately.

À la Grecque: It consists of rice (pilaf style) mixed with sausages, peas and peppers. It is used to garnish lamb and poultry preparations. Serve tomato sauce separately.

À la Japonaise: It consists of Japanese artichoke bound with veloute and placed in pastry case; croquettes of rice. It is used to garnish cuts and joints of meat and served with gravy from joints separately.

À la Mariniere: It consists of small mussels cooked in white wine then bearded; peeled prawns (shrimps). It is used to garnish Noisette and Tournedos. Serve Mariniere sauce separately.

À la Mexicaine: It consists of grilled mushroom (stuffed with chopped tomato, sauté peppers and eggplant) with tomato flavoured demi-glace sauce (contain finely shredded red peppers). It is used to garnish cuts or joints of meats and poultry. Serve tomato flavoured *Jus lie* separately.

À la Milanaise: It consists of macaroni with cheese, coarsely shredded ham, pickled tongue, mushroom and truffles. All blended in tomato sauce and garnished with parmesan cheese. It is used to garnish cuts and joints of meat. Finally, serve thin tomato sauce separately.

À la Nantua: It consists of crayfish or crayfish tails bound with Nantua sauce. It is used to garnish fish. Serve sauce Nantua separately.

À la Napolitaine: It consists of buttered macaroni or spaghetti in a tomato sauce or with peeled, chopped and seeded tomatoes, sprinkled with grated parmesan cheese. It is used to garnish cuts and joints of meat and poultry. Serve cooking juice separately.

À la Nicoise: It consists of tomato (stewed in oil and flavoured with garlic), buttered French beans or stewed courgettes (zucchini), small artichoke and Château potatoes for garnishing large cuts and joints of meat and poultry. While in case of fish preparations, garnish consists of coarsely chopped, peeled, seeded tomato, anchovy fillet, olives and anchovy butter. Serve Jus lie separately.

À la Normande: It consists of oysters, mussels, prawns (shrimp), mushrooms, truffles, fried gudgeon and crayfish in court bouillon. It is used to garnish fish preparations. Serve Normande sauce separately.

À la Parisienne: It consists of potatoes (cooked in *à la Parisienne style*), accompanied by braised lettuce and artichoke bottoms, juliennes of pickled tongue, mushroom (bound with veloute) and decorated with thin slices of truffles. It is used to garnish cuts and joints of meat and poultry. Serve demi-glace sauce separately.

À la Paysanne: *Fermiere* garnish with potatoes and lean salt belly of pork (cut into dices then blanched). It is used to garnish cuts and joints of meat and poultry.

À la Pimontaise: It consists of Risotto (containing grated white truffles) arranged in a variety of ways like Darioles, timbale moulds, etc. It is used to garnish cuts and joints of meat and poultry. Serve tomato sauce separately.

À la Portugaise: It consists of a whole tomato (stuffed with Duxelles mixture and Château potatoes). Serve Sauce Portugaise separately.

À la Printaniere: It consists of a mixture of vegetables (spring vegetables like carrots) tossed in butter. It is used to garnish sautés of meats and poultry.

À la Provencale: It consists of tomato and mushroom (stuffed with Duxelles – mixture contains little garlic). It is used to garnish joints of meat and sauce Provencale is served separately.

À la Romaine: It is made of tartlet case (filled with egg, spinach, anchovy), grated parmesan cheese; small bird casseroled with peas and ham; spinach loaf or soufflé. It is used to garnish joints of meat and sauce Romaine is served separately.

À la Sicilienne: It consists of small pieces of meat or poultry, which are fried and garnished with stuffed tomato, rice timbales and potato croquettes. It is used to garnish various food items and served in its own gravy separately.

À la Tyrolienne: It consists of fried slices of onion and tomato fondue (or crushed tomato) with Tyrolienne sauce. It is used to garnish grills of meat and venison. Serve sauce Tyrolienne separately.

À la Vert Pre: It consists of straw potatoes and watercress with Maitre D' Hotel Butter for grilled items. While items like white meat and duck are garnished with the mixture of peas, asparagus tips and green peas are tossed in butter. Finally, serve with its own clear gravy separately.

À la Vichy: It consists of cooked sliced carrots with fresh butter and parsley. It is used to garnish cuts and joints of meat.

À la Zingara: It consists of lean ham, slat ox tongue, mushroom and truffles cut in julienne forms and offered with Sauce Demi-glace flavoured with tomato and tarragon. It is used to garnish veal and poultry.

ADDITIONAL SAUCES

Aux Champignons: Mushroom liquor (reduced by half), add tomato sauce or Espagnole sauce then cook. Finish with butter cooked small mushroom.

Bercy: It is made with butter sweated chopped shallots, reduced white wine and fish stock and fish velouté. Seasoning and consistency adjusted. Finish the sauce with butter and chopped parsley.

Beurre Noir: Sauce made from black butter. This sauce is made with cooked dark brown butter, vinegar, chopped parsley and capers.

Bigarade: Orange sauce and braised duck liquor. Finish with fine juliennes of orange zest and lemon zest.

Bourguignonne sauce: Strain reduced liquor or juice (made up of red wine, sliced shallots, parsley, bay leaf, thyme and mushroom) then thicken it with Beurre Manie. Finally, finish with butter and cayenne.

Bretonne sauce: Reduced liquor or juice (made up of white wine, butter and chopped onion) with tomato sauce then cook and finish with coarsely chopped parsley.

Demi-glace: It means "half glaze". It consists of mixture of equal amount of brown stock and brown sauce that has been reduced by half.

Diable sauce: Demi-glace sauce with reduced white wine (containing chopped shallot) and seasoned with cayenne.

Duxelles: It is an apparel of finely chopped mushroom and shallots then sautéed gently in butter.

Essence: A concentrated flavouring extracted from an item, usually by infusion or distillation; items include vanilla and other extracts, concentrated stock or fumet.

Financiere: Reduced Madeira sauce flavoured with truffle essence.

Italienne: Tomato flavoured demi-glace sauce with Duxelles, dices of lean cooked ham and finish with chopped tarragon, chervil and parsley.

Jus: It means "juice" like *jus de viande* is meat gravy. Meat served as Au Jus means it is served with its own juice or Jus lie.

Mariniere sauce: It is similar to Bercy sauce made with mussels cooking juice and mariniere garnish (always include mussles; may also include prawns).

Matelote: Reduced red wine (containing Court Bouillon and trimmed mushroom) with fish Espagnole and finish with butter and cayenne pepper.

Moutarde: Butter sauce with English mustard.

Oriental: Reduced Americaine sauce flavoured with curry powder and finish with cream.

Poulette: Reduced mushroom liquor with Allemande sauce and finish with lemon juice, butter and chopped parsley.

Ravigote: Reduced white wine with vinegar, add veloute then finish with shallot butter, chopped chervil, tarragon and chives.

Regence: Reduced Rhine wine (containing butter cooked mirepoix and raw truffles) with Demi glace sauce.

Romaine: Dissolve caramel (golden colour caramel) into vinegar and add Espagnole sauce and game stock then reduce by half. Finish with toasted kernel seeds, sultanas and currants.

Sauce Aux Fines Herbs: Reduced white wine (containing parsley, chervil, tarragon and chives) with demi-glace or veal gravy. Finally finish with chopped fine herbs and lemon juice.

Talleyrand sauce: It is made by mixing chicken veloute sauce, Madeira, Mirepoix, truffles and pickled tongue.

Venitienne: Reduced tarragon vinegar (containing chopped shallot and chervil) with white wine then finish with green butter, chopped chervil and tarragon.

Villeroy: Reduced Allemande sauce (containing ham and tarragon essence) and cook till thick consistency (enough to coat the food).

Zingara sauce: It is a mixture of demi-glace and tomato sauce mixed with ham, pickled tongue, mushroom and seasoned with paprika.

KEY TERMS

Jus de viande	: Pan juice/drippings from meat preparations.
Chateau potatoes	: Parboiled then braised (in butter) potato balls.
Maitre D' Hotel Butter	: Parsley flavoured butter.
Choucroute	: Sauerkraut vegetable.
Tournedos	: A small beef steak cut from the tenderloin.
Noisette	: Hollandaise sauce finished with hazelnut butter.
Beurre Manie	: *Kneaded butter* (i.e., a mixture of flour and butter used for thickening sauces or soups).

Pomme Croquette	:	Mashed potato filled *croquettes* often served as a side dish.
Choron Sauce	:	Derivative sauce of Béarnaise sauce made by adding tomato paste to the standard Béarnaise.
Mirepoix	:	Roughly cut vegetables.

REVIEW QUESTIONS

1. What is a leavening agent? Classify leavening agents and explain each agent briefly.
2. Enlist any ten famous sauces with short description.
3. Enlist any ten famous garnishes with short description.
4. Differentiate between coating and marination.

42 CHAPTER

Herbs and Spices

Objectives

Students will be able to:

- enlist major culinary herbs and culinary spices;
- expound functions of herbs and spices; and
- explicate culinary uses of herbs and spices.

HERB AND SPICE

The word *herb* comes from Latin which means *grass*. Herbs are defined as the leaves and stems of soft stemmed wood plants. Fresh herbs are always preferred over dried herbs because the flavour of fresh herbs tends to be more complex and complete. Although there is little nutritive value in herbs with the exception of parsley, they form an important ingredient in almost every menu.

Spices are derived from the roots, buds, bark and fruit of plants. Spices have always been valued for their ability to add flavour, colour and aroma to dishes, but before the advent of refrigeration they were also an important means of food preservation, and in some cultures their medicinal and antiseptic characteristics are also revered.

CULINARY HERBS

The main groups of culinary herbs are those that fall into the French "Fines herbs" category as well as some other herbs that commonly enhance flavour and aroma of dishes. The main five "Fines herbs" are parsley, chives, tarragon, marjoram and chervil. These herbs are used extensively in French cuisine and are regarded by the French chefs as essential. Brief descriptions of these culinary herbs are as follows.

Parsley (from Apiaceae family; scientific name is *Petroselinum crispum*)

✓ A herb with long slender stalks, small curly dark green leaves and a slightly peppery and tangy fresh flavour (the flavour is stronger). It is the most commonly used herb. It can be used in fresh and dried form as a garnish.

✓ It can be added to salads or deep fried items. Fresh parsley combined with lemon juice makes an interesting sorbet. Its other uses are salad dressings, soups, casseroles, fish, cheese, potatoes, etc.

Herbs
- Aniseed
- Balm
- Basil
- Bay leaves
- Coriander
- Capers
- Capsicums
- Dill leaves
- Fennel
- Mint
- Lemon Grass
- Savory
- Rosemary
- Sage
- Oregano
- Angelica
- Rue
- Borage
- Dandelion
- Sorrel
- Horseradish
- Lovage
- Hyssop
- Woodruff

Chives (from Liliaceae family; scientific name is *Allium schoenoprasum*)

✓ This herb is a member of onion family. It has long, slender, hollow, green stems and purple flowers. Its flavour is like mild onion and generally used in fresh, dried and chopped forms. It is invaluable in flavouring hors d'oeuvre, fish, poultry and meat dishes.

Tarragon (from Asteraceae family; scientific name is *Artemisia dracunculus*)

✓ A herb native to Siberia having narrow, pointed, dark green leaves with tiny grey flowers. It has a distinctive anise-like flavour with undertones of sage and a strong aroma.

✓ It is available fresh as well as in dried forms. It is used fresh to flavour béarnaise sauce and vinegar. Coloured tarragon is put for decorative purposes in cold fish and chicken dishes.

Marjoram (from Lamiaceae family; botanical name is *Origanum majorana*)

✓ It is a Mediterranean herb of the mint family that has short, oval, pale green leaves with a sweet flavour (thus also known as sweet marjoram) like thyme and oregano with a strong aroma.

✓ It is a sweet/fresh herb which may be used fresh in salads, pork, fish, poultry, cheese, egg and vegetable dishes and when dried, it can be used for flavouring soups, sauces, stews and certain stuffings.

Chervil (from Apiaceae family; scientific name is *Anthriscus cerefolium*)

✓ It is a herb like parsley, with a slight taste of anise. It must be added late in the preparation of a dish to preserve its flavour.

✓ It is also called as cicely and sweet cicely. It can be used fresh or dry. Due to its attractive shape it is frequently used in decorating cold buffet dishes.

Note. The term "Fines herbs" is a mixture of fresh herbs usually chervil, tarragon and parsley and is added in many classical recipes. Coriander is also known as *cilantro*.

CULINARY SPICES

Depending upon which style of cooking chef does, or which type of dish chef is attempting, the use of one, two or more spices can make a huge difference to the overall flavour and aroma of the dish. Often it is the seeds of certain herbs that work as both herbs and spices. Some of the most common spices that we often use in culinary are as follows.

SPICES

- Ajwain
- Allspice
- Caraway seeds
- Cassia
- Cayenne pepper
- Cardamom
- Celery seeds
- Cinnamon
- Cumin
- Nigella
- Fenugreek
- Mace
- Dill seeds
- Nutmeg
- Paprika
- Poppy seed
- Saffron
- Sesame seed
- Clove
- Fennel

Pepper (from Piperaceae family, scientific name is *Piper nigrum*)

✓ A pepper has a hollow body with placental ribs (internal white veins) to which tiny seeds are attached (seeds are also attached to the stem end of the interior).

✓ A pepper can be white, yellow, green, brown, purple or red with a flavour ranging from delicately sweet to fiery hot.

✓ The genus includes sweet peppers and hot peppers. They are used whole as a flavouring agent or when ground for seasoning.

Salt (scientific name is Sodium Chloride)

✓ It is a substance resulting from the chemical interaction of an acid and a base, usually sodium and chloride. In simple terms, it is a white granular substance (sodium chloride) used to season foods.

Mustard (from Brassicaceae family; scientific name is *Brassica nigra*)

✓ It is a spice with a pungent flavour and available as seeds or ground or a condiment prepared with it. It is available in two forms/colours – yellow/white and brown/black.

✓ The *black seeds* contain myronic oil which gives the true piquant flavour but imparts them poor keeping quality while *white seeds* although have inferior flavour but better keeping qualities. It is used in mayonnaise, devilled dishes and Welsh rarebit.

Garlic (from Allium genus; scientific name is *Allium sativum*)

✓ It is a highly aromatic and strongly flavoured edible bulb-like food commodity and composed of several sections, called *flakes*. Each flake is encased in a papery covering. Garlic is used in most of the cuisines around the world for flavouring, for example, in salads, stews, sauces, etc.

Ginger (from Zingiberaceae; scientific name is *Zingiber officinale*)

✓ Ginger originated from a tropical plant from China and is used to flavour beverages and dishes in Asian and Indian cuisines. It has a taupe skin, ivory flesh and a peppery, sweet flavour with a hint of lemon. Ground ginger is used for baked goods and the whole root is used in curries, pickles and sauces.

Role of Herbs and Spices	
Herbs	Improve palatability, flavour, appearance of food; acts as a preservative; helps in digestion; cost effective and imparts nutritional balance.
Spices	Improve palatability, flavour, appearance of food; acts as a preservative and used for medicinal purpose also.

KEY TERMS

Fines herbs : A mixture of fresh herbs usually marjoram, chives, chervil, tarragon and parsley.
Cilantro : Coriander.
Flakes : Individual parts/section of any herb/spice like flakes of garlic.
Culinary herbs : Herbs that are mostly used for culinary purposes.
Culinary spices : All those spices that are mostly used for culinary purpose.

REVIEW QUESTIONS

1. Differentiate between herbs and spices.
2. Enlist any 15 spices and 15 herbs.
3. Elucidate the role of herbs and spices in cookery.
4. Write a short note on the medicinal values of herbs and spices.

43

CHAPTER

Basic Gravies, Curries and Sauces

Objectives

Students will be able to:

- expound culinary uses of different sauces;
- enlist menu examples/dishes made from different sauces; and
- explicate Indian masalas, gravies and their uses.

GRAVY/CURRY/SAUCE

Gravy is a kind of savoury sauce (but technically speaking gravy is not a sauce) often made from the juices that run naturally from meat or vegetables during the cooking process, often called *jus lie*. Typically, it is thickened with flour, corn starch or other congealing agents and mixed with water, broth, milk or wine. In North America the term *gravy* refers to a wide variety of sauces and often found thicker than British gravies. *Thin gravies* may contain only pan juices deglazed with liquid whereas sauces are made with the same technique but start with butter, lard or shortening or oil instead of meat or vegetable juices. Gravies are commonly served with roasts, meat loaf, rice and mashed potatoes. The French term *jus* is also used for gravy but primarily for the roast gravy, made by diluting the pan juices with water, clear stock or any other suitable liquid and then boiling it until all the flavours are absorbed into the stock. Remember, dishes described with *au jus* are prepared or served with this gravy.

USE OF BASIC SAUCES IN CONTINENTAL PREPARATIONS

Almost all continental preparations whether vegetarian or non-vegetarian are based on some kinds of sauces. It can be thin or thick, flavoured or plain, dark or light, but it is definitely based on the mother sauces or their derivatives. Sauce plays the same role in continental cuisine, that gravy plays in Indian cuisine. In continental preparations, a sauce is the crowning glory of any dish. From the basic "five mother" sauces, there are literally hundreds of variations of these sauces which may be used to dress, compliment, enhance and bring out the flavour of the food it is served with or as an add-on to the main dish. Some common/basic sauces used in continental preparations along with their base and menu examples are given below.

Sauce type	Mother sauce	Menu Examples (dishes made from given sauce type or mother sauce)
White sauce	Béchamel sauce	Lasagne, Croque monsieur, Moussaka, Pastitsio, Veal Prince Orlov, etc.
Blond sauce	Veloute sauce	Chicken veloute, Sole Veronique, Bisque d' homard, Oeufs Roland, etc.
Brown sauce	Espagnole sauce	Oeufs a l' Espagnole, Foie de veau a l' Espagnole, Cromesquis d' Amourettes à la Polonaise
Warm sauce	Hollandaise sauce	Filet de boeuf Bouquetiere, Filet de boeuf Brehan, Selle de veau Renaissance, etc.
Red sauce	Tomato sauce	Bourdeto (broth), Spaghetti milanaise, Vongole (pasta), Artichaut provencale
Cold sauce	Mayonnaise sauce	Fish mayonnaise (salad), Lobster mayonnaise, egg mayonnaise and in sandwiches.

Gravies in Continental Preparations	
Thick gravy	Leave tablespoon of fat in pan, add flour and cook it. Add stock/wine/water to this roux and reduce to achieve desire consistency.
Thin gravy	Remove fat from pan, add stock/wine/water and stir the mixture to deglaze until required consistency.
Flavoured gravy	Add extra ingredients (like onion, tomato, carrot, etc.) in pan gravy/*au jus*.
Plain gravy	Directly serve pan gravy or *au jus* (a gravy in which dish has been cooked) with the prepared dish.
Light gravy	For white meats (like poultry and fish), use light/golden coloured gravy.
Dark gravy	For red meats, gravy should be dark brown in colour.

INDIAN GRAVIES/CURRIES

Yakhni Gravy

✓ This Indian gravy is made with curd, gram flour (or besan), onion paste, nut paste, ginger-garlic paste and seasoning and flavouring agents/spices. Saffron and dried mint is also added to it, as they impart flavour as well as colour to the gravy.

White Gravy

✓ Indian white gravy is made with boiled onion paste and thickened with nut paste and curd; add seasoning and flavouring agents/spices. Its colour is usually between white to blond and may be modified by adding other ingredients like green chilies – it gives slight green tint.

Yellow Gravy

- ✓ It is available in two forms, i.e. Rajasthani yellow gravy and Mughlai yellow gravy. *Rajasthani yellow* gravy is made with curd, onion, seasoning, flavouring agents/spices and turmeric. Whereas *Mughlai yellow* gravy is totally based on white gravy with the addition of turmeric.

Brown Gravy

- ✓ Indian brown gravy is made with onion paste, chopped tomatoes, red chili powder, seasoning and flavouring agents/spices. Its colour is usually between brown and red and also popular by the name *Lababdar gravy* in Indian cuisine.

Green Gravy

- ✓ An Indian green gravy (*or palak gravy*) is made with cooked spinach, brown gravy, seasoning and flavouring agents/spices. Green chili paste enhances the green effect to this gravy. This gravy is also popular by the name *Hariyali gravy* in Indian cuisine.

Dry Masala

- Sambhar masala
- Molagai podi
- Garam masala
- Chaat masala
- Tandoori masala
- Buknu
- Panch poron
- Curry powder
- Meat masala
- Sabzi masala

Wet Masala

- Chana masala
- Korma masala
- Tandoori masala
- Vindalo masala
- Biryani masala
- Curry masala

Makhni Gravy

- ✓ *Makhni* means butter. This Indian gravy is made with cashew nut paste, *khoya*, tomato puree, milk cream, seasoning and flavouring agents/spices. Red chili powder gives the red hue to the dish. .

Kadhai Gravy

- ✓ This Indian gravy is made with chopped onion, dices of tomatoes, seasoning and flavouring agents/spices. Red chilli powder imparts red colour to the dish.

Achari Gravy

- ✓ This Indian gravy is made with onion, curd and achari masala, chopped tomatoes, seasoning and flavouring agents/spices. Add red chili powder, as it imparts red colour to the dish.

Korma Gravy

✓ Indian gravy made with brown onion, curd paste, seasoning and flavouring agents/spices. Add green chili paste, as it imparts green tint to the dish.

Salan Gravy

✓ Indian gravy made with paste of salan mirchi, tamarind pulp, seasoning and flavouring agents/spices. Add red chili powder, as it imparts red colour to the dish.

Vindaloo

✓ This Indian gravy is spicy in nature and was originally a Portuguese curry that was adapted by the indigenous people of Goa. It is made with wine, wine vinegar, garlic, lemon juice and made spicy by the use of more chili powder and black pepper.

Jalfrezi

✓ This Indian gravy is very much similar to Korma and is usually named for the way the food is cooked – literally it means stir fry or hot fry. It is saucy in nature and made with vegetables/roasted meat, potatoes, green peppers, onions and green chilies.

Other Gravies

✓ These include *masala gravy* (onion and tomato paste based gravy), *red gravy* (tomato puree based gravy), *paneer pasanda* gravy, *coconut gravy, rezala gravy, malai kofta gravy, mustard gravy* and so forth.

Gravy Usage		
White	North India	Malai Kofta, Navrattan Korma, Methi Matar Malai and so forth
Yellow	Rajasthan	Rajasthani Pakoda Kadi, Gatta Curry, Mughlai Paneer and so forth
Brown		Paneer Lababdar, Stuffed Babycorn (with aamchoori masala) and so forth
Green	North India	Saag Ghosht
Makhni	North Punjab	Murg Makhni, Daal Makhni, Paneer Makhni and so forth
Salan	Hyderabad	Mirchi Ka Salan, Baingan Ka Salan and so forth dishes.
Achari	Punjab	Achari Ghosht is a perfet example of it.
Korma	Uttar Pradesh	Often used in Korma preparations. Murgh Handee is an excellent example.

Yakhni	Kashmir	Dhaniwal Korma, Goshtaba, Heddar and so forth
Kadhai	North Indian	Kadhai Paneer, Kadhai Chicken, Kadhai Aloo, Kadhai Gobi and so forth
Jalfrezi	Bengal	Vegetable Jalfrezi, Paneer Jalfrezi, Chicken Jalfrezi, etc.
Vindaloo	Goa	Mutton Vindaloo and Fish Vindaloo are two excellent examples.

Note. *Gravy* is a type of sauce whereas *sauce* is a liquid or a cream or a semi-solid food. When meat is cooked plain or floured, the juice left over in pan is known as sauce which means sauce can be used to prepare food as well as to serve with food. On the other side, gravy contains meat or vegetable pieces and when flour is added to thicken the juice after the meat has been cooked, the resultant product is known as gravy. Gravy is used to prepare food thus it is considered a copartner in any prepared food.

KEY TERMS

Gravy : A kind of savoury sauce often made with pan juice/drippings.

Sauce : A wide range of flavoured liquids that serves (to mask flavour) as a part of the meal or dish.

Vongole : A pasta preparation tossed in butter with seafood and tomato sauce.

Korma : Term used for curry, but actually it is a cooking medium in which meats and vegetables are soaked.

Masala : Group/combination of Indian spices. It may be wet or dry.

Roux : Cooked thickening agent made from equal amount of fat and flour.

Rezala gravy : Awadhi traditional Indian white gravy.

Pasanda gravy : Indian gravy. Paneer Pasanda is an excellent example of pasanda preparations.

REVIEW QUESTIONS

1. What are the different Indian gravies? Explain any ten gravies briefly.
2. Differentiate between sauce and gravy.
3. Define the term sauce. Classify continental sauces and their uses in menu. Support each one with menu example.
4. Write a short note on Indian dry and wet masalas.

44

CHAPTER

Salad and Salad Dressing

OBJECTIVES

Students will be able to:

- expound salad types and their culinary role;
- reveal role of salad dressing in salad; and
- explicate parts of salad and qualities of good salad.

SALAD/S

Generally, *salads* are a combination of various cold ingredients which may be raw or cooked. Most salads are based on vegetables, especially leafy green vegetables but they also include fruits, meats, seafood, poultry, eggs, cheeses, etc. The term *salad* derives from the Latin word "Herba Salata" which means *salted salad*. Traditionally, simple and compound salads were served in individual or large crystal glass, china or wooden bowls. Some of the more expensive types of compound salads can be served on crushed ice. On a menu, salads often appear in different forms and served accordingly.

PARTS OF SALAD

- Base
- Body
- Dressing
- Garnish

As an Entrée Course

✓ Entrée salads consist of beef slices or chicken breast and are served as appetizer salads. Caesar Salad, Chef Salad, Greek Salad and Cobb Salad are some of the most popular entrée salads.

As an Accompaniment

✓ When serving salad as an accompaniment, it is served in side plate or in half plate. Remember, fruit and vegetable based *compound salads* can be served as a side dish (side salads) along with the main dish in place of vegetables. These salads usually consist of any one vegetable, which adds to the flavour of the main course.

As a Separate Course

- ✓ In 17-course French classical menu, the salad course is given separately after serving legumes. Nowadays, majority of salads are served pre-plated and most, whether green, mixed green, single or mixed and compound, are served on side or half plates.
- ✓ These salads are served after the main course in the French classical menu. They consist of green and savouring vegetables, hence, are light and refreshing.

As a Main Dish

- ✓ Salads that are served as a main dish consist of body building food such as meat, fish, eggs and cheese. The volume of this salad should be adequate to satisfy the normal appetite. *Salad bars* are an excellent example where a variety of salads is served.

As a Hors d'Oeuvres

- ✓ Generally, fish and meat based compound salads are served as a hors d'oeuvres or on all types of buffets because these salads arouse the appetite.
- ✓ These salads are often served on salad platters or in salad bowls. In 11-course French classical menus, salads are served as a hors d'oeuvre course.

Other Styles

- ✓ Salad can be served as a palate cleansing meal, dessert meal, etc. *Palate cleansing salads* are served after the main course in order to settle the stomach. *Dessert or sweet salads* (it contains whipped cream or gelatin) are served after the cleansing salads.

Food historians have stated that about 2000 years ago Romans ate greens topped with dressing and so did Babylonians. Salads were popularized in the United States in the late 19th century. It was in the later part of the 20th century when other parts of the world adopted salads as a part of their meals. *Readymade salads* are sold in the markets in countries like America, China, Australia and Japan. *Packaged salads* are even sold by popular food chains like KFC and McDonald's.

Classification of Salad

Meat and poultry salad

Meat and poultry based salads can be served as an appetizer, entrée or salad course or also placed on buffet table (in the starting) for self-service. In general, freshly cooked meat and poultry are used for salad making but often you will see that leftover products are also used in salad preparations. It is the responsibility of *garde manger* section to prepare all kinds of cold salad preparation whether it is based on egg, vegetable, fruits, meat, poultry or seafood. These salads can be prepared hot or cold but served only cold. Few examples of meat and poultry based salads are given below.

Hongroise	Salad made with bacon julienne, cabbage, potatoes, radish, lettuce and paprika. Finally, dress with lemon dressing.
Chatelaine	Salad made with hardboiled egg, truffle, artichoke, potatoes and tarragon. Finally, dress with vinaigrette dressing.
Viande	Salad made with brunoise of meat with chopped shallots, hardboiled egg, garnished with finely chopped parsley. Finally, dress with vinaigrette dressing.
Larb	Salad made with chicken, beef, duck, turkey, pork or sometimes fish, flavoured with fish sauce, lime juice and herbs.

Seafood salad

As the title suggests, these salad preparations are based on enormous variety of fishes and shellfishes with such a wide variety of fish and shellfish containing a wide spectrum of textures and flavours in seafood salads. Generally, seafood salad is made with shrimp, crab and grilled tuna which offer chance to chef to use pieces of small portions of fresh seafood that is often less expensive. But in all these cases, the high quality seafood will yield high quality results. Few examples of seafood based salads are given below.

Parsian	Salad made with fish, aspics, macedoine of vegetables, lobster, truffle, herbs and lettuce. Finally, dress with mayonnaise dressing
Fish Mayonnaise	Salad made with fish, tomato and parsley. Finally, dress with mayonnaise dressing.
Russian	Salad made with vegetables and decorated with tomato, egg, anchovies, lobster, ham and tongue. Finally, dress with mayonnaise dressing.
Nicoise	Salad made with French beans, tomato quarters, sliced potatoes, anchovies, capers and olives. Finally, dress with sauce vinaigrette dressing.

Raw Salads

(Fruits + Vegetables)

- Salade Celery
- Salade Turnips
- Salade Leeks
- Salade Cabbage
- Salade Apple
- Salade Astoria
- Assorted fruits
- Assorted vegetables

Cooked Salads

(Veg + Non Veg)

- Salade Beetroot
- Salade Andalouse
- Salade Viande
- Salade Japonaise
- Salade Mikado
- Salade Carmen
- Salade Artichoke
- Salade Cremone
- Salade Tosca
- Salade Lettuce

Fruit salad

Often, also called "dessert salad" as it is made with pieces of fresh fruits mixed (it must have at least three fruits to make a fruit salad) and finally served cold. These salads have both refreshing and good nutritive qualities, hence considered a healthy meal. It can be served as an entrée, appetizer or dessert salad. Fruit salad can range from a simple presentation to elaborate sliced or cut ingredients dressed with complimenting dressings. But before preparing any fruit salad, it is most important to check ripeness, texture and sugar level of raw fruits in order to produce a good salad. Few examples of fruit based salads are given below.

Creole	Salad made with scooped melon and ginger dice. Finally, dress with acidulated cream dressing.
Waldorf	Salad made with dice of apple, celery and bounded walnut. Finally, dress with mayonnaise dressing.
Japonaise	Salad made with tomatoes (in square pieces), pineapple and orange segments. Finally, dress with acidulated cream dressing.
Eve	Salad made with scooped out apple, filled with a dice of apple, pineapple and banana. Finally, dress with acidulated cream dressing.
Astoria	Salad made with grapefruit and orange segments with sliced red and green pepper on bed of lettuce leaves. Finally, dress with French dressing.

Vegetable salad

Firstly, all vegetables should be fresh when used to make salad. Vegetable based salads are one of the most common and basic salads; they are made with a single vegetable or by mixing together numerous kinds of vegetables. The vegetables that are commonly used to prepare salad include tomatoes, radish, cucumber, mushrooms, onions, beets, artichoke hearts and avocado. Even cooked vegetables like boiled potatoes are used to make salad. A variety of beans like black beans and green beans are also used for making salads, for instance, sprouted beans salad. Few examples of vegetable based salads are given below.

Tossed	Mixture of celery, lettuce, cabbage, herbs, onion and chives. Finally, dressed with vinaigrette or mayonnaise dressing.
Coleslaw	Salad made with juliennes of vegetables. Finally, dressed with mayonnaise dressing.
Verte	Salad made with lettuce hearts. Finally, dressed with vinaigrette dressing.
Lorette	Salad made with corn, julienne of beetroot, raw celery heart. Finally, dressed with vinaigrette dressing.
Gauloise	Salad made with lettuce leaves with strips of fresh nuts. Finally, dressed with mayonnaise dressing.

Saison	Salad made with lettuce hearts, salad vegetables in season. Finally, dressed with vinaigrette dressing.
Louisette	Salad made with lettuce hearts, quarters of tomato and skinned pipped grapes. Finally, dressed with vinaigrette dressing.

Egg salad

Egg based salads are usually high in protein and low in carbohydrates because they often include food mixed with seasonings in the form of spices, herbs and other foods and bound with mayonnaise based dressings. Its siblings include potato salad, seafood salad (such as crab salad and lobster salad), ham salad, chicken salad, fish salad, etc. Few examples of egg based salads are given below.

Aida	Salad made with chicory, tomato, artichoke, sweet pimentos and sieved boiled egg. Finally, dressed with mustard or vinaigrette dressing.
Mimosa	Salad made with lettuce hearts, filled orange, grapes skinned and stoned, sliced bananas and sprinkled with egg yolk. Finally, dressed with acidulated cream dressing.
Yam khai dao	A Thai spicy salad made with fried egg (khai dao).
Egg salad	Salad made with chopped hard-boiled eggs, mayonnaise, mustard, minced celery or onion, salt, pepper and paprika.
Piyaz	A salad made with hard-boiled egg, vegetables with the addition of any dry beans.

Rice salad

The essential element to a good rice salad is the proper preparation of rice before converting into salad. Rice salad is significantly affected by the quality, texture and flavour of rice. Generally, the best quality rice is a long grain polished rice. The texture of cooked rice will affect the rice salad because rice which is sticky or mushy will result in a salad which has a congealed (or solid) consistency when served. The flavour of the rice is affected by how it is prepared. Flavours can be infused in the cooking process such as using anything from slightly salted water to stocks or broths which will flavour the rice. Few examples of rice based salads are given below.

Glorified	Salad made with rice, crushed pineapple, egg, sugar, vinegar, flour and whipped cream. Finally, garnished with maraschino cherries.

Mixed Salads

(Compound + Composed)

- Salade Americaine
- Salade Windsor
- Salade Aida
- Salade Aurore
- Salade Catalane
- Salade Victoria
- Salade Russe
- Salade Creole
- Salade Dorzia
- Salade Italienne
- Salade Normande
- Salade Lorette
- Salade Polonaise
- Salade Oriental
- Salade Favourite

Oriental	Salad made with rice, tomato, garlic, French beans, pimentos and anchovy. Finally, dress with vinaigrette dressing.
Carmen	Salad made with rice, red pimentos, cold chicken and green peas.
Andalouse	Salad made with rice, quarter of tomatoes, sweet pimentos, garlic, onion and parsley. Finally, dress with vinaigrette dressing.

Grain salad

Grain based salads are usually high in minerals, vitamins and fibres. For instance, *three grain salad*, this is a delicious salad consisting of three separate grains—brown rice, pearl barley and wheat berries combined with the addition of crunchy apple, sweet raisins, red onion and toasted pecans. Finally dressed up with spicy honey based vinaigrette dressing. One can prepare enormous variety of cold and hot salads from different types of grains. Two examples of grain based salads are given below.

Three grains	A salad made with uncooked wheat berries, long grain brown rice and pearl barley.
Kisir	A salad made with fine bulgur, parsley, and tomato paste.

Pasta salad

Pasta based salads are prepared with one or more type of pasta, usually chilled and most often tossed in vinegar, oil or mayonnaise based dressings. It can be served as an appetizer, entrée or main course. The pasta salad can be as simple as cold macaroni mixed with mayonnaise, or as elaborate as several pastas tossed together with vinaigrette and a variety of fresh, cooked or preserved ingredients. These can include vegetables, cheeses, nuts, herbs, spices, meat, poultry or seafood. Few examples of pasta based salads are given below.

Bagration	Salad made with macaroni, celery, chicken julienne, artichoke, tomatoes, truffle, egg and parsley.
Macaroni	Salad made with cooked macaroni pasta. It is served cold and usually prepared with mayonnaise.
Assorted	Salad made with assorted pastas, most often tossed in vinegar, oil or mayonnaise based dressing.
Agrigento	Salad made with radiatori pasta, lettuce, tomatoes, roasted peppers, artichokes, mushrooms, olives and vinegar/oil.

Note. The ingredients used to make any salad must be distinct and neatly cut; not messy in appearance or mushy in texture. The size of the incorporated ingredients must be in balance with its position in the meal. Secondly, the flavour of salad must be well balanced, zestful or piquant, and not too strong nor bland.

Groups of Salads	
Broadly salads can be categorized as simple salad (raw and cooked salad) and mixed salad (compound, composed and warm salad).	
Raw salad	Salad made from raw fruits or vegetables without dressing (cut into fancy shapes like oval and round). It includes raw cucumber salad, raw tomato salad, raw onion, carrot, radish or beetroot salad, etc.
Cooked salad	Salad made from cooked/boiled ingredients like kidney beans, potato and sprouted beans. Dressing is must (either separate or on salad). Salad dressing may soft the grilled/roasted salad preparation, so be careful.
Compound	These salads are made by adding salad dressing like vinaigrette, mayonnaise or a similar dressing in any mixed salad.
Composed	In it, salad ingredients are arranged rather than mixed. The dressing is often added over the salad or may also be offered as an accompaniment.
Warm salad	In these salads, body and the dressing are served warm. Warm could mean anything from lukewarm (like *salade tiede*, a French luke warm salad) to piping hot.

Types of Salad Dressing

Salad dressing concepts vary from region to region. In North America there are plenty of commonly used salad dressings, for example, mayonnaise based ranch dressing, Caesar salad dressing, etc. *Crème fraiche* is the most commonly used dressing in Denmark. *Mayonnaise* is largely used as a dressing in Russia and Eastern European countries while *vinaigrettes* are used in Southern European countries. Light edible oils such as olive oil, safflower oil, soybean oil, and corn oil are often used in salad dressing. Some famous salad dressings are given below.

Role of Salad Dressing

- For flavour
- As lubricant
- To bind
- For nutrition

Vinaigrette dressing

✓ This salad dressing is prepared with the mixture of salad oil and vinegar (or lemon juice), enriched with herbs, spices and other seasonings. Other than being used as a dressing, it can also be used for seasoning and marinating purpose.

Mayonnaise dressing

✓ Mayonnaise is a rich creamy and smooth blend of vinegar, oil, salt and pepper with egg yolks and often mustard. All ingredients must be at room temperature. Mayonnaise based dressings are best used for cold food preparations.

Russian dressing

✓ It consists of a mixture of mayonnaise, pimentos, chives, ketchup and spices. The name comes from the earliest versions that included a distinctly Russian ingredient, i.e., *caviar*.

Thousand Island dressing

✓ It is made from mayonnaise sauce with the addition of bits of green olives, peppers, pickles, onions, hard-boiled eggs and other finely chopped ingredients. This dressing was invented in Thousand Island of New York.

Acidulated cream dressing

✓ Fresh cream and fresh lemon juice seasoned with salt. Various other items may also be included but in accordance with type of salad preparation.

Lemon dressing

✓ This salad dressing is made by adding salt, pepper, fresh lemon juice and olive oil to taste, with castor sugar.

French dressing

✓ French dressing is apparently an American invention. In the United States and Great Britain, the term French dressing is used for vinaigrette dressing. It is made with salt, pepper (mill), French mustard with one part vinegar to three parts of oil. It is also called French mustard dressing.

English dressing

✓ Salt, pepper, English mustard with two parts vinegar to one part of oil with castor sugar to taste (sugar will help in to "cut" the sharpness of vinegar). It is also called "English mustard dressing".

American dressing

✓ It is similar to English dressing with equal parts of oil and vinegar and sweetened with sugar.

Ranch dressing

✓ It is a condiment made of buttermilk or sour cream, mayonnaise, minced green onion, garlic powder, and other seasonings mixed into a sauce. This salad dressing owes its name to the fact that it was created on a ranch.

Italian dressing

✓ Italian dressing consists of a mixture of water, oil, vinegar or lemon juice, black pepper, minced onions and bell peppers. Often, it also includes sugar or high fructose corn syrup, and a variety of herbs and spices including garlic, oregano, fennel, salt and dill.

OTHER DRESSINGS

- Green Goddess
- Herb dressing
- Caesar dressing
- Chiffonade dressing
- Marseillaise dressing
- Blue cheese dressing

Wafu dressing

✓ It is a vinaigrette-type salad dressing based on soy sauce, popular in Japan. The name literally means Japanese-style dressing. The standard wafu dressing consists of a mixture of Japanese soy sauce, rice vinegar and vegetable oil. There are many variations of it.

Escoffier dressing

✓ In order to make it, add juice of half a lemon, dash of Worcestershire sauce, Tabasco sauce and sweet paprika powder into one litre of mayonnaise.

Roquefort dressing

✓ Similar to vinaigrette dressing but with the addition of Roquefort cheese (it is passed through a sieve). Sometimes this dressing is also called "blue cheese dressing" if Roquefort cheese is replaced with blue cheese.

Green Goddess

✓ A salad dressing that is a mixture of mayonnaise, anchovies, tarragon, vinegar, parsley, scallions, garlic, and other spices.

KEY TERMS

Salade tiede	:	Warm salads like Salade Tiède aux Oeufs en Meurette.
Compound salad	:	Mixed salads. And its texture and flavour can be improved by adding salad dressing.
Salad dressing	:	A liquid condiment used to enhance the flavour and texture of salad.
Mayonnaise	:	A cold sauce/dressing made with oil, dry mustard, vinegar and lemon juice mixed with egg yolks.

Vinaigrette	:	An acidic sauce/dressing made with vinegar, oil, mustard and seasonings.
Dessert salad	:	A salad made with fresh fruits.
Garde manger	:	A cold kitchen also known as larder section.
Crème fraiche	:	A salad dressing most commonly used in Denmark.

REVIEW QUESTIONS

1. What are the different parts of a perfect salad? Explain each part briefly.
2. Enlist any four qualities of a good salad. Classify salad into different groups and explain in brief.
3. What is salad dressing? Enlist any six and explain them briefly.
4. Explain the role of salad dressing in any salad preparation.

45 CHAPTER

Food Plating and Presentation

Objectives

Students will be able to:

- expound the role of good food presentation;
- explicate the techniques of food presentation; and
- expose standard guidelines for plating and presentation.

FOOD PLATING AND PRESENTATION

Plating and presentation is one of the most important things to consider when portioning and keeping the prepared dishes, as we all know that food is firstly observed by eyes then by eating. The term *plating* refers to the process and sequence of placing a meal on the plate or platter whereas the term *presentation* is related with appearance and arrangement of food in the plate or platter. A poor presentation of well prepared food lowers its value. Thus, whether presenting appetizers on a platter, soup in a soup bowl/ plate/consommé cup, main course in portion bowl, entrée dish (or directly in plates), or presenting dessert, make sure they are presented attractively. In pre-plated food service, the term plating also incorporates portion size. In kitchen, chef uses *spoodle* for correct portioning of food.

If food is to be eaten with the fingers (like in finger buffet) then make sure to offer small/bite size food items. Occasionally, diners may be given plates to place selected finger foods but they are generally eaten one at a time. Finger food is pre-portioned in such a manner so that each item can be consumed in one or two bites. Finger foods should be easy to eat and not messy in nature. When sauces, relishes and dips with finger foods are served to standing diners they should be served in such a way that the likelihood of someone dropping the sauce on him or her could be minimized.

Principles of Food Presentation

According to Escoffier Online International Culinary Academy, there are three primary elements of dish in specific parts of the plate, i.e., main protein, starch and vegetable based food items. The term *main protein* refers to main dish/key ingredient of the plate such as fish steak, whereas *starch* is concerned with starchy food preparations like French fries and *vegetable* reflects to side dishes often served as an accompaniment such as glazed vegetables. Apart from this, the placement of each of these food items is also a key component of food plating and presentation. A simple guide to classical plating is to consider a plate as face of a clock. The brief guidelines and focal points for food plating are given below:

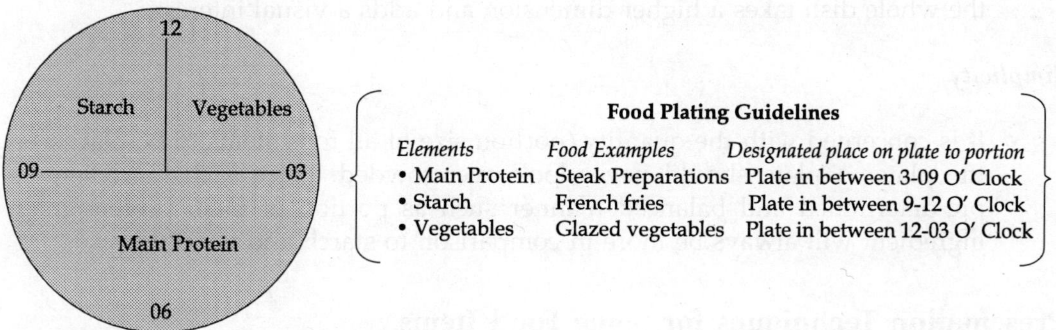

Food Plating Guidelines

Elements	*Food Examples*	*Designated place on plate to portion*
• Main Protein	Steak Preparations	Plate in between 3-09 O' Clock
• Starch	French fries	Plate in between 9-12 O' Clock
• Vegetables	Glazed vegetables	Plate in between 12-03 O' Clock

ESSENTIALS OF PLATING

- Balance
- Colour
- Shape
- Texture
- Portion
- Temperature
- Flavour

Emphasis

✓ It is concerned with placement of key ingredients onto the plate as it requires more space than remaining two food items on the plate thus its portion size must be pre-specified.

Balance

✓ It is concerned with placement of all three selected dishes onto the plate. All three primary elements of the dish must be carefully plated on their designated places and ensure that all sides are equal in terms of overall weight of the plate.

Contrast

✓ It is concerned with placement of dishes in a balanced manner according to their shape and colour for the purpose of attractive visual appearance of the whole plate.

Colour

✓ It is concerned with the selection of complementary colours or creates a focal point with a single burst of bright colour. A check can also start with drawings and sketches to visualize the plate.

Texture

- ✓ It is concerned with visualization of different textures of the dish in the components of the plate. By contrasting firm and soft, silky and rigid texture, the whole dish takes a higher dimension and adds a visual interest.

Simplicity

- ✓ It is concerned with the quantity/portion size of all food items to be placed on the plate. A plate should never look overcrowded. Place each ingredient in pre-determined and balanced manner such as portion of main protein/main ingredient will always be more in comparison to starch and vegetables.

Presentation Techniques for Some Food Items

The food presentation must have unique characteristics that will affect the overall *meal experience* of guests. The accompaniments for any platter can be included as part of the platter design or as part of the garnish. Accompaniments can also be served separately in small separate dish that has their own serving utensils. Buffet items should have signage (or *tent cards*) to identify main items and accompaniments. Some guidelines for presenting several food items are given below.

Cheese presentation

- ✓ A good cheese presentation will always demand a cheese trolley, as it gives a huge space in an attractive manner to display the enormous variety of cheeses. The cheese variety should always include cheeses from different categories and the layout of cheese should guide the order of tasting like milder to softer or younger to stronger/ripen cheese.
- ✓ When cheese is offered for tasting then some items should be served as accompaniments like assorted cheese biscuits/crackers, radish in season (in glass bowl), cruet set (salt, pepper and mustard), celery (in glass bowl on a bed of crushed ice) and water.
- ✓ But when cheese is served as a part of a buffet, the cheeses should be selected from a range of styles according to the guest demographics. The cheese should be cut appropriately in order to ease the self-service for guests.

Caviar presentation

- ✓ Caviar should be presented in such a way that clearly defines the portion that the guest should take. It is always good to serve the caviar from the original packing container, glass bowl or silver dish. Caviar is available in both raw and processed form and in two colours, red and black. Beluga, Sevruga, Sterlet, Starka and Osetrova are considered as best caviars in the world.

- ✓ In fine dine restaurants, caviar is mostly served pre-plated in half plate accompanied with hot breakfast toast, *Blinis* (Russian pancakes), lemon wedges, butter, chopped shallots, chopped parsley and sieved hardboiled egg. All accompaniments are served in separate bowls/plates by placing on underliner.
- ✓ In buffet service, place caviar on a large platter, elevate with ice pedestal and surround with small spoons or croutons that contain the portion of caviar that is intended for each guest. Remember, caviar should never be served by/in metal made material.

Fruit platter presentation

- ✓ While serving fruits, one should always select seasonal varieties that are sufficiently ripened but not over-ripe. Select fruits with different textures, colours and flavours, as it creates colour contrast plus taste variation.
- ✓ In fine dine restaurants, assorted cut fruits (or pieces of fruits) are served in half plate to table seated guest. Kitchen pantry is responsible for preparing and portioning assorted cut fruits. Often fruit trolley is also used which carries an array of fresh fruits.
- ✓ In buffet service, one may use whole fruit as it can be attractively arranged into designs or carved into interesting shapes for a centerpiece or focal point on buffet table. On the other side, fruits may also be peeled or partially peeled, portioned on attractive platters into bite-size pieces or slices.

Vegetable presentation

- ✓ Like fruits, always select seasonal, fresh and crisp vegetables. Vegetables may also be used whole like white gourds and squashes work well as whole and uncut or carved as the *pièce montée* as well as peel and cut into shapes that are easy to eat, as well as interesting to observe.
- ✓ Vegetables can serve as salad, main course and side dish. Consequently, its plating and presentation differs with intended purpose of serving.
- ✓ Chef may mix different shapes and colours to form attractive patterns. Lastly, offer appropriate dips and dressings as accompaniments.

Charcuterie presentation

- ✓ Charcuterie is the branch of cooking devoted to prepared cold meat products such as bacon, ham, sausage, terrines, galantines, patés, confit, etc., primarily from pork. The assortment of charcuterie items makes the platter attractive and eye appealing via different shapes, textures and flavours.

✓ In charcuterie, the focal point can be an arrangement of partial sausages and salamis positioned in the back centre area of the display. Slices can be shingled forward into lines that appear to have originated from a larger solid part. Accompanying chutneys, relishes, pickles and crusty breads should be served on the side.

Deli tray presentation

✓ The tray should contain a combination of sliced meats and cheeses, accompanied by relishes, salad items, condiments and breads. Food can be prepared in advance and dropped off at a location without the need of service staff.

Guidelines for Plating and Presentation	
For sauces	When offered separately – sauce is served in a sauce/gravy boat with sauce ladle (after placing on underliner) whereas when served on the same plate – it should be poured over, around or under the food; but usually not preferred to be scattered over the plate.
Accompaniments	Accompaniments should always be served separately in their own appropriate dish like butter in butter dish, bread rolls and sticks in bread basket, etc. Sauces and *au jus* is served in sauce/gravy boat.
For plate	Never pour any dish over the rim of the plate; food should always be plated inside the rim. Serve most of the pre-plated food in half plate and ensure that emblem should be on top (so that guest can clearly see and read it). Generally, side plate is not used for any pre-plated food serving.
Temperature	A golden rule of service to be remembered here: serve hot food hot and cold food cold. In order to maintain temperature, use hot plate for serving hot dish and vice versa.
Dishes	Arrange dishes attractively into the bowl, platter or directly onto the guest plate. Ensure proper garnishing of both pre-plated and pre-bowled/pre-portioned (into platter) dishes. Place food in the most attractive manner.
Garnish	A garnish is only added to a plated meal or platter for balancing the meal and it must be functional also. In simple terms, use garnish only when necessary.

KEY TERMS

Spoodle : A combination of a spoon and a ladle often used to guarantee portion sizes.

Cheese biscuit : It is also known as *cheese crackers* accompanied with assorted cheese.

Meal experience	: Series of occurrences that take place between staff and guest during the eating hours.
Consommé cup	: Twin handle soup cup mostly used to offer consommé soups.
Confit	: French word for various foods that have been immersed in a substance to flavour and preserve.
Finger buffet	: Buffet counter that consists of finger foods.
Pièce montée	: French word which means mounted piece. It is a kind of decorative confectionery centerpiece in an architectural/ sculptural form used for formal banquets.
Au jus	: Pan drippings or juice that comes from a roasting pan after deglazing.
Caviar	: Roe/egg of fish.

REVIEW QUESTIONS

1. Write down the importance of food presentation in menu pricing.
2. Elucidate the essentials of food plating and explain each briefly.
3. Write a short note on assorted cheese presentation.
4. What is deli tray presentation?

46

CHAPTER

Nutrition

OBJECTIVES

Students will be able to:

- expound the role of different nutrients in human body;
- explicate the source of different nutrients; and
- classify food into groups and their impact on body.

NUTRITION

Nutrition is the science of food. It is the study about the food you eat and how your body uses it to live, grow, support good health and, in general, make you look and feel well. Good health is impossible without good nutrition. Good nutrition allows you to function efficiently and resist infections and diseases. Nutrition influences the look, hair, eyes, complexion, teeth, gums, etc. Nutrition also affects the personality. Irritability usually occurs when a nutritional deficiency develops. Our physical and mental efficiency is affected by nutrition. *Nutrient* is a chemical component of food (called "food factor"). In the body, nutrients perform the following functions: produce energy, facilitate growth and repair of tissues and regulate body processes.

COMPONENTS OF NUTRITION

The food that we consume provides essential chemical compounds (like proteins, fats, carbohydrates, vitamins, minerals and water) called *nutrients*. Nutrients are needed by our body to stay healthy and grow. Various nutrients are required by human body to carry out its vital activities and to sustain life. Of these nutrients, micronutrients include protein, fat and carbohydrates. Good nutrition is a term synonymous with maintenance of healthy body. A brief description of various nutrients is given below.

Proteins

Much of the body's structure (e.g., muscles, skin and hair) is made up of proteins. Protein is the basic chemical unit of the living cell, essential for their nutrition, growth and repair, and to provide heat and energy. It also forms the enzymes that control chemical reactions throughout the body. It is considered an essential source of amino acids. Our body requires amino acids to produce new proteins (or protein retention) and to replace damaged proteins (or protein maintenance). It is required for basic structural unit, needed in metabolism, hormone, antibody and in DNA production. Major sources of protein include:

- Animal sources — Meat, game, fish, poultry, egg, milk, cheese, etc.
- Plant sources — Beans, peas, nuts, starchy vegetables and grains.

Carbohydrates

It is essential for providing energy to the body and works as building blocks for other nutrients. It can be divided into three sub-categories, i.e., monosaccharides (simple sugar), disaccharides (simple sugar) and polysaccharides {complex carbohydrates (C.C.)}, which mainly depend on the number of monomer (sugar) units they contain. They constitute a large part of foods such as rice, noodles, bread, and other grain based products. Major sources of carbohydrate include:

TYPES OF CARBOHYDRATES	
Sugar	Monosaccharides
Sugar	Disaccharides
C.C.	Polysaccharides

- Monosaccharides — Found in juices, soda and cookies
- Disaccharides — Found in juices, soda and cookies
- Polysaccharides — Found in starchy vegetables, pasta and bread

Fats

Fat is the most concentrated source of energy from all the food compounds. It is a molecule of dietary fat which typically consists of several fatty acids, bonded to a glycerol. They are typically found in *triglycerides* (three fatty acids attached to one glycerol backbone). There are two kinds of fats – saturated fats (remain solid at room temperature) and unsaturated fat (remains liquid at room temperature). Source of fats includes butter, margarine, oil, animal (like lard), milk, plants and vegetables, etc. Its basic functions include:

- It protects vital organs in the body and produces energy.
- It reduces the risk of heart attack and stroke.
- It aids in maintaining the body weight in the long run.
- It is also a good source of energy.
- Also works as a good source of heat, insulation and body protection.

TYPES OF FATS	
Saturated	Animal
Unsaturated	Vegetable

Fibres

Types of Fibre
- Soluble Fiber
- Insoluble Fiber

Fibre or dietary fibre is a carbohydrate (or a polysaccharide) and like all other carbohydrates, when it is metabolized it can produce four calories of energy per gram. There are two categories of fibre – insoluble fibre and soluble fibre. Whole grains, oats, low-fat nuts and seeds and fresh fruits and vegetables are good for building fibre in the body, as they are low in calories. Its basic functions include:

- It prevents cancers like colon and stomach cancer.
- It lowers the cholesterol level in the body.
- It helps digestive system and completes a diet.
- It prevents the harmful toxins hanging around the body.
- Insoluble fibre is found in whole wheat flour, nuts and vegetables.
- Soluble fibre is found in oats, peas, beans and in many fruits.

Minerals

Types of Minerals
- Macro minerals
- Trace minerals

It is a chemical element required by living organisms, other than the four elements – carbon, hydrogen, nitrogen and oxygen that are present in nearly all organic molecules. A large number of minerals are present in the body. Some of these form part of body structural components and some others act as *catalytic agents* in many body reactions. It is required for skeleton, protein synthesis, oxygen transport, fluid and acid-base balance in the body and for enzyme reactions. A brief description of different minerals is given below.

- Potassium — A trace mineral essential for growth and good health.
- Iron — It binds oxygen in the blood, giving it its red colour.
- Calcium — Found in bones, shells and limestone, among other materials.
- Phosphorus — Major component of bones and teeth and makes up part of DNA and RNA.
- Sodium — It helps to control the amount of fluid around the body's cells and regulate blood pressure.
- Others — Other or trace minerals include iodine, cobalt, chromium, selenium, copper, etc.

Vitamins

They are micronutrients which are required in small quantities, but their availability in our diet is vital. Like minerals, some vitamins are recognized as essential nutrients, necessary in the regular diet for good health. Its deficiency may result in diseased conditions like impaired immune system, disorders of cell metabolism, certain forms of cancer, eating disorders and premature aging whereas its excess may also be dangerous to health. Vitamins can be classified into two groups, fat soluble and water soluble vitamins. Its basic functions include:

CLASSES OF VITAMINS	
Fat soluble	A, D, E, & K
Water soluble	B & C

- Its deficiency or excess may lead to diseases.
- They have multiple functions like metabolism, enzyme reactions.
- They promote body growth and help in resisting several diseases.
- They aid in reproduction, digestion of food and maintenance mental alertness.

Water

Water is a source of life for everyone. It is excreted from the body in multiple forms including urine, sweating and by water vapour in the exhaled breath. Water is required for absorption, excretion, secretion, digestion, metabolism and finally to maintain body temperature. Pure ordinary water (H_2O) consists of hydrogen (11.1888 per cent) and oxygen (88.812 per cent). It has a slightly blue colour and is slightly compressible. Mineral water is perfect for drinking. Mineral water can be classified as:

- Artificial: These are manmade mineral waters. In it, all required minerals like sodium, salts, magnesium, etc., are incorporated in water in accordance with local governing laws of state.
- Natural: These are natural waters having refreshing qualities. They also contain minerals (naturally or gift of nature) that may have health giving properties.

Food Poisoning Diseases	
Salmonella	It produces mild or severe illness. Amongst them are bacteria that cause gastroenteritis, typhoid fever and enteric fever. It can be spread through meat, egg and milk based dishes.
Staphylococcal	These produce harmful toxins.
Botulism	It is caused by a powerful poison from *Bacillus botulinus* but fortunately occurs very rarely.
Hepatitis	It is caused by infectious or toxic agents found in raw clams and oysters that are taken from polluted water.
Dysentery	It is particularly prevalent in tropical climates.

FOOD GROUPS

Vegetables

✓ Fresh vegetables are an important part of a healthy diet. They include a large variety such as spinach, potato, cabbage, cauliflower, broccoli, carrot, turnip, etc.

They provide several vitamins, minerals, fibres and enzymes and are known for offering a number of health benefits.

- ✓ Green, leafy vegetables are rich in iron, which is an important constituent of blood. As vegetables are low in sugar and fats, they are included in weight loss diets. Generally, vegetables contain high amounts of fibres. Therefore, they are good for the digestive system.
- ✓ Most vegetables consist of photochemicals, which help to prevent chronic diseases such as diabetes, heart disease and some types of cancers. Consumption of vegetables in their raw form or in the form of juice is more preferable, so that one can get all their health benefits.

Vegetable Family	
Cabbage	Coloured cabbages, Brussels sprouts, cauliflower, broccoli, kohlrabi, etc.
Stalk vegetables	Asparagus, celery, Swiss chard, bok choy, etc.
Leafy vegetables	Spinach, kale, collards, sorrel and so forth
Salad greens	Endive and lettuce
Vegetable fruit	Cucumber, okra, eggplant, tomatoes, peppers, squash, etc.
Bulb	Onion, scallion, green onions, shallots, leeks, chives, garlic, etc.
Edible fungi	Truffles and a variety of mushrooms
Special vegetable	Artichoke and rhubarb
Others	Seeds, edible pods and shots like peas, bean sprouts, beans, corn, snow peas, etc.

Fruits

- ✓ Fruits such as orange, mango, grapes, lemon, peach, apricot, etc., are a rich source of vitamins, minerals, fibres and carbohydrates. They contain a high quantity of antioxidants, which protect the body from potentially harmful substances.
- ✓ Citrus fruits such as lemons, grapes and oranges are high in vitamin C. The fruits like apricot, cantaloupe, nectarine and peach are a rich source of vitamin A. One can consume these fruits whole or in the form of juice.
- ✓ Broadly, fruits can be classified as *fleshy fruits* and *dry fruits*. Fleshy fruits can be further classified as simple fleshy fruits, fleshy aggregate fruits and fleshy multiple fruits. Apart from it, fresh fruit can also be classified on the basis of their nature.

Classification of Fruits (based on their nature)	
Pome fruits	Apple, Asian pear, European pear, quince, etc.
Stone fruits	Apricot, cherry, nectarine, peach, plum, damsons, greengages, etc.
Small fruits and berries	Grape (European and American types), strawberry, raspberry, blueberry, blackberry, cranberry.

Citrus fruits	Grapefruit, lemon, lime, orange, pummelo, tangerine and mandarin.
Non-citrus fruits	Avocado, cherimoya, fig, kiwi, olive, pomegranate, etc.
Tropical fruits	Banana, mango, papaya, pineapple, carambola, cashew apple, durian, guava, longan, lychee, mangosteen, passion fruit, rambutan, sapota, tamarind, etc.

Starchy Foods

- ✓ Starchy foods such as cereals, maize, bread, pasta, cornbread and potatoes are an essential part of a healthy diet. They contain simple or complex carbohydrates, which are an important source of energy.
- ✓ Starchy foods are considered fuel for the body, providing energy. More fibre-rich foods in this category are the whole grain foods such as brown rice, whole wheat bread, grits or oatmeal.

Dairy Products

- ✓ Dairy products include milk, cheese, cream, butter, yogurt and other byproducts of milk. They are an excellent source of calcium and proteins. Dairy foods are also rich in vitamins A, B and D. Calcium is important for the health of bones.
- ✓ Vitamin D is required for building and maintaining bone health. Most milk products are high in fats, which help to build up the body and provide energy.

Egg, Meat and Fish

- ✓ They are the most important sources of proteins, zinc, iron and B vitamins. These nutrients are necessary for growth and repair of the body. Eggs are a rich source of iron and protein. Meat is a major source of vitamin B12.
- ✓ Fish is also a significant source of proteins. Some oily fish such as salmon, sardines, herring and mackerel contain high levels of omega-3, essential fatty acids.

Fats and Oil

- ✓ Oil includes groundnut oil, coconut oil, sesame oil, sunflower oil, safflower oil whereas fat could be vegetable fat or animal fat (like butter and ghee). Fat can be visible fat like oil. There is also invisible fat that cannot be seen but consumed. For example, nuts and oil seeds also contain fat.
- ✓ In fact, our body needs fats but it is important to avoid eating too much of it. This food group has more calories than nutrition so we should always use it sparingly; if we use them in excess, it may cause obesity.

✓ Fats such as butter, cheese, salad dressings and oils are high in calories. Unsaturated fats present in vegetable oils, seeds, nuts, olive oils, oily fish and avocados are beneficial for health, as they lower the cholesterol levels.

KEY TERMS

Nutrition	: Science of food.
Food factor	: Chemical components of food.
Catalytic agents	: Enzyme that produces a chemical reaction without itself changing.
Cobalt	: A metallic chemical element with a variety of uses.
Saturated fat	: Fats that remain solid at room temperature.
RNA	: It stands for Ribonucleic acid that is present in all living cells. Its principal role is to act as a messenger carrying instructions from DNA for controlling the synthesis of proteins.
Nectarine	: The fruit from *Prunus persia* tree; the fruit is a variant of the peach.
Food poisoning	: Illness caused by bacteria or other toxins in food, typically with vomiting and diarrhoea.
Cholesterol	: A fatty substance found in foods derived from animal products and in the human body.
Fibre	: A group of indigestible carbohydrates found in grains, fruits and vegetables.

REVIEW QUESTIONS

1. What is nutrition? Classify different nutrients and explain them briefly.
2. Describe the impact of food group knowledge in any menu planning.
3. Write a short note on food poisoning and its causes.
4. Enlist any five foods from every phase of food group pyramid.

47 CHAPTER Basics of Bakery

OBJECTIVES

Students will be able to:

- enlighten themselves about bakery essentials and famous breads;
- explicate the role of low/high bakery temperature; and
- expound methods used to make bread and quick bread.

BAKERY

The term *bakery* refers to the place/section/sub-kitchen where a range of baked products are manufactured through baking process. *Baking* is the process of prolonged cooking of food by dry heat, i.e., by convection; not by radiation, normally in an oven. It is primarily used for the preparation of bread, cakes, pastries and pies, tarts, quiches, cookies and crackers. Baking food involves the use of dry heat in an oven. The temperature range for baking is 130°C to 235°C. It is similar to roasting, but there is no liquid involved. Baking is both an art as well as science because baking is a process of bringing together a balanced quantity of ingredients in a proper form.

The baking process does not require any fat to be used to cook in an oven. Some bakers of snacks such as potato chips or crisps have produced baked versions of their snack items as an alternative to the usual cooking method of deep-frying in an attempt to reduce the calorie or fat content of their snack products. Flour, egg, leavening agents, fat, liquid (like water), sugar, flavouring agents, colouring agents, garnishing agents, etc., are a few basic bakery essentials/ingredients.

Technical Baking Terminology

Baker's dozen	Thirteen of anything, a bonus of one over the regular dozen.
Bloom	A white coating which appears on the surface of chocolate after variations in temperature over some time. Probably it is re-crystallized fat and sugar.
Caramelize	To heat sugar until it becomes brown.
Coddle	To poach gently in barely simmering liquid.
Conching	To process chocolate in conche in an attempt to refine flavour and texture by warming and grinding.

Crimp	To compress into small folds or ridges the ends or edges of something, e.g., pastry together.
Dot	To put small pieces of butter, fat or cheese over the surface of food to be grilled.
Dust	To sprinkle a powdery substance like flour, sugar or other substace over something, e.g., sugar over a cake.
Egg wash	A mixture of egg or egg yolk with milk or water to brush the food to be baked, to glaze and to give brown colour.
Floured	Dusted with thin layer of flour.
Flute	An indentation pressed into the edge of pie crust or pasty for decoration or to help seal two edges of pasty together.
Glaze	To apply a thick liquid over the surface of a food item in an attempt to give a final glossy sheen.
Knead	To press and fold dough to achieve smooth consistency like in making of bread.
Hot water bath	Cook in bain marie or double boiler.
Macerate	Tossing fruits in sugar, lemon, wine, liqueur or in any other liquid to absorb its flavour.
Lecithin	A natural substance found in egg yolk used as an emulsifier and antioxidant to reduce the viscosity.
Mask	Covering a surface of food with cream, icing, frosting, sauce or other substance.
Meringue	A whisked mixture of egg white and castor sugar. This mixture is beaten to a stiff consistency.
Mold	To make an attractive shape by filling a decorative container then it may be baked, steamed or chilled.
Pinch	The amount of powder held between the thumb and forefinger, roughly equal to one quarter of a gram.
Pipe	To squeeze soft food mixture through a small tube, so as to make decorative shapes.
Plump	To soak dried fruits in liquid until they swell.
Proof	To test the baker's yeast for potency before baking.
Refresh	To immerse boiled/blanched vegetables in cold water so as to cool them quickly and prevent further cooking.
Roll out	To spread a ball of dough flat by using a rolling pin.
Scald	To scald milk means to heat milk to a temperature just short of the boiling point where bubbles appear around the edges of pan.
Sift	To remove doable lumps of dry ingredients by using a strainer or sifter.

Tempering	It is a method used to establish proper crystallization of cocoa butter crystals in melted chocolate in an attempt to achieve a shiny, dark and hard finish.
Unmold	To remove a food from a mould; this mould is used to keep the prepared food in proper shape.
Whip	To lighten and increase the volume of a mixture by beating in a specified direction either with fork, whisker or blender.
Whisk	To beat the liquid with whisk or whip until well mixed.
Blind baking	A British term applied to pre-baking pastry cases for flans, pies, tarts, etc.

Baking Temperature	
Low temperature	It is required for those bakery products which bake on lower baking temperature (usually between 120 and 180°C). For instance, meringues (130°C), egg custard (165°C), cabinet pudding (170°C), ratafia biscuits (180°C), etc.
High temperature	It is required for those bakery products which bake on higher baking temperature (usually between 200 and 260°C). For instance, Genoese sponge (195°C), pudding soufflés (200°C), soufflés (210°C), vol-au-vents (215°C), croissants (220°C), bread rolls (230°C), savarins (235°C), etc.

BAKERY PRODUCTS

Bread and Yeast bread

Bread is a kind of food prepared from dough which is made from flour and water (or other liquid), usually by baking. Yeast is also an important component in bread making, as it makes the dough puffy. This puffy dough with yeast is fermented, kneaded and finally baked in oven. The action of raising agent gives bread its characteristic texture. It can be baked (in an oven or, as with pancakes, on a griddle), fried or steamed. Flavour, aroma and texture are the qualities that account for the popularity of yeast bread and rolls.

Yeast Breads

- Muffins
- Brioche
- Croissant
- Doughnut
- Danish pastry
- Baguette

Yeast breads are made from strong plain flour (or bread flour) which contains high gluten. It differs from quick breads in that they are leavened by yeast, a living organism, rather than baking soda and baking powder and are often lower in fat and sugar. When mixed with water and sugar, the yeast ferments to produce carbon dioxide, filling the bread dough with tiny air bubbles. Water also combines with the gluten (protein) in the flour to form the elastic structure of the dough that traps the air bubbles and makes the bread rise.

Standard Process of Bread Making

Raw material

- ✓ It includes flour, liquid (water/milk), yeast and salt. Measure all ingredients and sift the dry ones (like flour and salt). Side by side, dissolve the yeast in the liquid (all at once) and mix well the dry ingredients, until blended.

Kneading

- ✓ Now, knead the composed ingredients: water, yeast or leaven and flour, with a little salt to improve the final taste into a homogeneous mixture. Traditionally, kneading was done manually but nowadays, mechanical kneading is used.
- ✓ Due to kneading, the yeast or leaven is incorporated into the dough. It strengthens the gluten in the flour, thus making the dough elastic in texture.

Fermentation

- ✓ It occurs at a favourable temperature when a raising agent is mixed into the flour and water dough. The basic purpose of fermentation is to make the bread lighter; it also gives the bread its characteristic texture, appearance and smell.
- ✓ The process of fermentation acts on sugar in the damp hot dough to produce alcohol and CO_2, which forms gaseous bubbles that raise the dough. The first stage of fermentation takes place in the kneading dough then it is weighed and shaped into loaves and left to rise.

Make pans ready

- ✓ While the dough is rising, meanwhile make the baking pan ready by greasing and lightly flouring them. Size of the pan should be suitable to the dough. It should not be too big or too small. The ideal size for two pound bread loaf is 9 × 5 × 3 inches.

BREAD EXAMPLES

- Melba toast
- Babka
- Anadama Bread
- Sippet
- Pretzel
- Pita
- Panettone
- Oatcake
- Nutbread
- Zwieback
- Crispbread
- Wheat breads
- Rye breads
- Focaccia
- Fougasse
- Bagel
- Bap
- Vienna
- Frankfurter
- Cornell bread
- Water bread
- French bread
- Graham bread
- Garlic bread
- Raisin bread
- Herb bread
- Cheese bread

Punching and proofing

- ✓ In *punching*, the fermented dough is kneaded once again in order to knock out the air. For this, turn the lightly floured surface and knead for 2-3 minutes and turn it into desired shape and place in baking pan (on baking sheets) then cover with plastic wrap.
- ✓ In *proofing*, the shaped dough should be left at room temperature to rise again (until double in size).

Baking

- ✓ It may be done in a heated oven (basic breads are baked at 450°F). The loaves are put in fhe oven as quickly as possible. When cooked and obtained required colour, they are taken out and placed in the cooling-off room.

Cooling-off

- ✓ After baking, the bread is put into cooling-offroom. Due to it, the bread loses its humidity before being used. Once the bread or rolls are baked, they should be removed from the pan because pans retain heat after being removed from the oven.
- ✓ The resultant cooking is termed "carry over" cooking which means the heat from the pans gets transferred into the bread, consequently bread becomes dry. Perfectly baked bread can be ruined by *carry over* cooking.

Note. *Fine bread* is another category of bread, it includes bread sticks, French toast, etc. *Washing* is one more step (but optional) in bread making process. In it, most of the yeast products are brushed with a wash before baking. This brushing may be done either with egg wash, water wash or sugar based glaze.

Common Bread Preparation Faults

- Lack of volume
- Undue volume
- Lack of crust colour
- Excess crust colour
- Shell tops
- Rough surfaces
- Collapsing bread
- Seams
- Cores
- Holes in bread
- Streaks
- Condensation
- Damp clammy
- Crumbliness

Bread Making Methods

Sponge dough method

This method allows yeast to speedily and fully ferment and activate with part of the flour and water in the recipe and later be incorporated with the remaining ingredients. Some bakers feel this method offers a better texture, rise and taste for very rich or heavy yeast dough recipes compared to the straight dough method. Sponge doughs are prepared in three stages. This procedure gives the yeast an instant start.

Stage 1 Combine the liquid, the yeast and part of the flour (and sometimes part of the sugar).

Stage 2 Mix into a thick batter or soft dough. Now ferment the dough until double in size.

Stage 3 Punch down and add rest of the flour and the remaining ingredients. Mix to a uniform and smooth dough.

Straight Dough Method

In its simplest form, the straight dough method consists of only one step: combine all ingredients in the mixing bowl and mix. Many bakers make good quality products by using this procedure. However, there is a possibility that the yeast may not be evenly distributed in the dough. It is therefore safer to mix the yeast separately with a little water. In it, the following stages are involved:

Stage 1 Soften the yeast in a little water. Ideal temperature is 110°F.

Stage 2 Combine the remaining ingredients, including the rest of the water, in the mixing bowl.

Stage 3 Add the dissolved yeast, taking care not to let it come in contact with the salt.

Stage 4 Mix to smooth developed dough.

Modified Straight Dough Method

This method is for rich sweet dough. This method is the modification of straight dough method to ensure even distribution of fat and sugar. Following stages are involved:

Stage 1 Soften the yeast in part of the liquid, using a separate container.

Stage 2 Combine the fat, sugar, salt and flavourings and mix until well mixed, but do not whip until light.

Stage 3 Add the eggs gradually, as fast as they are absorbed.

Stage 4 Add the liquid and mix briefly. Afterwards, add the flour and yeast then mix well to make smooth dough.

MAJOR BREAD INGREDIENTS

- Flour
- Liquid
- Sugar
- Salt
- Shortening
- Egg
- Yeast

QUICK BREADS

Quick bread means bread that is quick to make because it does not require kneading or rising time. Quick bread is an American term used to denote a type of bread which is leavened with leavening agents other than yeast. The leavening agent in such a bread is usually baking powder or baking soda, which, when combined with moisture, starts the rising process immediately. In case of double-acting baking powder, oven heat causes a second burst of rising power. Eggs can also be used to leaven quick breads. Examples of quick breads include muffins, biscuits, and popovers along with a wide variety of sweet and savory loaf breads.

Types of Quick Breads

The type of quick bread produced is variable based predominantly on the method of mixing, major flavouring, and the ratio of liquid in the batter. Some batters will be thin enough to pour, and others will be thick and consequently be dropped. Therefore, quick breads are available in different consistencies.

Broadly, quick breads are grouped into two parts – *batter based quick breads* (like muffins and loaves) and *dough based quick breads* (like biscuits and scones). Batter based quick bread can be made from *pour batter* and *drop batter*, similarly, dough based quick bread can be made from *soft dough* and *stiff dough*. A brief description of both methods and their types is given below.

Quick Bread Examples

- Coffee cakes
- Pancakes
- Soda breads
- Fruit breads
- Cookies
- Corn breads
- Scones
- Muffins
- Tea breads
- Doughnuts
- Waffels

Pour batter

- ✓ As the name suggests, it is a batter of thin consistency, so that it can pour directly from mixing bowl into the baking pan. For instance, pancake batter, have a liquid to dry ratio of about 1:1, so it pours in a steady stream. Griddle cake, waffles and popovers are examples of pour batter based baked products.

Drop batter

- ✓ Drop batters are thick enough that require spooning into the baking pan. Drop batters such as cornbread batters and many muffin batters, have a liquid-to-dry ratio of about 1:2. Muffins, nut breads, coffee cakes, dumplings and drop biscuits are examples of a drop batter based baked products.

Soft dough

- ✓ Soft dough such as chocolate chip cookie dough has a liquid-to-dry ratio of about 1:3. Soft dough sticks significantly to work surfaces. This dough can be easily rolled and shaped into desired form (by hand, but it is slightly sticky). It is used to make biscuits, scones and shortcakes.

Stiff dough

- ✓ Sugar cookie and pie crust dough are considered stiff dough and are easy to work in that they will only minimally stick to work surfaces including hands. Stiff dough is produced with a ratio of approximately 1:8 (liquid to dry ingredients).

Methods for Making Quick Breads

Blending method (also called "Muffin Method, Stirring Method or Quick Bread Method")

- ✓ In this method, dry and wet ingredients are measured separately then quickly mix both separately (mixing is done by spoon or spatula to prevent the dough from being over beaten and deflating the egg's lift). Dry ingredients are mixed together in a bowl while all liquid ingredients are mixed together in another bowl.
- ✓ Often wet ingredients include beaten egg (it has trapped air to allow the dough to rise) and liquid fats (like cooking oil). Then, the liquid ingredients are poured into a hollow-well made in dry ingredients and stirred only until the flour is moistened. The batter looks very lumpy. The muffin method may also be used for loaves of quick bread.

Shortening method (also called "biscuit method")

- ✓ The term biscuit method is used because this technique is used for making biscuits, scones, and pie crusts. In this method, dry ingredients are sifted and stirred together.
- ✓ Then, the chilled fat (one may use lard, butter or vegetable shortening) is cut into dry ingredients (by blenders or food processor) until mixture resembles coarse crumbs.
- ✓ All the liquid is added and stirred to make soft dough. The layering from this process gives the rise and adds flakiness as the folds of fat melt during the baking process.

Creaming method

- ✓ This method is often used for *cake batters*. The butter and sugar are creamed or beaten together, until smooth and fluffy consistency is reached. Eggs and liquid flavouring are mixed in and finally dry and liquid ingredients are added.
- ✓ The creaming method combines rise gained from air pockets in the creamed butter with the rise from the chemical leaveners. Gentle folding of the final ingredients prevents destroying these air pockets. Quick loaf breads and many coffee cakes may be made from creaming method.

Standard Process for Making of Quick Bread

All quick breads rise quickly to become tender and light. The varieties of quick breads is almost countless. But almost all quick breads have similar preparation method with same basic ingredients (but in different quantities), i.e., leaveners, flour, eggs, fat (like butter, margarine, shortening, or oil) and liquid most prominently milk. Ingredients beyond these basic ingredients are included for variation in flavour and texture. A brief description of various steps involved in quick bread making process is given below.

Raw material

- ✓ Raw material for quick breads are composed of flour (all-purpose flour), baking powder, baking soda, salt and sugar (sugar is optional).
- ✓ Other ingredients like fat, eggs and liquid (milk or water) are used as per the requirement of the recipe. There are also a number of flavourings (like spices, fruits and nuts) which can be added to the recipe.

Mixing method

- ✓ First, mix the dry ingredients in a large bowl and if fat/shortening is used, cut it into the dry ingredients. Now take a second bowl and mix the wet ingredients into the dry ingredients and stir only until combined (but do not over-mix, as over-mixed batter creates tough and rubbery quick breads).
- ✓ Often *blending method* is used for making quick breads but one may also use other methods like *creaming method*, especially for making cakes.

Preparation method

- ✓ Now pour the batter into pre-greased (greased with butter) pans of muffin cups. Be sure to also grease the top of pan as muffins will expand making large tops.
- ✓ Now bake in preheated oven. When baked test for doneness with a toothpick and if properly baked then immediately remove from the pan and keep them on racks to turn cold.

PASTRY

Pastry is a general term for various kinds of baked goods made from ingredients such as flour, butter, shortening, baking powder or eggs. Small cakes, tarts and other sweet baked goods are also called *pastries*. Pastry may also refer to the dough from which such baked goods are made. Pastry dough is rolled out thinly and used as a base for baked goods. A general process for making pastry includes following steps:

Raw Material

- ✓ The basic ingredients for making any pastry include flour, fat, liquid, salt, sugar, leavening agent and eggs (optional).

FAMOUS PASTRIES

- Fleuron
- Linzertorte
- Profiterole
- Croque en bouche
- Éclairs
- Gougere
- St. Honore

Mixing of Ingredients

- ✓ Sift flour and salt together into a mixing bowl, as this helps to lighten the mixture. Additional air can be incorporated by lifting flour from the bowl by rubbing it with fingertips.

Adding Liquid

- ✓ It is always good to add very cold liquid but carefully because its excess makes the dough sticky.

Rolling and Baking

- ✓ Now lightly and firmly roll out the dough but do not roll more than required. Always use firm, light strikes and roll in one direction only. Finally, bake in preheated oven.

Note. Pastry shells are baked unfilled (if possible) because filling may cause the crust to become soggy and sometimes filling itself cannot be baked properly. But if recipe demands that filling is to be added and baked, then the shell should be partially baked.

Types of Pastries

Laminated pastry

These pastries contain solid fat which is repeatedly folded into the dough by a technique, called *lamination*. In simple terms, laminated dough is made by encasing butter in dough, and taking it through a series of folds then rolled and finally turned to produce layers of butter in between the sheets of the dough. The leavening in this dough is mainly derived from the steam generated by the moisture from the butter. The laminated fat traps water vapour and carbon dioxide formed during baking, and as steam expands in the oven, it lifts and separates the individual layers. Laminated pastries include:

Rough pastry

- ✓ It is also known as "flaky pastry or quick puff or blitz puff pastry". It is a simple pastry that expands when cooked due to sum of layers. It is a crisp and buttery pastry. The puff is obtained by beginning the baking process with a high temperature and lowering the temperature to finish.

- ✓ It is used to make pastries (or baked pastry), turnovers, savoury pies and sausage rolls and plaits. The chunks of fat keep the rolled particles of dough in the pastry plus separate from each other, so that when the dough is baked they become flakes.
- ✓ This creates a different texture from a puff pastry, where rectangles of dough and fat are rolled and folded together in such a way that the result is a number of uniformed sheets of pastry.

Puff pastry

- ✓ The French people call it "multilayered pastry or pate feuilletee". The puff pastry has many layers that cause it to expand or "puff" when being baked. These pastries are made by using flour, butter, salt, and water.
- ✓ It rises up due to the combination and reaction of the given four ingredients and also from the good amount of air that gets between the layers.
- ✓ Puff pastries come out of the oven light, flaky, and tender. It is used to make a variety of creations including Croissants, Napoleons, Palmiers and Allumettes.

Phyllo (filo) pastry

- ✓ The term phyllo is a Greek word which means leaf. Phyllo pastries are usually paper-thin, translucent and greatly stretched sheets of pastry. They involve several stretched out layers and are wrapped around a filling and brushed with butter.
- ✓ Phyllo can enclose a huge variety of fillings, both savory and sweet. These pastries are very delicate and can break easily, very much similar to strudel.
- ✓ These pastries are mainly used in Greek, Eastern European and Middle Eastern cuisines. The well known phyllo pastries include Baklava and Spanakopita.

Non-laminated Pastry

These pastries contain solid fat which is added by cutting it into the flour or added as melted or liquid oil. Like laminated pastry varieties, there are also enormous pastries that come under the category of non-laminated pastries. Some of them are as follows.

Short-crust pastry

- ✓ The short-crust or short pastry is the simplest and most common type of pastry. It is made with the ingredients flour (soft), fat (butter), salt and water. The process of making pastry includes mixing of the butter and soft flour, adding water, and rolling out the paste.

- ✓ The paste should not be kneaded, as rolling will compact the mixture. It is cooked at 180°C and the result is a soft, tender pastry. This may be prepared with or without eggs. It is also called "lining pastry". It is ideal for both sweet and savoury pies and tarts.
- ✓ A sweetened "sweet-crust pastry" is a relative type of short crust pastry. Sweet-crust pastry is made with the addition of sugar, which sweetens the mix and impedes the gluten strands, creating a pastry that breaks up easily in the mouth.

Choux pastry

- ✓ It is also called "cream puff pastry, choux paste or pate a choux". The choux pastry is a very light pastry that is filled with cream.
- ✓ The pastry is filled with various flavours of cream and is often topped with chocolate. Choux pastry paste is versatile and used to make many items, such as cream puffs, éclairs, profiteroles, croquembouche, Saint Honoré, etc.

What is hot water crust pastry?

The *hot water crust pastry* is made with all purpose flour, salt, lard and milk or water (or both). The prepared dough is heavy as it is made by heating water and fat (lard) together and mixing them into the flour. Because of the high quantity of water used, the pastry is quite hard and strong, making it suitable for encasing heavy mixtures such as veal, pork, ham or raised game pies without collapsing. In Great Britain, this dough is used for the raised meat pies. While still warm, the pastry is moulded into the desired shape and filled with demanded fillings.

KEY TERMS

Proofing	:	The process of yeast dough's growth leading to the final baking.
Punching	:	The kneading of fermented dough once again in order to knock out the air.
Baguette	:	It is a long bread stick, usually showing an evenly golden crisp crust with seven diagonal cuts across the top.
Pretzel	:	The brittle, hard, salted German bread that is formed into a looped shape resembling the letter B.
Fleuron	:	A small crescent shaped pastry made of puff dough that is used to garnish fish dishes and soups.
Linzertorte	:	An Australian pastry comprising short crust dough and flavouring agent.
Gougere	:	A French pastry (specialty of Burgundy) made with choux pastry, flavoured with cheese.
St. Honore	:	It is one of the examples of famous pastry.

Fine bread	:	It is another category of bread that includes bread sticks, French toast and so forth.
Scones	:	A small British quick bread of Scottish origin served with cream teas.

REVIEW QUESTIONS

1. Define pastry. Classify pastry and explain each one briefly.
2. Enlist any 25 types of bread.
3. Enlist any ten examples of low temperature and high temperature bakery products.
4. Define yeast bread/quick bread. Explain different methods used to make quick breads.

48 CHAPTER

Cold Kitchen

Objectives

Students will be able to:

- enlist the common terms used in cold kitchen;
- explicate the major preparations of cold kitchen; and
- expound the work profile of cold kitchen.

COLD KITCHEN

Cold kitchen is also known as *larder kitchen* or *garde manger*. Within the kitchen organizational structure, the garde manger is a hybrid position. Historically, the position was adopted to put a responsible person in charge of keeping food fit to eat. It means that a certain amount of understanding of sanitation and food preservation, coupled with training in meat butchery and food preparation is essential. In the modern commercial kitchen, the "cold kitchen, larder section or garde manger section" is responsible for preparing cold foods like hors d' oeuvres, cold canapés, cold meat, cold fish and other cold preparations. Apart from it, cold kitchen also prepares cold sauces, salads and salad dressings. In large properties, cold kitchen comprises the following sections.

SECTIONS OF COLD KITCHEN

Starter Section

Two Key Functions of Cold Kitchen

- Works as a cold store
- Prepares cold items

- ✓ This section of larder kitchen is responsible for the preparation of all cold starters or cold hors d' oeuvres. Cold starters are the assortment of foods which are well seasoned to stimulate the appetite and served as the first course.
- ✓ The food which can be used for preparing cold hors d' oeuvres includes meat, poultry, fish and shellfish, game, eggs, vegetables, salads, fruits and any other food that may be available in the kitchen.
- ✓ Often cold dishes made from these ingredients are termed as *deluxe hors d'oeuvres*. For instance, prawn cocktail, Pâté de foie gras, caviar, lobster mayonnaise, etc.

Salads and Salad Dressing Section

- ✓ This section is responsible for the preparation of a variety of cold salads which may be either vegetarian or non-vegetarian. Vegetarian salads can be served either raw or cooked (such as carrot, onion and tomato salad) or cooked (such as kidney beans, potato, etc.) but non-vegetarian salads can only be served cooked like *salade viande*.
- ✓ But remember all salads prepared in salad section must always be served cold, whether prepared hot or cold. Vegetable based cold salads are usually further classified as simple and compound salads. *Simple salads* include chopped celery salad, green cabbage salad, turnip tops and leeks salad. *Compound salads* include salade russe, salade oriental, salade astoria, salade waldorf and salade imperiale. On the other side, *salade viande* is a perfect example of non-vegetarian meat salad.
- ✓ The preparation of dressings for these salads is also the sole responsibility of this section. The major salad dressings include lemon dressing, mayonnaise dressing, vinaigrette dressing, etc.

Cold Sauces Section

- ✓ This section is responsible for the preparation of various cold sauces. For example, mayonnaise sauce and its derivatives (like Chantilly sauce, Cambridge sauce, Gloucester, Remoulade, Andalouse, Tartar sauce, Thousand Island dressing and Cocktail dressing).

Seafood Section

- ✓ This section is responsible for the preparation of various types of seafood based dishes like fish and shellfish based preparations, particularly for buffet froid and deluxe hors d'oeuvres. Consequently, these could be served as appetizer or cold buffet froid items.

Poultry and Game Section

- ✓ The section is responsible for the preparation of various poultry and game dishes. The term 'poultry' (volaille) applies in general to all domesticated birds (like guinea fowl), whether bred for table purposes or for their eggs.
- ✓ The term *game* (gibier) applies to various game birds which are considered fowl. Game birds would include pheasants, wild turkeys, quail, partridge and mallards. This section may also deal with dishes made from game animals.

Butchery Section

- ✓ The function of the butchery section (La Boucherie) is to prepare all raw meat for the kitchens. This involves the breaking down of wholesale cuts of meat, or carcasses, into joints and small cuts for entrées, such as stews, pies, minces, steaks, escalopes, cutlets, fillets, medallions etc., as required by the menus of the day or for banquets.
- ✓ Butcher has to prepare and trim each cut carefully so that it should be ready to make different dishes without any further trimming. This involves removing of all excess fat, all gristle and sinew, and any bones, which might interfere into table side carving; simultaneously butcher is also required to carry out correct food portioning of the meat.

Buffet Froid

- ✓ *Chef du Froid* is the in-charge of this section. The functions and duties of Chef du Froid and his/her team members include the preparation, dressing and often the serving of cold buffet items. For example, preparation of aspic, chaud-froid sauces, pies, galantines, terrines, pâtés, mousses or soufflés, pressed beef, brawns, boars head etc., as well as the various fillings for sandwiches and cold savouries, canapés and so forth.
- ✓ These buffet items can range from the elaborate display buffet set out in the restaurant or grill room or both, to the reception buffet, the cocktail party buffet, the cold luncheons for weddings or other banqueting functions, and the preparation of sandwiches for teas, dances, etc.
- ✓ This section must also be skilled in cooking and dressing of fish and shellfish, hams, tongues and other pickled meats, and in the dressing of smoked fish or meats, often showing a special flair and skill for artistic display and presentation.

Forcemeat Section

- ✓ This section is responsible for making of forcemeats. It is very important that only the best of meat or fish and other materials are used. All forcemeats should have a good binding but at the same time should be light and not too dry.
- ✓ To get a good binding, breadcrumbs are used for the simpler forcemeats and so-called *panadas* for the finer ones. To make them smooth, light and white, water, milk, or cream is used in accordance to the forcemeat made. There are numerous forcemeats, from the simple sausage meat to the finer forcemeats used for the making of hot mousses and soufflés.
- ✓ They are usually made from fish and shellfish, the white meats, like veal and pork, as well as from poultry, game, fish and certain vegetables and bread. To call the latter forcemeats would, in English, not be quite correct; those made of vegetables and bread are usually called *stuffing*, whereas, in French, all of these are known as *farces*. A wide variety of dishes for the outlet menus can be prepared from the various forcemeats.

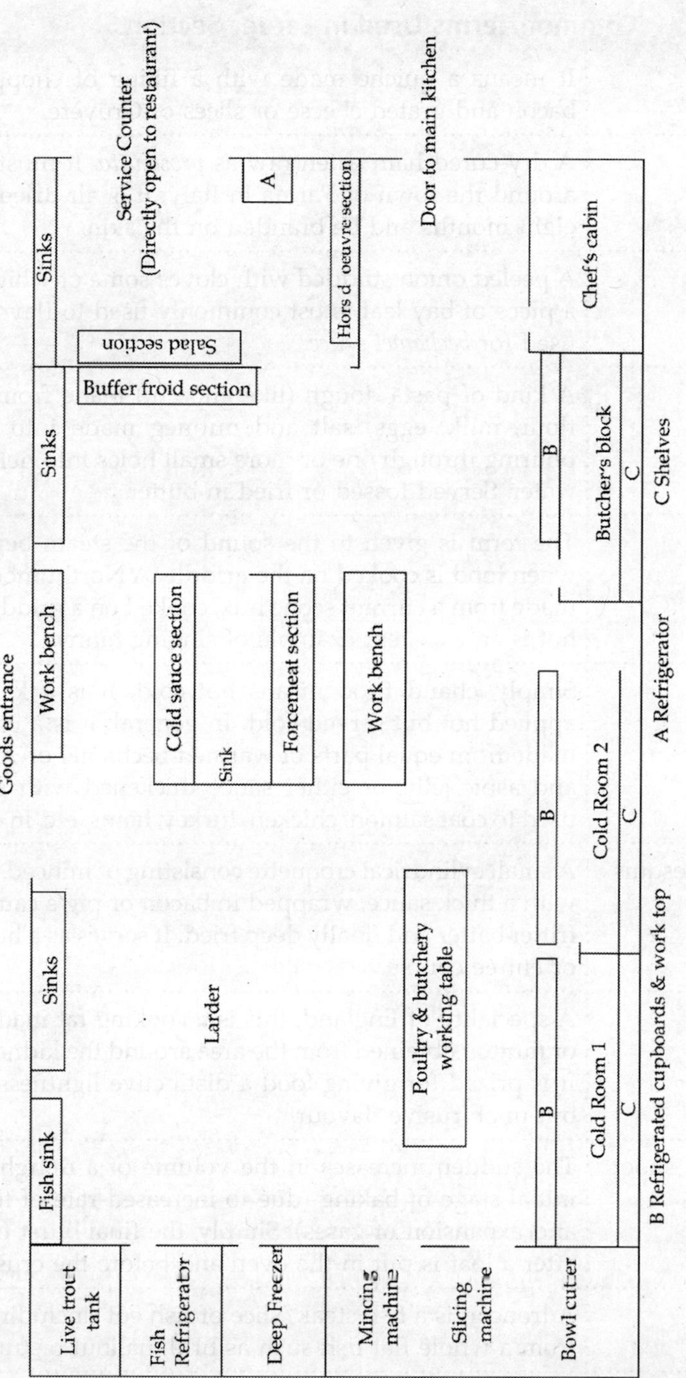

Fig. 48.1 Sections of Larder Kitchen

Common Terms Used in Larder Section	
Quiche Lorraine	It means a quiche made with a filling of chopped ham or bacon and grated cheese or slices of Gruyère.
Parma ham	A dry-cured ham eaten raw as *prosciutto.* It must come from around the town of Parma in Italy; it is air-dried for at least eight months and be branded on the skin.
Cloute	A peeled onion studded with cloves some of which may hold a piece of bay leaf, most commonly used to flavour the milk used for *béchamel sauce.*
Spätzle	A kind of pasta dough (like gnocchi) made from a batter of flour, milk, eggs, salt and nutmeg made into noodles by pouring through one or more small holes into fiercely boiling water. Served tossed or fried in butter.
Singing	The term is given to the sound of the steam being released when food is cooked on the griddle. A Northumberland cake, made from a currant scone mix, cooked on a griddle and eaten hot is an excellent example of singing hinny.
Chaud froid	Simply, chaud friod means hot cold. It is a kind of sauce applied hot but served cold. In general, it is a coating sauce made from equal parts of warmed béchamel or velouté sauce and aspic jelly, or either sauce thickened with gelatin. It is used to coat salmon, chicken, turkey, hams, etc. in cold buffets.
Kromeskies/Cromesquis	A small cylindrical croquette consisting of minced meat bound with a thick sauce, wrapped in bacon or pig's caul, dipped in fritter batter and finally deep fried. It serves as a hors d'oeuvre or entrée course.
Suet	A speciality of England, this is a cooking fat made from beef or mutton obtained from the area around the kidney and loins. It is prized for giving food a distinctive lightness, and a rich but unobtrusive flavour.
Oven spring/oven shoot	The sudden increases in the volume of a dough during the initial stage of baking (due to increased rate of fermentation and expansion of gases). Simply, the final burst of rising just after a loaf is put in the oven and before the crust hardens.
Troncon	A troncon is a fish steak/slice of fish cut (including the bone) from a whole flat fish such as brill, halibut or turbot.

Quenelles	Fish, meat or poultry meat processed to a very fine forcemeat, bound with eggs or fat, shaped with two spoons into small round or oval dumplings and poached in a cooking liquor. It is served as a garnish or as a main course with a sauce.
Bitok	It is a French name for a Russian meat loaf served with soured cream. It is prepared with a minced pork or beef patty with breadcrumbs and sweated chopped onions bound with egg, panéed, fried in chicken fat or lard. Finally served with ling-on-berry or cranberry sauce or the pan residues deglazed with sour cream.
Balsamic vinegar	It is also called "wine vinegar". It is a wine in which the alcohol has been biologically oxidized to acetic acid. The normal concentration is 3 to 4 per cent of acetic acid.
Larding	It is the process of threading strips of fat into the surface of meat in order to prevent it from drying out during the cooking process.
Darne	A darne is a thick fish steak/slice of fish that cuts across the backbone (including the bone) usually from a round fish like salmon, cod, hake and monkfish.

FUNCTIONS OF LARDER KITCHEN

Larder or garde manger is considered by many to be the most demanding station/job in any kitchen. Garde mangers need to be able to apply proper seasoning to food that is going to be served cold and in other cases, season food that is going to be served hot. A true garde manger has it all, including the ability to present beautiful plates and platters on an artistically arranged buffet accented with fruit, vegetable, tallow and ice carvings. A brief work profile of garde manger section is given below.

MAJOR COMPONENTS OF FORCEMEAT

- Meat/base agent
- Binding agent
- Seasoning agent
- Flavouring agent
- Garnishing agent
- Additives

To Prepare Forcemeats

✓ Forcemeats are ground up meat/s combined with seasonings and other ingredients and used for stuffing. Forcemeat is prepared in various types, it primarily includes *straight forcemeats, country style forcemeats, gratin forcemeats, emulsified forcemeats* and *moussline forcemeats.*

To Prepare Cold Preparations

- ✓ Cold preparations include a range of dishes like salads, gelatin, canapés, charcuterie, etc. A brief description of various cold preparations is given below.

Cold Hors d'oeuvres

- ✓ There are numerous cold hors d'oeuvres preparations like relishes, melon frappé, dolmas, olive, galantine, fruits, savoury jelly or aspic, carolines, cold sandwiches, dips, spreads, finger foods, etc. These can be served as single starter as well as part of assorted hors d'oeuvres.

Salads

- ✓ Salad is a dish of raw or cold cooked foods usually dressed and seasoned, served as an hors d'oeuvres, side dish and sometimes as an accompaniment and so forth. There are variety of salads which can be broadly classified into three parts: green salad, compound salad and composed salad.

Gelatin

- ✓ Gelatin is a colourless and odourless substance extracted from the bones and cartilage of animals and also from certain algae. Gelatin can be either in the form of powder, sheet or granular.
- ✓ The gelatin is soaked in cold water until it swells then dissolved either over or with a little boiling water. Finally, blended with the mixture for which it is intended.
- ✓ Gelatin is used for making jellies, numerous cold or iced desserts and also for the fining of wines and fruit juices. It is also used in industrial confectionery.

Types of Gelatin

Gelatin comes from a single strand of the protein collagen, which resembles a triple helix spiral. According to Pharmacopeia, there are two types of gelatin.

Type A Gelatin	It is made from collagen-rich tissue and bone pre-treated with an acid. The acid increases the amount of collagen converted into gelatin. Commercially pork skin is most commonly used for this purpose.
Type B Gelatin	It is made from collagen-rich tissue and bone pre-treated with an alkali. The alkali increases the amount of collagen converted into gelatin. Normally, beef bone and calf skin are most commonly used for this purpose.

Note.

- The strength and clarity of gelatin is measured with the help of "Bloom metre". A lower bloom normally has greater clarity while a higher bloom will have a lower quality of clarity.
- Gelatin can be used as a base (like in gelatin based dessert), binding agent (like in savoury cold mousse), to form structure (like in marshmallow), to form crystal (like in ice cream, crystal formation), etc.

Aspic Jelly

- ✓ Aspic jelly is a translucent savoury preparation which solidifies on cooling because of the gelatinous substance that it contains. Aspic jellies are prepared from basic white or brown stocks (of meat, poultry, game or fish). They are produced naturally when the stock is prepared with items rich in gelatin (like veal knuckle, fresh bacon rind, poultry or fish trimming).
- ✓ Aspic jellies are used in particular for preparing such cold dishes as aspics and terrines; as a garnish for cold dishes (chopped or cut into triangles) and to glaze cold preparations.
- ✓ Meat, poultry and game aspic stocks are reserved for aspics, terrines, etc., of which the dominant element is the same that of the jelly. For aspic fish or shellfish, gelatin in powdered or leaf form is dissolved in strained and clarified fish fumet.

Cold Sandwiches

- ✓ Again it is the responsibility of larder to provide variety of cold sandwiches in accordance to the guest order and outlet's menu. Sandwiches are the combination of two slices of bread enclosing a plain or mixed filling based on cooked meats, raw vegetables or cheese, then cut into thin slices or small pieces.
- ✓ Sandwiches are usually made with tin loaf bread (whole slices with or without crusts, sometimes cut into triangle or rectangular shape after filling).

Cold Canapés

- ✓ Canapés (cold canapés) are an appetizer, specifically a small piece of bread with a highly seasoned topping. The slice of bread is cut into various shapes and garnished. Apart from cold canapés, it is also available in hot version or hot canapés. Cold canapés are served at buffets or lunches or with cocktails or aperitifs.
- ✓ Few examples of cold canapés are canapés aux anchois (canapé with anchovies), canapés aux asperges (canapé with asparagus), canapés aux crevettes (canapé with shrimps or lobster), canapés au saumon fume (canapé with smoked salmon), canapés au cresson (canapé with watercress), canapés à la danoise (Danish canapé) and canapés arlequins (harlequin canapé).

Chaud Froid

✓ It is a dish which is prepared as a hot dish but served as a cold dish. Chaud froid preparations are usually based on pieces of meat, poultry, fish or game, coated with brown or white sauce then glazed with aspic. Typically, they form part of a cold buffet but are also served as an entrée.

Charcuterie

✓ Charcuteries are the food products based on pork meats or offal's. The word designates the place where this type of product is prepared. Charcuterie or pork butchery prepares numerous pork based preparations like cured meats, fresh and smoked sausages, patés, andouilles, hams, galantines, ready cooked dishes and ofcourse forcemeats.

Edible Displays

✓ Edible carvings include those items which can be used as decorative showpieces as well as one can also eat them. Its examples include carved fruits, nougat, chocolate, marzipan, decorated cakes, etc.

Inedible Displays

✓ The basic motive of inedible displays is same as the above – to use as decorative centerpieces, most preferably in buffet counter but it cannot be eaten.

✓ Its examples include thermocal carving, salt dough, pastillage, ice carving, etc. One most prominent benefit of most of the inedible carvings is that it can be reused in several subsequent occasions.

Quick Scroll on Larder Preparations

Forcemeats

✓ Forcemeat is a mixture of ground, *lean meat* emulsified with fat. The emulsification can be accomplished by grinding, chopping, sieving, or pureeing the ingredients. The emulsification may either be smooth or coarse, depending on the desired consistency of the final product.

✓ Forcemeats are used in the production of numerous items found in charcuterie like quenelles, sausages, pâtés, terrines, roulades, and galantines.

Galantine

✓ A traditional French dish made from poultry, meat or fish that is boned and stuffed with forcemeat, and often studded with items such as pistachio nuts, olives and truffles.

Ballotine

✓ A ballotine is a piece of meat, fish, or poultry that has been boned, stuffed and then rolled and tied into a bundle. It is then usually poached or braised. Menu dishes include the breasts of chicken pressed between cling films and 'hammered' with a variety of stuffing.

Pies

✓ It could be a sweet or savory dish made with a crust (it can be made with variety of mixtures like short crust or flaky pastry) and filling (such as fruit, pudding, meat or vegetable). There can be a range of fillings both sweet and savoury.

✓ The popular pies include beef steak and kidney, chicken and mushroom pie, veal and ham pie, etc. When pies are covered only on bottom and not on top, they are called "flans".

✓ When pies or flans are made smaller in size, they are called "tarts or tartlets". *Barquette* is a special tart made in the shape of boat.

Terrines

✓ It is a French forcemeat loaf similar to a pate, made with more coarsely chopped ingredients. Terrines are usually served cold or at room temperature. The term *terrine* is also used for a deep baking dish often made of glazed earthenware (terracotta, French *terre cuite*) in which dish has been baked.

✓ In simple terms, it is a cooking dish with vertical sides and a tightly fitting lid, generally rectangular or oval in shape. In larder kitchen, it is used to cook a forcemeat loaf.

Patés

✓ Paté is a paste normally made from chicken livers (goose livers and duck livers are considered best paté based preparations) and flavoured with things like brandy and cracked pepper. It has a layer of gelatin on top to cover it, and can be spread on crackers or bread. It has the same consistency as margarine.

Mousse

✓ A sweet or savory dish, mousse is usually made with egg whites or whipped cream to give the light, airy texture. In French, the word mousse means "froth" or "foam."

Mousselines

✓ The term mousselines can refer to several different things. The first is a family of sauces, and the second is a group of moulded dishes which are frequently served cold as appetizers. Both come from French cuisine, and they are beaten with eggs and whipped cream for a light, airy texture.

Soufflés

✓ It is a delicate, airy baked egg dish, with either savoury or sweet flavouring. For example, cheese soufflé and chocolate soufflé.

Timbales

✓ A high-sided, drum shaped mould that can taper towards the bottom. The food baked in the mould is usually based on custard, forcemeat or risotto combined with meat, fish, vegetables and cheese. It is un-molded before serving (it may be accompanied with béchamel sauce).

Chaud Froid Sauce

✓ Chaud-froid is a French word which means "hot-cold". Chaud froid is a cold dish covered with a sauce containing gelatin. It can also be prepared as a hot sauce then cooled to a syrupy consistency, and used to coat some seafood and meats that are to be decorated and served cold as chaud froid preparations.

Note. *Lean meat* is composed of muscles, which are numerous bundles of fibres held together by connective tissues. There are two kinds of connective tissues, i.e., elastin (yellow) and collagen (white).

KEY TERMS

Garde manger	:	Cold kitchen, also known as *larder section*.
Forcemeat	:	It is a seasoned mixture of ground meats and other foods, used as a filling/stuffing/base for terrines and pates.
Flans	:	Pies that cover only the bottom; not the top.
Flaky pastry	:	A rough pastry that expands when cooked due to amount of layers.
Panadas	:	A very thick sauce made from roux, mainly used to bind meatballs, quenelles, etc.
Farce	:	French term for stuffing.
Prosciutto	:	Air dry-cured raw ham that comes from Parma in Italy.
Pastillage	:	A paste made from icing sugar with gelatin and corn flour which can be molded into various shapes.
Terrine	:	A poached dish that is cooled in a mould lined with bacon/ pork strips; sliced and served like pate. Actually, the mould, originally made of earthenware, is called terrine.
Chaud froid	:	It means hot cold.
Oven spring	:	Oven shoot in which volume of dough increases during fermentation, consequently item burst.

REVIEW QUESTIONS

1. Enlist the functions of larder kitchen and explain them briefly.
2. What is garde manger? Classify its sections and give work profile of each section.
3. Describe the following terms páte, forcemeat, roulades, charcuteire, oven spring, timbales, soufflé, singing, etc.
4. Differentiate between mousse and mousseline; ballotine and galantine; canapé and sandwiches; aspic and jelly.

49
CHAPTER

Safety and Hygiene

OBJECTIVES

Students will be able to:

- enlighten to equipment and environment safety tips;
- explicate fire classes and their extinguishers; and
- expound the significance of food safety and hygiene.

SAFETY AND HYGIENE

The term *safety* is concerned with protection whereas *hygiene* is related with cleanliness. This chapter is based on food/kitchen safety and hygiene. *Food safety* is a scientific discipline describing handling, preparation and storage of food in such an appropriate way that prevents food-borne illness such as *food poisoning*.

According to World Health Organization, by implementing below mentioned five key principles of food hygiene, one can

- prevent contamination of food with pathogens spreading from people, pets, and pests;
- separate raw and cooked foods to prevent contaminating the cooked foods;
- cook foods for appropriate length of time and at an appropriate temperature to kill pathogens;
- store food at an appropriate temperature; and
- use safe water and raw materials.

SAFETY PROCEDURE IN HANDLING EQUIPMENT

The application of and adherence to strict safety rules in both food serving outlets and in all kitchen sections are of paramount importance. The department uses a variety of equipment which, if handled incorrectly or without expertise, can have very serious consequences. For this reason, there are hard and fast rules for the handling of sharp and potentially dangerous implements. Staff must follow all given safety procedures (or precautions) while handling manual or mechanical equipment. Equipment handling guidelines include following mentioned points.

Knives

- ✓ It is the most important tool in kitchen section without which a chef cannot do anything. Ensure that knives are sharp enough and be stored in racks or *knife blocks*.
- ✓ It is also preferable to give training to staff on how to handle a knife while doing different activities, for example, in carving, de-boning, cutting vegetables and fruits and so forth activities.

Machines

- ✓ It includes mechanically operated equipment like potato peeler, dough kneading machine, mixer, blender, slicing machine, etc. If possible, training should be provided for the correct use of these machines.
- ✓ Wherever possible, put the safety guards on highly dangerous machines such as slicing machine. All machinery should be repaired and maintained at regular intervals.

Heated Utensils

- ✓ Equipment containing hot fat or fluids (like electronically operated deep fryer) should be covered when not in use. Chef may also use the symbols or signs to judge the warmth of hot equipment.
- ✓ Staff training should be provided in the safe use of deep fryers and other hot items. Every staff member should keep himself protected from splash burns.

Gas/Fire

- ✓ All gas operated equipment must be located in a well-ventilated area. Training should be provided for an emergency drill. For instance, in the event of fire or gas leak: activate fire alarm, evacuate building and call fire brigade.
- ✓ At least one type K (Kitchen) fire extinguisher must be located in the kitchen. Training should be provided in fire safety and emergency procedures

Classes of Fire Extinguishers	
Class A	Used to control combustible material based fires, like fire caused by paper, wood, cloth, plastic, etc. Its symbol is *green triangle* with an "A" inside and *black square* with burning wood and burning trash can.
Class B	Used to control flammable liquid and grease based fires, like fire caused by kerosene, diesel, oil, paint, etc. Its symbol is "B" within a *red square* and a *black square* with a burning gas can.

Class C	Used to control electricity based fires, like fire caused by short circuit, fuse, etc. Its symbol is a *blue circle* with a "C" inside and a *square* with a burning plug and socket.
Class D	Used to control flammable metal based fires, like fire caused by sodium, magnesium or titanium. Its symbol is a *yellow star* with a "D" inside.
Class K	Used to control kitchen based (or oil based) fires, like fire caused by mustard oil, refined oil, etc. It is very rare to find, thus most of the hotels and restaurants still use the Class B extinguisher.

Electricity

- ✓ All electrical appliances must have safety switches and should be splash-proof or waterproof. Ensure that all electrical appliances are UL listed (Underwriters Laboratories). There should be enough power plugs/sockets to avoid use of multi-plug adapters and extension cords.
- ✓ All electrical equipment should be in good condition (no frayed or spliced cords, etc.) and regularly test, repair and maintain. Training should be provided in electrical safety also, if possible.

OTHERS

- ✓ Equipment like hoods, ducts and grease filters must be kept free of grease. Commercial cleaning is required on a regular basis, schedule depends on grease accumulation.
- ✓ Grease filters must be in place. The hood/duct fire suppression system must be tested and inspected semi-annually by a fire protection contractor.

Equipment Handling Guidelines	
Manual Handling	**Mechanical Handling**
Use trays and carts to carry armful of items	Always keep safety guards in place
Properly remove trash bins	Stop machine before making any adjustment
Use self-cleaning units for deep fryers	Electronic items should be unplugged before being cleaned
Dispose of oil waste properly	Provide training before being allowed to use a new machine
Use proper lifting and handling methods	Do not wear loose clothing when operating machinery
Wear-heat resistant gloves when handling hot utensils	Use only for its designed purpose; never make multipurpose use
Wear non-slip footwear, preferably with rubber soles	Always follow instructional manual/ guidelines

Work Environment Safety

Ventilation

- ✓ There should be adequate lighting at the working place, especially in the kitchen. Air change of a minimum of 30 times per hour for the cooking environment is usually preferred but a kitchen with low ceiling should undergo air change at least 50 times per hour.
- ✓ In general, to give three air changes per hour is usually necessary in any kitchen. The provision for replacement of extracted air with fresh air is essential in restaurant also.

Lighting

- ✓ The lighting may be natural or artificial or both but in proper proportion, for example, in restaurant usually 30% incandescent with 70% fluorescent light is a *balanced light*. The minimum legal lighting level in working area is 20 lumens per sq. ft. with upto 38 lumens preferable in all areas.

Noise

- ✓ Like ventilation and lighting, noise is also an important aspect of work environment safety in both restaurant and kitchen.
- ✓ The kitchen should be designed in such a way in which conversation should be possible within the area of approximately 4 meters (or 13 ft). In this stated gap, each and every staff can easily pass on information or talk.

Space

- ✓ There must be sufficient *access* aisle (1.5-2 ft) and *service aisle* (2-3 ft). Generally, kitchen should be at least 10 ft in height (from floor to ceiling). The ideal height for work top is about 2 ft 10 inches.
- ✓ The length of work area should be around 4 ft. A work top length of 8 ft would be suitable for two people working side by side (in kitchen). On the other hand, if two persons work back-to-back, the minimum work aisle space should be 4 ft.

Temperature

- ✓ In restaurant, the ideal temperature should range between 15 and 18°C. Ideally or no more than 20-26°C (or room temperature) is always a desirable temperature for kitchen environment with 16-18°C in preparation area (like vegetable preparation and pastry work).

- ✓ These stated temperatures make the staff comfortable to work efficiently and effectively. Below 16°C is preferable for meat and fish preparation areas while walk-in refrigerator works below zero or up to −20°C.

Humidity

- ✓ It is especially a problem of kitchen department. A humid atmosphere can create side effects such as food deterioration, infestation, condensation on wall and slippery floor.
- ✓ Generally, anything higher than 60% humidity lowers the productivity standard. Therefore, the provision for replacement of extracted air with fresh air is essential in every kitchen.

Floor cleaning

- ✓ Use those floor cleaning products that can remove oil and grease. Spills are cleaned up immediately in order to avoid any mishappening and accidents.

Linen and uniforms

- ✓ Linen like towels, curtains and other flammable cloths should be located away from the range (if used). Clothing with short or close-fitting sleeves should be worn while cooking like chef coat. Protective cloths are obligatory due to the purpose of safety.

FOOD SAFETY AND HYGIENE

Food safety is the care during preparation and service of food, so that it is clean, wholesome and free from contamination. All uncooked or unprocessed food carries organisms that have the potential to transmit illness. All cooked food has the ability to support organisms. Safe food handling is an important way of preventing illness to/from food. The safety and hygiene is required at various levels while converting raw material into final product.

When to wash hands?

- Before handling food
- Between preparation
- After handling raw foods
- After washroom and nose blowing or coughing/sneezing
- When hands are soiled
- After smoking

Pre-handling

- ✓ It means equipment should be thoroughly cleaned before starting food preparation/mise en place. It includes clean tongs or utensils that will be used when handling food.

✓ Minor cuts and sores must be covered with waterproof dressings when on arms or the face. Remember fingernails are kept short and clean and nail polish is not to be worn.

Preparing Food

✓ Clean equipment and clean surfaces are to be used when preparing food.

✓ Equipment requires to be washed between preparing food, clean surfaces and dry them after task has been completed. Staff must wash hands as and when required like before, during and after preparation.

Serving Food

✓ Hands are to be washed prior to food service. Utensils or gloves are to be used to handle food. The food is to be kept covered or in closed cabinets and stored at recommended temperatures for the recommended time period.

✓ Discard the foods that may exceed these time limits. Change gloves and wash hands if moving from food handling to any other task and back to food handling again.

Storing Food

✓ Meat and prepared food requires to be placed in the refrigerator immediately after delivery.

✓ Hot food should be placed in such a way (or in hot chamber) so that it will not get cold (when delay in service) and vice versa.

✓ Raw meat and chicken are to be stored in a separate refrigerator or at the bottom of the fridge in case of a juice spill. Stacked food must be covered at all times.

✓ Refrigerators are not to be overloaded.

✓ Hot food must be stored at above 60 degrees Celsius.

✓ Takeaway food brought in by visitors or guest (if any) must be served immediately.

✓ All sauces and gravies must be made daily and if not possible, then store properly.

✓ Food is to be served within two hours of preparation and if not used, discarded or stored properly.

Importance of Proper Hygiene

Good personal cleanliness, including proper and frequent hand washing, is vital to prevent food-borne illness. Food employees with the following symptoms must immediately notify their supervisor fever, persistent sneezing or coughing, diarrhea or vomiting, jaundice, sore throat with fever, etc.

Sick food employees should not be bound to report but if they are required then they must be assigned those duties that minimize the potential of contaminating food and equipment (including utensils, linens, single-service or single use items).

General Food Handling Safety Rules

Food tasting

- ✓ Chef requires tasting the food at regular intervals in order to ensure that food is correctly prepared. This tasting or sampling of food should always be done by separate spoon instead of stirring utensils.

Hot hot/Cold cold

- ✓ Ensure that hot food preparations should be served hot/piping hot whereas cold food preparations should be served cold/chilled.

Store food properly

- ✓ It is related with the proper storage of hot food and cold food. Perishable food should be kept out of the *temperature danger zone (TDZ).* Hot food should be kept hot (above 140°F) while cold food should be kept cold (below 45°F).

Clean utensil and surface

- ✓ After the completion of work (like processing of raw material), staff should clean and disinfect the utensils and surfaces in order to prevent cross contamination.

Proper thawing

- ✓ It means thawing foods under refrigeration, not at room temperature (i.e., about 65°F). It is a time consuming process. Remember, staff should never put frozen food in hot water in order to thaw immediately.

Cook to temperature

- ✓ It is especially important with potentially hazardous foods like meat, fish, milk, etc. These foods must be cooked to the recommended internal temperature to prevent the growth of bacteria.

Regularly rotate stock

- ✓ There are mainly two methods of stock rotation, i.e., FIFO (first in first out) and LIFO (last in first out). In food service industry, mainly FIFO system is followed due to perishability of materials.

Choose right supplier

✓ In order to produce quality dishes, a chef needs to choose good or approved food supplier who can supply wholesome food to the outlet. If there is any doubt in raw material, throw it out or return to supplier.

KEY TERMS

Hygiene`	: Conditions and practices that are followed to maintain the health.
Food-borne illness	: Diseases that happen due to food fault/bad food.
Balanced light	: Proper balance between incandescent and fluorescent light (in the ratio of 3:7).
Incandescent	: Filament light.
Fluorescent	: Soft and cool light, for example, CFL.
Thawing	: Melting something which is frozen under cold water.
TDZ	: *Temperature danger zone* which indicates to proper storage of hot and cold food.
Fire extinguisher	: Fire fighting appliances or fire control measures.
Class K fire	: Fire extinguisher used to control kitchen fire or kitchen oil based fire.

REVIEW QUESTIONS

1. Enlist major safety points that must be considered while handling electronic kitchen appliances.
2. Give step-by-step procedure for the safe handling of raw perishable ingredients.
3. Write a short note on food safety and hygiene.
4. What are the different components that affect kitchen workflow? Explain each one briefly.

50 CHAPTER

The Power of Skills

Objectives

Students will be able to:

- taxonomy the level and type of skill;
- explicate the role of soft skills in guest dealing; and
- expound guest complaint handling and job description.

SKILL

The term *skill* refers to the learned capacity (or possessed ability) of the person to carry out any pre-determined tasks often with the minimum outlay of energy, time or both. This skill can be classified into two broad categories - soft skills and hard skills. *Soft skill* is concerned with an individual's emotional quotient (EQ) or emotional intelligence. It is the cluster of personality traits, communication, language, attitude, friendliness and optimism that characterize relationship with other people. It compliments an individual's *hard skills*. These are the occupational requirements/technical skills (or intelligence quotient) of a job. While performing any tasks at workplace, an individual requires different level of skills, particularly technical, social and supervisory skills.

LEVEL OF SKILLS

Technical Skills

These skills are also called "operational skills" which involve the intricacy of the service trade, techniques of food and beverage preparation, presentation and service. Technical skills represent the following skills expected from service staff.

- ✓ Skill of preparing food in kitchen and handling or carrying trays and salvers in restaurant.
- ✓ Handling of kitchen utensils, glasses, cutlery, crockery, food and beverage, etc.
- ✓ Clearing of soiled plates, glassware and other equipment from table.
- ✓ Making different types of napkin folds.
- ✓ Lying of tablecloth and different styles of cover layout.
- ✓ Clearing of dirt and dust and crumbing of table.
- ✓ Mixing of drinks, their garnish and proper serving method

- ✓ Silver service procedures for all courses
- ✓ Service of specialty items like cheese, fish, etc.
- ✓ Guéridon and flambé techniques.

Social Skills

This skill is also called "human relation skills". As hotel industry is a guest service oriented industry, thus it is very important for any successful venture, to have the service staff with social and scheming skills to handle the guests in the best manner to achieve better guest satisfaction. Consequently, the following social skills are expected from service staff.

- ✓ They should be able to recognize their regular guests and know their likes and dislikes.
- ✓ They should have full knowledge of the local news, events and current affairs so that they can enter into a proper conversation with the guests.
- ✓ They should have scheming and leadership qualities to mold guests' choice.
- ✓ They should have tact to handle awkward and embarrassing situations in their stride.
- ✓ They should have pleasant and cheerful nature.

Supervisory Skills

- ✓ It is also called "managerial skill or conceptual skill" which is related with the ability to see beyond the technical aspects of a job.
- ✓ It includes skills like recognizing the interdependence of various departments and functional areas within the organization and understanding how the organization fits into the structure of the industry, the community and the wider world at large.

The above given different levels of skill for varying levels of job/management is determined on the basis of job analysis. *Job analysis* is also called job study which comprises two components: *job description* and *job specification*. Again it is the skill of job analyser that how he/she assesses and determines the portfolio of any job.

JOB ANALYSIS

Job analysis is the summary of the particular work or job. It shows what a person has to do after getting the job or what will be the portfolio of the work. It also enables the organization to fix the fair wages and salary structure for different sets of jobs. Job evaluation is concerned with rating the job but not the employee. Thus, it involves analysis of jobs for the purpose of writing *job description* and *job specification* and assigning a relative value to each job. A brief discussion on job description and job specification is given below.

Job Description

It is related with the requirement of the job in terms of time for completion of necessary activities and the expected performance standards. The job description should include:

- ✓ The position title
- ✓ The section of the hotel where the position is placed (if applicable)
- ✓ The remuneration
- ✓ The position to which this position reports
- ✓ Any other positions which report to this position
- ✓ Primary purpose and function/s of the job
- ✓ Description of the major tasks, duties and responsibilities
- ✓ The skills, knowledge, abilities, attitude and behaviour that are required in the person who will fill the position.

Job Specification

It means the study of specific technology and behavioural knowledge, skills and attitude needed among the personnel to meet the job requirements. Job specification concentrates on the characteristics needed by an employee to perform the job. It is a statement of minimum qualities which a person should possess to perform the job effectively. A criterion is determined in terms of the capacity and inclination of the person required for the job. These specifications may relate to:

- ✓ Aptitude and abilities
- ✓ Personality and related characteristics
- ✓ Educational qualification and training
- ✓ Experience and exposure
- ✓ Physical and mental requirements
- ✓ Decision making and judgment skills

HANDLING GUEST COMPLAINTS

Service sector (especially hospitality sector) is always vulnerable to guest/customer complaints due to the features of its products/services, i.e., perishability, inseparability, intangibility and invariability. So, in order to successfully handle these guest complaints, an employee must carry enormous skills which are reflected in the given complaint handling process.

Avoid Conflicts

- ✓ It means to avoid conflicts with the guest as it may spoil hotel's goodwill as well as loss of customer that ultimately the hotel's revenue and business volume.

Listen Carefully

- ✓ It means to pay attention to the guest complaint or listen to him/her carefully in order to understand the cause of complaint/dis-satisfaction/faults/root cause, without interrupting him or her while the guest is explaining.

Show Sympathy

- ✓ It means situation handler must have feeling of pity and sorrow for guest's inconvenience. Up to some extent it reduces the magnitude of guest's antagonism.

Do Not Justify

- ✓ It means do not try to justify who is wrong and who is right because it may create a convoluted situation. Staffs have to keep in mind the saying "Guest is always right" even when staff knows that guest is wrong.

Ask Questions

- ✓ It relates to clarifying the matter by asking questions in order to get an idea what actually happened with the guest due to which he/she feels offended/hurt.

Agree and Take Actions

- ✓ It means situation handler should try to sort out the matter as soon as possible plus ensure to agree with guests' opinion on their real dissatisfactory factors. Besides, take appropriate action as quickly as possible.

Follow-Up

- ✓ Even if the complaint was resolved by someone else, contact the guest to see if the problem was satisfactorily solved or not. Report the entire event, the actions taken and the conclusion of the incident to your senior/supervisor.

Note. You should always keep in mind that upto 50% guest's problem/complaint can be solved by careful listening because it reflects that you are cautious or careful towards the guests.

TELEPHONIC SKILLS/MANNERS

Identify Yourself

- ✓ The phone should be picked up within three rings. After picking up the phone, first greet the guest then identify yourself quickly and state your outlet clearly. For example, "Good morning, this is Manoj from room service, how may I assist you?"

Personalize the Call

- ✓ It is very good if you know the name of the guest. Due to this, you can personalize your call by using the name of the calling guest (if known) and project a tone of genuine warmth. For example, "Good morning Mr. Agarwal, how may I assist you?"

Write Guest Message

- ✓ Often, you may require writing down the message (like guest order in the room service department) of the guest in an appropriate register/message slip.
- ✓ After writing the guest message you should repeat the entire message on phone, so if there is any doubt or confusion, it should be clarified instantly.

Use Courtesy Words

- ✓ Use magic words or courtesy words during the conversation with guest. For instance, if you are not clear with given order, say "pardon". Similarly, when guest is busy with his/her family (in restaurant) while you are interacting on phone, say "excuse me" then take meal/beverage order.
- ✓ After the completion of order taking and recording process, it is again necessary to use courtesy phrases like – 'thank you, it's my pleasure, you are most welcome' and so forth.

General Telephone Etiquettes	
Phone pick-up	Telephone must be picked up within two or three rings.
Say sorry	If you are busy with some work and thus got delay in receiving the phone call then say sorry for delay.
Excuse me	While you are talking with guest on phone and urgently you need to excuse yourself due to any reason then say "Excuse me sir/madam, I will be back with you in a moment".
Clarity	Voice should be clear, phone must be handled correctly, speak distinctly and in your normal voice.
Careful	Pay attention to the mood of your caller, as well as to his message and give firm and undivided attention.
Repeat	Repeat all messages and instructions so that the caller can ensure that you have understood the message.
In business call	In business call, give a message of appreciation after the completion of conversation.

KEY TERMS

Soft skill	: An individual's emotional intelligence quotient.
EQ	: It stands for *emotional quotient* thus directly concerned with emotional intelligence.
IQ	: It stands for *intelligence quotient* thus directly concerned with intellectual intelligence.
Job description	: General job profile/job work.
Job analysis	: Summary of the particular work or job.
Job specification	: Specific/technical requirements of any job position.
Conceptual skill	: Managerial level skill thus directly associated with supervisory skills.

REVIEW QUESTIONS

1. Classify different types/levels of skill and explain each one briefly.
2. Give step-by-step procedure for handling guest complaints.
3. Write a short note on telephone etiquettes.
4. What do you mean by the term job analysis? Classify different components of job analysis and explain each one in brief.

Bibliography

Name of Books	Writer	Edition/Year	Publisher
• Successful Restaurant Operation	T.F. Chiffriller, Jr.	Second	Van Nostrand Reinhold
• The Complete Guide to the Art of Modern Cookery	H.L. Kracknell & R.J. Kaufmann	Seventh	William Heinemann Ltd.
• The Art and Science of Culinary Preparation (A Culinarian's Manual)	Jerald W. Chesser	First Edition	The Educational Institute of the American Culinary Fed.
• Larousse Gastronomique	Paul Hamlyn	1994	Butler and Tanner Ltd.
• Managing Service in Food & Beverage Operations	Paul E. Wise & Ronald F. Cichy	Second	AH&LA
• The Encyclopedia of Cooking		Second	Exeter Books (Distributor)
• Professional Beverage Management Lipinski	Bob & Kathie Third	Paul Gillette	
• Professional Table Service	Sylia Meyer	First	John Wiley & Sons
• Beverage Sales & Service	Brian K Julyan	Second	Butterworth Heinemann
• Management Skills in the European Hospitality Industry	Gamble, P, Lockwood	1994	
• Food Service : A Managerial Approach Lexington	B.H. Auxler	1979	
• Marketing of the Meal Experience: A Fundamental Approach	Graham Campbell – Smith	1989	

Book	Author	Year/Edition	Publisher
• Basic Food & Beverage Cost Control	Miller & Hyes	1994	John Wiley & Sons.
• Improving Food & Beverage	Waller	1998	Butterworth Heinemann
• The Catering Management Handbook	Ridgeway & Ridgeway	1995	
• Food & Beverage Control	Kotas & Davis	1990	Chapman & Hall
• Food & Beverage Service	Lillicrap & Cousins	Seventh	ELBS Edition
• Wine Global Encyclopedia	Peter F. & James	Second	Grange Books
• Food & Beverage Management	Jack D. Ninemeier	Third	AH&LA
• Bar Service	Hayte	1996	McMillian Press
• Food & Beverage Management	Davis & Stones	1994	Butterworth Heinemann
• Food & Beverage Service	Bamunnge & Karet	1989	McMillian Press
• International Guide to Drink	Compiled by UK Bartender	First	
• Food For Fifty	Grace Shugart	Eighth	McMillian Press
• Food Service Facilities & Planning	Edward A. Kaza	Third	Van Nostrand Reinhold
• Restaurants, Clubs & Bars (Planning, Design & Investment for F&B)	Fred Lawson	Second	Architectural Press
• Food & Beverage Management	John Cousins	Second	Pearson
• Food & Beverage Cost Control	Lea R. Dopson & David K. Hydes	Fifth	John Wiley & Sons.
• Food & Beverage Service	M.N. Ahmed	Second	

Title	Author	Edition	Publisher
• Introduction to Food & Beverage Service	Graham Brown & K. Hepner	Third	Longman
• Career Opportunities in F & B Industry	Kathleen Thomson H.	Second	Hospitality Press
• An Introduction to Food & Beverage Studies	Marzia Magris	Third	
• Introduction to Hospitality Industry	Gerald W. Lattin	Fourth	AH&LA
• Food & Beverage Service: A Text Book	Manoj Kr. Yadav	First	Aman Publication
(A base book for developing this book)			

Electronic References (Websites)

Wikipedia and Encyclopedia

Beverages	Wine, Beer, Fermenetation, Distillation, Rum, Gin, Vodka, Brandy, Cognac, Armagnac, Calvados, Tequila, Whiskey, Scotch Whiskey, Pomace, Mead, Fenni, Tea, Coffee, Water, Japanese whiskey, Indian Whiskey, Bourbon whiskey, Rusty wine, Hungarian wines, Pot Still, Patent Still & so on topics.
Foods	Soups, Sauces, Hors d'oeuvres, Accompaniments, Garnish, Egg dishes, Farinaceous, Legumes, Savoury, Entremets, Entrée, Releve, Roti, Buffet froid, Melon cocktail, Oysters, Lobsters, Pate de foie gras, Tisane, Herbal tea, CTC, Cigar, Cigarette, Tobacco, Bar, Cocktails, Mocktails, Pimms Cup, Pousse Café, Flips, Noggs & so on topics.
Other contents	Table Services, Crockery, Glassware, Hollowware, Silverware, Tableware, Dining Etiquettes, Table Linen, Napkin, Furniture, Sideboard, Lightening, Bar, Restaurant, Coffee shop, Coffee House, Café, Fast Food Restaurants, Banquets, Buffets, Cocktail Parties, Toasting, Banqueting Functions, Room Service & so on topics.

Electronic Dictionary

- A-Z food Dictionary
- Food Dictionary
- Beverage Dictionary

Index

N

O

P

Q

R